NOBODY BUT THE PEOPLE

To John Reynolds with
highest personal regards

John [signature]

Pell City,
Oct. 15/08

NOBODY BUT THE PEOPLE

The Life and Times of
Alabama's Youngest Governor

WARREN TREST

Best wishes to John Reynolds,
your friend,
Warren Trest

NEWSOUTH BOOKS
Montgomery | Louisville

NewSouth Books
P.O. Box 1588
Montgomery, AL 36102

Library of Congress Cataloging-in-Publication Data

Trest, Warren A.
Nobody but the people : the life and times of Alabama's youngest governor /
Warren Trest.
p. cm.
Includes bibliographical references.
ISBN-13: 978-1-58838-221-4
ISBN-10: 1-58838-221-4
1. Patterson, John, 1921 Sept. 27– 2. Governors—Alabama—Biography.
3. Alabama—Politics and government—1951- 4. Alabama—Race relations—
History—20th century. 5. Alabama—Social conditions—20th century. 6.
Lawyers—Alabama—Biography. 7. Judges—Alabama—Biography.
8. Alabama—Biography. I. Title.
F330.3.P27T74 2008
976.1'063092—dc22
[B]

2008003182

Design by Randall Williams
Printed in the United States of America

The human spirit. May it prevail.

Contents

A selection of photos follows page 112.

Nobody But the People

PROLOGUE

Inside the small country church in rural Cowpens, family and friends squeezed into the crowded pews to see Judge John Malcolm Patterson administer the oath of office to Tallapoosa County's newly elected state representative. It was a crisp Sunday morning in January 1995 when the trim seventy-three-year-old former governor swore in Betty Carol Graham, "a friend, a neighbor and a distant relative" who lived a mile or so down the road from where he was born. In his remarks, Patterson reminisced about his early childhood in nearby Goldville and talked about the importance of family and community ties. "You've always got to keep in mind your roots," he said with quiet conviction.[1]

The congregation knew where the judge was coming from. His family's roots, like their own, ran deep within the rolling red clay hills of north Tallapoosa County—a quilted landscape of lazy pastures, stands of timber, farm communities, and sinuous country roads winding down to where the Tallapoosa River and Hillabee Creek converge, barely an hour's drive southeast of Birmingham. There was a time when you couldn't pick up a rock in these parts and throw it without striking Patterson kin, some said. During the Sunday service the judge had joined in sotto voce when the minister led the congregation in singing "Onward, Christian Soldiers" and "Blessed Assurance, Jesus is Mine." He was saving his voice for the swearing-in.

Judge Patterson's reminiscences drew whispered amens. Some in attendance were as familiar with the ups and downs in his life as with their own. They knew that like his father before him young John had marched off to war when duty called. In 1918 the father, Albert, had been severely wounded in the Meuse-Argonne offensive on the Western Front and was awarded the Croix de Guerre with Gilt Star for gallantry by the French Government. During World War II the son had entered the Army as a private and rose to major, distinguishing himself in combat in North Africa and Europe and returning home with seven battle stars and the Bronze Star.[2]

Folks in these parts take their military obligations seriously. No one knows the times the haunting notes of taps have played for the fallen who sleep within these ageless hills, only that reveille sounds afresh in the morning dew. Not far down the river and through the trees lies the National Military Park at Horseshoe Bend where Andrew Jackson's frontier troops and U.S. regulars defeated Chief Menawa's braves in 1814 to bring the Creek Indian War to an end. Follow Highway 280 to the southeast and you come to the town of Camp Hill where Lyman Ward Military Academy keeps the tradition alive. Judge Patterson has long been a Lyman Ward supporter and served as chairman of the Academy's board of trustees. His son Albert is a West Point graduate and retired U.S. Army colonel.

INSIDE THE ROCKY CREEK Baptist Church even teenagers squirming in their seats knew the distinguished man standing in robes before them must be twice the age he was when Alabama voters swept him into office as the youngest governor ever elected in their state. What Tallapoosa schoolchild had not been taught that one of their own was the only man ever to beat George Wallace in a gubernatorial race? Who among their elders missed seeing *The Phenix City Story* about the brutal murder of Attorney General-nominee Albert Patterson in 1954 and how it propelled the grieving son into the maelstrom of Alabama politics?

"No star ever appeared on Alabama's political horizon so suddenly, glittered so brightly, and burned out so swiftly," wrote Bob Ingram, then the editor of *Alabama Magazine*, about the former governor in 1979. "Even now, but a couple of decades after the fact, Patterson's political career seems but a blur across the pages of history." Stepping reluctantly into his murdered father's shoes, Patterson's reputation as a crime-busting attorney general forged a statewide political following and set the stage for his successful bid for the governor's office in 1958.[3]

Television was just coming into its own in political campaigns. Candidates for governor still stumped up and down the state in motorcades, speaking to the crowds from flatbed trucks, kissing babies, slapping backs, and shaking hands. Adopting a catchy political slogan, "Nobody's for John Patterson . . . but the people," the Patterson campaign kicked off at the town of New Site, just down the road from Goldville, before hitting the trail with a popular bluegrass band, Rebe Gosdin and his Sunny Valley Boys.[4] Not unlike a scene from *O Brother Where Art Thou?*, the band warmed up the crowds by picking and singing before their candidate stepped up to the microphone and delivered his Sunday punch.

Three things all fourteen candidates running for governor in the 1958

Democratic primary had in common: they were residents of the state of Alabama; they were white Protestant males; and they were avowed segregationists. Otherwise, given the culture of the times, a candidate would have just been whistling "Dixie." Some were more moderate in their segregationist views than others, but race dominated the campaign as never before. Attorney General John Patterson planned for law and order to be his main issue, but he gleaned from his travels around the state and the flood of mail he received—he corresponded with more than fifteen thousand voters during the campaign—that people were more concerned about the federal government encroaching on states' rights and forcing the integration of Alabama's schools. In the wake of the U.S. Supreme Court's ruling in *Brown v. Board of Education*, the image of Little Rock Central High School being integrated at the point of a bayonet in 1957 was etched into people's minds.[5]

Patterson had become widely known as the defender of Alabama's segregation laws because of legal challenges he was involved in as attorney general to block court-ordered desegregation and to ban the NAACP from doing business in Alabama. A strategy of gradualism (resisting integration by legal maneuvering) was reaffirmed at a closed meeting of Deep South lawyers and public officials in Birmingham in December 1958. "We knew we couldn't reverse the Supreme Court's desegregation ruling, but we wanted to buy time, to delay integrating Alabama's schools until it could be done peaceably, without violence," Patterson said.[6]

During the campaign and after becoming governor, John Patterson— described as "articulate to a rare degree" by those who heard him—championed the traditional "separate but equal" doctrine of the Southern states.[7] Ironically, the stalling tactics of the segregationists helped to galvanize the civil rights movement and brought matters to a head sooner than might have been. The North, where racial bias was more subtle and less institutionalized, did not have the South's problems. Throughout the Deep South the righteous movement became a mighty storm of "sit-ins, demonstrations, Freedom Riders . . . it was a violent time."[8]

In the midst of this storm the young governor's friendship with President John F. Kennedy—they had met while Patterson was attorney general and JFK was a U.S. senator investigating the crime syndicate—hurt him politically. Relying on his own instincts that Kennedy would win the Democratic nomination and knowing it wouldn't hurt Alabama to have a friend in the White House, he endorsed Kennedy early in the contest and threw his support behind him at the

Democratic convention in Los Angeles in the summer of 1960. He backed the winning candidate in Los Angeles, but he paid a political price at home. His own pastor chastised the governor from the pulpit for joining forces with a Catholic, and a liberal Yankee to boot.[9]

In the spring of 1961 the governor had misgivings when the White House's bungling of the Bay of Pigs invasion against Fidel Castro's Cuba resulted in the deaths of four Alabama air guardsmen. On the heels of the Cuban debacle, Patterson's split with Kennedy's policies grew when two small groups of Freedom Riders—viewed even by moderate Southern whites as "outside agitators"—rolled into Dixie on Greyhound and Trailways buses to challenge segregation. Attorney General Robert Kennedy's heavy-handed approach when dealing with Southern governors and a widely held view at the time (later debunked by civil rights historians) that the Kennedys actively supported the Freedom Riders left many white supporters below the Mason-Dixon Line feeling outraged and betrayed.

A dramatic sequence of events—during which an embattled Governor Patterson refused to accept a phone call from President Kennedy—ended with the president's brother ordering federal marshals into the state to protect the Freedom Riders from mob violence, and the governor declaring qualified martial rule and breaking out the national guard to quell the disturbance and to save both the Freedom Riders and the ill-equipped marshals from angry mobs. Looking back on his differences with the White House during this volatile period, the governor speaks warmly of John Kennedy, but has few kind words for the president's brother. "It was hard to believe these two men had the same parents," he said to a reporter a few summers ago.[10]

THE CIVIL RIGHTS ISSUE was so dominant during Patterson's four years at the helm that history has almost overlooked the many positive accomplishments of his administration. Working with state legislators, he fought hard for economic and social programs to better the lives of all of Alabama's citizens—including huge increases in education funding, an accelerated highway program, higher old age pensions, more aid to farmers, and new industry with more jobs throughout the state. He put loan sharks out of business and got the laws changed so low- and middle-income families could borrow money without being gouged by usurious interest rates—legislation having special meaning for Alabama's black citizens. For the first time the state's black citizens had access to installment loans for automobiles, large appliances, etc., with monthly payments they could afford.[11]

Since Alabama's statutes then barred successive terms for governors, Patterson had to sit the next campaign out—looking on from the sidelines in 1962 as George Wallace (an old friend of his father's in the state senate) stole his political thunder. True to his famous promise after the 1958 defeat never to be "outnigguhed" again, Wallace took over Patterson's winning role as champion of the segregationists and played it for all it was worth. No one in Alabama history demagogued the race issue more than George Wallace—who years later asked forgiveness from Alabama's black citizens—and the voters loved it. They handed Wallace a victory in the 1962 primary with the most votes received by an Alabama gubernatorial candidate up to that time.

Patterson believed he could recapture the initiative when Wallace's term was up, but he had failed to take into account the political shrewdness of his opponent.[12] Wallace was not about to relinquish the advantage to Patterson or anyone else if he could help it. Failing in a bid to change the succession law so he could seek reelection, the governor came up with a stratagem to run his wife Lurleen in his place. With George by her side, Lurleen won hands down. Patterson—having lost his platform and his voters to Wallace—came in a distant sixth with only thirty-one thousand votes. Another four years passed before Patterson ran for public office again. In 1970 he opposed Howell Heflin for chief justice of the Alabama Supreme Court and was defeated. Having remained friends with George Wallace, Patterson worked in two of his old foe's presidential campaigns as well as two of his gubernatorial campaigns. In 1984 Wallace—then serving an unprecedented fourth term as governor—appointed Patterson to the State Court of Criminal Appeals.[13]

Reelected to the appellate court for two more terms, Judge Patterson retired from the Court of Criminal Appeals in January 1997, continuing to serve as supernumerary (retired active judge). During an interview before his retirement, a reporter remarked on the coincidence of his once being Alabama's youngest governor, and now the state's oldest sitting judge. "Isn't that a hell of thing?" the seventy-five-year-old Patterson said. "Now I'd like to be the youngest anything."[14]

DURING HIS HEYDAY, NEWSPAPERS described the youthful governor as handsome, bright, articulate, strong-willed, and untiring. Some editors warmly referred to him as "Governor John." Even detractors admired his drive and leadership, conceding that he had given Alabama four years of progressive government.

Patterson knows that history will sort out the successes and the failures of his administration, but as he told Bob Ingram twenty-five years ago, there was "a personal, inward satisfaction about some of the things we were able to accomplish which may be the best reward of all for public service."

The former governor admits to having made mistakes, none more regrettable than his handling of segregation. Turning the clock back to the racial demagoguery that helped get him elected governor in 1958, Patterson said, "In fact we were dead wrong. Black citizens were seeking their Constitutional rights and were trying to better their lives. We should have helped them." He has declared publicly on numerous occasions that his greatest mistake was not doing more as governor to bring Alabama's black citizens into the political process. "You start with the vote and everything else follows," he said. "If I'd done that I probably wouldn't have gotten reelected, but I didn't get reelected anyway."[15]

"Times change. We should remember that," he told a *Birmingham Post-Herald* reporter in 1984. "When you take an uncompromising position on something, you might live to regret it." As governor and attorney general he was responsible for upholding the laws that were on the books, but he would not have enforced them so rigidly if he had it to do over again. Particularly troubling to him was the mob violence against the Freedom Riders in Anniston, Birmingham, and Montgomery in 1961. City officials in the latter two cities had promised to provide security for the Freedom Riders, which was their job, but failed to keep their word. The violence not only gave the state a black eye, but embarrassed Patterson's administration.[16]

Today Patterson is gratified by the number of African Americans who have risen to positions of prominence in the Deep South and in the nation. He said in 1984, "I think the greatest progress we have made in Alabama . . . is in race relations. I think that is good."[17] On the desk in his home study is a photograph of him standing with a black man wearing overalls. "That's Earmon 'Wolf' Glenn," he said. "Wolf managed my farm for nearly thirty years. He suffered a stroke in 1991. Best friend I had in the world when he died."[18]

WHEN PATTERSON BECAME GOVERNOR, he bought the old homeplace consisting of eighty acres on Cowpens Road in Goldville from his uncle, Lafayette Lee Patterson, who had been active in politics in the 1920s and 1930s and served two terms as a U.S. Representative from Alabama. He subsequently acquired adjacent tracts of land, eventually expanding the original Patterson place into a twelve-hundred-acre farm and fulfilling a dream he had as a boy running barefoot through the hills at his grandfather's side.

About a mile back into the woods from his grandparents' deserted house—sitting right next to the road and beyond fixing up—the governor built a fifteen-acre lake and the Alabama conservation department stocked it with fish. He later added a hunting lodge-style house, with log siding, that was intended as a vacation home or family getaway from the fishbowl of state politics and capital-city lawyering. Then he acquired a registered Angus herd of sixty brood cows and some horses, and hired Earmon Glenn to manage the place for him.

Upon retiring from the Court of Criminal Appeals in 1997 Patterson and wife Tina sold their Montgomery townhouse and moved to the farm—described by a charmed visitor as a "lovely Shangri-La . . . hidden way back from the road . . . log-cabin like and surrounded by a large lake with squawking geese and abundant wildlife."[19] At that 1995 Sunday swearing-in ceremony in rural Cowpens he told about how he couldn't wait to get away from this place when he was growing up. When he finally did get away, he realized he'd made a terrible mistake. At critical points in his life he always came back here, whether it was to relish a victory, to nurse his wounds, or to gather his strength. "It took me a long time," he said. "Now I'm home for good."[20]

In the summer of 2007, veteran Alabama reporter Alvin Benn featured the eighty-five-year-old former governor and his wife in an article for *Cooperative Farming News*. The Pattersons were in good health and strong in spirit, and as they showed their guest around the farm their love for each other, for the land, and for the animals sparkled in their eyes. Patterson conveyed to Benn that this was where he was born and this was where he wanted to be when he died. And when that day comes he is not worried, Benn wrote: "He knows he's had an event-filled life most people can only dream of having."[21]

1

BAREFOOT IN TALLAPOOSA

W hen Mollie and Delona Patterson settled there in the 1890s, Goldville was just a wide spot in the narrow dirt road heading north
through Mellow Valley toward Talladega National Forest and the
Cheaha Wilderness. A few relics were still lying around to remind residents of
their community's roaring past as a boom town of some thirty-five hundred
inhabitants, mostly prospectors mining for gold, but you had to look for them.
During the 1840s the historic site had been the center of gold-mining activities
in east Alabama, and was incorporated with a mayor and council in 1843. Its lone
hotel and clusters of stores and saloons did a thriving business. Six years later the
budding metropolis became a ghost town overnight when prospectors and camp
followers packed up and headed west in the California Gold Rush of 1849.[1]

At the time, much of the region that is now east Alabama was still an untamed
wilderness. Before 1805 it was part of the Mississippi Territory, which included
the homeland of the Creek Indians. In 1814, Creek warriors rose to defend what
was left of their Nation, but were crushed by General Andrew Jackson. When
Mississippi became a state in 1817, Alabama became a territory, and two years
later it became the twenty-second state. Tallapoosa County was even younger,
having been created from land ceded by the Creek Indians in the treaty of Cusseta on March 24, 1832. The remnant of the once-proud tribe was herded off
to Oklahoma on the infamous Trail of Tears.[2]

A barefoot John Malcolm Patterson, playing across the road from the abandoned mine shafts on his grandparents' farm, wondered what life was like when
gold fever and the opening of Indian territory brought an influx of white settlers,
including his own ancestors, into north Tallapoosa County. His grandfather had
fired his imagination with tales about the early days and how "Old Hickory"
defeated the Creek warriors a few miles down the river at Horseshoe Bend.
General Jackson went on to win lasting fame against the British in the Battle of
New Orleans, and to serve two terms as president of the United States. He died
the decade before Delona Patterson was born in 1858.[3]

Delona and Mollie (her christened name was Mary, but everyone knew her as Mollie) had sharecropped in neighboring Clay County before moving to Goldville. Mollie's parents, Francis and Hollon Peters Sorrell, lived in the Goldville community and learned that some of the land abandoned by prospectors forty years earlier was to be sold for taxes. In 1890 Delona and Mollie bought one hundred and sixty acres—later losing half of the property when the original owners paid the taxes and reclaimed the land. The remaining eighty acres became the Patterson home place. Delona's father loaned him the money to buy the land and to build a one-room house; they built a larger house as the family grew.[4]

While building their new cabin in Goldville, Delona and Mollie lived a year on Timbergut Creek near New Site. It was at the interim residence on Timbergut Creek that John Patterson's father, Albert Love Patterson, was born January 27, 1891. Delona and Mollie already had two boys—five-year-old Edmon (Mollie's son before she married Delona) and two-year-old Lafayette, who was born while the couple was in Clay County. Delona was previously married to Mollie's sister, who had died along with their young son Lucius in a flu epidemic. Between 1893 and 1904, Delona and Mollie had five other children, all daughters, who grew up together on the Patterson farm.[5]

Prior to FDR's New Deal and World War II, raising cotton and bearing children was a way of life in rural Dixie. Three brothers and five sisters growing up under one roof, albeit not an unusually farm family in those days, made the Patterson household an active and crowded place. Their home, a typical farm dwelling in the early 1900s, was a weathered wood-frame structure of three fairly large-size rooms with floors that creaked when you walked and cracks in the walls that whistled when the wind blew. A dogtrot or breezeway ran through the middle of the house, and water came from a well off the back porch. Before rural America got electricity, kerosene lamps and wood-burning fireplaces were everyday essentials, as were long johns and heavy bed covers on cold winter nights.[6]

A GENERATION LATER, THIS humble dwelling was where John Malcolm Patterson was born on September 27, 1921. He was delivered by Dr. Dan Nolen of nearby New Site. Nolen and Dr. R. A. Foshee, also of New Site, were well-known country doctors who treated patients all over north Tallapoosa County, making their rounds on horseback or in a buggy. John was born the year after his father, hobbling on crutches, left the Army hospital at Fort McPherson, Georgia. Two years earlier a heroic Albert Patterson had lain near death on a bloody French battlefield for a day and night before the medics could reach him. John remembered his father telling about seeing a pear tree bear fruit twice outside his hospital window before the Army doctors finally released him.[7]

From a young age, Albert Patterson had shown the grit and the courage that saw him through that terrible day in France in October 1918. He was level-headed but adventurous. In 1914 he left home and went to work in the east Texas oil fields. While there he completed high school at Fairfield, Texas, and enlisted in the National Guard in May 1916 to earn extra money. The Guard division was called up eight days later, and he was sent to Brownsville to join in the hunt for Pancho Villa, whose bandits had raided towns across the U.S. border. Attaining the rank of sergeant, he returned home to Alabama when the division was demobilized.[8]

Before going to Texas Albert Patterson had met and courted Agnes Louise Benson, whose family moved down from Colbert County to the Sunny Level community on the outskirts of Alexander City. Albert and Agnes had corresponded while he was in Texas, and the courtship continued upon his return. Albert had his mind set on going to college, and his father let him plant a cotton crop on the farm to make enough money to pay tuition. He was in the field plowing when a letter arrived notifying him that his Guard division was being recalled because of the war in Europe and he was to report to Texas for duty.[9]

Following his return to Texas, Albert completed Officer Candidate School and was commissioned a second lieutenant. He was stationed at Brownsville when he sent for Agnes and asked her to marry him. She arrived in Brownsville by train on July 14, 1917. Following a brief reunion at the station they walked across the street and were married by a justice of the peace. In July 1918 Lieu-tenant Patterson was ordered to Camp Bowie at Forth Worth where the newly organized 36th Infantry Division, comprised of Texas and Oklahoma National Guard units, was assembling to go overseas. On their wedding anniversary he took Agnes to the railroad station where she left for home. A few days later he departed with the 141st Infantry Regiment for New York and Europe. Landing in France in August, the regiment trained briefly before moving to the front in the IV French Army sector in October.[10]

On October 8th Lieutenant Patterson led his platoon into battle against the German lines. Early that morning near the French village of St. Etienne he was wounded when a German bullet slammed into his helmet and creased his head, but he continued to lead his platoon in battle. Late that afternoon he was cut down by machine gun fire that riddled his left hip and leg. Helpless and bleeding on the battlefield, he was near death when the medics got to him the following day. For his heroic actions at St. Etienne he was awarded the Purple Heart and the coveted French Croix de Guerre with Gilt Star for gallantry. The commander-in-chief of the French Armies of the East cited Lieutenant Patterson as "a very brave officer" who "displayed audacity, valor and technical knowledge" on the battlefield. "By his excellent example he largely contributed to the success of the battle," the citation read.[11]

Albert Patterson was still recovering in an Army hospital in France when Agnes delivered a stillborn first child in November 1918. A daughter, Sibyl Maxine, was born in 1920, but an illness took her life when she was four years old. Born the year after Maxine, John Patterson barely knew her. "She died of a tumor, which is now curable," he recalled. Maxine's death left John as an only child until a younger brother, Maurice, was born in Alexander City in 1930. A third son, Samuel, was also born in Alexander City, and the youngest son Jack was born after the family moved to Phenix City, Alabama.[12]

After his release from the Army hospital in 1920 Albert Patterson attended the University of Alabama, graduating Phi Beta Kappa with a Bachelor of Arts degree in 1924. While teaching school he then earned a law degree from Cumberland School of Law in Lebanon, Tennessee, in 1927 and was admitted to the Alabama State Bar. He moved his family to Opelika where he practiced law for one year and then to Alexander City where he practiced law for nearly five years. In 1933 he opened a law office in Phenix City and moved his family there.

Until he was of school age John lived with his grandparents on the farm at Goldville, and afterward spent many of his summers there. Both of his parents were away teaching school and were staying at boarding houses in adjacent counties. Albert taught school in Tallapoosa, Clay, and Cullman counties in Alabama and in Fort Meade, Florida. He was principal of Clay County High School in Ashland and Coosa County High School in Rockford. During the summers John's parents furthered their education by taking classes at Jacksonville State Teachers College.

Delona Patterson was self-taught, but he knew the value of a good education and encouraged his sons to go to college. Albert's older brother Lafayette graduated from Jacksonville State Teachers College, Birmingham-Southern College, and later Stanford University. He was the superintendent of education of Tallapoosa County in 1924–26 before serving an unexpired term and two regular terms (1927–33) as a U.S. Congressman from Alabama's fifth district.

He later served as special assistant to the U.S. Secretary of Agriculture in the Roosevelt administration. He once described his duties as those of "a goodwill ambassador" for President Franklin D. Roosevelt, "selling his domestic programs across the nation."[13]

Delona once told his eldest son that he would starve to death if he had to farm because his nose was always in a book. Delona also accurately predicted that Lafayette would be a member of Congress by the time he was forty. Lafayette had to study at home because there was no school in the Goldville community until he was "about grown." Self-educated, he earned a teachers' certificate and "taught at a little country school when he was not farming." He started college when he was thirty years old without ever having been to high school. When he registered for college Lafayette said he backed out of the room so the officials wouldn't see the seat of his pants, which were almost worn out. His daughter later described the family's drive to Stanford University at Palo Alto, California, when they had to stop along the way and pick strawberries to help pay for the trip.[14]

SPENDING HIS FLEDGLING YEARS on the farm in Goldville instilled in young John Patterson an almost spiritual attachment to the land he grew up on and to his family roots. Being around grown-ups most of the time gave the inquisitive youngster a firm grounding in common sense and the work ethic. From his father and his grandfather he learned self-discipline and self-reliance. Grandfather Delona was a raw-boned man who stood about six feet two inches and weighed more than two hundred pounds. He had coal black hair when he was a young man but was gray-haired by the time John came along. He was a farmer who had worked hard all his life, a religious person who was strict, yet gentle in raising his family.

Albert Patterson was even more of a disciplinarian than his father. "You lived by his rules," his son recalled in later years. "My father was a little bit like me. He didn't play golf. He didn't hunt or fish. His hobby was work." After leaving the Army hospital Albert refused to let his war wounds hold him back. Determined to beat the disability, he traded the crutches in for a walking cane and eventually dispensed with the cane. One leg was shorter than the other, however, and by the time he was slain in 1954 he had gone back to using the cane and a built-up shoe. Unable to dress himself, he had to have help getting his pants and his shoes on.

John was inspired by his father's determination and integrity. When Albert

Patterson left the Army he was on record with the Veterans Administration as 100 percent disabled. For the rest of his life he was determined to reduce that percentage even though it meant a reduction in VA benefits. Periodically he petitioned the VA to review his case with the aim of lowering the percentage of disability. When he was murdered in 1954 his disability record with the VA was down to 35 percent. His son remarked that he had never known anyone else who would do that. "My father was a good man. A better man than me, that's for sure," he said.

His mother Agnes and his grandmother Mollie were positive influences on young John's life through the carefree days in Tallapoosa and beyond. Both were strong-willed women who faced triumph and tragedy with quiet strength and dignity. He was a more complete and more caring person because of them. Mollie outlived Delona, who died in 1937, by more than two decades. At age ninety-four, she attended her grandson's inauguration as governor and danced at the inaugural ball. John's mother Agnes lived for three decades after his father's murder in 1954. He was close to his grandfather, Robert Burns Benson, on his mother's side but never knew his grandmother Dixie Lavenia Hart Benson who died before he was born. He knew his grandfather's second wife Fannie Hanson Benson, but didn't spend much time with her. As a child he learned about his roots on both sides of the family, listening to stories told while sitting out on the front porch or by the fireplace at night inside the old Patterson place.[15]

From his elders he learned that the family's history was steeped in military tradition and public service going back to his Scottish ancestry. On his mother's side he descended from John Hart of New Jersey, one of the signers of the Declaration of Independence. Both great-grandfathers on his father's side had served with the Confederate Army. The family's Scottish heritage was traceable to an earlier John Patterson who lived in Argyleshire, Scotland, and was either killed in the Battle of Culloden in 1747 or was executed by the British shortly thereafter. His widow Catherine and their four children (three boys and a girl) left Scotland with other emigres and joined relatives in what is today Cumberland County, North Carolina. One of the three sons was named John for his father and served with a North Carolina infantry regiment in the Revolutionary Army.[16]

Surviving the American Revolution, John married Isabella McDuffie and they eventually raised ten children. One of the descendents, Daniel Patterson, was a prosperous miller and owned land along Buffalo Creek, which later became part of the Fort Bragg military reservation. "Buffalo Dan," as he was known locally, had

several offspring. Two, John Graham Patterson and Malcolm Patterson, migrated
to Alabama around the time the state expanded eastward to encompass the land
acquired in the Treaty of Cusseta in 1832. Buffalo Dan later sold his holdings in
North Carolina and moved to Alabama to live with his son Malcolm.[17]

After arriving in Alabama the brothers had settled in Coosa and Tallapoosa
counties only a few miles apart from each other. Malcolm settled in the Hatchet
Creek community just north of present-day Goodwater. John Graham moved
further east toward what is today the town of Hackneyville. Malcolm married
twice and had children by both wives. Three of his sons were killed in the Civil
War. His and John Graham's descendants eventually spread throughout north
Tallapoosa County and its environs. One of John Graham's sons, John Love Patterson, was about seven when the family came to Alabama from North Carolina.
This youngster, who grew up to become quite wealthy, was Governor John Patterson's great-grandfather.[18]

JOHN LOVE PATTERSON OWNED a large farm of more than seven hundred acres
and operated a grist mill on Town Creek. He was known throughout north
Tallapoosa County as "the miller" and as "Uncle John Patterson." In his later
years he was described as "a very tall man" who was well over six feet in height,
with white hair, blue eyes, and a ruddy complexion. While operating the mill
he always wore a white shirt, white trousers, and suspenders, and was "known
far and wide for the excellent quality of meal" which he ground for people in
the community.[19]

John Love Patterson's first child was a son Delona (Governor Patterson's
grandfather) born in 1858. Delona never knew his mother, who did not adapt
to life in the wilderness. According to family legend—the written record kept
in Delona's Bible was lost in a house fire in the 1920s—she left his father soon
after Delona was born and returned to North Carolina. The miller raised his son
alone with the help of a small number of slaves. When the Civil War erupted, the
miller was exempt from service for the first two years because of his occupation.
Called to duty with the Confederate Army in 1863, he left Delona in the care
of slaves. One of the stories Delona Patterson told his grandson was about going
to town for supplies with one of the slaves near the end of the war when they
heard the Yankee troops were coming through Tallapoosa County on their way
to Montgomery. The slave drove the mules and wagon out of town in a cloud of
dust to keep the Yankee soldiers from commandeering them.

After the Civil War, the miller married late in life to Mary Bryant of Hackneyville. They had five daughters. Delona was his only son, and they had a close father-son relationship. On the day his father died Delona was laid up in bed with the measles and was unable to attend the funeral. He told his family that he had not only lost a father, but the best friend he ever had.[20]

For young John Patterson, growing up on his grandparents' farm yielded a storehouse of memories. One vivid scene was his grandparents' house burning when he was about four years old. He and his grandmother were home alone when the fire started. His grandfather had gone to the mill in the buggy to have some corn ground. His grandmother was ironing clothes when she heard a loud crackling noise, grabbed him by the arm, and rushed out the back door. When they looked back at the house, the roof was covered in flames. She held onto his arm and ran toward Goldville yelling for help. A county road crew heard her and came running, but the fire was too far along to save the house. The ashes were smoldering when his grandfather returned.[21] The Pattersons spent the night with the Burnette family, who lived a couple of miles away. Owen and Willa Burnette had a daughter Sibyl who was John's age. Since his clothes were destroyed in the fire, he slept in one of her nightgowns. "She lives in New Site, and still talks about how the governor of Alabama once slept in her nightgown," Patterson recalled in the fall of 2002. "She and her folks were like family. They worked hard for me in the governor's race."[22]

The Pattersons and the Burnettes were close friends. Sibyl called Delona and Mollie Aunt Pat and Uncle Pat. "We loved Aunt Pat and Uncle Pat," she said. "I can remember quite well seeing them walking down the road to our house to visit on a hot summer afternoon. She was carrying an umbrella, and I remember how dusty that road was." She remembered playing with John when they were children, and said he used to stand on an upturned bucket under a shade tree in their front yard and act like he was preaching. "I guess that's where he developed his oratorical skills," she laughed.[23]

The day after the fire his grandparents cleaned out the cotton house across the road from their burned-out home and moved in until they could rebuild. The home place fronted a one-lane dirt road that was barely wide enough for a horse-drawn buggy to stay in the ruts leading from Goldville to Cowpens. On the rare occasions when two parties met coming and going, one had to pull off the road to let the other one pass. A barn sat on a rise back up from the house where it was closer to the pasture and fields. The drainage sloped away from the house. There was a large chicken coop located closer to the backyard. Other outbuildings included a log crib and a small garage across the road next to the cotton house. Delona built the garage for his son Albert who purchased a new Ford automobile with the money saved up while he was hospitalized at Fort McPherson.

Automobiles were a rare sight on the unpaved back roads of Tallapoosa County at that time. Some parts of the county were so far back in the hills the old-timers swore they had to lobby the politicians on Goat Hill in Montgomery to pipe in daylight. "In my early time here when grandma and grandpa went anywhere, they traveled in a buggy," John Patterson said. "Of course when it rained, it got so muddy you couldn't go nowhere on these one-lane dirt roads."[24]

The twenty or so families residing in the Goldville community were a close-knit group. Patterson was fond of the people he grew up around while staying with his grandparents. One special neighbor he would always remember was a well-known bootlegger named Malvin Jones. Making whiskey was an accepted practice around north Tallapoosa in those days, according to Patterson. "We were way back in the country, no paved roads anywhere," he explained. "In fact there wasn't a paved road running in and out of Alexander City in any direction. If you went from Alex City to Birmingham in a car, it would take all day, a dirt road and just a cloud of dust all the way. But up here it was really isolated, and a lot of people made whiskey for a living around here."

Patterson remembered Malvin Jones as a caring person who looked after Delona and Mollie after they became elderly and were living by themselves. "Nobody was left there but grandma and grandpa, and they had trouble cutting wood and doing chores like that," he recalled. Every Sunday morning Jones came by the house early going down the road to his still hidden in the woods. "He'd come by whistling and singing with jugs and stuff in a white meal sack on his back, and he'd wave at grandpa sitting on the porch. Late that afternoon you could hear him coming back drunk. He'd be hollering, and he'd have a couple of jugs of whiskey in that sack on his back, and he'd pitch headlong when he was going downhill, and sometimes he'd run in the ditch."

Patterson recalled that when Malvin got near their house, "grandma would go in the kitchen and wash out a quart fruit jar and get it ready." When Malvin came by and saw Delona Patterson sitting there, he'd come to the house and say, "Come on Uncle Pat, let's have a drink." He'd pull a jug of whiskey out of the sack, and they'd go back into the kitchen and get some glasses. "Grandpa liked toddy," Patterson said. "He'd put a couple of ounces of whiskey in the bottom of a glass and add some sugar. That's the way he drank it. As soon as they'd get through, they'd have another one, and another one." Then Malvin would say to Mollie, "Aunt Pat, pour yo'self a little out." "Here she'd come with that quart fruit jar," Patterson laughed.

"That bootlegger looked after them, cared for them, cut wood for them, furnished them some whiskey in their old age that made their life more comfortable," he said. "I was crazy about that fellow, and I kept in touch with him." When Patterson became governor, Jones still lived in the Goldville area and still made whiskey. The governor told his ABC administrator, who oversaw the liquor laws in the state, about Jones and asked that he be left alone. "Malvin ain't doing no harm to nobody. Leave him alone," Patterson said. "If you were to catch him, we'd have to put up the money to bail him out. Just tell your folks to stay away from him."

One day the governor's secretary came into his office and said, "There's a man out here to see you. He's wearing overalls, don't have no socks on, and needs a shave." "Well, who is he?" Patterson asked. The secretary replied, "Well, he says his name is Malvin Jones from Goldville." The governor got up from behind his desk, walked out into the anteroom, and brought Jones into his office ahead of everyone else. Patterson canceled his other engagements and spent the day with his unexpected guest. They had lunch together in the governor's mansion. Afterwards, the governor got Malvin a job where he wouldn't have to work hard, but could make a little extra money to live on. "I was sort of paying off a debt for all he done for grandma and grandpa," he said.

When Jones died, his funeral was at Bethel Church, back in the country about two miles from Goldville. It was obvious at the funeral that the former governor wasn't the only person who had a special place in his heart for Malvin Jones. "Here was a fellow who had been a bootlegger all his life, and that was the biggest funeral I've ever seen in this community," Patterson said. "Several acres of people came to pay their respects. There was so many people that three-fourths of them couldn't get in the church. Beat anything I ever saw."[25]

LIKE OTHER SMALL FARMS around Alabama, Delona Patterson's eighty acres were largely self-supporting. The principal cash crop was cotton. There was always plenty to eat. He raised corn and had a vegetable garden. There were chickens and milk cows. There was a fruit orchard in the backyard, along with scuppernong vines and beehives. Occasionally he would slaughter a calf so the family would have fresh meat. They canned the fruit and vegetables. There was no refrigeration. They hung the meat in the smokehouse and kept perishables like milk and butter from spoiling by letting them down in a bucket into the well.

The same was true of their neighbors. "We raised everything we ate," Sibyl Burnette recalled. "If beans were in season we ate beans till the beans was gone." It was a hard life. The Piedmont soil around Goldville was not the best for agriculture. "The bottoms are fairly good, but cotton don't grow well here," John Patterson explained. "Grows about knee-high, and you have to bend over to pick it. It's terrible to pick that stuff. You've got to pay to fertilize it, and if you got a bale to the acre you could consider yourself fortunate." His Uncle Lafayette said about growing up on a hardscrabble farm, "You just plowed and hoed . . . you have no idea."[26] Their description of hoeing out a living on Piedmont soil brought to mind a tune by a banjo-picking Grand Ole Opry star of that era, Uncle Dave Macon, that went something like this: "eleven-cent cotton, forty-cent meat. How in the world will a po' man eat."

Small Piedmont farmers were one crop away from ruin. A drought could have wiped them out. Banks weren't going to loan them money. "There was no economic safety net in those days. You made it on your own or went to the poor house," Patterson pointed out. He was proud of the fact that his grandparents had raised seven children on the home place, and all but two went to college and all were reasonably successful. Just surviving under those conditions was no mean accomplishment. But, as the title of a more recent song made famous by Hank Williams, Jr., says, "A Country Boy Can Survive." Patterson credits his growing up on the farm with helping him tough it through five major campaigns in World War II.[27]

His Aunt Grace, who was living at home when her nephew spent his early years there, recalled that he took naturally to rural life and work on the farm. "He wanted to be just like his grandfather," she said. After he became of school age and joined his parents, he returned each summer to the farm until he was in his late teens. He learned to shoulder responsibility early in his life, and helped his grandparents with the plowing, planting, and harvesting. "His grandparents depended on him to do many of the chores on the farm and sent him on errands normally requiring older boys," she said. "On days when the work was caught up or it was too wet to work in the fields, John rambled in the woods or whiled the time away around the farm house."[28]

Patterson described the farm regimen: "Grandpa would get up about three in the morning. And I would get up around four. Then we'd have breakfast—a couple of boiled eggs, biscuits, jam, and butter. He'd have coffee. I'd drink a glass of milk. Then we'd go to the field. In the summertime, he'd knock off about ten o'clock, come to the house, and we'd have lunch. Then he'd take a nap, and he'd sit on the front porch in his rocking chair and read his Bible. About four in the afternoon we'd go back to the field and work until about dark. Then we'd come back in and get a bite and go to bed." They had no outhouse. "You did your business in the barn," he said.[29]

His grandmother dipped snuff, which was a common practice in those days, although not in public. She preferred Brewton snuff when she could get it. "She used a little brush made out of twigs from a black gum tree to stir and moisten the snuff before putting it in her mouth," he recalled.[30] "She was very petite, and very gentle," one of her granddaughters said. "I never heard her raise her voice, except to call the men from the field or to call the children to supper." She was a good seamstress who made lace curtains for the windows and sewed the family's clothes.[31]

His grandfather chewed Lucky Joe tobacco. Sometimes when he was sitting in his rocking chair on the porch reading his Bible he would drop off to sleep. When he did, tobacco juice would drool from his mouth onto the Bible. Later in life his grandson John had the Bible rebound and used it to administer oaths of office, conduct marriage ceremonies, and in other official ceremonies. "You can look through the Bible and see the spots where his tobacco juice drooled down onto the pages. You can tell from these spots his favorite parts of the Bible, the parts he read the most," he said. "I wouldn't take nothing for that Bible."[32]

FOR A YOUNG BOY, the farm was an isolated life. "You'd hear a car coming, you could hear it a long way off, and you'd run to the road just to watch it go by," he remembered. His grandparent's mail was delivered to a relative's house in New Site two miles away. They would walk down on Sunday and pick it up. The rolling store came around on a regular basis, every week or so. "Grandpa and grandma would save their eggs and sell them to Mr. Allen who ran the rolling store. They used the money to buy coffee and sugar and things they needed from him. We'd all go out there and grandpa would buy me a nickel box of Cracker Jacks."[33]

Allen operated the rolling store out of New Site from the 1920s until around 1937. His son Hoyt used to make the rounds with his father. They peddled their wares all week, then drove to town on Saturday and restocked the store. "We put up coffee in pound-and-a-half sacks and weighed out sugar in five-pound brown bags," Hoyt recalled. "He got five cents a quart for kerosene. I forget what he got for a gallon." Everybody in north Tallapoosa County knew his father. "My daddy's name was Marvin, but nobody called him that," Hoyt said. "They just called him 'Peddler.'"[34]

He remembered stopping by the Patterson farm once a week. They usually stopped down on the road, but sometimes drove up to the house to load corn they bought from the Pattersons. "Mr. Patterson traded eggs to my father for coffee, sugar, pepper, and things he couldn't raise on the farm," he said. "Sold us a lot of corn too. He was a good farmer and neat. Used to clean up the corn and put it in sacks. Had it just so. We brought it back and shelled it, put it in sacks and sold it to wholesale houses."[35]

Sometimes the rolling store would have copies of newspapers or magazines for sale. Patterson said his grandfather loved to read and sometimes bought magazines or the *Grit* newspaper. His favorite magazine was the *Country Gentleman*, which was published in Birmingham, but occasionally there were copies of *True Confessions* and other magazines around the house. They didn't own a radio. Mr. William Hand bought the first radio in the community, and neighbors would sometimes go up at night and listen to his radio. When Lafayette Patterson was a member of Congress he mailed copies of the *Congressional Record* to his parents. After reading the *Congressional Record* they used the backs of the pages, which were blank, to write letters on. Nothing went to waste.[36]

They heated bath water by letting it sit in the sun during the week so they could take a bath on Saturday night. John Patterson recalled that every time he'd drink water out of the well, he'd pour a couple of bucketfuls into a washtub they kept on the back porch for that purpose. The rest of the week, his grandmother made him sit down on the back steps and wash his feet in a pan before going to bed. His grandmother grew lots of flowers, and during dry spells he drew buckets of water from the well and watered the flower beds. On rare occasions when the well went dry, they would tote water from a stream and a spring located over the hill approximately a mile away from the house.[37]

His Aunt Grace, whose married name was Harry, recalled that as her nephew grew older he shouldered more and more of the farm work every summer. "He made a pet out of almost every animal on the farm," she said. "He and his grandfather knew where just about every bird nest on the farm was and watched them carefully until the young birds hatched and left the nest. He wouldn't destroy a bird nest for anything." He kept a 410-gauge shotgun at the farm, which he used for squirrel and rabbit hunting. He learned how to trap animals, but did not use traps that would snare or maim. "I found out how cruel it was," he said. Instead, an uncle taught him how to build a trap to catch quail without harming them. He would set the traps where the quail entered the cornfields. "The quail would stay together bunched up, and you could trap the whole covey at one time," he explained.[38]

He sometimes attended church services with his grandparents, either the Bethlehem Primitive Baptist Church in New Site or the Valley Grove Primitive Baptist Church north of Goldville. "The churches were a big gathering place for everybody in the community," he recalled. "They'd usually have services once a month, and there would be mules and horses and buggies all over creation." Everybody would bring food and they would have dinner on the grounds. In the back of the buggy, there was a built-in box where fodder and corn were kept. When people arrived at the church, they would unhook the mules and tie them to the rear wheel so the mules could eat the fodder and corn while their owners were attending church.[39]

Aunt Grace described young John as "an unusually bright child." She said he could talk plainly when he was eighteen months old and could read and write at an early age. Before starting to school he printed legible letters to his father, who was away at college. When he last wrote a letter to his parents from the farm in Goldville, he was fifteen years old. In the summer of 1936 he wrote them that he had arrived at his grandparent's house just in time for dinner. He had ridden the train from Phenix City to Alexander City, where he got off and started walking. "I caught a ride about a mile out of town and rode to New Site and walked the rest of the way (four miles)," he wrote. "Grandma and Grandpa are alright. The weeds have took the place."[40]

His grandfather suffered from a chronic kidney infection, was in failing health, and could no longer keep the place up. He died of kidney failure in November of the following year. Sixteen-year-old John was there at the time. In the years ahead he often thought his grandfather's death had marked the end of an era. The war clouds were already building over Europe and Asia, but his grandfather did not live to see the great changes that World War II would bring or those already underway at home by the Roosevelt administration. The promise of rural electricity—FDR established the Rural Electrification Administration in 1935 to bring electricity and telephone service to farmers—and paved farm roads were but two of the advancements that would dramatically alter postwar rural life in America.

John Patterson's close ties to his grandparents and the old home place could not repress the curious nature and adventurous spirit he had as a child. Growing up was a healthy blend of learning to be responsible, independent, and self-reliant, while nurturing a natural curiosity for the larger world. Many were the times he roamed the fields and thought how in the world was he going to get away. "I plotted that all the time," he recalled. "Finally, when I did get away, finished high school and joined the Army, and escaped from it, I always wanted to come back."[41]

Up the road from the old Patterson place there is a clearing that delights passersby with a breathtaking view of verdant foothills unrolling northward as far as the eye can see. On some mornings a stubborn mist clings to the faraway tree tops, waiting to burn out in the noonday sun, or rises mystically to be borne away by the wind. On a rare day when the air is still and the view unobstructed, the sprawling Cheaha wilderness reaches out for miles in the direction of Alabama's highest peak hiding in the distant forestland. To a barefoot boy stuck on a lonely farm with only dreams and a vivid imagination, this vista inevitably became more than a portal to the mysteries of the lower Appalachian chain. It was his window to the world.

2

WHEN ALL THE LEAVES WERE GREEN

In the late summer of 1927 a new world opened up for five-year-old John Patterson when he enrolled in the first grade in the town of Rockford, thirty miles down the road in neighboring Coosa County. To the excited youngster who rarely traveled far from his grandparent's farm, it was the start of a grand adventure. Not only was he attending school for the first time, but he would be living full-time with his parents. His mother taught the sixth grade in Rockford, and his father was the high school principal.

The Rockford grammar school was in a new, sturdy wood-frame structure on Nixburg Road. The school closed in the early 1960s, but the old building was restored and today serves as a community center. Three quarters of a century have passed, but the former governor recalls his first year of school in the friendly town as if it were yesterday. His teacher was Mrs. Nell McEwen, whose husband John was raised on the old McEwen homeplace on Hatchet Creek north of town.[1]

Miles further up Hatchet Creek the woods and fields were rich in Patterson family history. In the northeast corner of Coosa County, where the creek flows down from Talladega National Forest, a heartbeat beyond present-day Goodwater, was where John Love Patterson's brother Malcolm settled in the 1830s and where their father Buffalo Dan lived out his final years. Their graves rest in a cemetery beside the Presbyterian Church that Malcolm helped found when he moved to Hatchet Creek from North Carolina.[2]

The year that John attended the first grade in Rockford, the family boarded and lived in a hotel owned and operated by the King family on Main Street (they later roomed in the King residence next door to the Methodist Church). He remembered eating at the large family-style tables at the hotel. "They served great, great food there," he said. "I had the run of the town." He recalled an amusing story about his father standing in as a football coach. The high school had trouble hiring a coach, so his father, without any prior coaching experience, put a team together. To give his players more confidence, his father arranged a practice game with some of the larger boys from the grammar school. "In those days a lot of fellows went to grammar school who were grown, chewed tobacco and stuff," he explained. "The grade school went over to play the high school and beat them. My mother ragged my daddy about that for the rest of his life."[3]

Everybody walked to school, and the rooms were heated by pot-bellied wood stoves. There were no water fountains or indoor toilets since the town had no running water. The students brought their own cups and drank from a spring near the school. Behind the school there were separate outhouses for the boys and the girls. Some of the older boys got John in trouble one time when they tricked him into going inside the girls' outhouse. After seeing girls enter the outhouse the boys told John it was empty and dared him to open the door and look inside. When the girls went running and screaming to the teacher, he got his first and only paddling from Mrs. McEwen.[4]

A man who always used time judiciously, John's father earned a law degree by correspondence from Cumberland Law School while serving as school administrator. Cumberland was then in Lebanon, Tennessee, a good day's train ride from Rockford (today the school is at Samford University in Birmingham). In 1928, after passing the bar exam, Albert moved his family to Opelika and started a law practice with attorney O. P. Lee, a classmate from the University of Alabama. Lee, also a WWI veteran, was a couple of years younger than his law partner. He was so eager to serve in the Army during the war that he had lied about his age. The two men remained close friends for life.

When the Pattersons moved to Opelika they rented an apartment in the middle of town. Soon afterward they bought a three-bedroom stucco house in a residential area named Alta Vista. It was the first home Albert Patterson ever owned. John attended the second grade in Opelika. The family made many friends in town, but his father soon found there was not enough legal business to support another attorney. In early 1929, with his wife expecting another child, Albert Patterson sold the house in Opelika and moved his family to Alexander City, where he opened his own law office.

The family's brief stay in Opelika coincided with the first presidential election John Patterson remembers. The race was between Republican Herbert Hoover and Democrat Alfred E. Smith. Al Smith, four-time governor of New York, was unpopular in Alabama because he was Catholic. This had not discouraged Albert Patterson, who was a dyed-in-the-wool Democrat and campaigned hard for Al Smith anyway. "I remember wearing an Al Smith button myself," John said. He learned a valuable lesson from his father that a man's race or religion was not what counted, but the cut of the man himself.[5]

WHILE ALEXANDER CITY HAD fewer residents than Opelika, the Russell Mills area outside of town more than made up the difference. According to 1930 census figures, Alexander City claimed a population of 4,500 people compared to Opelika's 6,100. But when the families living in Russell's mill villages were counted, Alexander City had just under 7,500 residents within a mile and a half from the center of town. The population of the town itself had more than doubled since the end of World War I.[6]

In January 1929 Albert Patterson leased an office over the Alexander City Bank. The family joined him soon afterward. The *Alexander City Outlook* reported that attorney Patterson had expressed "deep appreciation" for the many courtesies that the citizens of Opelika had shown him and the family. He stated that he "never expected to reside in a finer city or among better people." In neighboring Rockford the *Chronicle* also announced that the town's former school principal had opened a law practice in Alexander City. When he made a brief visit back to the Rockford community in March, the *Chronicle* reported, "His friends here are always glad to see him and hope that he will be a more frequent visitor."[7]

At the end of their first summer in Alexander City, John's father moved his office from the Alexander City Bank building to the courthouse where he leased space formerly occupied by the county sheriff and where he practiced for the next four years. The move to Alexander City brought the family nearer to Goldville where they could help look after Albert Patterson's aging parents Mollie and Delona. Also John's mother Agnes had grown up on the outskirts of town, and still had siblings living nearby. After her mother's death, her father had eventually remarried and moved back to north Alabama.

Albert Patterson's return to Tallapoosa County was not without adversity, however. The family had been back only a few months when the stock market crash of October 1929 sent economic shock waves around the globe. The collapse of the U.S. economy and the onset of the Great Depression brought hard times to the Deep South and across the nation. Even those banks that survived the crisis had no money to lend. Unable to purchase another home, the Pattersons rented houses in Alexander City (on Semmes Street and Marshal Street) during the five years they resided there. While the family struggled to make ends meet, they were better off than some of their neighbors. Albert's small disability pension helped put food on the table during this bleak period.[8]

Albert and Agnes Patterson did not let the hardships spoil their plans to have more children. In March 1929 Agnes gave birth to their second son, Maurice.

The following year she bore a third son, Samuel, in the house on Semmes Street. John attended the third and fourth grades while the family lived there. Among his playmates were the two young daughters of the Dean family living next door. They learned to roller-skate together on the sidewalk in front of their houses. John also suffered through two life-threatening childhood illnesses—scarlet fever and diphtheria—in the house on Semmes Street. A stern official from the health department posted a large quarantine sign on the house. "That was embarrassing for the family," John recalled.[9]

The Pattersons attended the First Methodist Church located a couple of blocks from their residence. The prominent red-brick structure, with some renovations, still stands today. John's parents took him to church every Sunday, and saw to it that he attended vacation bible school during the summer as well as all revivals held at the church. The hellfire-and-brimstone revivals of that era were community events, and regardless of denomination the churches were packed. One visiting evangelist left a lasting impression on the young boy, teaching him a lesson he never forgot.[10]

Arriving late on the first night of the revival John had to sit in the front pew. No sooner had he taken his seat than the evangelist fixed his gaze on the faithful flock sitting down front and in a kindly voice wanted to know how many in the congregation had read the twenty-third chapter of John. When the hands of the grownups around him went up, young John did not want to be left out so he hesitantly raised his hand, too. The clergyman's cherubic demeanor changed dramatically. With piercing eyes and furrowed brow, shaking beads of perspiration from his shock of silver hair, he glared straight at young Patterson seated in front and shook his head in mock reproach. Then he lifted his arms to the congregation, closed his eyes and prayed, "Heavenly father, forgive these sinners who lied about reading the holy word. Worshipers who truly read the good book know there is no such thing as the twenty-third chapter of John."

"You never saw hands drop so fast," Patterson said. A gasp went through the congregation like letting air out of a balloon. As everyone turned to see whose hand was raised, the organist began to play a resounding "come-to-Jesus" hymnal and the preacher exhorted the congregation to heed the words of his sermon—that the eternal fires of hell burned with the souls of sinners who bore false witness and told lies. "That preacher had us all squirming in our seats," he laughed. The experience not only impressed on him the virtue of telling the truth, but also taught two other lessons that would serve him well in life. One lesson was to never blindly follow the crowd. The other was to arrive early and not have to sit on the front pew.[11]

PRACTICING LAW IN THE county where he grew up held obvious advantages for Albert's budding political aspirations. His brother Lafayette, whose residence was in Alexander City, represented Alabama's Fifth District in the U.S. House of Representatives. Lafayette was a respected congressman, and his campaign for a second term in 1930 went unchallenged. That same year Albert made his first bid for elective office when he ran for one of Tallapoosa County's two seats in the Alabama House of Representatives. He lost the election, but made a respectable showing by receiving 1,262 votes against 1,725 and 2,441 that were cast for the two winners.[12]

Albert Patterson remained active in politics, and in November 1931 he organized and led a delegation comprised of Judge C. J. Coley and several other prominent citizens to call on Franklin D. Roosevelt who was vacationing in Warm Springs, Georgia. In a thirty-minute chat with the New York governor, the group asked his assent to form an organization in north Alabama to support his nomination for the U.S. Presidency. Roosevelt gave the standard response that he was too busy at the moment being governor of New York "to think of national politics," but thanked his Alabama supporters and did not discourage them from working for his nomination. They returned home convinced that Roosevelt was the right person to lead the nation out of the Great Depression, and that he would be the next President of the United States.[13]

Agnes Patterson shared her husband's strong sense of civic duty and social consciousness. She and her husband, by word and by example, instilled these values in their children. One of her prized possessions was a small book listing the bylaws for a club that her son John organized when he was ten years old. He had printed the bylaws on Blue Horse tablet paper and bound the pages in cardboard. "If you are asked to do a thing on a program or anything else, don't deny it, but do it," one of the rules read. Other rules were: "Do not cuss or it will make the whole club go wrong. Obey the president and other officers of the club. If elected as an officer don't quit on anything, but do it. Make good grades in school, and you will rank high in the club. Never disobey the laws of the club."[14]

Family values were the core of young John's upbringing. His parents taught him to work hard and to be a responsible member of the community. Once when the youngster missed the payment on a bicycle he had purchased on an installment plan, his father admonished him not to let dark come without the payment being made. The money was in the proper hands before sundown. "You must earn and pay for everything you get," his father lectured him. "The world doesn't owe you a living."[15]

John took his father's words to heart. The enterprising youngster got his first paying job when he was ten years old. Major H. R. Wiseman gave John a paper route delivering the *Birmingham News* after school. The newspapers sold for a nickel a paper. When they had a few papers left over, he and the other paperboys would go downtown and sell them to guests staying at the Russell Hotel. The two-story brick hotel down from the railroad station was a busy place, he recalled. "People trading with the Russell Corporation would come and stay there," he said. "The management didn't want us in there, but we'd sell our papers real quick in the hotel dining room and reception area, and slip out before they caught us."[16]

By the time he was twelve John had established a credit account in his name at Frohsin's Department Store. "Mr. Ralph Frohsin was the first person who ever extended credit to me," he recalled. "I'd buy my clothes, shoes and jackets and things, and pay for them at a rate of fifty cents to a dollar a week from the earnings from my paper route." He saw that as an important part of growing up, for a young person to learn to take care of their personal business. He had the highest respect for Frohsin, and continued to buy clothes there after he grew up and became governor. "He was always my friend," he recalled. "I never had a stronger person working for me when I ran for governor."[17]

What he didn't learn at home John picked up in school, in church, or in other community activities. He attended the third through the eighth grades while living in Alexander City. When he was in the eighth grade he got his second whipping, for misbehaving in school. I. I. Fox, who was coach and principal, was a strict disciplinarian. "He swung a lot harder than Mrs. McEwen," Patterson said. "He taught me a real lesson, and I never acted up in school after that." In later years they became friends, and when Patterson became governor Coach Fox never let him forget the whipping. "I told him that whipping was probably responsible for my being governor," Patterson laughed.[18]

"Alex City was a special place to live as a young boy," he said. "You couldn't ask for better people or a better town." As a boy growing up there, John was described as being independent as well as friendly and outgoing. "He walked with his head high, shoulders straight, looking everybody in the eye," a family friend recalled. "In some ways he was unyielding. He wouldn't bow to anyone. He'd ask for something just one time. If he didn't get it he'd walk away." A relative stated that Albert Patterson taught his sons not to be afraid of anyone or anything. Their father did not know the meaning of fear, the relative said. The word was not in his vocabulary.[19]

Young John got to know everybody in town, including Ben Russell, the founder of Russell Mills who also owned the Russell Hotel and the First National Bank, and whose brother T. C. Russell was mayor. Every morning except Sunday, Russell would go to his office at the textile mill, and then about nine or ten o'clock he would leave and walk down the middle of the railroad track to the center of town where he would cut across and go in the back door of his bank. On Saturday mornings John would go down that same railroad track when he was collecting from customers on his paper route. Their paths sometimes crossed in the middle of the railroad track.

"Mr. Ben Russell would always stop and talk to me," he recalled. "The first time I ever met him, he stopped and asked me who I was and who my folks were? From then on he knew my name. He would stop and talk to me, call me by name. Man, that made me feel important, I'll tell you. He was the biggest fella' in town and knew my name. I would go home and tell my folks that, and they wouldn't hardly believe it." They were impressed that the town's most influential citizen would take the time to stop and talk to him. "We never know whose lives we touch," he said. "As grown-ups we need to think about that."[20]

No ONE WHO LIVED in Alexander City in those days would ever forget the sights and sounds of the railroad. The dual tracks of the Central of Georgia Railway Company ran through the middle of town, and the handsome red-brick railroad station next to the town square was the hub of business activity. There was no end to passenger and freight trains passing through. Most people walked wherever they were going in Alexander City, but when going out of town they rode the trains. Bus service in rural Alabama in the 1920s and early 1930s was neither popular nor reliable. Dealers had new automobiles for sale—they ranged in price from about $500 for Chevrolet Phaetons and Roadsters to over $1,000 for a Hupmobile Six four-door sedan—but few could afford them and the rutted dirt roads and streets shook them into disrepair after only a few years. The only filling station in town pumped Woco Pep gasoline, a Wofford Oil Company product containing a benzol additive that was a byproduct of Birmingham steelmaking. The company advertised Woco Pep as the "King of Motor Fuels," but Patterson remembered it having a purplish color and smelling like "rotten eggs."[21]

The area's economic development had been so reliant on the railroad that grateful citizens had changed the town's name from Youngville to Alexander City in honor of Edward Porter Alexander, president of the Savannah and Memphis Railroad, when the S&M laid its lines westward into the county from Georgia through Opelika in the early 1870s. Delona Patterson told his grandson about being there in 1874 when large, jostling crowds gathered from across the county to see the first excursion train loaded with dignitaries steam into Alexander City. Around noon that day, the train came chugging around the bend from the direction of Dadeville and blew its whistle. When it did the buggies and horses and wagons went flying in every direction, like a scene out of an early western movie.[22]

The bustling train station was one of the places where boys used to hang out when they had nothing else to do. "We'd come down here and sit on those tall baggage carts and watch the trains come through," John recalled. "There were double tracks here then, and there would be five or six passenger trains going north and five or six going south every day. And there were two express trains going each way—north to Birmingham and on to Chicago and south to Savannah, Jacksonville, and Miami." When the trains came through the boys would stare in awe at the well-dressed people in the dining cars with their fancy tables, shining silver, spotless tablecloths, and waiters in tails. "We used to wonder if we'd ever get to travel on a train like that," he said. "I remember that very, very well."[23]

The hoboes who rode the rails also held a fascination for John and his friends. "When I was a boy there were a lot of hoboes on the trains. Sometimes a train would go by, and there would be a hundred or more hoboes on the train. It was during the Depression and people didn't have money. So they'd just hobo, get on the trains and ride them. I ran into some pretty famous hoboes who came through Alex City. I remember one whose name was Montana Slim. He and the others led interesting lives."[24]

On Fridays and Saturdays boys sometimes ambled across the railroad tracks and hung out around the large parking lot that came alive shortly after daybreak with wagons and mules and buggies and people who had come to town to trade and shop. "People would come from all over and bring their animals to trade," he said. "They'd bring goats, chickens and everything else and haul them down there. They'd just camp out there all day and do their trading. I liked to go down there and wander around and visit with people and look at their animals."[25]

Another place he frequented was a huge mule barn located around the back of the other stores. A man named Burton sold and traded mules there. John and his friends spent some interesting and entertaining hours with Mr. Burton and his mules. When they had spare change they might stop after school at Carlisle's Drug Store. Still in business today, Carlisle's was a landmark that existed before he or his schoolmates were born. "They served the best milk shakes you ever tasted and still do," he said. At the time the high school hang-out was across the street at Nick's Cafe. "The mark of becoming a man," he said, "was to walk in there by yourself and get up on a stool and order a hot dog and pay for it yourself."[26]

Less than a block away stood the Strand Theater, owned and operated by Mr. Mack Jackson. "We ended the week in the make-believe world of the Saturday matinees," he said. "All of us boys would go and see the westerns—Tom Mix, Buck Jones, and Johnny Mack Brown—and then go back and play cowboys and Indians around town." They could not afford tickets every week, though the movies only cost ten cents on Friday and fifteen cents on Saturday. So they pooled their pennies to purchase a single ticket for one member of the group. After he entered the theater and they dimmed the lights to start the movie, he went around behind the stage and took the bar off the back door to let the others in. They always figured that Mr. Jackson knew what was going on but let them get away with it because times were hard for everybody during the Depression years.[27]

John enjoyed all the westerns, but his favorite was MGM's 1930 silent film *Billy the Kid* because it starred Johnny Mack Brown in the title role along with Wallace Beery as Sheriff Pat Garrett. Johnny Mack Brown was from Dothan, Alabama, and had been an All-American running back on the Crimson Tide football team at the same time John's father attended the university. One season the football star was in danger of losing his scholarship because he was failing his math class. Albert Patterson, who was an honor student and later taught math, tutored Johnny Mack Brown in math so he could pass the course and play football.[28]

The tutoring paid off when Brown led the Crimson Tide to victory against the favored Washington Huskies in the 1926 Rose Bowl. He scored two of the Tide's three touchdowns, and his rugged good looks caught the eye of Hollywood agents. He went to Hollywood in 1927 and became a star at MGM. After World

War II when John Patterson attended the University of Alabama, he met Brown's daughter on campus but did not know her well. Then in 1960, while he was governor and heading up the Alabama delegation at the Democratic National Convention in Los Angeles, he had a visit from the aging movie star himself.[29]

"I was staying in a suite at the Ambassador Hotel in Beverly Hills," Patterson recalled. "One day I got a call from Johnny Mack Brown saying he wanted to come up and see me." The governor was delighted to see the former matinee idol, but could tell that he was down on his luck. Brown was only in his late fifties, but looked older and his health was bad. "He asked me for a job," Patterson said. "He caught me completely off guard. I didn't have any jobs readily available. I told him so, and I turned him down." Patterson said he regretted that for the rest of his life. "Looking back on that, I should have given him a job even if I had to create one. I could have done it, and I regret very much that I didn't do that. That's been on my mind for many, many years."[30]

WHILE LIVING IN ALEXANDER City John visited his grandparents in Goldville as often as he could. Delona and Mollie were getting on in years, and his grandfather's health was failing. They came to stay with their son Albert and his family for awhile in the house on Marshal Street. The house was on a lot that had enough acreage for Delona to do a little farming. He kept his cows and chickens there, and grew corn and vegetables that were so good they received special mention in the *Alexander City Outlook*. The old folks soon became homesick for their farm and friends, however, and insisted on returning to Goldville.

On one of John's visits with his grandparents, he and his grandmother were the innocent victims of a police raid on a neighbor's house just up the road. "Grandma and I would walk and visit neighbors when I was there," he explained. "One day we were visiting Malvin Jones and his wife Elsie who lived with their three daughters in a little unpainted house up the road when federal and state revenuers busted in looking for moonshine." It was no secret that Malvin made liquor for a living because he had no other obvious means of support, Patterson said. [31]

Even as a young boy John knew that being raided was the chance Malvin Jones took by breaking the law, but he was disturbed by the way the agents carried out the raid—discourteous, bullying, practically tearing the house apart, and trampling on people's rights. "Suddenly these automobiles pulled into the yard, men jumped out of them and came busting into the house. They started going through the drawers throwing things around, opening trunks and throwing the contents out, and just trashed the whole place," he recalled. The revenuers didn't find any liquor because the only moonshine in the house was a half-filled jug on the kitchen table where John and his grandmother were seated with their hosts and Elsie Jones got rid of the evidence before the men reached the kitchen.[32]

Beside the table was a slop bucket where the family discarded scraps from the table to be fed to the hogs. Elsie grabbed the jug and emptied the contents into the bucket. She then poured kerosene on top of it to kill the smell of the moonshine. When the revenuers didn't find any illegal liquor, they stomped back out to their cars and drove away, not bothering to straighten up the mess they'd made inside the house. "I remembered that all my life," Patterson said. "I thought it was an awful way to treat somebody who was poor and had no way to defend themselves and nobody to look after their interests. It's not like that today, but back then you were completely at the mercy of the law."[33]

"We've come a long way since then, but we still have a way to go," he said thoughtfully. "The law has to be tempered with compassion. We do a pretty good job of that today. But we have to guard those rights carefully, and not backslide." Many families in Tallapoosa County back then were like Malvin and Elsie Jones. They were neighborly and mostly law-abiding with the exception of eking out a living in hard times by making moonshine. "Malvin and Elsie had a lot of character, and people around there liked them," he said.[34]

Another fact of life growing up in a small town is that friends you make are friends for life. "Everybody knows everybody, and people take care of each other," Patterson reflected.[35] One of his grammar school friends was Floyd Mann, who later served in his cabinet as head of the department of public safety. Mann's associates in Montgomery remembered him as a first-rate lawman who was mischievous and good-humored. Folks from Tallapoosa County said he came by those traits naturally.

The Pattersons and the Manns were related through marriage. In 1914 John's Uncle Lafayette had married Nancy Jane "Nannie" Mann of Daviston, Alabama. The first year they were wed the couple lived on her father's Sweetwater farm between Daviston and Dadeville. Their oldest daughter Geraldine ("Gerry"), was born there in 1915. She described her grandfather Mann as a jovial, caring person who loved to kid around and make people laugh. "Grandpa Mann's family were wonderful people," she said.[36]

One member of the Mann family who was known throughout the county for his good humor and country wit was Floyd's Uncle Perry. "Folks in Alex City could of written a book about Uncle Perry Mann," Patterson said. "He was sort of the town wit. Almost every day when the weather was good you'd find him over across the street from Carlisle's Drug Store in front of Mitchell's Barbershop where I got my first haircut." One day a well-dressed stranger pulled up in front of the barbershop and asked where he could find the Church of God in town. Uncle Perry stroked his chin and said, "Well, let me see now." He pointed to the First Baptist Church where the Russell family worshiped. "Now you see that church up yonder, that's Mr. Russell's church." He then pointed toward two other churches attended by prominent families in town. "Now that church over yonder is the Carlisle church, and that one over there, that's the Coley church." He scratched his head and grinned. "You know, come to think of it, God ain't got no church in Alex City."

Another Uncle Perry Mann story poked fun at the *Alexander City Outlook*, the town's only newspaper since the 1890s and still in print today, and the Climax Cafe, a popular eating place that has long since closed down. One day Uncle Perry got sick and went to see Doctor Street whose office was in a little white frame house where the post office was later built. Doctor Street prescribed some medicine and said, "Perry, I tell you what I want you to do. I want you to go home and I want you to stay there until you get better and I don't want nothing on your stomach or nothing on your mind." Uncle Perry said, "Well that'll be easy, Doc. I'll eat at the Climax Cafe and read the Alex City *Outlook*." After a couple of weeks he got better and showed back up at Mitchell's Barbershop. A friend said, "Why it's good to see you Uncle Perry. I'd heard you was dead." "Yeah, I heard that, too," Uncle Perry replied. "I knew it was a damned lie the minute I heard it."[37]

Uncle Perry's repartee exemplified the easygoing way of life in Alexander City and other small Southern towns of that era. Life was idyllic for the young people growing up, the hardships of the Great Depression notwithstanding. "Folks didn't have nothing, but they didn't want for nothing either," Patterson recalled. "Our folks couldn't afford store-bought toys and stuff, so we made our own. We whittled out wooden guns that had clothes pins for triggers and cut-up inner tubes for ammunition."

He couldn't afford a stamp collection, so he foraged through the trash bin outside the post office collecting postmarks off discarded junk mail. "Things we had to play with might not of been as good as store-bought stuff, but they had more meaning. Kind of a spiritual thing, you might say. A rite of passage of sorts."[38]

But the idyll couldn't last. Stirred by the lonesome sound of a train at night, the dining cars with their fancy clientele, the hoboes, the movie screen, photographs in a book, the shape of a cloud, a shooting star, the town's young people dreamed of faraway places and grown-up things. Family breadwinners wanted more for their children when Franklin Delano Roosevelt became the thirty-second president in 1933. FDR's New Deal started the nation on its journey toward recovery and gave people hope. John Patterson's father began to look elsewhere for a more lucrative law practice. In 1933 he made a fateful decision to move his family to Phenix City, Alabama, which enjoyed a profitable military trade from soldiers stationed at Fort Benning, sitting across the Chattahoochee River near Columbus, Georgia.

IF THERE WAS A blight on life in small Southern towns when he was growing up, it had to be the social injustices of the Jim Crow laws that were on the books at the time. Other regions were guilty of *de facto* racial discrimination, but the *de jure* segregation practiced in the Deep South was more of a cultural phenomenon. The term "Jim Crow" (the name of a song sung in a blackface minstrel show) was in itself a disparagement of blacks in Southern states. The first laws applied to railway passengers, but spread over time to every facet of Southern life. The U.S. Supreme Court validated the early Jim Crow laws in 1896 when it ruled in *Plessy v. Ferguson* that "a Louisiana statute requiring 'separate but equal' accommodations for white and black railroad passengers did not conflict with the Fourteenth Amendment clause guaranteeing all citizens equal protection of the laws."[39]

In the Patterson home there was never any discriminatory talk "against anybody because of their religion or their race or anything else." His parents would not tolerate it. They always insisted that their children be kind and respectful of everybody. He believed the same was true of most families living in the Alexander City area. There was no organized Ku Klux Klan activity present, or if there was he didn't know about it.

In small towns and rural communities of the pre-WWII period few people questioned racial segregation. Patterson said he rarely saw black people in white neighborhoods or in the center of town when he was growing up. The passenger trains had separate compartments for whites and blacks and the railroad station had separate waiting rooms. Everything in town was segregated down to the water fountains and rest rooms—one marked for Whites and one for Colored. Black patrons at the Strand Theater had to sit in the balcony. Even blacks who were thrown in jail were segregated. "We used to pass by the city jail on the way home from school," he recalled. "It was a one-story brick building with two doors opening to the outside. Whites were put in one side and blacks in the other. We'd come by there and peek through the bars to see who was in jail. Sometimes we'd tease the drunks and they'd cuss us out."

Black families lived in black communities, worshipped at black churches, and attended black schools. When they died, they were buried in black cemeteries. Patterson said he never realized until he was campaigning for governor that the separate but equal mantra surrounding black schools in Alabama was a myth. He found that the facilities at most black schools and some white schools were a disgrace, a problem that he worked with his cabinet to try and improve.[40]

In 1933 his Uncle Lafayette found out what it meant to be out of step with the "lily-white" political culture in his home state. Lafayette Patterson, according to his nephew, held "liberal, populist views at a time when being a friend of education and welfare was unpopular in state government circles." "Probably his greatest interest was public education, trying to get public education to everybody," his nephew said. He was far ahead of his time on issues like civil rights and voter rights, and told voters he wouldn't run "on a platform of abuse of Negroes and Yankees." "Voters liked him fine, but Alabama politicians didn't," an admiring reporter wrote.[41]

The Alabama legislature was dominated by "Big Mule" and "Black Belt" conservatives in the 1930s, and they were at odds with the congressman because of his populist views. Consequently, when Alabama lost a congressional seat after the 1930 census, the legislature reapportioned the state's congressional districts and "gerrymandered" Lafayette Patterson out of office. He had represented nine counties in east central Alabama, but the new district gave him only three of those counties. By contrast, his opponent in the next election, Miles Allgood, who had been in Congress for almost ten years, retained 70 percent of the voters from his old district. Allgood won the election by 231 votes.[42]

Politically, Lafayette Patterson never recovered from that loss, even though he later held a key position in the Roosevelt administration during WWII and made a quixotic run for the Democratic presidential nomination in 1951—a candidacy "that never really got off the ground." He had stayed true to his populist beliefs at a time when those beliefs were out of favor in his state, and it cost him dearly. At the time, his uncle's politics held little meaning for John, whose thoughts were more on both families moving away from Alexander City. One of his cousins, John Delona, was the same age, and they wouldn't be seeing each other as often as before. A decade later, aviation cadet John Delona Patterson was killed in a plane crash near Douglas, Arizona, five days before he was to receive his commission in the Army Air Forces. The funeral was held on the day he and his fiance were to have been married in Birmingham.[43]

In an interview after his uncle's death in 1988, John Patterson looked back on the time when he was attorney general and the NAACP was in noncompliance with a court order to produce its membership list in Alabama. Birmingham attorney Arthur Shores had suggested he might want to be careful about what he wished for since his Uncle Lafayette's name was on that list. He also recalled that when he was running for governor his uncle came to him and said he ought not to be using race as an issue in the campaign. "If I'd listened to him I wouldn't have been governor," he said. "But you know what. He was right."[44]

3

ACROSS THE CHATTAHOOCHEE

Phenix City was a wide-open gambling town when Albert Patterson moved his family there in October 1933. Two illegal lotteries had been licensed by city hall and operated in plain view on Dillingham Street across the lower Chattahoochee River bridge from Columbus, Georgia. A dozen or more casinos, honky tonks, and night clubs openly violated state laws by trafficking in various forms of gambling and vice, including B-girls and prostitutes. The jingle of nickel, dime, and quarter slot machines—taking in more profit than the cash drawers—could be heard in stores and shops all over town. John, who had just turned twelve, described the Phenix City of his youth as a "poor man's Las Vegas" preying mostly on soldiers from Fort Benning, Georgia, and college students from Auburn.[1]

"The Fort Benning payroll was large enough to pump up the economy on both sides of the Chattahoochee River," he explained. Counting the artillery units and students attending the infantry schools, Fort Benning housed the equivalent of three full regiments—including the white 29th Infantry and the black 24th Infantry. The nightly parade of GIs crossing the Fourteenth Street Bridge and the lower river entrance to Dillingham Street looking for a good time was why "there was plenty of cash floating around Phenix City even during the Depression."[2]

That the Phenix City area had a history of lawlessness going back many years was a matter of public record in libraries and old newspaper morgues around Alabama. Portrayed before the turn of the century as "those cutthroats across the river," the crime-ridden community of Girard had given the northeast corner of Russell County a bad name long before being consolidated with Phenix City in August 1923 by Governor William W. "Plain Bill" Brandon. An infamous haven for bootleggers and the illegal liquor trade, unruly Girard was an eyesore in Phenix City's backyard with only the line between Lee and Russell counties separating them.

In 1916 the lawlessness and illegal liquor activity had become so rampant in Russell County that citizens petitioned Governor Charles Henderson to intervene. When the governor failed to act, Attorney General Logan Martin sent a trainload of armed deputies to Girard to clean the place up. Judge A. H. Alston impaneled a grand jury, and Attorney General Martin picked a young Birmingham attorney named Hugo Black to serve as special prosecutor. They not only successfully convicted and jailed the illegal liquor dealers, but convicted the city marshal for accepting bribes, forced the resignations of the mayor and board of aldermen, and impeached Russell County Sheriff Pal M. Daniel for conspiring with the lawbreakers.[3]

The cleanup forced the criminal elements underground, but they reemerged during the roaring twenties more brazen and defiant than before. In January 1923 Russell County thumbed its nose at the Alabama attorney general's office by reelecting Pal Daniel as sheriff. When murder and mayhem ensued, Governor Brandon sought to resolve the crisis by consolidating Girard and Phenix City in Russell County. The criminals merely repeated their tactic of suspending operations until the heat was off.

By merging the municipalities Governor Brandon had hoped that Phenix City, as the larger and more law-abiding of the two, would change Girard for the good. But at the start of the 1930s Phenix City citizens awoke to find things the other way around. The hard times of the Depression had given local vice lords the edge they needed at city hall. A three-man city commission comprised of Homer Cobb, Dr. Ashley Floyd, and C. L. Gulatt ran city hall. Faced with the prospect of defaulting on Phenix City's bonded debt, the commission licensed gambling and other illegal enterprises to keep the town solvent.[4]

Two local syndicates controlled gambling in Phenix City. The kingpin was Hoyt Shepherd, a shrewd, ruthless Georgia drifter who had teamed up with Jimmie Matthews, the soft-spoken son of an American GI and his English bride, to form the S&M gambling syndicate. The pair ran the Old Reliable Lottery, known as "the bug," and other gambling enterprises out of the Ritz Cafe on Dillingham Street. A third partner named Clyde Yarbrough was a notorious Phenix City figure, allegedly Shepherd's mentor.[5]

Hoyt Shepherd had a shady past, but not the "repeat-offender" rap sheet of his rival C. O. "Head" Revel. A hoodlum who grew up in Phenix City, Revel was a fugitive from Florida and had served time on a Georgia chain gang. He and another Phenix City tough with a long police record, squat, cigar-chomping Godwin Davis, Sr., ran the National Lottery Company and other illegal enterprises, also on Dillingham Street. The lottery operated out of the Bridge Grocery, where not so much as a can of beans could be bought. The phony grocery even housed an underworld classroom, complete with blackboards and visual aids, where petty crooks learned safe-cracking and other tools of the trade.[6]

The flouting of state laws by the criminal elements drew citizen complaints, but no public outcry. Residents were still reeling from the Depression and had yet to fathom the depths of corruption between the vice peddlers and city hall. Phenix City's breadwinners were trapped in the age-old predicament of "going along to get along." They were too concerned with keeping their families clothed and fed to worry about the illegal gambling or what many perceived as a bit of hanky-panky at city hall. By the time FDR and the New Deal led the nation out of the Depression, it would be too late. Phenix City had cast its lot with the gamblers and was now in the clutches of a criminal empire that the syndicates would go to any length to protect.

ALBERT PATTERSON HAD COME to Phenix City seeking a better life for his family. Thirteen years had gone by since the Army doctors released him from the Fort McPherson hospital on crutches, and he was now approaching his fortieth birthday. He had struggled to overcome his crippling war injuries, but still needed help dressing himself and hobbled with the aid of a cane. The handicap had not held him back, however. He set a vigorous pace, working late into the night at the office and at home while giving generously of his time to church and civic activities.

The house the family rented on Broad Street was near the center of town, in walking distance of local businesses, churches, and city hall. Down the street was a Catholic church and on the corner Curt Lakey's service station attendants pumped gas, wiped windshields, and changed tires. A couple of blocks away John's father hung his shingle over the door of a cramped cubicle inside Johnson's Printers on Line Street, a ribbon of narrow pavement straddling the county line between Lee and Russell counties. A short stroll over to Fourteenth Street led down to the rock-strewn banks of the muddy river and across the bridge to Georgia.[7]

Albert's law practice in Phenix City got off to a good start. Within two years he could afford to move his family into their own home, a three-bedroom brick house with a basement apartment, a detached garage, and goldfish ponds out front. The house was located on Pine Circle in a forested hillside residential area not far from Central High School. The owners who lived next door sold the property for $2,400 to avoid foreclosure on the mortgage. Business was good enough for John's father to relocate his law practice from the small printing shop on Line Street to the Phenix-Girard Bank building, and later into a suite of offices on the second floor of the newly constructed Coulter Building near the Russell County Courthouse.[8]

The Phenix-Girard Bank was the only bank in town, and it was owned by C. M. Mullins, a Columbus banker. Mullins had a reputation for being tight-fisted. People who needed to borrow money knew not to go to the Phenix-Girard Bank. They went to the loan sharks on Dillingham Street where they paid exorbitant interest rates. John once heard his father say that Roy Dickinson (a notorious Depression-era bank robber) was the only fellow who ever got any money out of the Phenix-Girard Bank.[9]

The Pattersons joined the Trinity Methodist Church where Albert later served as chairman of the board of stewards. The church was down the street from the Coulter Building and the Elite (pronounced E-Light) Cafe, a block over from Smitty's Grill and the Palace Theater, close to Dobbs Funeral Home. Albert was active in numerous Phenix City civic organizations, including the Lion's Club, the Shriners, the Masons, and was a member of the VFW and American Legion posts. In 1937 he was named to the city school board where he served fifteen years, six as chairman. He also served eleven years as chairman of the Russell County Selective Service Board.[10]

While his passion for politics had not diminished, the elder Patterson put off running for public office again until he got his law practice going and became better established in Russell County. He had followed Franklin Roosevelt's 1932 presidential campaign enthusiastically and sat by the radio when FDR gave his inaugural address in March 1933. He had been in Phenix City only a few months when the telephone rang one day and the voice on the other end said, "Mr. Patterson this is Franklin Roosevelt over at Warm Springs, Georgia. How about getting a carload together and driving over to see me Sunday afternoon."

"You can imagine, that put my father in solid with the party faithful in town," his son stated. "He was a great supporter of FDR, and you couldn't say nothing critical of the President around him. He thought FDR was one of the greatest men who ever lived."[11]

TWELVE-YEAR-OLD JOHN FOUND PHENIX City exciting. They drove on dirt roads to get there from Alexander City, but the streets in downtown Phenix City were paved. "When we got down here Phenix City was a great big place compared to anything I'd ever seen," he recalled. Across the river, Columbus still had streetcars until 1935, with old tracks embedded in the middle of the Fourteenth Street Bridge where they used to come across into Phenix City. "With the Fort Benning soldiers and the gambling and everything, it was an exciting place for a young fellow to live," he said.[12]

John "had the run of the town" for the two years the family lived on Broad Street. He bought his first bicycle on credit from the Sears and Roebuck store in Columbus, and got a job after school and on Saturday delivering groceries for King Grocery located down the street and around the corner from their house. As he got older he worked as a clerk in the store and drove a bread route for Craig's Bakery. "I got to know most of the people in town. I delivered groceries and stuff to the nightclubs and bars and gambling places." He sometimes took his spare change and played the slot machines.[13]

There were no age restrictions on gambling in Phenix City. "When we were growing up, we all played the slot machines. They even had stools for the kids so they could reach them." Some children used their lunch money to play the lottery.[14] Across from the grocery where John worked, a pool hall had betting in the back room and slot machines up front. Unbeknownst to their parents, the pool hall owner let boys hang out there and play the slot machines.[15]

Some Saturdays he would stop by the pool hall before it opened. "I'd come to work before daylight and they'd be cleaning the place up getting ready for another day," he said. "I'd go over there and put one coin in each of the slot machines. Some nights people quit playing them just as they were ready to pay off. I made money that way." He also bought lottery tickets for a penny each, and won seven dollars once.[16]

Dorothy Johnson, a classmate of John's, recalled that her younger brother Fred hung out at the pool hall with the other boys, but he got caught. Fred also worked as a delivery boy at King Grocery. Leland Jones, the manager of the store, had married a Johnson cousin, which could be how Dorothy's mother heard that her son was in the pool hall across the street. Their family attended the same Methodist church as the Pattersons. "My mother called the preacher. We had this preacher that we thought whatever he said was gospel. He went over to the poolroom and got my brother out," Dorothy said. "Fred told me he never went back in there after that."[17]

"[Girls] didn't have the freedom that boys had back then," Dorothy said. Good girls didn't go out alone at night, and their parents shielded them from the vice in Phenix City. One of the few places her mother let the girls go unaccompanied was the Columbus Public Library located just across the Fourteenth Street Bridge near the mill. The Johnsons' house was on "Floyd's Hill," named after city commissioner Dr. Ashby Floyd whose large house was located there. Walking to the library took them by the gambling dives and night clubs. "My mother let us walk over there in the daytime, but told us 'you better not be looking in those doors when you go down that way,'" Dorothy said. "So we didn't look. We wouldn't dare look when we were told not to."[18]

She belonged to the Methodist Youth Fellowship, and was allowed to socialize at church-sponsored group functions, like singing in the choir and going up to Pine Mountain on picnics. John participated in some of these church activities. They were friends at church and at school, but never dated each other. "I couldn't date until I was sixteen years old, and then had to double-date with my older sister," Dorothy said. She also knew John's family, and later worked at his father's law office. She sometimes looked after John's youngest brother Jack after he was born in January 1938. She reminisced, "Mrs. Patterson and other mothers brought their babies to church. They didn't have a nursery back then so they brought a basket and laid a quilt down on the floor and put their babies on it."[19]

Up from King's were two other grocery stores—Rogers' Grocery and an A&P. Next to them was a fruit stand owned by John Freeman, a colorful character who was also a justice of the peace. It was said that couples just pulled up to the curb beside Freeman's fruit stand and he would get in the back seat and marry them. For couples who did have time to get out of their cars, some people also claimed that Freeman rented out the couch in his upstairs office so the newlyweds could consummate their marriage. Years later after John came home from WWII he would stop by the fruit stand and chat with Judge Freeman. "He drank Early Times and kept a bottle under the counter. I'd come by and he'd ask if I wanted a drink. I'd go around behind the counter and have a drink with him."[20]

One day John was at the fruit stand when a woman came in and asked, "How much are your bananas?" Freeman said they were fifteen cents a dozen. She became indignant. "They got them down there at the A&P for ten cents a dozen," she grumbled. Freeman asked, "Then why don't you go down to A&P and buy them there?" "I would, but they're out," she replied. Freeman scratched his head and said, "Lady, if I was out I'd sell 'em for ten cents, too."[21]

A little further up the street was Mayor Homer Cobb's barbershop, which had five or six chairs busy all the time. Mayor Cobb (one of the three commissioners served as mayor) transacted city business over a telephone on the wall beside his chair. "I've had him cut my hair, and the phone would ring," John recalled. "He'd stop and get the phone and keep right on cutting hair." Mayor Cobb, like other politicians in Phenix City, was put in office and kept there by the syndicate bosses. Said to have rued the day the city gave in to the gamblers to keep from going under, he allegedly became wealthy, not from cutting hair but from his connections to the gamblers.[22]

John was close to the same age as the mayor's son and visited their home, which was also in the center of town, many times. He remembered there being a lot of pictures on the wall showing Mayor Cobb with the local syndicate bosses and high-level political figures at Democratic fundraisers in Washington. One traditional event was the annual Jefferson-Jackson Day banquet. "Hoyt Shepherd, Jimmie Matthews, and that crowd would buy two or three tables at this banquet by contributing a thousand dollars a plate or whatever," he explained. "They would get the mayor and other local officials and take all these people up to the Democratic banquet."[23]

Even as a teenager John said he could read into those pictures how the gamblers worked the political system. "You'd see all these senators and congressmen hobnobbing with the Phenix City mob. There were dollar signs in their eyes. They weren't tied into the mob, but had to make an appearance at those fundraisers. In every election the syndicate would hit their people up for big contributions and raise money for the candidates. State candidates didn't have to campaign in Russell County, because the syndicate could guarantee the outcome of any state or local election held there."[24]

It was not always easy to distinguish between the syndicate crowd and the general public in Phenix City because they lived in the same neighborhoods, sent their children to the same schools, pooled their efforts in sports and civic events, and even attended church services together. Hoyt Shepherd's residence was next to Central High School. Head Revel's wife lived next door to the Patterson's home on Pine Circle, although her husband was rarely seen there. Everyone knew who the big shots were, but all the people who worked for them or were in their debt were hard to spot. Even residents who didn't have direct ties to the gamblers had an uncle or a cousin or knew someone who did.

The same could be said for Ku Kluxers in Phenix City. Unlike in Alexander City, the Ku Klux Klan was visible throughout Russell County, which had a large urban black population. Gambling and vice were as wide open in the predominantly black side of south Girard as it was in downtown Phenix City. The illegal black establishments were under the thumb of the white syndicate bosses—who owned the slot machines and gaming equipment—and the white sheriff's deputies who did the bosses' bidding. In addition to helping keep south Girard under control, the Klan provided another means of intimidating black soldiers coming over from Fort Benning.

While John was still in high school, he witnessed several Klan parades through the middle of town. They didn't march on foot, but rode through downtown Phenix City in a procession of cars with white-hooded klansmen on the running boards, brandishing rifles and handguns. The string of cars wound through the streets and up a large hill known as Ku Klux hill outside of town. They held Klan meetings and burned crosses on top of the hill that could be seen for miles. Watching the klansmen go by he found that the white sheets did not mask their identities. "You could tell who they were by their shoes and the way they walked and everything. The folks in city hall were right in there with the store owners and the local toughs. Some were Phenix City's prominent citizens."[25]

TRANSFERRING INTO THE EIGHTH grade when the family moved to Phenix City, John was a student at Central High School until he graduated with the class of 1939. He made good grades in high school, mostly A's and B's with an occasional C. His favorite subjects were English and history, but he did well in mathematics, too. When the family moved to Pine Circle in 1935, the high school was just down the hill from their house. "We had a lot of good times here," he reminisced when visiting the school decades later. "They were great years. Great people here. My senior class, all of them did well."[26]

John said he really had to watch his step after his father became chairman of the school board. Albert Patterson and the superintendent of schools, Lucien P. Stough, were good friends, and if John got out of line it was reported to his father. He told a story about his eighth-grade math teacher, Mrs. Williams, who had a paddle she called her "board of education." "If you didn't keep your lessons up, you had to face her board of education," he laughed. When he went into the Army, he credited the fundamentals of math taught at Central High School for helping him become an artillery officer.

Students would rather face Mrs. Williams and her board of education than the school principal, Mr. Langley, he said. Langley kept a copy of "Invictus" by William Ernest Henley in the bottom left-hand drawer of his desk. The poem was pasted on a piece of cardboard. "He'd get you in his office and have prayer meeting with you, and read that poem to you. You know the words: 'I am the master of my fate; I am the captain of my soul.' He'd have you crying, and he'd cry with you. Didn't have to use a paddle to get his point across. He used that poem."[27]

John played sandlot baseball with his neighborhood friends. Their team was called the Pine Hill Panthers. The only varsity sport he participated in was basketball, but he was too small to make the first string. There was no gymnasium; the team practiced and played in the auditorium. Sometimes when the boys weren't working after school, they would go down to the river and fool around. "If the river was just right, you could catch fish with your hands. Get up on the rocks and catch them with your hands. Carp. Red Horse. Catfish. We used to fish the river all the time."[28]

His teen years saw John's horizons expand. Under FDR the highways were improved and cars became more plentiful. His father owned an Essex automobile—"a lemon if there ever was one"—built before 1932 and after WWII purchased an Oldsmobile with an automatic transmission. The family traveled some, driving back to Tallapoosa County to visit with his grandparents or to Birmingham where Uncle Lafayette and his family had moved. Lafayette's daughter Gerry remembered those visits, and her visits with the family in Phenix City. She said her father and uncle were very close, and that Uncle Albert "was fun to be around." "He was always helping out members of the family," she said.[29]

Gerry's daughter Nancy remembered her great-uncle as "friendly," "kind to children," and "always good to his sisters." When his sister May's first husband walked out on her, Albert drove up, brought her back to Phenix City, and got her a teaching job. She stayed with the family for awhile at the house on Pine Circle, and when she remarried the wedding was held there. May and her second husband had a long, happy marriage.[30]

In the summer of 1937, when he was almost sixteen, John and classmate Sidney Pelham experienced wanderlust. Hoboes had fascinated John since his Alexander City days when Montana Slim and others rode the rails through Tallapoosa County. During the school year he had read a library book which told about hoboing from the east coast to California on a dollar and a quarter. The author wrote about the colorful characters he had met up with while riding the rails and about the hobo jungles where they camped out until another freight train came by. John had ridden the passenger train to Alexander City the previous summer to visit his grandparents in Goldville, but that was dull compared to the lives the hoboes led.

John told Sidney about what he had read. The two teenagers put their heads together when school was out and decided they would be hoboes that summer. Knowing their parents would not approve, they caught a freight train out of Columbus without telling them. They rode down to Mobile in a gondola car and then back up to Birmingham on another train, going all the way to St. Louis before deciding the hobo life wasn't for them. By that time they had been gone for several weeks "living on fruit and tomatoes out of people's gardens, a nickel loaf of bread, and a can of sardines or pork and beans." If they tired of hoboing, they hitchhiked for awhile.

The freight trains were full of people, he said. "We'd get on a gondola car and climb up over and look down and it would be full of men, women, and children." One morning after sleeping on the ground, they walked out to the highway and decided to hitchhike. "Which way are we gonna go?" Sidney asked. John thought for a moment, shrugged his shoulders, and said, "Well, let's just thumb both ways. The first one that stops, that's the direction we'll take." He said in later years he thought about that a lot. "I believe that was the only moment in my entire life that I ever felt completely and totally free."

One night it was cold and raining when the train pulled in on a siding at Chapman, Alabama. Next to the railroad track was a big lumber yard, the W. T. Smith Lumber Company. They crawled through a hole in the fence and got under the lumber stacks to get out of the misting rain. "We spent a terrible night in those stacks," he recalled. Unknown to him at the time, the lumber company was owned by Earl McGowin who had served in the legislature as far back as the Frank Dixon administration and was one of the richest men in Alabama.

Years later when John Patterson became governor he appointed Earl McGowin as state docks director. "Everybody was pleased about that because he was a fine, fine man," Patterson said. One time he told McGowin about hoboing and sleeping in his lumber yard one night. McGowin just smiled and said, "You want to be careful about these young men you run into because you never can tell what might happen someday. Can you?"

When the boys wound up in St. Louis "cold and wet and hungry" they decided they'd had enough, so they turned around and headed back home. He didn't know what to expect when he got back, but his parents acted as if nothing had happened. "We walked in and they never to this day ever said one word, where have you been, or anything like that. Never said a word. They handled that just right." He laughed. "Every man in his life ought to experience being a thousand miles from home, broke, hungry, cold and wet, and have no friends."[31]

When his grandfather died that November, John also thought about how badly he would have felt had something happened to his family while he was away and nobody knew how to reach him. He grew up a little more that summer, and walked a little taller when school started back in September. In his junior year he began to go out on more dates and to party more around town. He bought his first car, a black 1929 A-model Ford coupe with a rumble seat, in 1938. Jimmie Matthews sold him the coupe on credit for one-hundred and twenty-five dollars. That same year he had begun to pay attention to one special girl, Gladys Broadwater, who lived nearby. They became high school sweethearts.[32]

Following graduation he wanted to go to college, but didn't have the money. He didn't want to impose on his father, because he felt the money was needed at home. His brothers Maurice and Sam were growing up, and Jack had just been born the year before. Having been a guest at Fort Benning on several occasions, he was impressed by the gun parks of the 83rd Field Artillery and by the food served in the mess halls. He began to think seriously about joining the Army and seeing some of the world. One day in March 1940 he walked across the Fourteenth Street Bridge to the post office in Columbus and enlisted.

The recruiter said the Army would take him, but not without his father's permission. They gave him a form for his father to sign. Without having consulted with his father about joining the Army, he took the form back to his office in Phenix City and presented it to him. Albert read it and asked, "John, is this what you want?" He replied, "Yes, sir, that's what I want." Albert said, "I'll sign it on one condition. That you stick it out to the bitter end, come what may." "That's a deal," he said. So he took the form back to the recruiting office and spent that night at Fort Benning as a raw recruit.

John said there were a number of times during WWII that he had occasion to remember what his father said. "I was very much concerned that I never do anything that would reflect discredit upon me or my family. I thought about what he said a lot of times. He was absolutely right. When my own son left to go to West Point to be a student, I told him essentially the same thing, that he never do anything to dishonor his name or his family."[33]

WHEN JOHN PATTERSON JOINED the Army in the spring of 1940, the die had been cast in Phenix City. A decade had passed since the city fathers joined forces with the gamblers to keep from defaulting on the town's bonded debt. When the Depression ended the city officials were in so deep with the syndicates and the town was so dependent on a corrupt economy, there was no turning back. Attracting new industry was not a consideration, since the gamblers didn't want the competition and no legitimate business wanted to cope with Phenix City's growing reputation for vice and crime.

The lure of gambling and vice was not only a deadly attraction for Phenix City's young people, but left them with few choices following graduation. Those who couldn't afford to go to college could move away, seek a nine-to-five job across the Chattahoochee, or go to work at the bars and gaming tables. Shoppers couldn't find most brand-name items they wanted to purchase in Phenix City. They had to go to Columbus where the large stores and new car dealers were.

As FDR's federal work programs got underway in the mid-1930s, Fort Benning experienced a construction boom extending through the buildup during WWII. The impact of this on Phenix City, other than providing job opportunities on the military base for a few of its residents, was to pump up the illegal profits as more soldiers and civilian workers squandered their paychecks in the garish neon jungle across the Chattahoochee. "On a payday night the soldiers coming across from Columbus were shoulder to shoulder on both sides of the street," Patterson recalled.[34]

A tragedy on April 21, 1938, could have put the gamblers out of business had the city fathers been so inclined. On that date the building which housed the Ritz Cafe and the Old Reliable Lottery collapsed as hundreds of ticket holders were jammed inside waiting for the winning lottery number to be called. Twenty-four people were killed in the disaster and eighty-three others were badly injured. "Cries and groans filled the air as hundreds from both sides of the Chattahoochee River began the gruesome task of digging out the dead and injured," a reporter wrote. "For a full day workers pulled masonry, heavy rafters, slot machines and other debris from crushed bodies. Everywhere there were lottery tickets tinged scarlet with the blood of the players."[35]

Shepherd and Matthews had been warned by a city building inspector that construction of a new addition to the two-story structure was faulty. The day before the disaster, ten other lottery players were injured when a section of the new construction gave way. Relatives of the disaster victims filed lawsuits, but nothing came of them. A hearing into the tragedy was called off because witnesses were reluctant to testify. The next day the Ritz Cafe reopened at another location, and the gambling and lottery operations never skipped a beat. According to reporters "lottery slips were available to workers digging into the debris still seeking bodies." "The tragedy slipped into limbo," one wrote. "Nothing was done about it."[36]

On the eve of WWII the town across the river from Fort Benning—now known to GIs as "Sin City"—was rougher and rowdier than ever. Shepherd and his cronies had watched greedy-eyed as Fort Benning geared up for wartime expansion. When war clouds gathered over Europe and Asia, FDR ordered the war department to rearm in preparation for contingent military operations on two world fronts. If the United States declared war, the Phenix City crowd knew that Fort Benning would be busy. More dives popped up and more hustlers drifted into town as Hoyt Shepherd and his boys got ready for the flood of GIs into Phenix City.

Within weeks of the Japanese attack on Pearl Harbor, new second lieutenants and raw recruits being rushed through Fort Benning's schools and training facilities numbered in the thousands. Their first time away from home made many of the GIs easy pickings for the hustlers and prostitutes across the river. They were routinely cheated, mugged, drugged, arrested if they complained, and one or two even murdered. The names of Phenix City's notorious dives—Chad's Rose Room, Ma Beachie's, Coconut Grove, Bama Club, and more—soon became as much a part of wartime GI lore as General George Patton's threat to send his tanks across the river and flatten the town to avenge the outrages perpetrated against his soldiers. Patton's threat and Secretary of War Henry L. Stimson's declaration that Phenix City was the "wickedest city in America" brought to a close one more chapter in the town's sordid past, and the start of another.[37]

4

MARCH TO THE SOUND OF THE GUNS

At the completion of recruit training in the spring of 1940, the lieutenant called him to the orderly room and said, "Patterson, I see where you requested field artillery. I have two vacancies. One's at Fort Ethan Allen in Vermont. The other's at Madison Barracks, New York." "Sir, I'll take New York," Patterson blurted, thinking he would be stationed close to New York City.

The lieutenant neglected to mention that the New York unit, the 5th Field Artillery Regiment, had recently come down to Fort Benning to support the newly assembled 1st Infantry Division and was camped in the woods in the Harmony Church area. He had Private Patterson get his duffel bag, and a truck dropped him off in the woods at regimental headquarters. "All this time I thought I was leaving for New York," he laughed.

"Patterson, you was so small when you reported in, we thought you was the paperboy," a noncom from the regiment kidded him. He was thin at five feet, ten inches and a hundred and thirty-five pounds, but he had worked since he was ten and never let size hold him back. He adapted quickly to the discipline of Army life. From his initial assignments as a lineman and a switchboard operator, he learned the ABCs of the artillery mission. The vintage artillery pieces and their history fascinated him. The 5th Field Artillery was equipped with older Schneider-model 155-mm howitzers. "Some of the tubes had actually fired in World War I," he recalled.

From Fort Benning the 5th Field Artillery accompanied the 1st Infantry to the Louisiana maneuvers, and then convoyed up through the midwest, eventually winding up at the regiment's home in upstate New York. There he found out that Madison Barracks, on Lake Ontario near Sackets Harbor, was about as far removed from the Manhattan skyline as one could get without leaving the Empire State.

He spent the winter of 1940–41 at Madison Barracks, the "coldest place" he'd ever been. "Nothing in the world ever equaled the cold and misery of that winter on Lake Ontario," he wrote in a letter home, conceding that it had been good training. His mentor in the 5th Artillery was First Sergeant Jacob Weinberg, a White Russian emigre who had served in the Army of the Czar. He described Weinberg as a strict disciplinarian who was "tough as nails" and respected by everyone in the unit.[1]

Patterson said he made the mistake of admitting he could type, and Weinberg had made him the battery clerk. He took the job grudgingly, but admitted it was good experience and broadened his knowledge of administrative matters. He also had more time off. One payday he and a couple of his buddies went to nearby Watertown and bought a 1926 Nash four-door sedan for twenty-five dollars. "We drove that Nash all over the country, until we wore the engine out."[2]

In the summer of 1941 the 5th Field Artillery moved to Fort Devens, Massachusetts, and later to North Carolina to take part in the great GHQ (General Headquarters) maneuvers across Louisiana and the Carolinas. When the maneuvers were over in early December, the 5th Artillery packed up and headed back to Fort Devens. But Patterson requested ten days leave so he could go to Phenix City and see his family. He had been home two or three days when news of the Japanese attack on Pearl Harbor shattered the Sunday calm. Unable to get through to the orderly room by phone, he caught a train back to Fort Devens early Monday morning.

"That was some ride in those days," he recalled. "You'd catch a train in Columbus, change in Atlanta, and ride overnight to Washington. Change again there, go into Pennsylvania Station, take the subway across midtown to Grand Central, and catch the New York, New Haven, and Hartford Railroad to Boston. From there you'd ride the bus from Boston to Ayer, Massachusetts, and Fort Devens. That was a long damn journey. They didn't have a Pullman, but I didn't care. I was too excited to sleep much anyway." He got back to Fort Devens early only to find the place deserted. "People were going on Christmas leave. They had a big laugh over my coming back early. But I had honestly believed that we would be shipping out right away, and I didn't want to miss the boat."[3]

He liked the Army and thought about becoming an officer as his father had in WWI. At Fort Devens he had applied to officer candidate school, but was not accepted. He was promoted to corporal, however, and was reassigned to the instrument section. In February 1942 he wrote home with exciting news. His unit had received orders to move with the 1st Infantry Division to Camp Blanding, Florida, to train in the Everglades prior to shipping out. "I guess I'll get to kiss this Yankee country good-bye," he wrote to his mother.[4]

While at Camp Blanding the battery commander asked him one day, "Why don't you put in again for OCS?" He stammered, "Well, I don't know." The commander prodded him, "Go ahead and put in. I believe you'll make it this time," failing to mention that one of the officers on the selection board was a friend of his. So he reapplied to OCS, thinking he didn't have much of a chance. Knowing his unit would soon be going overseas with the 1st Division, he went home on furlough and married his high school sweetheart Gladys Broadwater. They had little time together before he had to report back to Camp Blanding.

He had not heard from the OCS selection board when the 5th Artillery was ordered to go with the Big Red One to Indian Town Gap, Pennsylvania, the staging area for overseas deployment to England. En route, they stopped at Fort Benning to put on firing demonstrations for the Infantry School. While there he received orders to report to OCS at Fort Sill, Oklahoma. A few more days and he would have been on a troopship steaming across the Atlantic. In those days they didn't bring you back.

In late May 1942 he entered OCS with Class 27 at Fort Sill. He was twenty years old. While others in the class were older and had more formal education—two of his five roommates had law degrees—he believed his two years in the Army and his practical knowledge of artillery gave him "a distinct advantage over some of the fellows." He also showed a lot of grit and determination. "Well, I will take you up on what you said," he wrote his father. "If I fail this course I'll be so disgusted with myself that I'll never come home again."[5]

He graduated with his class on August 27th, received a commission as a second lieutenant in field artillery, and traveled to Fort Hamilton, New York, for onward shipment to England as a replacement artillery officer. He completed the course with a 90 percent average, and out of a class of five hundred was one of forty new lieutenants whose "high grades and experience" singled them out for foreign service. In a letter home he noted with pride that the 1st Division had taken part "in the Dieppe raid on France the other day."[6]

His new Army ID revealed a handsome young officer with inquisitive hazel eyes, neatly brushed brown hair, and a trim, athletic build. Nobody would mistake him for the paperboy again. He now weighed 170 pounds and was in top physical condition. Fellow officers remembered him as being bright, studious, and affable with a strong sense of purpose and direction. He was also fun-loving and enjoyed an occasional drink of whiskey, while eschewing the use of tobacco. He had tried smoking a cigarette or two and once sneaked a chew from his grandfather's plug of Lucky Joe tobacco, but never took up the habit.[7]

"EVERY DAY WAS A great experience for a fellow like me," Patterson said of shipping out from New York in September on the Norwegian freighter *Samuel Bakke*. The *Samuel Bakke* had accommodations for only eight passengers—Patterson and seven other artillery lieutenants from Fort Sill. The eight thousand-ton freighter took sixteen days to cross the North Atlantic—in a thirty-ship convoy zigging and zagging to dodge German Admiral Karl Doenitz's deadly U-boats.[8]

During the days at sea the eight young lieutenants grew close to the ship's captain and his forty-man crew. They ran into two heavy storms that rocked the freighter and sent waves crashing over the bridge—doing minor damage to a few P-38 Lightning fighters and other heavy cargo lashed onto the deck. During one of the storms a tanker broke up and sank. A British destroyer dropped out of the convoy to rescue survivors, while the other ships plowed ahead through the stormy waters with their precious war cargo.

Lieutenant Patterson spent his twenty-first birthday aboard the *Samuel Bakke*. Captain J. Olsen treated the eight lieutenants as his guests. They dined with him each evening in the captain's mess. There was only one brand of beer and one brand of whiskey on board the freighter. Captain Olsen told them they could drink as many bottles of Rupert's beer as they wanted without charge, but if they drank Black and White Scotch they had to pay $1.25 a quart. For dessert they routinely had sliced peaches and whipped cream which the captain ladled out from a huge bowl brought in from the ship's galley. On Lt. Patterson's birthday, the captain served dessert to the others as usual, but had the steward place a much larger bowl in front of the honored guest.

When the voyage ended the eight lieutenants went to the bridge as a group and filed by the captain one by one to thank him and to bid him farewell. Captain Olsen was a proud and stalwart seaman whose native Norway was now under Nazi occupation. As he watched the young American officers disembark, for a fleeting moment his blue eyes misted. He knew their voyage across the Atlantic on his ship was part of a much larger journey that would see his country freed. For the young lieutenants it was the start of a great battle from which some would not return—an experience that would be etched into their memory for all time.[9]

THE EIGHT LIEUTENANTS DISEMBARKED at Liverpool on England's northwest coast. They lugged their heavy bags down to the railway station and took a southbound local to Crewe, where they changed trains to Lichfield, north of Birmingham. There they bummed a ride on a British Army truck down to Whittington Barracks, located about seven miles outside Lichfield. The barracks were empty because the North Staffordshire Regiment was in North Africa with General Bernard Montgomery's Eighth Army fighting the Afrika Korps. To the delight of the Americans, the Army Territorial Service (British equivalent of the Women's Army Corps) was quartered nearby.

While at Whittington Barracks, Lieutenant Patterson was posted on temporary duty to Sutton Coal Fields and put in charge of the guards for Post Office No. 1—a bottleneck in the overseas mail system where rail cars filled with unsorted letters and packages from home sat idle on the tracks. His spirits were lifted two days later when ordered to report to HQ Allied Forces (General Dwight D. Eisenhower's headquarters) in London to pick up his assignment.

Eager to get back with field artillery, he took a staff car to Norfolk House on Grosvener Square where HQ Allied Forces was located. While walking down the second floor corridor looking for the personnel section, he passed an open door and heard someone call his name. He stepped back, looked inside, and saw Colonel H. V. Roberts who had been one of his superiors in the 1st Division. "Patterson, you're just the man I'm looking for," the colonel ordered. "Take off your hat and coat. I'm putting you to work."

"Oh no, colonel. I'm going to the field artillery," he protested.

"Oh hell no, you're not. You're staying right here."

The colonel brushed aside his protests, called the personnel section, and had the orders changed. "I felt like I'd been shanghaied right off the street," Patterson said. "I didn't know enough to realize what a wonderful opportunity it was."

He rented a room in a flat owned by an elderly lady on the west end of London and took the underground to Grosvener Square every day. For the most part the trains ran on time and the underground stations were clean, although occasionally marred by British graffiti or an American reminder that Kilroy had been there. Instead of destroying British will, the Luftwaffe bombing starting in the Autumn of 1940 had steeled their resistance. People went about their lives with "a stiff upper lip," uninterrupted by the war's many inconveniences. Patterson liked the British people and their customs. To this day he wakes up in the morning to a cup of hot tea rather than coffee.

Colonel Roberts assigned him a staff car and driver. Every morning and every evening he delivered top-secret dispatches from Eisenhower's headquarters to high-level British officials—to addresses like 10 Downing Street, the Admiralty, and the War Office. He also kept "agitating and agitating" for a field artillery assignment. One morning he went to work as usual and Roberts called him into the front office. He told Patterson to close the door. "You want to go to North Africa?" he asked.

"Hell, yeah. When?"

"We leave tonight."

"Tonight?"

Roberts nodded. "This is top secret. Don't breathe a word." He gave Patterson the rest of the day off, and told him to go home and settle up with his landlady. "Take all your baggage to 63 Saint James Place. Be back here tonight at ten sharp in dress uniform, without hand luggage."

This was the first he had heard about Operation Torch, the invasion of North Africa. Plans for the invasion had been closely held. When he reported back that night the British officers were dressed in field uniforms and had all their gear, while the Americans were "in their pinks and greens and had no luggage." A British major he knew asked, "Where's your gear?" He repeated the instructions Colonel Roberts had given him. "You're going to be sorry as hell about that," his British friend laughed.

They were taken to Paddington Station and loaded aboard trains. Riding all night they pulled into the Glasgow, Scotland, harbor the following afternoon. After dark they boarded ships and sailed for North Africa. Lt. Patterson sailed with the Allied Force Headquarters contingent aboard the *H.M.S. Durban Castle*, a former British Orient Line vessel that had been converted to a troopship. Standing on deck before the ship weighed anchor, he shut his eyes to a pungent breeze blowing in off the Firth of Clyde. Or was it a downdraft coming off the Highland moors? Somewhere a foghorn sounded. Then the mournful wail of bagpipes in the distance. Or had he imagined it? Before going below his thoughts turned, for a fleeting moment, to another vessel and another time when a bereaved widow and her four children set sail for America from these ancestral shores.

THE *DURBAN CASTLE* DOCKED at Algiers on December 8 without incident. The Vichy French defenders had laid down their arms when Admiral of the Fleet Jean Louis Darlan ordered a cease-fire soon after Allied forces landed in Algeria and Morocco. Patterson and his fellow officers were still in dress uniforms. The only luggage they had was a ditty bag with a toothbrush, toothpaste, and a razor given to them by the Red Cross. He didn't see the luggage he left at 63 Saint James Place until 1946; he was a student at the University of Alabama when he received a letter that the Army had located his personal belongings at Fort Leavenworth, Kansas.[10]

Allied Forces Headquarters took over the fashionable Hotel St. Georges, a grand old structure on a hill overlooking Algiers. Since only a few American junior officers were assigned to the headquarters, Patterson was billeted with British staff officers in the Hotel Feminina in downtown Algiers. As the name implied, the hotel's residents were the daughters of fashionable families who were students at the University of Algiers along with their entourage of maids and governesses. The students and their attendants had been squeezed into the bottom five floors to make room in the three floors above for Allied officers.

As the only American living in the hotel, Patterson became friends with the British officers, all of whom were senior to him. They rode to work every day on a streetcar and ran around together in the evening. After the Allies occupied Algiers, German bombers flew raids over the city almost nightly. Sometimes the officers went up to the roof of the Hotel Feminina to watch the planes attacking the port and the airfields. The port was only a few blocks away, but surprisingly the German bombers never targeted the hotels, not even the Allied headquarters in the St. Georges.[11]

The nightly raids reminded him how much he missed the field artillery and wanted to be where the action was. Colonel Roberts didn't help the situation by putting him in charge of awards and decorations. Sometimes he commiserated with General Eisenhower's British driver, Kay Summersby, who had an office on the third floor and came down nearly every morning for a cup of coffee and to chat for a few minutes. She was fun to be around, and seemed to be a nice person. As for postwar claims of an affair between Summersby and her boss, Patterson said no such rumors drifted down to the second floor while he was there. "I had tremendous admiration for General Eisenhower, and I never heard anything like that the entire time I was in Allied Force Headquarters."[12]

Algiers was a city of intrigue. Patterson was there on Christmas Eve when a young antifascist Frenchman assassinated Admiral Darlan, a scheming little man who was mistrusted by all sides. Patterson and a colonel from G-1 (Personnel) were attending a dinner party at Villa Mirador, home of the Mollar family on the Rue Micheliet, when the news came that Admiral Darlan had been shot. "They didn't know what else might happen, so they just shut the whole city down," he recalled. The Mollars were a wealthy French family with two lovely daughters, Annie (seventeen) and Edith (twelve). Annie became an ambulance driver with the French Army during the war. He corresponded with the Mollar family long after the war was over.

He had been in Algiers less than a month when Roberts notified him that he was receiving an early promotion to 1st lieutenant in January. He was elated, but suspected the promotion was a way of enticing him to stay in the headquarters. If that was the colonel's intent, it didn't work. One evening Patterson went into the hotel dining room and found all the tables taken. The only empty chair was at a table occupied by two general officers. One of the generals saw him looking around for a place to sit and motioned for him to join their table. He introduced himself and sat down.

The generals were on a staff visit from Washington. One was the Inspector General and the other was the Surgeon General. "What's a young man like you doing in a place like this?" the IG asked. Lt. Patterson knew there was a regulation against higher headquarters proselyting young officers from line units, as Roberts had done to him in London, and that it was frowned upon. He answered truthfully and explained that he wasn't happy with the situation. He was thinking of making the Army a career, and wanted to get back to field artillery.

There was "hell to pay" the next morning when he arrived at the office. He passed by the colonel's door and heard him yell, "Patterson, get in here!" He went in, and Roberts shut the door. He was livid. "You son of a bitch," he ranted. "You go down to the message center and get your orders and get your ass out of here. I don't wanna ever see you again."

As he cleaned out his desk, General Eisenhower's chief of staff, Major General Walter Bedell "Beetle" Smith, sent for him. He later recalled that when General Smith's attractive young French secretary came and said the general wanted to see him, it "liked to have scared him to death." When he entered Smith's office, the general got up, came around the desk, shook his hand, and said: "I admire you. I'd give anything in the world if I could take your place. Good luck to you."

THE FOLLOWING MORNING, JANUARY 22, 1943, 1st Lt. Patterson went out to Maison Blanche and hopped a flight on an Army transport plane to Tafaraoui airfield outside Oran. A truck from his new unit, the 13th Field Artillery Brigade, drove him to brigade headquarters. One of the Army's last active artillery brigades, the 13th had arrived in Algeria in early December and had begun training intensively in the desert south of Oran awaiting orders to join the campaign in Tunisia.

Patterson had done his homework and knew that the 13th Brigade had three regiments of artillery (17th, 36th, and 178th Field Artillery regiments) and the 1st Field Observation Battalion. The 17th Regiment and the 178th, which was a National Guard outfit, each had two battalions of 155-mm howitzers. Each battalion had three batteries of four 155s, for a total of twelve guns per battalion. They also had some 37-mm antitank guns known to the men as "pop guns" and "squirrel rifles." The 36th Regiment had the same number of battalions as the other two regiments, but its batteries were equipped with 155-mm guns known as "Long Toms" rather than howitzers. The howitzers could not match the range of the Long Toms, which were mounted on large carriages and had longer and larger tubes.[13]

When the truck dropped him off at brigade headquarters, he heard the guns firing in the distance and stepped a bit livelier as he walked inside to meet the commanding general, Brigadier General John Alden Crane. The general talked with him about his new assignment with the 17th Field Artillery Regiment. Afterward they had dinner at the officers' mess together. Then Patterson loaded his gear in the truck, and the driver took him to the regiment.

Along the way he looked out on the bleakest landscape he'd ever seen. He'd always thought of the African climate being tropical, but January in Algeria was shivering cold. The driver pulled up to a campsite in the middle of nowhere. "See that tent up on the hill?" the driver pointed. "That's the headquarters of the 17th Field Artillery. That's where you're going." Patterson lugged his bags up a small trail to the headquarters tent, and stood in the doorway until his eyes adjusted to the dim light inside. He walked in and looked around.

A captain with a wool-knit cap pulled down over his ears stood in the center of the tent warming his hands over a potbellied stove. Patterson handed him the orders. The captain looked them over, and then studied Patterson's face. "Where are you from, Patterson?"

"I'm from Alabama."

"What part of Alabama?"

"Phenix City."

"You wouldn't be Albert's boy would you?"

"Why, yeah. Who are you?"

"I'm Woodrow Barnes from New Site."

Patterson had heard what a small world the Army was, but until now had never met anybody in the service he'd known before. He didn't know Woodrow well, but had heard his parents mention him and knew he was related by marriage.

Woodrow's wife was Patterson's cousin. "I had to watch my step after that," he laughed. He'd get letters from home saying, "John, we've been hearing all about you through Woodrow."

Woodrow was an interesting fellow. They called him "Country" Barnes. He had played basketball at Auburn (then Alabama Polytechnic Institute) and was awarded the university's first basketball scholarship. He got his Army commission through the Auburn ROTC. He had come over with the 17th Field Artillery from Fort Bragg, North Carolina, and now commanded the regimental headquarters battery. He was a favorite of the regimental commander, Colonel "Hooks" Howell. After the war Barnes became probate judge and sheriff of Tallapoosa County. "Woodrow and I remained friends for the rest of his life. A fine, fine fellow," Patterson said.[14]

Colonel Howell assigned Patterson to the 1st Battalion and Headquarters Battery, where he commanded the antitank platoon. His primary duty was to train the troops to fire the platoon's six 37mm pop guns. "I had to train myself, too, because I'd never fired one either," he said. The 1st Battalion was off in the desert training when he reported for duty. Colonel Howell sent word that he was going out to the training area at three the next morning, and that Patterson could ride out with him. "I didn't sleep that night because I was afraid I would be late. I was already full of coffee and there waiting on him when he came out to the command car."

"Sometimes a fellow just doesn't know when he's well off," Patterson recalls that he thought as he looked out over the bleak landscape on the drive to the training area. Colonel Howell naturally was curious about his transfer from a plush desk job in General Eisenhower's headquarters. The colonel also showed an interest in his background. That interest, Patterson would later surmise, was all that saved him from the slaughter of the bloody Battle of Kasserine.[15]

THE 2D BATTALION WAS the first element of the 17th Field Artillery to take part in the Tunisian campaign. When ordered to the front in early February, the 2d Battalion was short of forward observers. General Crane's headquarters tasked the 1st Battalion for three lieutenants to augment its sister battalion. Patterson's name was on the list. When Colonel Howell was told of this, he said, "Naw, don't send Patterson. He hasn't been here long enough to know anybody. Send someone else."[16]

By February 12th, after completing the long road march across Algeria, the 2d Battalion had moved up to Faid Pass in southern Tunisia to support elements of the 1st Armored Division and the 168th Infantry Regiment of the 34th Infantry Division. The battalion barely had time to get its artillery pieces into position before "all hell broke loose." The Battle of Kasserine opened in the early morning hours of February 14 when the German 10th Panzer Division struck without warning, quickly overran the outgunned American positions in Faid Pass, and scattered the defenders.

The crushing armored assault on the pass was well coordinated with supporting artillery fire, screaming Stuka dive-bomber attacks, and strafing runs by Luftwaffe fighters. The 10th Panzer's sixty-ton King Tiger tanks and other armor drove through the pass with lightning swiftness. Twenty miles to the south the 21st Panzer Division pushed through Maizila Pass to complete a double envelopment against the American defensive positions. The German armored columns sent the widely scattered defenders reeling fifty miles back to the Western Dorsal, rolled triumphantly into the abandoned village of Gafsa, and took the strategic Kasserine Pass.

A week into the Battle of Kasserine the 1st Battalion of the 17th Field Artillery got its orders to move up to the front with the regimental headquarters. The march started on the 21st and took five or six days. Two days into their march, they received intelligence that German Field Marshal Erwin Rommel, not wanting to overextend, had pulled his forces out of Kasserine and was racing back to the Mareth Line. While moving out of Algeria into the Thala area of Southern Tunisia, the 1st Battalion came upon the survivors of the 2d Artillery Battalion, which had lost about half of its men and all of its guns and vehicles. All of the forward observers had been killed or captured.[17]

It was a sobering moment for the men of the 1st Battalion. Patterson would have been one of those dead or missing forward observers if not for Colonel Howell. He was never told why the colonel took his name off the list of men being sent to the 2d Battalion, but he wondered if Woodrow had something to do with it. "Of course, it might have intrigued that West Point colonel how a man from Allied Forces Headquarters had shown up in his battalion, you know. I'm sure that was an odd thing to him." He never asked Woodrow about it.

Hearing the survivors' stories of "the invincible German Tiger tanks and the terror of the Stuka attacks" was unnerving for the men of the 1st Battalion, but they tried not to show it. Word spread fast that General Eisenhower had relieved the II Corps commander, Major General Lloyd Fredendall, after the rout at Kasserine. Fredendall's headquarters was inside an impregnable tunnel he ordered his engineers to blast out of rock near Tabessa, located on the Algerian side of the border sixty to seventy miles from the winter front in Tunisia. He was too isolated from the fluid Tunisian battlefield and had made grave tactical errors in the disposition and commitment of frontline troops. The Allied positions—extending "over a very wide front" running north and south along the Tunisian mountain ranges known as the Eastern and Western Dorsals—were too shallow and too weak to withstand a massive armored thrust like the one at Kasserine.

The Kasserine engagement was the first major test for the American forces in the Tunisian campaign, and they had been badly bloodied. The 2d Battalion, one of two artillery battalions overrun that day, had been destroyed in its first engagement. Patterson noted that "the 2d Battalion had been improperly deployed in the Faid Pass and simply abandoned." The battalion "ultimately was refitted and rejoined the Regiment; however, it was a long time before it recovered from its harrowing experience."[18]

The 1st Battalion took defensive positions at Bou Chebka, waiting to be ordered into battle. The troops figured they wouldn't have to wait long when they heard that General Eisenhower had named Major General George S. Patton, Jr., as the new II Corps commander. "Everything changed when Patton took charge," Patterson recalled. "I didn't like the S.O.B. Most of the people in the regiment didn't like him. One of the guys he slapped in Sicily was in the 17th Field Artillery. But when Patton took charge you knew it. There was no doubt in anybody's mind."

He remembered how discipline had stiffened overnight under Patton. "Everybody had to wear leggings and helmets. They still had lace-up leggings in those days. The officers had to wear ties. He ordered the MPs to write tickets on those who didn't comply—fifty bucks if you were caught without a helmet or without leggings and fifty bucks for an officer without a tie. Of course we didn't make much money. We made only about $125 a month, as a lieutenant. That damned tie got to be like a black rope out there in the desert. I understood the reasons and thought it was wise myself. That damned uncomfortable tie all day long, you know that reminded you of something. I tell you I was more afraid of Patton than I was of anybody.

"One thing's for sure. You wouldn't find Patton hunkered down behind the lines. He's the kind of son of a bitch who'd get you killed, now. But he'd be there chewing on your rump when it happened."[19] Not even the swaggering commanding general of the 1st Infantry Division, Major General Terry Allen, was spared Patton's bullying. Patton rode his subordinates mercilessly, on one occasion urinating in a slit trench outside Allen's tent to show his "contempt for passive defenses."[20]

Orders came down on the night of March 15. The battalion commander, Lieutenant Colonel Lloyd Mulholl, took Major George Kenmore and a driver out on reconnaissance. They drew fire from German artillery and returned to camp, where Mulholl held officers' call. "Boys, the blue chips are down," he said. He laid out the battalion's plans to support the 1st Infantry Division in retaking Gafsa, a remote oasis south of Kasserine which had changed hands four times in as many months and was lightly defended.[21]

The next day they moved up to the oasis at Fairiana, where General Patton had set up his command post in a bullet-riddled sandstone hotel. He and General Eisenhower visited the battalion briefly on the 16th before it moved out that night. Patterson recalled that the battalion moved its batteries of artillery into position under the cover of darkness, dug in "real good," and waited until the predawn hours to commence firing. The battalion's first combat rounds of the war quickly silenced the lone defending artillery battery at Gafsa. American bombers then flew over and blasted the enemy positions. By noon the 1st Division moved in to quickly secure the abandoned oasis. The German and Italian defenders had fled.[22]

The Big Red One's advance was coordinated with the British Eighth Army's main attack on the Mareth Line, located to the southeast on the Libyan border. Fresh from the victory at El Alamein, General Bernard Montgomery's Eighth Army had pursued Field Marshal Rommel's retreating panzer divisions across Libya into Tunisia. Montgomery's orders were to break through the Mareth Line in Tunisia and capture the port city of Gabes.[23]

Patton had instructions not to become heavily engaged, but this was ignored after Rommel's panzers stalled the Eighth Army advance south of Gabes. To relieve pressure on the Eighth Army, Allen's Big Red One moved out of Gafsa and pressed the offensive up Highway 15. Passing through El Guettar, already captured by Colonel William Darby's famed 1st Ranger Battalion, the division moved beyond the mud huts and palm fronds of the oasis into the rugged ridges along the Gafsa-Gabes road. They didn't get far before the forward columns came under intense enemy fire. "That's where we hit the German lines and began to take our first casualties," Patterson recalled.[24]

A northern approach by the 1st Armored Division over Highway 14 to raid the airfield at Mezzouna and take the sting out of the Luftwaffe's local air superiority was blocked by German forces in the hills east of Maknassy. Allied tactical air power ultimately defeated the Luftwaffe in North Africa, but the enemy planes owned the Tunisian skies during the early stages of the conflict. "It was not uncommon to see twenty-five to thirty warplanes overhead at one time. They worked us over with those Me 109s and the Focke-Wulf 190s strafing and bombing, and those damned Stukas (JU 87s). That damned Stuka was a terrifying thing."[25]

By the night of March 22 the Big Red One's three infantry regiments and supporting artillery had taken up blocking positions behind the ridges east of El Guettar. Patterson had twenty-five to thirty men and six 37mm "pop guns" (two to a section) in his antitank platoon. Since the 37mm guns proved ineffective against armor, he ended up placing them around the battalion for position security.

Their positions were flanked by two mountains. In front of them sprawled the great open plain to Gabes, with a trail dubbed Gum Tree Road running along the ridge line to Mahares and the Gafsa-Gabes road splitting the valley floor down the middle. "Looking out over that plain was like viewing a 3-D movie or a panorama. That desert floor had a thin layer of sand, but was hard as a rock underneath. We knew they could come at us from any direction."[26]

The men of the 1st Battalion spent much of the night hardening the gun emplacements, laying wires to the observation posts and the fire direction center, and readying for a German attack. What little sleep they got was fitful. What would tomorrow bring? They knew their strength and their skills were about to be tested. More than that, their courage. All were familiar with Colonel Darby's chilling phrase, "Give them some steel!" Patton's orders rang in their ears. "Everybody would stand and fight where they were."[27]

5

Long Road Home From El Guettar

The Battle of El Guettar was more than a baptism of fire for Lt. Patterson and other members of the 17th Field Artillery. A relatively small engagement in the annals of military history, the battle held special meaning for the artillerymen—validating all they had been taught about the timely and accurate massing of fire against the enemy. When the smoke finally cleared on the field of battle, their massive artillery barrages and the Big Red One's tank destroyers had saved the day. Together, the untested American soldiers reversed the loss at Kasserine and proved they could hold their own against the battle-hardened Wehrmacht.

The daunting armored onslaught in the predawn hours of March 23 stirs their memory with haunting clarity. "We awoke to see the entire 10th Panzer Division looking down our throat," Patterson recalled. The armored formations had advanced under the cover of darkness along the Gafsa-Gabes road from the east. They poured out onto the valley floor like an army of ants, looming ever larger as they approached. "There were about a hundred tanks. Just before daylight they launched their attack."[1]

At first it looked as if the panzers would repeat their stunning victory at Kasserine. By sunrise the tanks had breached the perimeter of two infantry regiments, overrun two division artillery battalions, and penetrated to within three hundred yards of Patterson's position. He described the ineffectiveness of the small antitank guns. "We got two guns in action, but it was ridiculous to shoot the things. We were lucky they didn't pulverize us. When they broke off the action, they had rolled right up in front of us."

The 10th Panzer Division lost thirty to forty of its tanks, mostly to the tank destroyer battalion and heavy artillery barrages, before pulling back. They had come perilously close to breaching the defensive lines, however, and had inflicted heavy damage. The 1st Division's organic tank destroyer battalion, the 601st, was almost wiped out. "They went out there and met that thing head on and blunted that attack. At the end of the day the 601st had only three half-tracks left," Patterson recalled.[2]

The burned-out tanks and half-tracks were still smoldering on the valley floor when General Patton received British "Ultra" intelligence that six German battalions (two each of tanks, infantry, and artillery) would renew the attack before sundown. Knowing when the attack would come gave the Big Red One time to improve its positions and get ready.[3]

"Just before the sun went down, they came again," Patterson recalled. "Heavy bombing and strafing of the American positions . . . was immediately followed by an all-out frontal assault by German tanks and infantry."[4] Colonel William Darby, in his memoir *Darby's Rangers*, described looking out on the plain at the Germans preparing to attack "in parade-ground formation": "I was never so wildly excited as when watching this mass of men and vehicles inching toward us. The caterpillar-like force rolled irresistibly forward."[5]

Uncommon acts of valor became commonplace that day. Patterson told about a radio operator who stayed at his post in the back of a command car while bombs blasted craters all around him. A bomb fragment took the lapel off his coat, but he stayed on the radio and didn't budge. Another soldier, "just a young kid," braved the barrage of incoming rounds walking up and down in the open area, checking for breaks in the telephone lines and repairing them.[6]

One of Patterson's friends, Lieutenant Paul Frank, manned the A Battery observation post overlooking the battlefield. Before the battle got underway, Major Joseph Couch from regimental headquarters showed up and took charge. Captain Hirens was with him. The observation post had been a hot target for the Germans all day long. Waves of Luftwaffe planes came close to knocking out both the observation post and the fire direction center.

The Germans had even used a captured American half-track pulling a light howitzer to try and take out the observation post. The half-track came down the road from the east, stopped, turned around, and pointed the howitzer at the observation post. Captain Hirens saw an infantry platoon with mortars nearby. "Those your mortars?" he asked the grizzled sergeant.

"Yessir."

"Can you put one on that half-track?"

"I believe I can."

"Then do it!"

The belch of the mortars echoed along the ridge line. One round hit the half-track, disabling it, and the gun crew broke and ran.[7]

Major Kenmore kept the fire direction center in operation and Major Couch, having taken over the communications and the instruments at the observation post, adjusted the time fire over the advancing enemy. Moving up on the open plain the German formations were easy targets for the time fire of the artillerymen. Patterson witnessed the deadly effect of the time-fire shells as they "burst just over the heads of the waves of advancing German infantry and cut them down like wheat falling before a sickle."[8]

In *An Army at Dawn*, Pulitzer Prize-winning author Rick Atkinson depicts the carnage on the open plain as "something between war and manslaughter," with massive and accurate artillery barrages "raining down on the enemy formations."[9] "The time fire tore great gaps in the lines of the oncoming Germans," Patterson recalled. "They closed the gaps and kept coming, but their ranks were thinning. Finally, they faltered, and those left began falling back."

"The 1st Battalion fired more than three thousand rounds that day, and at times, the gun tubes were so hot it was difficult to stand near them. Cooks, mechanics, medical aids, clerks and drivers joined the cannoneers . . . carrying ammunition and cooling the gun barrels by throwing wet towels, rags, and blankets on them." The defenders remained alert. Through the night they watched as German Dornier bombers dropped flares and bombs, but the great open plain grew eerily quiet.[10]

They didn't realize the extent of their victory until the following morning. Patterson said he'd never been so happy in his life when he stared into the rising sun and saw the Germans were gone. A feeling of great elation spread through the ranks as reality sunk in that they "had stood, fought, and defeated one of the enemy's finest divisions." It was the most exciting day of their lives, Patterson said. "The thrill that went through that battalion when that thing was over, the excitement of that thing, you couldn't have bought that with money. When the guys got together for years and years after that, all they wanted to talk about was that day."[11]

THE 1ST BATTALION REMAINED in the El Guettar area for several more days. While there, the battalion turned the antitank guns in, broke up the antitank section, and assigned the men to the various batteries. Patterson became a forward observer with A Battery. He and Paul Frank maintained observation posts at El Guettar, and during the subsequent drive north to take Tunis and Bizerte.[12]

Major Couch was awarded the Silver Star for his actions at El Guettar, promoted to lieutenant colonel, and replaced Mulholl as commander of the 1st

Battalion. (The night after the big battle, Mulholl had gone to the mess truck for a cup of coffee and something to eat. He slipped on grease, fell off the back of the truck, and fractured a vertebrae. The surgeon evacuated him the next day.)[13]

Both regimental commander Colonel Howell and Couch were West Pointers. Patterson noted that Couch had gone from captain to lieutenant colonel in a matter of weeks, and was promoted over Majors George Kenmore and Tom Shackleford, two Reserve officers who had played football for Auburn. Kenmore was also awarded the Silver Star for his actions at El Guettar. "It was a little Army politics. Didn't bother me none, but I observed it with great interest," Patterson noted. "Of course, Couch was a fine artillery officer. He knew his business. I liked him and thought he was an outstanding commander."[14]

On April 7, Patton's forces joined with the British Eighth Army in the drive north. Rommel had pulled his legions out of the Mareth Line and Gabes overnight.[15] Patterson wrote his father, "We are closing in on the Jerrys and the going is slower and tougher. Lots of my buddies aren't ever coming home and this war is now something 'personal' to me."[16]

Serving as a forward observer was dangerous work, but Patterson loved it. He was assigned a jeep with a driver and radio operator. When the battery moved forward, they were out on their own a lot and sometimes in recon parties with the battery commander. "You're constantly trying to find a location where you can get a better view of the German lines," he said.

"One never knew what to expect to see from those forward positions," he noted. One night on the drive toward Tunis and Bizerte, he spotted both British and German patrols going in and out of this huge French colonial estate known as Anserine Farms. Closer observance revealed that artillery shells had destroyed most of the buildings, but there were huge wine vats, "as big as oil tankers," still standing. The patrols, after drinking their fill, were leaving with jerrycans and buckets overflowing with sloshing red wine. "Both sides avoided contact simply by waiting until the opposing side left before they went in to get their wine. Of course, our troops soon joined in the nightly parade."[17]

After the Germans pulled back, the battalion's recon parties assembled at Anserine Farms before going out to pick new gun positions. Colonel Couch saw groups of GIs hanging out around the wine vats. He noticed that "lined up at the spigot was a long queue of American infantry soldiers happily filling their canteens, helmets, and ration cans," even though incoming rounds were shaking the earth nearby. Viewing the wine as a distraction, Couch ordered his soldiers to take axes to the bottom of the vats. Wine soon ran freely down the ditches on both sides of the road. The men left "grumbling and bitching," but went back to fighting the war.[18]

THE 1ST BATTALION OCCUPIED firing positions around Mateur when the Allies declared victory in the Tunisian campaign on May 13. When the campaign ended, the Allies accepted the surrender of about 250,000 German and Italian prisoners, many having been trapped on the Cap Bon peninsula. In mid-April, with victory in Tunisia all but assured, Eisenhower had pulled Patton out to prepare for Operation Husky, the forthcoming invasion of Sicily.[19]

For nearly two months the 1st Battalion bivouacked near the town of Herbillion, Algeria, training and awaiting further orders. Colonel Couch recalled an incident concerning Patterson that he said "should have told all of us that one day he would make a great politician." There was a small French convent for little girls aged eight to twelve in the town of Herbillion. One day the mother superior invited the battalion's officers to a music and dance revue. The colonel asked for volunteers, and Patterson volunteered. Executive officer Major Shackleford challenged him, "C'mon Pat, you're not interested in that form of entertainment. Besides, none of those girls are more than ten or twelve years old." Patterson smiled and explained, "Little girls often have big sisters."[20]

On July 7th, the 17th Field Artillery moved to the staging area in Tunis for the invasion of Sicily. Patterson was still with A Battery of the 1st Battalion. Shortly before they began to load the landing craft, he obtained maps of Sicily from the regimental headquarters. He was put in charge of 150 men on the landing craft, with instructions to land at Gela, Sicily, with the 1st Infantry Division. His group made the overnight run across the Strait of Sicily, landed on the beach at Gela, and went up the steps through the town out to a predesignated area. He then sent guides back to the beach for the guns. "It was an exciting, but relatively uneventful thing except they were strafing and bombing the boats and the beach when we went ashore," Patterson said.

The 1st Battalion was "in the front lines with the leading elements" in the Sicilian campaign, which lasted from July 10 to August 17. Couch described the campaign as "short, hot, and bloody." The Allied forces secured Palermo and other strong points before taking Messina, which was to be the jumping-off point for the invasion of Italy. The 1st Battalion was attached to the 45th Infantry Division in the drive to the north shore, and then supported the 3d Infantry Division in its main effort eastward from Saint Agata to Messina.[21]

Couch had assigned Patterson as the reconnaissance and survey officer after the landing at Gela. He was working around the clock, getting no sleep, and doing night surveys, too. "Patton was pressing toward Messina, wanting to get there before [British Field Marshal B. L.] Montgomery, and we were moving two and three times a day," he recalled. Each time he had to do a survey and coordinate the results with corps headquarters.

One of the hazards in doing reconnaissance and surveying was mines. Patterson had read up on mines and had conducted classes in North Africa on mines. He wasn't afraid of the mines, but had a healthy respect for them. The Germans had just withdrawn, and the area was full of mines. "I've crawled along on my hands and knees at night and felt with my hands trying to find mines on these little old roads where we pulled off. That's where they planted the damned things."[22]

In the village of Saint Agata, about thirty-five miles from Messina, he came down with malaria, but didn't know what he had or how severe it was. Each night around sundown he would come down with chills and high fever. He tried to ride it out, and didn't report it. He got in the back of a truck or under a vehicle until the chills were gone without anyone seeing him. His survey crew, Sergeant Moran and the others, covered for him, and made sure the surveying was done. He kept getting weaker and weaker, later learning that he'd lost nearly twenty pounds in five days.

Finally, he got so weak he couldn't stand. After spending the night lying on the ground behind a rock wall "with artillery fire going in both directions and a helluva firefight raging nearby," he woke up to find his legs wouldn't hold him. Another officer in the battalion offered a tin of grapefruit chunks he had received from home. Patterson ate about half the grapefruit chunks, and dragged himself to the medical section across the street.

His temperature was 106 degrees. The doctors gave him medication to bring down the fever, and sent him down to a collecting station in the local cemetery. He lay on the ground between two tombstones until an ambulance came and took him to a railhead, where he was put aboard an Italian hospital train to the port at Palermo. Boarding a hospital ship, he and the other patients were told to strip off all their clothing. A nurse gave them each a new pair of GI underwear and a Coca-Cola. "I'll never forget that. That was the best CocaCola I ever had," Patterson said. What impressed him most was that sick and wounded German soldiers were brought aboard and were treated just like the Americans.

During the night the ship weighed anchor and went to Oran, where trucks and ambulances took the patients about fifty miles south to a hospital in the Moroccan desert. He volunteered to participate in a new treatment for malaria that took three weeks and two days. "It was one week of quinine, one week of Atabrine, and one week of a new drug called Plasmochin, and then two days of blood tests, one right after the other. Then I was discharged," Patterson said.

He was weaker when he got through the treatment than when he started, but he never had a recurrence of malaria. He and a couple of infantry lieutenants rode a train six days and six nights across North Africa to Tunis, where they got rides on an 82d Airborne plane to Licata, Sicily. The transportation officer in Licata issued them train tickets to Palermo. Before rejoining their units outside of Palermo, the three lieutenants drew partial pay from the finance officer and took a few days R&R.

"We had a good time in Palermo until one evening it came to an abrupt halt," he said. They were in the officers club when they met up with a group of Scottish officers who were dressed in their kilts and were out for a night on the town. The Scotsmen were "a pretty rowdy bunch," and the more they drank the rowdier they became. Two generals, an American and an Italian, came in together and were seated at an adjoining table. The Italians on Sicily had surrendered and changed alliances, but the Scottish officers didn't care for them. They began heckling the Italian general.

Becoming annoyed, the American general called the waiter over and had him place a folding screen between their two tables. This offended the Scots. There was a large bowl of fruit on the table. They began throwing the fruit back and forth among themselves and then, with a shout of "Tallyho", they emptied the bowl of fruit over the screen into the Italian general's lap. Patterson and the two infantry lieutenants jumped up and ran from the club. They never looked back. The next morning they rejoined their units.[23]

PATTERSON RETURNED TO THE 1st Battalion just in time to make the landing at Salerno, Italy, on September 23. Three weeks earlier, while he was recovering from malaria, the 1st Battalion had fired a two-hour barrage across the Straits of Messina in support of the British Eighth Army landing on the toe of the Italian peninsula. The long arduous struggle to wrest control of Italy from the Wehrmacht was underway.[24]

Major General Mark Clark, the U.S. Fifth Army commander, led the invasion. Patton was taken out of the action. Eisenhower temporarily relieved him because of the slapping incidents in Sicily. A prearranged armistice with Italy was little comfort to the Allies advancing up the war-ravaged peninsula. The Wehrmacht's occupation force of fifteen to sixteen fighting divisions commanded by Field Marshal Albert Kesselring was formidable and gave ground grudgingly. To make matters worse, the coming winter promised to be a hard one.

In the drive north from Salerno the 1st Battalion was in direct support of the 34th Infantry Division. The Allied forces were under continuous air and artillery bombardment as they took Naples and crossed the Volturno River. Kesselring pulled back and massed his defenses for the winter along the Gustav Line running south of the Liri Valley to hold the high ground against the advancing Allied forces. Dominating the winter line was Monte Cassino, the hilltop site of a sixth-century Benedictine monastery that towered over the approaches from the south. Failed attempts to break through the heavily defended Gustav Line and take Cassino were costly for the stalemated Allied forces through the winter of 1943–44.

As the line stabilized in December, the 2d Moroccan Infantry Division replaced the 34th Infantry Division at the front. The 17th Field Artillery then supported the Moroccan division which had no medium artillery. Trained in North Africa before being brought to Italy, the 2d division was an element of the Corps Expeditionnaire Francais which commanded three-plus divisions of colonial troops with French officers. The 17th supported the Moroccan division through the winter, during the drive on Rome in the spring, later when the line stabilized just south of the Arno River at Florence, and until they landed in southern France in September 1944.[25]

A few days after the Moroccans arrived Patterson was on duty in the battalion command post when a three-star French general entered the tent unannounced. Patterson recognized the visitor as the French Corps commander, General Alphonse Juin. He had seen pictures of Juin, and had read that the general lost an arm in WWI and was the only man in the French army authorized to salute with his left hand. Patterson reported to Gen. Juin, who spoke English, and said, "Let me get the colonel."

"No, no. Don't worry about that," Juin protested. "Just let me look at the situation map and tell me a little about what you're doing here."

Patterson explained that the unit was a medium artillery battalion assigned to support the Moroccan division, then turned and told his sergeant to find

Colonel Couch quickly and bring him to the command post. The sergeant took off running. "There's no time. I'm in a big hurry," Juin insisted.

Patterson pleaded with him. "General, please don't leave. If the colonel don't get to see you, he'll kill me." Juin started laughing. Then here came the colonel running down the hill.[26]

Patterson was impressed with Juin. He would see the general again under different circumstances. Recalled to duty during the Korean War, Patterson was with the 4th Division when it docked at Bremerhaven, Germany. General Juin commanded NATO at the time, and conducted a formal review of the division's officers on the docks. There was a steady downbeat of rain. Raincoats had not been prescribed, so the officers were standing unprotected in the rain waiting for Juin to speak. "Juin took off his raincoat and spoke to us in the rain. I won't ever forget that."[27]

"THE WINTER FIGHTING IN the mountains of Italy was the worst thing any of us ran into," Patterson recalled. The 1st Battalion, which had been re-equipped with new 155-mm howitzers in October, was in the line around Cassino the entire winter. "It is getting rough up here and the mud is up to our knees," he wrote home around Thanksgiving. ". . . Mud, mud, mud, the damnedest stuff you have ever seen. My outfit has been through three campaigns now and this one has turned out to be the roughest."[28]

"We ate turkey Thanksgiving, standing knee deep in mud, raining, and shells flying overhead and all around," he wrote. Christmas Day was a little better. "With all the inconveniences of the front we had turkey with all the trimmings. We topped off the meal with two bottles of champagne that the Italians gave to us. The sun came out Christmas day but today it is snowing. The mountains are all very white and beautiful."[29]

An avid reader, he read everything he could get his hands on "during those long damned winters in Italy when we'd sit there in that hole around a little old stove trying to stay warm." They lived in holes and bunkers dug out of the ground with the "biggest rats you ever saw." "Just made themselves right at home with us. I tell you, that was a helluva way to live. The rats even got to where they liked us. And with all that incoming artillery, bombing, and strafing, we were sorta' sympathetic toward them."[30]

Around the time he became the Assistant S-2 (intelligence officer) in January, he wrote home and asked for a copy of *Lee's Lieutenants: A Study in Command* by

Douglas Southall Freeman—thinking the book's insights into Lee's leadership might make him a better officer. Not only was he considering making the Army a career, but wanted to be the best officer he could be. His father sent him the book, which Scribner's published as a single volume of over nine hundred pages. "I read every word in that book and passed it around," he said. "The last time I remember seeing that thing it had been rained on in the jeep, and had swollen up. It was about twice as thick as it was before it got wet, and people were still reading it."[31]

Like GIs the world over, the men of the 1st Battalion found ways of taking a few hours off from the grime and gore of war. Weather permitting they occasionally got away for short periods of time by driving to Naples, about fifty miles south of their positions. Patterson described the routine. "You could crawl out of your dugout or foxhole and get your jeep and driver and drive forty-five miles, go to the Red Cross and get your clothes pressed, go to the public bath and get you a bath, and then go to a nightclub and have a string orchestra and waiters with tails, living it up like no war ever existed. Then about 2 o'clock in the morning, crawl back in the jeep and head back to the front again. That was a helluva life, wasn't it?"[32]

Patterson was promoted to captain in April 1944, the month before Allied forces made a decisive breakthrough at Cassino. Soon afterward he was given command of Service Battery. Both sides had suffered staggering losses in the battle for Cassino. Massive formations of B-17 Flying Fortresses, B-25 Mitchells, and B-26 Marauders had leveled the centuries-old monastery atop Monte Cassino. The Italian Campaign was far from over, but the gates of Rome were only a hundred-odd miles and approximately three weeks away.[33]

Patterson said that when the final offensive against Cassino came, it took about three days for the French Corps to punch through the German lines. "The Germans began to retreat and fall back. The only way out was a single narrow mountain pass with a two-lane road. An observation plane spotted the Germans funneling through the pass, and all of the corps artillery was directed against the target. A little later Captain Patterson went up on reconnaissance and drove through the pass. He described the carnage:

"You've never seen so many dead Germans in your life. They were piled everywhere. They were in the ditches. They were in the road. When the French and our armor came up they didn't even bother to move them out of the road.

Just ran over the bodies in the road. I'd ride through that pass and look down, and there would be a German body smashed flat in the middle of the road. You'd look down and your jeep would be running over a German body, still in uniform, mashed flat as a pancake. That's awful, isn't it?[34]

The harsh realities of war followed them on the push to Rome. Abandoned equipment and ammunition littered the roads behind the retreating German forces who fought "a delaying action with strong rear guard at selected key points."[35] "We didn't just speed down the highway to Rome. We were fighting a rear-guard action all the way."

A brutal experience during the drive north was the night that rampaging Moroccan soldiers raped and pillaged the small Italian town of Ausonia, located near the 1st Battalion's positions. "We could hear the screams of the women and children all night long. It appeared to us that the French officers weren't doing anything to control the situation, and might even have encouraged it."

Some of the troops—there were Italian-Americans from New York in the battalion—wanted to go into town and confront the Moroccans, but Couch stopped them. As the only American unit in the French Corps, an armed confrontation was out of the question. The next morning they awoke to find hundreds of Italians (old men, women, and children) hiding in a wheat field around their gun emplacements. They had gathered around the Americans for protection from the Moroccans.

Couch and the Catholic chaplain, Major McCormick, were determined to put a stop to the atrocities. Chaplain McCormick got in his jeep the next morning and drove nearly seventy-five miles to Caserta over muddy, torn-up roads to make an official complaint to Fifth Army headquarters. He reported the incident to General Clark personally, and the atrocities stopped. "I always liked McCormick and Couch for their stand on that thing," Patterson said.

He recalled that McCormick and a Protestant chaplain named Rognus often drove up to the battery positions, under all kinds of difficult conditions, to hold Sunday services for the troops. The chaplain set up an altar on the hood of his jeep and conducted services. The driver passed out hymnals and played a portable organ. "I thought the chaplains played an important role. It always seemed to me that the men of faith fared a little better than the others."[36]

When the Allies reached Rome, they would not allow the Moroccans to enter the city because of their earlier atrocities. The 1st Battalion moved into the area on June 4, and took up positions in the railroad yards on the city's edge.

Patterson decided to take his jeep and slip off downtown to see what was going on. "I figured, well if I don't go into Rome, we're going to have to leave here with the Moroccans. I might not get to see it," he said.

There were huge demonstrations in the public squares and around the Venezia Palace, which housed Benito Mussolini's Fascist headquarters in the 1920s and 1930s. "Must have been a million people there. Four or five American GIs were up in Mussolini's famous balcony. They were drinking wine out of bottles. One could speak Italian. He was speaking to the crowd, mocking Mussolini, sticking his chin out, and the crowd was going wild."

He drove over to the Vatican. No one was there. Leaving the jeep at the curb, he strolled through the entrance into the plaza and walked across to St. Peter's Basilica. He went past the Swiss guards into the cathedral wearing his helmet and holstered Colt .45 automatic, looked around, came back out, got in his jeep and drove over to an elaborate old hotel where a crowd of American soldiers were going in and out. He elbowed his way into the main ballroom packed shoulder-to-shoulder with steel-helmeted GIs with rifles slung over their shoulders, dancing with the girls off the street to the music of a string orchestra beneath the crystal chandeliers. Patterson recalled:

"That was the damnedest thing I believe I ever saw in my life. Several American divisions had a part in taking Rome. When the Germans pulled out, and the Americans flowed into the city, there was a lot of them. They say it took weeks to get them all out. I can understand why."[37]

A couple of days later the battalion moved into bivouac two miles west of Frascati and stayed until June 10th. While there, Patterson and the other officers drank a toast to the June 6 D-Day landings at Normandy. They were still drawing a liquor ration from the British army. When the 17th Field Artillery was in North Africa, the supply officer somehow got them included in the British army liquor ration. Patterson explained:

"The ration was one bottle per officer per month, so each month we got a bottle of whiskey. Either Johnny Walker Red Label or a bottle of Irish whiskey. We drew that thing the rest of the war, and we weren't even with the Brits. We had Waggoner in my battery, and he was a teetotaler. There was four of us in a battery. Three of us got Johnny Walker. We gave Waggoner the Irish whiskey. We'd drink ours up and then chisel the bottle off him and drink it, too."

Lieutenant John Waggoner was the ammunition officer in Service Battery. "He was a busy guy, let me tell you," Patterson said. The battery was in charge of getting all of the supplies for the battalion—food, gasoline, clothing, ammunition, etc. "That was a hell of a job, going to the rear and finding those ammo dumps and getting that stuff up to the front."[38]

While at Frascati, Chaplain McCormick arranged to hold a service in St. Peter's Basilica for Catholic members of the 17th Field Artillery. He said mass there, and obtained an audience with the Pope for the men in attendance. On June 11, after a sixty-five-mile march, the battalion rejoined the 2d Moroccan Division in a rendezvous two miles south of Viterbo. From there they moved out toward the ancient city of Florence, the Arno River and the peaks of the northern Apennines.[39]

For a couple of months Patterson passed back and forth through Viterbo every day or so making sure that ammunition and supplies got to the front lines. He didn't learn until after the war that his father's old friend O. P. Lee from Opelika was the military mayor of the town. Having been recalled during the war to serve in the Army's military government branch, Lee was installed as military mayor of Viterbo soon after the Germans pulled out.

Patterson wrote his father that he was confident that "the critical times" were near at hand. During July his battalion met heavy enemy resistance as the French Corps swept northward. The battalion came under intense enemy fire from guns and planes nearly every day. One battery reported losing its kitchen vehicle and cooking utensils to enemy shells. By August the Allies had taken Florence and reached the south banks of the River Arno. The Germans had fallen back to the Gothic Line.[40]

The Italian campaign was over for Patterson and the 17th Field Artillery. In late August they were pulled out of the line at Florence and moved to Naples where they staged for the Allied landing in southern France. They loaded aboard the USS *Dickman* and set sail September 7, 1944, in a convoy for the beaches at St. Tropez.[41]

THREE DAYS LATER THEY arrived at St. Tropez. There was no fighting on the beaches since the Germans had withdrawn. From St. Tropez the battalion traveled 470 miles inland and bivouacked at Vesoul below the Vosges Mountains. From Vesoul the battalion moved a few miles north to St. Loup in support of the 45th Infantry Division. On September 21, in the vicinity of Girancourt, the battalion fired its first rounds in the French Campaign.[42]

A few days later battalion commander Colonel Couch was badly injured when his jeep was blown up by a land mine. Patterson was in a jeep nearby and witnessed the incident. They were on reconnaissance about fifteen to twenty miles north of Epinal near a little town called Rambervillers at the time. Corporal Waters was the commander's driver, and the S-3 Major Mulcahay was in the back. Couch had Waters pull off the main road onto a cow trail leading into a field when they hit the land mine.

"The left front wheel and the right rear wheel hit mines simultaneously," Patterson said. "The blast threw the jeep up into the air fifteen or twenty feet, turned it upside down and it came down on its top. Blew Couch and the major out into the field. Waters apparently held onto the steering wheel and rode the vehicle down and was underneath the vehicle." The medics gave the commander and the major emergency treatment and took them away in an ambulance. Everybody thought the driver was dead. "While they were working on Couch, all of sudden Waters comes scratching out from under the jeep and wasn't hurt at all."

After about three days, Mulcahay was back on duty. Couch, however, was severely wounded. "We never expected to see Couch alive again, but he survived and got through it. His Army career was over. Went with the CIA for twenty-five years after that. We never saw him again during the war." Major Charles L. Haley replaced Couch as battalion commander.[43]

Action in support of the 45th Infantry was sporadic as winter set in. At the end of November he wrote home that he was "still in the line and winter is here." The mud had been bad in Italy, but he wrote, "You have never seen mud until you see the mud of the Rhine valley." That day he had received mail from home, including packages from his mother, two gifts from Gladys, and one from Aunt Judy. "They were perfect. You could not have selected any thing better than a fruit cake. You should have seen me and my two lieutenants go for that cake."[44]

A touch of homesickness showed in his letters. "I think everyday how wonderful it would be to be at home with you all," he wrote his mother. He and Gladys corresponded, but things had changed. He'd been away more than two years now. They both had grown. They had grown apart. Their lives were different now. They had different experiences, developed different interests. They would remain friends.

Through the winter of 1944–45 and into the spring, the battalion moved around a lot providing fire support for cleanup operations but was involved in no heavy firefights. General Patton, meanwhile, was in a mad dash to be first to cross the Rhine. On the night of March 22, the first Third Army elements crossed the Rhine into Germany at Nierstein. Two days later Patton stopped halfway across a pontoon bridge at Oppenheim and urinated into the river. He followed up with a terse message to higher headquarters: "I have just pissed in the Rhine. For God's sake, send some gasoline."[45]

WHEN THE WAR ENDED in Europe in May, the 17th Field Artillery was twenty miles deep into Austria helping clean out pockets of German resistance. Captain Patterson had been given command of A Battery. They had crossed the Rhine in March with the 10th Armored Division, driven toward Heidelberg, south to Ulm, and on to Fussen on the Austrian border. They were still on the move in Germany in April when the news reached them that President Roosevelt had died at Warm Springs, Georgia. Patterson thought of his father. He knew his father would be touched personally by the president's death.

There was quiet elation in the battalion when word came down that the war was over, but no noisy celebrations. Patterson went down and pulled the lanyard to fire the last round of A Battery. "We began to realize, I think, that this great experience was over. A lot of us thought we might go to the Pacific." Everyone wanted to go home, of course, but they had lived and fought so long together that their unit had became a home of sorts, too. There were about 650 men in the battalion, and most had been with the battalion all the way through the war.

From Austria the 17th returned to Germany for occupation duty south of Munich around Starnberger See. Under the Army's rotation system, nearly all of the soldiers in the 17th were eligible to go home. The command immediately began shipping people back, stripping the battalion of experienced personnel. Patterson and some of the other officers volunteered to help train new personnel. As much as he had looked forward to going home, he felt compelled to stay and "see the thing through." He planned to go home on leave before shipping out to the Pacific.

"We got a lot of new men and moved up to a range near Regensburg and started training a new battalion," he recalled. They no sooner "got the new battalion trained" and fired a demonstration for General Patton in early August than two modified B-29s named *Enola Gay* and *Bock's Car* dropped the atomic bombs on Hiroshima and Nagasaki. The weeks following VJ Day were a blur as the greatest army the world had ever seen rushed to demobilize.

Patterson's orders came through immediately. He was ordered to Augsburg to return home with the 103d Division. Motoring across Germany to France to an abandoned airfield near the port of Le Havre, they parked all the division's equipment, got in the trucks, and drove to the waiting troopship. They just left everything and shipped out. The division arrived in New York on September 21, processed through nearby Camp Shanks, and was deactivated.

There was no band playing. No ticker-tape parade. They came up the Hudson River to Camp Shanks just after daylight. The morning rush-hour traffic jammed the streets going into New York City. "I remember seeing all those brightly colored cars honking their horns and inching along. The different colors of all the cars fascinated me. Things sure had changed since we'd been gone. Wasn't nothing like that in North Africa and Europe."

Alongside the ship a colorful fireboat shot geysers of water into the air. On the deck a bevy of bathing beauties waved, welcoming them home. Standing back from the ship's railing, he found himself alone in the crowd of cheering soldiers. All of sudden, melancholy struck him. He missed his old unit and all they had been through together. The great adventure was indeed over.

He was held over a couple of days at Camp Shanks to help deactivate the division, and was then put in charge of a troop train to Fort McPherson, Georgia. Arriving at the station, he found a disorganized crowd of soldiers milling around on the platform. He recognized a sergeant in the crowd named Lowry who was from Georgia. They had served together in A Battery of the 5th Field Artillery before the war. "We had a little reunion," Patterson said. "I told him I was in charge of the train going to Fort McPherson and needed some help."

"What can I do?" he asked.

"You know some of these other sergeants, don't you?"

"Oh yeah."

"Let's get them here and have a little meeting. Let's organize this train so we can go home."

THE NONSTOP TRAIN RIDE to Georgia was an overnight run. Patterson closed his eyes, but couldn't sleep. Gazing out the window he watched the olive drab countryside pass in review. Droplets of rain burst against the coach's tinted glass. His fingers drummed a marching beat against the arm of the seat. The new diesel engine hummed a well-oiled melody as they sped through the night. He tried to read, but wasn't in the mood. At Camp Shanks he had picked up a copy of Thomas Wolfe's, *You Can't Go Home Again*. There's a title for you.

He studied his rain-washed reflection in the window. An Army captain at twenty-two. Not bad for a high school grad. He would be twenty-four in three days. Promoted ahead of his contemporaries. Chalk that up to character and the way he was raised—working and accepting responsibility at an early age. He was thinking of staying in the Army, making a career of it. He was about as close to being a professional soldier as a person could get. It was a big decision. Things were moving too fast. He wanted to go home and think on it first.

The rush to demobilization was not the Army he had known. If the 17th Field Artillery had come home as a unit, it would have been different. The disorganized mob at the train station wasn't the real Army. All they had on the troop train to eat and drink was cold C-rations and five-gallon cans of water. What a way to come home.

One thing for sure, that captain in the rain-drenched window was not the eighteen-year-old boy who reported to the 5th Field Artillery at Fort Benning six years ago. That captain, who would make major in another month, was old beyond his years—not callous or hard, but tough, resilient, and ready and able to take charge when the situation called for it. The Army had made him a leader, taught him how to get things done, and how to work with others in getting them done. The array of ribbons on his chest included an arrowhead for the beach landing in Sicily, eight battle stars for the North African and European campaigns, and the Bronze Star. Whether he stayed in or got out, after his experience in Eisenhower's headquarters and all he had gone through in North Africa and Italy, he figured he was prepared to deal with just about anything that came his way.

HE WASN'T EXPECTING THE stiff-necked bureaucracy awaiting at Fort McPherson. When he reported to the headquarters the morning after they arrived, he found hundreds of other officers already in line to be processed. He walked to the end of the line—the first he ever had to stand in as an officer—and waited in the hot sun. He finally reached the front of the line and was greeted by a square-jawed master sergeant from personnel who asked for his 201 file. The sergeant thumbed through the file and asked, "Whataya' wanna do captain? Stay in or get out?"

He couldn't believe what he was hearing. He explained to the sergeant that he had been overseas for three years, and wanted to take a thirty-day leave before deciding what to do. "Naw, captain, you can't do that," the sergeant said. "You gotta' decide right now."

His eyes flashed with anger. "The hell you say."

"That's right, captain."

"In that case, I'm out. I'm gone."

Just like that it was over. What a hell of a way to end this great adventure, he thought as he waited for his mother and father to drive over from Phenix City to pick him up. He had called the night before. His father knew Fort McPherson well—having spent two years in the hospital there after WWI. They would meet him in front of the headquarters building. He waited outside with his luggage. He looked up and saw his father's old maroon Oldsmobile turn the corner. He was home.[46]

6

ANOTHER LAWYER IN THE FAMILY

J ack Patterson's first distinct recollection of his brother John was when he returned from the war. "When John came home in his Army uniform with all the ribbons, I thought that was one of the most marvelous things I'd ever seen," he said. "I was old enough to know we had been at war, who we were fighting against, and that we had won. I was very proud of my brother having participated. So when he returned I just thought that was the grandest experience in my life up to that point."

He remembered his mother serving dinner that evening. It was the first time he had seen the whole family together around the dinner table. His other brothers, Maurice and Sam, were there. Maurice was in high school, and Sam soon would be. John remarked that he couldn't get over how grown-up they were. Their mother brought out the main course. John commented, "Spam. Hmmm. That looks familiar."

On the home front there were shortages of just about everything. "Spam was the best meal my mother could put on the table at that time," Jack said. "During those war years we didn't have a lot of sugar. My parents didn't have a lot of coffee. We used syrup to sweeten our cereal." The family had done its part for the war effort in other ways. He and his brothers participated in drives to collect scrap metal, tin cans, and newspapers, and the family saved tinfoil. "That wasn't much, but it meant a lot to us. We all wanted to do our part."

"That first dinner after John got home, he started sharing his war stories," Jack recalled. "He was a good storyteller. Still is. The whole family was absorbed in his war stories. We must have sat there a couple of hours after dinner listening to his war experiences. While he was living there with us, we repeated the same scene night after night after night."[1]

JOHN WAS HOME ONLY a few days. During his brief stay in Phenix City, he and Gladys mutually agreed to dissolve their marriage. His father filed the court papers for them and the divorce decree became final in January 1946. "She was a very fine person," he said. "We never really had a marriage." They parted friends.[2]

93

Patterson immediately left for Tuscaloosa and the University of Alabama. He had decided during the drive from Fort McPherson that he would get a law degree. His father encouraged him. Classes had already started for the quarter, and he had only a few days to register or he would have to wait another three months.

Enrolling as a freshman, he was one of the first veterans to attend the University of Alabama after the war. There were only about twenty-five students to a classroom. They were mostly girls. "There would be two men and the rest would be girls. It was a very interesting place, to say the least. But then the veterans began to come in rather rapidly."

The first year he roomed in Mrs. Cummings's boarding house on Thomas Circle, less than a block off University Boulevard. He couldn't keep a roommate because he insisted on the room being neat and orderly, and he had nightmares about his war experiences. This problem resolved itself during the second quarter when he found a new roommate, Joseph G. Robertson, who was also a veteran.[3]

Joe Robertson had served with the Army Air Forces. He had attended the U.S. Military Academy at West Point for a term, but decided to go to college on the GI bill instead. Before transferring to the University, he had taken classes at Birmingham-Southern College where he was an active member of the Alpha Tau Omega fraternity. During their second year at Alabama he convinced Patterson to join the fraternity, and they roomed together in the ATO house.[4]

The scarcity of automobiles and civilian clothing was an inconvenience faced by most Americans during the war and the immediate postwar years. Patterson had about $7,000 in savings. This was more than enough to purchase an automobile, but there were no new cars in the showrooms and few used ones on the market. Students walked, rode the bus or train, or hitchhiked.[5]

"You could walk up and down University Boulevard and you wouldn't see a car nowhere," Robertson recalled. "Nobody had one." He said they elected a fraternity brother as president because his father bought him a new '46 Buick. "He parked it in front of the fraternity house, and that was the only car on University Boulevard."

They often borrowed each other's clothes. "I had only one white shirt," Robertson said. "The rest of the time I wore khaki shirts and GI clothes." He remembered one problem with his roommate always borrowing his clothes. "John would borrow my shirt and he'd go out on a date and he'd come in and have lipstick all over my white shirt."

He said the professors and the house mother were impressed with Major Patterson, who proved to be "a good influence" on him while they roomed together. "I was an average student until I moved in with John Patterson. John would say, 'Now, we're going to sit down and study for the next two hours. Then we'll go out and kick up our heels.' He helped me bring my grades up. John was a straight-A student. Through his influence I got to where I made some A's and B's, when I'd been making C's before."

Robertson recalled that under the GI Bill veterans got their tuition and books free, and received a monthly check for $50 to pay room and board. This was increased to $65 in 1946 and to $75 in 1948, with a slightly higher allowance for married veterans. For spending money, they worked at odd jobs. "John and I did everything. I had twelve different jobs at one time. I graded papers. I worked at the funeral home. I developed pictures in a darkroom. I sold birthday cakes. Anything that wouldn't get us busted. And one that almost did."

He came up with the bright idea of going to Bessemer and picking up a suitcase of liquor from the ABC store. He rode the Greyhound bus back to the campus. They sold the bottles of whiskey out of the fraternity house, planning to double their money. "One night we had a knock on the door long after everybody was asleep. We said no, we're out of business. They kicked our door in. We sold them everything we had, and we didn't buy anymore. That put us out of business."

Causing a ruckus was not their style. Because of their military backgrounds they kept the beds made and the room in order, which was rare around the fraternity house. The two men roomed together until the fall of 1947 when Patterson entered law school. They remained lifelong friends. Robertson later became executive secretary to Patterson during his four years as governor.

He was to have been best man at Patterson's marriage to Mary Joe McGowin (known as "Tuti" to family and friends), an undergraduate student from Clanton, Alabama, but appendicitis a few days before the wedding changed their plans. He was recuperating in a hospital in Birmingham on the Sunday when John and Mary Joe were married in Clanton. John's father filled in as his best man.[6]

WHEN HE ENROLLED AT the university, Patterson was determined to make up for lost time by going straight through school, including summer classes, until he got a law degree. Looking back, he said, "I would not do that again. I think a fella needs to live a little bit along the way."

Two of his favorite professors nearly convinced him to change course. They offered a teaching fellowship if he would switch his major to public administration and then go to Syracuse University to get a master's degree. "Public administration interested me, and I seriously toyed with the idea," he said, but his father was saying the opposite: "Get your law degree as fast as you can and come home. I need you." His father won the tug of war.

Dr. John V. Masters was one of several law professors who influenced him. An older man who was "very formal, and wore dark suits and little bow ties," Masters taught "trusts, sales law, things of this kind . . . I don't suppose I ever spoke ten words with him. He did not socialize. He was very thorough, however, and I liked him very much."

On the first day of class, Dr. Masters always brought out a little black book and announced that the uniform for his class would be coats and ties. There would be no exceptions. He spoke in a low, but stern voice. "You hope to be a lawyer some day soon. When you get to be a lawyer and represent your client in court you will have to wear coats and ties. You'll be expected to. So you might as well get in practice."

Fortunately, by the time Patterson got to law school, more goods were for sale in the clothing stores and he no longer had to wear his Army uniform. There was no air conditioning, however, and the classrooms were saunas during the summer sessions. Invariably, a student would show up in class without his coat and tie. When he did, Dr. Masters stared straight ahead, without saying a word. Everyone started looking around until they spotted the guilty party. When the embarrassed student slunk out, the professor took out his black book and made a notation. Patterson said he got his name in that black book only once, and that was enough. They had double seating in the classroom, and he was talking to the student in the other seat when the roll was called. "Dr. Masters, I don't believe you called my name," he said. Bad mistake. "Oh, yes, Mr. Patterson, I called your name. You were talking. You weren't listening." Out came the black book.

Masters had a teaching technique that kept the students on their toes. He assigned the class five or six cases from the text each day. The students had to study each case and be prepared to recite the case if randomly called on. Patterson said the students were afraid not to study all of the cases, because they were afraid he would flunk them. "And he was tricky. You knew that one day he'd skip you and then get to you second or third, so you had to be ready for all of them. It was a tremendous technique."

Using this technique Masters led the class through every case in the book—starting on the first day and finishing the last case on the final day of the course. "On the day he finished the last case, he said to the class, 'As the shoemaker said to his wife, this is the *last*.' That was the extent of his humor. But I was crazy about that old man."[7]

SHORTLY BEFORE FINISHING LAW school in August 1949, he began closing out the apartment in Tuscaloosa and moved Mary Joe to Phenix City, where they had rented a house in the Summerville area on Essex Drive. She was expecting their first child. On the 26th, the day he graduated, he stopped in Montgomery to be certified by the Alabama Supreme Court clerk's office. In those days a certificate proving that an individual had earned a diploma from the University of Alabama law school was all the State required for admission to the bar.

From Montgomery he drove to Phenix City and went to work with his father. They had "a pretty good-sized" suite of offices in the Coulter Building. Their offices were at opposite ends of the suite. His father immediately began assigning him cases. There was an intercom system, but his father never used it. He shouted down the hall. "He'd say, 'John, come here!' I'd go back there and say, 'Yes sir.' He'd say, 'Here. Take care of this." And he'd throw me a file." Patterson was almost immediately trying cases in court.

He also took on "some of the drudgery of law practice like searching land titles in the probate office." He said they had a terrible record system in Russell County, and still do. "Every time I would have to go over there and go down in that dusty basement and pull out those old deeds and mortgages, and work on the titles, I would get headaches," he said. Some things never change. He said he recently went down to the basement of the probate office for a visit, and got a headache.

His father's law practice had grown steadily over the years. The Pattersons handled all types of cases, from traffic violations to capital murder. They closed loans, and handled mortgages, deeds, wills, and estates. They had a fairly large probate practice. "We were trial lawyers in the sense that we handled a lot of cases of personal injuries rising out of automobile accidents, train wrecks, and things like that. There was plenty of work to do, and a full docket all the time. It was hard work, and my father was making a pretty good living. Right from the start, I made a pretty good living out of it, too."

During the years he had been away from Phenix City, his father's interest in civic affairs and politics had never waned. He was the first chairman of the Russell County draft board, and had served in that role all through the war. He was a member of the school board, the chamber of commerce, the Lions Club, the American Legion, and the VFW. He was active in church affairs and was on the board of stewards of the Trinity Methodist Church. He had also stayed active in the Democratic Party. He was a delegate to the Democratic National Convention twice, and served four years (1946–1950) in the Alabama Senate from Lee and Russell counties.[8]

When he ran for the Senate in 1946, Maurice drove for him. Maurice graduated from Central High the next year and enrolled in the University of Alabama. He majored in business administration and received a bachelor of science degree in 1951. Receiving his commission through the ROTC program, he served two years in the Army during the Korean War. His brother Sam attended high school at Marion Military Academy in Marion, Alabama.[9]

As the youngest son, Jack came along at a good time to help his father and to grow with the experience. He helped out at his father's law office "licking stamps, making mail runs, and going to the courthouse, which was across Fourteenth Street from the Coulter Building, to file papers in the clerk's office." His father also took him to political meetings. He got to know a lot of the lawyers and public officials around town.

When his father was elected to the Alabama Senate, Jack went with him to Montgomery as a Senate page. Eight years old when he started, he served as a page for the full four-year term. He stayed with his father at the old Exchange Hotel located near the fountain at the foot of Dexter Avenue. Still crippled from his war wounds, his father couldn't put on his trousers or his shoes by himself. Jack helped his father dress and did minor chores, but more importantly the experience helped him come out of his shell—he was shy as a child—and developed his social skills. At the time he was the youngest page in the legislature and the only one with a perfect attendance record. "That was my father's doing. His idea was that you have a job to do. You've been hired and are being paid to do your job, and you have a duty to perform your job the best you can. I'd be the only page up there at one o'clock in the morning. . . . If the session started at midnight, by one o'clock I was sound asleep in my chair. He never woke me up. It didn't matter to him that I slept. What really mattered to him was that I was on the job doing the best that an eight-year-old could do . . . He had a tremendous sense of duty and responsibility.[10]

John and Maurice occasionally visited their father in Montgomery. John remembered the first time he met George Wallace was one Friday when he caught a ride (from Tuscaloosa) to Montgomery to go with his father to Phenix City for the weekend. Wallace was a member of the House of Representatives from Barbour County. He and Senator Patterson had worked on legislation together and had become good friends. "We had a late lunch in the afternoon at the Elite Cafe, which used to be the watering hole for all of the legislators," John recalled. "This young guy comes in and he looked like he was about fifteen or sixteen years old. My father introduced us. I guess George must have thought I was awful young too. At that time I was twenty-four, and he would have been twenty-six."[11]

Jack had met a lot of his father's friends in Montgomery, but George Wallace stands out in his memory more vividly than others. He was impressed with the future governor and liked him. "I don't remember any particular thing that he did for me, but I do remember that he was always very nice to me," Jack said of Wallace. "Kids generally remember folks that are nice to them."[12]

John did not share his father's passion for politics in those days, but did help out with his campaigns. While a student at the university he stumped for his father in Tuscaloosa County when he ran for convention delegate to the 1948 Democratic National Convention in Philadelphia. "I went all over Tuscaloosa County making speeches for him. In those days, every high school had political rallies at various times during the elections. They'd have box suppers and raffles. All the candidates would put their names in a hat. They'd draw the names out, and they'd speak to the crowd. You'd go and pass out literature. There was one nearly every night, and I used to work them and make speeches."

He said supporting his father's campaigns at these rallies helped him improve his own public speaking skills, recalling that when he was taking speech classes at the university, his teacher "thought my speeches were terrible . . . I used these political campaigns and these country crowds at these high school auditoriums to hone my skills. I enjoyed that thoroughly, and I did a lot of that. I learned a lot."[13]

Campaigning for convention delegate was a learning experience for his friend Ralph Williams as well. He had known Ralph since high school. Ralph was a little older, had already finished law school, and was practicing law in Tuscaloosa. Since Ralph too was running for convention delegate, they handed out literature and spoke at the same rallies.

Wanting to make a good impression, Ralph had cards printed with a profile portrait that showed his best side. One of the first couples to arrive at the rally was an elderly farm couple. Ralph shook the farmer's hand and gave him one of the cards. As they walked away the farmer squinted at the card and then tossed it on the floor. Turning to his wife he grumbled, loudly enough for the novice candidate to hear, "I can't stand a man who won't look you in the eye."[14]

By the time John joined the law practice in 1949, his father was faced with a political quandary over the growing influence that Phenix City's gambling kingpins had in the corridors of power in Montgomery. Albert Patterson had no quarrel with the gamblers. He had represented them in court. He had always believed in the basic rule of law that every defendant was presumed innocent until proven guilty, and that he was obligated to defend any client to the best of his ability regardless of who they were or their station in life.

He patiently explained this to his friend Hugh Bentley, who had lashed out at him three years earlier for representing Hoyt Shepherd in a sensational murder trial. Bentley, a local businessman who owned a sporting goods store in Columbus, had crusaded for years against Phenix City's rampant crime and violence. He now headed the Christian Laymen Association, a small group organized in the churches to oppose the criminal element and to clean up the city. While sympathetic to the group's aims, Albert Patterson had yet to join their cause. A man of faith and strong beliefs, he was also a pragmatic man not known for rash judgments or decisions. He did not tilt at windmills.

It was strictly business when he joined Hoyt Shepherd's defense team in the gambling boss's trial for the murder of Fayette "Fate" Leebern, a rival from across the river. Leebern was shot to death at the Southern Manor nightclub on a sweltering September night in Phenix City. Hoyt's brother Grady confessed to killing Leebern, claiming that it was done in self-defense. Witnesses implicated Hoyt, however, and a grand jury indicted both brothers for the murder.[15]

Hoyt hired every lawyer in town plus Jacob "Jake" Walker from Opelika to defend him. The lawyers went down to the jail as a group to meet with their client and discuss trial strategy. Shepherd asked Albert Patterson, who had a reputation for "helping the downtrodden and cutting clients a lot of slack on fees" to set the attorney fees for the group.

Patterson shocked all present, with the apparent exception of the defendant, when he said, "Five thousand dollars." Someone asked, "Is that five thousand dollars total?" He replied, "No. That's five thousand dollars each."

Five thousand dollars was a lot of money in the postwar period, more than double a year's wages for any of Shepherd's jailers. The jailhouse conversation between the lawyers and their client was privileged, but one of the jailers was listening in when Patterson named the fee. When the meeting broke up and the lawyers started to leave, he was overheard to say, "I think we got the wrong man in jail."[16]

AT SHEPHERD'S TRIAL ALBERT Patterson was the chief strategist for the defense, while Jake Walker (a close friend of Patterson's) was chief counsel and made the closing arguments. Roderick Beddow, a famous Birmingham defense attorney, was brought in by the Leebern family to assist the prosecution. The defense was granted a speedy trial. The case was tried in Phenix City during the second week of October. On the fourth day the case went to the jury. After four hours the jurors came back with a verdict of not guilty.[17]

When Hugh Bentley rushed down to Patterson's office before the trial, he had confronted his friend with the argument that Phenix City could never expect to see justice done if respected and admired men like him defended the criminal causes. Patterson told him patiently, but firmly that Hoyt Shepherd had hired his services, not bought his soul.[18]

He looked at politics the same way. From his perspective there was no quid pro quo when Hoyt Shepherd rallied Phenix City's underworld figures behind him in the Alabama Senate race held on November 5, less than three weeks away from his notorious client's acquittal on the murder charge.[19] The Senate seat represented both Lee and Russell counties, and Patterson had strong support among both constituencies. He had not courted the Phenix City machine's support, but would hardly have turned down votes from any quarter.

As Senator he coauthored a bill with Representative Jabe Brassell to separate Russell County from the four-county judicial circuit and make it a separate circuit. When the bill passed in August 1947, the county became the Twenty-Sixth Judicial Circuit. The change pleased Hoyt Shepherd, who had little or no political influence in the other three counties. Patterson insisted that the bill was passed solely on its merits—that a separate circuit was needed to handle the overflow from Columbus and Fort Benning. Nevertheless, the bill's passage strengthened the political machine in Russell County.

Senator Patterson had supported Folsom for governor, as had Hoyt Shepherd.

Big Jim had stayed overnight in the Patterson home on occasion. Jack remembered the six-foot-eight governor bumping his head on the door facing when he came in the house. John recalled that the bed in the guest room was too short for Big Jim, and his mother put chairs at the end of the bed for their guest's feet to rest on, and covered them with a separate blanket.[20]

On most of his visits to Phenix City, however, the governor's limousine was seen parked outside Sam's Motel, the only motel in town, where he was wined and dined at Hoyt Shepherd's expense. After signing the Patterson-Brassell bill, Governor Folsom appointed Julius B. Hicks as the new circuit judge and Arch Ferrell as the circuit solicitor (forerunner of today's district attorney) until the general election was held in May 1948. Not long afterward, Senator Patterson broke ranks with the Folsom administration. The newspapers said the senator was embarrassed when the governor failed to accept his advice on appointing a probate judge in Lee County. There are also suggestions that Patterson believed the administration had sold out to the political machine in Phenix City.[21]

Albert Patterson did more soul-searching after representing Head Revel in 1948. He lost the case when the State of Georgia succeeded in extraditing the gangster on a murder charge. Where Hoyt Shepherd had been accused of killing a rival gambler, the case against Head Revel was murkier and involved the cold-blooded slaying of a U.S. government witness and burying his body in the Okefenokee Swamp. Patterson was said to have vowed after the Revel case never again to accept payment for services from the Phenix City mob.[22]

In 1950, any remaining questions about Patterson having ties to the Phenix City machine were answered when he and his son John represented Gloria Floyd Davis in her suit for divorce from William R. "Bubba" Davis. Gloria was the daughter of Dr. and Mrs. Seth Floyd, a prominent family in town. Bubba was the son of racketeer Godwin Davis, who gloried in his tough-man image as "one of the meanest bastards that ever lived in Phenix City." When Bubba kicked her out, Gloria wound up at the Coulter Building seeking counsel. No other lawyer in town would take her case.

Bubba contested his wife's suit for alimony, custody of their small child, and child support. The divorce hearing was held before Circuit Court Judge Julius B. Hicks, who was in office because the Phenix City machine put him there. Judge Hicks was a "likeable fellow" who spent more time on his farm in Florida than he did in his office. John Patterson said that he never saw law books in the judge's office, but on the top of his desk were "these big ears of corn" that he had grown on his farm. "In an ordinary case where the mob had no interest in the thing, Hicks was a pretty good country judge," Patterson said. "But if the mob had an interest he did their bidding."

Judge Hicks ultimately ruled in Bubba's favor, but not before details about Phenix City's illegal gambling activities came out in open court. In seeking an equitable alimony settlement for their client, the Pattersons had to determine the husband's net worth. Not only had Gloria kept the books for the family's gambling enterprises, but she was entitled to copies of joint tax returns filed during their marriage. The gamblers were meticulous about obeying the tax laws to keep the federal and state authorities off their backs. Having fallen out with his former partners, Head Revel took the stand and testified against them. When the juicy details spilled out in court they became part of the public record, and citizens across the state were soon digesting them with their morning coffee. Phenix City's gambling bosses were not pleased.[23]

Gloria had married and divorced an Army captain before her marriage to Bubba. Judge Hicks ruled that she was not legally divorced from the Army captain, and this invalidated her marriage to Bubba. Albert Patterson pointed out to the judge that his ruling made the Davis child illegitimate. Hicks's face flushed. "Well, I'll take care of that." Slamming the gavel down, he decreed the child to be legitimate.[24]

John Patterson argued the appeal before the Alabama Supreme Court. He said it was the only case he'd ever known where the Alabama Supreme Court ruled from the bench. Before arguments began, Chief Justice J. Ed Livingston asked, "Who's that judge over there?" "Judge Hicks," Patterson replied. When the arguments were over, the justices whispered among themselves. "We can't let this thing stand," Livingston stated. "Something's got to be done about this." He told everyone to hang around while they prepared a temporary order and worked out a formal decree. They ruled in favor of the appellant and granted the attorneys a $750 legal fee. "We were never able to collect it," Patterson said. "The gangsters still controlled the courthouse, and the sheriff wouldn't enforce a judgment."[25]

Albert Patterson's repudiation of the Phenix City machine did not help his statewide campaign for the lieutenant governor's office in 1950. John campaigned for his father in east central and north central Alabama. His father lost to Jim Allen, a prominent Etowah County attorney who had served in the state senate with Patterson. Allen later served as a United States senator from Alabama from

January 1969 until his death in June 1978. Although Albert Patterson lost his bid to become lieutenant governor, the campaign gave him exposure across the state and set the stage for his bid for the office of attorney general four years later.

AFTER PRACTICING WITH HIS father for awhile, John noted an obvious shift in political power within the Phenix City machine. Hoyt Shepherd still pulled the strings, but inside the machine itself the power had shifted from the city fathers to the Russell County Circuit Solicitor's office. From his office on the second floor, Arch Ferrell had rapidly become a dominant figure in Phenix City politics. A few years later the *Birmingham News* revealed that anonymous wiretaps on Hoyt Shepherd's phone calls supported allegations that the county solicitor was both the "brains" of the machine and the "tool" of the local racketeers.[26]

One reporter described Arch Ferrell as "a lean, hard man of thirty-seven" who came from "a well-established family of lawyers" in Seale.[27] His father, H. A. Ferrell, had been deputy county solicitor before the 1947 creation of Russell County as a separate circuit had abolished his job, and his brother Pelham was also a local attorney. Arch had attained the rank of captain in the Army during WWII, and afterward served as state commander of the American Legion.[28]

Around Phenix City people knew the county solicitor as a ruthlessly ambitious man who had a drinking problem and a violent temper. He described himself as "tough and mean," and "bragged about his involvement in the Phenix City rackets, claiming that he was in charge of it all" and that he "had the power to prosecute or excuse anyone he wanted to." When he had too much to drink he boasted about having powerful friends in the state capital who took care of him.[29]

The wire taps on Hoyt Shepard's conversations also implicated Russell County Sheriff Ralph Matthews and Chief Deputy Albert Fuller in the Phenix City rackets. Fuller, a swaggering bully whose WWII service entailed pulling Navy shore patrol duty in Texas, strutted around town in a Stetson hat and cowboy boots with a pearl-handled six-gun strapped to his leg. Whether intimidated or just inept, Sheriff Matthews let Deputy Fuller do whatever he pleased. Fuller was more than just a tool of the racketeers. He was a partner with Cliff Entrekin in Cliff's Fish Camp, a bustling house of prostitution, and he ran a protection racket taking a cut of the profit from rival brothels around the county.

Albert Fuller added a notch to his tough-guy image in March 1946 by pouring five slugs into a small-time bootlegger while accompanying federal and state agents on a raid. The wife of the slain man, Guy Hargett, claimed that her husband was asleep in a chair and unarmed when Fuller burst through the door and shot him. Matthews and Ferrell backed up Fuller's claim that he had fired in the line of duty after Hargett had pulled a gun. Suspiciously, Hargett had been fingered by the gambling bosses for trying to muscle in on the lottery business.[30]

The killing didn't stop. In September 1950, Fuller and big Ben Scroggins (another deputy present when Fuller shot Hargett) trapped a wounded robber hiding in a cemetery and shot him thirteen times. Clarence Franklin Johns had been wounded in the leg while robbing Godwin Davis's Manhattan Cafe, and hid out in the cemetery after a local doctor patched him up. The getaway driver told authorities where to find Johns. Again it was ruled that the killing had been done in the line of duty. Fuller's cowboy image continued to grow. This time, however, stolen money was not recovered—creating suspicion in Davis's mind and opening a rift between the gambling kingpin and Fuller.[31]

If the phantom wiretaps had surfaced at this juncture, they might have raised more eyebrows. Time after time in the recordings Hoyt Shepherd referred to "the big boss" and "the man upstairs," making clear references to Solicitor Arch Ferrell. The tapes revealed that Fuller did Ferrell's bidding, and was at times a go-between for the solicitor and the crime bosses. Corruption was so pervasive that one Russell County grand juror sought to "work a shakedown" with the solicitor, but was warned off by Fuller. More troubling, the tapes revealed that the oil-slick of corruption in Phenix City had spread to the heart of state government in Montgomery.[32]

In the wiretapped discussions Shepherd's pet name for Governor Folsom was "Big Foot." The discussions implied that the gambling bosses had connections within the Folsom administration. In one recording, Shepherd told Sheriff Matthews that they got word from the governor's secretary to "go ahead and run your damn politics like you want and don't worry about no one over here." In a later reference to the conversation Shepherd said, "The word didn't come from Big Foot himself, but from mighty close to him."[33]

Also revealed in the wiretaps was that Shepherd and his friends were never sure where Albert Patterson stood. In a wiretap made in 1948 Shepherd admitted, "I ain't never been no great admirer of his. They put him on the ticket and there ain't much I can do about it." In another discussion about Patterson, he said, "I tried to get him kept off the ticket once, but they put him on there anyway." Shepherd sounded bitter when telling a friend that Patterson "walked by with some big shot" and "failed to speak to him, but merely nodded his head."[34]

When asked how he thought Albert Patterson would fare in his race for delegate, Shepherd said he didn't know but believed he would win "because of his popularity with voters both in and out of Russell County." He also thought the machine would be wasting its time to try and defeat Patterson in a multiple county or statewide election. The only way the machine could beat him, Shepherd said, would be if he ran for office in Russell County alone, or in a race involving no more than one or two additional counties. The gambling czar admitted that neither he nor the political big shots in Phenix City had ever "been able to do much" with Albert Patterson.

John's law practice with his father was interrupted in March 1951 when he returned to active duty during the Korean War. In May he shipped out from Fort Benning to Germany with the 4th Infantry Division. He was later joined by Mary Joe and their young son Albert. Named after his grandfather, Albert was born in September 1949 at the hospital in Columbus, Georgia, just after John graduated from law school and joined his father's practice.

There had not been much social life for the young couple while they lived in Phenix City. John was busy starting out practicing law, and there wasn't much in town for a young couple to do. Phenix City didn't have a golf course or a country club in those days. Columbus had these things, but there was little socializing back and forth across the river.

They belonged to the Trinity Methodist Church, where his father was on the board of stewards. "We went to church often . . . and did everything we could to be a part of the community, to be friendly to people, and to promote our law practice," he said. John sometimes gambled a little, and they occasionally went to the better nightclubs in town. He recalled that Hoyt Shepherd had a fine Chinese restaurant in his gambling hall south of Phenix City. It was there as a come-on to get people out to gamble, and the food was inexpensive. (The Chinese chef's name was George Chin. He and Patterson became friends, and Patterson entertained him in Montgomery after becoming governor. While John was still at the university, Albert had purchased a new Oldsmobile with an automatic transmission. He gave John the old maroon Olds. After he and Mary Joe moved to Phenix City, John traded in the Olds on a new Buick. When he got orders to Germany he sold the Buick to George Chin. The car must have given Chin good service, because their friendship remained steadfast for many years.)

After fighting broke out in Korea in July 1950, the armed forces had drawn from resources in Europe and other areas to build up U.S. troop strength in the combat zone. This left Western Europe vulnerable to invasion if the Soviets decided to strike while U.S. forces were engaged on the Korean peninsula. The Army had reassembled the 4th Infantry Division at Fort Benning as one of the divisions that would defend Western Europe in the event of a Soviet attack.

A Reserve major, Patterson voluntarily accepted an active-duty assignment in the lower grade of captain. He was promoted back to the grade of major in January 1953. With the 4th Division, he was assigned to the 42d Field Artillery Battalion as the battalion adjutant. Upon arrival in Germany, the battalion was stationed with the 12th Infantry Regiment at Gelnhausen. War plans tasked them to block the Fulda Gap to stall a Soviet advance if the Red army invaded Central Europe. Major Patterson didn't care for the monotony of the battalion adjutant's job. He had a bright young private named Fred Rothstein working in the office as a clerk, and left the routine duties to him. Rothstein's father had been a Berlin banker who escaped just ahead of the Nazis and made his way to the United States. Fred spoke fluent German and was indispensable as an interpreter with the local authorities.[35]

What impressed Rothstein about Patterson as an officer was that he was always interested in the soldiers and tried to help them if they got into trouble. "He was known by the soldiers as an officer who truly had their best interests at heart. Even if they committed some violation they wanted Captain Patterson to defend them. He gave his utmost professionally to present the soldier's case, whatever it would be. I mean that's the reputation John Patterson had."[36]

The two men became great friends and stayed in touch after leaving the Army. Rothstein later became president of Manhattan Shirt Company in New York, and helped finance Patterson's campaign for governor in Alabama. "Today he travels all over the world," Patterson said of his old friend. "He's a consultant for a number of textile firms. He has clients in China and all over the world. He travels all the time, and occasionally comes down here. It's an amazing world, isn't it?"

The Pattersons loved living in Gelnhausen, a beautiful old German town in the forest northwest of Frankfurt. They mixed well socially within the military and the local community. The year they spent in Gelnhausen was almost like an extended vacation, he said, with excellent fishing and hunting. "We had a nice apartment there. A lot of fine people live in Gelnhausen, and we had quite an interesting social life."

The 4th Division headquarters was at Frankfurt. After a year at Gelnhausen, Patterson was brought to the headquarters to join the Judge Advocate General's office, which was short of lawyers. For his professional development in criminal law, he couldn't have asked for a better assignment. There were about eighteen thousand men in the division, and no shortage of criminal cases. "I started out either defending or prosecuting three serious general courts-martial a week," he said.

The criminal investigation division (CID) had an excellent crime lab in Frankfurt. Also located there was a general hospital with a battery of psychiatrists who assisted with criminal cases when needed. "All kinds of expert witnesses, fingerprint experts, document experts, and the like" were available. Patterson viewed it as "a great educational experience." It didn't take long for him to gain a reputation as a winning criminal attorney.

Most of the cases were criminal in nature. Patterson prosecuted a number of deserters who had crossed over into East Germany and asked for political asylum. At any given time there were a hundred or so GIs in the east zone who had deserted, he explained. Some were going over, while others were coming back. "In those days we didn't have the Berlin Wall, but we had the fence. A nut would walk across, not knowing what he was doing, and ask for political asylum, or he might be a criminal running from the law. Sometimes a fugitive who committed a bad crime would flee across into the east zone and ask for political asylum."

None of them knew what they were getting themselves into. The Russians would imprison them for several months and interrogate them. If the interrogators bought their story, the deserters would be given a job in the interior somewhere, usually in construction work or common labor. After a few months of this, the deserter realized he'd made a mistake. "He'd catch the train to East Berlin and get on the subway—the subway went back and forth at that time—and ride across into the west zone, leave the station, and turn himself in to the first MP he saw. They'd put him on a plane, fly him to Frankfurt, and lock him up in the municipal jail. If he was a 4th Division man, they'd turn him over to us for prosecution."

As a general rule, the turncoats were convicted and received long prison sentences—usually about seventy-five years in the penitentiary and a dishonorable discharge. They were flown immediately to the United States and confined at Leavenworth. One interesting thing about those deserters, Patterson recalled,

"Our intelligence was good and we knew at all times just about where every one of them was being held in East Germany."

When representing defendants he sometimes had to put the system on trial, a tactic that did not sit well with the top brass. An example was his defense of a lieutenant charged with burying serviceable equipment and other materials behind the military installation. One of the soldiers on the burial detail had become disgruntled and turned him in. "When CID agents investigated the charges, they found that the ordnance unit had been burying stuff out there for years. They dug up a mountain of stuff and charged the lieutenant with all of it."[37]

Patterson successfully defended the lieutenant by pointing the finger at his superior officer. The lieutenant was ordered to get rid of the equipment before an inspection by headquarters. "What am I going to do with it," he asked? "They won't take it back because it's serviceable. I can't turn it in." "That's your problem," he was told. "Just get rid of it. Don't let it be here on inspection day." He did the only thing he knew to do. He followed orders. He couldn't destroy the equipment. So he buried it.[38]

A CRIMINAL CASE THAT stood out in Patterson's trial dossier was the court-martial of Private Charles W. Poor Thunder for raping a fifteen-year-old German girl. Poor Thunder had been drafted into the Army off the Sioux reservation and was shipped out to Europe as soon as he completed basic training. On the night he arrived at division headquarters in Frankfurt, he went out and bought his first legal drink of whiskey. He got "wild drunk and chased down a girl in a wheat field and raped her."[39]

The top brass decided to showcase the trial and to make an example of the defendant by setting up a special court comprised of hard-nosed senior officers. A tough sentence would have the dual effect of placating the local populace and sending a message to other GIs that the command would come down hard on criminal behavior. Patterson opposed the special court, urging instead that the private go before the regular court set up each month to try cases. Then there could be no question about fair treatment. He lost the argument.

Then Patterson was told that the higher ups wanted him to defend the accused. "Naw, you don't either. You don't want me to defend him."

"Why?" he was asked.

"Look. You can't stack the court on this man with me knowing about it and expect me to defend him without bringing it out."

He lost this argument, too. "Okay. But the book says I'm supposed to do my duty. He'll get the best defense I can give him."

He went down to the Frankfurt jail to see the defendant. Charlie Poor Thunder was buck naked, sitting cross-legged on a bare mattress on the floor. He had confessed to the crime three times while he was still drunk. Patterson told him that he had been assigned as his defense lawyer. "Do you want me to represent you?" he asked.

"Yeah, I reckon," Poor Thunder mumbled.

Patterson explained the charges and said, "You got no friends here. I'm your only friend, and I'm asking you to do something for me."

"Whut's that?"

"I want you to shut your mouth and don't open it again unless I tell you to. Will you promise me that?"

"Yessir, I'll do that."

At a preliminary hearing, the defendant was asked if he had anything to say. "Private Poor Thunder, you've got a right to make a statement. Would you like to say anything?"

His jaws were clamped shut.

"Do you understand?"

Patterson answered for him. "He understands."

"I think it would be in his interest to make a statement. Don't you think so?"

Silence.

"I really believe you ought to make a statement."

Patterson smiled. "Private Poor Thunder has nothing to say."

The court trying Poor Thunder was top-heavy. A brigadier general and seven field-grade officers had been selected to try the case. To Patterson's knowledge, the court was the first of its kind in the 4th Division to have a general officer sitting on it. The defendant had a right to enlisted representation on the court, so Patterson asked that four enlisted members be appointed. Four top sergeants—the sergeant majors of the three infantry regiments and the division artillery—were then appointed to the court.

In voir dire Patterson moved to strike two colonels for cause—questions of fair play had been raised—but was overruled. The defense had one peremptory strike, which Patterson decided to use to maximum advantage after all else had failed. "I strike the general," he said. The general got up, slammed his books together, stuffed them into his briefcase, and stormed out of the courtroom.

During breaks in the trial, an enlisted clerk overheard the four sergeant majors discussing the case and reported to Patterson that the enlisted men didn't think the officers were giving the private a fair trial. "When I found that out, I did everything I could to drive that wedge between the officers and the enlisted men," Patterson said.

Deliberations lasted much longer than anyone expected. They didn't have to spend time deliberating over Poor Thunder's guilt. Evidence of his guilt was strong and he had confessed. "They were in there for hours deliberating over how long a sentence they would give him," Patterson said. "You could hear them in there arguing and carrying on. They finally compromised on a sentence. A colonel named Hess, who had come up through the ranks and had won the Distinguished Service Cross, and the four master sergeants were on one side, and the rest of them on the other. They sentenced that private to twelve years. And they had set out to hang him."

"Well, the commanding general got madder than hell," Patterson said. During voir dire one of the colonels, responding to questions from Patterson, disclosed for the record that the general had chewed the colonel out because the court handed down what he deemed to be a light sentence in an earlier case. The general was in line to take over one of the top posts in NATO. When the verbatim record of the Poor Thunder trial got back to Washington, he was called home, given another star, and put in charge of the Army's troop information and education program.[40]

PATTERSON CONSIDERED STAYING IN the Army JAG program, but decided it was time to go back into civilian practice. "It wasn't the same Army I had known in World War II. It had become too political. And didn't have the same discipline and all. I just didn't fit there any more."

At one point he had also seriously considered staying in Europe and practicing law privately there. He became friends with some prominent American civilian lawyers in Germany, and they had discussed the possibility of him returning as a civilian attorney. The opportunities were appealing, but he decided that he was needed more at home.[41]

The Pattersons enjoyed their tour in Europe and made many new friends in the Army and in their host country. He kept in touch with several of his JAG associates after leaving the Army. One fellow officer, Edmon L. "Ted" Rinehart, a New York-born attorney and Princeton and Harvard graduate who had been a POW in WWII, later served as assistant attorney general and commissioner of the State Insurance Department in the Patterson administration and afterward became Patterson's law partner in Montgomery. The Patterson and Rinehart families were close through the years.

Mary Joe gave birth to their second child, a daughter, in May 1953 at the Army general hospital in Frankfurt. They named her Barbara Louise, but she became known to family and friends as "Babel," a nickname she was given while in Germany. A German nurse had called her "Barbel," and this was shortened to Babel.[42]

In August 1953 Patterson asked to be released from active duty so he could return to civilian practice in Phenix City with his father. The Army granted the request, and he returned from overseas in December. He stayed in the active U.S. Army Reserve until the 1960s when he transferred to the inactive reserve as a lieutenant colonel. He would have traded nothing for the time he spent in the Army, and he had a deep and abiding interest in the armed forces throughout his life.[43]

Mary Joe and the children came home before he did, because of a family emergency. Her father died of a heart attack a few weeks before they were scheduled to return from Germany. She flew back to Clanton with the children, while Patterson stayed behind and cleared out of family quarters in Frankfurt. When he came back in December, they set up housekeeping again in Phenix City and he went back to practicing law.

While John was away a chain of events convinced Albert Patterson that Phenix City had to be cleaned up and the only way it could be done was for him to become attorney general. John was not aware of these events or that Phenix City's sordid history was moving inexorably toward denouement. His father filed to run for attorney general in the 1954 Democratic primary and had pledged to clean up Phenix City if he was elected. The vice lords and the crooked politicians had thrown down the gauntlet, and Albert had picked it up. There would be no turning back the clock.

Above: Family of Delona and Mollie Patterson, Goldville, about 1910: (front) Delona, Grace, Mollie, Callie Mae; (back) Carrie, Alice, Lafayette, Edmon, Hollon, and Albert.
Left: Lt. Albert and Agnes Louise Patterson, Brownsville, Texas, in 1917. *Below:* Albert after release from Army hospital, 1920.

Clockwise from top left: Two-year-old John Patterson on the steps of Dougette Hall, Jacksonville State College, in 1923; Patterson growing up in Alexander City, 1932; Patterson and the Sears and Roebuck bicycle he purchased with his own earnings in Phenix City, about 1936.

Clockwise from top left: John Patterson with A Battery, 5th Field Artillery, 1st Infantry Division during North Carolina maneuvers in 1941; Patterson, while on furlough in 1941, drawing water from the well on the back porch of his grandparents' home in rural Tallapoosa County; Capt. Patterson in 1945 at the end of WWII; Patterson with fellow officer, Captain Tommy Thompson, at Battalion headquarters, Cavalle, Italy, 1944.

Left: Recalled to active duty during the Korean War, Patterson was photographed crossing the English channel to Germany. *Above:* back home, Albert Patterson, Hugh Bentley and other concerned citizens formed the Russell Betterment Association to fight corruption and vice in Phenix City. A wave of gangland violence ensued. Among other outrages thugs dynamited Hugh Bentley's home. *Below:* Albert Patterson, Jim Folsom, Mayor Homer D. Cobb, and Rep. Jabe Brassell at a political luncheon in Phenix City.

Albert and Agnes Patterson listen to election results in the state attorney general's race in the 1954 Democratic primary.

Above: Albert Patterson's automobile at the murder scene. *Below:* Albert Patterson was gunned down outside his office on the night of June 20, 1954. Arriving at the scene, John Patterson learned of his father's murder from sheriff's deputy Aaron Smith and Phenix City policeman Leon Sanders.

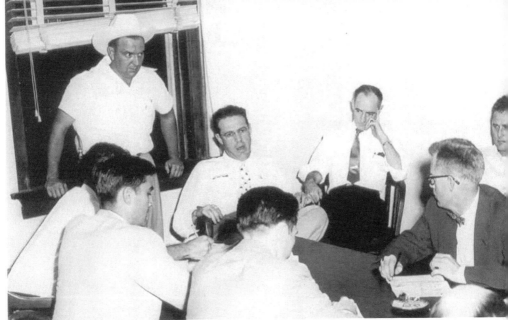

Top: Attorney General Silas M. Garrett III holds a press conference in Phenix City announcing he is taking charge of the Patterson murder investigation. Deputy sheriff Albert Fuller leans against the window sill behind Garrett. Mayor Elmer Reese is seated on the other side of Garrett. Within months Deputy Fuller was convicted of murdering Albert Patterson, while Garrett escaped prosecution by checking himself into a mental institution in Texas. *Bottom:* Major General Walter J. "Crack" Hanna reads proclamation of martial rule in Phenix City signed by Alabama Governor Gordon Persons in July 1954.

Above: Judge Walter B. Jones ordered national guardsmen to retrieve deputy Albert Fuller from his sickbed and bring him to court to answer corruption charges. *Right:* Russell County Circuit Solicitor Arch Ferrell, under indictment for vote fraud, was jailed for public drunkenness in July 1954. Escorting Ferrell to city hall were national guardsmen F. G. Hughes (right) and Douglas Chandler, both of Birmingham. *Below:* Ferrell (hands clasped), was indicted December 9, 1954, with Attorney General Si Garrett and Fuller for the murder of Albert Patterson. Ferrell was arrested by Sheriff Lamar Murphy and booked at the county jail.

Above: Chief Justice Ed Livingston swearing in John Patterson as Alabama's Attorney General in January 1955. *Left:* Attorney General Patterson escorted his mother to the Jefferson County courtroom where she took the stand as the leadoff witness in the Fuller murder trial.

Above: Albert Fuller, right, with Birmingham lawyer Roderick Beddow at the disgraced deputy's trial for the murder of Albert Patterson. Fuller was convicted, but indicted co-conspirator Arch Ferrell was acquitted. *Below:* Ferrell (center) with defense attorneys George Rogers (left) and Drew Redden (right) at his trial in Birmingham.

Top: Gubernatorial candidate John Patterson on the campaign trail in 1958.
Bottom: Kickoff rally for Patterson's 1958 campaign for governor inside the
school auditorium in New Site, Alabama.

Above: Rebe Gosdin and the Sunny Valley Boys warm up the crowd at a Patterson rally. *Below:* Patterson had the audience's attention as he hammered home his theme of good government and respect for the law.

Above: Patterson speaks at a political rally at the Alexander City airport featuring the full slate of candidates in the 1958 primary.

Above: Inaugural Day, January 19, 1959, outgoing Governor Big Jim Folsom rode with Patterson up Dexter Avenue. Patterson wore a too-small top hat borrowed from Earl McGowin. *Right:* The incoming governor and the first lady on the reviewing stand.

Above: In a photo printed even in foreign newspapers, five-year-old Barbara Patterson stuck her tongue out at a photographer, as her brother Albert waved to the crowd. The caption in the *San Franscisco News* was "Sugar'n Spice'n Everything Nice . . . Whoops!" Patterson's grandmother, Mollie, and wife, Mary Joe, are behind. *Below:* Judge Walter B. Jones swears in Patterson as Alabama's forty-ninth governor.

Left: Governor John Patterson's official photograph, 1959. *Below:* The first family on the staircase inside the governor's mansion, 1959.

Above: The Patterson cabinet, January 1959. Seated, from left: Edward Azar, Floyd Mann, Charlie Meriwether, Ralph Williams, Governor Patterson, Harry Haden, Leland Jones, E. M. McCollaugh, and Olin Brooks. Standing: Harry Cook, Sam Engelhart, Ralph Smith, Major General Henry V. Graham, Joe Robertson, Roy Marcato, Alvin Prestwood, Joe Foster, Claude Kelley, Edmon L. Rinehart, William Younger. *Left:* Patterson addressing the joint session of the Alabama legislature in 1959.

Above: Governor Patterson on the front porch of the old home place in Goldville (1962). *Below:* News reporters accompanied state officials on a raid of an illegal gambling establishment in Shelby County. From left: Edward Azar; unidentified man; Joe Robertson; Patterson; Floyd Mann; unidentified state investigator; Billy Vickers; and Rex Thomas of the Associated Press.

Right: Patterson welcomed President Eisenhower to Redstone Arsenal, September 8, 1960, for the dedication of the George C. Marshall Space Flight Center. *Below:* Democratic presidential nominee John F. Kennedy and Patterson at a campaign rally in Warm Springs, Georgia, on October 10, 1960.

Above: Patterson and Robert F. Kennedy comparing notes on roll call of delegates to the 1960 Democratic National Convention. Robert Bradley and Joe Robertson look on. *Below:* Patterson joined former President Harry S. Truman, in Decatur, Alabama, in late October 1960 at a Democratic rally supporting the Kennedy-Johnson ticket.

Right: Patterson campaigned for John F. Kennedy in Walker County in 1960. *Below:* John F. Kennedy accepted his Party's nomination for president at the Democratic National Convention in Los Angeles, July 1960.

DEMOCRATIC NATIONAL CONVENTION
1960

Above: With vice-presidential nominee Lyndon Baines Johnson aboard the "Democratic Victory Train" ride through Alabama are Patterson, State Representative Roland Bounds of Clark County, and Jefferson County Democratic Party leader George Lewis Bailes, Jr. *Below:* Lady Bird Johnson pins a carnation on the governor, as they prepare to disembark from the "Democratic Victory Train" and meet the throng of enthusiastic supporters awaiting them in Montgomery.

Above: Patterson was a special guest at the inaugural of his friend Louisiana Governor Jimmie Davis in Baton Rouge in 1961. *Right:* Groundbreaking for the University of Alabama Research Institute, Huntsville, December 20, 1962. From left: Patterson; Dr. Hermann, Institute director; Dr. Frank Rose, president, University of Alabama; Dr. Wernher von Braun, director, George C. Marshall Space Flight Center; Maj. Gen. Francis J. McMorrow, U.S. Army Missile Command, Redstone Arsenal.

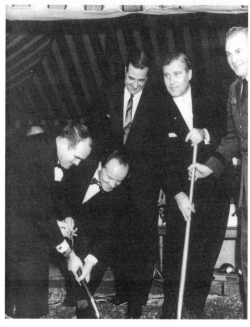

Top: A Greyhound bus goes up in flames outside Anniston, Alabama. State plainclothes officer E. L. Cowling was credited with saving the Freedom Riders on board from the thugs who set the bus on fire. *Bottom:* The Freedom Rider crisis stole the headlines in May 1961. At the height of the crisis, assistant U.S. Attorney General Byron "Whizzer" White met with Governor Patterson and state officials on the morning of Sunday the 21st of May in the governor's office. Seated around the conference table are, from left, Floyd Mann, White, Patterson, MacDonald Gallion, and Robert Bradley.

At a ceremony on the Capitol grounds, a statue of the late Albert Patterson was unveiled by his grandson and namesake, twelve-year-old Albert Patterson II, and Bob Harry of New Site.

"I love Alabama! I'm proud that it's my state and I will fight for it! It can become a better state and I ask your prayers and your help in working toward that goal."

May 3 is a day of decision for Alabama and *you*! Shall we move forward together in peace and harmony or shall we continue to live from crisis to crisis, defeat to defeat. Young or old, your future opportunity and security depends on your vote. For law and order . . . for full time dedication to Alabama . . . vote **JOHN PATTERSON** for Governor . . . a *proven man* for a *man-sized* job!

Patterson campaign poster in 1966 gubernatorial race.

Four Alabama governors: John Patterson, Jim Folsom, Albert Brewer, and
George Wallace, about 1969.

John and Tina Patterson in downtown Montgomery, about 1975.

Right: Patterson and Earmon "Wolf" Glenn together at the farm a few years before Wolf's death in 1991. *Below:* Patterson with Belvedere Lass and his herd of Angus brood cows sometime in the 1960s.

The judges of the Alabama Court of Criminal Appeals, 1988: seated from left, John C. Tyson, Sam Taylor (presiding), and William M. Bowen, Jr.; standing, John Patterson and Bucky McMillan.

NOBODY
BUT TH
PEOPL

Facing page, top: Judge Patterson and Tina greet U.S. Supreme Court Justice Sandra Day O'Connor at a Law Day reception in Anniston, May 9, 1986. *Bottom:* John and Tina Patterson at a dinner celebrating the twenty-fifth anniversary of the Patterson administration.

Above: On the fiftieth anniversary of the Phenix City tragedy, Alabama Governor Bob Riley presented posthumous Distinguished Service Medals to the families of Albert Patterson, Major General Walter J. "Crack" Hanna, and Judge Walter B. Jones. On the same occasion, Riley honored the Alabama National Guard for its part in cleaning up Phenix City. In this photo, Riley is pictured with Albert Patterson's four sons, Jack, John, Sam, and Maurice Patterson.

John and Tina Patterson at their farm in Goldville, May 2007.

No More Darkness, No More Night

John Patterson had looked forward to coming home, resuming law practice with his father, and getting on with his life. He and Mary Joe moved temporarily with their two young children into the basement apartment of his parents' house. They had purchased a house near Fort Benning before going overseas, but rented it out while they were gone and the occupants still had six months on their lease. John started to work immediately. Occupying his old desk in the Coulter Building he handled most of the cases so his father could concentrate on the attorney general's race.

He had not anticipated the volatile situation he found upon his return to Phenix City. The alliance between gambling kingpin Hoyt Shepherd and county solicitor Arch Ferrell had existed in 1951, and had already spun a web of political graft and deceit that would perpetuate the darker side of Phenix City's history. Knowing this, however, had not prepared him for the tapestry of fear and intimidation hanging over the Alabama side of the Chattahoochee River when he returned at the end of 1953. Inside the county courthouse and in the dives and gambling dens clustered around the Fourteenth Street Bridge and on Dillingham Street there was seething rancor and hostility toward the town's "bible thumpers hell-bent on reform" that was not apparent when Mayor Homer Cobb held the keys to city hall.[1]

While overseas he was unaware that his father was embroiled in the movement to clean up Phenix City and had become a prime target of the local politicians and their gangster friends. By opposing the machine his father had crossed Hoyt Shepherd and made a mortal enemy of Arch Ferrell. The county solicitor had expressed an intense dislike for the elder Pattterson and publicly vented his rage about how much he hated "that sonuvabitch" in the Coulter Building. John Patterson was not told about the dangers his father faced or the machine's retaliation against the Russell Betterment Association until he got home because the family had not wanted him to worry.

Once he returned it didn't take long to put the story together about his father's troubles with Ferrell and his cronies. He learned that for months there had been nearly as many anonymous telephone threats as there were legitimate business calls. The callers seemed to know his father's every move. From the windows in the county courthouse they could monitor his father's comings and goings at the Coulter Building. According to the secretary, Albert shrugged off the threats. If the calls bothered him, he didn't let it show. Around the house the family talked openly about the situation. They took necessary precautions. They locked the doors at night and stayed clear of the windows. His father wouldn't let family members go near his car in the mornings until he got in and started the engine.

John said his mother sometimes lay down inside the front door with a shotgun so her husband's rest would not be disturbed. "Now I wanna tell you, that ain't no way to have to live," he recalled in later years. But his mother never complained. Throughout their marriage Agnes Louise (called "Skeet" by her husband and friends) had been a tower of strength in support of her husband's endeavors. She was no less now.[2]

Phenix City politics, although corrupt, had been sugarcoated when Homer Cobb was alive. Mayor Cobb had become a wealthy man off his mob connections, but he had not lusted for power nor run roughshod over the opposition like the new wheels in town. John Patterson was still at home in August 1950 when Cobb suffered a heart attack and died while celebrating Cobb Memorial Hospital's third anniversary at a festive barbecue in Idle Hour Park. The mayor's death marked the end of an era when his neighborly style of politicking with "a wink and a nod" had sustained at least a modicum of propriety between bureaucracy and bossism in Phenix City. His two decades of keeping the city solvent through "accommodation and compromise" as councilman and mayor had died with him.[3]

Phenix City's residents generally believed that the former mayor had their interests at heart, and that his underlying concern in accommodating the gamblers was not to line his own pockets, but to fill the public coffers and to pay the city's bills. Cobb Memorial Hospital was a proud monument to that legacy, even though it was whispered around town that the facility was a handmaiden of the rackets and did their bidding. The hospital's alleged shady practices were unproven, but no one questioned that legitimate business and industry had shied away from the city's tawdry history of vice and violence.

Albert Patterson had been friends with Homer Cobb since moving to Phenix

City in 1933. For nearly two decades he got his hair cut at Cobb's barbershop, and he spoke with the mayor almost every day. Cobb had confided to friends that he feared the racketeers and power-hungry politicians in Russell County were out of control and would move in and take over completely when he was gone. His fears were well-founded.[4]

By John's return in 1953 the Russell County officeholders had become caricatures that a casting director might have hired for the villains in the Saturday matinees he had watched as a young boy in Alexander City. With Homer Cobb out of the way, county deputy Fuller wasn't the only lawman in town who owned a piece of Phenix City's lucrative sin palaces. The town's hulking assistant police chief Buddy Jowers (the new mayor's nephew) was half-owner in an illegal enterprise similar to Fuller's. Jowers kept the soldier boys in line when they got rowdy, and had a cut of Fuller's protection racket as well. Hoyt Shepherd not only pulled the strings above every dangling politician in town, but had filled the public offices with his henchmen. He controlled the law, and he controlled the system of justice in Phenix City and Russell County.

JOHN'S YOUNGEST BROTHER JACK, a sophomore at Central High, was the only one of the four sons still at home. Maurice had returned from an Army tour in Korea, and now lived and worked across the river in Columbus. Sam worked for Kinnett's Dairies in town and lived nearby. Fifteen-year-old Jack, who went nearly everywhere with his father, knew more about his father's political life than all the other brothers put together.

While overseas, John had listened proudly to his father's voice over the radio when he addressed the Democratic National Convention in Chicago in 1952. Back home Jack had accompanied his father to Chicago, where they stayed at the Roosevelt Hotel on Michigan Avenue. He recalled that the convention hall was packed with delegates, but few ventured outside where the pungent odors from the nearby stockyards were as sharp as the images in a Carl Sandburg poem.[5]

The primary reason Albert Patterson had become a delegate to the 1952 Democratic Convention was to lobby for federal help in cleaning up Phenix City. It was not surprising that his personal choice for president was Senator Estes Kefauver who had gained national prominence as chairman of the Senate crime investigating committee in 1950 and 1951. Kefauver's election to the Senate in 1949 was credited with having ended "Boss" Edward H. Crump's control over politics in his home state of Tennessee.

Jack recalled that Kefauver's 1951 book on the Senate committee's investigation, *Crime in America*, was one of his father's favorites. Albert studied the book, quoted from it in his public addresses, and loaned the book to his son to use in writing school papers. Prior to the convention, Jack had attended a campaign dinner with his father "at a club in Vestavia, over the mountain from Birmingham" where Kefauver was the guest of honor.

Not sure that his father had a commitment from Kefauver, Jack was confident that he worked on behalf of the Senator "with at least some hope of federal support" if elected. He remembered that during the convention, a campaign worker for another candidate solicited Albert's vote and was asked, after explaining the Phenix City situation, whether the candidate would lend federal support to cleaning the city up. The worker replied that such support was doubtful because the cleanup was a local matter, not a federal one.

Lafayette Patterson, who also attended as a member of the Alabama delegation, was squarely behind the nomination of Adlai Stevenson of Illinois. Unlike today, candidates were not selected beforehand, so the convention halls were filled with lively debate and campaign workers lobbying for delegate votes. Jack witnessed a heated discussion in their hotel room between his father and Uncle Lafayette, who was the only Alabama delegate to vote for Stevenson. Albert, solidly behind Kefauver, stood his ground with his older brother only to end up on the losing side when Stevenson became the party nominee.[6]

John Patterson later met Senator Kefauver, who spoke warmly of Albert. Describing him as "a warm friend" who had "tremendous courage and ability," Kefauver said he "respected and admired him very much." He told a *Birmingham News* reporter that he got to know Albert Patterson well. "He talked to me many times about Phenix City and his determination to wipe out crime there. He was most concerned about it."[7]

JOHN PREFERRED THAT HIS father stay out of the fight to clean up Phenix City. They talked about it, but things had gone too far. Another hard-fought political campaign would be taxing for the fifty-nine-year-old Albert, still badly crippled from his war injuries, but he was not about to back down. Among numerous outrages committed while his eldest son was away, the machine had retaliated against Albert for having exposed the syndicate's lottery profits to IRS scrutiny in the Bubba Davis divorce case, and for representing a young mother victimized by the baby rackets and a black man brutally beaten by the police. From

the shadows Ferrell and Shepherd led a vicious smear campaign against Albert
Patterson and plotted to have him replaced in community positions he had held
for years on the school board, the draft board, and in his church.[8]

The machine and the mob had conducted campaigns of intimidation and
violence against Hugh Bentley and other reformers. If the opposition couldn't
be bought off, they set out to ruin them. Even clergymen were not spared their
mockery or their wrath. No one who lived in Phenix City at the time would
forget the monthly prayer vigils that Reverend R. K. Jones ("a robust, powerfully
built man whose sermons shook the rafters") and other local ministers conducted,
where the various church congregations came together and read scripture, sang
hymns, and prayed through the night. The organist played the old country
spirituals and newer ones like Hank Williams's huge hits, "Wait for the Light to
Shine" and "I Saw the Light":

No more darkness, no more night. Now I'm so happy,
no sorrow in sight. Praise the Lord, I saw the light.

While delivering knee-trembling, hell-fire-and-brimstone sermons the ministers called on the Lord to remove the gamblers and the corrupt public officials
from their midst as the Lord saw fit, and they prayed for the heavens to give them
a sign. When Mayor Cobb died just hours after one of the all-night vigils, the
faithful wondered was this the sign? The vice mayor took Homer Cobb's place.
Within a year he dropped dead after one of the hallelujah camp meetings had
rocked the night away. Even non-believers began to wonder. Rumors abounded
that the mob had put a contract out on R. K. Jones, but the fearless reverend
never faltered. When he was transferred to a church in Lee County, the Phenix
City congregation figured it was payback from Satan and the mob.

The story didn't end there. The displaced preacher was still a legal resident
of Phenix City, and he continued to vote in Russell County. After the cleanup
the state legislature passed an act requiring a re-identification of all voters in the
county. Individual voters had to appear at the courthouse and sign a sworn affidavit that they legally resided in Russell County. As the story goes, R. K. Jones
complied with the requirement and was spotted by a parolee who was part of
the old Phenix City crowd and had done time for murder. Not realizing that
Jones was still legally domiciled in Russell County, the parolee signed a warrant
against the minister for perjury.

The week before Jones was to appear in Judge Harry Randall's court on Monday morning, the complaining witness was sitting on his sofa at home watching television when he suddenly pitched forward and died. On Sunday afternoon Randall, who had been Russell County judge for sixteen years, was fishing at his cabin on the backwaters of the Chattahoochee River when he fell out of the boat and drowned in water that was no more than knee deep.[9] When a new judge was appointed to the court, his first order of business was to dismiss the perjury case against Reverend Jones.

After John Patterson was elected governor in 1958, the reverend brought his wife and the youngest of their twelve children to Montgomery and came by the governor's office to pay his respects. Ending their visit with a few words of prayer, Jones turned to the governor on the way out and said with conviction, "Brother John, I've lived my life for Christ. And it works."[10]

THROUGH THE SUMMER OF 1951 the Phenix City bosses treated the "meddle-some ministers" and Hugh Bentley's small band of reformers (now known as the Citizen's Committee) with contempt—decrying them as public nuisances. They scoffed when the reformers invited the Kefauver Committee to investigate crime in Phenix City and when they petitioned Governor Gordon Persons, who had been in office only a few months, to do something about the situation. Kefauver was busy campaigning to be the next Democratic presidential nominee and declined. Governor Persons sent a state investigator to look into the matter, but the Phenix City crowd was tipped off in advance. As usual, nothing came of the state's investigation.

A turning point in the reform movement came on a brisk October night in 1951—about six months after John Patterson had been recalled into the Army and shipped overseas with his family. His father, having watched the political machine outmaneuver his friends Hugh Bentley, Hugh Britton, John Luttrell, Charlie Gunter, Howard Pennington, and other reform-minded citizens at every turn, decided he'd seen enough. If the Phenix City machine was to be defeated, someone with an intimate knowledge of the law and the political system had to get involved.

On the night of October 26, the boisterous crowds going in and out of the honky-tonks down near the river were oblivious to a late-night meeting taking place in the Patterson law offices just up Fourteenth Street at the Coulter Building. Any passersby who saw the second-floor lights still on would have thought nothing of it, since Patterson nearly always burned the midnight oil. Even the night deputies were too busy looking out for their interests inside the sin palaces to notice the steady arrival of men at the Coulter Building and their nervous glances around before trooping up the stairs to the suite of law offices.

That night Albert Patterson had called the leaders of the reform movement together and laid out a plan for defeating the Phenix City machine through legal means. He warned that it would be an arduous undertaking, and a dangerous one. By winning the battle they would be risking their lives. As an initial step the group formed the Russell Betterment Association, led by ten stalwarts known as the "Gall Club." Only the names of the stalwarts were to be made public. The names of other members were kept secret for their protection. The newly formed RBA put the mob and the machine on notice in a front-page story in the *Columbus Ledger* the following morning.[11]

The *Birmingham News* followed up two days later with a story about the RBA's plans to impeach Russell County's laidback, do-nothing sheriff by bringing up neglect-of-duty charges against him before the Alabama Supreme Court. Hoyt Shepherd, described in a *Look* magazine article as "a dapper, soft-spoken, gum-chewin' gamblin' man who hung out in the office of his good friend H. Ralph Matthews, sheriff of Russell County," responded quickly to the news. The gamblin' man hurried over to the Coulter Building and arranged to meet privately with Hugh Bentley in Albert Patterson's outer office.[12]

Hoyt Shepherd, if taken at his word, wanted out of the rackets. Since the Fate Leeburn killing, he'd become a marked man and had barely survived two attempts on his life. He promised Hugh Bentley any public office in the county if the RBA would "call off their dogs." When Bentley scoffed at the offer, Shepherd informed him that he was quitting the rackets and was going to lead a respectable life for the sake of his family. Shepherd apparently kept his promise and disposed of his gambling properties, but only to remain in the background and mastermind Phenix City's political intrigue from the shadows.[13]

After a conspicuous interval, during which the gamblers made a pretense of closing down and the RBA proceeded with plans to impeach Sheriff Matthews, the mob decided to teach Hugh Bentley a lesson. Around midnight on January 9, 1952, the RBA leader arrived home from a trip to Augusta, Georgia, to find his house had been blown to smithereens by dynamite. Miraculously, no one in the family was seriously injured, although Bentley's teenage son Hughbo had been thrown more than thirty feet into the yard by the force of the explosion. The blast completely destroyed the dwelling.[14]

Word on the street alleged that Deputy Fuller had instigated the bombing and served as a lookout while Tommy Capps, a local hood known in the gambling community as "Dynamite" Capps, planted the explosives. As with so many other Phenix City crimes, these suspicions were never proven.[15] Ordnance experts from Fort Benning concluded that an amateur had planted the dynamite. Had the job been done properly, they said, there were enough sticks of dynamite under the structure to "have blown the Bentleys' house clear out of Russell County."[16]

Governor Persons made a hurried visit to Phenix City to inspect the bombing wreckage, and offered a $1,000 reward for information leading to the arrest and conviction of the perpetrators. He told local authorities that he wanted no stone left unturned in finding those responsible, while expressing regret to reporters that the bombing had exposed the state to undeserved publicity. Attorney General Silas M. Garrett III, accompanied by Sheriff Matthews and Police Chief Pal Daniel, called a press conference after investigating the crime scene—an obvious smoke screen in light of later events. Garrett, a crony of Arch Ferrell's and his guardian angel in Montgomery, stated to the press that he saw no connection between the RBA's complaints, which he claimed were totally without basis, and the bombing of Bentley's house.[17]

Circuit Judge Hicks called for the convening of a grand jury to investigate the crime. A rigged jury, made up of racketeers and their friends, found no evidence linking the vice lords or public officials to the bombing and returned no indictments. Ugly rumors spread through town that Hugh Bentley had dynamited his own house to give the RBA more phony evidence supporting its charges of corruption against duly elected officials in Russell County. Bentley was so shocked that people would think he could do such a thing to his own family that he traveled to Birmingham and took a lie detector test to prove it was a lie.[18]

At a stormy public hearing, attended by Jack Patterson with his father, the RBA members vowed to stay on the offensive until the criminals and the corrupt officials were thrown out. Jack described it as "a very heated meeting," where an enraged Arch Ferrell "got into an argument with the people in the audience." To a chorus of boos, Ferrell declared that Phenix City was one of the cleanest little towns in America. He angrily shouted a challenge to the RBA members to get on with their impeachment proceedings, that he wasn't afraid of them. A fistfight almost broke out when Ferrell's sister slapped a man who called her brother a liar. Ferrell lost his temper, and had to be restrained from charging into the audience after the man.[19]

The *Columbus Ledger*, to its credit, was the only newspaper to cover the RBA's struggle from start to finish. Newspapers throughout Alabama were conspicuously silent. Outraged by the cowardly bombing of Bentley's house, the *Ledger* went on the attack with hard-hitting investigative reporting on the violence and political corruption on the other side of the Chattahoochee. The paper's hate mail shot up overnight and two of its reporters, veteran Tom Sellers and Ray Jenkins (a young journalist on the rise who would one day become editor of the *Montgomery Advertiser* and the *Baltimore Sun*), were attacked at the Phenix City polls during the 1952 elections. Hugh Britton, Hugh Bentley, his son Hughbo, and other RBA members, who were there as poll-watchers, were also kicked and beaten by the local toughs while a state trooper looked on with his arms crossed.[20]

Early one Sunday morning, within a few weeks of the bombing of Bentley's house and the stormy public meeting, the fire chief called Albert Patterson to tell him that his office had been torched. The janitor had arrived at the Coulter Building before sunrise, saw smoke coming from the upstairs office, and sounded the alarm. Had the janitor not discovered the fire, Patterson's office and the RBA files would have been destroyed. An arsonist had broken in through a window and drenched the office area with flammable liquid before setting it ablaze.[21]

John Patterson said that once more the finger of suspicion pointed to Deputy Fuller and an accomplice, but the arsonist was never caught. "They were trying to scare off the RBA," he said. "but they didn't know Hugh Bentley and Hugh Britton and the other stalwarts, and they didn't know my father."[22] In a scathing editorial the *Ledger* condemned the string of criminal acts against the RBA and excoriated "the bastard who desecrated the Sabbath by this crime." The paper stopped short of implicating Phenix City and Russell County lawmen, but suggested they bore "a measure of responsibility" for having failed to act.[23]

Since the impeachment trial against Sheriff Matthews was more than a year away, Albert Patterson sought immediate relief before the U.S. District Court for the Middle District of Alabama in Montgomery. Although the RBA presented the U.S. attorney with solid evidence of federal crimes, a grand jury didn't call for the testimony of a single RBA member. The only witnesses called were federal, state, and local officials—the very people who were charged in the complaint.

The grand jury reported finding no evidence of organized criminal activity anywhere in the Middle District. This was another setback for the RBA and a foretaste of what the group would be up against in the upcoming trial to try and unseat Russell County's well-entrenched sheriff. Higher-ups in state and federal law enforcement had rallied behind the Phenix City and Russell County lawmen during the grand jury hearing, and there was no reason to believe things would be any different in an impeachment trial. If they lied under oath once, they could be expected to do it again.

Albert knew not to look for help from the state inspectors, state troopers, or the attorney general's office. Attorney General Si Garrett and Solicitor Arch Ferrell were "two peas in a pod," and the state troopers and inspectors had shown they would go out on a limb in protecting their own. Governor Persons had sounded sympathetic and said the right words, but words were cheap. Now, the federal authorities had gone before the grand jury and twisted the facts. Going forward with the impeachment process, Patterson could only hope that honorable men would feel compelled to speak the truth before the Alabama Supreme Court and that the RBA's evidence would be judged on its merits.

Some members of the group, including Albert Patterson, wanted to go after Ferrell first, but the majority believed that Matthews was more vulnerable for having failed to perform his duties and that a case against him would be easier to prove. At Patterson's suggestion the RBA retained Roberts Brown, a respected lawyer from nearby Opelika and speaker of the Alabama House of Representatives, to bring the impeachment charges against Matthews. Patterson helped prepare the case, and Brown filed the charges with the Alabama Supreme Court in July 1952.[24]

With a year to wait for the Supreme Court to hear the charges, both attorneys were under constant pressure from the Phenix City machine to drop the case. When Brown turned down an anonymous caller who tried to buy him off, he awoke one night to find his house in flames. He and his wife barely escaped with their lives. Some people suspected Dynamite Capps of setting the fire, as well as the earlier one at Patterson's law office, but there was not enough evidence. Brown heard rumors that the Phenix City gamblers were giving odds that he wouldn't be around to argue the case against Matthews, but the gutsy attorney refused to back off.[25]

When his father told him what had transpired during the impeachment trail, John Patterson's brow wrinkled in anger. He had pressed his father for information because he knew that the trial had been the final straw behind his decision to run for attorney general. The trial had opened before the seven Supreme Court justices on June 8, 1953, and ended five days later with a unanimous vote clearing Sheriff Matthews of the impeachment charges. The Supreme Court's ruling left his father no choice but to accept when the RBA members came to him and asked that he become a candidate for attorney general.[26]

The impeachment trial was a mockery of justice in Alabama. Hugh Bentley, Hugh Britton, and several others had driven over from Phenix City to present evidence against Matthews. They introduced investigators who testified to the wide-open gambling and vice they had witnessed in Russell County just the day before the trial. Everybody knew that Phenix City was a gambling town—two members of the Supreme Court had been there and gambled—and the RBA's witnesses presented substantiated evidence to that effect. Along with this evidence their attorneys had built a solid case against the sheriff's failure to close down the vice and gambling operations.

Not surprisingly, given the history of the state's tolerant attitude toward Phenix City's lawlessness, the plaintiff's attorneys were stonewalled by the very men who were sworn to uphold the law and to protect the citizens of Alabama. Just as they had done at the federal grand jury hearing the year before, a parade of high-level state and federal law officers testified for the defense. Among those praising Matthews and his enforcement of the law in Russell County were Attorney General Garrett, state public safety director L. B. Sullivan, state highway patrol chief Tom Carlisle, chief criminal investigator Joe Smelley, and ABC board agent Ben Scroggins. All testified that they were familiar with Russell County, and knew of no organized gambling or racketeering there.[27]

Particularly galling to Roberts Brown and Albert Patterson was the sworn testimony of federal officials. The U.S. Attorney for the Middle District testified that he and the FBI had conducted a grand jury investigation into claims of organized gambling and prostitution in Phenix City and had found no evidence to support such claims. He presented the Supreme Court with the grand jury report from the year before. The FBI agent for the district followed him to the stand and swore that he too knew of no organized gambling and vice in Russell County.

How could the federal officials not have known when 223 of the 238 federal gambling stamps issued in Alabama after the gambling tax act went into effect in 1951 were to Phenix City establishments? In fact there were more than 350 outstanding federal gambling licenses in effect in Phenix City on the day the two officials testified. Even the Alabama Supreme Court, in its ruling against impeachment, felt compelled by "the realities" to acknowledge Phenix City's "unsavory reputation . . . acquired because of alleged gambling operations there through years past."[28]

Had the state and federal law officers testified truthfully instead of protecting one of their own, they might well have forestalled the tragic events that were to unfold in Phenix City. John Patterson, for one, viewed the untruths sworn to that day and upheld by the Supreme Court's decision as a black day in the history of jurisprudence in Alabama. He said he often thought that "had the court done their duty that day . . . and if the federal government had done what they were supposed to do . . . we might never have had the trouble we had in Phenix City and my father probably never would have been killed."[29]

THE BATTLE LINES FOR the attorney general's race in the 1954 Democratic primary were drawn between Albert Patterson and the machine-backed candidate, Lee "Red" Porter from Gadsden. A third candidate, MacDonald Gallion, a young Montgomery attorney and WWII Marine Corps officer, didn't make it into the run-off and threw his support behind Patterson. The Phenix City crowd backed a slate of candidates that they wanted to see win in the May 4 primary, including "Big Jim" Folsom for governor, but no vote count concerned them more than seeing that their candidate for attorney general defeated Albert Patterson. The stakes were so high in the attorney general's race that the gambling bosses and their political friends were willing to go to any length to see that their man came out on top.

The outgoing attorney general had his own reasons for not wanting Albert Patterson to succeed him. Si Garrett and his cronies had big plans for the future that would be "shot to hell" if Patterson acceded to the office. They didn't take Albert Patterson lightly. The former state senator had not only taught school and lawyered in several counties, but had made friends and was highly respected all over north and central Alabama. His relatives and his wife's kin were well-established across the state, and would support his candidacy. He also had a strong political base throughout Alabama from his earlier campaigns and his service as state senator. He was a seasoned campaigner, whose crime-fighting message had popular appeal. He would be hard to beat, and they knew it.

With the Phenix City machine's backing, however, Garrett was confident that Porter would defeat Patterson. While Porter couldn't match Patterson's years of experience, Garrett knew that he was a tough opponent because the Gadsden attorney had given him a scare in the 1950 attorney general's race. Besides being a respectable family man with four young children, the shrewd but affable Porter had an "unblemished record as a U.S. commissioner and civil attorney." He had political savvy that would serve him well with the insiders down in Montgomery. Moreover, he had been Arch Ferrell's classmate at the University of Alabama law school and was open to Ferrell's counsel and support.[30]

The RBA members and the ladies in the auxiliary all pitched in and campaigned for their candidate. The auxiliary, headed by Hilda Coulter, a young Phenix City housewife, had become a vital force in supporting the RBA's cause. They all knew the dangers they faced. At one of their meetings, a newcomer to the group enthused about the glory that would come from cleaning up Phenix City. Patterson gave the individual a stern look and said, "There'll never be any glory for anybody out of this. About the only glory you can expect is when they chisel the word on your tombstone."[31]

Howard Pennington, a young carpenter who succeeded Hugh Bentley as RBA president, accompanied Albert Patterson on his campaign swings across the state. Others raised funds for his campaign and stumped for him. John Patterson recalled that Pennington carried a pack of his father's campaign cards in his right pocket, and about halfway through the campaign he had to switch the cards to the left pocket. He'd worn the right pocket clean off the coat shoving his hand inside to pull out campaign cards and give them to people. John, whose time was mostly taken up with the law practice, traveled some with Hugh Bentley around east Alabama (from Phenix City over to Montgomery and north to the Tennessee line) making speeches and talking to people about his father's candidacy.[32]

From the time John returned in December until the following June his father stayed out on the road most of the time. It was a hard-fought, grueling campaign. Some nights his father would come home worn to a frazzle, his voice gone and his bad leg swollen twice its normal size. His mother would rub his father's leg down with liniment, and he'd be up and dressed the next morning when Howard Pennington came by, and off they'd go again. His mother worried herself sick about him, but tried not to let it show. She had gone back to teaching for a spell when Jack reached school-age, but had since retired. She never actively participated in the campaigns, but John knew that his mother was intensely interested in them. Her husband and her family were her life.[33]

Albert was well aware that the machine would use every dirty trick in the book to defeat him and would steal the election if that's what it came to. The late Bob Ingram, elder statesman of political reporting in Alabama, recalled that tombstone ballots were "not an uncommon practice" in the old Phenix City. He illustrated the point with a story that he swore Albert Fuller had told him. It seems that Fuller and another deputy were in the cemetery one night copying names "off tombstones to vote in an upcoming election" when the other lawman spotted the marker of a deceased man who had three first names. He shouted to Fuller that they could get two votes from this one tombstone. With a straight face Fuller replied, "We can't do that. It would be illegal."[34]

Albert wouldn't stoop to their level, but knew he had to make every vote count. He and the RBA placed campaign ads in every newspaper they could afford. One of their ads appeared in a local "rag" published by Parson Jack Johnston, a fundamentalist lay minister in the Columbus-Phenix City area known for his fiery rhetoric and his espousal of far-right causes. When Hugh Britton saw the ad, he rushed down to Patterson's office and tossed a copy of the paper on his desk. "Pat, what's this? What's this heah?" he asked. "Why're we spending money on a rag like this heah?" Patterson looked up patiently and said, "Hugh, calm down. You know we have to win this race. I'd welcome Beelzebub's vote if that's what it took to beat these people." Hugh Britton thought for a moment and said, "Well, Pat, if you see Beelzebub you give him my regards. But when you see Parson Jack Johnston you tell him for me, I think he's a sonuvabitch."[35]

FROM THE OUTSET PORTER and the machine tried to smear Albert Patterson with mud from their own conspiracy. When the candidates squared off at their first campaign rally in Gadsden, Porter caught Patterson off-guard by snidely referring to him as that "lawyer from Phenix City" before a hooting partisan crowd. From that point it became clear to Patterson that Porter was the machine's candidate, and that their "devious strategy" (probably concocted by Hoyt Shepherd) was to divert attention from this fact by brazenly hanging their label on him.[36]

Their strategy didn't work. Drawing huge crowds at rallies up and down the state, Patterson hammered away at organized crime in Phenix City, and told how the mob's political corruption had not only taken control of Phenix City but was a cancer spreading across the state. He told hushed crowds the story of their struggle against crime in Phenix City, about the violence and injustice, and that he was "coming to the people in a last-ditch appeal for help in this battle." Howard Pennington said Patterson not only received a warm welcome at rallies across Alabama but got "a standing ovation" after every stop they made.[37]

Patterson's crime-fighting message resonated with the voters, who went to the polls on May 4 and gave him a seventy thousand-vote plurality over the other two candidates. The wide margin was not enough for him to win the Democratic nomination outright, so a runoff against Lee Porter was set for June 1. Gallion threw his support behind Patterson. Since the state's Republican party did not have a foothold in Alabama politics in the 1950s, the victor in the runoff between Patterson and Porter would be the state's next attorney general.[38]

Patterson had led in the 1954 primary without the support of the state's major newspapers. For some unknown reason Alabama's editors and reporters, apparently taking the position they "didn't have a dog in that fight," failed to capture the drama of the battle for attorney general until it was over. Even the *Columbus Ledger*, which had covered the classic conflict between good and evil in Phenix City since the RBA's inception, all but ignored the attorney general's race. Part of the reason, the editors claimed, was because they questioned Patterson's motives.[39] This could have come from the candidate's earlier handling of Shepherd's and Revel's legal defenses or from the smear tactics by his adversaries. Did it also reflect the cynicism of the press toward anything political?

Jefferson County circuit solicitor Emmett Perry set the record straight about Albert Patterson's motives "in his late-starting battle against the criminal forces in his hometown." Perry knew the Phenix City story as well as, and perhaps better than most. As circuit solicitor in Jefferson County, he conducted the extensive post-election probe leading to indictments against Garrett, Ferrell, and Birmingham attorney Lamar Reid for vote fraud in the attorney general's race. Perry declared that Albert Patterson's nature was "to be sincere in whatever he undertook." He said that when Patterson decided to "dedicate his life to bringing about law and order, his knowledge and his rugged tenacity of purpose made him the most feared enemy of the mobsters."[40]

As for the *Columbus Ledger*'s position, the editors might have thought it prudent not to interfere in another state's elections. Exposing political corruption just across the river was one thing, while showing partiality in a statewide election was quite another. The paper's impartial coverage of the Alabama elections focused primarily on the gubernatorial campaign where Big Jim Folsom trounced seven other candidates to win his second term as governor. Folsom captured more than 50 percent of the vote on May 4, winning without a runoff. The former governor had endorsed Lee Porter for attorney general. The Phenix City machine had thrown its support behind both Folsom and Porter.[41]

Even critics who didn't think much of Folsom's record as governor conceded his genius at grassroots politicking. His campaign in 1954 perfected the automobile caravan, later put to good use by John Patterson in his successful run for governor in 1958. Folsom lost stature, however, by hanging onto "political friendships with leaders in Phenix City" after they were implicated in Albert Patterson's murder. This continued show of support for the old Phenix City crowd by a few diehards within the administration created difficult working relations between them and the attorney general's office when John Patterson took his father's place.[42]

The mudslinging and dirty tricks against Albert Patterson in his runoff with Porter were a low point for postwar politics in Alabama. Lee Porter, sticking to the duplicitous slogan "Beat the Phenix City Machine," came out swinging against his opponent. He repeatedly charged that Patterson was backed by money from the Phenix City gambling bosses and was their tool, while Porter's campaign was the one actually being financed by the machine. Pouring "incredible" sums of money into the runoff, Porter's backers financed "an elaborate advertising campaign" which the state's premier news magazine *Alabama* claimed had "easily established a new high for outlay in a campaign for attorney general."[43]

The Phenix City gamblers came up with a slush fund of over $200,000 in an all-out effort to defeat Patterson in the runoff. Porter later admitted to receiving "$22,600 in contributions from one Phenix City gambler alone, Godwin Davis, Sr." Porter had also conferred with Shepherd and Davis during the campaign, but denied that he had known they were connected to the rackets in Phenix City. John Patterson said he believes that Porter was innocent of any actual mob connections, but had shown "poor judgment in allowing himself" to be used by the Phenix City machine and "surely would have wound up their servant" if he had won the election.[44]

Porter's heavily financed campaign cut into his opponent's lead, but Patterson still led by a 1,104-vote majority in the unofficial count reported the morning after the election. Particularly rewarding for the RBA members, their candidate had carried Russell County by 204 votes—sending a message to the machine that voters who were not connected to the rackets wanted their county cleaned up. Patterson was the presumptive Democratic nominee for attorney general, but he could not declare victory until the official tabulation. Claims of vote fraud had already surfaced in Russell County and elsewhere, and he was wary of what the machine might try next.[45]

When they couldn't buy the election they tried to steal it. A later probe into election irregularities uncovered an elaborate scheme to change the election results. Before the polls closed Attorney General Garrett, with the help of two assistants and Arch Ferrell, kept their office telephone lines tied up calling election officials across the state trying to get them to hold off reporting their returns until it could be determined whether Porter needed additional votes to win the election. If they found that Porter was losing the election, they would know how many votes he needed and could doctor the tabulations accordingly.[46]

John Patterson told how his father first got wind of the plot. Becoming frantic in their last-ditch efforts to steal the election, the conspirators gave little thought to caution or to covering their tracks. At Ferrell's insistence the Phenix City mob had dispatched carloads of hoods, their pockets stuffed with cash, around the state trying to convince local officials to change the vote count. Hoyt Shepherd said Ferrell told him "that if it was necessary to steal ten or fifteen votes in every county, that was going to be done."[47]

Two of the hoods went with a prominent Tuskegee citizen to Sheriff Preston Hornsby's house late that night, got him out of bed, and offered him a bribe to alter Macon County's election returns. Hornsby told them, "Hell no!" He said there was no way he was going to the penitentiary for them, and anyway the returns had already been reported and posted on the bulletin board down at the courthouse in Tuskegee. No one thought to ask, but Sheriff Hornsby was a friend of Albert Patterson's and had supported his campaign. This scene was repeated all over Alabama and word, of course, got back to Patterson. In some counties the plotters succeeded in altering the vote count in their favor, but the total still was not enough to swing the election for their candidate.[48]

In a smoke-filled suite at the Molton Hotel in Birmingham, a brash act born of desperation on Si Garrett's and Arch Ferrell's part proved their undoing. Lamar Reid, the chairman of the Democratic Executive Committee in Jefferson County, later admitted under oath that he had taken the runoff tabulation sheets to the Molton Hotel at the request of Garrett. He testified that he had been duped into letting Garrett and Ferrell alter the numbers, claiming that he had been out of the room at the time. By changing 1s into 7s and 0s to 6s with a ballpoint pen, they stole six hundred votes from Patterson and gave them to Porter.[49]

John Patterson, who taught a class in political science at Troy State University in later years, used the experience to illustrate the pitfalls graduates would have to look out for in their careers. Lamar Reid had been a classmate and friend of Patterson's in law school. He was a bright young attorney who had married into a prominent Birmingham family and had become a partner in his father-in-law's prestigious law firm. The Molton Hotel scandal ruined his career. He threw it away by ingratiating himself to men who were drunk with power just because one of them held a high public office. Had he but known that one of these men had a history of manic depression and the other was in bed with the Phenix City rackets.[50]

Adding an ironic twist to the story, Albert Patterson's brother-in-law Roy Cole was the night manager at the Molton Hotel. Roy was married to Agnes Patterson's youngest sister Ruth. Having worked in his brother-in-law's campaign, Roy knew Ferrell and Garrett and became suspicious when he saw Lamar Reid go up to their suite. Ferrell and Garrett had been drinking heavily all evening. Whenever they ordered drinks, Roy posed as the waiter and carried the tray up to their suite. He paid close attention to what they were doing and saying, and fed this information back to his brother-in-law.[51]

An alert *Birmingham News* reporter broke the story on the conspiracy. Circuit Solicitor Emmett Perry later told how Ed Strickland, an "ace reporter for the *Birmingham News*," came to him on the afternoon of June 8, 1954, the day state election officials were to certify the runoff tabulations, with suspicions that someone had altered the Jefferson County vote count in the attorney general's race. The numbers on the tabulation sheets given to the state election officials were not the same as the ones he had seen on election night. He had written the correct totals down, and still had his notes.[52]

Solicitor Perry took the charges to the Jefferson County grand jury, which was in regular monthly session at the time. The grand jury called in the tabulation sheets, saw where the numbers had been altered, and began a probe into the transparent attempt to steal the votes in Jefferson County. That same day, June 10, state election officials declared Albert Patterson the winner by 854 votes out of 382,678 cast. The conspiracy to steal the election had failed. He would have to go through the motions of facing a Republican challenger in the general election, but the Democratic nominee had already done all that was required of him to be recognized as Alabama's next attorney general.[53]

ALBERT PATTERSON WAS SLAIN before he could take office. On the night of June 18, as a heat wave engulfed Alabama, he was gunned down outside the Coulter Building in an alleyway where he'd parked his car every day for the past twenty years. It was Friday evening around nine o'clock. Not a breeze stirring, not even off the lazy Chattahoochee. Cruising down Fourteenth Street a CoOp Cab had stopped for a red light when the shots rang out. The fare, an Army captain from Fort Benning, jumped at the sound of the shots. He laughed nervously. "We must be in Phenix City," he said.

"The bastards shot my father in cold blood," John Patterson swore that night between clinched teeth. "They never gave him a chance." Amidst the trauma of ensuing grief and the clamor for justice he retraced his father's steps that fateful day "to find out who he saw and if there was anything that might help lead us to whoever killed him." The haunting clarity of the day's events stirs memories yet of his father's tragic, senseless death. When he arrived at the office that morning "the old man" had already been there and left. He had driven to Montgomery to help out a friend and to take care of some business matters while he was there.

Albert had mentioned to his son the previous day that Reuben Newton, a lawyer from Jasper who was a friend and supporter, had called several times and asked him to appear at the Montgomery County Courthouse and testify as a character witness in his behalf. The Alabama Bar Association had scheduled disbarment hearings against Newton, and the troubled attorney's career hung in the balance. Although he didn't have the time to spare, Albert Patterson felt he had no choice. "When your friends are in trouble, you have to be there for them," he had said to his wife the night before.[54]

John worried about his father, as did the whole family. Albert refused to carry a gun even though the faceless telephone threats had become uglier and more menacing. The day before his murder a caller warned, "You've got to change your mind or you won't be here over the weekend." This was interpreted as a warning for him "not to appear before the grand jury in Jefferson County with the information he had about the vote fraud in the attorney general's race." On Thursday night he had spoken at a Methodist men's club in Phenix City where he told the audience "the odds were something like 100-1 that he would not be alive to take office in January." Despite the threats against his life, he had agreed to go to Birmingham the following Monday and tell what he knew.[55]

On Friday he faithfully appeared at the county courthouse in Montgomery and testified for his friend Newton, as he had promised. Afterwards he went around the courthouse shaking hands and talking with people. From there he dropped by Walker Printing Company on Dexter Avenue to settle a printing bill run up during his campaign. He had trouble raising money during the campaign and had mortgaged his home for $15,000 to help defray expenses. (For some reason he didn't pay the printing bill that day, and shop owner Tilly Walker wouldn't accept payment from the family after his death.)[56]

Next he went over to the judicial building nearby to see Mollie Jordan, deputy clerk for the state court of appeals. "Miss Jordan was a great friend of his, and she later became a real friend of mine," John Patterson recalled. Miss Mollie said Albert talked with her about the campaign, and they discussed the attorney general's office which was only about a dozen steps down the hall. He didn't go by the attorney general's office. He just talked to Miss Mollie and left.[57]

Before leaving Montgomery, Albert stopped by the Exchange Hotel where he and his son Jack had stayed when he was in the Senate. Among friends he saw there was Jabe Brassell, who also had driven over from Phenix City that day on business. Brassell had troubles of his own with the Phenix City machine, and had brought vote fraud charges against them after he was defeated for reelection as Russell County's state representative in the May 4 primary. As they sat in the lobby of the Exchange Hotel "waiting out a rainstorm," Patterson mentioned to Brassell, as he had to several other acquaintances in Montgomery that day, that he had the goods on Garrett and Ferrell and he was going before the Jefferson County grand jury on Monday to tell them all he knew.[58]

When the rain let up he left the hotel and started home. On the way out of town on Highway 80, he pulled off the road and stopped at the Parkmore Restaurant. He was the only customer at that hour. The waitress, a young English girl who was married to an airman stationed at Maxwell Field, said Albert sat in a booth and ordered a vanilla milkshake. He asked her to mix an egg into the milkshake, a common practice in the fifties. When she later read about his murder, she distinctly remembered another man coming in while Patterson sat in the booth drinking the milkshake. She couldn't give a description of the man, but had the distinct feeling that he knew Patterson and was following him.[59]

John had left the office before his father got back. Mary Joe and the children were at their house at 24 Mason Drive near Fort Benning, and he drove there from work. The tenants had moved out, and they were moving in. Mary Joe had worked all day getting the house in order. After supper John lay across the bed to read *Scottsboro Boy*, an expose of the Alabama prison system. Albert, meanwhile, had arrived back in town and gone directly to the office. It had been a long, hot drive from Montgomery. The afternoon rainstorm hadn't even settled the dust. Instead of cooling things off, the rain had left the air hot and sticky.[60]

He parked in the first parking space in the alley beside the Coulter Building and went up to his office. He signed some letters, came back down, and went around the corner to the post office to check his mailbox. Sometime around eight o'clock, after he returned to the office, his friend Leland Jones dropped in. They chatted for a few minutes, and Jones left. His wife was waiting in the car. They were on their way to dinner, and thought Albert Patterson might like to join them. But he was worn out and said he was going straight home after he finished up at the office.[61]

Roughly an hour later, Albert Patterson turned off the lights and locked up. The lights going out could be seen as far away as the courthouse, and the tap of his cane on the steps would have alerted anyone lurking in the dark alley that he was coming down. When he opened the door to the Olds and sat behind the wheel, the killers were standing outside the car. He knew them. One leaned with his hand on the edge of the window to talk. One of the killers pulled a gun. Three shots rang out. The killers ran from the alley. Their defenseless victim staggered out of the car onto the sidewalk where he fell mortally wounded in a pool of blood.[62]

At the house on 24 Mason Drive, John was still reading in bed when the killers ambushed and murdered his father. No telephone had been hooked up yet, and John had left word that he could be reached at a next-door neighbor's number in an emergency. The neighbor came over about fifteen or twenty minutes after nine with a message that something had happened at the office, and John needed to get down there as soon as he could. "They didn't tell me what it was," he recalled. "So I tore me a piece of paper, and stuck it in that book and laid it down. I ain't never finished it. Every time I see the book I think about that."[63]

Today, that unread book is locked away in a bottom drawer of the desk in Judge Patterson's study. He can't bring himself to resume reading the book, but he can't bear to part with it either. Keepsakes of his father's and his family's sacrifice are always around to remind him of that night of endless sorrow. Among them the book is all that ties him to the moment his father was struck down. The slip of paper he stuck between the pages is still there.

8

BIG TROUBLE IN RIVER CITY

O n that grim Friday night he had driven as fast as he could across town, not knowing what he would find at the Coulter Building. As he crossed the bridge and came up Fourteenth Street, he saw the flashing lights of the police cars before he topped the hill. He slowed and turned right onto Fifth Avenue, slamming on the brakes and pulling over to the curb when clusters of bystanders blocked the way. He jumped out and dashed across the street to the alley where his father's blue Olds was parked. Deputy Aaron Smith came over to him and said, "Your father's been shot. He's been taken to the hospital."

The door to the Olds was open. He looked inside and saw the cane on the floorboard behind the driver's seat. His father obviously had been behind the wheel when shot, and had stumbled out and across to the sidewalk before collapsing in a pool of blood—a Herculean effort for a man who hadn't walked without the cane for more than thirty years. The thick pool of blood on the sidewalk told Patterson the wounds were serious. Rushing back to his car he pulled away from the curb and raced to the Cobb Memorial Hospital emergency room where his father's lifeless body lay beneath a sheet on a gurney. A Catholic priest who was a friend of his father's was there to comfort the family.

Across the room Sheriff Matthews, Deputy Fuller, and a couple of their cronies were standing around. Matthews mopped his face with a red bandana. Ferrell dropped in later, his face flushed from drinking. They were a nervous group. Only Fuller looked cool, cocksure. His smirk was a trademark. So were his fast guns. There was something different about Fuller that night. His holster was empty. Patterson noticed this, but said nothing about it at the time. Others who did ask Fuller about the missing revolver got no satisfactory answer. Patterson shot a glare in their direction before walking over and lifting the sheet from the gurney.[1]

"I saw he'd been shot in the upper part of the body and in the mouth. I went through his pockets and removed his wallet and keys and things, and his Phi Beta Kappa key which he always wore." His father had been dead on arrival at the hospital. He fought back the anger and the tears, keeping his emotions under control. His mother had broken down after viewing the body. The couple who moved into the basement apartment when he and his family moved out had driven her to the hospital. Maurice was there. Sam was on the way. They had sent someone for Jack, who was performing in a play at the high school.[2]

William Benton, a younger member of the RBA, arrived with a friend, Harry Barr. They drove his mother and Maurice back to the Patterson home on Pine Circle. John had someone drive his car to the house so it would be available if his mother needed it. He stayed behind to watch over his father's body. He wanted to be with the family, but he was not going to leave the body alone until the state toxicologist came to do an autopsy. The toxicologist, Dr. C. J. Rehling at Auburn University, had been called, but was out of town. His assistant, Dr. Wendell Sowell, had been notified and was on the way.[3]

Shortly after midnight Morgan Reynolds drove in from Clanton. John asked Morgan to stay at the hospital while he went to see about his mother. A prominent attorney in Clanton, Reynolds was married to Mary Joe Patterson's sister. Mary Joe had called and asked them to come for the children and keep them for a few days. Arriving in Phenix City, Morgan dropped his wife off with her sister, and then came to the hospital to see if there was anything he could do to help. "If you'll just stay here till I get back," Patterson said. "Don't let nobody touch the body until the state toxicologist gets here. I want him to do the autopsy and preserve any evidence that he may find."[4]

He walked over and told Ferrell and Matthews that he didn't want anyone touching his father's body until Dr. Sowell got there. As he turned to leave, he remembered that his car was no longer at the hospital. Albert Fuller offered him a ride. "C'mon, I'll give you a lift over to your mama's place," Fuller said. So he got in the deputy's car and rode with Fuller to the house which was only about six blocks up the hill. On the way over Fuller turned to him and said, "John, when we catch the man who done this, I'll bring him to you." "I appreciate that," Patterson said.

He had known Albert Fuller since grade school and knew he could not trust the swaggering deputy or his cohorts Ferrell and Matthews. Their dawdling around the hospital showed they were in no hurry to catch his father's killers. They were more likely scheming to cover up the crime. From his father's and the RBA's experiences he also knew he couldn't blindly trust state law enforcers. His father's murder, to all appearances premeditated and committed by people he knew, cried out for justice. Come what may, John promised to see that justice was done. His immediate concern was to protect the family. The people who did this were capable of anything.

WHEN PATTERSON RETURNED FROM his mother's house Dr. Sowell had just arrived at the hospital. Sowell's professional demeanor, his handling of the autopsy, and his subsequent inspection of the crime scene convinced Patterson there was at least one state office he could rely on to help bring his father's killers to justice. Having placed the items taken from his father's pockets in a sealed envelope, he turned them over to Sowell to be examined as evidence in the case. During the investigation and the prosecution of the crime, the two men became "great friends." Sowell later served as the state toxicologist in Texas. "He was quite a fellow," Patterson said.

Sowell examined the crime scene before Chief Joe Smelley and the team of state investigators got there, and he did not like what he found. The police had roped off the alleyway, but not before onlookers had trampled all over the place. There was reason to believe that someone had tampered with evidence. A muddy footprint, possibly the killer's, had been discovered in the alley near the car soon after the murder. The police on the scene had not made a plaster cast of the footprint, but had placed a board over it. Overnight the board had been removed, and someone had deliberately destroyed the evidence.[5]

When the investigators dusted his father's car for prints they discovered that the door and window on the driver's side had been wiped nearly clean. The only retrievable prints on the door were a thumbprint lifted from the rain guard above the ventilator window and a partial palm print on the door itself. Suspecting that someone with access to the crime scene had deliberately destroyed evidence, the lead investigator took the thumbprint across the river to the Columbus post office and mailed it to the FBI in Washington before reporting to Chief Smelley what they had found.

"There's always an honest man shows up," John Patterson said when talking about what the lead investigator did. That lone thumbprint and the .38 slugs the toxicologist recovered from his father's body proved to be vital physical evidence in prosecuting the case. Employees in the Elite Cafe next door and other people around town heard four gunshots that night. His father had been struck three times at close range. The first bullet, intended to silence him, was to the mouth. A bullet in the back tore through vital internal organs. He had tried to shield himself from a third shot that shattered his arm. A fourth bullet missed and pierced the brim of his hat before ripping through the door on the passenger side.

While the physical evidence pointed to a single trigger man—the four .38 slugs had come from the same gun—two men were seen running from the alley after the shots were fired. The presence at the crime scene of someone other than the man who pulled the trigger was presumptive evidence of a thicker plot. Eyewitnesses recognized the two men fleeing the scene, but were too frightened to come forward. When finally given state protection, witnesses identified Arch Ferrell and Albert Fuller as the men they saw leaving the crime scene. The rumor mill, however, did not waste time on tongue-tied witnesses. Within twenty-four hours the talk on the street had already pointed an accusing finger at Ferrell and Fuller. Word also leaked out that Ferrell had been seen wiping prints from the door of the victim's car while ostensibly investigating the crime scene.

Ferrell gave more credence to the rumors by repeatedly professing his innocence before being accused of the crime. He admitted to hating Albert Patterson, but swore he had nothing to do with the murder. Drinking heavier than usual, Ferrell acted as if he had something to hide, as did Attorney General Garrett and Deputy Fuller. Garrett's and Ferrell's behavior became more irrational as the week wore on. Bob Ingram, who covered the murder for the *Montgomery Advertiser*, recalled an uneasy night he and his managing editor spent with the two men soon after the slaying.

Ingram had been camped out all week at the Russell County courthouse with other members of the press corps covering the state Democratic Committee's hearings into legislators Jabe Brassell's and Ben Cole's charges that the Phenix City machine had stolen the May 4 primary election from them. Even larger numbers of newsmen had sweated it out in Birmingham on Friday when Attorney General Garrett testified before the Jefferson County Grand Jury about the vote fraud case there. Ingram recalled how relieved he and the other reporters were when Judge Frank Embry recessed the Phenix City hearings that Friday morning. Sweltering inside a crowded, un-airconditioned courtroom during one of the hottest summers on record had made for an unpleasant week.

In Montgomery the record heat wave was even harder on Ingram's wife, Edith, who was pregnant with their second child. Ingram drove back to Montgomery, and after work he and the family headed north for Cherokee County where his mother and Edith's parents lived. When they arrived at his in-laws' farm in the Tate's Chapel community, his wife's father was waiting on the front porch. "Bob, your paper wants you to head back to Phenix City right this minute," he said. "Mr. Patterson's been murdered."

The news jolted Ingram, as it did the whole state. Earlier in the week the young reporter had spoken briefly with the attorney general nominee when he dropped by the courtroom to catch up on the proceedings and to pay his respects to Judge Embry, who was presiding from St. Clair County. Ingram turned the car around and headed back to Montgomery. After dropping the family off he returned to Phenix City and checked into the Ralston Hotel in Columbus during the predawn hours on Saturday morning.

That evening he and his managing editor, Fred Anderson, along with other newsmen, ended up in "a wild night on the town" with Garrett and Ferrell. Garrett kept reminding the reporters that he was in charge of the murder investigation. The day before he had thrown his weight around when he testified in Birmingham, at one point telling Solicitor Emmett Perry that as attorney general he didn't have to testify and that he had the power to dismiss the grand jury hearings altogether if he so chose. He seemed at the time to be unaware that Lamar Reid and Lee Porter were prepared to implicate him and Ferrell in the vote fraud conspiracy.

Ingram said he was uncomfortable being around the two men that night. "Arch was drunk as a skunk and raising hell," he recalled. "Already the word on the street was that Arch was involved in this thing, that he'd probably killed him or had it done along with the others, and I was a little uneasy."[6] While they were gathered in a room at the Ralston drinking, his managing editor bluntly brought up the fact that some people thought Ferrell was involved in the murder. Ferrell slurred a drunken denial. Garrett jumped to his defense claiming that Ferrell was talking with him on the phone at the time Patterson was killed, and that attorney Frank Long, head of the Young Democrats, would verify that.[7]

After midnight Garrett invited the newsmen to join them for steaks at the CoCo Club located on the way to Fort Benning. The club, which was rumored to have connections to the Phenix City mob, was closed when they got there. Garrett pounded on the door until the manager came and let them in. "They opened it just for us, and we were the only people in there," Ingram recalled. "Arch Ferrell was so drunk he threw up on the table. He stood up in the booth and shouted that he would do anything for this man Si Garrett. And I'm saying to myself, oh God, he already has. He killed a man last night." No one thought to ask how Garrett could be so sure he was on the phone with Ferrell at the precise time when Albert Patterson was murdered. Even Ferrell in his drunken state was said to have listened "spellbound" as Garrett spun the story giving him an alibi.

The reporters had already asked themselves who had most to gain from Albert Patterson's death? The timing of the murder led logically to the suspicion that he was killed to stop him from testifying before the Jefferson County grand jury during the coming week. He had agreed to appear in Birmingham on Monday and tell them what he knew about widespread vote fraud in his run-off election with Lee Porter, and had stated publicly that his testimony would ruin those responsible for the voting irregularities. Those were the men who had the most to lose if Albert Patterson lived out the weekend.

The only other plausible motive—keeping the attorney general nominee from taking office and carrying out his pledge to clean up Phenix City—did not fit the reckless nature of the crime. The swearing-in was seven months away, giving Phenix City's crime lords more than ample time to lay plans that were not so flagrant and were less likely to stir up the kind of trouble they must have known Patterson's murder would bring down on them. The slaying of Albert Patterson just off a well-lighted street at an hour when the night owls were on the prowl was not the mark of a professional hit, but a reckless act committed by desperate men.

EVEN SO, THE MURDER had repercussions the killers could not have foreseen. Over the weekend local citizens awoke to find that the entire state of Alabama and half of Georgia had descended on their town, or so it seemed. Reporters from every major newspaper within a hundred-mile radius, and some from as far away as London and Tokyo, poured into town to give readers around the globe up-to-date news about the murdered crime-fighter and "the wickedest city in America." The limelight and the public outcry from across the state created a demand for action that state officials could not ignore.

Early Saturday morning the local authorities were caught off guard when a big green Lincoln Continental pulled up to the Russell County courthouse and out stepped Alabama's Adjutant General Walter J. "Crack" Hanna, a major general in the National Guard. With him were his seventeen-year-old son Pete, a private in the guard, and Colonel Jack Warren, the guard division's provost marshal. Standing five-foot-seven and built like the bantamweight fighter he once had been, Crack Hanna let nothing stand in the way of carrying out a mission. Before the weekend was over the old time gamblers were complaining bitterly about "that badass soldier boy marchin' in heah kickin' butt and takin' names."

Governor Gordon Persons had sent General Hanna to Phenix City to find out how bad things were and to close down the gambling and vice. He had responded to a frantic call from Representative Jabe Brassell urging him to send troops to Phenix City to keep from having anarchy in the streets. Badly shaken by his friend Albert Patterson's murder, Brassell feared for his own life. Brassell had heard that he too was on a hit list for having challenged the election results in Russell County. The governor got Hanna on the phone and asked him to get over to Phenix City as soon as he could. He then called General Joseph H. Harper, the commanding general at Fort Benning, and got him to place Phenix City off limits to his soldiers.

Persons flew into Phenix City later on Saturday to offer his condolences to the Patterson family, and to confer with Hanna and the local authorities. At a press conference Persons told reporters he had given Sheriff Matthews and Solicitor Ferrell instructions that there would be no more gambling in Phenix City as long as he was governor. "Make it clear to the boys that this is the end of the line," he told them. "There's not going to be any more of it." Ferrell was overheard telling the governor to "get his ass and his soldier boys" back to Montgomery and leave Phenix City's problems to them. Persons told Ferrell that he'd let them have free rein in the past, but this time they'd gone too far.

The governor flew back to Montgomery, but Hanna and his guardsmen remained in Phenix City. Hanna's troops patrolled the hostile streets, and kept a lid on crime for the first time in recent memory. He posted a guard at the Patterson residence to protect the family from further harm, and brought John Patterson's close friend and former college roommate Joe Robertson down from Birmingham to help look out for the family. Before Governor Persons left that Saturday, Patterson had reminded him of past empty promises to clean up Phenix City. He figured the racketeers and the machine would just bide their time until the heat was off, as they had always done. Persons reassured him that he meant business. "Not this time, John," he said. "Not this time."

ALBERT PATTERSON'S MURDER ROCKED the conscience of Alabamians like nothing before or since. In the wake of the slaying there were days of eulogy and sorrow, public outrage, and rising demands for a time of reckoning. Each day local citizens waited for the next shoe to drop as newspaper headlines heralded new developments in the case. On Monday the Garrett faction's plans for runner-up

Porter to fill the breach left by the slaying were upset by an announcement that thirty-two-year-old John Patterson had declared himself available as a candidate to take his father's place. Friends of his father's from across the state had urged him to seek the nomination, but he was reluctant to do so. The law was his chosen profession, not politics. He made up his mind to seek the nomination at his father's funeral on Monday.[8]

Eulogized in sermons across the state on Sunday (Father's Day), Albert Patterson was laid to rest on Monday in the place of his birth, the small country town of New Site about eighty miles from Phenix City. Funeral services had been held at the Trinity Methodist Church a half-block from the blood-stained alley. The church overflowed with the throng who came to pay their final respects to the fallen hero. Ed Strickland, the reporter for the *Birmingham News*, had formed a special bond with Albert Patterson after breaking the story on the Jefferson County vote fraud. He reported from Phenix City that the slain attorney general nominee "became today, in death, a martyr and rallying point in the battle for a new way of life here."[9]

The Reverend R. K. Jones heaped blame on indifferent state officials for his friend's death, excoriating them for ignoring "the pleas for help in this crime-ridden city." "Brother Patterson could be with us," he declared, had these officials not failed. "We pled on ears of indifference and we've come to this." Reverend T. E. Steeley called on God to "come in His mighty power" against the men responsible and to bring them to justice. "Oh, God, put your finger on the men behind the crime as well as the murderers," he prayed. "Let this crime make for a stirring battle for righteousness."[10]

A mile-long line of cars in the funeral procession wound their way northward to the country graveyard at New Site. "Services at the cemetery lasted only a few minutes, but friends filed by the casket for more than an hour, disregarding the punishing heat of the sun and the stifling dust that rose from thousands of feet," Strickland reported. "The farewell to the quiet courageous man was a tribute to his life, and it was as sincere as he was sincere about all he undertook."[11]

After the graveside services Charles Meriwether, president of the Dewberry Drug Company in Birmingham and a political ally of Albert Patterson, approached the bereaved elder son about taking his father's place on the Democratic ticket in November. "Without the power of the attorney general's office you might not ever be able to solve these cases over here, or clean up this place," he said. Meriwether believed the nomination was John's if he wanted it, and was prepared to support his candidacy. Patterson thought for a minute, and said, "All right, let's go for it." Entering the political arena was not something John Patterson wanted to do. It was something he had to do.

By making the announcement he had put the killers on notice. Word got back that Matthews and Fuller had made up preposterous theories about the crime to throw suspicion away from the sheriff's office. They had even accused Albert of having an affair with one of the secretaries, suggesting that a jealous husband might be the guilty party. John thought about this when he was back in the office on the day after the funeral. The office window provided an unobstructed view of the county courthouse across the way. In a paper sack on his desk was a German .32-caliber Walther automatic he had brought back from the war. He didn't think he would need the gun but wasn't taking any chances.

He noticed that Joe Smelley, the state's chief investigator, spent most of his time either parked in front of the courthouse or inside the sheriff's office hanging out with his friend Fuller. That Tuesday the two lawmen came by his office without giving a reason for the visit. He saw them coming up the sidewalk as they approached the Coulter Building. "They obviously came over to find out what I knew, if anything," he said. He was already suspicious of the two men. Their visit served only to heighten his suspicions. He later learned that Fuller had even tried to implicate him in his father's murder.

Still uneasy about whom he could trust, he flew to Washington the following day to try and see J. Edgar Hoover—unaware that the FBI director had already turned down a request from Governor Persons for assistance—but received the same brush-off. Both were told it was a state matter. Making the bureau's crime lab available to state investigators was about all the FBI had to offer. Patterson arrived at National Airport on Wednesday evening and was met by Colonel Neil Keller, a friend who had served with him in Germany and was now with the National Security Agency. The next morning Colonel Keller drove him to the Justice Department building where they were met by "some of the most aggressive reporters" he'd ever encountered.

The Scripps-Howard reporter at the scene described Patterson as a "polite, slender man with a youthful face and not much to say." "He wants official Washington to do something about the murder of his father . . . without blowing any trumpets," the reporter wrote, emphasizing that Patterson "was not interested in manufacturing headlines." The only words the reporter attributed to Patterson were, "Look, I can't go around shooting off my mouth. You know my father was killed and I want to find out who did it. But all I want to say now is that I'm up here on business."[12] The reporters had already talked to a Justice Department spokesman and knew that Patterson was in town on "a tragic and, probably, futile errand." "They'd be glad to talk to John, and so would FBI men," the press reported, after meeting with the spokesman, "but said they could not see how they could help him. Murder is not a federal offense, even when the slain man is a prominent politician."[13]

Patterson didn't get in to see Hoover, but was handed off to an assistant named Hannigan. The assistant was "nice and courteous" and listened to what he had to say. "I told him what I was doing there, that I was very concerned about the people who were the most logical suspects in killing my father being the ones in charge of investigating the murder," Patterson recalled. "I explained that all they were doing was to try and cover it up, and that I would like for the FBI to get involved and help us with the investigation." Hannigan spoke bluntly. He said the FBI had no jurisdiction in the case, and could not get involved.

Patterson rose to his feet. "Well, you know, I appreciate it," he said. "I thank you for what you've done."

"What do you mean?"

"You've made me a smarter man." He left Hannigan's office and Colonel Keller drove him back to National Airport where he boarded a plane and came home. In Columbus, a dozen or so reporters and cameramen were waiting for him in the terminal. They asked where he'd been. "Well, I've been to Washington," he replied.

"What for?"

"I went there to see J. Edgar Hoover."

"Why'd you go see Mr. Hoover?"

"Well, I wanted them to know that the men I think are the most logical suspects for killing my father are the ones in charge of the investigation down here, and they are covering it up. I wanted them to know that, and I asked for FBI help in the investigation."

"What'd he say?"

"Well, he refused to see me."

At breakfast on Friday, a smile crossed his face when he opened the morning paper and saw the headline, "Patterson accuses investigators." The trip to Washington was not a failure after all. The press could send a shot across the bow as surely as a cannon or a gun.

ANOTHER BANNER HEADLINE THAT was splashed across Friday's front pages captured his atttention. The lead story in the *Birmingham Post-Herald* reported a surprising turn in the overall direction of the state's probe into his father's murder. After the funeral on Monday, shock and grief had turned to anger throughout Alabama, with a chorus of cries from an outraged public for the state to appoint a special prosecutor. Attorney General Garrett insisted that he would personally lead the investigation, however, declaring that "under no circumstances" would he replace solicitor Arch Ferrell with a special prosecutor.[14]

Governor Persons and Chief Justice J. Ed Livingston met with the intractable attorney general to try and change his mind, but to no avail. Garrett remained defiant even when advised that Justice Livingston "had the authority to empanel a special grand jury which, in turn, could commission a special prosecutor." After conferring with the chief justice, Governor Persons decided to force the issue by releasing a statement to the press that he "would request the early organization of a special grand jury."[15]

Meantime, the grand jury in Birmingham had expanded its inquiry to look into allegations of a link between the Patterson murder and the vote fraud case in Jefferson County. Garrett, having testified two hours before the grand jury on Friday, was called back on Wednesday to give more testimony. The hearings were closed, but the deeply troubled attorney general was reported to be the main witness of the investigation. According to the *Birmingham Post-Herald*, Garrett "testified late into the night on Wednesday and then announced he was leaving the state 'for health reasons.'"[16] Soon thereafter, the Garrett family issued a statement that the attorney general was "a very sick man, mentally" and had been admitted to the John Sealy Hospital in Galveston, Texas, on the advice of his physician.[17]

Without Garrett to prop him up, Arch Ferrell was left swinging in the wind. Overnight he fell from a position of influence as "machine boss" and county solicitor to being a person of interest in the Patterson murder investigation. Witnesses testifying at the State Democratic subcommittee hearings in Phenix City the week before had already identified the county solicitor as the ringleader of the machine. This was backed up by tapes of Hoyt Shepherd's telephone conversations that an unidentified individual (who became known as the "phantom wiretapper") mailed to the RBA. Also under investigation in the Jefferson County vote fraud case along with Garrett, Ferrell had said that he would voluntarily testify before the grand jury in Birmingham, as Garrett had done. He sent a prepared statement instead, never making a personal appearance before the grand jury.[18]

On Friday, the thirty-six-year-old assistant attorney general, Bernard F. Sykes, announced that he was taking over the investigation of the Patterson murder with the full cooperation of Governor Persons and Chief Justice Livingston. One of Sykes's first official acts was to bar Arch Ferrell from further involvement with the investigation. The governor and the chief justice also anticipated having to relieve Russell County's Circuit Judge Julius B. Hicks from the case and bringing in replacements for both Ferrell and Hicks. Judging from the mountain of evidence compiled by the RBA, the Democratic Party subcommittee, the grand jury in Birmingham, and General Hanna's guardsmen, they knew they might have to wipe the entire slate of local officials clean in Phenix City before the matter was done.

A FEW DAYS AFTER Patterson's Washington trip, the State Democratic Executive Committee met in special session in Birmingham to decide what to do about a replacement for the slain attorney general nominee. The options before the executive committee were whether to call a special primary and elect a Democratic nominee to run in the November general election or to simply handpick the nominee. Also on the executive committee's agenda was what to do about a replacement for Haygood Paterson, who had died a few days after receiving the nomination for Commissioner of Agriculture.[19]

The committee chairman was Ben Ray, a lifelong friend of the Patterson family who had grown up in Tallapoosa County on a farm adjoining the land owned by John Patterson's great-grandfather. There were other Patterson allies on the committee. One was attorney Ralph Smith from Guntersville. Smith and John Patterson were friends in law school at the university, and had roomed together for a time. They had remained friends and had kept in touch.

Fortunately, there were as many allies as enemies in the Folsom camp, which had a plurality on the executive committee after Big Jim swept the Democratic primary without a runoff. Folsom was set to start his second term as governor in January. John Patterson's father had friends among the Folsomites, even though he broke ranks with Big Jim during his first term. Albert's friends included party stalwarts like Senator Broughton Lamberth of Alexander City, Fayette's Fuller Kimbrell who was to be Folsom's finance director, and rising political star George Wallace who had his sights set on succeeding Folsom in the governor's office. These men respected Albert Patterson, and they deeply resented his murder.

There was a groundswell of support across Alabama for John Patterson to take his father's place in the November elections. If the executive committee called a special election, the winner was not in doubt. A few committee members, realizing that a handpicked replacement offered better odds for putting their candidate into the attorney general's office, argued against calling a special election. Some members wanted to appoint Lee Porter, a proposal that died in committee when Porter (who was in hot water because of accepting large campaign contributions from Phenix City gamblers and then trying to cover it up) withdrew his name from consideration.[20]

John Patterson had said he might run as an independent if the committee handpicked Porter or someone else. His supporters on the committee pointed out that if he got elected as an independent, the Democratic Party might have a problem on its hands. George Wallace was among those who stood up and fought for holding a primary election. Some warned Wallace that he could be "creating a monster" for himself in future elections. Wallace shrugged off the advice, and followed his own conscience in the matter.

The consensus of the executive committee was to hold a special primary to elect the Democratic nominee. Before adjourning, members set the date for the election and set a deadline for candidates to qualify. That afternoon John Patterson borrowed five hundred dollars from Ralph Smith and paid the qualifying fee. No one else met the deadline for qualifying. After all the earlier talk of other candidates, Patterson ran unopposed in the special primary and became the party's nominee in the November general election. He faced a token Republican candidate in the general election, but Alabama was still a one-party state in the 1950s and the outcome of general elections was rarely, if ever, in doubt.

Patterson was sworn in as attorney general on January 15, 1955, in Montgomery. At thirty-three years he was one of the youngest men elected attorney general in the state's history, but his maturity and his qualifications were not in question. He had proven his leadership abilities in WWII. His law partnership with his father and the seasoning of his courtroom skills while defending and prosecuting cases with the Army JAG in Europe made him uniquely qualified to be the next attorney general. He was poised and self-confident, and was determined not only to bring his father's killers to justice, but to finish the job his father had started. In his first speech after being named the Democratic nominee, John Patterson told the Dothan Rotary Club that he was going to carry on his father's fight against "the alliance of law enforcement officers and political leaders" with the crime lords in Phenix City and wherever that alliance existed in Alabama.[21]

Patterson warned that the fight against crime in Phenix City could not succeed "until the guns and badges [were] stripped from the law enforcement officers in Russell County." He called on Garrett to stay in Alabama and to remove "his political confederate, Arch Ferrell, from his office as solicitor of Russell County." He also urged that the outgoing attorney general "not be allowed to leave the State of Alabama." Almost from the outset he had charged that the investigators themselves were the logical suspects in his father's murder, and the evidence continued to build against Ferrell, Fuller, and Garrett.[22]

THE CORDON OF JUSTICE began to tighten around the three suspects after Sykes took charge and removed Ferrell from the murder investigation. Soon thereafter, Governor Persons appointed McDonald Gallion as his special counsel in the case. Gallion, who had thrown his support behind Albert Patterson after dropping out of the attorney general's race, joined the Phenix City investigation as the governor's personal representative.

Sykes operated out of the Ralston Hotel in Columbus until he obtained office space down the hall from the Patterson law offices in the Coulter Building. In addition to members of his own staff, Sykes brought in veteran homicide investigators Robert A. McMurdo and Maurice House, who were on loan from the city of Birmingham. He also retained the services of Willie Painter and two other state investigators who had no prior connection to the Phenix City crowd and were believed to be impartial. Sykes then had Police Chief Joe Smelley removed from the case along with other state investigators who were known to be Albert Fuller's friends and had shown favoritism toward the sheriff's office in the past.[23]

Smelley bitterly resented being taken off the case and charged that the Russell Betterment Association was "trying to make a goat" of him. Public Safety Director L. B. Sullivan, who had spoken up for Sheriff Matthews at his impeachment trial in 1952, praised Smelley and the other dismissed investigators. Sykes tried to smooth the situation over by issuing a statement that he too had "complete confidence" in Smelley. The dismissed investigators continued to befriend Albert Fuller, however, and reportedly worked to undermine the state's case against the renegade lawman.[24]

Persons had asked Patterson to serve as special counsel in the murder probe, but John declined.[25] The job paid $18,000 a year plus expenses—$8,000 more than Persons himself made. "That was a lot of money, and I was broke and needed it bad," Patterson said. "But I didn't need it that bad." He figured that would have been asking for a conflict of interest complaint against the state when the case came to trial. "Governor, I'm flattered that you would want me to do this," he said. "But I want an unbiased investigation, and I want it to be accurate. I want it to appear that way too. I'm sorry, but I can't accept your proposition."[26]

Newsmen reported at the time that Patterson had turned down the governor's generous offer, but planned to "continue to work in close harmony with law enforcement efforts on a statewide front."[27] He had a law practice to run and could get more done if he remained independent until being sworn in as attorney general in January. His father had even mortgaged their home to finance his campaign to win the attorney general nomination. Many friends and businessmen forgave the debts after Albert was murdered, but there were a lot of loose ends that needed tying up.

Patterson brought in attorney Jack Miller, a WWII pilot from Phenix City who had worked for the FBI after graduating from law school, to be his law partner. They had a lucrative practice during their short time together, and Miller continued to practice law in Phenix City after Patterson became attorney general. Patterson also developed close ties to Sykes and Gallion. Both were fine attorneys, he said, and they did "a magnificent job under very difficult circumstances" in their investigation of his father's murder. His father had thought highly of Gallion. In January John kept the promise Albert had made to bring Gallion into the attorney general's office as first assistant.[28]

The officials who were dispatched to Phenix City to clean out the "rat's nest" of racketeers and crooked politicians were among the best the state had to offer. "They don't make enough medals to reward Major General Crack Hanna's and the Alabama Guard's role in cleaning up Phenix City," Patterson said. He also praised Judge Walter B. Jones (president of the Alabama Bar Association and the son of a former governor) for his role in the cleanup. Chief Justice Livingston named Jones to replace Judge Julius B. Hicks after ousting Hicks from his circuit judgeship in Russell County. Livingston cited "the public good" as the basis for removing Hicks.[29]

The caliber of people sent to Phenix City to represent the state showed that Persons and Livingston meant business. John Patterson came to admire both Hanna and Jones, who were men of honor—tough, principled, incorruptible, and at the top of their professions. Walter B. Jones was the antithesis of the ousted circuit judge. For years under the control of Judge Hicks the jury boxes, the grand juries, and the verdicts had been stacked in favor of the crime bosses and the machine. Judge Jones, with the machine insiders fighting him every step of the way, gave Phenix City's citizens back the system of justice they had before it was corrupted by Hoyt Shepherd and his political cronies in the 1940s.

Persons was under increasing pressure from the press and the public to declare martial law in Phenix City, but this was an extreme measure he hoped to avoid. General Hanna argued fervently for a declaration of martial law, which he believed was the only way to get to the bottom of the Patterson murder and to clean up Phenix City once and for all. As long as the machine remained in power, he argued, the city fathers could intimidate witnesses and block the state's investigation. In late July, Governor Persons relented and imposed qualified martial law on the troubled city.

With the declaration, the press reported that General Hanna (as military commander) had installed National Guard officers in key law enforcement positions and "went after the gambling joints with vim and vigor." "In one day sixty-seven arrests were made. Most of the night spots now were dark." According to *Alabama* magazine, John Patterson called the governor's crackdown "mighty fine but a bit late." "He contended troops should have taken over immediately after the murder, but the governor said numerous details, legal and otherwise, had to be ironed out in advance of the drastic step," the magazine reported.[30]

What was not made public was the fire that the governor's office was taking from all sides, and that no matter what action Persons took, "he was damned if he did and damned if he didn't." He and General Harper had both received calls from congressional and White House staffs expressing interest in lifting the off-limits restrictions on Phenix City. At a public meeting General Harper told Phenix City's business leaders he would rely on John Patterson to make the call whether to put the town back on limits or not. Patterson had served with the general's command in Europe, and Harper knew he could trust John's judgment. The restrictions stayed in force as long as they were needed.

In typical mob fashion, when hush money and political influence didn't show results, the Phenix City machine fell back on threats and intimidation. Everyone who had anything to do with the case—from witnesses off the street to Hanna and Persons—received threats of bodily harm to themselves or to family members. McDonald Gallion's wife was threatened by an anonymous caller. Governor

Persons received anonymous threats against his teenage daughter's life, and one night the governor's mansion was targeted in a drive-by shooting. When the life of Hanna's son was threatened, the general enrolled him in a private school in Tennessee, and kept on about the business of enforcing martial law in Phenix City. The state of Alabama would not be intimidated, the governor declared.[31]

All the while the demand from the press and public for the state to solve the Patterson murder had risen "to an impatient pitch." The *Birmingham Post-Herald*, publishing an open letter on its front page, called on the governor "to exert the full powers of your office" toward solving the case. Persons remained silent amidst the storm of criticism, but Sykes issued a blunt statement that he was not "letting newspapers run the investigation." While progress was being made in the probe, Sykes cautioned that premature arrests could only jeopardize the state's case. He called on witnesses who had information about the murder to come forward. "If it's just talk it won't help us," he said, "but if it's facts it would help a lot."

Ferrell and Fuller still topped the list of suspects. The FBI had identified the thumbprint found on the rainguard above the window of Albert Patterson's Oldsmobile as Albert Fuller's. This gave Sykes sufficient cause for a warrant to search Fuller's residence, where additional evidence tying the deputy to the crime scene was discovered. The slugs recovered from Albert Patterson's body and at the crime scene were fired by the same .38 revolver, and were a mix of regular bullets and wadcutters sometimes used by police officers. Underneath Fuller's bed the investigators found a half-empty box containing a mixed batch of bullets matching those used in the slaying. Unfortunately, the murder weapon was not found on the premises, and more evidence of Fuller's guilt was needed before Sykes could make the charges stick.

The investigators had been told there were witnesses who could pin the murder on Ferrell and Fuller, but were still afraid to come forward. Fear of retaliation had long been a deterrent to going up against the crooked system in Phenix City, and anyone on the street with knowledge of the crime would likely remain anonymous as long as they felt threatened. This was why John Patterson and others knew that his father's killers might never be brought to justice unless the gamblers and the machine were crushed once and for all. General Hanna's enforcement of the governor's martial law decree, the indictments rising out of the Birmingham and Phenix City election-fraud hearings, and the principled system of justice that Judge Jones imposed on the circuit court came together to produce a climate more conducive to a probative investigation of his father's murder.

MacDonald Gallion knew the gamblers were feeling the heat when he got a call one night that Hoyt Shepherd wanted to see him. The person on the other end of the line said that the gambling kingpin would talk to no one but the governor's special counsel. He was given precise directions to a country crossroads outside of town and was told to come there alone and wait for a signal. Gallion realized the caller might be setting him up but decided it was a chance he had to take. Shepherd had been threatening to break his silence, which was said to have "many higher-ups in a dither," and this just might be the time. Shepherd had maintained all along that the gambling bosses were not responsible for the Patterson killing because they "knowed there'd be nothing but trouble in River City."

After driving out to the countryside and pulling off the gravel road at the designated rendezvous point, Gallion waited several minutes and then saw car lights up ahead flash on and off. He flashed his lights back at them. The other car eased toward him and did a U-turn in the middle of the road. An arm came out of the window and signaled for him to follow. They drove up a narrow dusty road to a rambling farmhouse, where he was ushered inside to hear what the gambling kingpin had to say.

Shepherd was seated at a table in the middle of the room. He was flanked by two thugs, one standing on each side. The gambling man was in a playful, hazing mood. "Yur' the one who put that wanted flyer out on Head Revel," Shepherd said to his uneasy guest. "Head swore he was gonna' git the guy that done that." Shepherd jerked his head toward a closed door, and said loudly, "Y'all kin come on out now, Head. We got him heah fer yuh." Gallion shifted his feet nervously, grasped the .38 revolver he had stuffed into his pocket, and looked expectantly toward the door. Shepherd burst into laughter. The two thugs laughed with him. Their employer's crude practical jokes entertained them almost as much as an evening of poker and scatological banter with the boys or breaking in the fresh merchandise out at Cliff's fish camp.

Now that he had center stage, Shepherd's expression turned serious. He said he had some "straight dope" to give Gallion about the murder of Albert Patterson. The only reason he was telling what he knew, Shepherd said, was because the National Guard was tearing the town apart and causing everybody grief. He wanted the governor to know that he was cooperating with the investigation.

"We gotta' git things settled down," he said. "Quiet and peaceful like. Sunday on the farm." He raised his voice, and slammed his hand on the table. "Yew can cut my heart out and lay it on this table if Albert Fuller ain't involved in this thing." That was as far as the informant would go in naming Fuller, but insisted that he was "dealing off the top now," and it was up to the governor's man "to take it from there."[32]

Gallion realized that all he had for his trouble was another finger pointing to Fuller's guilt. Shepherd had provided no evidence and his word alone wouldn't stand up in court. They still needed solid proof of the deputy's involvement. The next day Gallion dropped in on Fuller to question him and found him laid up in bed. "Fuller looked like he'd been run over by a truck. Said he'd been thrown by a horse, but the truth was that big Buddy Jowers had beaten the hell out of him," Gallion said.[33]

The questions for Fuller would have to wait. Gallion went looking for Buddy Jowers, but "the amazing hulk" had skipped town. Jowers and Fuller had both been served with subpoenas. They were under indictment for voting irregularities and other charges, and had been ordered to appear in court before Judge Walter B. Jones. The state's crackdown had precipitated a falling out among thieves, and the gambling czar's readiness to give up one of his crooked lawmen was a sign that Hoyt Shepherd's house of cards was falling.[34]

WHILE GENERAL HANNA AND the guardsmen were dismantling the gambling empire in Russell County, the reports from the Jefferson County grand jury and the Democratic Committee's investigation spelled big trouble for Si Garrett, Arch Ferrell, and the Phenix City machine. First to be handed down were the grand jury indictments of Garrett, Ferrell, and Lamar Reid for manipulating the Jefferson County vote count in the attorney general's race. Garrett and Ferrell were also charged with having directed a campaign against Albert Patterson that was financed by Phenix City's gamblers and vice lords. While not accusing the two officials of involvement in Albert Patterson's murder, the grand jury did conclude that the slaying "was the climax of dirty politics, financed by a gang of unlawful men and engaged in by persons with unlawful motives."[35]

Garrett's family retained Birmingham's vaunted courtroom wizard Roderick Beddow to represent him. The self-exiled attorney general returned from Texas briefly and appeared with Beddow before the Jefferson County sheriff to post bond. Then, still professing innocence, Garrett left the state again for an undisclosed destination. Beddow suggested that his client's return to the mental hospital in Texas was likely. Solicitor Ferrell, meanwhile, had been relieved of all duties, and was ordered by Bernard Sykes to "devote his full time to writing a report on what he had done toward solving the ambush slaying of Albert Patterson." A laconic press report stated that "none of the officials now in charge of the inquiry thought this would require much writing." Ferrell never turned in the report.[36]

Patterson called Garrett's "continued inaccessibility" preposterous, and urged that the evasive attorney general be questioned about developments leading up to his father's assassination. He told a reporter for the *Montgomery Advertiser* that he was "morally certain" he knew who murdered his father. He did not point to Ferrell by name, but the description fit. "This man is a known drunkard with an uncontrollable temper. He is deeply enmeshed with the Phenix City criminal element. He had both the motive and the opportunity. I don't believe his alibi is worth a damn."[37]

Making him more inaccessible, Garrett was hospitalized in Waynesboro, Mississippi, for an extended period after wrecking his car on a family vacation. His attorney and his family kept interrogators from questioning Garrett during his lengthy recovery in Mississippi, and afterward when he reentered the psychiatric hospital in Texas. Attorney Beddow and his client played a cat-and-mouse game with reporters and prosecutors about their possible use of an insanity plea. Garrett's voluntary confinement in Texas shielded him from Alabama prosecutors, but when informed that Jefferson County solicitor Emmett Perry had filed lunacy proceedings against him, Garrett assured reporters that he was "as sane as [Solicitor] Perry."

Unlike their wily co-defendant, Ferrell and Fuller had no place to run. When he appeared before the grand jury in Birmingham, Garrett had reasserted the alibi he had given Ferrell for the night of Albert Patterson's murder. That seemed to offer little comfort to Ferrell, however, when the state committee threw out the results of the primary election in Russell County and he was indicted for vote fraud in Jefferson County. Ferrell, Sheriff Matthews, and the slate of machine candidates lost their jobs when the primary election was overturned, and many faced the prospect of indictment. Attorney George C. Johnson, "a vigorous, resourceful young upstate circuit solicitor" from Athens was brought in as acting solicitor of Russell County until new elections could be held. He was aided in the prosecutions by circuit solicitors Conrad "Bully" Fowler of Columbiana and Julian Bland of Cullman County who assisted in preparing and presenting the cases to the special grand jury when it was impaneled.[38]

The ousted city and county officials didn't go quietly. Tempers flared. Hotheaded city clerk Jimmy Putnam became front-page news after jostling a young Birmingham reporter named Harry Cook and damaging his camera. Two national guardsmen who witnessed the incident arrested Putnam and booked him for assault. Patterson remembered the young reporter from their days at the University—Cook had been highly visible as editor of the campus newspaper—and later picked him to be press secretary when he became governor. Jimmy Putnam's day in the sun was not just his assault on Cook, but included a previous incident in 1953 when his jaw was broken in an altercation with his friend Arch Ferrell.[39]

Ferrell, unlike Putnam who was yesterday's news when the sun went down, had trouble staying away from the limelight. Nothing depicted the Phenix City machine's utter defeat or the ousted county solicitor's fall from grace quite like a photograph of two Alabama guardsmen arresting a disheveled Ferrell for public drunkenness. The lopsided grin plastered on the fallen solicitor's face tells the story. "Give these Boss Crump wannabe's some wildcat whiskey and a little rope, they'll hang themselves," one of the guardsmen said.

Judge Walter B. Jones had come to Phenix City to do the hanging. Within the mountain of evidence the Democratic subcommittee and General Hanna's guardsmen had piled up was enough dynamite to bring down the lot of local "wannabe's" and their racketeering friends. Mixed in with the sleaze and dirt were a few priceless gems such as the testimony of an RBA poll-watcher who saw Albert Fuller drive up with a carload of familiar faces from Cliff's Fish House. When his passengers got out and went inside to vote, one painted blonde came back to the car and asked sweetly, "Deputy Fuller, honey, what'd you say my name was this time?"

Fuller's entourage had never heard of Judge Walter B. Jones. For all they cared he could have been another one of their faceless johns or boring one-night stands. Before Cliff's or Ma Beachie's girls could treat their Fort Benning regulars and Auburn's frat brothers to another New Year's blast, however, they were out of business, Ma Beachie had a cameo role in *The Phenix City Story*, and every drunk in Russell County and farmers from miles around knew who Judge Jones was. To the gamblers and misfits he was that black-robed S.O.B. sent by the Capitol City big mules with deep pockets to clean up their mess, who quoted from the Bible in a croaking voice and beat the pants off the Phenix City high-rollers right in what used to be their own courtroom. The *Columbus Ledger-Enquirer* called Jones the "prophet of a happier day in Russell County" and said his words were "like mountain thunder rolling across the sinful plain."

Judge Jones was a large man, but not an imposing one. The portly, balding sixty-six-year-old jurist impressed those who met him as a soft-spoken, courteous Southern gentleman. He was an Alabamian through-and-through, a Christian gentleman, a scholarly man of means basking in the sunshine of Southern charm—the only distraction being a conspicuous voice impediment, a condition that led to his death of throat cancer in 1963. Born into Southern aristocracy and raised in the shade of the state capitol—his father, Governor Thomas Goode Jones, as a Confederate officer had carried General Lee's flag of truce to General Grant at Appomattox—Judge Jones had attained a status among his peers that was singular in distinction and achievement.[40]

The judge had authored some forty-five books on legal, historical, and biblical subjects. He served as president of the Alabama Bar Association, president of the Alabama Bible Society, and editor of the *Alabama Baptist Society Quarterly*. In 1928 he founded the Thomas Goode Jones School of Law where he served as president, dean, and faculty member. His scholarly bearing and gentility in social settings belied a commanding presence in the courtroom, as Phenix City's toughs soon found out.[41]

Through the years since his father's murder and the cleanup in Phenix City, John Patterson spoke often of the drama in the courtroom the day Judge Jones opened court in Russell County. On that day the ruffians were out in force: the "courtroom was packed with hostile mobsters, racketeers, brothel operators, prostitutes, and the like, as well as citizens hoping for a return to law and order." Hoyt Shepherd and his crowd were seated or standing up front, some sprawled in the jury box or leaning on both sides of the railing. Deputy Fuller slouched with his guns holstered and his arms crossed in the witness chair. A murmur rippled across the courtroom as Judge Jones entered "flanked by guardsmen," and "a military bailiff called the court to order."

The judge lifted his arms high, and a hush settled over the room. After he explained courtroom procedure to the spectators, he had the bailiff move everyone from in front of the rails and ordered Deputy Fuller to remove himself and his guns from the court. Up front near the bench was a state flag, but no American flag. Jones kept the spectators waiting while he sent a guardsman to bring one back. When the guardsman returned, Jones led them in the Pledge of Allegiance.

He then delivered a prepared address in which he assured "the good people of Russell County" that the State of Alabama was going to restore law and order there and "all the powers of hell won't be able to prevent it."

Jones dismissed the sitting grand jury made up of political hacks and relatives, and then purged the rigged jury box containing only names that were acceptable to the machine. He impaneled a new grand jury comprised of citizens who were known to be honest and upright members of the community. For them not to do their duty, he instructed the jury, they would be better off giving their county back to "the bats and the owls." One of the youngest jurors was William Benton, a twenty-eight-year-old family man who had served four years in the Army, taught school and coached afterward, was active in church and civic organizations, and was presently working with the Boys' Clubs across the river in Columbus. Benton later got his law degree, practiced law in Phenix City, and served for sixteen years as the district attorney of Russell County.

Benton recalled the dedication of the citizens who served on the grand jury with him. Judge Jones asked Benton to be the backup in the event the elderly foreman, Cloyd Tillery, needed a replacement. The grand jury worked at an exhaustive pace through the end of the year. Tillery tired easily, and Jones had a cot brought into the jury room so the foreman could lie down and rest for an hour in the morning and an hour in the afternoon. When their work was done the jurors had "returned 741 indictments against 144 defendants," of which "all but two either pleaded guilty or were found guilty." Among those indicted and convicted were Hoyt Shepherd, his partner Jimmy Matthews, and other gambling kingpins.[42]

Albert Fuller was still recovering from the beating Buddy Jowers had given him when the grand jury returned indictments against him for vice and corruption. When Judge Jones convened court on November 19, the date of Fuller's trial on bribery charges, the ailing former deputy was absent. His attorneys Joe Smith and Arch Ferrell's brother Pelham explained that their client's severe spinal injuries, suffered nearly four months earlier, had prevented him from appearing in court. Judge Jones ordered the attorneys to produce their client forthwith, and Fuller was brought to court on a gurney to hear the charges against him.[43]

Fuller's troubles had only begun. A few weeks later, on December 9, the grand jury handed down indictments against Fuller, Arch Ferrell, and Si Garrett for the murder of Albert Patterson. William Benton said there was "not a bit of doubt" among grand jury members that they had indicted the right people for the Patterson slaying. There was "a little speculation" about whether it was Fuller or Ferrell who pulled the trigger that night, but Benton and his fellow jurors were convinced that all three men were involved in the assassination.[44]

From the desk drawer in his father's office John Patterson had retrieved a card inscribed with a quote by English statesman Edmund Burke: "The only thing necessary for the triumph of evil is that good men do nothing." His father often cited Burke in his speeches. Following the lead of Albert Patterson, the RBA members, the ministers, General Hanna, and Judge Jones, the grand jury's dedication and courage showed the good people of Phenix City that they could overcome the evil in their town. Fifty years down the road, William Benton looked back with pride: "You know, we became an all-American city. Good things began to happen. We began to get industry. People found out they could have decent government. They didn't have to rely on the underworld. And to their credit some of them developed a better way of life and became good citizens."[45]

Benton noted that as a young man he had found in Albert Patterson's life a challenge for shaping his own. "The courage and decency of the man was so extraordinary," he said. Benton was a few years younger than John Patterson, but they became close in the wake of Albert's assassination. "I was with John the night he became attorney general," Benton said. "When the votes came in we went into his office and talked. We've been good friends ever since." He thought for a moment before continuing. "He's been a good friend. I'll always love him and his family for what they've gone through to help provide a better way of life here. They paid a terrible price for this community."[46]

Patterson spoke admiringly of the grand jurors and the importance of their contribution to cleaning up Phenix City and bringing closure to his father's assassination. The grand jury's findings resounded far beyond the courtroom. Their indictments, for instance, went a long way toward removing the fear of retaliation that had long held the community in bondage to greedy politicians and the underworld. Witnesses who had been reluctant to talk to investigators broke their silence when they no longer felt intimidated. Their statements became critical to prosecutors in building the state's case against the men accused of murdering his father. As seasoned prosecutors knew, however, building a solid case against defendants was one thing, getting a conviction was something else altogether.

9

BITTERSWEET REFRAIN IN BIRMINGHAM

John Patterson is as convinced today as he was in 1955 by the evidence the special grand jury weighed when it indicted the three men accused of murdering his father. Half a century has gone by since the fatal shots rang out in the alleyway between the Coulter Building and the Elite Cafe. Books have been written about the cowardly crime and movies made, the ink long dry on the pages now yellowed with age. No one is closer to the history of the murder or has pored over the old evidence and new leads more times than the eldest son. Nothing he has seen or heard over the past fifty years has shaken his confidence in the state's case or in the prosecution's theory of who committed the crime and why it was done.[1]

That confidence endured shock and disappointment when only one of the accused, Russell County's former chief deputy sheriff Albert Fuller, was convicted of his father's murder. Patterson's first weeks as Alabama's attorney general were under way when Fuller's capital murder trial opened in Judge J. Russell McElroy's court in Birmingham on February 16, 1955. A change of venue had been granted in both Fuller's and Ferrell's trials because of the strong feelings the assassination and its aftermath had aroused in Phenix City. Both defendants entered not-guilty pleas. Fuller's trial was to have started on Valentine's Day, but was delayed until the 16th while prosecutors rounded up a missing witness, taxi driver James Radius Taylor.

Circuit Solicitor Emmett Perry was busy with the Jefferson County vote-fraud case, so his assistant Cecil Deason prosecuted the capital murder trials. Fuller's chief counsel was Roderick Beddow, Sr., who had his son and a corps of other attorneys assisting him with both Fuller's capital murder trial and Silas Garrett's mental sanctuary in Galveston, Texas, to evade prosecution. The high drama, the international press attention, and the anticipated clash between topflight lawyers packed the courtroom. Beddow—Albert Patterson had aptly called him "the battering ram from Birmingham"—and his assistants fought hard to win an acquittal for Fuller, but the weight of evidence against their client prevailed.

When the trial ended on March 11 the jury deliberated for only six hours and fifty minutes before returning a verdict of guilty. The jury fixed the sentence of the fallen deputy, once the "cock of the walk" around Phenix City, at life in prison.[2]

Ferrell's capital murder trial began in April. In what could have been a calculated move to unlink his trial from the co-defendants, Ferrell had retained Birmingham defense attorneys George Rogers and Drew Redden rather than the more colorful Beddow. Ferrell's defense team gained an unexpected advantage when Solicitor Perry first tried their client on the misdemeanor charge of election fraud (while the Fuller trial was still underway) and, "by an incredible quirk of Jefferson (County) jurisprudence," the jury acquitted him. This surprising turn, along with the convenient alibi that Ferrell had been on the phone with Si Garrett when Albert Patterson was murdered, was apparently enough to raise doubts in jurors' minds about the motive, the prosecution's conspiracy theory, and Ferrell's involvement in the murder.[3]

Prosecutors and spectators sat in shocked silence when the jury came back with a not-guilty verdict. According to *Alabama* magazine," the stolid, staring defendant himself was almost speechless," but "finally framed a murmur of deep gratitude for the justice" he received. "Instead of going manacled to join Fuller (who was stunned by the news) in jail he went voluntarily to pay his old friend a nervous visit before departing for home with tearfully joyous Mrs. Ferrell."[4]

Ferrell's acquittal quashed hopes of winning a conviction against Garrett on the murder charge or for the lesser count of vote fraud. Judge McElroy refused to force Garrett to submit to a sanity hearing sought by the attorney general's office—a ruling upheld by the state supreme court—and he was never brought to trial. A decade after Albert Patterson was murdered, Attorney General Richmond Flowers dismissed the charges against the ailing former attorney general. Three years later the man who prosecutors believed had masterminded the slaying of Albert Patterson was dead of a massive stroke.[5]

The only punitive action taken against Garrett and Ferrell came from the Alabama State Bar, which revoked their licenses (along with those of Lee Porter and Lamar Reid) to practice law in Alabama. This was little consolation to Alabama's new attorney general, who believed that his predecessor had manipulated the justice system to save himself and his cohort Ferrell from prison. Winning a conviction in Albert Fuller's trial, while the other two accused men went free, was for John Patterson a textbook case of "justice done, and justice denied"—a bittersweet refrain that burdened his thoughts as the trial docket on his father's murder came to a close in Birmingham.

THE MEN INDICTED FOR his father's murder proclaimed their innocence to the bitter end, but they acted as if they had something to hide from the start. For John Patterson and the prosecution, the state's evidence pointed to their culpability. Prosecutors, having reconstructed the crime from witness statements and other evidence, reasoned that the three indicted men had plotted to assassinate Albert Patterson when he could not be stopped any other way. He had beaten them in the election and now threatened to ruin them by telling the grand jury in Birmingham what he knew. A call from Big Jim Folsom, in the role of peacemaker, had failed to dissuade Albert from testifying.[6]

Prosecutors believed that Garrett, on the morning of that treacherous Friday, instructed Ferrell to go ahead with plans to assassinate Albert Patterson. They were desperate men. In their warped thinking Patterson had become too dangerous to live. He had to be stopped now, to keep him from going before the grand jury. Garrett was on the way to Birmingham that morning to face the grand jury himself. He was suspected of making the call to Ferrell before leaving Montgomery, while stopped along the way, or after arriving in Birmingham.[7]

Accompanying Garrett to Birmingham was heavy-set attorney Frank Long, a staunch Folsomite and former head of the Alabama Young Democrats from Jasper, Alabama. On the way out of Montgomery they stopped at the Stockyards Cafe where Garrett made some last-minute telephone calls. Telephone records established that one of those calls was made to Ferrell. A witness overheard Garrett say "that's thirty" (an expression used by journalists to end a story) just before hanging up the phone. Prosecutors believed that call could have sealed Albert Patterson's fate.[8]

After dropping the attorney general off at the courthouse in Birmingham, Long had gone to the Redmont Hotel and registered for Garrett. Long's presence in the Redmont suite at the time of the Patterson murder would be a godsend for Ferrell since Garrett could not return from Texas to testify at Ferrell's trial without compromising his own defense strategy. Long would be ready and available to take the stand in Garrett's stead.[9]

While Garrett and Long were en route to Birmingham, Albert Patterson was preparing to leave his office in Phenix City to drive to Montgomery. Patterson's trip would have given the conspirators all day to lay plans for waylaying their victim following his return to the office that evening. Monitoring his movements was a simple matter for them since the courthouse was only a hundred yards or so across Fourteenth Street from the Coulter Building. The only obstruction between them was the post office and it did not block the view of Patterson's law offices. When their intended victim turned off the office lights that evening, the conspirators knew how long it would take for him to lock the door and hobble with his cane down the steps to the parking lot.

Prosecutors believed the evidence was conclusive that Ferrell and Fuller were both standing next to Albert Patterson's car when the shots were fired. Witnesses placed the two men outside the Coulter Building that night, and saw them fleeing the scene of the crime. Witnesses indicated that Fuller and Ferrell "broke and ran" from the alleyway around the Coulter Building. Fuller jumped into a waiting car that took off down Fourteenth Street, turned off to a parallel street, came back, and pulled in behind the jail. Fuller jumped out and ran inside, claiming later that he had been in the jail at the time of the murder. The getaway car kicked up a cloud of dust as it pulled away from the jail and was seen leaving Phenix City at high speed. At the same time Ferrell was seen running from the direction of the Coulter Building and down Fourteenth Street in front of the post office, toward the parking lot on the other side of the building where he always left his car.

If General Hanna and the Alabama Guard, with the help of Judge Jones and the special grand jury, had not cleaned out the dregs of Phenix City—making it possible to hold honest elections, the state might never have made a case against the alleged conspirators. When Matthews was forced to resign, the new sheriff, Lamar Murphy, pitched in to help prosecutors build their case. Murphy was a former boxing instructor from Troy, Alabama, who had run his own gas station in Phenix City for many years and was well-liked and respected within the community. When he became actively involved in solving the Patterson murder, informants began coming to him with what they knew.

Sheriff Murphy had tracked down the state's principal witness, Johnny Frank Griffin, after a mechanic informed him there was a man in town who claimed to have seen Fuller and Patterson together outside the Coulter Building around the time of the murder. Murphy convinced Griffin to tell prosecutors and the grand jury what he knew. Griffin's testimony before the special grand jury was the linchpin in the state's case. He had not witnessed the actual slaying, but testified that on the night of the murder he was walking toward Smitty's Grill, a couple of doors down from the Elite Cafe, when he saw Fuller arguing with Albert Patterson at the entrance to the Coulter Building. Fuller's gun was in his holster at the time, Griffin said. When Patterson hobbled away, the deputy followed him into the alley where the Oldsmobile was parked. Then Griffin heard gunshots and saw the victim stumble from the alley without his cane and collapse on the sidewalk.[10]

After the grand jury handed down the indictments other witnesses opened up to prosecutors. Bill Littleton, a former Phenix City taxi driver, told them that he was driving his cab along Fifth Avenue on the night of the slaying and saw Ferrell and Fuller standing near the Coulter Building. He testified at Fuller's and Ferrell's trials that he had "waved at the two men, both known to him for a number of years, and Ferrell waved back." He said that he had been afraid to tell authorities what he knew before the grand jury indicted Ferrell and Fuller.[11]

Another cab driver, James Radius Taylor of Columbus, testified that he had stopped at a traffic light at the intersection of Fourteenth Street and Fifth Avenue when he heard gunfire and saw a familiar figure running out from around the First Federal Building toward a car parked in front of an adjoining empty lot. The fleeing man was Deputy Fuller, who jumped into the waiting car and sped off in the opposite direction. Taylor's fare, an Army lieutenant from Fort Benning, could not be found to corroborate the story, but the dispatcher recalled announcing the news of the murder over the radio and Taylor then blurting out Fuller's name. Like other witnesses Taylor had been afraid to identify Fuller when he first talked to investigators.[12]

Arch Ferrell had been spotted leaving the scene of the crime by another witness, courthouse janitor Quinnie C. Kelley. After checking the courthouse to see that everyone had gone, Kelley had locked the doors to the building and was standing on the front steps smoking a cigarette when he heard three pistol shots. As he walked down the sidewalk to get a better view Kelley saw the county solicitor come hurrying out from between the post office and the Coulter Building. The last he saw of Ferrell he had turned right at the post office and was moving "between a fast walk and a run" down Fourteenth Street in the direction of the courthouse parking lot. Kelley, too, when first questioned, had failed to name the man he had seen. Asked about this at Ferrell's trial, Kelley responded: "I was scared the night it happened, and I don't feel the safest in the world now."[13]

Prosecutors had back-up witnesses and other evidence to support their case. The physical evidence against Albert Fuller (his thumbprint under the rain guard on the Oldsmobile, the empty holster, the box of mixed ammo recovered from his apartment) was particularly strong. Eyewitness statements together with the physical evidence supported the prosecution's theory that Ferrell and Fuller were both present when the fatal shots were fired. They concluded that Fuller had confronted Patterson as he came out of the Coulter Building and followed him to his car, while Ferrell had approached from the other direction. Ferrell was believed to have used a telephone located on the wall inside the back door of the Elite Cafe to call Garrett at the Redmont Hotel in Birmingham and establish an alibi.

Perhaps the two assailants made a final attempt to warn Albert Patterson off from testifying before the grand jury in Birmingham on Monday. When he refused, prosecutors argued, Fuller either pulled the pistol and shot Patterson or Ferrell, in a blind rage, had jerked the pistol from Fuller's holster and fired point blank at his unarmed adversary behind the wheel. The accused murderers then fled the scene—Fuller running to a waiting car and Ferrell heading toward the courthouse parking lot when he was spotted by Quinnie Kelley. The inquisitive janitor had put out his cigarette and walked down the sidewalk to see what all the commotion was about over at the Coulter Building.

WITNESSES AGAINST THE ACCUSED men had good reason to be afraid to tell what they knew. Men had been killed for less. Even special grand jury members and their families had been threatened by unknown callers. More ominous was the suspicious death of the state's star witness, Johnny Frank Griffin, who died on the operating table at Cobb Memorial Hospital within twenty-four hours after telling his story to the special grand jury. Griffin had been under protective custody before he testified. Sheriff Murphy had slipped him into the grand jury room disguised as a janitor carrying a mop and a bucket. After testifying he slipped away unnoticed and wandered out onto the streets alone. He caught a bus to a place called Five Points, where he had an altercation with a black youth and was stabbed in the neck with a pocketknife.

After the stabbing incident Griffin was taken to the emergency room at Cobb Memorial Hospital where he was treated and held overnight for observation. When word of the stabbing reached him, John Patterson rushed to the hospital where Sheriff Murphy was waiting. Griffin was sitting up in bed. The wound did not appear to be life-threatening. "He had a piece of cotton over the wound in his throat. There was a little bowl beside his bed, and he would clear his throat now and then and spit a little blood in the container there." While Murphy stayed with Griffin, Patterson drove over to his mother's house where he was eating dinner when the call came that the state's star witness was dead.[14]

Returning to the hospital he was told that the patient had a heart seizure and was rushed into emergency surgery. The doctor performed an open-heart massage to try and save the patient, but he had died on the operating table. They had no proof of foul play in Griffin's death, but Patterson said that he and Murphy both suspected that the state's star witness was murdered by someone in the hospital. The monument to Mayor Homer Cobb's blend of machine politics and public service had a less than stellar reputation in those days. There was a saying on the streets of Phenix City at the time: "If anything happens to me, don't let them take me to Cobb Memorial Hospital."[15]

Prosecutors had an affidavit from Griffin but couldn't use it at trial because the defense would be denied the right of cross-examination. Fortunately for the state's case, other witnesses like Quinnie Kelley, Bill Littleton, and James Taylor overcame their fears after Ferrell and Fuller were indicted. Murphy, meanwhile, continued to dig for more evidence. He knew from questioning Johnny Frank Griffin that another man had been on the street the night of the murder and may have witnessed the crime. Murphy kept digging until he found the man, a thirty-year old construction worker named Cecil Padgett.[16]

Padgett told Murphy that he and his wife Edith had driven downtown on the night of the murder and were thinking about going to a movie. They had parked on Fifth Avenue opposite the Coulter Building. While his wife waited in the car, he crossed the street in front of Smitty's Grill and walked up to the Palace Theater to see which movie was showing. As he passed in front of Smitty's Grill, Padgett said he saw Fuller and Patterson going into the parking lot beside the Coulter Building. He recalled that Fuller was wearing his pistol.

After checking the movie schedule, Padgett had walked back to his car when he heard the pistol shots. He turned quickly and saw Fuller leaning against Patterson's Oldsmobile with one hand above the driver's window. With Fuller was another man. Padgett was "almost certain" the other man was Arch Ferrell. He watched as the two men ran from the alleyway. Padgett's wife confirmed his story. John Patterson was convinced that Sheriff Murphy had come up with the eyewitness the state needed to nail down its case. Cecil Deason grilled Padgett at length before agreeing to prosecute the case. When Deason was convinced that Padgett was telling the truth, the state was ready to go to trial.

AT FULLER'S TRIAL BEDDOW, his white hair flopping over his eyes, went after Padgett and the other state witnesses with everything he had to try and impeach their testimony, but the witnesses stuck to their stories. Beddow also put witnesses on the stand to rebut them, and brought in others to shore up his client's alibi that he was in the jail behind the courthouse at the time of the murder. With one exception, Fuller's alibi witnesses (Sheriff Matthews and others) were longtime friends from Sin City's impeachable past. There were contradictions about the precise time the witnesses were supposedly with Fuller at the jail. The one witness who was not a member of the jailhouse clique and gave some credibility to Fuller's alibi was George Phillips, a highway patrolman with the driver's license bureau who sometimes slept at the jail when he was in Phenix City.

To bolster the state patrolman's testimony, Beddow put public safety director L. B. Sullivan and highway patrol chief Tom Carlisle on the stand as character witnesses. Their sworn testimony attesting to Phillips's moral character and truthfulness was reminiscent of the 1953 impeachment trial when these same state officials appeared in court to support Sheriff Matthews. With high-level state lawmen and investigators in the defendant's corner, the public safety directorate was acting at cross-purposes with the attorney general's office in the Patterson murder case. Had it not been for an alert citizen in Centreville, Alabama, the brotherhood might have put enough doubt in jurors' minds to set Fuller free.

Responding to the intense public interest, the *Birmingham News* gave the Fuller and Ferrell trials maximum coverage, including the printing of verbatim testimony of witnesses. Roberta Oakley of Centreville, like many Alabamians, followed the newspaper accounts of the trial religiously. She had more than passing interest in the news since she helped her husband Jim publish the town's weekly paper, the *Centreville Press*. When she read about the highway patrolman testifying that he had been with Fuller at the jail when Albert Patterson was murdered, she exclaimed, "Why, that's not true!"

"What's that?" her husband asked. She reminded him that the highway patrol officer had been transferred to Centreville after the Patterson murder. He had told a different story then from the one he was now telling on the witness stand. The newspaper office was across from the courthouse, and the officer had dropped in to chat with the Oakleys when he first came to town to give drivers' tests. They were discussing the Patterson murder case when Phillips remarked that he had been in Phenix City the night the slaying occurred.[17]

Mrs. Oakley asked who he thought committed the murder, and Phillips replied that he didn't know the killer's identity. Ferrell's and Fuller's names came up in the conversation. She recalled Phillips saying "that he didn't know about Fuller, but he was having a cup of coffee with Ferrell at the time of the murder." She was positive that the state patrolman had told her "he was unaware of the whereabouts of Fuller that evening." Now he was testifying under oath that he was with Fuller at the jail when Patterson was slain. A person who overheard Mrs. Oakley's discussion with her husband informed the attorney general's office, and she was called to testify as a rebuttal witness.[18]

When Mrs. Oakley took the stand, she was described by reporters as "a soft-spoken bespectacled woman" who was very direct in her testimony. Beddow's questioning was aimed at discrediting her. He prefaced his questioning with a reference to Mrs. Oakley's "alleged conversation" with the veteran highway patrolman. Mrs. Oakley corrected him. "This isn't an alleged conversation, Mr. Beddow. This is an actual conversation."[19] "Old Roderick Beddow got madder' than hell and attacked that woman trying to break her story," Patterson recalled. "He implied she was a friend of mine."

"How long have you known John Patterson?" Beddow snapped.

"I don't know Mr. Patterson."

"You don't know Mr. Patterson. Then how did you meet?"

"I never met Mr. Patterson."

"You didn't talk with him?"

"No, sir."

"How did they know about you? How did they find out about this?"

"I don't have any idea."

Beddow backed off and started to walk away. The witness was imperturbable, but he noticed that she tightly clutched something in her lap. He turned on his heels and demanded, "What's that you've got in your lap? What're you holding out on us?" Mrs. Oakley opened her hands and smiled softly. "It's my Bible," she said.

"I wouldn't have took nothin' for that moment," Patterson recalled. "The defense had been caught with its trousers down, and old Beddow knew it."[20]

There were other dramatic moments in Fuller's trial, but none to match the audacity of the defendant's testimony in his own defense. Beddow had promised the jury that he would put Fuller on the stand, and he didn't disappoint them. As John Patterson listened to what he knew was "a web of lies" being spun from the witness stand, he remembered the night of his father's murder when the deputy had driven him over to his mother's house. He marveled at the ease with which "bald-faced lies and deceit" became second nature to Fuller's kind. Not only did the defendant insist that he was innocent of the murder charges, but testified that he had been "a close personal friend" of Albert Patterson and had supported him politically.

On cross-examination Deason tripped the defendant up by asking if it was his testimony that he had supported Albert Patterson in his "successful campaign for attorney general of Alabama last spring." Fuller said that it was. Then Deason asked how he had voted in the attorney general's race. Fuller admitted after an embarrassing pause that he had voted for Patterson's opponent. Knowing that prosecutors could verify how he had voted, Fuller had no choice but to answer the question truthfully.

At another point Fuller claimed that it couldn't have been him that prosecution witnesses saw running from the murder scene because he suffered from a severe leg injury that wouldn't let him run. But then he testified that "he ran out of the jail when he heard about the shooting and ran across the street when he arrived at the murder scene."

The contradictions didn't seem to bother Fuller, whose demeanor on the witness stand was described as ranging "between a blank expression and a frown." During questioning by Beddow, Fuller seemed to suggest that drug injections taken for the back injury suffered at the hands of Buddy Jowers were to blame for his memory lapses.[21]

At Ferrell's trial he, unlike Fuller, made no pretense of being friends with the man he was accused of murdering. Ferrell had been too vocal in his hatred toward the slain crime-fighter, and had threatened in public that Patterson would never become attorney general. Although admitting that he had hated Patterson, Ferrell vehemently denied any part in his murder. The state believed it had a solid case against Ferrell. He had been tied to the scene of the murder by reliable eyewitnesses, while his thin alibi hung on a telephone call made to Garrett's hotel room in Birmingham.

Garrett, after an exhaustive day in front of the Jefferson County grand jury in Birmingham, had invited a small group of guests to his suite at the Redmont for dinner and drinks. His companion Frank Long was present.[22] This was no victory party. Did Garrett need the support of friends or were they invited there to be witnesses, prosecutors asked? Their presence gave some legitimacy to the telephone alibi Garrett later provided to Ferrell in front of reporters on the weekend after the murder. Prosecutors argued that the murder was premeditated, and the alibi could easily have been staged.

When Frank Long took the stand as Ferrell's alibi witness, he testified that he had taken a call from the Russell County solicitor at the Redmont Hotel around 9 P.M.—ten minutes before the fatal shots were fired in Phenix City. The call had come into Room 718 where Garrett was holding a dinner party. Long said the noise interfered with his hearing the solicitor so he had the call transferred to an adjoining room. After they talked for three or four minutes, Ferrell asked to speak to Garrett. Long turned the phone over to Garrett and went back to the party. He stated that Garrett left the door to the other room open and "was in view throughout the conversation with Ferrell."[23]

During cross-examination Deason got Long to admit that he had been drinking all afternoon on the day he accompanied Garrett to Birmingham. When asked how well he knew the solicitor, the witness said that he and Ferrell were acquaintances and had talked a couple of times on the telephone.[24]_ Deason pressed Long about whether he could say with certainty that he recognized Ferrell's voice on the telephone. The witness responded that it was "his considered best judgment" that the caller was Ferrell—a lawyer's way of saying "don't quote me on that" or "I'm not really sure."[25] Long's statement was similar to the one that key state witness Cecil Padgett had made about recognizing Ferrell as the other man with Fuller at the crime scene. It was on the thin thread of Frank Long's testimony that the jury apparently acquitted Ferrell.

JOHN PATTERSON WAS GUEST of honor at a banquet in the Essex Hotel when he learned of Ferrell's acquittal. An assistant came in and whispered the news in his ear. His jaw tightened perceptibly. "It was a great shock," he said. He knew that men had been sent to the electric chair in Alabama with less evidence. Unable to finish the meal, he pushed the plate aside. He took a sip of wine and set the goblet down, his forehead furrowed in thought. The wine was bitter to the taste. He wondered how his mother would take the news. She had been first to testify at the trials, but was not in court when the jury came back in. He knew that she too would be devastated by the not-guilty verdict.

The young attorney general also realized that he had to put the best face he could on an improbable situation, and he was glad to have a little time before the banquet ended and the doors were opened to reporters. An adage from his law school studies kept coming to mind. The saying was appropriate for the occasion, and when reporters came rushing in, he quoted it to them. "Those of us who seek redress for the wrong done us may console ourselves with this thought. No man is ever acquitted at the bar of his own conscience."[26]

When *Alabama* magazine reported the Patterson quote, the editor added his own blunt observation: "Though legally exonerated of murder, Arch Ferrell would still endure substantial punishment for notoriety gained in connection with Phenix City's uprooted filth."[27] From all accounts Ferrell's personal life went downhill fast following his acquittal for the Patterson murder. His attorneys appealed his permanent disbarment by the Alabama Bar Association, but he lost the appeal.[28]

Less than three years after his trials for election fraud and murder, the former county solicitor's infamous bouts with alcohol and violence were back in the headlines. In August 1957 Ferrell was arrested on a reckless driving charge after leading deputies on a high-speed chase through Phenix City's streets and ending in Seale. A year later, at the family's request, Russell Probate Judge Shannon Burch twice had Ferrell committed to Bryce State Mental Hospital in Tuscaloosa for tests and treatment. More than once Sheriff Lamar Murphy had been called to the Ferrell home to protect the family. On one of these occasions in May 1958 Ferrell had "barricaded" himself in the house when Murphy and a deputy drove up with a warrant for his arrest on assault and battery charges.[29]

Ferrell had a pistol and a sawed-off shotgun in the house, but gave himself up to the sheriff without resistance. The Georgia man who swore out the warrant told officers that Ferrell had pistol-whipped him and threatened to kill him at a service station in Seale. At the time of his arrest Ferrell was free on bonds from two other warrants signed by a Seale grocer charging him with assault and carrying a concealed weapon.[30]

In later years Ferrell seemed to have put the past behind him. He went to work for his brother-in-law selling Bardahl oil supplies. Then, in 1969, he applied to the state bar association to get his law license back. When William Benton was district attorney, Ferrell's brother Pelham came to him and asked if he would sign a petition for Arch to be readmitted to the bar to practice law. Benton refused to sign. "My feeling at the time was that I didn't take it away from him and I wasn't going to be party to trying to give it back to him," Benton said.[31]

Benton and the brother had words. "Some of yo' friends will sign," the brother said.

"Maybe so," Benton replied. "But some of my friends may not have had those calls in the middle of the night from a drunk threatening his family." Those calls had come when William Benton served on the special grand jury that indicted Ferrell and the others for the Patterson murder.

A few days later Arch Ferrell called and asked Benton if he would speak with him. "My door's always open," Benton said.

Ferrell came to the DA's office and apologized to Benton. He claimed not to have remembered making the calls. With tears in his eyes, he admitted that he had been an alcoholic and when he was drunk had "done a lot of things he shouldn't have done." He begged Benton's forgiveness.

"Well, I thought about that," Benton recalled. "I'm a Christian and shouldn't carry a grudge. I'm a lawyer. I believe in the system, and the system says he's not guilty. Where does that put me other than being vindicative. So I sat down and wrote a letter . . . that I would have no objection if they saw fit to license him."

After being readmitted to the bar, Ferrell practiced law in Phenix City until his death in 1993. Those who believed that one day he would confess to the Patterson murder or implicate others were disappointed. Until the day he died of a heart attack in his sleep, Ferrell maintained that he had no part in the murder and had no knowledge of who committed the crime.[32]

FERRELL'S SURPRISING ACQUITTAL LEFT the attorney general in a quandary as to what the state could do about bringing Si Garrett to the bar of justice. The matter came to a head on a brisk October day in 1955 when the crafty former attorney general (five months after his accused partner in crime had been aquitted) emerged from confinement and surrendered to Sheriff Lamar Murphy in Phenix City. Murphy, who was not told beforehand that Garrett would give himself up, lodged his unexpected guest in the county jail pending a habeas corpus hearing scheduled by Judge McElroy for Friday morning. Garrett announced through his attorney Roderick Beddow that he was completely cured of his mental illness and was ready to prove his innocence in the Patterson murder case.[33]

Plans for a habeas corpus hearing were put on hold when attorneys for both sides agreed to Garrett's release on $12,500 bond, the same bail previously set for both Ferrell and Fuller. After posting bond Garrett walked out of jail, having spent less than forty-eight hours behind bars. Unshaven and unsmiling, he entered a waiting car with two of his brothers, T. Watrous and Broox Garrett, and was whisked away to his hometown of Grove Hill to await word on whether or not the state would try him on the murder charge.

Patterson knew as well as Beddow did that his office would be "pissing in the wind" trying to convict Garrett when a jury had already found Arch Ferrell not guilty. Consequently, the attorney general—contending that the question of the defendant's sanity "should be cleared up before he was tried for murder"—filed a motion to have Garrett committed to Bryce Hospital at Tuscaloosa for a mental examination. The basis for the motion was a statute allowing a judge to order a mental examination for a defendant accused of capital murder if there was reasonable doubt as to his sanity. In support of its motion the attorney general's office produced a statement from Dr. J. S. Tarwater, head of the Alabama hospital for the insane, that he had examined Garrett while he was in the mental hospital in Galveston, and concluded there was "reasonable doubt" about the man's sanity "at the time of the crime or at the present time."[34]

The defense objected vigorously, contending that the law under which the state filed its motion was unconstitutional. Beddow argued that his client maintained he was innocent of any connection with the slaying, and would never enter a plea of innocent by reason of insanity. Garrett claimed he was "completely cured" of the illness which kept him confined for nearly a year, Beddow said, and now "demanded a quick trial to clear his name." Following a weekend recess Judge McElroy ruled that he did not have the authority to order a mental examination for Garrett if the accused man was unwilling to submit to the tests. At the same time he suggested that the attorney general's office appeal his ruling "to test the constitutionality of the state law."[35]

His office's strategy blocked by the ruling, the young attorney general was too savvy and had too much respect for Judge McElroy to be upset about it. "We always knew when Judge McElroy was going to rule against us," Patterson said. "He would call and ask me to bring MacDonald Gallion and Bernard Sykes up to Birmingham and discuss the case." When they were gathered in the judge's chambers to receive the bad news, McElroy greeted them congenially by taking out a bottle of Early Times and pouring a round of drinks. When his guests were comfortable the judge passed the bottle around and they poured another one. "We knew then that old bastard was getting us prepared to rule against us," Patterson said. "You get a couple of drinks in you and you couldn't get mad, you know."[36]

In the Garrett case the attorney general asked the state supreme court for a writ of mandamus to force McElroy to comply with the statute. Although the supreme court ordered McElroy to show cause why he should not commit Garrett for a mental examination, a scheduled hearing before the justices in April 1956 was cancelled and the matter dragged on for months. Eventually the court upheld McElroy's decision not to force Garrett to undergo mental tests before facing trial, thus throwing the burden back on the attorney general's office. Putting his personal feelings aside was not easy for the attorney general, but it was not in Patterson's character to put his office and the state through a costly trial that he knew could not be won. The jury that acquitted Ferrell of the murder charge had destroyed the case against Garrett.[37]

Neither Patterson nor MacDonald Gallion, who succeeded him as attorney general, would drop the charge against Garrett as long as there was a chance that Ferrell or Fuller would talk or that new evidence might come to light. New evidence was not forthcoming, however, and in July 1963 Attorney General Richmond Flowers filed a motion before Circuit Judge James Caldwell in Phenix City to discontinue the indictment against Garrett. Judge Caldwell, having been circuit solicitor when the Phenix City grand jury handed down the indictment in 1954, recused himself and appointed attorney Frank Samples to hear Flowers's motion. Samples signed the order nol-prossing the Garrett indictment.[38]

Patterson recalled his path crossing either Garrett's or Ferrell's only on two occasions after 1955. Once after he was governor, he was on a fishing trip with friends when they stopped at Grove Hill to gas up. "By God, I ran straight into Si Garrett at that little country store. He showed no sign of recognition, just walked right by, got in his car, and drove off." On another occasion John and Tina attended a banquet in Phenix City honoring attorney Roy Smith's sixtieth anniversary as a member of the bar. The hosts had seated them at the head table next to Arch Ferrell.

When the Pattersons entered the room Ferrell came over and stuck out his hand. They shook hands, and Ferrell went on his way. Tina asked, "Who was that?" "That's Arch Ferrell," her husband replied.

Recalling the awkwardness of that evening, Patterson said, "I played the role out because I wasn't going to make no goddamn scene you know." Pausing, he added thoughtfully, "But I have to say that either the devil or the Lord worked on those guys for all that time, because they lived wretched lives. They really did."[39]

ALABAMA POLITICS HAD A front-row seat at the Fuller and Ferrell trials, and

Albert Fuller (who deported himself at pre-trial "as though he were running for sheriff, rather than bracing for the state's effort to electrocute him")[40] had political angels watching over him while he was a guest of the state at Kilby Prison. A state senator "kept inquiring about him all the time and kept everybody on their toes at the prison system."[41]

That the convicted former deputy sheriff would receive preferential treatment while incarcerated was apparent from the time the jury came back with the guilty verdict. After the verdict was read Fuller and his wife Avon had nearly an hour together in the privacy of the judge's chambers before the convicted murderer was escorted by a "cordon of deputies" to a jail cell on the seventh floor of the county courthouse.[42] Any ordinary citizen under similar circumstances would have expected to be taken straight to the lock-up in leg irons.

Fuller began his life sentence at Kilby Prison in June 1955 after Judge McElroy denied Beddow's motion for a new trial. Complaining that he had lost twenty-six pounds since March because of "close confinement" in the county jail, Fuller had asked to be transferred to Kilby Prison while appealing his conviction to the Alabama Supreme Court.[43] Fuller eventually lost the appeal, which the supreme court justices deferred ruling on for nearly five years,[44] but gained his weight back and then some while serving time in prison.

The first anniversary of Fuller's incarceration gave "Kilby Prison's most famous inmate" a public forum for reasserting that he was not guilty of murdering Albert Patterson and that he wanted to find the real killer. When Bob Ingram interviewed Fuller for the *Montgomery Advertiser* in June 1956, he found "inmate No. 67315" wearing white prison garb, a light tan, and a broad smile. Ingram talked with Fuller in the privacy of the deputy warden's office, where they were left to themselves after Deputy Warden O. H. Dees and Prison Commissioner J. M. McCullough exchanged pleasantries and excused themselves.

When asked how he found prison life, Fuller said he had no complaints. He kept busy "sort of" doing clerical work in the classification office. Oddly, he volunteered the information that everybody was treated alike at Kilby and there were no "heavies" who got "special treatment and privileges." Out of the blue he inquired about Ingram's boss, the *Advertiser*'s executive editor Grover C. Hall, Jr. "How's Mr. Hall getting along?" he asked.[45] For reasons known only to himself, the *Advertiser*'s executive editor had taken a special interest in Fuller's plight, one that led to visits with the prisoner and an exchange of correspondence with both him and his wife Avon about the case.[46]

Hall, who wielded a sharp pen and enjoyed special relations with the capital city's power brokers, had attacked John Patterson from the day he was sworn in as attorney general. Printer's ink, politics, and privilege were in Hall's blood. He walked in the shadow of his father's reputation (Grover Hall, Sr., had garnered power and prestige as the paper's editor and had won the Pulitzer Prize for exposing the Ku Klux Klan in Alabama), while harboring ambitions of his own. Hall Jr. kept his finger to the wind of Alabama politics and sat behind his cluttered desk dreaming of the big story.

Hall Jr. was pals with one of the rising stars in Alabama politics, thirty-five-year-old legislator George Wallace. Might he have resented the rose petals lavished on young Patterson after his father's murder? Did he sense in the newcomer's popular appeal a rival for the capital city's and Alabama's affections? Or, was Hall's grudge purely political? His pal's toehold in Alabama politics was challenged by the elder Patterson's legacy and by the ease with which his son had captured the imagination of old and young voters across Alabama. If Hall could prove that the upstart attorney general had convicted the wrong man for murdering his father, it would be a coup for him and for the *Advertiser*. If young Patterson's political capital suffered in the process, so much the better.

The curious interest in Fuller's plight may have given the convicted murderer false hope when he opened up to reporters in 1956. In an interview with a *Birmingham News* reporter, Fuller repeated his claim that he "didn't kill Mr. Patterson . . . and don't know who did kill him." The reporter's story drew a comparison, perhaps unintentionally, between Fuller and other white convicts who were serving time for murder and death row where "eight prisoners, all Negroes, were awaiting the electric chair." When taken on a tour of death row, no one laughed at the gallows humor when they came to the room where "Yellow Mama"—the electric chair—waited and the guard asked, "Would anybody like to sit down?"[47]

Even though the "chummy" interviews likely did more harm than good, Fuller kept talking to reporters until his lawyers shut him up. Puzzling at the time were reports by a columnist in the *Columbus Ledger* that he had visited Fuller in November 1956 and found him in high spirits and "sure of his freedom." The source of his confidence, according to the *Ledger*, had to do with new evidence purportedly unearthed by two New York private detectives (Bernard Spindel and a man named Varris) who had been in Phenix City for two or three months working on his case. Fuller described their detective work as an "official" investigation.[48] By mid-1957, however, Fuller's outlook had changed. He was said not to "have much to smile about."

"My lawyers told me I shouldn't talk to a reporter," he groused, when approached for an interview. "You get it squared away with them, and it's okay with me."[49] Fuller was in low spirits because the supreme court ruling on his appeal for a new trial had slipped, and the hoped-for results from the two New York detectives had not materialized. The detectives not only failed to come up with new evidence that might help Fuller, but were in trouble themselves for illegal wiretapping back in New York. Their activities around Phenix City and Columbus led authorities to conclude that they were con men working for no one in particular and willing to shake down anybody they could.[50]

Sheriff Murphy knew the two New Yorkers were nosing around in his jurisdiction and that Head Revel's name had come up in connection with the two men. Revel had not been seen around Phenix City for months. He was a wanted man and had been on the run down in Florida. Murphy talked things over with his friend John Patterson, and they agreed that it was time "to shake the bushes on Revel and see what ran out." So Murphy spread a rumor through the remnants of the Phenix City underworld that Albert Fuller was trying to pin the Patterson murder on Revel. The scheme worked. Revel came running back from Florida and turned himself in to the authorities.

"I know something that'll help you," Revel said to the sheriff, looking for a deal. "That .38 pistol Albert Fuller used to shoot Mr. Patterson ain't never been found. I know where the gun come from. And I know what he done with it." Revel claimed that Fuller got the murder weapon from Phenix City's safecracking "professor" Johnny Benefield, and that Benefield also got rid of the "hot piece" for Fuller afterward. Revel told Patterson and Murphy that if they wanted information about the murder weapon they ought to go see Benefield who was serving time in the state penitentiary in South Carolina. Benefield too had left Phenix City when the cleanup started and was arrested for cracking a safe in the Palmetto State.[51]

On New Year's Day 1957, after making arrangements with the attorney general of South Carolina, Patterson and a group from his office drove over to Columbia to meet with Benefield at the penitentiary. They took Head Revel with them. Benefield was cooperative, stating that he had "never put the finger on nobody" before, but wasn't going to stand by and see Revel framed for something he hadn't done.[52]

Benefield told them that Fuller had come to his house outside Phenix City "a few days before Mr. Patterson was murdered" looking for a pistol that could not be traced. When he laid out the pistols he had on a table, Fuller selected a unique piece that had been stolen from a safe in a daylight burglary near Jonesboro, Georgia. The pistol was a rebuilt .38 revolver on a .44 frame. Fuller came back late on the night of the murder, according to Benefield, and wanted help getting rid of the pistol. Benefield said he laid the pistol on the concrete floor of his toolshed and cut it up with an acetylene torch. After cooling the pieces down he dropped them in a burlap sack, and Fuller took them away.[53]

There were elements of truth to Benefield's story, as investigators soon discovered. Benefield gave them directions to the Georgia farmhouse where he had stolen the pistol. Ted Rinehart and Noel Baker from the attorney general's office found the place and verified with the owner that he had a pistol like the one described by Benefield stolen from his safe a few years back. The burglar had taken the pistol, and left the holster. The owner still had the empty holster. The heavy firearm had been built according to his specifications. He was a railroad detective out of New Orleans for many years, and had wanted a handgun that could be used as both a firearm and a club.[54]

At Patterson's request Benefield sketched a map depicting the exact spot in the toolshed where he cut the pistol up with an acetylene torch. The attorney general had that section of concrete dug up and sent to the metallurgical laboratory in Mobile. Found embedded in the concrete slab were metal particles that tended to bear out that aspect of Benefield's story. They still had only Benefield's word about the part Fuller played in his story, but in the end his word was not needed. Fuller's attorneys failed to come up with the new and compelling evidence that was required to overturn their client's conviction or to get him a new trial.[55]

Even after losing his appeal to the supreme court in 1959, Fuller's political friends (perhaps fearing he might tell what he knew) never gave up on winning his release. Patterson had become governor that January, and during the summer Warden Frank Lee contacted the governor and said that Senator Roland Cooper had been to see him on Fuller's behalf. The senator, who had strong ties to the Folsom camp, wanted to set up a meeting for Fuller with Governor Patterson and the prison officials. The warden said Cooper had expressed an interest in Fuller for many months and frequently asked about him.[56]

Instead of agreeing to such a meeting, Patterson had Ted Rinehart and Floyd Mann, his director of public safety, go out to Kilby and see Fuller privately. Mann and Rinehart advised Fuller that if he had anything to talk over with the governor that he had to tell it to them. He refused to talk with them, insisting that he wanted a personal meeting with the governor. As they were leaving, Mann, who had been the police chief in Opelika and had known Fuller for years, lagged behind. Fuller winked and nodded at Rinehart, as if to say that he did not want to talk in his presence.[57] Princeton-educated and urbane, Ted Rinehart still had traces of a "Yankee" accent, which would have made him an outsider in Fuller's book. The prisoner never got his personal meeting with the governor.

In discussions with the prison officials Governor Patterson was told that Fuller had been quartered in the trusty barracks since arriving at Kilby. While the governor would have preferred seeing his father's murderer serving "hard time" and put behind the wall with other maximum security prisoners, the warden advised against it. He was told that the reason Fuller had not been put with the other prisoners was to keep him from being killed. "If you start leaning on Fuller, it will only make you look bad," the warden said. "It will harden Fuller's resistance, and he will never tell us what he knows." Having become friends with Lee, the governor took his advice on the matter.[58]

Three years after Governor Patterson left office, to his consternation the pardon and parole board approved Albert Fuller's application for parole. He had served only ten years—the minimum time "life-termers" had to serve before they could be considered for parole. The board consisted of three members, two of whom were appointed by Patterson while he was governor. One of those was W. N. "Uncle Mac" McKathan, whose wife Mae was the youngest sister of the governor's late father. When pressure was put on the board to parole Fuller at the end of ten years, two members voted for parole and Uncle Mac abstained. "My mother was so upset with the board over Fuller's parole that she never spoke to my uncle after that," Patterson said.[59]

As a condition of his parole, Fuller was forbidden from going back to Phenix City. Patterson, who was in private practice at the time, believed the board was wrong about this. He thought the board should have made Fuller "go back there and live among the folks he'd done wrong all those years." Fuller got a job working at the sewage plant for the city of Theodore below Mobile. Four years after being paroled, in the spring of 1969, he sustained critical head injuries and underwent brain surgery at a hospital in Mobile. He had reportedly fallen from a ladder while on the job.[60]

In June 1969, his parole officer did not object when Fuller returned to

Phenix City by ambulance to stay with his old friend Ralph Matthews. The former sheriff, who was now employed as a car salesman and had been listed on hospital forms as Fuller's next of kin, agreed to look after him. A number of times Sheriff Murphy went out to question Fuller about the Patterson murder, but could never get him alone. Fuller notified the *Montgomery Advertiser* "that he was willing to talk about 'unknown facts' surrounding the murder," but always lapsed "into periods of rambling conversation" when reporters saw him.[61]

Then Fuller's health began declining rapidly, and he was admitted to a private hospital in Columbus for brain surgery. He underwent two more operations, but remained in critical condition in the intensive care unit. On September 16, 1969, he died without ever admitting his own guilt or telling what he knew about the guilt of others in the Patterson murder case.[62]

JOHN PATTERSON WAS SATISFIED then and he is satisfied now that the state met its burden in the Birmingham trials. McDonald Gallion, Bernard Sykes and his investigative team, and all of the prosecutors who worked on the case did a thoroughly professional job bringing the men accused of murdering his father before the bar of justice. When Governor Persons and Chief Justice Livingston sent them to Phenix City, they took over an investigation that was fraught with lies and deceit, blinded by misguided loyalties, and intentionally thrown off focus by corrupt public officials who themselves were prime suspects in the murder.

Under new direction the investigation focused on the logical suspects, the ones who had motive, opportunity, and the most to gain from his father's death. They still might have failed to build a case if not for honorable men like state investigator Willie Painter, since the department of public safety's investigative division fought them every step of the way. Mindful that others besides those who were indicted had abetted the crime, Patterson stated: "We know of at least one accomplice who was never identified. The person who drove the getaway car for Albert Fuller."

On the night his father was gunned down, the getaway car with Fuller inside was seen pulling away from the curb and racing down Fourteenth Street. Witnesses described the car as "a large, dark green or black Buick or Pontiac-looking automobile." Not long afterward a car fitting that description was spotted heading out of town on Highway 80, and later was seen speeding through downtown Tuskegee toward Montgomery.[63]

Lee Porter, Albert Patterson's opponent for attorney general, had a car like the one described. He reportedly pulled up in front of the Jefferson Davis Hotel in Montgomery where he was registered that night, rushed inside and checked out, and "burned rubber" taking off for Birmingham. Arriving there he had checked into the Redmont Hotel where Garrett was staying. Garrett had talked Porter into contesting the election, but that was overtaken by events.[64]

Porter's actions that night brought him under suspicion, but none of the witnesses could identify the driver of the getaway car or had thought to get the tag number. He was not named as an accomplice in the murder, but was in enough trouble for accepting campaign money from Phenix City mobsters and for trying to steal the election. There was no future for him in Alabama. He closed his law office in Gadsden and moved with his family to Houston, Texas.[65]

With the Birmingham trials over, it was time for Patterson to get on with other pressing business of the attorney general's office. This included keeping the racketeers from regaining control in Phenix City and hammering away at organized crime wherever it was found in Alabama. In March 1955, two weeks after Fuller's conviction, Patterson warned that "underworld elements" had been meeting in an apparent attempt to regain control of local government in Phenix City. He also charged that racketeers were bent on "undermining the state's success in cleaning up and obtaining convictions for crimes committed in the community." As a first order of business, he was going to see that this did not happen. "The attorney general's office will not tolerate a renewal of the vice and racketeering that once dominated Phenix City."[66] He knew that if his father was alive, he would be the first to agree.

10

New Blood and Old Political Wars

P olitics is everything, and everything's political. He couldn't remember who said it, but the thought crossed John Patterson's mind on that cold January 1955 inaugural morning when he and Mary Joe left the house on Cloverdale Road and drove downtown. It was that jazzy time in the capital city—that quadrennial hiatus when work shuts down, streets are blocked off, and lamp posts shimmer in bunting and dew. The grand old city was gussied up. Over on South Perry Street the people's mansion was jumping. Up Dexter Avenue the Cadillac floats and the Dixie darlings passed in review, while the bands played on. It was the next biggest thing to football fever in the capital city. Governor Persons had quietly packed up and gone home. Big Jim Folsom was back in town.

The Pattersons arrived at the stately old Judicial Building early. The swearing-in ceremony for the thirty-three-year-old attorney general was a contrast in styles to the victory dance that had wound through the downtown streets to crown the returning governor. The convivial top-hatted giant—rewarding those who got up close with a faint whiff of Good Old Guckenheimer—had won in a landslide to clinch his populist hold on state politics. In the later ceremony down the street a resolute Patterson—the youngest attorney general in the nation and one of the youngest to ever hold the state's third-highest office—was all business.

Among the well-wishers from around the state, a thirty-seven-car motorcade of family and friends had driven from Phenix City to show their support. After Chief Justice J. Ed Livingston administered the oath of office, Patterson spoke briefly. He pledged to be "a credit to the people of the state of Alabama and to my father." He was ever mindful, he said, that "the credit for this office and the honor that has been bestowed upon me I owe to my father, Albert Patterson."[1]

In making himself available as the state's top legal officer, he had affirmed that the reasons were "because he felt it was his duty, because he wanted to assure himself that the campaign against crime would be carried on, and because he wanted to see his father's killers brought to justice." For the next four years a portrait of his father would hang in the attorney general's office to remind him of that pledge. Unlike his father and his Uncle Lafayette, who had been active in politics most of their adult lives, the younger Patterson had previously taken no interest in holding public office. He had "just wanted to be a good lawyer."[2]

Although reluctant to enter politics Patterson was a natural campaigner and a well-schooled public administrator. He had developed poise and self-confidence trying cases with the Army JAG in Europe and practicing law in Phenix City, and had polished his oratorical skills stumping for his father around the state. Having worked all his life, he could relate to the needs and the aspirations of working families throughout Alabama, and he spoke their language. A consummate storyteller with a warm, down-home sense of humor and a genuine interest in people, the youthful attorney general was bright, articulate, and much in demand as a public speaker after he entered the political arena.

In the booming fifties youth was an asset for public service, not an encumbrance. Across the nation older politicians clung to power but many were celebrating their last hurrah, and promising younger candidates, having learned what leadership was all about in World War II and the Korean War, were eager to take their places. Patterson and his contemporaries had developed disciplined leadership and administrative skills in the armed forces and brought these qualities to bear on civilian life after their wartime service. At the University of Alabama Patterson was torn between law school or a graduate degree in public administration. Equally at home with both fields of study, he was well prepared for public service when he stepped into the breach left by his father's murder.

In 1955 newspapers were already speaking of the young attorney general as a candidate to beat in the next governor's race. Before the year was up he had begun to think seriously about seeking the state's highest office, but that information was closely held until he announced for governor in early 1958. The Phenix City story and his news-making exploits as attorney general would make him a household name when the time came to run. On that first day in the Justice Building, however, the bemused expression on a prison trusty's face reminded him that he was journeying into unfamiliar territory.

The swearing-in ceremony was held in the Supreme Court hearing room on the first floor of the majestic old building. Mary Joe was at his side. His mother looked on proudly with two of his brothers, Maurice and Jack. After the crowd thinned out he wanted to show the family his new office, but didn't know where it was located on the upper floors. Prison trusties were working in the building, and he asked one if he knew where the attorney general's office was.

"Yessir," the trusty said.

"Would you show me where it is?"

"Lawsy, boss. Don't you know?"[3]

THE SPRAWLING OFFICE ON the second floor was nothing like he had imagined. He had not seen such extravagant trappings since his brush with wartime high command in London and North Africa. Behind his predecessor's enormous polished mahogany desk was the largest overstuffed leather executive chair he'd ever laid eyes on. "I couldn't believe a man would sit in a chair as nice as that. It was a tremendous thing. That had been Garrett's chair. He just walked out of there and left the thing." Before having the furniture replaced, Patterson rummaged through the desk drawers and found all kinds of things, including a half-empty jug of wine, but nothing incriminating. "Call somebody to come and get that stuff out of here," he told the secretary.

The in-basket held letters of resignation from two of the eighteen assistant attorney generals. He had received reports that three had let themselves be used by Si Garrett in the foiled attempt to steal the election from his father. Accepting the two resignations, he decided to take a chance on the third assistant who had not resigned but was also an alleged member of Garrett's inner circle. He was an eager young attorney named Bob Bradley from Brewton, Alabama, who never gave Patterson cause to regret keeping him on as part of the team.

"As a matter of fact Bradley became the best assistant in the office," Patterson said. "He handled more special projects than anyone else, and I picked him to be my legal adviser when I became governor." Bradley later served on the Alabama Court of Civil Appeals, and was at one time the state prison director. Patterson said that if he had it all to do over again, he would not have accepted the resignations of the two other assistants. "I believe in giving deserving people a second chance. One of the fellows I accepted the resignation from is today one of my closest friends. I've learned a lot since those days."[4]

Patterson brought in only three people from outside. He kept his father's promise to MacDonald Gallion to make him senior assistant attorney general. Two other new assistants appointed by Patterson were Noel Baker, a friend of his father's from Opelika, and New York-born lawyer Edmon L. "Ted" Rinehart, who had family roots in Alabama and the Deep South. Rinehart, a prisoner of war in WWII, and Patterson had served together in Europe and were close friends.

Patterson appointed his former college roommate Joe Robertson as executive assistant. Joe was like family, and had been at his side since General Hanna ordered him down to Phenix City with the National Guard.[5]

A first order of business was assisting Circuit Solicitor Perry's office in Birmingham with the murder trials of Arch Ferrell and Albert Fuller. At the same time the new attorney general was determined to follow through on the crime-fighting program that had cost his father's life. His contacts in Phenix City informed him that remnants of the Phenix City syndicate were already trying to regain a foothold there, and he was not going to allow that to happen. Through Sheriff Murphy and others he kept a watchful eye on the situation and monitored the local elections.[6]

Support from the governor's office was crucial. Patterson and the Russell County legislative delegation met with Governor Folsom to discuss their concerns and to ask that he reappoint the jury commission put in place by Governor Persons. Rumors abounded that the Folsom administration would oust the commissioners and appoint "men more friendly to the rackets." Patterson left the meeting, however, reassured that the governor would "definitely do the right thing about the Russell County situation." Folsom publicly denounced "blue-ribbon juries" and promised his administration's "full cooperation" in keeping Phenix City clean.[7]

The lessons from Phenix City's troubled past were a recurring theme in Pattersons speeches around Alabama and outside the state. He described for audiences how the gambling syndicate had wormed its way into city hall when the town faced bankruptcy during the Great Depression, and eventually corrupted the political process and the judicial system of Russell County. By the onset of the fifties the moral fabric of the community was so threadbare that the lawless were indistinguishable from those sworn to uphold the law. Their tentacles had spread to the halls of justice in Montgomery and beyond, leading ultimately to the murder of his father to keep him from exposing the corrupt politicians and uprooting the criminal empire.

He talked about the intimidation of citizens who had spoken out against vice and corruption in Phenix City—the beatings at the polls, the bombing of Hugh Bentley's home, and the burning of the Patterson law office in the Coulter Building. Sometimes he took along a copy of a soot-stained law book rescued from the office fire and brandished it to emphasize his message—the crux of which was the power of the vote in America and what could happen when citizens forfeited that birthright. "There will always be someone out there willing to steal the vote from you," he warned.[8]

When his mother was in New York that November to accept the LaGuardia Award for her late husband she too addressed those lessons. The fifth annual award for outstanding achievement in municipal affairs was made posthumously to Albert Patterson for "his leadership, courage, love of community and country and for his tenacity in the face of vicious opposition." Newsmen reported that "the slender, soft-spoken widow" talked "with nervous intensity . . . about the fight for clean government having passed to the younger generation." She stated that her son John felt as she did "that voting regularly is one of the best defenses against the sort of thing that happened in Phenix City."[9]

The first post-cleanup Phenix City elections were held in September 1955. To guard against fraud, a special legislative act introduced by State Representative Homer W. Cornett required that Russell County voters reidentify themselves before going to the polls. Asked by the Board of Registrars for a reading on the law, Patterson ruled that voters had to reidentify themselves before casting their ballots in the city elections. On election day the attorney general "cleaned out his office and moved everyone to Phenix City." He and his assistants were there when the polls opened, "threatening vigorous prosecution" of violations of election laws.[10]

On the previous day he had mingled with the crowd at a courthouse rally where Arch Ferrell's younger brother Pelham delivered "a scathing attack" on the attorney general's office, the Alabama National Guard, and the political opposition. Spotting Patterson in the crowd, Ferrell yelled out that he knew why the state attorney general was in town, but it would be to no avail. Taunting them with Spiro Agnew-like barbs, Ferrell called the attorney general and his staff "a paltry little palace guard of scummy, crummy gun-toters," but Patterson refused to take the bait.[11]

On election night he was with the reform candidates in Sheriff Murphy's office where the returns were trickling in. When their lead appeared to be insurmountable Ray Jenkins of the *Columbus Ledger* had his cameraman taking victory shots of the exultant winners. Patterson cautioned the group against posing for the cameras until the last vote was counted. "That was a trait Patterson inherited from his father," Jenkins said.[12]

The anti-reform candidates blamed everybody but themselves for losing the election. One of the losing candidates was former Mayor Reese's nephew,

Dr. W. B. Mims, who was defeated in his bid for a seat on the city commission. (The ex-mayor's other nephew, Buddy Jowers, now ran a country store.) Mims accused the attorney general and his staff of influencing the election. He complained that the attorney general had come to Phenix City "not to check on certain election violations . . . but to frighten numerous people away from the polls on election day."[13]

The complaint from the disgruntled candidate drew a wry smile from Patterson. He was well aware that the only people who were afraid to come near the polls because he and his staff were there were the dregs of the old Phenix City mob looking to stuff the ballot boxes or to intimidate legal voters. He continued to keep a watchful eye on the elections in Phenix City as long as he remained in office.[14]

A curious public, fascinated with the revelations of Dixie's modern Gomorrah, never tired of stories about the reforming border town and its sinful past. That summer, as the controversy surrounding the Ferrell and Fuller murder trials died down, Allied Artists released *The Phenix City Story*, a romanticized movie filmed on location and using local extras such as popular club owner Ma Beachie in a cameo role. Taking dramatic license the movie exploited John Patterson's image as a crime-fighter bent on avenging his father's murder. That same year Birmingham reporters Ed Strickland and Gene Wortsman published *Phenix City: The Wickedest City in America*, which would stand the test of time as an accurate, unbiased account of events surrounding the murder. At year's end his mother and RBA members brought suit against CBS for an hour-long Studio One TV Show entitled *Short Cut*, a thinly disguised distortion of the Phenix City tragedy that held his late father and the RBA up to ridicule. The suit for damages was settled out of court.[15]

Patterson knew better than to turn his back on the Phenix City bosses who deeply resented giving up power and would try to return to the old ways when no one was looking. They had done their best to keep him from taking his father's place as attorney general. Arch Ferrell, before being indicted by the grand jury, had led a futile attempt to dig up dirt to use against him. Ferrell had hired a private detective to smear Patterson, but the only thing he came up with was a phony charge that his ownership of property in Georgia made him ineligible to hold public office in Alabama. Patterson had been an Alabama resident all his life, and the house he purchased outside Fort Benning did not change that.[16]

The young attorney general knew also that the old Phenix City crowd had sympathizers within the community. Sheriff Murphy, a "straight-shooting" lawman who never talked around an issue or talked one to death, said that was "the sad part . . . they have so many sympathizers." The transient gamblers and drifters had pulled up stakes, and the ones whose pictures decorated post office bulletin boards had fled the state or were making car tags behind prison walls. Those with roots in Russell County and not in jail, however, had laid low until the heat was off. They had "cousins and in-laws" in church congregations and on every street corner in town who disparaged the cleanup as much as their embittered kinfolk did.[17]

When Governor Persons pulled the National Guard out in December, local resentment turned inward with neighbors snubbing neighbors when passing on the street or sitting in adjoining pews. Within his own family, his brother Jack (who had two years of high school ahead of him) was at an age that made him more sensitive to snobbery and antagonism from some thoughtless teachers and parents. Declining an offer from his older brother that he move with them to Montgomery and complete high school there, Jack chose to stay at home so he could look after his mother and graduate with his classmates. After graduation he followed the path taken by his father and older brother, and enrolled at the University of Alabama to pursue a law degree.[18]

The witnesses who testified for the state at Ferrell's and Fuller's murder trials were subjected to a more vicious form of harassment. Courthouse janitor Quinnie Kelley, whose life was threatened numerous times, lost his job after he obtained a pistol permit and persisted in wearing a holstered weapon to work. Cecil Padgett, also harassed on the job and then laid off by his employer, couldn't find work as a carpenter. Feeling sorry for these men and their families the attorney general got them out of harm's way by securing jobs for them in Montgomery. Kelley hired on as a laborer making a dollar an hour at the state capitol. Padgett worked at a number of jobs, including as an Alabama liquor agent. Predictably, Patterson's helping Kelley and Padgett led to charges by political enemies that the jobs were payoffs for their having testified against the men accused of murdering his father.[19]

From talks with the new city commission, Patterson was confident that most residents who opposed change could be won over if they were assured of a better future for themselves and their families. Before the mass cleanup there was no future other than illegal gambling or vice open to Phenix City's young people unless they left home. The election returns in 1955—the first legitimate political contest the city's younger generation had ever known—were proof that the voters wanted honest government and a reformed economy. The winning candidates had pledged to keep the rackets from coming back and to turn the economy around. By mid-1956 the attorney general could tell reporters with confidence that they were succeeding on all fronts.[20]

In January of 1956 the League of Municipalities and *Look* magazine presented Phenix City with the All-American City Award in recognition of the progress the town had made. The *Columbus Ledger*, which won the 1955 Pulitzer Prize for exposing the vice and corruption on the other side of the river, made the nomination. More than 180 cities had competed for the honor. Tom Sellers reported in the Sunday *Ledger-Enquirer* that "the old border town" accepted the honor "with humble spirit," but "was due for a celebration . . . and she had it." "Old timers cannot remember a day when the city had seemed so gay, so neat and clean, and so resplendent," he wrote.[21]

Dr. George Gallup, the public opinion expert and president of the National Municipal League, presented the award to Mayor Clyde M. Knowles at a ceremony in front of city hall. Governor Folsom headed a large delegation from the state capital that included Chief Justice Livingston, Attorney General Patterson, General Hanna, and Judge Jones. Following a stirring address by Gallup, the national commander of the Veterans of Foreign Wars conferred the VFW's highest award posthumously on Albert Patterson.[22]

In an interview with reporters the attorney general praised the local officials. He said the city's finances were better than ever before, and the progress of the past year was only the start. He pointed proudly to "a huge slum clearance program" that was underway, with federal help, "to replace the once brightly lighted nightclub district near the two bridges that span the Chattahoochee River." Organized crime had tried to move back in, he said, but "we've beaten them at every turn."[23]

While the Phenix City underworld was in disarray, the resurgent political rivalry was rooted in the bitter feuding of the past and would bear watching. The clumsy snooping by New York private eyes Spindel and Varris, for instance, and their ties to arch-criminal Head Revel in Phenix City and convicted murderer Albert Fuller in Kilby Prison, kept the attorney general and the local authorities alert to the axiom that a beheaded rattler writhing in the dust is still venomous. As the state's chief legal officer Patterson stood fast with city and county officials against any revival of organized crime in Phenix City, and he supported their goals of honest government and economic progress. He hoped to be in a position to do more when the time came to announce for governor in the 1958 campaign.

FORMER STATE FINANCE DIRECTOR Fuller Kimbrell recalled that relations between the Folsom administration and the attorney general's office "worked really well" until Patterson decided to run for governor. Patterson had voted for Folsom, and liked Big Jim and his family, but he soon found himself at odds with the administration over its political patronage and spending practices. Shortly after becoming attorney general he learned that a number of the state's leases to private companies were made without competitive bidding which violated the intent if not the letter of the law. He investigated the most egregious cases and filed injunctions to overturn them in Judge Walter B. Jones's court.

"Jim Folsom used to rib me about having 'injunctivitis' because I enjoined him so many times," Patterson said. "But we were always friendly, and never got to where we couldn't talk. I think that's a great compliment to him—that with all of our political differences we could be cordial and work to get the job done." Folsom had that down-home charm and Southern drawl, and he had a disarming way of getting his point across without offending people or ruffling feathers. An example cited by Patterson occurred early in the administration when he was commissioning private lawyers to work on the interstate highway program.

The right-of-way acquisitions for the cloverleaf and highway inside the city of Birmingham alone involved the condemnation of huge tracts of prime real estate and the expenditure of millions of dollars. The attorney general appointed lawyers from the private sector to represent the state in these acquisitions, but the governor had to approve the appointments before they could be paid. These were lucrative commissions, and they were eagerly sought after by competing law firms.

Patterson, as a routine administrative matter, made the appointments and sent the forms to the governor's office for signing. Soon he noticed that the paperwork wasn't coming back from Folsom's office. "Didn't take me long to figure that one out, so I went over and explained the situation to him," Patterson said. Folsom grinned, leaned back, and crossed his feet on the top of the desk. "John, I've got some friends that are lawyers. They need to make a little money too," he drawled. "Tell you what I'll do, John. I'll split 'em right down the middle with you."

Patterson reached over and shook his hand. "That's a deal," he said.

"From then on, we didn't have any trouble at all," Patterson recalled. "He had every reason to be mad as hell at me when I was going after his administration over their spending practices, but he never showed it." Folsom, whose first term was rocked by accusations of selling pardons and paroles, rolled with the punches. Patterson said there was only one time when Folsom was too busy to see him. That was one morning after the governor had partied late into the night. Folsom looked up and groaned when Patterson walked into his office. "John, I've got this awful hangover. Turn off the light and close the door when you go. You'll have to come back tomorrow."

Patterson chuckled on the way out. Just the other day, at the urging of the state's chief examiner, Ralph P. Eagerton, he had looked into the question of money being transferred from the governor's emergency fund to pay for lavish parties at the mansion. At that time the governor had $40,000 a year allocated to run the mansion, and a fund of approximately $150,000 to spend on emergencies. For weeks Eagerton had been in a running battle with the governor over a proposed audit of the emergency and mansion fund books. Patterson, whose office worked closely with the examiners in uncovering spending irregularities by the state, ruled that the audit of the mansion and emergency funds was required by law. Folsom declared that he wouldn't permit "a political audit" unless the examiners had "bigger guns and tanks" than he did.[24]

Folsom threatened to have Kimbrell order an audit of the chief examiner's records, but finally opened his books to the examiners after agreeing to repay a $5,180 error discovered by a private CPA firm he had hired. Patterson, meanwhile, had dropped over to see the governor's legal adviser, Uncle Bud Boswell, and talked with him about the situation. "You've got to stop transferring that money from the emergency fund to pay for those big parties over at the mansion, spending it on booze and everything."[25]

A quizzical look crossed Boswell's face. "I don't understand, John. I've got an attorney general's opinion saying that's legal."

"The hell you do."

"Yes, I do have one. It's right here." He rummaged through his desk drawer and pulled out a letter signed by assistant attorney general Billy McQueen when Gordon Persons was governor, authorizing transfers from the emergency fund to the mansion fund. McQueen had served as legal adviser to Governor Persons and was now an assistant in Patterson's office.

"Well, Uncle Bud, you got me," Patterson said, and went back to his office and forgot the incident until he moved into the governor's mansion in 1959 and ran short of money to keep the place up. He called his legal adviser into the office and told him, "Find me that letter signed by Billy McQueen authorizing the transfer of those funds."[26]

While they remained cordial, Patterson's battles against spending abuses and patronage deals by the highway and conservation departments during his second year as attorney general did strain his relations with the administration, as Kimbrell noted. The statute governing competitive bids "had holes you could drive a freight train through." The way the law was written only new construction in excess of $500 was subject to competitive bidding, while all repair work regardless of cost was exempted. "If the conservation department built an outhouse costing over $500 at one of its camps, it had to be let under competitive bidding," Patterson explained. "But resurfacing a long stretch of highway for millions of dollars was exempt because it was not new construction."[27]

This was a loophole the attorney general set out to block in the fall of 1956. He started by petitioning the circuit court for an injunction against a $13,000 purchase order with Glencoe Paving Company of Gadsden. The Glencoe deal, one of several large highway jobs that were let without competitive bidding, served as a test case for the others. The injunction was also a wedge for having the competitive bid laws changed. Circuit Judge Walter B. Jones found in Patterson's favor and blocked the state from paying Glencoe the $13,000.[28]

Patterson then obtained restraining orders holding up payments totaling $1.5 million to three other construction companies who had done road work without competitive bidding. He knew that this was only round one, however, because there was too much at stake for the administration or the construction companies to concede defeat. Glencoe's lawyers appealed Judge Jones's ruling to the Alabama Supreme Court, and the lower court's decision was overturned in early 1957.[29]

The rhetoric from the two sides had heated up at the Supreme Court hearing and in the media. Glencoe's attorney, John Harris of Montgomery, charged Patterson with "playing politics" and acting against his client because of "avowed ambitions" to run for governor in 1958—a drumbeat that higher-ups in the administration continued to bounce off reporters.

When they asked who he was backing in 1958, Folsom said he didn't have a dog in that fight but might put one in if the attorney general and the state examiners didn't leave him alone. Patterson said those who opposed competitive bidding apparently did so "because they fear that under such an arrangement they could not give state business to their political friends."[30]

Patterson had not yet disclosed that he might announce for governor in 1958. When the high court overturned the circuit court decision in the Glencoe case, jubilant cabinet members quipped that the attorney general was now "the leading candidate in the state for the office of lieutenant governor," rather than the governor's office. Most newspaper editors didn't see it that way. The high court's reversal came on the heels of a year when papers reported that John Patterson had "forged into the limelight as one of the most-mentioned prospects for the gubernatorial race in 1958."[31]

The young attorney general took the potshots in stride. Sometimes you can lose the battles and still win the war, if you get lucky and don't back off. His goal was not to try each and every case in court, but to convince the state legislators that changing the competitive bid statute was not only the right thing to do, but was to their political advantage. "We lost that case, but as a result of the publicity . . . we were able to get the legislature to rewrite the law. When I left we had a good competitive bid law if it was enforced."[32]

The spoils of office were not confined to the highway department. The conservation department, its budget fattened by a bond issue, had new park facilities under construction without competitive bids. The attorney general enjoined these as well. He also set out to stop the letting of long-term leases to political cronies at little or no financial gain to the state. "The only pockets these fellows were interested in filling were their own." Some leases overlapped several administrations, tying the hands of future governors. "We won some and we lost some, but we got these problems aired and made known to the voters so their legislators would be pressured to do something about them."[33]

One of the long-term leases had been awarded to Folsom's father-in-law to manage the new 250-acre public fishing lake in Tuscaloosa County. Various concessions at the lake were an added bonus. The state had already paid $35,000 to build a "luxurious lakeside cottage" for the father-in-law, but the attorney general successfully petitioned Judge Jones for a temporary injunction to halt improvements to the property that would cost another $17,719. The suit to nullify the contract had to be filed in Tuscaloosa County, however, and "got nowhere fast." The circuit judge there was a friend of the Folsom family, and he took the case under advisement. It was still under advisement when Patterson left office.[34]

He ran into another hostile circuit judge in Baldwin County when he tried to stop the leasing of state land on the Mobile causeway. There were problems across the state with squatters and leaseholders living on public land and using up natural resources without compensating the government. So he assigned a small group in his office to work on the problem, and the office had some success in protecting state land from encroachment and in reclaiming land from earlier encroachers. The office also put a stop to the practice of allowing logging companies to clean out huge tracts of prime timber without concern for conservation or reforestation.[35]

One "sweetheart deal" would have bilked the state "big time" if the attorney general had not taken the parties to federal court. In 1956 he learned that the state had leased 2,700 acres of prime real estate (appraised at more than $1 million) at Gulf Shores, including miles of beachfront property, to a shadow company owned by two Florida businessmen. The two Floridians had formed the Tri-State Corporation (an obvious front rumored to hide a silent partnership involving prominent officials in the Folsom administration and a Florida congressman) and filed a certificate in Bay Minette, the county seat of Baldwin County, to manage the leased property.[36]

The terms of the lease, which gave Tri-State exclusive rights to the property for fifty years with an option to renew for forty more years, would still have the property tied up today had Patterson not contested it. All the lease required of the corporation was a $25,000 down payment, $150,000 in improvements over the next five years, and payments to the state of 4 percent of gross income from use of the property. The actual improvements to the property consisted of cutting the timber and constructing a "no-tell" motel comprised of a few ramshackle cabanas.[37]

When the lease arrangements came to Patterson's attention, he had them investigated and found that Tri-State, not satisfied with just "getting something for nothing," had schemed to swindle the state out of its 4 percent share of income from the property. By subleasing to one of its own officers and stipulating that he pay the company only 5 percent of the gross income, Tri-State reduced the state's income from the property to a mere 4 percent of 5 percent, an amount that was "less than the property tax on the place if the state had given it away." The individual who subleased the property used the state land as collateral to obtain a loan from the Reconstruction Finance Corporation (a federal agency later taken over by the Small Business Administration) to build the motel.[38]

The federal loan proved to be their undoing. When Patterson brought suit to enjoin the lease, the case was transferred to federal court where it was tied up until after he became governor in 1959. U.S. District Judge Frank M. Johnson, Jr., finally heard evidence in the case in August 1962. Two Montgomery lawyers, Nick Hare and Joe Phelps, were hired to represent the state and to continue the case. Patterson knew they would get a fair hearing before Judge Johnson because he "was a straight shooter from way back." Had the case been litigated in state court, Patterson believed there was a good chance of winning a favorable decision from Judge Jones, but his experience with earlier appellate reviews had made him leery about the case being reversed on appeal.

The tract sat idle for several years as the case made its way through the courts. In January 1963, as Governor Patterson was leaving office, Judge Johnson ruled that the lease was invalid. His ruling was based on "gross abuse of discretion" by state officials in leasing the property and on "decisive evidence of fraud" by the parties involved. He returned all of the property, including improvements, to the state, but made the state liable for repaying the federal loan. Questioning the state's liability, Patterson raised the point in a meeting with Johnson.[39]

"You're not happy about winning?" Johnson asked.

"Yeah, I'm happy about winning."

"Then pay off the debt and get the property back."

Johnson awarded $25,000 attorney fees to Phelps and Hare, but they had a hard time collecting. George Wallace was in the governor's office by then. He balked at paying the fees, but eventually signed the checks.

The property was later designated as a state park, and the 144-room Gulf State Resort motel and convention center built there in the early 1970s soon became "the most successful of the state-owned resorts, bringing $1 million a year in profits to Alabama." Only a small fraction of those profits would be going to the state each year had Patterson not acted fifty years ago to stop a few dishonest public servants and their scheming friends from stealing prize public land.

PATTERSON HAD COME INTO the attorney general's office fighting crime and he would carry the crime-buster image into the governor's race four years later. As attorney general he used the powers of his office to fight crime throughout Alabama—not just lecturing to law enforcement and civic groups about the problems, but actively assisting local officials in doing something about them. As part of this effort the office opened an investigation into a possible link between local criminal activity and organized crime on a regional or national level. The illegal gambling paraphernalia in Phenix City—the hundreds of slot machines busted up by General Hanna's men and the punch boards removed from every counter in town—wasn't manufactured in Alabama, so there had to be an interstate connection.

As a teenager allowed into the billiard parlor across from where he worked, Patterson had bet on the ball games and watched while sipping a bottle of cola with his fingers crossed as the proprietor posted the results coming in on telegraphic ticker tape. There were several of these wire-service machines in betting establishments around town, with an obvious connection to out-of-state gambling operations. On a hunch that the use of wire-service lines for illegal gambling in Alabama was not limited to Phenix City, the attorney general put his investigators to work.

Their investigation disclosed that Continental Press, a Mafia front organization out of Chicago, had leased lines from Western Union and was using them to transmit gambling information. In Alabama these lines were feeding gambling results into 150 or so ticker-tape outlets around the state. Patterson figured the best way to attack the problem was at the source. He couldn't go after the Mafia, so he called New York and got the Western Union president on the phone. He explained who he was and why he was calling. "Do you know that your company is involved in the illegal dissemination of gambling information in Alabama?" Patterson asked. There was stony silence on the other end. He then requested that Western Union provide his office with a complete list of the ticker tape outlets in question, with the names and addresses of the persons leasing them.

"Oh, Mr. Patterson, I can't do that. That's confidential information."

"You sure about that?"

"Oh, yes. That's company policy."

"Then you leave me no choice."

"How's that?"

"We'll seek an injunction against you in Judge Walter B. Jones's court."

"Not sure I understand."

"We'll enjoin Western Union from doing business in Alabama, because you're abetting the violation of our gambling laws."

There was another long pause on the line. "Somebody will be in touch with you," the Western Union man said.

When Patterson got back from lunch, a Western Union courier had delivered the list and it was waiting on his desk. Subsequent raids, coordinated with local authorities and carried out simultaneously, closed down the gambling operations and confiscated all of the equipment. "We shut them down in a matter of hours," Patterson said. "But then we had all those ticker tape machines on our hands for months, and nobody would come forward to claim them."[40]

In the spring of 1957, their mutual interest in fighting organized crime brought Patterson and boyish-looking U.S. Senator John F. Kennedy together in Birmingham. Kennedy, who was in town to address the Alabama League of Municipalities convention at the Thomas Jefferson Hotel, spoke on the problem of labor racketeering. Afterward the two men talked briefly about Albert Patterson's murder and organized crime. Their talk blossomed into friendship, and whenever Patterson went to Washington he was a guest in the Kennedy home. He knew that JFK's Catholic background and liberal views on racial integration were a political liability in Alabama, but he strongly supported the Massachusetts Democrat's candidacy in the 1960 presidential election because he had confidence in Kennedy and believed he was the best man for the job. Besides, it wouldn't hurt for Alabama to have a friend in the White House.[41]

ONE OF THE BATTLES that gave him the greatest satisfaction as attorney general was "cracking down on the loan sharks." Before he was sworn in, two of his father's friends—Will Sadler, an attorney in Birmingham, and another young lawyer named Goodlow Rutland—came to see him in Phenix City and urged him to do something about the small-loan problem in Alabama. They convinced him that Alabama's small-loan businesses were a blight on the state because usurious lenders were preying on Alabama's underprivileged citizens, particularly poor blacks who could not afford legal counsel. An archaic small-loan statute (the Harris Act) protected money lenders from criminal prosecution for usury and made the state a party to the scourge.[42]

There were some eight hundred small loan companies in Alabama—many had operated for years without a license. The money lenders had fomed one of the most powerful lobby groups in the state—the Alabama Finance Institute had about five hundred members—and had successfully lobbied against the enactment of laws that were unfavorable to them. Alabama law set the absolute interest rate on loans at 8 percent per annum on a written contract and at 6 percent per annum on an oral contract, but loan sharks operating under the protection of the Harris Act gouged their borrowers without fear of penalty. "We found that it wasn't uncommon for some of these small lenders to charge five hundred to a thousand percent interest on loans," Patterson said. "Sometimes a poor man who needed money would get in the clutches of one of these loan sharks and would be paying on a three hundred-dollar loan for the rest of his life. It was an outrage."[43]

The low fixed interest rates and the toothless law penalized all Alabama consumers because large national lending corporations were discouraged from doing business in the state. The holders of large, secured loans (banks and mortgage companies) could make money at the low rates, but the companies who lent smaller amounts for items such as home appliances and automobiles could not compete with the loan sharks. It was the state's loss and the people's loss when reputable finance companies would not come into the state because they were unwilling to break the law, leaving the loan sharks free to charge exorbitant rates in defiance of the law and to flourish.[44]

Soon after taking office Patterson hired an investigator and put some of his best people to work on the small-loan problem. The investigation uncovered widespread abuse of the usury laws all over the state, but the protective provisions of the small-loan statute blocked the attorney general's office from bringing charges against the violators. Finding their hands tied by the statute, Patterson and his legal staff found a way around the problem by filing a petition for injunctions against the most flagrant violators (Tide Finance of Montgomery and two other money lenders) as public nuisances.

In this test case of the public nuisance doctrine, the attorney general's petition had precedents dating from old English court rulings to a modern-day Alabama Supreme Court decision (the Bynum case). The petition was guided by the principle that perhaps "the best way to get a bad law off the books is to enforce it."[45]

In September 1955, acting on the attorney general's petitition, Judge Walter B. Jones issued an injunction against Tide Finance enjoining the small loan company from collecting more than 8 percent interest per year from borrowers. On loans already made in violation of the usury statute, the judge's order prohibited the company "from filing suits to collect more than the actual amount of the loan." "Payments already made, including interest, must be credited against the original amount of the loan," he decreed. Finding Tide Finance's loan methods "evil and repulsive," Judge Jones censured the company for conducting "its leading business with studied contempt for our usury laws."[46]

For two years the case was tied up on appeal. In July 1957 the Alabama Supreme Court upheld the decision, ruling "that Judge Jones was right in issuing the injunction and that loan companies charging more than the legal rate were 'public nuisances.'" The loan company's lawyers asked for a rehearing, but the Supreme Court denied the request in November. Meanwhile neither the attorney general's office nor the lobbyists had been sitting idle awaiting final word from the court.

While the attorney general had won an additional injunction against five usurious loan companies in Birmingham, the finance institute had lobbied successfully to defeat new legislation. During the 1957 legislative session State Representatives Roscoe Roberts of Huntsville and John Tyson of Mobile introduced legislation to regulate the illegal loan companies, but opponents held the bill in committee and kept it from coming up for a vote. Patterson then expanded his crackdown into Anniston and Calhoun County—laying more groundwork to have the small-loan law changed.[47]

The quest for new legislation gained support from the U.S. Senate in the fall of 1957 when Senator William Langer (R-ND) opened hearings in Montgomery with a statement that Alabama had "become notable and distinctive as the bankruptcy and small-loan capital of the nation." Langer, a member of the subcommittee on anti-trust and anti-monopoly, stated that Alabama appeared "to be competing with Texas for the title of The Loan Shark State." Patterson appeared as a lead-off witness and testified that the loan companies "operated openly and notoriously" because they were protected by state law.[48]

Patterson explained how the loan firms, after they were enjoined from charging usurious interest rates, had turned to credit insurance as a subterfuge to get around the law. The firms started charging the legal rate of interest, but made up the difference by requiring lenders to take out insurance on the loan and pay a premium that was sometimes in excess of the amount of the loan itself. Another firm provided the insurance but was directly tied to the company making the loan. "They were insuring their own loans," Patterson said. "And they were making a killing doing it."[49]

The president of a Birmingham firm which specialized in credit insurance testified that his company was allowed the right to examine loan company books, but that written contracts with the loan companies were rare. When asked why written contracts were not required, he said with a straight face that it was because "We are dealing with Southern gentlemen and take their word for it."[50]

Witnesses for the lobbying group (Palmer Keith, Birmingham attorney who was vice president of the finance institute, and Wallace Johnson, Mobile attorney for the institute), while not invoking their Fifth Amendment rights, volunteered little information. The indignant attorneys complained to reporters that the committee was "usurping" state rights by coming to Alabama. Senator Langer concluded the three-day hearing with a warning that his subcommittee "certainly found a situation which needs remedying, and we're going to remedy it if we possibly can." The senator said that he was in favor of the state taking care of its own problems, but might have to recommend federal legislation "as a last resort."[51]

Additional federal support for changing the small-loan statute came in early 1958 when the Armed Forces Disciplinary Control Board announced that it too was looking into the usurious loan practices in Alabama. The board was concerned about military personnel stationed in the state, particularly those in the lower grades, being charged illegal interest rates on short-term "payday" loans. The staff judge advocate at Fort Rucker stated that the problem was "somewhat limited" to Alabama since neighboring states had stringent laws concerning the small loan industry.[52]

Patterson had more support from federal authorities than from the governor's office in his war against the loan sharks. Part of the reason for this was his campaign against "graft and corruption" in the Folsom administration. The governor took a position diametrically opposed to the attorney general's office by standing firmly behind R. W. Rosser, the superintendent of the state department of loans, in 1957 when Folsom opposed legislation to regulate the small-loan industry. Rosser also had the governor's support in opposing the attorney general's injunction against the forty-one loan companies in Anniston.[53]

MacDonald Gallion took up the fight against the loan sharks when he became attorney general in 1959, and finished the job by enjoining all small loan companies in Alabama from charging illegal interest rates. "This forced the small-loan companies themselves to help us get the legislature to rewrite the small-loan law and put some teeth into it, so people could borrow money at reasonable rates in Alabama," Patterson said. "And once we got the law passed the big companies such as Household Finance and Beneficial came into Alabama because they could operate legally here."[54]

Patterson made some powerful enemies by taking on the loan sharks and defeating them. They were not able to stop him in the campaign for governor in 1958, but their leverage was surely felt in his later bids for public office. He believed the fight was worth it. "I honestly believe that one of the best things I ever did as attorney general was to clean up this small-loan racket in our state. It was a terrible situation, and I'm glad we were able to do something about it."[55]

Over time the hard-won victory has been set aside by the money lenders and their political allies. This has disappointed the former governor. "We've gone back to the usurious practice of charging these poor people huge amounts of interest in Alabama. The legislature has permitted a rewriting of the law for the lender, at the expense of the borrower. And the people who are really hurt are poor people, people that work for wages, have to spend everything they make, and have to borrow money. It's a terrible thing."[56]

Political battles that he professes to have taken no pleasure in were those against the civil rights movement in Alabama. Patterson entered office knowing that as attorney general he would have to deal with the legal aspects of public school desegregation in Alabama, but he had not anticipated the issue would create years of racial unrest across the Deep South. He had grown up in a home where racial and religious tolerance were virtues, and racial slurs were forbidden. The family had friends of diverse ethnic backgrounds, and their law firm provided equal representation to all clients, regardless of race or station. Many of their poorer clients were accepted as pro bono cases.[57]

The U.S. Supreme Court's ruling in May 1954 that racial segregation in public schools was unconstitutional, in *Brown v. Board of Education*, had come as no surprise. Patterson's tours as an Army officer, especially while serving with the Truman-integrated armed forces of the Korean War era, had prepared him for desegregation's inevitability at home. The high court's ruling was handed down the month before his father's murder. They had no time to discuss the ruling, but he knew his father thought as he did that racial integration, while inevitable, portended far-reaching political and socioeconomic consequences for Alabama and other Southern states. Desegregation was a sensitive, potentially explosive change which had to be administered judiciously and within the letter of the law.[58]

Patterson gave little thought to school desegregation during his first weeks in office. His time was taken up with Fuller's and Ferrell's murder trials and other pressing business. Overlooked on the editorial page of the *Montgomery Advertiser* was an oddity reported by Grover Hall, Jr., while covering the trials, that the nearest water fountain to the courtroom happened to be the one marked "Colored" and it was freely used by white spectators. Could Hall in an oblique way have been suggesting that the time had come to remove the Jim Crow signs? Or was he merely saying that white Southerners took segregation for granted and thought nothing of crossing the color barrier? But what if you were black and the fountain was marked "White"? There was the rub. Removing that social injustice and burying the "separate but equal" myth institutionalized in 1896 by *Plessy v. Ferguson* was what the Supreme Court's *Brown* ruling was really all about. The myth had spawned a deluge of outdated state laws that had to be enforced or taken off the books. It's easier to make new laws than to rescind bad ones, and so it was with the shameful Jim Crow signposts.[59]

Initially, Patterson was reluctant to get involved in civil rights litigation. He watched the Montgomery bus boycott (growing out of the arrest of Rosa Parks in December 1955 for refusing to give up her seat on the bus to a white man) with growing interest, but steered clear of the legal proceedings. "This was a boycott of the city bus lines in Montgomery. L. B. Sullivan was one of the commissioners of transportation. It was under his watch, and they had their own lawyers. They didn't want any interference from the attorney general or the governor. Folsom and I were eager to accommodate them. We didn't want to get involved in it, either."[60]

In the spring of 1955, the U.S. Supreme Court followed up on its 1954 ruling and ordered "all deliberate speed" in racially integrating the public schools. Across the Deep South the segregationist rhetoric from white public officials (there were no black ones to speak of) was high, KKK recruitment was up, and White Citizens' Councils (which first appeared in Mississippi in the summer of 1954) sprang up like milkweed. The clamor for resistance to the high court's desegregation rulings and the bumper stickers sporting slogans such as "the South will rise again" reflected the frustrations of Southern segregationists who felt themselves betrayed. Out on the speaking circuit Patterson soon found that his audiences were more interested in hearing what the attorney general's office was doing to save the public schools from forced mixing of the races than they were about his dedication to fighting crime and rooting out corruption in public office.[61]

These were tumultuous times in the Deep South. A rash of violent acts against blacks—ranging from the bombing of the homes of civil rights leaders including Martin Luther King, Jr., and E. D. Nixon in Montgomery, to the murder of fourteen-year-old Emmett Till in Mississippi—left no doubt that the KKK and hotheaded racists would go to any length to preserve segregation. Moderates on civil rights, with the exception of a few remarkable people such as Clifford and Virginia Durr of Montgomery, were more inclined to keep their views to themselves. Anxieties reached fever pitch in September 1957 when President Eisenhower sent federal troops to Little Rock to enforce a court order to integrate black students into an all-white high school.

Patterson and his staff joined other Southern states in seeking legal relief from the Supreme Court's ruling on desegregation. He coordinated closely with neighboring attorneys general and had his assistants study what sister states were doing in the way of litigation. His evolving strategy for dealing with desegregation was formulated from those early discussions, particularly those he had with Attorney General James Lindsay Almond, Jr., of Virginia. Almond's service as his state's top legal officer, like Patterson's, became a springboard to the governor's office in upcoming elections.[62]

Patterson, who spoke warmly of his friendship with Almond, described the Virginia governor as an insightful elder statesman and a "kind and gracious" companion. He worked closely with Almond throughout the desegregation crisis, either visiting Richmond himself or sending Rinehart, Smith, or Bradley to discuss the legal aspects with Almond's staff. Patterson could always count on there being a fifth of Virginia Gentleman waiting for him in the hotel suite. "I'm a Scotch person," he said. "But Virginia Gentleman is sipping whiskey and sure goes down smooth."[63]

The desegregation issue was of continuing interest at the national conferences of attorneys general. Most conferees showed genuine concern for defining their roles in the crisis. Few treated the matter cavalierly. Patterson could recall only one occasion when a discussion was over the top. The breach of protocol occurred one evening when some attendees were living it up at the bar and Lindsey Almond came in and said U.S. Attorney General Herbert Brownell wanted to meet informally with all the Southern attorneys general in his suite. One member of the group was a huge assistant from the Carolinas who was standing in for his boss. No one suspected that the burly Carolinian, who looked as if he never missed a meal, had trouble holding his liquor.

The diminutive Brownell, who was instrumental in convincing Eisenhower to run for president in 1952, carried a lot of weight with the White House. When the Southern conferees gathered in his suite that evening, Brownell had them seated in a horseshoe arrangement in front of him. "Gentlemen, I know you're wondering why I asked you here," he said in a small voice. "I want you to tell me about the progress you're making on integrating the public schools." The drunken Carolinian was seated next to Brownell. He stood up and grabbed the U.S. Attorney General in a bear hug and slurred, "We don't call that progress in my state. Tell you what, Mr. Brownell. You forget about that and we will too." Brownell was not amused. Almond laughed and said that was the only smart thing he heard during the entire conference."[64]

When Patterson began to think that he might run for governor in 1958, he knew from his visits around the state that school desegregation was certain to be an election-year issue in the campaign. Both he and Folsom had taken "flak" for standing by and doing nothing in the Montgomery bus boycott and Autherine Lucy cases. Folsom's political fortunes had plummeted when he ridiculed the White Citizens' Councils and welcomed Harlem's congressman Adam Clayton Powell, Jr., to the governor's mansion when he came to Montgomery in a show of support for the bus boycott.

Southern whites in general, and politicians in particular, tended to blame their racial problems on the NAACP (National Association for the Advancement of Colored People). From his discussions with Almond and others, Patterson decided to preempt the NAACP by bringing suit against the civil rights giant. If other states took similar action, which many did, they could put the NAACP on the defensive and diffuse the organization's legal resources. The maneuver not only struck at the core of organized desegregation, but gave heart to disgruntled whites who viewed the NAACP as a monolith of outside agitators bent on fomenting racial strife among Southern blacks.

Partly because of outside agitation and fear of reprisal, the voices of Southern white sympathizers were mostly muted during the emerging civil rights struggle of the 1950s. Even Governor Folsom, who was accused of being "soft" on the race issue, played politics with school desegregation. He yielded to the thousands of constituents who wrote to protest racial integration—many of them quoting scripture to support their hardline opposition. In his folksy, disarming way, Folsom told reporters "that he certainly would not think of forcing those nice Negro children to go to school with those whites."[65]

Patterson had his people take a close look at the NAACP's operations in Alabama. They found that the national organization of the NAACP, which had a regional headquarters and state offices in Birmingham, was incorporated in New York. Loosely interpreted, this made it a "foreign" or out-of-state corporation, according to Alabama statutes. Further study revealed that the NAACP had been conducting business in Alabama (soliciting members, collecting dues, financing lawsuits, seeking plaintiffs for lawsuits, etc.) for decades without having qualified under the state's domestic corporation law to do business in Alabama. The organization had filed none of the statutory documents that were required, and therefore, Patterson concluded, had been operating outside the law since coming into the state.[66]

Giving the case an ironic twist, the attorney general's office found a similar situation from the turn of the century, in which a Ku Klux Klan group (also a non-profit entity) incorporated in North Carolina had been conducting business in New York in violation of that state's corporation laws. The New York attorney general had sued to enjoin the KKK group from operating in the state because of their non-compliance with New York law. The court entered an order prohibiting the KKK from doing business in New York. The Klan appealed the case to the supreme court, which affirmed the lower court's ruling.[67]

In June 1956, using the New York case as a precedent, Patterson filed a petition with the circuit court in Montgomery seeking an injunction to halt the NAACP from continuing to operate in Alabama. The attorney general charged the NAACP with helping to organize and finance the six-month-old bus boycott in Montgomery and with paying two black coeds to seek enrollment at the University of Alabama. He said these and other actions by the NAACP had breached state statutes and local ordinances, and in some instances had created a breach of the peace. Judge Walter B. Jones, a staunch segregationist, issued a temporary injunction outlawing the NAACP in Alabama.[68]

While the NAACP's lawyers studied the petition, White Citizens' Council members applauded the injunction. State Senator Sam Engelhardt of Macon County, executive secretary of the Alabama Association of Citizens' Councils and also a staunch segregationist, hailed the injunction "as a step toward our goal of race harmony." Governor Folsom told reporters he thought "some Negro leaders (were) hurting their own cause by pushing too hard for integration," but he didn't think the injunction against the NAACP was "likely to accomplish anything." The governor repeated his pledge that there was "not going to be any race mixing in our public schools."[69]

Patterson followed up in July with a petition to compel the NAACP to produce records on its activities in Alabama. The state needed the records, he said, to respond to a motion by the NAACP asking that the temporary restraining order be lifted. The attorneys for the NAACP contended that the law was not applicable to their client since its operations were strictly interstate in character. They also denied that the organization had financed the bus boycott or the black college applicants at the university. In the petition seeking a court order to open up the NAACP's records to the state, Patterson requested specific documentation including its charters in Alabama, membership lists, names of persons who had contributed money within the past year, records of property ownership, bank statements, and correspondence dealing with civil rights activities.[70]

At the court hearing the lead attorney for the NAACP, Arthur D. Shores of Birmingham, described the state's petition as "a fishing expedition." He argued that compelling the NAACP to comply would be the same as forcing the organization to give evidence against itself, which was prohibited by the constitution. Judge Jones decided in favor of the state, and set a date for Shores to produce the requested documents for the inspection of state authorities. When the NAACP defied the court order, Jones cited the organization with contempt and fined it $10,000, warning that the fine would automatically increase to $100,000 if the records were not produced in five days.[71]

NAACP Executive Secretary Roy Wilkins of New York announced that the group would fight the court order to name its Alabama members. The membership list was not relevant to the case, he said, and state authorities could not "guarantee that the list would not be misused." Wilkins was concerned that the organization's 14,566 Alabama members would be subjected to "economic pressure and personal threats and acts of violence" if their names were revealed. Through the attorneys handling the case, he offered to produce some of the records in court, but he refused to make public a list of members.[72]

When Jones and the Alabama Supreme Court denied requests to modify or stay the contempt fine, the NAACP attorneys appealed to the U.S. Supreme Court. A brief filed in September 1957 cited the hostile legal climate in Alabama. The NAACP legal team, headed by Thurgood Marshall and Robert Carter of New York, charged that Judge Jones, as an avowed segregationist, should have recused himself and that Alabama officials had "committed themselves to a course of persecution and intimidation of all who seek to implement desegregation." The attorney general fired back accusing the NAACP of making unfounded charges against state authorities and undermining race relations in the South.[73]

The U.S. Supreme Court agreed to review the case and heard final arguments in January 1958. Robert Carter argued the case for the NAACP. Assistant attorney general Edmon Rinehart argued for the State of Alabama, with Patterson in attendance. Rinehart contended that the NAACP's deliberate noncompliance and contempt for state law was plain, and that there was "nothing for the high court to decide." Carter conceded that the NAACP's integration aims were "at variance with state policy," but contended that the state had no jurisdiction over the group's work "to protect constitutional rights of Negroes who are unable to look after their own rights as individuals."[74]

Justice Felix Frankfurter, at one point in the proceedings, observed that the NAACP was given "a death sentence pro tem" even though its position might be upheld. He further noted that the organization, after being found in contempt, had agreed to register with the state and pay the fifty-dollar fee, but the state refused to accept the post hoc registration. Before adjourning the 1957–58 term, the high court overruled the contempt judgment and the $100,000 fine imposed by Judge Jones. Justice John Marshall Harlan said the court regarded Jones's order "as substantially restraining the exercise by NAACP members of their right to freedom of association." The court refused to rule on the request to set aside the 1956 order barring the NAACP from operating in Alabama, however, which allowed the state's injunction to stand.[75]

Patterson recalled that he and Rinehart, who had practiced law in New York, had earlier tried to hire a New York firm to collect the $100,000 fine, but were turned down. This was fortuitous since the high court's ruling meant the money couldn't be collected anyway. The court's reluctance to rule on the constitutionality of the order barring NAACP operations in Alabama was a procedural decision since the case first had to go through the appellate system. Litigating the appeal bought more time for the state, which was Patterson's aim in bringing the suit in the first place.

The U.S. Supreme Court ultimately reversed Jones's decision, but not before the long appeals process had put the NAACP out of business in Alabama for nearly nine years. The final decision in the case came down after Patterson left the governor's office in January 1963. The Supreme Court justices ruled that the NAACP's case was not the same as the earlier New York suit against the KKK because the two litigants were not comparable. The ruling, in effect, said that the state's refusal to let the NAACP operate in Alabama equated to denying the oppressed minority their constitutional rights.[76]

An NAACP spokesman admitted at the end of 1957 that Alabama had been "more successful than any other Southern state in fighting the NAACP." The NAACP board of directors met in New York "to take stock of their battle-scarred organization." The directors reported that membership had dropped by 48,000, or 14 percent, and the operations budget showed a $52,000 deficit for 1957. This was directly attributable to the court fights in Alabama and Virginia, and to other states that followed suit. For those whose strategy was to go slow on integration, executive secretary Roy Wilkins said: "Our reply is that we're already going slowly, according to law and order, that ninety-three years have passed since Emancipation and that we think the time is long overdue for us and our children to enjoy these rights."[77]

HOMEGROWN CIVIL RIGHTS ACTIVISTS were not without their own legal and strategic resources. Patterson acknowledged that while his office had the NAACP tied up in litigation the civil rights movement had opened up new fronts in the state. "Having the U.S. Constitution and the federal government at the table makes a powerful friend of the court," he remarked, in later years. "Even without the NAACP the movement in Alabama had an excellent coterie of attorneys who were well-schooled in the law and knew their way around the courtroom. They were worthy adversaries, and were getting better all the time."[78]

The black attorneys he faced in the courtroom won Patterson's respect— particularly Arthur Shores of Birmingham and Fred D. Gray, a young Montgomery attorney who began his legal career with the 1955 bus boycott. For his part, Gray stated that Shores was "the dean of black lawyers in this state and had been handling civil rights cases since the late 1930s." Gray had just turned twenty-four when Patterson was sworn in as attorney general in January 1955; by the end of the year Gray was representing Rosa Parks after she was arrested.[79]

The ensuing years found Gray's reputation rising rapidly as he won case after case for the civil rights movement. In 1956 the Supreme Court ruled in the young attorney's favor by affirming the lower court's ruling in the Montgomery bus boycott case that segregated seating on city buses was illegal. He was just twenty-eight years old when he argued his first case before the U.S. Supreme Court in *Gomillion v. Lightfoot* "challenging the Alabama legislature's gerrymandering of Tuskegee for the purpose of denying blacks the right to vote." Patterson later told a friend and historian that without Fred Gray, "the movement for desegregation perhaps could have been stalled or put on hold for a generation or more . . . Gray just kept getting the people out of jail."[80]

In June 1956, Gray had drawn up the papers incorporating the Montgomery Improvement Association (formed six months earlier to support the bus boycott) as a nonprofit corporation. The *Alabama Journal* quickly printed the street addresses of the MIA's founding members, including Ralph D. Abernathy, J. W. Bonner, Martin Luther King, Jr., E. D. Nixon, Solomon S. Seay, Sr., Moses Jones, and Erna Dungee, thus exposing the civil rights icons and their families to harassment or worse.[81]

That same day newspaper headlines across Alabama announced that "cheering Negroes" hailed a new organization in Birmingham "designed to replace the outlawed NAACP." Founder Reverend Fred Shuttlesworth stated that the Alabama Christian Movement for Human Rights was dedicated "to wiping out racial segregation" and was opposed to "gradualism in seeking to do away with segregation." He emphasized that the movement was organized by Alabama citizens and had no connection to the NAACP. "We are insiders. There should be no charge of outside interference."[82]

Members of the new organization passed a resolution praising participants in the bus boycotts in Montgomery and Tallahassee, Florida, for "conducting themselves in the struggle so valiantly, and without rancor, hate and smear, and above all, without violence." Five months later the U.S. Supreme Court affirmed a decision of the U.S. District Court in Montgomery that segregation on city buses violated the federal Constitution's guarantees of due process and equal protection of law. Reverend King called the decision "a glorious daybreak," while white officials across Dixie branded it as "unlawful interference with rights of states." That night carloads of robed KKK members drove through black residential areas in Montgomery, horns blowing, but police said there were no reports of violence.[83] (The violence came a few weeks later, when on January 10, 1957, dynamite bombs exploded at four black churches and two homes in Montgomery; no one was ever convicted in these incidents.)

Feelings still ran high in the summer of 1957 when the Tuskegee Civic Association retaliated for the Tuskegee gerrymandering act by sponsoring a boycott of the town's white merchants. The president of the association was Dr. C. G. Gomillion, dean of students and a professor at Tuskegee Institute. The gerrymandering act, which was passed by the legislature unanimously and without debate, was designed to break up a heavy concentration of black votes in Tuskegee and Macon County where black residents outnumbered whites seven to one. Six weeks into the boycott the attorney general's office opened an investigation into whether the TCA had violated Alabama's anti-boycott law.[84]

Patterson was put in a quandary by the gerrymandering bill. The bill's sponsor,

Senator Engelhardt, had been a political ally of his father's and had befriended Patterson after he became attorney general. Engelhardt's bill conflicted with Patterson's championing of voting rights in Phenix City and across the state since his father's murder. Gerrymandering, albeit legal, was just another way of stealing the vote without a fist or a gun. He had not forgotten that the state legislature had gerrymandered his Uncle Lafayette out of his congressional seat in the 1930s because of his liberal views. Yet, the Tuskegee Civic Association and similar groups were alter egos of the NCAAP whose purpose, most whites believed, was to stir up racial unrest in the state. He stayed on the sidelines of the controversy until Bunny Kohn, a Jewish friend who owned two stores in Tuskegee, and other merchants filed complaints that the TCA had used coercive tactics and intimidation to keep black customers from trading with white businesses.[85]

With the deadline to announce for the governor's race only six months away, the attorney general's political aspirations were an obvious consideration in his deciding to intervene. He obtained a warrant and led a raid on the TCA's campus headquarters, during which investigators confiscated a list of members and other documents, including NAACP membership rolls. Responding to a petition from the attorney general, Circuit Judge Will O. Walton issued a temporary injunction enjoining the TCA from "using any force, threats, intimidation, and coercion to prevent any person from trading with or buying goods and services from any merchant in Tuskegee and Macon County." Attorney Fred Gray, whose services had been retained by the TCA, countered that the attorney general's heavy-handed actions were "an act of intimidation" against his clients. Gray brought Arthur Shores in on the case.[86]

An economic tug of war ensued with Tuskegee's white merchants promoting a huge sales campaign and the city's black leaders forming a new organization to promote trade for black merchants and to help set them up in business. The sales promotion gave white merchants a short-lived boost when black customers poured back into their stores. Gomillion stated that reports accusing him of leading the boycott were erroneous. "I have not stopped trading with the white merchants because I never started," he said, defiantly.[87]

The following January the attorney general went back to court seeking a permanent injunction against the civic association. He knew from Judge Frank Johnson's ruling in the Montgomery bus boycott, which the high court upheld, that even if he won the injunction the case would be lost on appeal, but he proceeded with the suit anyway. This at least put the matter before the court, where he thought it belonged. In a bold move, after the state rested its case, the defense called the attorney general to the stand as a witness. Attorney Gray later wrote that he used this opportunity to probe Patterson's motives for bringing the suit. Gray hoped to make a case that the attorney general's legal actions against the NAACP and the TCA were for political gain, that he was using them "as stepping stones . . . towards the governor's mansion."[88]

Patterson acknowledged that he had not taken steps to shut down the KKK as he had the NAACP, but pointed out that his office had the Klan under investigation for the past two years and would bring charges anytime the evidence supported it. When Shores asked if Patterson planned to run for higher office this year, Judge Walton warned that the line of questioning was going too far afield. Patterson smiled and responded anyway, saying that if he were to announce for governor, he wouldn't be doing it from the witness stand.[89]

Walton took the case under advisement, stating that he was "in no particular rush" to hand down a ruling "because of the importance and serious nature of the issues involved." Gray pointed out in his book *Bus Ride to Justice* that it was election time, and the judge had "a great deal of politicking" to do. After he was reelected, Walton ruled against the atttorney general's office, saying that the black residents of Tuskegee "were within their constitutional rights to trade with whomever they pleased." Patterson did not appeal the ruling.[90]

Patterson recalled that some of the white merchants supported his actions, and some didn't. "Some of them said I was over there because of my political ambitions, which was partly correct." Even though the state lost the case, his actions "put a damper on the boycott, and some of the white merchants were able to survive." He later said the crux of the matter was that the black citizens, even though the gerrymandering act had taken away their voting power, proved by the use of their economic power they could still have some persuasion in the white community. "But anyway, by getting involved over there, I didn't hurt myself with the rest of the state."[91]

AT THE END OF January, a few days after closing arguments in the Tuskegee case, Patterson announced at a press conference that he had officially entered the race for governor. Friends and supporters had been after him to run, and he had talked it over with Charlie Meriwether who agreed to be his campaign manager. This is what his father would have wanted him to do. Albert Patterson had confided to Ray Jenkins of the *Columbus Ledger* in 1954 that he intended to stay eight

years in Montgomery, interpreted by Jenkins to mean that he planned to run
for governor in 1958 had he lived.[92]

John Patterson was no longer the angry young man he had been when his
father was murdered in 1955. There were still occasional flashes of anger when
things got screwed up, and he was quick to strike back when he felt he was treated
wrongly by the press. But his good humor and keen wit never left him. He had
never been more sure of himself or his purpose. His aim if elected governor
was to make a better life for all of Alabama's citizens. He had definite plans for
promoting industrial and economic development, constructing new highways
and airfields, building new schools and improving education, increasing old age
pensions, and waging war on poverty in Alabama.

The racial problem was a critical issue facing the state and weighed heavily
on his mind. His temporary success in outlawing the NAACP and his resistance
to desegregating public schools had made him a champion to Alabama's white
voters. To ignore the message in the upcoming campaign for governor would
relinquish that advantage. He proposed instead to articulate the state's position on
school desegregation in a reasoned, dispassionate way which would not inflame
already overheated emotions. There were a host of other problems that had to
be resolved to make Alabama a better place to live for all of its citizens, and he
did not intend for the racial issue to become an overreaching concern or for it
to define his campaign or his term in office, if elected.

The year 1957 had started off with a bang for the attorney general's political
fortunes when the U.S. Junior Chamber of Commerce announced his selection as
one of the ten outstanding young men in the nation. Lauded as "the most active
attorney general in Alabama's recent history," Patterson had won a large following for his stand concerning state expenditures and his crackdown on crime and
corruption. He had also made some powerful political enemies, such as the loan
sharks and the old Phenix City crowd, who had scores to settle and wanted to
bring him down. As the year drew to an end it appeared that his candidacy might
be in trouble when State Banking Superintendent Lonnie Gentry leaked to the
press that the hard-hitting attorney general was himself a "partner" in a Phenix
City firm recently indicted for making small loans without a state license.[93]

Gentry, who had resisted Patterson's efforts for effective small-loan legislation,
denied allegations that he was engaged in a smear campaign against the attorney
general. When the full story came out, however, doubts were raised about the
political impetus behind the leaks. Columnist John Temple Graves described

"the smear attempt [as] too visible, simple and thin." "John Patterson's worst enemies wouldn't believe him so stupid as to make war on usury while practicing it. Obviously the stupidity is in his would-be smearers."[94]

In the wake of his father's murder and the Phenix City cleanup, a group of leading citizens headed by Jack Gunter (local real estate man and one-time leader in the Russell Betterment Association) had formed Investors, Inc., with the goal of establishing a second bank in Phenix City to help rebuild the broken economy. Patterson and his law partner Jack Miller (along with Sheriff Lamar Murphy, Solicitor James Caldwell, State Representative Homer Cornett and some forty other local residents) had been invited to become stockholders and had each invested one hundred dollars with a pledge to purchase another ten dollars in stock monthly over the next three years. Patterson was not on the board of directors, and had no knowledge of the operation.[95]

While causing no lasting damage to Patterson's campaign plans, the leaked information created a press frenzy. In Montgomery, the *Advertiser* called the incident "an acute embarrassment" to the attorney general. The usually more friendly *Columbus Ledger* ran a front-page story describing the situation's effect as crippling, and perhaps fatal, to Patterson's candidacy in 1958.[96]

The furor over the leaked story had given the Patterson camp a bit of a scare, but in the end it left the candidate better prepared to handle media bombshells in the rough-and-tumble campaign that lay ahead. If ever there was a "tempest in a teapot" this was it, Patterson's campaign manager said. Once the overdone story dropped off the front pages, all interested parties knew that the first shot fired in the upcoming governor's race had fizzled and missed the target. They could hardly wait for the real fireworks to start, however, in what promised to be "an old-time barn burner" in the race to be Alabama's next governor.

11

THE JINGLE, THE RUMBLE, THE ROAR

The Democrats had as many dark horses running for governor in 1958 as there had been party faithful elected to the state's highest office since the turn of the century. When John Patterson announced his candidacy in January 1958, eleven other fired-up Democrats had already qualified for the May 6 primary. By post time the field had risen to a total of fourteen, and they were off and running.[1]

Patterson had kept the press guessing for months. Small-town newspapers around the state had urged the popular young attorney general to run, but none at this early stage dared predict he would win. Only a self-proclaimed political oracle who worked for a meat-packing company in Pickens County stuck his neck out. A year before the Democratic Primary, in May 1957, the *Pickens County Herald* reported that a local man named Ward Price had predicted Attorney General Patterson would be the next governor. Price, by his own count, had not "missed predicting the outcome of an election in this county since he began making his forecasts way back in 1934."[2]

Patterson, when told about Price's prediction, smiled and said, "If I'd known about him, I might've hired that fellow. We could've used a man like that in my administration." He was more heartened by a straw vote in *South* magazine in September 1957 that showed him with a wide lead over ten other Alabamians "prominently mentioned" as gubernatorial contenders. Of 10,000 questionnaires mailed to a cross-section of voters, the magazine had received 3,641 responses by press time. Patterson led with 1,087 votes, totaling slightly more than 30 percent. George Wallace was the runner-up with 496 votes, followed by Laurie Battle with 459 and Jimmy Faulkner with 401.[3] Other straw polls, depending on the source, came up with different winners.

The public recognition Patterson had gained as "the most active attorney general in Alabama's recent history" accounted for his statewide popularity and gave him a fast start out of the gate. The constant exposure had helped him build on his father's political base to organize an effective grass-roots campaign and to attract new supporters across Alabama. Not a week went by without newspapers running stories of him being in one small town after the other speaking to civic groups or traveling out of state to address some convention.[4]

The straight-talking attorney general cultivated new friends wherever he went and corresponded with them on a regular basis. "I just systematically covered the state, going into every county spending the night with people, speaking to civic clubs, and making friends," Patterson said. He kept them advised of new initiatives by his office, "so they would know what was going on and would feel like they were part of what we were doing." In August 1957, he told a group of Gadsden business men that he was receiving "a half-bushel of mail a day" commending his office for what they were doing and urging him to run for governor.[5]

From this correspondence he had developed an extensive file system listing supporters in every county. Red tags were placed on the files of those who were willing to actually help in his campaign. He referred to them as "Red Men." When he announced his candidacy in January 1958 he was corresponding on a regular basis with some fifteen thousand supporters. "This was the basis for my organization. It was purely grass roots. They were mostly people who had never gotten involved previously in any campaign. These are the best kind of people to have for you."[6]

Patterson had a seasoned pro managing his campaign. The *Montgomery Advertiser*'s Bob Ingram wrote that Charles Meriwether, a Tennessean, had come to Alabama in 1947 "as a perfect stranger, armed with nothing more than his own talents," and in a few years had become one of the state's "foremost political figures." Meriwether was an executive with the Dewberry Drug Company (one of the oldest and biggest pharmaceutical firms in the state) in Birmingham. In Memphis he had worked for an insurance firm owned by "Boss" Crump. Although not connected to the Crump political machine, he had studied Crump's methods and said that he had "learned as much about politics from observing Crump than any other man."[7]

The friendship and mutual trust between Patterson and Meriwether was obvious. The tall Tennessean, having worked in Patterson's father's campaign in 1954, was first to convince the son that he was "in a position to become governor" when he agreed to take his slain father's place as attorney general. Patterson valued his political counsel, but Meriwether's major contribution was managing the campaign's organization and finances.

Patterson's own political instincts, unaffected and at times impetuous, were rooted in common sense and sensibility. "What you saw was what you got." He genuinely liked people, and his sincerity won converts on the campaign trail. "John had the background, the color, the record, and the drama," Meriwether said, and "he made a record as attorney general which he could run on." He emphasized that a candidate had to have "horsepower" to win an election, and that Patterson had "more horsepower" than any candidate he'd ever seen.[8]

Two years before he announced his candidacy, Patterson and Meriwether met privately with a select group of "Red Men" at Birmingham's Molton Hotel (which later became Patterson's campaign headquarters) on March 29, 1956, to discuss his plans to run for governor. The people in attendance at the planning session were the first to contribute to the campaign chest. Irby Keener, a pal from law school who now had a practice in Centre, Alabama, made the first contribution, a $200 check.[9]

One of the decisions made at the meeting was to hire his and his father's former secretary in Phenix City, Lucille Smith, to handle the administrative workload for the campaign. They set up an office for her in Montgomery, so correspondence and other matters relating to the campaign would be completely divorced from the attorney general's office to avoid giving even the appearance of misusing the attorney general's office to run for governor.[10]

Later, after he announced for governor, Patterson turned the attorney general's responsibilities over to Jim Screws who was senior to others in the office and had worked there for twenty years. He had complete trust in Screws, and knew he wouldn't do anything to embarrass the office and would let him know if his decision was needed on any matter. "And it worked perfectly," Patterson said. "Jim was an old hand and knew what to do. He kept us all out of trouble."[11]

MacDonald Gallion was not available because he had entered the race for attorney general soon after Patterson made his formal announcement. Gallion and Patterson agreed it would be a good idea for him to step down as first assistant until the campaign was over. Non-state funds were used to compensate him for the lost pay.[12]

MOST POLITICAL CAMPAIGNS ARE family affairs. Four generations of Pattersons contributed in some way to his run for governor—from his grandmother appearing with him at the opening rally to his brother Maurice working full-time to get him elected. Mary Joe frequently joined her husband at campaign events—taking Albert (eight) and Barbara Louise (four) with her on special occasions.

His mother attended some rallies, and spoke to civic groups in support of her son's candidacy. Jack stumped for his brother in small towns around Tuscaloosa, where he was still enrolled at the university. In the summer of 1957 Maurice gave up his position with Proctor & Gamble in Atlanta and moved to Montgomery to devote his full time and energy to the campaign. Relying on his brother's list of contacts Maurice moved around the state organizing supporters and making new friends well in advance of the campaign's kick-off in early 1958.[13]

Patterson's core support came from the same contributors and voters who had clinched his father's nomination in the 1954 attorney general's race, i.e. the underpaid laborers, the mom and pop businesses, the one-mule farmers, and wage-earners across Alabama who made up the "silent majority" in state politics. Their pockets were not deep, but they paid their bills on time and bore more than their share of the tax burden. All they asked in return was a fair wage, good government and reliable, uncorrupted law enforcement.

The candidate said his brother Maurice understood the constituency better than others, and proved to be the best vote-getter in the campaign. He carried every county in northeast Alabama, the area where Maurice served as campaign coordinator. Maurice, sometimes mistaken for his older brother despite their difference in age, hit the road during the week, calling on people in towns from Opelika north to the Tennessee border. "If I had a dollar for every sign I put up, I'd be a rich man today," he said. "In Heflin, George Wallace had a Chevrolet dealer handling his campaign. I had a cab driver running ours. We ended up polling more votes in Cleburne County than anybody ever had. Go figure. The key is who is going to work the hardest and get you the most votes."[23]

Maurice found campaigning to be "just a lot of fun" as he made new friends everywhere he went and stayed overnight in their homes. "Got a lot of free meals out of the thing," he said. Sometimes when he stayed overnight with folks, he got his brother John on the phone and let them talk with him about the campaign. "That made a fellow feel awfully important, you know." He went from door-to-door all over northeast Alabama, returning each weekend with a list of the contacts he'd made. His brother would write them a personal letter, and Maurice would be back on the road the following Monday working new towns. "All the way up to the Tennessee line, we carried every county."[24]

The southeastern part of the state, the Wiregrass, was Wallace country. "George carried that easily," John Patterson said. "I didn't do well down there, and I didn't do well up in the Tri-cities area. Jimmy Faulkner had that sewed up. I put a lot of effort up there and got very few votes in return for it." Perhaps his greatest coup was carrying Mobile, despite solid opposition (or because of it) from the "silk stocking crowd." Bill Clark was Patterson's man in Mobile. He put together a working class coalition of stevedores, dock workers, waitresses, bartenders, cab drivers, store clerks, and wage earners of every sort.[25]

"Bill Clark knew how to do it," Patterson said. When he won the campaign, Patterson showed his appreciation by driving to Mobile and holding a victory rally in Bienville Square "right downtown at high noon." Red Jernigan, an ardent supporter who owned a business named "Collards and Everything" in the suburban town of Whistler, wrote a poem to celebrate the event. Across from the square there was a popular nightclub called "The Metropolitan" which was run by a Greek friend of Patterson's. When he addressed the crowd Patterson invited everyone over to the Metropolitan for a round of drinks on him. Joe Robertson went over ahead of the crowd and bought out the bar.

They held another rally in the nightclub. The crowd called on Patterson to speak again. Shorty Price, who had brought up the rear in the Democratic primary, had supported Patterson in the runoff and was present at the rally. Patterson, expecting his loquacious former rival to liven up the party, introduced Shorty and asked him to say a few words. Shorty got up on a barstool and lifted his schooner of beer in a toast. "Now old John is the guv' and I ain't nobody. But iffen' I'd been elected instead of him, then I'd be the guv' and he'd be nobody." Shorty then turned up the schooner and chug-a-lugged the beer.[26]

Patterson said it was unfortunate that while public figures learned from their mistakes, few ever had the opportunity to put what they'd learned into practice. This he found to be generally true during the 1958 campaign and during his four-year term as governor. Therefore, he believed it in the public interest for officeholders to learn from their predecessors' experiences, rather than plowing over old furrows and replanting the mistakes others before them had made.[8]

He made a point of reading the histories of past administrations to learn what their problems had been and how they dealt with them. He discovered that since the beginning of Alabama as a state, successive governors had been confronted with essentially the same issues. Not surprisingly, these core issues (education, roads, revenues, taxes, old-age assistance, new jobs and the race issue) were the cornerstone for his campaign platform and the four-year plan he drafted as a road map for his administration.[9]

Whether it was running the campaign or getting ready to take the reins as governor, the Patterson organization was not "sitting around waiting for the light to shine." The campaign was a well planned, highly organized, and efficient operation. Nothing was left to chance. Patterson said he didn't believe there was another candidate in the race who had as smooth an organization as the one he and Merriwether put together. The whole thing had been mapped out months in advance. Starting with the kick-off at New Site the candidate knew where he would appear at every stop on the campaign trail through the end of the primary in May.

"These political rallies don't just happen. To be successful, to do seven, eight, or nine speeches a day over 150 miles and draw huge crowds, it has to be carefully planned and organized." They would send out people days in advance to let communities know that John Patterson would be there on a certain day. They put up handbills on telephone poles and in store windows, put ads in newspapers and spots on the radio, increasing the tempo right up until the candidate made his appearance. "Our caravan had ten or fifteen cars filled with people, so we were sure to have a crowd everywhere we went."[10]

Every detail of the campaign trail was worked out well in advance, and went like clockwork. People stayed behind at each stop to assess the reaction to Patterson's message. They mingled with the crowds and listened to what they were saying about him. That night they huddled with the candidate wherever he was staying and filled him in on what they had learned. "You need that feedback," he said. "You don't want them to come back and tell you what they think you want to hear. You need them to tell you the God's honest truth."[11]

Patterson's campaign workers had instructions to stay away from city hall and the court house at every whistle-stop. They had supporters campaigning for him in each town, but for the most part they were not local officeholders. Since the 1930s the mayors throughout the state had traditionally belonged to the Alabama League of Municipalities based in Montgomery. Ed Reid, the league's founder and executive director, was a power in Democratic politics "going back to the days when he worked with Governor Bibb Graves in the thirties," and he had "connections throughout the federal government and the state governments, not only in Alabama but all over the country." Like his friend Grover Hall, Reid made no secret of the fact that he was a Wallace man.[12]

McDowell Lee, who has served eight years in the state legislature and more than four decades as Secretary of the Senate, has long been a respected figure in Alabama politics. Lee comes from Wallace's hometown of Clio in Barbour County and was Wallace's campaign manager in the 1958 race. "George handled legislation for the League of Municipalities when he was in the House," Lee recalled. "He got close to them and had connections with all the mayors. They were the core of his support when he was running for governor that first time."[13] This alone was reason for the Patterson campaign to bypass local officeholders and to appeal directly to the people.

Patterson learned quickly that he could not afford to "spin his wheels" going after the wrong votes or to "get boxed in" by empty promises. Early in the primary, when he was having difficulty raising funds, Patterson had an encounter with hardball politics that threatened to derail his campaign. Partly because he had taken a stand as attorney general against the NAACP and school desegregation, some of his father's former colleagues from the Black Belt (big landowners like Sam Engelhardt, Senator J. Bruce Henderson of Miller's Ferry in Wilcox County, and Sen. Walter Givhan of Dallas County) promised to support him in the governor's race.[14]

Candidates for state office coveted the Black Belt's support, which traditionally carried with it the backing of big business and industry as well. Throughout Alabama history a political alliance had existed between the land barons in the Black Belt rural regions (where lucrative timber and mining interests lived side-by-side with King Cotton) and the so-called Big Mule business and industrial giants in Birmingham. That these centers of gravity shared a community of interest politically and worked together to control the legislature was well known around the state. Patterson had been schooled in the history of the odd-couple coalition while taking political science classes at the university.[15]

One weekend Senator Henderson invited the youthful candidate out to his estate and offered to support him in the governor's race: "John, we can get the Big Mules in Birmingham to finance you, and between the two of us you should have enough backing that you won't have to go out and make commitments to people you'd rather not be obligated to." Patterson was flattered by the offer. Henderson was twice his age and one of the Black Belt's wealthiest landowners. During the second Folsom term, Big Jim and the Miller's Ferry senator had become bedfellows as strange as any in Alabama politics. Big Jim put aside his contempt for the Black Belt land barons to choose Henderson as president pro tem of the senate.[16]

Henderson showed his guest around the vast estate, encompassing thousands of acres of plantation land. Patterson later learned that his host's father had fought with the Union Army in the Civil War. When the war was over he had moved from Ohio to Alabama, where he became active in Reconstruction politics and acquired vast land holdings in Wilcox County. Touring the estate was like stepping back in time to an antebellum past. You could drive for miles or walk all day without leaving the premises.[17]

The Henderson place dwarfed most other large plantations, such as Sam Engelhardt's sixty-five hundred acres of rich farmland in Macon County. The sprawling operation was huge and self-sustaining. The hundred or so workers on the place were mostly blacks. A few, along with poor whites, scraped out a living by sharecropping. A person could easily be born and buried there without ever stepping off Henderson land.[18]

Many of the Black Belt plantations were microcosms of the Jim Crow world outside, a step up the ladder from the shameful rung of slavery. Not unlike the "owe-your-soul-to-the-company-store" practices of big mine owners, railroad czars, and mill towns across America, the sharecroppers and indentured farm workers labored under the yoke of endless sweat and endless debt. Large, well-stocked commissaries provided the families with food and supplies, and payment was collected from the workers' wages or when the crops were sold. The black workers were not allowed inside the commissary, but had to make their purchases through an outside window. These cradle-to-the-grave enclaves exemplified the extremes inherent in the so-called separate-but-equal doctrine. Critics said everything was segregated but the work. Even the pond on the Henderson estate had separate times posted for blacks and whites to fish there.[19]

Senator Henderson promised to bring the Big Mules on board, and he invited Patterson to speak at three meetings he arranged in Birmingham. At one meeting were the insurance and banking executives. Members of the state manufacturers association and the mining institute were at the second one. The third group consisted of the chamber of commerce and business leaders. The senator introduced the candidate, who spoke to the groups about their shared concerns for good government and law enforcement. He made a pitch for their financial backing, stressing the point the senator had made that he needed their support and that it would relieve him of having to raise money from special interest groups wanting something in return.[20]

He could tell his talks had not impressed the Big Mule audiences, even though they listened politely and promised to come through for him. Later he said they must have thought he was the most naive person they'd ever heard. "The more I reflect back on that, can you imagine how ridiculous I must have looked, and how ridiculous I must have sounded to them." But he needed the money badly—the campaign was hard pressed to come up with $200,000 just to buy time on television—and their promise of financial aid could not have come at a better time. Only, the money never came.[21]

Patterson was convinced that he had been set up—not by Henderson who he believed was sincere about helping him, but by the Big Mules who had obviously committed to other candidates in the race, either Faulkner or Wallace. He and Meriwether suspected that the financial giants in Birmingham might be stringing them along, perhaps hoping that his campaign would recover too late to raise enough money to stay in the race. They decided to play along, while going ahead with plans to raise campaign contributions from individual supporters and from firms that traditionally did business with the state.[22]

SOUTHERN POLITICAL CAMPAIGNS, BEFORE the rise of TV's scripted duck-and-dodge debates and Jimmy Swaggart's come-to-Jesus televangelism, were live entertainment and drew crowds as large as the throngs at any of Alabama's old-time brush arbor revivals. Guitars and fiddles and rousing political speeches blaring out over radios and on street corners across the South had long made regional campaigning a celebration of Southern expression and Southern roots. In the 1946 gubernatorial race Big Jim Folsom had bounced back from his losing effort four years earlier with a winning campaign strategy of motorcading through the branchheads making speeches nearly as crowd-pleasing as the sweet strains of country music heralding his arrival. Traveling with Folsom and the Strawberry Pickers band down the lost highway, when his schedule permitted, was the legendary Luke the Drifter, Hank Williams.[14]

Patterson had seen Big Jim's road show when he was a student at the University of Alabama in 1946. Folsom held a political rally one night in the auditorium at Graves Hall. As the Strawberry Pickers began to warm up the crowd, a group including Patterson and Joe Robertson had drifted over from the fraternity house more out of curiosity than serious interest in what the candidate had to say. They had no spending money left from their monthly GI Bill checks, and the picking and singing at Graves Hall offered free entertainment. The talk around the fraternity house had been, "Let's go over to Jim Folsom's rally, and have a little fun."[15]

Folsom, who had a talent for sizing up his audiences and talking directly to them, quickly got their attention. When the picking and singing stopped Folsom stood up and started to talk:

> Now look, I'm travelin' all over the state, goin' back into the branchheads and talkin' to the real people of Alabama. You know who I'm talkin' about, them folks back in the branchheads.
>
> Now I know y'all are college students and you're a cut above everybody else. You're intelligent people, and I probably ought to talk to you on a higher plane than what I'm doin' out in the branchheads. But I thought about that, and figured I'd just give you what I'm givin' them out in the branchheads so y'all will know what I'm tellin' them out there. You fellas are smart, and can make your own judgment about what I'm sayin'.[16]

On cue, Folsom's helpers brought out a suds bucket and a homemade mop put together from corn shucks, the kind that country folks used to scrub floors. He described to the audience how, as governor, he planned to use the suds bucket and the shuck mop to clean up the state capitol and scrub the "big mule" power brokers out of office. When he told the students their dollars and dimes were needed to give the big mules a good scrubbing, his helpers passed the bucket among them to collect donations. The students had to dig deep to come up with pocket change, but they responded enthusiastically to Folsom's message.[17]

Patterson recalled that Folsom "put on a real show and when he was done, he'd sold every one of us." Folsom was looked upon "as a veteran too" because he had made the perilous Murmansk run with the merchant marine on more than one occasion during the war. Folsom had volunteered for army service in 1943, but was released after six months because the quartermaster didn't have shoes or uniforms large enough to fit him. Patterson recalled that on the way back to the fraternity house that night all the veterans were singing Folsom's praises. "I don't know if they all voted for him, but I sure did," he said.[18]

While planning his own campaign in 1958 Patterson had not forgotten how the Strawberry Pickers warmed up Folsom's crowds. He had his eye on a local country music group, Rebe Gosdin and the Sunny Valley Boys, to join him on the campaign trail. He had met Rebe, a cousin of Grand Ole Opry star Vern Gosdin, and had seen the group performing on WSFA television in Montgomery. When he kicked off his campaign in early February at the New Site school, just down

the road from where he was born and a few hundred yards from the Bethlehem
Cemetery where his father, grandfather and other relatives were buried, Gosdin
and the Sunny Valley Boys were on hand to entertain the overflow crowd of
fifteen hundred supporters.[19]

Two older men from a nearby county told reporters they "came in" to the
rally because they had known "John's daddy" and "wanted to see what this boy
has." Some folks had driven from as far away as Huntsville to show their support. Backers from Opelika and Phenix City rolled into New Site on two special
buses and a caravan of cars. The six hundred seats in the school auditorium filled
up fast. People stood along the walls and in the hallway outside, while others
were seated inside the gymnasium to hear the speech piped in on the school's
auxiliary sound system.[20]

In the days leading up to the New Site rally Patterson had meticulously
drafted a speech, only to conclude afterward that his delivery suffered from relying on the prepared draft to jog his memory while at the podium. The *Advertiser*,
which opposed Patterson in the governor's race, reported that "his delivery in
the main was smooth," but "it was apparent at times that he was reading, rather
than speaking." The paper conceded, however, that the crowd "remained attentive and apparently interested throughout the speech," and responded at the end
with a standing ovation. Patterson learned from the experience and returned to
his natural style of speaking without notes.[21]

He stuck to his guns on the core issues, never wavering from the platform
that was spelled out in his opening speech. He pledged to give the people of
Alabama honest, efficient government that would "stop up the holes and get a
dollar's worth of goods and services for every dollar spent." The money saved
from greater efficiency would allow him to expand every program and to put the
savings to work "building modern, segregated schools for both races, and paying
teachers the higher salaries they deserve." As governor he would continue "an
all-out fight against outside agitators like the NAACP," and would see to it that
there would "be no mixing of the races in the public schools."

While insisting that public schools "must be segregated," Patterson believed
the state had a responsibility for seeing that "both white and colored" Alabama
children were provided a public education and had equal school facilities. Raised
by parents who were educators he learned that the "separate, but equal" rule as it
applied to the public school system below the Mason-Dixon line was a myth. All
a person had to do to be enlightened was to step inside one of the substandard

black schools. Most, if not all, were a disgrace to their communities and to the state. Patterson was intent on correcting this injustice, only to find that not even governors stepped on the prerogatives of school boards. "You were expected to mortgage the farm to fund their budget, but you didn't dare tell them how to spend a dime of that money."[22]

Patterson pledged to support programs for farmers and organized labor, assuring workers that labor would get "a fair deal" with his administration. He emphasized the need for industrial growth in Alabama, and promised to bring in new industries of the kind that would promote "healthy economic growth." He promised to expand and develop waterways and dock facilities, along with an expanded highway building program that would include farm-to-market roads "to meet the needs of rural communities." "I will work to improve the living and working conditions of the Alabama farmer and see that he has a market for his products and that he gets a fair price."[23]

The candidate interrupted his talk to introduce his elderly grandmother, a lifelong resident of Tallapoosa County. "She's ninety-three years young," he said, as he turned to the subject of old-age pensions for Alabama's senior citizens. The average old-age pension in the state was around $33 a month, compared to a national average of about $55 a month. "As your governor I will see to it that those who qualify for old-age pensions will be paid at least $75 a month, and more if possible," he stated.[24]

Law and order remained a cornerstone of his platform. "I have known from personal experience that gangsters and public officials cannot be partners in decent government. During my administration there will be no room for gangsters to operate in this state." He declared that he would enforce the laws fairly and impartially, but assured the audience that he would "stamp out vice and corruption wherever it rears its head."[25]

At the conclusion of the forty-minute address, Gosdin and the Sunny Valley Boys played and sang a medley of tunes as Patterson shook hands with departing friends and supporters. The rally opened and closed with the group's rendition of "The Wabash Cannon Ball," a country classic made popular by Grand Ole Opry legend Roy Acuff and adopted as the theme song for Patterson's campaign. To this day the former governor can recite every line of the haunting railroad melody that carried Daddy Claxton home to Dixie and John Patterson on to victory on the Wabash Cannon Ball.[26]

The slogan for the campaign, "Nobody's for John Patterson, but the People," was the brainchild of an early Patterson supporter, Robert Nahrgang of Fairhope, Alabama. The phrase spread rapidly through the state in April when the *Greene County Democrat* ran an editorial entitled "Nobody's For John Patterson But The People." The gist of the editorial was that an "insidious alliance" made up of "professional politicians, loan sharks, organized racketeers, political grafters and influence peddlers" were working day and night "spreading lies and smears against John Patterson" to try and defeat him. "The history of this campaign will some day be written in a single sentence: 'Nobody's for John Patterson but the people!'"[27]

The editorial was reprinted throughout Alabama. That same week a political ad in the *Montgomery Advertiser* invited readers "to tune in to WABT Channel 13 tonight" to find out why "Only the People Are for Patterson." A timeless political slogan was born and has since become as much a part of the Patterson lore as the official record of his administration or the multidimensional life (soldier, statesman, lawyer, teacher, farmer, jurist) of the man himself.[28]

THE OPENING RALLY IN Tallapoosa County on that cold, windblown Monday night in February set the pattern for his campaign. The long lines of friends and neighbors, more than double the size of New Site itself, instilled in him the confidence needed to break out on top in the roller-coaster ride that lay ahead. As a whole, the slate of thirteen candidates he faced was an uneven lot. Formidable opponents among the group could be counted on one hand, but these included such well-known figures as Circuit Judge George Wallace of Clayton and State Senator Jimmy Faulkner of Bay Minette. Wallace had been in politics since he wore knee pants. Faulkner was the runner-up to Jim Folsom in 1954. They were veteran campaigners and would make it a tight race to the finish line.

Patterson followed up with a smaller but no less enthusiastic rally at Central High in Phenix City. His camp had made a few adjustments since opening night in Tallapoosa County. The Sunny Valley Boys not only warmed up the crowd before Patterson spoke, but Rebe Gosdin introduced the candidate. The campaign had figured out that having a local political figure introduce Patterson ran the risk of losing voters who disliked the person or were on the opposing side of the community's political fence. In Gosdin's introductory remarks, described by a reporter as "a little gem of a political talk," the popular band leader made the point "that several other candidates had tried to get his services but he chose Patterson because he was for him."[29]

In his Central High address, the candidate did not dwell on Phenix City's lawless past. His speech capped a "John Patterson Day" celebration proclaimed by both the city and county commissions. He hammered at themes he introduced at New Site, but reminded the approving crowd of the special interest he had in his hometown and pledged, if elected, to "work night and day to improve and build Phenix City."[30]

The *Columbus Ledger*'s Millard Grimes wrote that Patterson talked sense at his political rallies. He pointed out that the hometown candidate had borrowed some of Folsom's innovations, but had no desire to emulate the style of the former governor.

> Patterson will never be a stump performer such as Jim Folsom—nor should he really want to be. Folsom is a magnificent figure waving his long arms before a crowd. His entertainment value is high but his gubernatorial value has been consistently low.
>
> Electorates have a distressing habit of being swept up in the excitement of a wild-shouting rally. They give no thought to the time when the bands will be gone and only the responsibility remains.[31]

Patterson wasn't the only one to borrow from Folsom's campaign techniques. Ben Knight of the *Florence Times* observed that all of the major candidates and a few of the lesser ones were employing country music stars to boost attendance. Grand Ole Opry star Minnie Pearl was traveling over the state with George Wallace (Wallace signed the Opry's pint-sized guitar-picking singer Little Jimmy Dickens for the runoff). Jimmy Faulkner had the Blackwood Brothers gospel quartet, while A. W. Todd of Russellville brought in the Sons of Song and the Chuck Wagon Gang. C. C. Owen used a variety of performers and Roy Acuff joined him at one rally. Musically talented candidate Shearen Elebash of Montgomery hauled a piano around on the back of a truck and provided his own music.[32]

Knight wrote, tongue-in-cheek, that there was about as much interest around Nashville's Ryman Auditorium (home of the Grand Ole Opry) in Alabama's race as there was on Montgomery's Capitol Hill. He noted that one of the candidates who couldn't afford paid entertainers had commented that there might "be a lot of confusion among the voters when they go to the polls on election day and won't be able to find the names of their Grand Ole Opry stars on the ballot." The leaner the budget the sourer the grapes, for "the lure of the entertainment was drawing more folks out to see the candidates than ever before."[33]

Folsom's landslide victory in 1954 had been the first effective use of television by Alabama gubernatorial candidates. In the early fifties television was in its infancy in Alabama—Montgomery got its first local station in 1953—and state politicians were eager to exploit the new medium. Some candidates in the 1958 race hired television consultants. Patterson's team brought in an expert named Roy Marcato to film Patterson's campaign for the local TV stations. Marcato worked with the stations to get the film clips (crude by today's standard, but avant-garde at the time) shown on the six o'clock news nearly every night.[34]

An innovation by the Patterson camp that was popular with voters was the use of pocket-sized comic books to tell his story and get out his message. The booklets were handed out by the hundreds at his campaign rallies, many distributed by teenage Patterson support groups which had sprung up over the state. Newspapers reported that teenage girls were holding "Patterson" placards aloft at almost every rally. The comic books were popular with supporters of all ages. "When we cleaned up the place after the rallies, there wouldn't be one of those booklets left on the ground," Patterson recalled. "Folks always took them home."[35]

Another Patterson initiative was to keep a record of comments made by people he talked to on the campaign trail. As he stumped throughout the state, he took every opportunity to discuss state issues with "the man on the street—farmers, factory workers, salesmen, and housewives." In his room at night he took out a notebook and wrote down some of the things people had told him. Patterson said he did this "to help me be the kind of governor that all of the people want."[36]

Despite earlier warnings when Patterson had been attacking his administration, Folsom stayed on the sidelines in 1958. He also instructed his cabinet to stay clear of the race. Some cabinet members disregarded Folsom's instructions, according to the *Advertiser*'s Bob Ingram, and spread their support around once the race got underway. Most candidates welcomed their support and carefully avoided saying anything that might "incur the wrath of Folsom." "The only exception has been John Patterson, and he can afford to be brash," Ingram wrote. "He wouldn't get Folsom's support anyway."[37]

The incumbent governor was displeased, Ingram said, because major candidates other than Patterson—Wallace, Faulkner, and Todd, in particular—had courted the old warrrior's support, but did not want his public endorsement. Wishing to be seen as their own man and not Folsom's handpicked successor, the candidates feared that muck from the scandal-plagued administration might rub off on them. An investigation into allegations of selling pardons and paroles during Folsom's first term was old news, but Patterson's multiple charges against the administration were still fresh in the minds of voters.[38]

More compelling for most of the candidates in the wake of *Brown v. Board of Education* was the urge to distance themselves from Folsom's image of being soft on the race issue. In the fall of 1955, when angry whites protested a visit to Montgomery by Harlem congressman Adam Clayton Powell, Jr., Folsom had tried to defuse the situation by sending his limousine to the airport for Powell and having him over to the governor's mansion for a Scotch and soda. Afterward Powell told the press about his warm reception at the mansion, announcing that he and Big Jim had a drink together and had found common ground in denouncing the evils of segregation.[39]

After this breach of Southern protocol, Big Jim's popularity plummeted among whites. Gun-shy political allies ran for cover. A prominent Southern historian noted that the White Citizens' Council members had grown "from a few hundred to twenty thousand" in Alabama around the time of the Powell incident. By the spring of 1958 their ranks had expanded to more than eighty thousand members, a powerful voting bloc to be ignored at a candidate's peril if he was in the race for governor.[40]

The most conspicuous defector from the Folsom camp was Patterson's strongest rival, George Wallace. The bantam judge from Barbour County had been a south Alabama Folsom campaign manager in 1954, and had stumped for the candidate. Historians are divided over who deserted whom. Some argue that Big Jim accepted Wallace's help during the campaign, but saw him as a political opportunist and dropped him after winning the election. Others make the case that Wallace broke with Folsom because of the Powell affair. It seems likely that Wallace (nicknamed "Wishy-washy Wallace" by candidate Ralph "Shorty" Price) had his eye on the 1958 election and repositioned himself politically to run as a dyed-in-the-wool segregationist.[41]

All fourteen candidates in the Democratic primary had sworn to uphold Alabama's tradition of segregation, particularly in the schools. Wallace vowed "to maintain segregation in Alabama completely and absolutely," but said it could be done without "violence or ill will." He boasted "time and again that if federal agents came into his judicial district, he would jail them." Jimmy Faulkner was less strident but said he would go to jail himself before he would allow the integration of the races. Winston Gullatte, a Selma insurance man, drew more nervous laughter than applause with an outrageous declaration that he would shoot himself to keep Alabama segregated.[42]

Patterson's record as attorney general had convinced white voters he was more than just talk on the race issue. Teenagers frequently attended Patterson's rallies, and some brought fruit jars filled with coins to contribute to his campaign. While they couldn't vote, the teenagers said they wanted to help because they had seen the soldiers and bayonets at Little Rock on television and knew Patterson wouldn't let it happen at their schools. An elderly man in overalls came up to Patterson after a speech and pressed a crinkled hundred dollar bill in his hand. "This is for what you've already done, not what you're gonna' do," he said as he shook the candidate's hand.[43]

The conventional wisdom was that Patterson had forfeited the black vote when he outlawed the NAACP in Alabama and raided the offices of the group responsible for the boycott of white merchants in Tuskegee. Patterson was realistic about his chances of winning over black voters, but was unwilling to write them off. At many rallies, a group of attentive blacks would be standing apart from the larger white audience. Patterson made a point of going over to them, shaking their hands, and soliciting their support—a gesture that was criticized by hardline opponents.

A few weeks into the campaign, the *Phenix City Citizen* ran an editorial in response to articles in the larger dailies giving Patterson little chance of winning black votes "because of his fight against the NAACP and his solid stand against segregation." The *Citizen* accused the large dailies of assuming that black voters would mark the ballots the way they were told, rather than making up their own minds. Reminding colleagues that black citizens would benefit from Patterson's stand against loan sharks and his promise of increased old-age pensions, the *Citizen* reasoned that in a race where no candidate was for integration the best governor for black citizens was the same as the person who would be best for white citizens. And in the *Citizen's* judgment, that person was John Patterson.[44]

While the attorney general expected to get few minority votes because of his stand against the NCAAP, a different segment of Alabama's neglected minorities came out solid for him. In April, Creek Chief Calvin McGee of Atmore, near Mobile, called on sixty thousand Indian descendants in Alabama "to stand by

John Patterson in this race." McGee announced that "after careful consideration of all candidates," the newly formed Indian organization KILROL (Kinsmen of Indians for Liberty, Reform, Opportunity and Instruction in Civic Affairs) had unanimously endorsed John Patterson for governor. The Indian group pledged support for "segregation, states' rights and liberties of the individual."[45]

FROM THE ENTHUSIASTIC SEND-OFF in Tallapoosa County, Patterson's campaign moved into high gear. For nearly four months, from February through the May 6 primary and into the runoff on June 1, he campaigned six days a week with Rebe Gosdin and his band crisscrossing the state by caravan. Meriwether organized the campaign schedule. Joe Robertson, "who doubled as a bodyguard and wore a snub-nosed revolver in a holster under his coat,"[46] stayed by Patterson's side throughout the grueling campaign and drove him everywhere they went.

They traveled up to one hundred and fifty miles a day, stopping and speaking "off the back of a lowboy truck" at eight or more towns along the way. Campaign workers went out ahead of the caravan putting up signs, handing out leaflets, and using loudspeakers to announce the arrival time of their candidate and his band. When the sun went down, they pulled up stakes and moved on to the last stop of the day, where they held a night rally and met afterward until midnight or one o'clock in the morning with local people to try and raise money. Patterson's eyes light up when he talks about the 1958 campaign: "I gotta' be honest with you. I got a kick out of traveling with Rebe and the band, and meeting all those wonderful people. I thought the band was great. You have to psych yourself up to do that sort of thing. It would kill me today to do that. It really would. I'd wind up at the Molton Hotel on Saturday night, just crash on Sunday, and try to wind myself up to head out again on Monday."[47]

Everyone in the Patterson caravan did their part. Rebe and the band arrived in town ahead of the candidate, set up their equipment, and began to play. Rebe's wife Carrie, who often traveled with the band, handed out campaign literature and talked to people in the crowd until Patterson arrived and Rebe introduced him. After making his speech, he went down into the audience shaking hands and talking to people. "While he was doing that, we'd take down the instruments and move on to the next town," Carrie said. "We did that eight or ten times a day, traveling from one end of the state to the other."[48]

She recalled "the really, really big crowds" at the Patterson rallies. More than once Patterson told her with a twinkle in his eye that he wondered "who they were coming to vote for, Rebe or me." People came out in all kinds of weather. One bitterly cold morning snow was falling when they rolled into the town of Oxford just south of Anniston after daybreak, and a crowd of two hundred people had already gathered in the town square waiting for them. More people poured into the street when Patterson started speaking. From there the caravan drove east to Heflin, where the snow was still coming down. There were no electrical outlets available, so they struck up the band without amplifiers. Heflin's residents—it seemed like the whole town was there—roared their approval.[49]

The crowds grew larger when the campaign began to make headway, and as the race came down to the wire the Patterson caravan was surrounded by acres of people in some of the towns where they stopped. In York, he made a speech from a lowboy parked beside the railroad station. "My god, there was two or three acres of people there. Beat anything you ever saw." They were spread out as far as you could see on both sides of the railroad tracks running through the middle of town. Patterson was halfway through his speech when a heavily loaded freight train chugged into town, parting the crowd and drowning out the candidate. He stood on the lowboy and waited until a mile of freight cars and the red caboose cleared the station and moved on down the line. The crowd closed back together and everything got quiet. Suddenly an enthusiastic supporter jumped up and yelled, "I'll bet that engineer's a Wallace man!"[50]

When Rebe Gosdin missed a beat before introducing Patterson at a rally in Tallassee, he was upstaged. An enterprising young student at nearby Auburn University jumped onto the lowboy and introduced "the next governor of Alabama" to his friends and neighbors. That student was Sonny Hornsby, who grew up in Tallassee and was an avid Patterson supporter. He graduated from Auburn, got his law degree from the University of Alabama, and accepted a position with the Patterson administration as assistant superintendent of insurance—launching a distinguished career as lawyer and businessman that thirty years later led to his being elected chief justice of the Alabama Supreme Court.[51]

The *Advertiser's* Bob Ingram described some lighter moments at Scottsboro, where a huge political rally was held in conjunction with the town's "First Monday Trade Day." Upwards of ten thousand people braved the elements—it was miserably cold with fierce winds dropping temperatures to forty-two around noon—to make trades and to hear a half-dozen candidates for governor and other office-seekers appeal for votes and exchange barbs. After gubernatorial candidate Jack Owen spoke, his musical group, the Confederate Colonels, "let go with an old-fashioned hoedown." "The tempo was too much for a sixty-nine-year old Jackson farmer," Ingram wrote. "He leaped up on the rear of the truck and did a buck dance routine which would have made today's rock 'n' rollers look like squares."[52]

State legislator Karl Harrison chided Owen and the other candidates who campaigned with "high-priced" hillbilly bands and gospel singers. "You can't get this singing stuff and noises for free," he declared. "And I didn't want to be obligated in that manner." Ingram reported that Harrison "got a bad break in the middle of his address." "A fire alarm was sounded, sending a siren-screaming fire truck down main street," he wrote. "The siren had its usual effect on literally hundreds of dogs brought there for trading purposes. The hounds howled, the beagles bayed; Harrison was silenced."[53]

Other gubernatorial candidates speaking at the event were George Hawkins, Laurie Battle, Wallace, and Patterson. Battle's hand was bandaged from shaking hands up and down the state. He said he "shook hands with one thousand farmers and one hound dog" during the day-long Scottsboro event.[54] Patterson and Wallace had by far the largest audiences of the day. Patterson stayed on message and ignored barbs thrown at him by Wallace. He recalled that his father had carried Jackson County by a margin of two-to-one in his race for attorney general in 1954, and he hoped to do at least as well. At this point in the race he felt good about his chances, noting that "When the opposition starts attacking you personally, you know you're doing something right."[55]

PATTERSON HAD KNOWN BEFORE entering the governor's race that the strongest competition would come from Faulkner and Wallace. Former governor Persons might have been strong but had suffered a heart attack near the end of his administration and a light stroke kept him out of the running in 1958. Other major contenders (Battle, Harrison, George Hawkins, Owen, Todd) did not have the statewide organization and resources they needed to catch up to the frontrunners. Bringing up the rear were Reverend Billy Walker, W. E. Dodd, John Crommelin, Elebash, Gullatte, and Price. Walker, Dodd, and Elebash were political novices. Price was the clown prince of Alabama politics. Gullatte said he ran "just for the fun of it." Crommelin, a WWII naval air hero and retired admiral who campaigned as a white supremacist and John Bircher looking for Jewish conspirators and Red spies behind every tree, had already lost three times for the U.S. Senate.[56]

A political candidate draws strength from the size and enthusiasm of the crowds who come to hear him. Straw polls and headlines make nice scrapbooks, but can be misleading. In the 1958 race polls nearly always favored the candidate endorsed by the news agency doing the polls or writing the headlines. As Easter came and the campaign entered the final stretch, the pace became near-frenetic as the last-minute voters scurried to make up their minds. The month started with a new poll that had Wallace leading Faulkner and Patterson by 42,000 and 62,000 votes respectively. On the 1st of May, as the race came down to the wire, the *Advertiser*'s ace political columnist Ingram declared that it was a Wallace-Faulkner-Patterson race.[57]

The *Anniston Star* had Wallace ahead, but noted that Patterson had been "coming to the front in a very spectacular way in the last few weeks" and some forecasters believed he would "get in the runoff." Ingram agreed that Patterson had made "considerable strides," but doubted that he had overcome the initial lead of the top two candidates. The candidates pressed so hard during the final week of campaigning that their motorcades didn't even stop for lunch. Ingram reported that Patterson's box lunch "on Highway 24 between Halltown and Belgreen was cold chicken, cold bread, cold drink and cole slaw." In between bites campaigners counted bumper stickers. Ingram noted that en route from Tuscumbia to Cherokee with Patterson's caravan they met thirteen cars with gubernatorial bumper stickers headed in the opposite direction, and not one was for Patterson. Wallace and Faulkner had the most stickers, he said, but one of the automobiles with a Wallace sticker bore a Mississippi license plate.[58]

Ingram wrote in a late April issue of the *Advertiser* that Patterson had "improved tremendously as a campaigner" and it showed in the faces of the huge crowds that came to hear him speak. On an oleander-scented Saturday night, the candidate for the first time brought his caravan of more than two hundred cars to the Capital steps—speaking to a cheering throng estimated by police at seven thousand strong, that covered the Capitol grounds and overflowed into the streets below. "At that one rally he spoke to more people than Faulkner attracted in seven daytime stops in Montgomery earlier in the week," Ingram wrote. A Patterson rally in Selma had "attracted more than twice the number who heard Faulkner in the same auditorium a week earlier."[59]

The *Advertiser* and other pro-Wallace papers refrained from comparing Patterson's drawing power with that of their candidate, even though Wallace's rallies had also drawn huge crowds. Patterson's surge had obviously changed the momentum in the race. Caught off guard, the Wallace camp barely had time to alter its strategy and go on the offensive against Patterson before the polls opened on May 6. Ingram reported in April that Wallace had begun "to fire a few shots in the direction of the attorney general." "One of those shots misfired when Wallace offered to debate any candidate in the race on the issue of law enforcement. This challenge was meant for Patterson, but George Hawkins gummed up the works when he called Wallace's bluff."[60]

The Wallace camp dodged when Hawkins offered to pay half the costs for a thirty-minute television debate. Then Reverend Walker challenged Wallace to debate the "entire segregation" issue with him. There was nothing the two trailing candidates would have liked more than the public exposure of debating the front-runner. Wallace had nothing to gain, however, and let one of his campaign managers claim prior commitments as an excuse not to debate.[61]

Meanwhile, the Patterson camp sensed victory. Clarke Stallworth of the *Birmingham Post-Herald* caught up with the Patterson motorcade in Gadsden in late April and found "a trim, slightly sunburned" candidate dressed in a dark conservative suit and brimming with confidence. "We're on the rise and gaining steadily by the hour," Patterson told Stallworth. "We're going to reach our peak on May 6, and so help me, I think a majority of the people of this state will vote for me and good government."[62]

Stallworth observed little of the "air of desperation" which seemed to pervade other candidates' camps. "His backers weren't yelling about it, but they seemed absolutely convinced they were with the next governor of Alabama." The campaign delegation had been eating lunch between stops and when they finished eating they moved out for the town of Altoona, but not before Patterson shook hands with everyone in the cafe. "We sure need your help," he told them. The candidates eyes sparkled "with enthusiasm."[63]

Stallworth noted that Patterson's strongest appeal was his sincerity—"people apparently believe what Patterson tells them." He observed that after one rally in Etowah County an overalls-clad elderly man, his face leathery from years of wind and sun, came up to Patterson and shook his hand. "You could see he believed in Patterson. In his face was a mixture of hope, confidence and almost reverence. He pumped Patterson's hand and looked him in the face. 'I hope you all the good luck in the world,' he said."[64]

Patterson surprised the experts when he upset Wallace on May 6 by 34,424

votes and led Faulkner by 105,347 votes. The vote count for the top three candidates was Patterson 196,859, Wallace 162,435, and Faulkner 91,512. The other
eleven candidates pulled in 167,656 votes—ranging from a low of 655 for Price
to a high of 59,240 for Todd. The outcome threw Patterson and Wallace into a
June 3 runoff. History favored Patterson. Only three times in Alabama's political past had runoffs selected the Democrats' nominee for governor. Two out of
the three times the candidate who led in the first primary was victorious in the
runoff.[65] The Molton Hotel was jumping the night Patterson won the primary.
He had to slip out the back through the coal chute to keep from being mobbed.
With family and friends, he had watched the election returns on the TV set in a
sixth-floor suite. The hotel staff had worked through the afternoon readying the
ballroom for the star-spangled celebration. "I was very confident, because you
can tell when you're going to win," Patterson said. The early returns from the
Wiregrass had Wallace leading. Then Patterson closed the gap and pulled steadily
ahead as the totals from other counties trickled in. By 9:30 P.M. he was far enough
in the lead that the party faithful knew they were headed for a Patterson-Wallace
runoff with the Barbour bantam trailing by a wide margin.[1]

The refurbished halls of the fashionable Molton hadn't been rocked by such
a gala celebration since the doors opened in 1913. Squad cars had to be called
out to control the jubilant throng converging on the corner of Fifth Avenue and
Twentieth Street with blaring horns and champagne laughter. Amid the rising
excitement Meriwether took a call from the *Birmingham News* asking the winning
candidate to come over to the newsroom for an interview by Fred Taylor. Patterson
said hell no he wasn't going to give the *News* the time of day. The paper had not
only opposed him, but Taylor's pen in particular dripped with acrimony and he
had taken "some cheap shots." Meriwether insisted, saying it was traditional on
election night for the *News* to interview the winner. "You couldn't get through
the mob in the front of the hotel," Patterson said. "So I crawled out through the
coal chute in the basement to go down to the *Birmingham News*."[2]

He figured half the people at the Molton that night had voted for other
candidates. Some, he knew, were blatantly opportunistic and had come down
"to buy tickets after the thing was over" in hopes of lining up lucrative state
business. "I didn't like that one damned bit," he said. A Ford dealer brazenly offered to make him a half-owner in his dealership if the state leased its cars from
him. "The fella actually got mad when I turned him down," Patterson laughed.
"When I said he could put in bids like everyone else, he said, 'Goddamn, I've

heard everything now,' and he got up and stormed out of the hotel."

PATTERSON SAID HE BELIEVED in helping your friends first, as long as it was legal and aboveboard. Meriwether agreed in principle, but reminded him that "we ain't won yet" and "you've got to let these other folks get on board." The tall, affable Tennessean was already on the phone negotiating for the votes of losing candidates. He placed calls to the Wallace camp urging the runner-up to drop out of the race by offering to support him next time and to raise money to help defray his campaign debts. Wallace's own people suggested he might want to concede the nomination since the candidate who led in the primary historically won the runoff anyway. But Wallace was a fighter, and insisted on staying the course.[3]

The May 6 votes for the twelve other candidates totaled 259,168. This was 100,126 votes less than Patterson and Wallace compiled together, but it was a critical bloc of uncommitted voters. Faulkner, whose bloc was the biggest prize, said he had been contacted by both Patterson and Wallace seeking his support in the runoff. The Bay Minette publisher admitted "to being very disappointed" at the outcome. "I knew Patterson had gained some ground. I thought he was taking votes away from Wallace but from the looks of things he was taking them from me." Faulkner planned to be active in the runoff, and a few days later threw his support behind Patterson.[66]

Patterson never warmed to the business of raising campaign funds and making deals with other candidates in return for their support. He left most of these matters in Meriwether's agile hands. While Meriwether failed to get the Wallace camp to concede, he did the next best thing when he quickly sealed a deal for Jimmy Faulkner's help in the runoff. Faulkner had run a well-organized, highly efficient race—"the slickest you ever saw"—and had run up a campaign debt of approximately $45,000." In return for Faulkner's support, Meriwether made a deal to let the defeated candidate raise funds for Patterson and keep the first $45,000 to pay off his own campaign debts. Gaining the backing of Faulkner's "smoothly run organization" not only meant more campaign cash and more votes for Patterson, but kept both out of his opponent's pocket.[4]

In politics, the art of the deal could be a minefield. "Emory Folmar, General Hanna, and the whole Faulkner organization crossed over and campaigned hard for me," Patterson said. "And when the runoff was over we made sure Jimmy got the $45,000 we'd promised him." In November, after the general election, a special agent for the IRS came to see Patterson one day and asked, "Did you give

Jimmy Faulkner $45,000?" "Yes, I did," Patterson said. The agent thanked him and left. He later heard that the IRS charged the $45,000 to Faulkner's personal income tax. "All I had to do was say no, and I would have been charged with a federal crime. They would have been all over me like a swarm of mad hornets and I would have never served out my term."[5]

Patterson and Meriwether accounted for every dollar contributed to his campaign. "You had to watch your back when you took money from some of these high-rollers. They were all looking for a return on their money and often hedged their bets by backing more than one candidate." When the campaign first started a well-known wheeler-dealer from Mobile said he wanted to make a contribution and handed Patterson a paper sack containing $5,000 in small bills. A few days later when Patterson's popularity temporarily dipped in the polls, the contributor came up to him at a rally in nearby Fairhope and said, "John, you understand that $5,000 was just a loan, don't you?" Patterson said no, he thought the money had been a contribution. "Naw, naw, I couldn't afford to do that," the fellow said. "I just loaned it to you. I expect it back."[6]

Later, when his poll numbers were back up, Patterson ran into the man while campaigning in Mobile. "John, you remember me telling you about that $5,000 being a loan?" he said. "Just forget I said that. I didn't mean that. You just keep that money." Patterson told him no, he was going to pay the money back. He was in Mobile after the election and sent for the fellow. "I gave that money back the way he gave it to me, stacks of fives and tens in a paper sack. I paid that S.O.B. back his $5,000, and showed him the door."[7]

Wallace said he too had been offered help by other candidates and their supporters, and he promised "to take the gloves off" against his opponent in the runoff. He came out swinging "with a big television speech" that flailed away at Patterson for being "weak on segregation." Wallace blasted his opponent for not actively supporting university officials in the Autherine Lucy case and for not going to the aid of the city in the Montgomery bus boycott—failing to mention that the attorney general had no jurisdiction in either situation. Wallace emphasized that he would not be drawn into a "smear campaign," but said facts were facts, and they proved that he was the candidate to maintain segregation in Alabama.[67]

For his part, the attorney general "humbly thanked the people of Alabama for giving him the lead in the governor's race." Patterson said he thought voters had favored him because they wanted "good, honest government." "I think there were three issues mainly. In my speeches I promised the people good law enforcement. I promised to maintain segregation of the races, and I said I would plug up the holes in the state treasury. Everywhere I went, people were vitally interested in the third part—about the waste in government." He repeated his long-standing commitment to maintain segregation "by legal methods rather than by approval of force and violence."[68]

Patterson refused to let Wallace bait him into a contest of charges and counter-charges. Adjusting their strategy for the runoff, he and Meriwether decided on a plan to win new supporters across the state without risking his substantial primary lead. The plan, dubbed "hide-and-seek campaigning" by reporters, entailed going back into the small towns throughout Alabama meeting and talking to the people, while making as few scheduled speeches as possible and avoiding face-offs with the opponent at all costs. Patterson thus hoped to control the exposure he got between the primary and the opening of the polls on June 3 for the runoff.[69]

The week after the primary, Patterson set the Wallace camp on its heels when he made an unannounced appearance on Ralph Edwards's nationally televised program, "This is Your Life." Hugh Bentley was the guest of honor on the show, which paid tribute to the pre-cleanup Russell Betterment Association in Phenix City. No mention was made on camera of Patterson's candidacy for governor, but he obviously gained added exposure from the appearance. The Wallace side cried foul and demanded equal time on Alabama television.[70]

In private Wallace grumbled, "I'm running against a man whose father was assassinated. How'm I supposed to follow an act like that?"[71] He lashed out in televised remarks that the attorney general had "the benefit of ten million dollars' worth of free publicity" growing out of the tragic death of his father. Alabama TV stations granted Wallace free time to make up for Patterson's exposure on network television. Then Wallace chided his opponent for leaving the state in the middle of the runoff and going to Los Angeles to appear on the TV show. "Mr. Patterson, with only two weeks of the campaign left, was so confident that he had the election won that he was out in the state of California."[72]

When he flew to Los Angeles, Patterson was unaware that the *Montgomery Advertiser* was about to go to press with a sensational story linking his campaign to Robert Shelton, the rawboned twenty-eight-year-old grand dragon of the Ku Klux Klan in Alabama. The attorney general had been introduced to Shelton as a political supporter, but did not recall anyone saying that he was affiliated with the Klan. Some of the thousands of routine letters mailed by campaign workers in Birmingham soliciting votes under the candidate's signature had mentioned Shelton as "a mutual friend." The Klansman, who had a big "Patterson for Governor" sign on his lawn in Northport, across the river from Tuscaloosa, was spotted hanging around the campaign headquarters at the Molton Hotel, but not in the candidate's company.[73]

While Patterson was a guest at a cocktail party hosted by Ralph Edwards after the TV program aired, a reporter with the *Los Angeles Times* called and asked for a comment on the Klan's connection to his campaign for governor. That was the first Patterson had heard about a story that would appear in the next day's *Advertiser* exposing a political alliance between his campaign and the KKK grand dragon. "This is amazing," Patterson replied. "I am not a member of the Ku Klux Klan. I have never been a member. I don't know anyone named Shelton."[74]

Patterson had to retract his denial upon returning home and being reminded by the staff that Shelton was a supporter from Tuscaloosa whom he had met during the course of the campaign. He then issued a retraction, but still maintained that he knew nothing of the man's affiliation with the Klan. Asked to denounce the Klan's support, Patterson responded cautiously, "If any person in Alabama is a member of any organization and believes in John Patterson, what he stands for, and good government, I solicit his vote."[75]

The Klan represented only a few thousand votes, which the Patterson camp estimated were split between the two candidates. The greater concern was whom the White Citizens' Council members supported. Neither the Klan nor the White Citizens' Council organizations comprised a solid voting bloc. There were five Klan groups in Alabama, and the citizens' councils were divided as well. Sam Engelhardt, state senator from Macon County who resigned as executive secretary of the Alabama Association of Citizens' Councils to make a losing bid for lieutenant governor in the first primary, supported Patterson in the runoff. A virulent group of council members in north Alabama was led by Birmingham-based Asa Carter, a violent anti-Semite and Klansman who was a Wallace supporter and later became his speechwriter.[76]

Wallace harped on the alleged Klan-Patterson alliance in his speeches until his camp became concerned the attack was backfiring. He charged the attorney general was "rolling with the new wave of the Ku Klux Klan and its terrible tradition of lawlessness," and warned there would be a revival of the Klan if Patterson were elected governor. The Patterson side, unwilling to risk any votes at this stage of the campaign, refused to answer the charges. Wallace's friend Grover Hall wrote that Patterson neither defended himself nor recoiled from the attack. "It was Wallace who recoiled." He had lost ground since the story broke. Hall believed the man on the street either had new-found empathy for the Klan because of the racial turmoil or viewed Wallace's attack as a smear tactic against his opponent.[77]

Perhaps the worst damage the Klan story caused was to distort the future governor's image under the national spotlight. The week before the votes were cast in the Alabama runoff, *Time* magazine featured the story and exaggerated the Klan's support for Patterson. By the time the story reached syndicated muckraker Drew Pearson's column, it had become a journalistic pretzel with the truth twisted and torn. Pearson's column egregiously portrayed KKK grand dragon Shelton as Patterson's "lifelong friend," and warned that a Patterson victory would mean "a Klan revival throughout the South."[78]

Wallace, meanwhile, was frustrated by his failure to goad Patterson into a heated exchange. That frustration was reflected by editor Hall who wrote, "Patterson is now so serenely confident of victory Tuesday that he is doing an unprecedented thing—circulating over the state shaking hands but refusing to make a speech." Patterson was not going to let his opponent dictate the pace of the campaign and saw nothing to gain by talking to reporters. Except for the *Birmingham Post-Herald* and the *Dothan Eagle*, the large dailies in Alabama had endorsed Wallace, and their coverage was slanted in his favor. So Patterson kept the opposition off-balance by ducking reporters and avoiding a head-on collision with his opponent. Accompanied by Joe Robertson he spent the two weeks before the votes were cast on June 3 taking walking tours of the small towns around Alabama and talking to voters about their problems and asking for their support.[79]

To flustered reporters Patterson became a will-o'-the-wisp, popping up anywhere and everywhere around the countryside and never being where he was expected to be. Ingram ran across him by chance in Clanton, the hometown of Patterson's wife, on a day his headquarters said he would be in another county. Ingram and a reporter were headed to the other location when they stopped in Clanton for a cup of coffee. Patterson did move into the other county late in the afternoon, but only after touring three other small towns along the way. That was the pace the candidate set for the next two weeks, until he had taken a walking tour through virtually every county in Alabama.[80]

The attorney general was reported to be "a confident, smiling candidate as he went from store to store at every crossroads" talking to folks and asking them to vote for him on June 3. "I am meeting thousands of people," he said. "This is a good way to contact the people." A supporter in Clanton advised Patterson "not to accept any of the challenges being hurled at him by Wallace." "What do you think I should do?" Patterson asked. "Just ignore him," the supporter urged.

Wallace himself had no illusions about how the election was going. Two days before voters went to the polls, his friend Hall noted with a gray sigh of finality "the betting is that Patterson will be Alabama's forty-seventh governor." Wallace had known his campaign was in trouble when he gambled on making an issue of the Klan's support for Patterson, and he knew as soon as the returns started trickling in on the evening of June 3 that he had failed to cut into his opponent's lead. Said to be inconsolable, a dejected Wallace refused to concede the race when he went before the television cameras with his wife and children. He later congratulated Patterson in a midnight telegram from Montgomery "offering his wholehearted support for a better Alabama." Hall and other friends had ridden with Wallace from the TV station to the Greystone Hotel where he went inside and greeted supporters with the caustic slur, "Well, boys, no other son-of-a-bitch will ever outnigguh me again."[82]

THIRTY-SIX YEAR OLD JOHN Patterson made history on June 3, 1958, when he swept to victory by almost 65,000 votes. The official count was 315,353 votes for Patterson to 250,451 for Wallace. The surprisingly heavy turnout of more than a half million voters set a new runoff record for gubernatorial elections in the state.[83] Patterson still had to face Birmingham Republican William L. Longshore, Jr., in the November general election, but that was a formality. The Democratic Party had dominated politics in Alabama for more than eighty years, and it would be another three decades before the Republicans could break that hold.[84]

Other losers in the governor's race were the state's large daily newspapers— proving once again that even those who can't gulp down their first cup of coffee without the morning paper don't want someone else telling them how to vote. Alabama's fourth estate, for the most part, was gracious in defeat. An exception was Grover Hall who penned a grudging editorial conceding "the razzing" he was taking because Patterson won. Hall found some redemption in having been one of "those lying newspapers" Jim Folsom had bashed during his campaign four years earlier. Look at Big Jim now, Hall seemed to be saying in a smug way.

In his obtuse piece, Hall conceded that Patterson's victory (like Folsom's) was "on the scale of mandate," and that he "enters the next phase of his dazzling career with many assets." "He is young, strong and evidently quite decisive," the unrepentant Hall wrote. "He has a stiff neck, but he also has a stiff back." What the editorial did not say was that if the new governor stumbled, Hall would be there to write the obituary, not to pick him up.[85]

Veteran *Birmingham News* staffer Ed Strickland (who had discovered the vote tally change in Albert Patterson's race in 1954) painted a more admiring portrait of the young governor-nominee. He described Patterson as "quiet, soft-spoken and handsome." "Steely eyes peer sharply from under heavy brows," the reporter wrote. "His hair is receding, his smile quick and his handshake firm." He had found Patterson to have "a shrewd mind and quick wit," but could be "easily underrated at first acquaintance" and had a stubborn streak. "He is not a man who dominates a crowd," Strickland observed. "He speaks sparingly but makes his presence felt."[86]

Acerbic *News* reporter Hugh Sparrow, after interviewing the winning candidate, reported that many troublesome problems faced the next governor and "no one realizes it more than Atty. Gen. John Patterson himself." He observed that "Patterson apparently wears his new laurels gracefully." "Although he has just won a fight for high stakes which could turn the heads of less balanced fellows, he does not appear to have been changed in the least. All of which could mean well concerning a good state administration."[87]

Perhaps the most revealing comments came from the man whom Patterson had oratorically kicked "from one end of the state to the other in his race for governor." Jim Folsom had not taken the attorney general's political attacks on his administration personally, and when finally breaking his silence on the governor's race he told the press he wasn't surprised at Patterson's victory. "He ran the same kind of campaign I did," Folsom said. "He went to the branchheads, talked about old-age pensions and had a string band." Folsom wished Patterson well and predicted that he would "make a good governor."[88]

12

Sweeter Than Muscadine Wine

On the night he won the runoff the celebration at the Molton Hotel was another gala affair and "sweeter than muscadine wine." A *Columbus Ledger* reporter, who was in Patterson's suite when the returns carried him over the top, wrote, "Below on the fifth floor hundreds of followers from every county in the state had also gathered to celebrate the victory they felt was certain." Their candidate had pulled it out—he had defied the powerful machines and won the nomination.[27]

Winning had put the youthful governor-nominee in a relaxed mood—a flash of anger crossing his face only once, when *Time, Life,* and *Look* reporters and photographers attempted to crash the victory party. "Patterson didn't want them in and he said so," the hometown journalist reported. "He was understandably perturbed at a particularly vicious article which *Time* magazine had run last week in which it stated that election of Patterson would mean a return of the Ku Klux Klan to power in Alabama." Earlier that evening a writer for *Look* had cornered the candidate's younger brother Jack and badgered him about the Klan story. The newshounds were disappointed when they found no klansmen at the celebration.[28]

Alabama's newsrooms had concluded that the Klan story was politically contrived, had been overblown, and was more problematic for the opposition than it had been for Patterson. The people had spoken and local post-election coverage focused on the caliber of the man, his campaign promises, and what kind of governor he would make. The *Birmingham News* "bent over backwards" in its coverage. "Patterson told a television audience that while the runoff campaign had been bitter, he would enter the governor's office holding no grudges. He called upon the people of the state to join him in what he said would be an administration of good, honest government for the state, and one devoted to the state's welfare."[29]

The *News* conceded that Patterson had concentrated his campaign on the major issues and vowed to keep the promises he made to voters. The campaign had been grueling, but the nominee "skipped a summer vacation" so he could concentrate on wrapping up the affairs of the attorney general's office while preparing to take over the reins as governor. "Although the attorney general at times was critical of newspapers which opposed him during the campaign, and declined to hold news conferences during the later stages of the runoff, he promised an open-door policy during his administration."[30] "Everything will be open and above board," Patterson said. "I will have nothing to hide from the press."

Two main concerns before taking office were to choose the leaders he wanted to work with in the legislature and to put together an administration that would best serve the people of Alabama. He believed that a few self-serving department heads within the Folsom administration had betrayed their trust to the governor personally and to the state, and he did not want that mistake repeated during his term. He was determined "to surround himself with competent advisers and department heads and give the people a clean and honest administration."[31]

Patterson unveiled his four-year plan at a NewSite homecoming and in speeches around the state. The homecoming was attended by an estimated five thousand people. W. D. "Billy" Vickers, a local businessman and family friend, chaired the homecoming committee, with Albert Barnes serving as co-chairman. W. B. Sowell of Alexander City was coordinator. At a later meeting of Alabama's county commissioners in Mobile, Patterson repeated his promise to give the state "decent, honest government" and "mighty good times in Alabama in the next few years." He told reporters he would announce all his major appointments before the November general election. He was opposed in the November general election by Republican William L. Longshore, a Birmingham attorney, but no Republican had won statewide office in Alabama since Reconstruction.[32]

Patterson said he expected to move ahead with developing Alabama's highway system and doubling old-age pensions without having to raise taxes. Folsom had had a progressive highway program, including the start of the interstate system in Alabama. With the federal government providing 90 percent matching funds to the state's 10 percent, the interstate project was the linchpin in Patterson's program. "Of course that meant a lot of money coming into Alabama, and that primed the economic pump too," Patterson said. He intended "to pick up on that thing and travel with it."[33]

With Folsom's cooperation he was able to move forward on the highway program before taking office. In early January he called a special session of the legislature to float a bond issue for highways and bridges. "We got a $60 million bond issue passed very quickly to continue the highway program. When we took all the tax money earmarked for roads, took the bond money and maximized the federal matching funds that went along with it, we had a half-billion-dollar road program."[34]

The highway program, the improved management of the state docks and the expansion of airfields across the state were incentives for bringing more industrial development into Alabama. Patterson said he would also mount "a concerted effort to bring about some form of reapportionment of the legislature on a population basis." Working with the legislature he expected "to get a lot accomplished for the betterment of Alabama."[35]

Education was another centerpiece of Patterson's program. He was determined to raise standards, to raise teachers' salaries comparable to other Southeastern states, and to provide state aid (through a $100 million bond issue) in building new classrooms." He later called the state's first special session of the legislature for education and raised revenues by lifting the exemptions off sales tax and off heavy machinery. "Anyway you look at it, that's raising taxes on somebody," he said.

Sticking his neck out for the educators didn't endear him to them when he was forced to order a proration of the funds. Proration was necessary because a hundred-day steel strike and the Eisenhower recession had cut into revenues from the new measures. "It hurt me politically. The education folks got three quarters of a loaf, but when they didn't get the whole loaf they jumped on me and gave me hell. Anyway, we did have a fine education program, and it helped a lot of people and did a lot of fine things."[36]

Patterson flew to Washington in July to confer in closed session with Alabama's two senators and nine congressmen about his program and the problems that his administration would face. Senator John Sparkman hosted the luncheon, which was restricted to the Patterson party of four and the Alabama congressional delegation, so they could "discuss freely" matters of importance to their state. Patterson said the purpose of the trip was to establish "close liaison between Montgomery and Washington" to benefit the people of Alabama.[37] This spirit of unity would guide the administration's approach to dealing with state business following the inaugural in January.

The question on everyone's mind was what lay in store for their state with respect to federally ordered integration of the public schools. As governor, he intended to honor the commitment he had made during the campaign to uphold the state's segregation laws. He placed the blame for racial trouble on "interference from the federal government" and "a handful of racial agitators," and pledged to continue his fight in the courts to keep them out of Alabama. "The people of Alabama must work together to solve our race problems," he said.[38]

An Alabama statute enacted in 1957 empowered local school boards to close any school threatened with integration. The statute also provided for the transfer of school property to private individuals, and for the use of tax funds to pay tuition to private schools. The statute survived its first court test before a three-judge federal panel but was on appeal. Patterson proposed a stiffer law patterned after legislation in Virginia, which would cut off state funds to any integrated school and close automatically any school where federal troops were sent to enforce integration.[39]

Speaking to community leaders at Huntsville's Russell-Erskine Hotel, he "renewed his request for strengthening state laws to close the schools automatically in face of federal integration efforts." Lieutenant Governor-nominee Albert Boutwell also assured the audience that he would help carry out the program outlined by Patterson. The *Birmingham News* reported that Patterson "was applauded repeatedly, particularly when he stressed he would help make certain school segregation is maintained."[40]

Patterson watched developments in the Arkansas and Virginia school integration cases closely to see what Alabama could learn from their experience. It had become apparent that Arkansas and Virginia were to serve as the federal government's test cases. A decision by Federal Judge Harry J. Lemley to postpone integration at Central High School in Little Rock for two and one-half years showed "a consideration for peace and order in the school" and an awareness that more time and understanding was needed to lay the groundwork for integrating public schools in the South.[41]

Judge Lemley's reprieve was shortlived, however, when the U.S. Supreme Court overturned his ruling and ordered immediate integration of Little Rock's Central High School. Patterson issued a statement condemning the high court's decree, stating that it would "increase strife and turmoil between the races" and would "destroy our public school system in areas where it is enforced." "I want it clearly understood that we are going to maintain segregation of the races in the public schools of Alabama," he added. Newsmen reported that Governor Folsom was not available for comment.[42]

Senator Sparkman called the reversal "tragic," pointing out that the Supreme

Court had done an about-face on its 1954 integration decree which contained a provision that "the matter of putting the ruling into effect would be left up to the district court." The reversal showed intent "on the part of the court of ramming this thing on through." "The Supreme Court ought to soon know that the people of the South are determined to set their way of life, even at the cost of closing schools," he warned.[43]

The Little Rock crisis stirred strong passions in Alabama. Newspapers across the state described the foreboding that the crisis had cast over the state's white majority. The *Mobile Press Register* warned that "the ordeal faced by the people of Arkansas today may come to Alabama tomorrow." Patterson, as incoming governor, would then become the front line of defense "against flagrant sabotaging of state sovereignty" just as Arkansas Governor Orval Faubus was today. "All Alabamians are hopeful that no Little Rocks occur within the confines of their state. But they cannot be blamed for feelings of apprehension when they look at the record of impatience shown by the integrationists."[44]

BY LATE SUMMER PATTERSON had announced most of his cabinet appointments. "Filling key positions with the right people was not easy because I had a lot of people who wanted jobs. You want people who will be a credit to you. By and large I was pretty successful. If you are right half the time in judging people, you are lucky. I thought we had a much better record than that."[45]

Some cabinet selections fell into place more readily than others. Meriwether's executive experience and his masterful job managing the state campaign made him a natural choice as finance director for the new administration. Because of his brother's business acumen and his effective work in the campaign, the governor-nominee had already decided on having Maurice Patterson serve as assistant finance director. Roy Macarto, who put together the TV advertising for the campaign, was named state publicity director. Not unexpected was the appointment of Joe Robertson as the incoming governor's executive secretary. Robertson had been at Patterson's side since the Phenix City tragedy, and had served as executive assistant in the attorney general's department.[46]

Patterson's appointment of Floyd Mann to be his director of public safety was another coup. The Patterson and Mann families had been close for years in Tallapoosa County. John and Floyd had gone to grammar school together in Alex City, and had been friends since. After serving with the Army Air Corps in WWII Floyd had joined the police force in Alex City, and then served eight years as the police chief in Opelika. Patterson knew there was no better man anywhere to put in charge of public safety. "Floyd was rock solid, unflappable and absolutely fearless," Patterson said. "Excelled in everything he did. Wasn't no doubt in my mind, he'd make Alabama proud."[47]

Patterson's opponents had attacked his pledge to raise the old-age pension from $30 to $75 as "pie-in-the-sky" campaign rhetoric, but he was determined to keep his promise. Responsibility for attaining this goal fell to the commissioner of the Department of Pensions and Securities, who oversaw a budget in excess of $100 million. Patterson surprised many old timers when he named twenty-nine-year-old Alvin Prestwood to be the new commissioner. Prestwood, who received a battlefield commission in the Korean War, had impressed Patterson with his mature judgment and managerial skills while serving as an assistant attorney general. "Nobody was more dedicated or more capable, or had the interest of the people of Alabama at heart more than Alvin," Patterson said. "He would get the job done."[48]

Another appointee with great promise was press secretary Harry Cook, who had covered the Phenix City story as a young reporter for the *Birmingham News*. Cook then joined the staff of Birmingham's Congressman George Huddleston in Washington before returning to Alabama in 1958. Patterson remembered Cook from the university when he was editor of the campus newspaper. He referred to Cook as the intellectual in his administration, and Bob Ingram later dubbed him "Patterson's Pierre Salinger."[49]

The youngest person on the staff was the state photographer, Daniel "Tommy" Giles, who turned twenty a few days after the inaugural in January 1959. The talented Giles had caught the eye of Patterson and Joe Robertson when he worked on assignments for the *Montgomery Advertiser* and the attorney general's office. Among older cabinet appointees was former state legislator Sam Engelhardt, who accepted the highway director's post. "Sam had some engineering experience. He knew a lot of the probate judges and county officials. He was an ideal fellow for highway director and did a fine job there."[50]

Investigations of the Folsom administration while Patterson was attorney general had found no evidence of corruption being widespread, as alleged, but did uncover isolated abuse such as the Gulf Park case and pockets of mismanagement where loose practices and neglect of state property were rampant. Two agencies causing the most concern were the state docks and the conservation department. Patterson began a search to find the best managers available to straighten out the two agencies. "The state docks in Mobile were the ninth port in the country in tonnage. Big business down there. Had their own railroad. Also had some big problems. Folsom's people hadn't run the docks very well."[51]

Problems at the docks ranged from shakedowns of commercial vessels by stevedores and dock workers to losses of more than $77,000 in state revenue during the first five months of 1958. A group of Mobile businessmen who had an interest in the docks convinced the incoming governor that Earl M. McGowin of Chapman was the man he needed to head the troubled organization. Patterson didn't need a lot of convincing—his wife Mary Joe was a McGowin and Earl had supported him for governor—but the busy lumber company executive did.

McGowin was one of Alabama's distinguished citizens. In 1905 Earl's father, J. Greeley McGowin, had joined with his brothers and a brother-in-law in purchasing the W. T. Smith Lumber Company (where a teenage John Patterson took shelter from a storm while hoboing with a friend decades later) in Chapman, Alabama. When Earl returned from England in 1925, after attending Pembroke College at Oxford University as a Rhodes scholar, he joined his brothers Floyd and Julian as the second-generation managers of the lumber company. Julian later left the company, while Earl and Floyd stayed and presided over its growth into the largest lumber processor east of the Mississippi.

Earl had forged a remarkable second career in public service. He served twenty years in the state legislature as a representative from Butler County, and four years as conservation director (1951–55) in the Persons administration. During WWII he volunteered as an officer with the U.S. Navy, charged with supervising lumber procurement in Memphis and New Orleans.

McGowin had retired from public life and was devoting full-time to the family business. "So I went to see Earl," Patterson said. "He didn't want to do it. So I had to talk him into it. He finally agreed to take over the docks, and that took care of one of my biggest headaches as governor."[52]

Patterson thought he had the right person to head the conservation department when he appointed Atmore's influential Claude D. Kelley to be director, but quickly changed his mind when Kelley spent more time touring the country in his private role as president of the National Wildlife Federation than he did at home taking care of state business. When Kelley came on board Patterson had given him a list of problems that needed his immediate attention. He was told that he had "a blank check," and "to get the job done without delay." A month went by and a legislator from Mobile called on the governor: "John there hasn't been a goddamn thing done. Just like the day you was inaugurated."

"I can't believe that."

"It's true."

Patterson sent Willie Painter (the resourceful investigator in his father's murder case) to check out the legislator's complaint, and he came back with photographs revealing that nothing had been done to correct the problems. The governor sent for the conservation director, but he had flown out to California on private business having nothing to do with the state of Alabama. Calling Joe Robertson into his office Patterson said, "Joe, Claude Kelley's not our man. Go over there and bring me some of his letterhead stationery."

Patterson then dictated a letter of resignation: "Joe, when Mr. Kelley gets back from California, have him sign this and bring it back to me."

"Joe handled that thing to perfection," Patterson recalled. "Claude Kelley disappeared. I got Bill [William C.] Younger who I'd known for a long time to take the job." Younger had little "active background" in conservation, but was a first-rate manager. After completing law school at the University of Alabama, he served as an assistant attorney general under Patterson who knew he would make a first-rate director of the conservation department. "Bill was just what the doctor ordered," the governor said, "and he got that place cleaned up straightaway."[53]

Another agency of high interest was the Alabama Alcoholic Beverage Control Board. The governor-elect named Morgan Reynolds (whose wife Barbara was a sister of the new first lady) of Clanton as chairman of the board. He filled the other two positions on the board with businessmen Charles Enslen of Birmingham and J. C. McDowell of Piedmont. The board, at his request, appointed Edward J. Azar of Montgomery to serve as ABC administrator (the executive overseeing beverage control operations in the state) and W. D. "Billy" Vickers as the assistant administrator.[54]

In his mid-thirties, Ed Azar was a native Montgomerian and had been a member of the law firm of Azar and Campbell for the past decade. He had headed Patterson's campaign in Montgomery County, and agreed to serve as general chairman of the inaugural committee. Vickers, a prominent New Site businessman and civic leader, was a former president of the Tallapoosa County Board of Education.[55]

Among other key appointments, Patterson selected Gunterville's Ralph Smith, a former classmate and trusted friend, to be his legal adviser. Birmingham real estate executive and National Guard Colonel Henry V. Graham was picked for the adjutant general's post and promoted to major general. Prominent Montgomery banker John C. Curry, who was Alabama's first commissioner of revenue when the post was created by former Governor Frank Dixon, was picked to head the state banking department. Rounding out the cabinet were Ralph R. Williams, industrial relations director; Harry H. Haden, revenue commissioner; Joe S. Foster, civil defense director; Olin Brooks, labor commissioner; Leland Jones, industrial development director; and Edmon L. (Ted) Rinehart, insurance commissioner.

Few Patterson appointments raised more eyebrows than "the transplanted yankee" he put in charge of the insurance department. Not only was Ted Rinehart a close confidant of the governor, but their families had been friends since serving together in Europe at the start of the fifties. Bob Ingram interviewed Rinehart and devoted a full column in the *Advertiser* to introducing "the brash yankee" to the public. Ingram assured readers there was more to the "converted Rebel" and WWII prisoner of war than the stuffed-shirt image an alumnus of Princeton University and Harvard Law School might project to his new neighbors.

At his acerbic best, Ingram pointed out that Rinehart, despite "brisk, blunt and brash" mannerisms Southerners normally associated with yankees, had come from "some of the very best Southern stock." Rinehart's paternal great-grandfather served in the Army of Virginia under General Robert E. Lee. His mother's family had settled in Alabama, and she was born in Mobile. Besides, Rinehart's legal work on the NAACP case was living proof that not all yankees practiced what they preached when it came to racial integration. Ingram wrote that Rinehart, when the interview was over, had "fastened the top two buttons of his Ivy League suit, hiked up his Ivy League breeches and departed for a lunch of corn pone and blackeyed peas."[56]

PATTERSON KNEW THAT HE had to have the support of state legislators to realize the ambitious program he had projected for the next four years. Soon after winning the June runoff, he began lining up support to get an early start on the program when he took office in January. "One of the most important things a governor does is work with the legislature. It's not written down anywhere, but the governor is charged with the responsibility of coming up with a program for his four years in office and for presenting that program to the legislature, getting it passed and getting a budget to support the program."

Patterson said he was fortunate to have friends in the legislature he had known for years and who had supported both him and his father in their campaigns for public office. This was particularly true of the House, where he had close working relations with lawmakers such as Homer Cornett and Joe Smith of Phenix City, Charles Adams of Tallapoosa County, Virgis Ashworth of Bibb County, Pat Boyd of Troy, Bo Torbert of Opelika, and Kenneth Ingram from Clay County, and a host of others including McDowell Lee and Pete Turnham. Patterson endorsed Adams for speaker of the House and recommended Ashworth for House speaker pro tem. As chairman of the Ways and Means Committee, Smith was the second-ranking man in the House.[57]

In the Senate he named Vaughn Hill Robison of Montgomery as floor leader and president pro tem. Senators Ryan deGraffenried of Tuscaloosa, Bob Kendall of Conecuh County, and others helped push his program. He started meeting with members of the legislature to see what they wanted and how they could help each other. There was as much give as take in the relationship.

He recalled a particular meeting with Robison, deGraffenried, and Kendall where their counsel kept him from getting off on the wrong foot in the governor's office. Just before the inaugural, word got around that he might terminate the jobs of all employees in the governor's office and bring in his own people. The three senators came to see him, and Robison said, "Now, John, you've asked us to head up your program and to work with you in the Senate. We're going to do that, but there's something we want you to do for us. You're going to keep Miss Mabel Amos and Miss Kate Simmons in your office, aren't you?"

"Tell you what I'll do, Vaughn Hill," Patterson said. "I'll give them every consideration."

"Naw, that won't do. They stay or your program's in trouble."

"Well, since you put it like that, they stay."

He gave the matter some thought when the meeting broke up, and was glad that the senators had come to see him about keeping Miss Mabel and Miss Kate. He thought back to the time in Folsom's first term when his father was in the Senate and had taken him over to the governor's office. A friend had given him a ride down from the university so he could drive home with his father for the weekend. Even then Miss Mabel and Miss Kate cast a spell over the governor's office. "For a college student like me, they really made me feel important. I never forgot that."

The more he thought about it, the more he realized that "a man would've been a damned fool to let them go from the governor's office." Half a century later he would reminisce: "Miss Kate and Miss Mabel, they knew how to do it. They knew all the players. They looked after me. Kept me out of trouble. You walked into the governor's office in those days, you thought you were really somebody. They made you feel important. It was a wonderful feeling."[58]

THE CHAIN OF EVENTS leading toward the inaugural in January was interrupted by an announcement that the new U.S. Civil Rights Commission had ordered an investigation into charges of discrimination against African American voters in Alabama, Florida, and Mississippi. The probe was a first test of the powers of the commission created by the federal civil rights law enacted the previous year. Advocates had lobbied for broader civil rights legislation, but settled for a compromise bill limited essentially to the protection of voting rights to appease filibustering Southern senators.[59]

Complaints of voter discrimination in a handful of Alabama counties were under review, but the federal probe spotlighted Macon County where famed Tuskegee Institute was located. Professor and civil rights activist C. G. Gomillion, president of the Tuskegee Civic Association, acknowledged to reporters that he had filed complaints with federal authorities for the past ten years about voter discrimination in Macon County. In the years before the civil rights commission was formed, Gomillion had complained directly to the U.S. Justice Department. He had bypassed local grievance channels because history had taught him not to expect favorable resolution of African-American grievances without federal intervention.[60]

At the heart of Gomillion's complaints about voter discrimination was the fact that twice as many white residents as blacks were registered to vote in Macon County, though blacks outnumbered whites nearly six to one. Of a population of 27,000 African Americans, only 1,070 were on the voting register, while there were 2,100 registered white voters out of a population under 5,000. This disparity in voter registration existed in other counties. Montgomery County, for instance, had 89,000 white and 62,000 black residents with approximately 27,000 whites and 2,300 blacks registered to vote.[61]

The gerrymandering act passed by the state legislature in 1957 exacerbated the grievances of Macon County black citizens by redrawing the municipal boundaries of Tuskegee so that predominantly black residential areas were placed outside the city limits. Of 420 African Americans who resided in Tuskegee prior to the gerrymandering legislation, only 10 were eligible to vote in city elections after the new boundaries were imposed. The 600 white voters in Tuskegee were unaffected by the change.[62]

When officials in Macon and other counties refused to give federal agents access to their voter registration records, the civil rights commission scheduled a hearing in Montgomery for December 8, only six weeks before Patterson was to be sworn into office. The commission revealed that six counties were under investigation—Macon, Bullock, Barbour, Lowndes, Dallas, and Wilcox. Fourteen white officials were subpoenaed from the six counties and were ordered to appear with their voter registration records.[63]

The commission ran into a wall of resistance by state and county officials, and abruptly ended the hearing after only two days of testimony. Governor-elect Patterson, leading the resistance, charged that the commission "had unlawfully invaded the rights of county officials and had violated the U.S. Constitution." He stated that Alabama officials could not "legally and conscientiously comply with commission subpoenas and orders." "In fights of this nature there can be no surrender of principle to expediency," he declared. "The time for retreating has come to an end."[64]

Six public officials refused to testify about voter registration procedures on the first day of the hearing, and five declined even to be sworn as witnesses. Their resistance kept the commission from seeing voter registration records in any of the six counties where the files had been subpoenaed. The records had been taken over by state courts or state officials. Probate Judge William Varner brought in voting records from Macon County, but they contained no information about prospective voters who had been turned down. Circuit Judge George Wallace defiantly refused to appear at the hearings and ordered the voting records impounded in Barbour and Bullock counties, which were in his jurisdiction.[65]

Testimony by African American witnesses revealed that discrimination in Macon County was worse than previously reported. Only 1,110 African Americans were registered to vote out of a population of approximately 27,000 black residents, according to witnesses. This compared to just over 3,000 registered white voters out of a population estimated at between 4,000 and 5,000. Other witnesses testified that no black voters were registered in Lowndes County, and that none had attempted to register in recent years because of "economic pressure." Without the voter registration files, the commission was unable to confirm witnesses' complaints.[66]

Commission chairman Dr. John A. Hannah, president of Michigan State

University, abruptly closed the hearing with a dramatic announcement that the Justice Department had been asked "to seek a federal court order against registration officials who refused to testify or surrender voter records." The 1957 act empowered the attorney general "to seek court orders when necessary to compel witnesses to testify or to have records brought before the fact-finding body." Anyone refusing to comply would be held in contempt of court. Attorney General William P. Rogers said he would have a U.S. attorney in Montgomery take the matter before the district court.[67]

Former Virginia Governor John S. Battle, the only avowed segregationist on the commission, made a futile plea that state officials "cooperate a little more." The tall, white-haired Virginian and another commission member, former Florida Governor Doyle Carlton, expressed concern that the lack of cooperation would lead to stronger civil rights legislation. Ernest Wilkins, former assistant secretary of labor and the only African American on the commission, said that actions by white officials gave the impression they had something to hide.[68]

Attorney General Patterson issued a statement clarifying the state's position in the matter. He contended that registering and determining the qualifications of voters was left to the states under the U.S. Constitution, and that circuit courts and boards of registrars were judicial officers carrying out those responsibilities under the state's constitution and laws. Under the separation of powers guaranteed by the Constitution, he maintained that an agency of the legislative branch of the government such as the civil rights commission had no more right to interfere with state courts and judicial officers than they would to subpoena members of the Supreme Court of the United States.[69]

Given their past unreliability, Patterson didn't put much stock in the FBI or the Justice Department doing the right thing in the state's standoff with the federal government. He recalled the disappointing reception from the Justice Department when he went to Washington seeking help with the investigation into his father's murder. Earlier, when his father and the Russell Betterment Association initiated impeachment proceedings against Sheriff Matthews, a federal agent and the U.S. Attorney for the Middle District of Alabama took the witness stand and blatantly lied to help save the corrupt sheriff's job. Those experiences didn't instill much confidence in what he could expect from the federal authorities.

He found it ironic that Attorney General Rogers, who had recently published a lengthy article in the *American Bar Association Journal* on the separation of powers doctrine to justify why he denied Congress access to records in his department, now sought to enforce the legislative branch's encroachment on the state's judicial authority. History had once more recorded that everything rests "on whose ox is being gored." Patterson contended that the registrars had carried out their duties "in a legal and constitutional manner" and had treated all citizens of the state "equally and impartially."[70]

Alabama's editors, with few exceptions, supported the governor-elect's stand on the voting rights issue. Even the *Montgomery Advertiser*, whose editor went after Patterson tooth-and-nail in the campaign, found "that our Attorney General is on sound ground in resisting the Commission's action toward our state judiciary as illegal" and "in defending the right of a state to decide who is qualified to vote and who is not." The *Advertiser* denounced Battle's patriarchal "voice of surrender," although "plausible on its face," as having been "a great disappointment to defenders of segregation." Based on the experience of the past four years with school integration, the paper reasoned: . . . whatever we do in Alabama is still going to be unpleasantly debated, reported and misrepresented in the North, primarily for the reason that up North politicians consider it good politics to abuse the South."[71]

The *Mobile Press*, while defending both the right of African-Americans to vote and the doctrine of interposition to preserve "the rights, the honor and dignity of the sovereign state of Alabama," applauded the governor-elect for sounding the rallying cry of "no retreat." "The task at hand is to get big government off the neck of Alabama," the paper declared, "then to proceed from there with our own state program to give Negroes the privileges to which they are entitled."[72]

In later years, a retrospective John Patterson, who took a lot of abuse from the Northern press for his defense of Alabama's laws and state sovereignty, regretted that he had not done more to secure the voting rights of Alabama's black citizens. His father had lived and died by a set of principles that embodied civic duty and responsibility, and valued the ballot box as the bedrock of freedom in our nation to be kept safe at all cost. Without voting rights, the road to equality for African Americans would have been more tortuous and more cluttered with Jim Crow roadblocks and other debris. The long, drawn-out journey, without the engine of the civil rights movement and the federal courts, would have sputtered and died to the misery and the detriment of all.

During the unfolding voting rights drama, which extended past the early weeks of the Patterson administration, Circuit Judge Wallace's actions rekindled some of the rivalry of the Democratic primary. Wallace's refusal to appear at the federal hearing was clearly designed to upstage other subpoenaed witnesses and the attorney general. Both Patterson and Wallace threatened to jail any federal agent attempting to seize registration records. Wallace had boasted during the campaign that he would "refuse to go to jail" if the feds came after him. In the December standoff he came close to having to make good on that boast.

Wallace's defiance was setting the stage for his next run at the governor's office four years down the road. Wallace said he didn't think the civil rights commission could jail him for ignoring its subpoena, but he was prepared for it anyhow. "I don't care who they call in. They can call in the Justice Department or airborne troops as far as I'm concerned. I'm going to test any move they make in the courts of the land." The newspapers loved the "grandstanding," as did their readers. When Wallace opened an anonymous gift that came in the mail, inside the box was a necktie with a hacksaw blade sewn inside.[73]

It was said in jest that lawyers who tried cases in Judge Wallace's court were silently pulling for the feds to win. They liked Wallace, but hated having him on the bench because "he wouldn't tend to business." A lifelong friend said, "He would not rule on cases before him. He just wouldn't do it. He wanted to politic." Once after he'd been on the bench for about a year, friends asked him, "Say, George, how'do ya' like being circuit judge." He replied, "I like it just fine except for all the damned decisions I have to make."[74]

A political pundit wrote that Wallace had emerged as the central figure in the voting rights case and had won "widespread new acclaim" because of his "absolute refusal" to capitulate to the federal authorities. Wallace's new-found prominence had made him even larger in the public limelight than he would have been had he won his political race, the pundit said.[75] Another wrote that recent political rivals John Patterson and George Wallace were now shoulder to shoulder in defense of states' rights and that both represented "the solid sentiment of all [white] Alabama."[76]

At the U.S. District Court in Montgomery, Judge Frank M. Johnson, Jr., issued an order instructing Wallace and the rebellious voter registrars to surrender the contested records and to submit to questioning by the federal commission. Johnson, a Winston County native, was an anomaly among Southern white jurists of the era. His court was one of few in the South where civil rights cases received an impartial hearing. He was said to be "mean, but fair," a backhanded compliment that he treated "all lawyers equally mean." His fearless decisions striking down Jim Crow laws—starting with a ruling against segregated buses in 1956 following the Montgomery bus boycott—made him an outcast in the city and put him and his family at risk.[77]

Johnson and Wallace were classmates in law school and had been friendly, but this didn't stop Wallace from vilifying the federal judge when it suited his political purposes. Wallace, in his successful bid for the governor's office in 1962, laid into Johnson calling him an "integrating, scalawagging, carpetbagging liar." Patterson had no quarrel with Johnson and respected his legal opinions even though they were on opposite sides in the federal versus states' rights struggle. Johnson was sometimes called the "most hated man in Alabama." A cross was burned in the yard of the judge's Montgomery residence in 1957, and his mother's home was later bombed.

Minutes after Johnson issued the order requiring Wallace and the others to testify and to produce the voting records, both Macon County registrars—E. P. Livingston (brother of Alabama's chief justice) of Notasulga and Grady Rogers of Tuskegee—resigned their positions but were still subject to the court order. Acting for the state, Attorney General Patterson filed a motion (and a separate petition for Wallace) asking that the court order be vacated and the commission's subpoenas be quashed. He asked for a hearing before Judge Johnson and a stay of the court order pending the outcome. Johnson granted the stay and set a date of January 5 for a hearing.[78]

An impressive array of legal talent led by Patterson appeared at the hearing for the State of Alabama, Judge Wallace, and the county registrars. Included in the group were former Governor Chauncey Sparks (who was 79 and still practicing law in Eufaula), former Supreme Court Justice Preston Clayton, State Senator L. K. "Snag" Andrews, Assistant Attorney General Ralph Smith, and Circuit Solicitor Seymore Trammell. The latter, a sharecropper's son from Barbour County who had clawed his way up from poverty with the help of FDR's New Deal, WWII service, and the GI Bill, Trammell became a Wallace ally late in his career—he supported Patterson in 1958—eventually carving out a reputation as the "meanest son of a bitch in the Wallace administration."[79]

In discussions prior to the court hearing on the 5th, the attorneys for the state determined that since there was nothing detrimental or embarrassing in the voting records, it would be easier on everyone concerned to open the files to the commission. The state had made its point, but had not swayed Judge Johnson who was likely to come down hard on the spokesmen for the state if they tried his patience. They convinced Wallace, who was facing contempt charges and possible jail time if he refused the court order, that allowing the commission to see the records was the best course of action. Wallace had driven to Montgomery for the occasion, and was staying at the Exchange Hotel. With his concurrence, the group met with the attorneys for the civil rights commission and worked out a compromise settlement to let the commission review the records without removing them from the custody of the county registrars. Judge Johnson sanctioned the agreement.[80]

After the attorneys represented to the court that the commission could see the voter records for Barbour and Bullock counties (impounded by Wallace prior to December 8), Wallace reneged on the agreement. Huddled with Wallace at the Exchange Hotel following the hearing, Trammell and others convinced him that the compromise made him look weak and would hurt him politically. With his client in open contempt of court, Patterson went to the federal courthouse and had his name struck from the list of lawyers representing Wallace because he had gone back on his word. When Patterson arrived at the clerk's office he found that former Governor Sparks had already been in to withdraw from the case.[81]

Wallace defied the court until a mutual friend convinced him that Judge Johnson would "lock his ass up and throw away the key" if he remained in contempt. The friend, Glen Curlee, arranged a meeting with Johnson. Wallace drove up from Clayton and went to Johnson's house around midnight. He said his "ass was in a crack," that he couldn't turn over the records because they were no longer in his possession. The Barbour and Bullock grand juries had custody of the records and would make them available to the commission.[82]

Johnson saw through the subterfuge, but let Wallace off the hook when assured of compliance with the court order. Wallace went immediately to the papers to publicize the fact that the grand jury had caved in, but that he had defied the federal authorities to the bitter end.[83] Alabamians weren't aware they were being fed a preview of the sleight-of-tongue politics that would rule the state for most of the 1960s and 1970s. The artful dodge reached its zenith in 1963 with the stand in the schoolhouse door, which the University of Alabama oddly commemorates today as being of historic consequence, rather than the P. T. Barnum stunt it really was.

WHILE THE DRAMA PLAYED out in Judge Johnson's court, workmen were constructing the viewing platform for the incoming governor's inauguration. Governor Folsom, who cooperated fully with his successor, was said to have spent his final days as chief executive throwing farewell binges at the mansion. He stayed out of the state's run-in with the civil rights commission, but his deeply held populist beliefs put him in the commission's corner. Nobody asked his opinion in late December when the *Montgomery Advertiser* announced that no black school bands had been invited to march in Patterson's inaugural parade.

Attorney Ed Azar was in charge of plans for the inauguration. He spoke to reporters and said that the decision to have only white schools represented in the parade was not intended as a slight against the black community. To the contrary, Azar said, the incoming governor decided against "inviting Negro bands to march" because he did not want to put them in an embarrassing position. He was sensitive to the fact that black leaders might be reluctant to participate in his inaugural because he opposed racial integration in public schools and had the NAACP banned from operating in Alabama. The incoming governor offered assurances that he was going "to be governor for everybody."[84]

Behind the decision was the specter of confrontation which seemed to gain friction with each new flexing of federal power in the civil rights struggle. Patterson said the decision to exclude African Americans from the inaugural parade was not done as an intentional slight against them, but had been made hastily on advice from Floyd Mann and local authorities. They feared that klansmen and other hoodlums might cause trouble if the black bands were present.[85]

The last thing the incoming administration wanted was to have the inaugural marred by protests or outbreaks of violence. The election year had seen a reprieve from racial violence, but indignant public reaction to the civil rights hearings in Montgomery had tensions running high. With the inaugural only two weeks away, an announced plan by Reverend Martin Luther King, Jr., to end segregation of Montgomery schools brought an ominous threat from Klan leader Robert Shelton in Tuscaloosa. King said if school leaders did not accept the plan, lawsuits would follow. Shelton warned that klansmen were "ready to maintain segregation and our Christian ideals in the State of Alabama," adding that "we mean business." "We are warning the Negroes and white manipulators who have no regard for either race that if Martin Luther King's statement and announced plans of last week are carried out it will bring bloodshed to Alabama."[86]

The political rhetoric, meanwhile, stopped short of stirring the waters, but did nothing to calm them either. Patterson intended to keep his campaign promise of using legal means to delay the desegregation of Alabama's public schools and facilities. He concurred in a proposal by Albert Boutwell to form "a solid Dixie

front in the fight to maintain segregation and other states' rights," and accompanied
Boutwell to an informal meeting of public officials and constitutional lawyers
in Birmingham to discuss "Southern unity" and "some of the legal problems in
the segregation fight."[87]

The meeting was held in the law offices of Joseph H. Johnston over a cold,
rainy weekend in early December. Johnston, whose grandfather served as governor
of Alabama from 1896 to 1900 and as a U.S. Senator from 1907 to 1913, was
head of the Alabama Constitutional Commission. Attending the meeting with
Patterson and Boutwell were Attorney General-nominee MacDonald Gallion,
Ted Rinehart, and Ralph Smith. Johnston had helped draft the "Freedom of
Choice" amendment and the Alabama School Placement Law which Boutwell
had sponsored in the state legislature. Johnston's father, Forney Johnston, and
Birmingham attorney J. H. Willis were also in attendance.[88]

Governor-elect Ernest Vandiver of Georgia was unable to attend the meeting, but was represented by a committee of attorneys including Griffin Bell and
Charles J. Bloch. Bell, an Atlanta lawyer who went on to a distinguished career
as U.S. attorney general and legal adviser to three presidents, has been credited
with "educating segregationists on the inevitability of public school desegregation"
and saving Georgia's public school system. Bloch, a prominent Jewish lawyer
from Macon, was a leading authority on constitutional law.[89]

Nothing new or innovative came out of the meeting. The discussions ended
in a consensus that Southern states did not have a constitutional leg to stand on
in resisting the high court's order, but delaying compliance would give citizens
and institutions time to adjust to the change. The absence of a firm timetable
and the high court's stipulation of "all deliberate speed" gave the states some
leeway. Delaying desegregation had its pitfalls, however. Any delay perceived as
foot-dragging ran the risk of provoking federal intervention and inviting more
lawsuits from civil rights groups, whose struggle had been too long and too hard
to see the prize slip away.[90]

Patterson continued to confer with other Southern governors as he moved
into his first days as Alabama's chief executive. Although he would give ground
when he had to, as shown in the compromise in Judge Johnson's court, Patterson advocated "a positive unified program to preserve segregation and no
further appeasement or cooperation with integration groups." In an address to
the Alabama Association of Citizens' Councils, he laid out a four-point program
of resistance: to present a common, united front; to get out the white vote and

push registration of white voters; to bloc vote "against them as they do us"; and to speak out boldly "every chance we get to defend out position."[91]

In early 1959 the new governor noted that racial agitation had quieted down since "the NAACP was put out of business in Alabama," but said there were signs that black leaders were "seeking to make Alabama another battleground for integration as they did in Virginia and Arkansas." He asked state legislators "to consider a complete overhaul of laws requiring separation of the races in schools and other public facilities." The segregation laws needed strengthening, he said, "to meet an expected onslaught by integration forces."[92]

While anticipating that civil rights leaders would test the waters during his administration, the young governor took no pleasure in their adversarial relationship or in the racial strife of the times. He cautioned all parties against agitation or violence, and promised to come down hard on those who violated the law. At the same time he neither addressed the desegregation issue in the context of the forward-looking state program he had outlined for the next four years nor perceived of it as a defining element within his administration.

At early staff meetings Patterson laid down the law that he wanted everyone treated fairly and equitably. He later instructed department heads not to let racial strife impact on their services to all of Alabama's citizens. Alvin Prestwood recalled that while he was commissioner of pensions and security, Governor Patterson had called him in to talk about his department's services during periods of racial unrest, such as the later ugly outbreak of violence greeting the Freedom Riders' arrival in Alabama. Prestwood said the governor wanted his assurance that all pensioners and families on welfare got the funds they had coming to them and wouldn't go hungry during these unsettling times.[93]

Twenty-nine year old Prestwood had already earned a reputation for fairness, honesty, and integrity, which had influenced his appointment as commissioner by Patterson. Early in the administration an influential political supporter from Mobile approached Prestwood about doing a special favor for a friend. He wanted the friend moved ahead of hundreds of other couples on the waiting list so he and his wife could adopt a child whom the courts had ordered removed from the natural parents. Since this would subvert the adoption process, Prestwood refused. "I'll go see the guv'ner and have your goddamn job," the supporter threatened.

Prestwood went to the governor and explained what happened. "When I asked you to take the job, did I ask you to do anything against your conscience?

Anything illegal? Anything improper?" "No sir." "Well, what makes you think you have to come and ask me about this. If you know something's wrong, all you've go to do is say it's wrong, and I'll back you up. Then if the person threatens to come see me, you tell them to kiss your ass."

"What if they still don't listen?"

"Then you tell them John Patterson said they can kiss his ass because he told you to do what you know is right."[94]

Prestwood said he left the governor's office, and from that day on he stuck by that principle. "Governor Patterson was a man, I think, of significant principle, and that became the bedrock for his administration."[95]

13

The People's Governor

Just yesterday, or so it seemed, the family had moved to Montgomery and John Patterson was sworn in as attorney general. Leading the inaugural parade up Dexter Avenue his thoughts drifted back to that pivotal time in their lives and to Big Jim Folsom's celebrated return to the governor's mansion. Over the ensuing months his office's investigations had exposed widespread waste and fiscal irregularities within the Folsom administration. Alabamians witnessed a drop in Big Jim's popularity, as an overblown Adam Clayton Powell affair, the governor's chronic problems with alcohol, and the attorney general's injunctions took their toll. Before his numbers in the polls bottomed out, even the governor's beloved constituency in the branchheads had soured on bunkum, pork, and politics *ad hominem*.

Here the two men were, four years later, the outgoing populist governor—cuddling a half-pint of Old Guckenheimer in his hip pocket and craving a hair of the dog—and his harshest critic, the crime-busting attorney general, seated side-by-side in an open Cadillac DeVille rolling past the waving throng to the capitol steps and the beribboned reviewing stand. Decked out in the traditional cutaway coats and top hats (Patterson had borrowed his from Earl McGowin) the incoming and outgoing governors smiled and waved back to the bundled-up, shivering crowds. Monday, the 19th of January 1959—what a bone-chilling day for a parade! An alabaster sky streaked with jet contrails from nearby Maxwell Field greeted the thousands of people lining the downtown streets. With temperatures in the high forties through the morning and the wind chill dipping into the thirties, brrr it was cold.

Ed Azar had done a "marvelous job" putting the inaugural together. The only shortcomings were the conspicuously absent black marching bands and the snail's pace of a four-hour parade. "We were so elated over winning that we gave each county three units, and three times sixty-seven is one helluva parade," Patterson said. Marching proudly at the head of the long, winding procession were high school bands from New Site, Alexander City, and Dadeville representing Tallapoosa County.[1]

In keeping with custom, the chauffeur-driven convertible had driven the incumbent governor over to pick up his successor, and then to the foot of Dexter Avenue where the front of the procession awaited them. When it reached the capitol steps, the Cadillac pulled over and Folsom escorted the incoming governor to the inaugural stand. Behind them the strutting majorettes turned onto Decatur Street, led the grand procession in a U-turn back toward the capitol steps, and awaited the signal to pass in review. Folsom and Patterson had conversed pleasantly during their brief ride. They had their political differences, but never took them personally. Patterson asked if there was anything Folsom would be needing from him. Folsom said he might want to borrow the state yacht sometime. "You got it," Patterson said.

The only advice Folsom offered, with a sheepish grin, was a down-home bon mot that "a buzzard never fouls his own nest"—taken to mean that a governor should do nothing to disgrace the office.

Joining the incoming governor on the reviewing stand were his wife and two children, his mother Agnes, and his grandmother Mollie, whose ninety-fourth birthday was just days away. "The eldest of the three Mrs. Pattersons stood smiling near her grandson while he saluted the crowd." Four hours can be an eternity to a precocious child. Nine-year-old Albert remained attentive through the ceremony, but his sister Babel, half his age, grew bored and restless. Tired of having her picture taken she showed her displeasure by sticking out her tongue at a pesky news photographer. The next morning the governor arrived at the office to find that his five-year-old princess had stolen the show when her picture appeared widely on front pages near and far.

When the last float passed in review, Governor and Mrs. Folsom slipped away. It was customary for the outgoing governor to leave before his successor's inaugural address and the swearing-in ceremony. The Folsoms went by the office to say good-bye to the governor's staff, which was assembled there, and left through the back entrance to the chauffeured car waiting to take them back to the mansion and then home to Cullman.[2]

Patterson was sworn in by Judge Walter B. Jones. Both were students of history and appreciated the significance of this being the third inaugural held on Robert E. Lee's birthday—January 19th (the others were of Benjamin Meek Miller of Wilcox in 1931 and Chauncey Sparks of Barbour in 1943). Like other governors before him Patterson took the oath of office while standing on the capitol steps where Jefferson Davis had been sworn in as president of the Confederate States of America in February 1861.[3]

The inaugural address was notable for the governor's resolve to make good on the promises he made to the people of Alabama during his campaign. He reiterated earlier statements of the problems facing the state, his administration's program for dealing with them, and what he proposed to do to move the state forward and to make a better life for all the people of Alabama. Tommy Giles, state photographer and the youngest member of the Patterson team, said one of the governor's strong points was saying what he meant during the campaign and meaning what he said after taking office.[4]

In step with the inaugural's historical theme, Patterson vowed to defend and preserve "the rights, customs, and traditions of our state." Racial problems were a sign of the times in Alabama and the Deep South, and had to be addressed. His position, as stated during the campaign, was that the problems would never be solved "by court decrees, injunctions, and federal troops," but only through "mutual understanding and good will between the races without outside inter-ference and agitation." He sought to reassure Alabama's black citizens that he was interested in their welfare, and that his administration would be working to protect their interests as well as the interests of all of the citizens.

He did not intend for the public school system, a high priority of his admin-istration, to be held hostage to the threat of forced desegregation by the federal government. He pledged to do all in his power to improve school facilities for all Alabama students and to raise teachers' salaries commensurate with other states, but said the schools must remain segregated. He repeated the call for legislation authorizing him to close schools forced to desegregate by the federal government and to cut off public funds to any school which was integrated.[5]

A misconception prevalent among white Southerners at the time—wishful thinking in light of later events—was that the black community thought as they did and shared their concerns about the federal government's desegregation of public schools. Patterson stated in the inaugural address that he believed an "overwhelming majority of the Negro citizens in the state [were] opposed to integration of the races." He called on them to "stand up and speak out" against the agitators of their own race whose actions could result in a dismantling of the state's public school system.[6]

Most white newspapers in the state supported the governor's stand on segregated schools. A black newspaper published in Tuscaloosa took issue with the governor's message, suggesting that the white majority had misread the silence from black communities to mean consent. An editorial appearing in the paper scoffed at the image of a "stereotyped Negro" who was content with living as a second-class citizen and going to second-class schools. The editorial in turn, however, misinterpreted the governor's words as an "extended effort . . . to frighten the Negro citizens of his state."[7]

The progressive program Patterson had proposed to move the state forward educationally, industrially, and economically, and to improve the well-being of all Alabama citizens, won universal appeal. He planned to build on the "tremendous industrial expansion during recent years" to bring new industry into the state and encourage local industry to expand. To head this effort he brought Leland Jones, experienced businessman and close friend from Phenix City, into the administration. To encourage industry to come to Alabama, he believed it was imperative to provide a climate of "good law enforcement, honest government, good schools and an administration that people have confidence in."[8]

Another high priority was to follow through on "the great strides in road building" made by Governor Folsom. These included the farm-to-market roads (called "mailbox roads" by Folsom) and the federal interstate highway program, which was barely underway in Alabama. "During my administration we will have available for matching purposes, approximately 379 million federal dollars for the building of roads," he explained. "275 million dollars of this sum will be for the interstate highway system for which the state matches one dollar to every ten of the federal government." To take full advantage of available federal funds, his program called for issuing bonds to raise the money the state needed to match them.

To keep from levying an additional burden on Alabama taxpayers, he planned to finance the bond issue from gasoline taxes and other revenues. There were ample funds coming into the state treasury, the governor said, to finance the entire road-building program through the end of his administration without having to levy additional taxes. "With money from this bond issue and other funds coming into the highway department we can take full advantage of every federal dollar available during the next four years and leave the Highway Department in excellent financial condition when I go out of office four years from this day."[9]

Other campaign promises he intended to keep included the continued development of the state's rivers, docks, and harbors; maintaining strong law enforcement; working to improve the lives and working conditions of Alabama's farmers; supporting organized labor and improving labor-management relations in Alabama; working to expand the tourist trade; incrementally raising the average old-age pension payment to $75 a month and substantially increasing payments to the blind, dependent children, and disabled persons. As made clear during the campaign, he planned to finance these programs with savings from cutting out graft, corruption, and waste in state government.[10]

Thunderous applause rang out across the capitol grounds when Patterson delivered the inaugural address and took the oath as Alabama's forty-ninth governor and the youngest ever elected to the office, but the day's festivities had only begun. Receptions were held at the mansion and elsewhere around the capital city, and the inaugural ball attended by thousands that night at the coliseum was a gala affair. The governor's grandmother Mollie, who seemed energized by the day's events, attended the ball and danced with her grandson. Two weeks later she dropped off to sleep while seated in a chair at home and didn't wake up. She had been so vibrant and had such a joyful time at the inauguration, her family found it hard to believe that she was gone.[11]

Less-celebrated political dramas were being played out around the capital city on inaugural day. One was an internal party dispute in which former state senator Sam Engelhardt nosed out popular Montgomery attorney Frank J. Mizell, Jr., for the chairmanship of the State Democratic Executive Committee. Patterson had worked to get Engelhardt elected because he believed, as governor and titular head of the state party, that he needed a stronger voice in the decisions of the executive committee. The incoming governor thought highly of Mizell and considered him a friend, but he wanted a savvy politician and trusted administration insider to head up the committee. Getting Engelhardt elected caused some friction, but gave the governor leverage he felt he needed at the time within the executive committee.

WHEN THE PATTERSONS MOVED into the governor's mansion, the servants were busy cleaning up from a party Folsom had thrown on his last night in residence. "Most of the people in Big Jim's crowd were likeable people, and I enjoyed drinking with them and going hunting with them," Patterson said. "But they partied hard. There was such a big bash at the mansion the night before they left office, there was some of them still in bed upstairs on the morning we moved in."[12]

"The place was a shambles," he recalled. A perennial problem at the mansion had been the lack of security between the time one governor left and the next governor moved in. "There wasn't enough silverware and plates in the mansion to make six settings," Patterson said. The next morning when he got up to go to the office, the black limousine was missing. He had Joe Robertson track down the limousine and do an inventory.[13]

Robertson checked around and learned that the chauffeured limousine had accompanied Big Jim in his old 1951 Nash back to the Folsoms' "elegant fourteen-room house" in Cullman.[14] He also discovered there were two convicts missing from the pool of trusties assigned to the governor's office. When he called the Folsom home in Cullman, one of the trusties answered the phone. Robertson asked what he was doing there. "Guv'na Jim said to git myself in the car, so I'se up heah in Cullman," the trusty said.

Robertson asked him to put the governor on the phone. When Folsom came on the line, Robertson said, "Governor, you've got a couple of our convicts up there. You know you can't take 'em home with you."

"Aw, you got plenty of 'em. You won't miss a couple."

"Naw. We can't do that. We'll send the sheriff by to pick 'em up."

Robertson hung up and called the Cullman sheriff's office. The sheriff sent his deputies over to pick up the limousine and the trusties, and delivered them back to Montgomery.[15]

In addition to those assigned to the governor's office, all but one of the ten servants who worked at the mansion were trusties. The exception was the head cook, who was a state employee. The trusties at the mansion included a butler, a valet, a downstairs maid, an upstairs maid, a gardener, and four cooks and servers in the kitchen. Their quarters (converted horse stables) behind the mansion were substandard but it was better than being locked up in the trusty barracks at Kilby Prison.

All the servants at the mansion were black. "Most of them were serving time for murder. Crimes of passion," Patterson said. "People who are imprisoned for a crime of passion are the best risk because they are not likely to commit murder again." The butler and the valet were both serving time for murder. The valet was Eddie White. "I really liked Eddie. He was in prison because of a big mistake. He had shot at his brother-in-law and accidentally killed his sister. He thought he shouldn't have to serve time for that."[16]

Patterson's personal aide and chauffeur was a giant state trooper named Tom Posey. Public Safety Director Floyd Mann had handpicked Posey for the job and he stayed through Patterson's four years in office, driving the governor everywhere he went and watching over him. Other members of the team were carefully screened security guards who manned the gates at the entrance to the mansion. They became a close-knit family. "For four years I grew up with them (the servants and security guards) as my immediate friends," the governor's son said. "They ran the world that I lived in."[17]

Albert fondly recalled a trusty named Rosalie King who often looked after him and his sister. She worked at the mansion as a cook and was serving time for capital murder. The story he heard as a child was that Mrs. King had killed her husband, a preacher, for coming home one night and urinating on the organdy curtains she had spent all day washing and cleaning. Albert said he never felt ill at ease around any of the trusties. He also recalled the security guards who walked him and his sister to school and to other activities. The black servants and the white security guards were part of the family.[18]

A week after the inaugural a reporter caught up with former Governor Folsom in Cullman and asked if he planned to run for office again. Did he have his eye on the U.S. Senate race in a couple of years? Admitting he'd made some mistakes, Folsom said he didn't believe he could run for any office right now, not even justice of the peace or constable, and get elected. Certainly not to an office in Washington, D.C. "Besides, I don't want to take my chillun up there in all that whang-dang anyhow."[19]

In his waning days as governor Folsom had gone soft on "them lyin' news-papers" and was more accessible to the capitol press corps. He repeatedly dodged questions from reporters aimed at drawing him into a controversy with his succes-sor, however. Patterson, too, even when he was attacking administration officials, always had something nice to say about the big man from Cullman. Folsom told the reporter who came to see him in Cullman he thought John Patterson was going to make a good governor. "Of course, we crossed swords once in awhile, but I'm the main preacher for his road program and old-age pensions. You can't go wrong on a good road program and old-age benefits."[20]

ON HIS FIRST DAY at the office Governor Patterson held a staff meeting where all cabinet members and department heads were sworn in. Mabel Amos, recording secretary in the governor's office, administered the oath. The portrait of his father had been moved from the attorney general's office and now hung on the wall behind the governor's desk. He discussed the ground rules for their administration with the cabinet—reminding them of his pledge to be the governor of all the people, not a political front for the Big Mules in Birmingham or any other special interest group. He wanted an honest administration. He wanted the law enforced. He wanted competitive bidding. Most of all he wanted to keep the promises he had made to the people of Alabama.

"Old timers at the Capitol watched in silent admiration," a reporter wrote, as the new governor "and the forces at his command took control of the state government in the quietest and most orderly transition in years." The governor told cabinet members he wanted them to take complete charge of their departments immediately, to "operate their departments with economy and efficiency," and to "put an immediate halt to all non-essential programs." "Let's show the people of Alabama that we mean business," he said. "The people want more than words."[21]

The new governor cautioned against being too rigid, however, saying he didn't want there to be any early sign of rigor mortis. Before the sun went down, he was reminded of a lesson he had learned many times in North Africa and Europe—i.e., when you're receiving incoming rounds or they're tossing grenades at you, flexibility becomes the order of the day. After the cabinet meeting broke up, he had called Floyd Mann back into the office for a chat. They had been friends since grammar school. Floyd was a decorated tail gunner on B-17s in WWII and had flown twenty-seven combat missions, including the first daylight raid over Berlin. He was fun-loving, at times a prankster, but dead serious when it came to doing what was right and enforcing the law. They briefly discussed the administration's philosophy on law enforcement.[22]

"Floyd, we got to read from the same sheet of music on enforcing the law," the governor said. "Make sure your people know they have to be tough on lawbreakers, but I want everybody treated the same. There's not going to be any tickets fixed in our administration. I don't care who gets a ticket, everybody pays just like everybody else. We got to treat everybody the same on everything down to traffic tickets. Is that understood?" Floyd said he understood that.

That very afternoon a U.S. Senator from Missouri passing through south Alabama with his family was pulled over by a state trooper for speeding. The family had been vacationing in Florida and were on their way back to Missouri. In those days the rules required that traffic violators who were nonresidents go before a justice of the peace and pay a fine on the spot. With the trooper leading the way, the irate senator drove around looking for a justice of the peace but couldn't find one. "Well, they drove all over south Alabama, and this senator was hot under the collar. He was hoppin' mad."

The senator got on the phone and called Washington. In a matter of minutes the phone was ringing off the hook in the governor's office. "I got calls from Senator Lister Hill and Senator Sparkman. President Eisenhower's chief of staff, General Guenther, called. They wanted me to know that we had a very important senator on our hands." Then a call came in from Frank Boykin, Alabama's flamboyant congressman from Mobile. Boykin said, "Guv'na, you got to do sump'n 'bout this thang. This fellow's the chairman of the appropriations committee that puts up all the money for the development of rivers and harbors. John, you know everthang's made for love. You don't do sump'n, you can kiss the Tennessee-Tombigbee canal good-bye."

"Nice of you to call, Frank," Patterson said. "We'll straighten the situation out. Thank you for calling."

He got Floyd Mann on the phone. "Floyd, you remember this morning me telling you about them tickets?"

"Yeah."

"Ol' buddy, I didn't mean that."

The trooper let the senator go on his way, and the Tennessee-Tombigbee project survived in the U.S. Senate.[23]

Not long afterward Floyd Mann called the mansion one night to let the governor know they had Fred Taylor, star reporter with the *Birmingham News*, locked up in the Clanton jail. Taylor was on his way back to Birmingham when troopers stopped him. "He's too drunk to drive," Mann said. "What do you want us to do with him?" He knew that Taylor and the *News* had been tough on the governor since before the 1958 campaign. Patterson thought for a second and said, "Don't charge him with nothing. I'll call Morgan Reynolds in Clanton. He'll take care of it."

Patterson called his brother-in-law, who was a prominent lawyer in Clanton and had been his campaign manager in Chilton County, and explained the situation. "Morgan, they got Fred Taylor in jail there. Could you go down and see that he's not charged? Take him over to your house, sober him up, and have somebody drive him and his car to Birmingham."

"I'll drive him myself," Morgan said.

After pouring black coffee down Taylor and sobering him up, Morgan and his wife Barbara (the first lady's sister) drove the reporter and his car home that night. "We never had any trouble out of Fred Taylor after that. He became a supporter of the Patterson administration." The governor laughed, and added, "You see, it pays to stay flexible."

While the governor was strong on law enforcement—influenced to a great extent by his father's murder and Phenix City's lawless past—experience had taught him not to go through life beating a dead horse. "If you overdo law enforcement, pretty soon people don't want it, you know. You have to use a little common sense. Listen to that voice in the inner ear."

He was mindful of this on another occasion when Peter E. Xides, the prominent, fatherly owner of the Elite Cafe came to see him about a problem with the ABC Board. He was distraught. "Governor, Ed Azar's trying to put me out of business. Said I might go to jail."

"What're you talkin' about, Mr. Pete?"

"They said to stop selling that whiskey on Sunday."

"The hell you say."

"You know, Governor, you been coming in my place since you was in college and drinking that whiskey on Sunday."

"That's a fact, Mr. Pete. It sure is. We gotta do something about that."

Patterson told Azar he wanted the ABC Board to leave the Elite Cafe alone. "We gotta have a place on Sunday to get a drink."

This put the new administrator of the Alabama Alcoholic Beverage Control Board in an awkward position. Just recently he had called ABC district supervisors to Montgomery and declared that there would be "no political influence" in the way the agency operated. Azar told the supervisors, "Governor Patterson is dedicated to good, honest, and efficient administration, and as long as I am administrator of the ABC board that is exactly what Governor Patterson is going to get from this department."[24]

A devout Catholic who attended Notre Dame prior to earning a law degree at the University of Alabama, the straight-shooting Azar was the ideal person to head the troublesome ABC Board. He initially balked at making an exception for the Elite Cafe, not understanding what all the fuss was about. He rarely drank liquor himself and had never purchased a drink there or anywhere else on Sunday. He was quoted as saying that he did not object to liquor on moral grounds, but didn't like the taste of it and would "much rather have a cup of coffee." He complied with the governor's wishes, however, and declared a truce with the Elite Cafe over the time-honored tradition of serving surreptitious booze in teacups to its regular Sunday customers.[25]

The governor said Ed Azar was the person the ancient Greek philosopher Diogenes searched for. "Most honest fella you ever saw," Patterson said. Nobody who knew the ABC administrator questioned his honesty and integrity. At midterm, Azar's forthrightness was on full display in a speech to the East Montgomery Exchange Club. While liquor sales had netted almost $20 million for the state in the past year, Azar said candidly that the "real purpose of the ABC, as stated in the act establishing it and stressed in the Patterson administration, is control of legal alcoholic beverage sales and elimination of moonshine manufacturing and sales."[26]

"Our first and chief purpose and justification for existing," he said, "is in exercise of the state's police power to promote the public safety, health, welfare and morals, to promote temperance in the use and traffic of alcoholic beverages, and to suppress the evils of intemperance." Stressing that revenue was secondary, he said, "If we never make another dime, yet continued to do our duty well of enforcing the beverage laws, we will be a complete success so far as I'm concerned."[27]

Considering that the $20 million in ABC profits made a vital contribution to state solvency (including $7.5 million to pensions and security), the governor must have blinked at the last statement. His ABC administrator's candor in an appearance before a legislative committee in 1959 about the state's customary practice of employing liquor agents made even seasoned reporter Bob Ingram wince. Ingram wrote in the *Advertiser* that Azar "made no bones about the fact that the first and foremost qualification to become a liquor agent in the Patterson administration was to have voted and worked for the election of John Patterson. The only thing surprising about the confession was that Azar made it."[28]

Words, like deeds, usually have a way of balancing out. Ingram added that "looking back over his two years in what has long been a hot seat in politics, Azar said most gratifying was the support he had received from the Governor." He had no objection to the liquor agent system because it provided $500,000 in income for Alabamians at no cost to anyone. "This agency has had a history of being involved in politics, but that has not been the case during this administration. I have been exceptionally unhampered in the direction of the board. I have had a free hand most of the time. I have never been pressured to put certain brands on the list or to take others off."[29]

The governor asked nothing from his people that he wouldn't do himself.

He set the tone and the pace for his administration. The *Advertiser's* Ingram, equally tough on friend or foe, wrote admiringly after the first two months: "Gov. John Patterson has set a remarkable example of diligence since he took office in January. Not only has he been on the job every day, but he works three or four nights each week, usually staying at the office until midnight. Further, he has been at the office every Saturday and almost every Sunday."[30]

Ingram noted that Patterson was "the direct opposite of the two chief executives he succeeded—Gordon Persons never made an appearance in public. Folsom seldom made an appearance at his office." He suggested that Patterson had probably "spent more time on the job in his ten weeks in office than Folsom did during his last ten months."[31]

He was there to do the people's business. On taking office he had declared an open-door policy. His executive staff, Ruth Richardson and particularly Joe Robertson, tended to be over-protective of their boss, however. Legislators who showed up without an appointment began to complain that the governor was too busy to see them. The governor knew that would never do. The legislature was no bargain basement where you got something for nothing, but a bargaining table where deals were cut or lost.[32]

When he addressed the joint legislature at the start of the regular session in May, Patterson strayed from his prepared speech "to throw in a comment concerning his desire to meet with the lawmakers." The following day a number of legislators who were waiting in line to call the governor's bluff quickly found out that Patterson wasn't bluffing—he saw them all." "It was just like a barbershop," one was overheard to say. "The ones who got there first got in first. That's the way it should have been all the time." The governor smiled and nodded his head in agreement.[33]

PATTERSON HAD USED THE six months between the Democratic primary and the inauguration to fill key leadership positions in the legislature, to cultivate friends among legislators, and to line up support for his programs. The resulting partnership paid huge dividends for the state in the first year of the new administration. Together the administration and legislature put through historic legislation and programs that would transform the landscape of public education and the economy in Alabama for years to come.

His brain trust in the legislature was comprised of some of the ablest and most dedicated men in Alabama politics. Among the governor's closest advisers were lawmakers such as Senate floor leader Vaughn Hill Robison of Montgomery; Senator Ryan deGraffenried of Tuscaloosa; House floor leader Virgis Ashworth of Centreville; House speaker Charles Adams of Alexander City; Ways and Means chairman Joe Smith of Phenix City; and Representatives A. L. Boyd of Troy and Ira Pruitt of Livingston. Without them the administration could not have led off with the "most productive legislative year in Alabama history."[34]

Twice during his first months in office, Patterson called the legislature into special session. At that time, the legislature met in regular session only biennially, convening in odd-numbered years on the first Tuesday in May. Not wanting to risk losing a dime in federal highway funds the governor had been in office two weeks when he called the legislature into special session to authorize issuing $60 million in bonds to finance the state's contribution to a comprehensive four-year highway construction program. When added to revenues from gas taxes and other sources, the matching funds from the bond issue brought in over a half-billion dollars in federal funding without having to raise taxes.[35]

The four-year highway program dwarfed those of previous adminstrations. Patterson had set out to improve on the highway constructon started under Folsom, who had claimed his "mailbox or farm-to-market road program got folks who lived in the country "out of the mud." "There's a lot of truth to that," Patterson said. "Jim Folsom had a great road program. We just wanted to continue the program and improve on it."[36]

Patterson described the $60 million bond issue and the half-billion dollar federal funding as the capital he needed to prime the economic pump during his administration. Political pros explained that putting the $60 million bond issue at the forefront of his legislative agenda had provided the governor with "a formidable tool for eliciting support from legislators" for his other programs. His commitment to the essentials of his program and a willingness to compromise on non-essential elements made it possible to pass key legislation in the regular session. Patterson praised the lawmakers for their diligence and their courage.

One editor wrote that "courageous" was "an appropriate term for most of the measures passed, and some that were rejected," because they "were not the kind . . . conducive to winning popular support at the polls." There was even speculation that a few legislators, "by sponsoring and supporting some of the bills that were passed," might have made themselves an endangered species. One of the most bitterly contested bills of the 1959 session was a historic small-loan regulations act, which passed "at the governor's insistent prodding of the legislature" and had been sought by him since his first days as attorney general in 1955.[37]

The 1959 regular session, however, did not start auspiciously for the administration. There were signs before the session convened that "the summer-long grind" promised to be "a political tempest of considerable proportions." Patterson knew there were disgruntled legislators, nearly all of them representing the big-money interests, and he had no illusions about his full program yielding the same "prompt and enthusiastic approval" given to his "multi-million dollar road bond issue." He was expecting a battle royal, but remained confident the session would be productive despite rumblings to the contrary. "Something good usually comes from controversy," he said to a reporter.[38]

The foremost challenge facing legislators was "a financial crisis in education," the governor declared at the opening session on May 5. Funds were urgently needed to raise teachers' salaries and to construct new buildings and expanded classroom facilities, he stated. He proposed $42 million a year in new taxes to finance the education program, plus a $100 million bond issue for school construction, with equal consideration given to white and black schools. The governor suggested that the legislators pass the general appropriations bill first and then recess, at which time he would call a special session to bring up the school funding proposals.[39]

Other urgent business he put before the legislature included a property tax equalization proposal, reapportionment, legislative regulation of the small-loan businesses, and substantially increased public assistance funding. He wasn't surprised when a House faction, led mostly by Black Belt legislators, revolted against the program with a "lazy man's filibuster" on the first day. Rather than taking the floor themselves and talking to kill time, the insurgents demanded that a 387-page proposed insurance code be read word for word. The House, to keep from listening to the technical jargon, adjourned for two days while the clerk read the document. When members returned on Friday, only thirty-four pages had been read because of frequent interruptions. Defying an admonishment from the governor "to quit stalling and get to work," the unruly minority insisted that the clerk finish reading the voluminous code.[40]

The Black Belt factions in the House and Senate were not only opposed to "the most ambitious educational budget in the state's history," but had fought legislative reapportionment for years. The governor's property tax equalization program met wider resistance in the legislature, even among supporters of his program, but vested interests were behind this fight as well. He refused to be goaded into a war of words with legislators, friend or foe, however, and told newsmen he was pleased with the way things were going and wasn't worried about the slowdown.[41]

In a TV-radio "report to the people" Patterson praised the legislature as "one of the best" and expressed confidence that legislators were "heading into a highly constructive session in which the best interests of all the people of Alabama will be paramount at all times." He assured legislators and the public that "we are going to crisscross Alabama with fine, modern roads—with every county getting its share." Reminding his audience that the roads to good legislation were paved with "compromise," Patterson said that his administration was seeking "reasonable compromises in the public interest."[42]

The governor was confident that his administration wielded more power over the compromises in key legislation than the special interest groups did. Passage of the $60 million road bond issue in the February special session had bolstered his bargaining position. The power to build roads or not to build roads was a strong incentive for legislators to do things the administration's way. About all the leverage left to the special interests rested with passage of the general appropriations bill. Patterson didn't expect legislators to hand him everything he asked for in the regular session and was willing to give a little to get a lot.[43]

When rebellious House members (faced with the threat of a gag rule) called off their filibuster after the first week, their Black Belt brethren in the Senate immediately "cranked up" one of their own. Senators who were opposed to the filibuster conferred with Patterson and gave written notice they would attempt to end the shutdown. Finally, on 3 June, the House "weathered a brief storm of protest" to pass the $74 million general appropriations bill with only two dissenting votes. For the general appropriations bill (supporting non-school state functions for the next two years) to clear the House on the ninth legislative day of the 1959 session was in itself exceptional. It usually took much longer.[44]

Governor Patterson congratulated the House and appealed to the Senate for "the same prompt and fair consideration" of the bill so they could get on with the urgent business of doing something about education. It took a compromise on the governor's tax equalization program to break the logjam in the Senate, and the Senators passed "the huge general appropriation bill in record time" on June 19. One hour after the Senate had passed the $74 million bill, it was on its way downstairs to the governor's office.[45]

The governor had worked behind the scenes to move the appropriations bill along. He wanted to get the general appropriations out of the way before calling a special session (where he controlled the agenda) because legislators on the other side, after a rough and tumble fight over education, might be less inclined to cooperate on the state's budget requirements. One thing he did was to encourage educators to flood the mail with demands that legislators pass the general appropriations so they could get on with the important business of dealing with the state's education problems. The strategy had worked.[46]

The legislature recessed that Friday, and Patterson called for a second special session the following Wednesday to deal exclusively with the state's education problems—the first Alabama governor ever to do so. During his travels around the state he had seen that the education system was "in terrible shape" and decided to do something about it. "They said that children were going to school in chicken coops. In some places that was literally true. I saw that with my own eyes. So I decided we would do something to improve the quality of public education."[47]

In his address to the special session Patterson asked for an appropriation that would give public schools an additional $42 million per year, and for enactment of a bill authorizing a $100 million bond issue for school construction. Press secretary Harry Cook pointed out that the governor had put his political future on the line to get this increased funding for education. "This was one of the roughest fights I ever got into," Patterson said. "Of course we used road money to get people to support the school program. We had to change a lot of the program, but we finally got it through."[48]

When it was over, the special session had taken longer than anticipated. Not that legislators were opposed to helping the schools—no politician wanted to be portrayed as anti-education, but they were hung up on how to pay for it. Legislators were into their tenth week when they came together and passed the biggest school appropriation bill in Alabama's history—authorizing $148 million to operate the public schools and higher institutions for the coming fiscal year and $155 million the following year. They also approved the governor's $100 million bond issue, the highest ever authorized for the construction of new school facilities.[49]

The appropriation bill not only afforded a 15 percent pay raise for Alabama's 25,000 teachers, but provided funds for hiring 1,000 new teachers for the coming school year. The staggering bond issue earmarked $74 million for the construction of public schools, $23.5 million for colleges, and the rest for trade schools, including a $1 million facility in Montgomery. The legislature enacted

$30 million in new taxes to finance the record appropriation.[50]

Patterson had fought hard to get the education appropriation passed without raising the sales tax and imposing a hardship on daily breadwinners and families with low or no incomes. He supported a measure to lower the sales tax from 3 percent to 2.5 percent and remove the tax exemptions on industrial machinery and other high-priced items. This brought the administration squarely into the crosshairs of the big landowners and big business. While labor leaders favored the legislation, the governor accused the Big Mules and their coalition of lobbying to kill it.[51]

From the outset the battle lines in both houses were clearly drawn. "The Patterson forces were on one side while the opposition was made up almost entirely of legislators from Jefferson, Mobile, and the Black Belt counties." In a speech before a legislative committee, a Birmingham board chairman compared the governor's assault on the big corporations and the "Got Rocks" to the branchhead politics of his predecessor. Patterson struck back at "the big business people" in a speech before the state American Legion convention at the Tutwiler Hotel: "The poor man of the state . . . the average citizen . . . doesn't have a lobby. But every big business has a battery of paid lobbyists doing their work night and day . . . and most of it at night."[52]

The governor had conferred often with the leaders in the legislature and took every opportunity to promote the education program. He and the first lady hosted receptions for state educators and legislators at the governor's mansion. Hundreds of Alabama alumni attended a reception honoring Dr. Frank A. Rose, president of the University of Alabama, who told the guests that the state would be denying itself for years to come if it failed to follow the governor in his program to improve education. The governor mended fences with former adversaries to win them over to his program. He invited Ed Reid, longtime executive director of the League of Municipalities, to the governor's office, and Reid arranged a visit with columnist Drew Pearson in his home during a trip to Washington, D.C., to elicit his support.[53]

The governor's extraordinary efforts paid dividends. Over a late July weekend, legislators blocking the education program were shocked to hear Drew Pearson laud the Alabama governor's "courageous" sales tax fight on his regular Sunday afternoon broadcast. Maligned by Pearson when he was elected governor, Patterson once described the syndicated muckraker as the only man he knew who could peep through a keyhole with both eyes at the same time. The normally ultra-critical columnist now praised Patterson's courage "in battling for equitable taxes despite pressures from big business, the big plantation owners, and lobbyists." He said he hoped "the people of Alabama will stand behind a man who is trying hard to make economic democracy live."[54]

When Patterson succeeded in pushing his education program through in August, he credited his "brain trust" in the legislature for the victory. These close advisers and other legislators met with Patterson regularly and offered him ideas. "Patterson took some of their ideas, rejected others, and came up with some ideas of his own," reported the *Post-Herald*'s Clarke Stallworth. "But whether the political maneuvers were Patterson's—or his adviser's—the credit must go to Patterson."[55] State legislators applauded the governor's "sturdy leadership." State educators were effusive in their praise of his "outstanding" and "untiring efforts" to improve educational opportunities in Alabama.[56]

When the gavel came down on the regular session in mid-November (it had reconvened in September after a two-week layoff), Patterson could look back with pride on a nonpareil start for his administration. Making it all the sweeter for the administration was knowing that previous administrations hadn't fared nearly as well. Even the *Birmingham News* conceded that Patterson had "drawn from the legislature more than many governors have been able to do in a much longer time." Governor Folsom, by comparison, had all of his major bills defeated in the opening regular session of his first term in 1947. These included reapportionment of the legislature and his $40 million bond issue.[57]

The legislators had been put through their paces in the 1959 session, which "continued for eleven months with only an interruption here or there," and "was the costliest" the state had ever known. More than $1.7 million was spent on salaries for House and Senate members and employees, and for printing and other expenses. Franklin County's Representative Emmett Oden cited the cooperation between the governor and the legislature as the primum mobile of the "progressive" session. Governor Patterson sent the House and Senate "warm words of appreciation" for what he called a "notable record of progress . . . a record which will long be remembered in gratitude."[58]

AMONG HITS THE GOVERNOR had taken, when the curtain came down on the 1959 session, was the defeat of his calls for reapportionment of the legislature and property tax reform. Both were thorny issues with roots in post-Reconstruction politics and sweetheart alliances between big landowners, industrialists, and railroaders at the expense of blacks and poor whites. Folsom had wrestled with the twin issues through his two terms as governor before throwing his hands up in resignation and disgust.[59]

The 1901 constitution had resulted in legislative malapportionment favoring the Black Belt and south Alabama. For more than half a century afterward, the top-heavy governing body on Goat Hill failed to redress the imbalance by simply ignoring census results and a stipulation in the constitution that the legislature would reapportion itself every ten years. The big landowners and their allies stood to lose too much if they allowed the heavily populated and poorer urban areas to gain a fair and balanced apportionment in the legislature. Governor Patterson warned legislators that if they didn't reapportion themselves the federal government would step in and do it for them, but he had to put the argument off for another day.[60]

The property tax muddle in Alabama was just as impervious to reform. The big landowners and the industrialists who pulled the strings in the legislature were the same people who benefited from the inequitable tax laws. It was simple arithmetic that as long as the legislative body was controlled by big money and was unwilling to correct the imbalance in representation, they had the votes to defeat tax reform. The Folsom administration had fought for a more equitable tax system, but in the end had ceded victory to the power-elite in Alabama politics.[61]

When Folsom's first term started in 1947, Patterson was learning the rudiments of tax law from the person he would later select to be his state revenue commissioner—fifty-one-year-old Harry H. Haden, professor of law at the University of Alabama. Patterson's choice of the brilliant, diminutive professor to head the revenue department was greeted as a masterstroke when he announced the appointment a few weeks before the inaugural. Haden, an authority on tax law, accepted the appointment with the understanding that he was "to run the department free of politics and in accordance with the law."[62]

Haden convinced the governor that getting county tax assessors to assess property across the board at 30 percent of its market value would generate the additional revenues needed to fund all of his programs—"the highways, the schools, everything." Equalizing the ad valorem taxes at 30 percent of true value over the state—which was half what the law required, but more than double the assessments in many counties—was settled on as a fair and equitable solution for all property owners. The commissioner explained that ad valorem (by value) taxation—"the property tax on which Alabama's government is based"— "was at greatest variance with the law and the constitution."[63]

"Utter inequality in assessments exists in every one of the sixty-seven counties," the commissioner asserted. The assessments varied from county to county, but the holdings of the wealthiest landowners (banks, big businesses, industries, mining, and timber interests, etc.) were generally assessed at a small fraction of their value. The governor was convinced of the wisdom of the Haden proposal, but ran into "a hornet's nest" when he presented it to the legislature. "From the moment he outlined the plan the governor was under constant and heavy fire," the *Advertiser* reported.[64]

The commissioner had high ideals, but his years at the university seemed to have left him with a tin ear for politics outside the lethal rivalries of academe. He implemented the plan without waiting for the legislature to convene in regular session. On April 7 he issued a directive to county tax assessors— "which the majority chose generally to ignore"—that they must equalize ad valorem assessments at 30 percent of the fair market value for all property subject to taxation. His authority for the directive was a stipulation in the law that the Department of Revenue could make the evaluation and assessment of property if the county tax assessor or the Board of Equalization failed to do so.[65]

Haden later said he had decided that if he was going to equalize the taxes, he was going ahead with it and do it right, with "the downtown property owners and the big corporations and industries" being hit first. Alabama Power Company, at the pinnacle of corporate land barons in the state, had litigated against higher tax assessments in the courts and won. "If I was going to be stopped at all, they would be the people who would stop me," Haden said, "and if I was going to be stopped I wanted to be stopped right at the first rather than halfway through when maybe all I would have succeeded in doing would be to raise taxes on some householders."[66]

Commissioner Haden got his wish. First, the commissioner "received brusque treatment when he got around to talking tax turkey with the finance committee." Then the legislature introduced a bill to take away the revenue commissioner's "authority to set local property tax assessments aside and reassess them as he saw fit." Newspapers reported that Haden's campaign had "antagonized the powerful farm bloc in the legislature along with large timberland owners and big industry," and had much to do with the governor's fight with Black Belt legislators during the regular session.[67]

When the bill's sponsors got enough signatures in both houses to pass it, they went to the governor with an ultimatum that if the commissioner didn't back off the plan to equalize property taxes, they were going to take the authority away from him. This threatened dire consequences for the state, perhaps resulting in losses of millions of dollars in revenue annually, and might have even bankrupted some counties suffering losses from taxes on public utilities. Patterson "decided that the better part of valor would be strategic retreat."[68]

Patterson said he hated to lose that fight, because fair and equitable ad valorem taxes would have been better for the state, the counties, and the people of Alabama. The county tax assessors couldn't be expected to resolve the problem themselves because they would be defeated in the next election if they raised property taxes. Haden rationalized that the failed effort was not a total loss. He had seen a gradual rise in county assessments resulting from his department's interest. More importantly, he said, the public had been educated about the problem. "The money is there, it is legally due and they can have it whenever they make up their minds to collect it." "It was the right thing to do, but we were unable to pull it off politically," Patterson said.[69]

Another battle the governor lost was his bid for the emergency power to close Alabama's public schools when threatened by forced desegregation. He was not "too disappointed" by this since the governor had "the inherent power to close schools to preserve order and peace anyway." Segregation, although still a front-row issue on the floor of the legislature, was reported to be "not as bombastic as in past years," which was a good sign.[70]

Fustian outbursts weren't dead on the House and Senate floors, however. When the House passed and sent to the Senate a bill cutting off welfare payments to mothers with more than one illegitimate child, the bill's author, H. B. Taylor of Butler County, thundered, "We must stop those Negro women from raising bastard children who some day will grow up and outvote us!" The House overrode vigorous opposition from Etowah Representative E. K. Hanby, who maintained that "an unfortunate child should not be punished for the mistakes of a mother."[71]

The governor agreed with Hanby and told legislators who came to him about the bill that he could not support it. As governor, he wasn't about to let this happen because of the repercussions. The lion's share of the welfare costs were defrayed by Washington, and the federal agencies would have cut off the state's funding before allowing such a discriminatory law to be put into practice.

Whenever legislators associated with White Citizens' Councils introduced one of their warmed-over "bastard bills," Patterson thought about his grandfather being raised by a single parent. Each time one of these bills was introduced he worked behind the scenes to have it defeated. One day a group of Black Belt legislators who supported the bill went to the governor's office seeking to win him over to their side. "You fellows shouldn't be jumping on these single-parent kids," Patterson said. "Alabama had a governor one time that was illegitimate, you know." The legislators expressed disbelief. "That's right," he continued. "He was from down there where y'all come from." On their way out, Patterson chuckled and said, "If all the single-parent children were organized and could vote, you fellows wouldn't dare be jumping on them."[72]

He also instructed Commissioner Alvin Prestwood to make certain families on welfare did not suffer as a result of Alabama's racial problems. He did not have to veto the "bastard child" bill, however, because it was killed along with others when the Senate finished the historic 1959 session locked in a filibuster—leaving scores of bills to die on the calendar.[73]

The governor had made it clear at the start of the regular session that he wanted "one of the finest, most progressive public assistance programs during the next four years that this state has ever had." "The benefits now paid to our aged citizens, blind, dependent children, orphans and physically handicapped persons are woefully inadequate," he told legislators. "It is our duty to adequately provide for these people." When a 10 percent increase in liquor taxes was proposed, he forced a compromise in which the estimated five million dollars a year in new revenue would be split 50-50 between mental care and old-age welfare programs.[74]

Neither the administration nor the legislature could have asked for higher tribute than the one bestowed by the *Tuscaloosa News* when it stated that their efforts were "more dominated by a keen realization of need and the general welfare of the state than by political expediency." Their record was described as "one of progress if not one of overwhelming popularity."[75]

GOVERNOR PATTERSON'S WORLD WAR II and Korean War background had given him an insider's perspective on military service and a lifelong commitment to the men and women in uniform. Many of his department heads and close advisers were former military officers, and for the most part were bright young up-and-comers with a promising future ahead of them. This affinity showed in the interest the governor took in the Alabama National Guard and the Air Guard during his four years in office.

One task awaiting him as governor was to appoint senior officers to serve in key positions with the Alabama Guard. He objected to politicizing the Guard appointments, and made a studious effort to see that only the top officers in line for promotion were given key assignments. Two of his initial nominees were Major General Henry V. Graham of Birmingham as adjutant general and Brigadier General Jack Parsons of Montgomery as deputy adjutant general. Graham, a war veteran who commanded the Dixie Division's 167th Infantry Regiment when Patterson nominated him for promotion from colonel to major general, had a stellar record. The legislature rapidly approved the Graham and Parsons nominations when the regular session convened in May.[76]

The governor's goal of basing senior officer assignments on qualifying criteria created a political brouhaha when he nominated Major General Walter "Crack" Hanna to command the famed Dixie Division (31st National Guard Division). The 31st Division was made up of Alabama and Mississippi units, with the two states alternating in the appointment of commanders. It was Alabama's turn when Major General A. G. Paxton, a cotton man from the Mississippi Delta, retired after eight years as commander. Governor Folsom had recommended Colonel Joseph N. Langan, Mobile city commissioner, to replace Paxton, but left office before Langan's name could be submitted to the Senate for approval.

Patterson spoke well of Langan, whom he considered to be "an able officer" and deserving of promotion, but there were others who were more qualified. Judging from their records Patterson concluded that no Guard officer was more qualified to be division commander than Crack Hanna. He had a long association with the Dixie Division and had commanded the 155th Infantry Regiment in WWII. While serving as adjutant general in Governor Persons's administration, Hanna had led the National Guard troops in the Phenix City vice cleanup in 1954 following the murder of Patterson's father. Hanna, a successful Birmingham businessman, already wore two stars and was the senior National Guard officer in the state.[77]

Patterson knew Hanna was a controversial figure, but for all the right reasons. The general subscribed to the principle that "you have to break eggs to make an omelet," and if there was a tough job to do Hanna was your man. At five feet, seven inches, he "was built like a bulldog and twice as pugnacious." His toughness rubbed some people the wrong way, but as he proved in Phenix City the disgruntled folks were usually on the deserving end of the bayonet or got in the way of the thrust. Patterson had grown close to Hanna and the guardsmen during the Phenix City cleanup, and believed he was the right general at the right time to command the Dixie Division.[78]

The governor didn't think of it as a political appointment. During the race for governor Hanna hadn't supported him in the Democratic primary until the runoff with George Wallace. The general had already committed to Jimmy Faulkner, and joined the Patterson camp only after Faulkner's defeat. Hanna hadn't asked the governor for the command. The governor relied primarily on the records available to him and his personal knowledge of other eligible officers to make his decision in favor of Hanna.[79]

Patterson found out how deeply ingrained politics was in the Guard when Mississippi Governor James P. Coleman objected to the appointment, saying he would "never concur" in naming Hanna division commander. Coleman would not say why he opposed Hanna, only that he did so "for excellent reasons." Sources close to the governor revealed that the reason for Coleman's objection was bad blood between Hanna and Paxton, when Paxton commanded the division and Hanna was deputy commander. Both were strong-willed men, and intense rivalry had built up between them after Hanna criticized Paxton's appointment as commander.[80]

The feud was irrelevant, in Patterson's view. Commanders didn't pick their successors in the Army he served in, and Coleman's objection to Hanna was purely Mississippi politics. He handled the situation with diplomacy, not wanting to ruffle more feathers, but couldn't get the Mississippi governor to change his mind. Federal recognition was required in the acceptance of division commanders, but the National Guard Bureau would not interfere in the dispute unless either of the two states requested intervention—something neither governor was willing to do.[81]

Patterson stressed that until the matter was resolved, it was imperative that Alabama Guard leaders not let the dispute spill over into the Guard's operations. It was a critical time for the Alabama Guard for a comprehensive reorganization was underway to bring units in line with the active Army's new pentomic divisions. The governor announced the change in the make-up of the Guard in April, stating that the biggest problem confronting Alabama was a reduction in total units. Under the realignment, the Dixie Division was being "converted from the triangular-type division of three regiments into a more flexible pentomic division of five battle groups. Three of the groups would be located in Alabama, the other two in Mississippi.[82]

Two months later General Hanna "executed a soldierly withdrawal" by taking his name out of contention for the division commander's post. He, like Patterson, feared that dragging the dispute out longer would do the Alabama Guard more harm than good. Governor Patterson made the announcement "with sincere regret," reiterating that General Hanna was "the best qualified man for the job." The state was indebted to Hanna for his exemplary service and unselfish endeavor "to reach a solution to the problem with Mississippi," Patterson said.[83]

The governor subsequently announced the promotion of Brigadier General John D. Sides, a native of St. Clair County, to two stars and appointment as commander of the 31st Infantry Division. Brigadier General Rex D. Roach of Geneva was named assistant commander. Both officers were combat veterans, and had fought together in the Pacific during World War II. Coleman readily concurred in the appointments.[84]

When Sides retired a year later Patterson appointed Roach to serve as interim commander of the 31st Division and nominated Colonel Joseph Langan for promotion to brigadier general and assignment as assistant commander. Roach subsequently retired in September 1961. The governor, with the concurrence of Mississippi Governor Ross Barnett, then announced Langan's promotion to division commander, and the appointment of state adjutant general Henry Graham to be assistant commander. Patterson said both Langan and Graham excelled in their respective command assignments.[85]

POLITICAL FALLOUT, IF ANY, from the Patterson-Coleman dispute fizzled in comparison to the furor over the Alabama governor's support for Senator John F. Kennedy (D-Mass.) for president of the United States. Even his minister who was Methodist took the governor to the woodshed for supporting a Catholic and a Yankee one at that. The minister paid a visit to the governor's office to protest the apostasy and preached a sermon on Sunday morning against the nation's highest office having ties to the Roman Catholic Church.[86]

While he was attorney general, Patterson had met Senator Kennedy briefly at an Alabama League of Municipalities convention in Birmingham. At a banquet that evening, attended by Patterson, the visiting senator spoke on the government's fight against organized crime. Patterson was seated at the head table, and when the speech was over, he went up to Kennedy and introduced himself. They chatted for a few minutes. "Yes, I know you," Kennedy said. "You knew what I was talking about, didn't you?" "Yes, sir, I sure did," Patterson replied.[87]

Patterson had read about Kennedy and the statements "he had made concerning various problems in the country," and had some knowledge "of the kind of person he was and the things he stood for." He found the senator's book *Profiles in Courage* interesting and looked forward to the opportunity of meeting him personally. Patterson later recalled at that first meeting with Kennedy having a feeling "this was probably the next president of the United States."[88]

After that first meeting, whenever Patterson was in Washington, D.C., and had an opportunity, he dropped by Kennedy's office to visit. On a trip in February 1959 he and Charlie Meriwether were invited to breakfast with the senator at his residence in Georgetown. They discussed the political situation in Alabama, and politics in general. Patterson expressed an interest in Kennedy's plans for becoming the Democratic candidate for president. By that time it was generally accepted that Kennedy would seek the nomination. Patterson told Kennedy that he would help him in any way that he possibly could.[89]

Patterson was joined on a weekend trip to the nation's capital in June by members of his staff (Meriwether, legal adviser Ralph Smith, Robertson, highway director Engelhardt) along with the municipality league's Ed Reid and Hubert Baughn, editor of *South* magazine. It was on this visit that Reid arranged for Patterson to meet with Drew Pearson at his home, where they patched up past differences and the governor subsequently received a plug for his education program. The more important thrust of the trip, however, was a long session over breakfast with Senator John Kennedy at his Georgetown mansion. With Kennedy was the assistant charged with getting the nomination, Stephen Smith.[90]

Patterson again pledged his support to Kennedy and agreed to help the senator win the Democratic nomination in 1960. When the meeting broke up, unknown to Patterson, Ed Reid got on the phone to his friend Grover Hall and broke the story to the *Montgomery Advertiser*. Reid told Hall that Coleman of Mississippi was expected to be Kennedy's Southern campaign manager, but Alabama's governor would be "the pivot man" in the South for Kennedy. "He will be heading not a holding operation—as those favoring Senator Lyndon Johnson will be doing—but an operation planned to ride with a winner all the way," Reid stated.[91]

Breaking the story—Hall's scoop was picked up by the wire services and flashed across the nation—was premature for both Patterson and Kennedy. Criticism of the Massachusetts senator for "accepting the backing" of the Alabama governor came fast and furious from civil rights groups such as the NAACP, still smarting over its banishment from the state. Congressman Adam Clayton Powell, Jr., blasted the breakfast alliance, lashing out at the governor and Engelhardt as "these two Negro-hating Alabamians." Kennedy, walking a tightrope to get all the delegates he could from the North and the South, played down the relationship and said he had promised Alabama's governor nothing in return for his support.[92]

Governor Patterson said it was true that they had not discussed the racial situation (then or later), or anything along those lines, and that Senator Kennedy "never promised him anything." Admitting that it might have been naive of him, Patterson said he had sought no political favors when he endorsed Kennedy for president. He had given some thought to how having a friend in the White House might benefit the people of Alabama, but that was the extent of his thinking about any advantages to be had from his support for JFK.

"I liked the man personally," Patterson said in a 1967 interview, expounding on the theme. "I considered him a friend." The country was ready for change, and he believed JFK was the right person to lead the country in a new direction. He liked what Kennedy had to say about solving America's economic problems and his statements on foreign relations. "I think that we need a complete reevaluation of our foreign policy in this country and I think that if he'd have lived that it might have been a little different, as far as our foreign relations are concerned," Patterson said. "Also I think he disliked organized crime as much as I did, and this was something I was very interested in, too."[93]

Back home the mocking tone of Grover Hall's story—Patterson pledged "all the king's horses and all the king's men to the Kennedy-for-President movement, while shaking hands "across the bacon and eggs" at the senator's home in "Georgetown where dwell the high and mighty of Washington"—reemphasized that he was neither a Patterson nor a Kennedy man. The *Advertiser* editor must have taken pleasure in any discomfort caused the governor by the tone of the story or its untimely publication.[94]

Patterson told Kennedy his Catholic faith would not "hurt his chances in the South" and that if it was made an issue it would "backfire and help the senator." Now he wondered. Not only did he and his minister have words over his support for Kennedy, but other denominations protested as well. The bitterest denunciation came from the *Methodist Christian Advocate*, the official publication of the Methodist Church in Alabama. The editor, Dr. T. P. Chalker, said Patterson would discover "to his sorrow that the people of Alabama whose attitudes are basically Protestant, do not intend to jeopardize their democratic liberties by opening the doors of the White House to the political machinations of a determined power-hungry Romanist heirarchy."[95]

The governor answered his critics by saying, "A man's religion is his personal business." He still didn't feel Kennedy's religion was going "to seriously affect his chances for the presidency," and asked that the public be tolerant of Kennedy's religious views. "I think the state of Alabama is in a good position to play a leading part in national affairs and I want to see us play this part," he said. "He has a good chance to win and the people who are with him early will sit at the front table. I want Alabama to be up front."[96]

Late one afternoon, in the shimmering heat of summer, when it looked as if passions had cooled over the Kennedy affair, a delegation of three dozen irate citizens descended on the state capitol demanding an audience with the governor. They called on the chief executive as a group because individually they had been unable to get past Joe Robertson's desk at the front office. A spokesman for the group was later identified as a railroad man and local klansman. Self-styled white Christians who were "former supporters, rooters, and workers for John Patterson," the delegates wanted to know "if the governor was being used as a guinea pig by Communist-Jewish integrators to sample Southern political sentiment" for Senator Kennedy?[97]

Governor Patterson snapped back that he was not being used by anybody. "Senator Kennedy is a friend of mine," he said. "and I have no apology to make to anybody for my stand." Neither did he have any apology to make for his record on preserving segregation. He was angered when the group asked about his Jewish friends Bunny Kohn of Tuskegee and Fred Rothstein of New York City. His friends were none of their business, the governor retorted. During the 1958 campaign Rothstein came down for a visit and was introduced to United Klans grand dragon Robert Shelton at a rally in Tuscaloosa. Afterward Shelton asked a campaign worker what that New York Jew was doing in Alabama? He was told that Rothstein was an old Army buddy of John Patterson's, and he'd better not say anything derogatory about him. When Rothstein got back to the Big Apple, he smiled and said "Mama, you'll never guess who I shook hands with down in Alabama."[98]

The delegation also expressed concern about a Jewish firm, Herbert Lehman of New York, being connected to the sale of the state's road bonds. Patterson curtly explained that the bonds went to the low bidder, as required by law. The New York firm, referred to by the protesting group as "the arch-integrationist and avowed enemy of the South," had purchased only a small part of the bond issue. Alabama banks and investment firms made larger purchases. The governor called the session to a halt, and the confused delegates left in a stew.[99]

A non-supportive editor opined afterward: "There are some awfully sore people in Alabama today who are just hoping that John Patterson will have the temerity to offer himself again for office."[100] The editor was referring, of course, to the governor's unflinching support for Senator Kennedy's presidential aspirations. Only time would tell what his support for Kennedy would mean to Patterson's own political future at home. He would deal with that later. For now the thought hadn't crossed his mind.

14

ALL THE WAY WITH JFK AND LBJ

Governor Patterson did not waver in his support of John F. Kennedy's campaign for the presidency. He backed the Massachusetts senator's successful bid for the Democratic nomination at the national convention in July, and threw his wholehearted support behind the Kennedy-Johnson ticket in the November general election. He had not asked for anything in return, and he was not promised anything.

Political reporters are incurable skeptics. They follow the creed that says show me a political favor, I'll show you a political plum. At the national governors' conference at Glacier National Park, Montana, in late June, a Patterson associate, weary of being hounded by reporters looking for the nonexistent plum in the governor's support for Kennedy and by political opponents trying to get him to switch sides, complained: "Those fellows don't understand that . . . friendship is the reason Patterson is sticking with Kennedy. Patterson certainly has nothing to gain. Kennedy wouldn't dare appoint him to any important federal job; the Northern liberals wouldn't stand for it."[1]

The governor could not have been more open about his reason for being first on the Kennedy bandwagon. He genuinely liked John Kennedy, both as a person and as a public figure. Convinced that JFK would be the next president of the United States, he wanted Alabama to have a friend in the oval office. That many people in his state opposed him on Kennedy's candidacy did not bother Patterson, but their hang-ups over the senator's religion did. He too was a man of faith, had grown up in a God-fearing home, and had Tallapoosa brush-arbor gospel in his blood. But he was no zealot and tried not to let piety cloud his judgment or constrict his views.

Still, he did not hold others' prejudices against them. "My parents taught me that bitterness makes the medicine go down harder," he said. As a rule he simply did not carry a grudge. "I can honestly say that the only grudge I ever had was against the men who murdered my father," he said.[2]

Patterson saw in Kennedy the same ideals that guided his father's quest for "good government." As a lasting reminder of the price he paid, a statue of slain crime fighter A. L. Patterson was erected on the state capitol lawn in 1961. State Representative W. L. Vickers, the governor's friend and supporter, gave the dedicatory address on behalf of the New Site Masonic lodge which had put the statue on the capitol grounds. The governor and his eleven-year-old son Albert pulled the cloth covering away, as he reminded scores of onlookers his father's memorial was "a symbol of man's never-ending search for good government."[3]

The statue going up in the midst of the JFK-related criticism brought back memories of the elder Patterson's active support for Alfred E. Smith's (also a Roman Catholic) unsuccessful bid for the presidency in 1928. The Pattersons were living in Opelika then, and his father "took a lot of flak" for supporting a candidate who was Catholic. The governor said he thought "we'd gotten over all that" until he too "caught a lot of hell" over John Kennedy. "I could not believe people would feel the way they did about a fellow running for president who was a Catholic at that particular time in our history. Anyway, it was pretty rough to carry the Kennedy banner in Alabama because of his religion."[4]

In his father's home and in his home there was never any talk of discrimination against anyone "because of their religion or their race or anything else." It was not allowed. Albert had always insisted, as did he, that "we all be kind and respectful of everybody." "I guess that's one reason why it never dawned on me that I'd catch so much hell when I endorsed John Kennedy," Patterson said. "But I did. Anyway, Al Smith lost, but Kennedy won. That helped us get over that anti-Catholic thing. Once and for all, I hope."[5]

PATTERSON SAID THE SLUMPS in his popularity over the Kennedy affair were not a concern, but he didn't want to lose friends to political differences. For awhile it looked as if the news media would blame politics and the JFK-connection anytime his administration stubbed its toe. One incident hyped by the media and causing the governor some remorse was a policy dispute arising between himself and a close friend and supporter, prominent Alabamian Winton M. (Red) Blount.

Blount, from Union Springs, was the same age as Patterson and they had come back from WWII around the same time. Blount purchased some surplus Army construction equipment and started a construction company with his brother Houston (who left the business in 1948). Ten years later, when Patterson ran for governor, Blount was on his way to building one of the top construction companies in the world. He contributed $10,000 to Patterson's campaign.

"That amount of cash money bought you two new cars and was larger than most folks' bank accounts in those days." Blount even footed the bill for the inaugural bleachers and scaffolding. They were pals, and when Patterson moved into the governor's office he named Blount to a non-salaried position as chairman of the licensing board for general contractors. Both men were concerned about the Folsom administration's laxity in general contracting, and moved quickly to regulate contractor licensing in the state.

The governor came to rely on Blount's business acumen and counsel and prized their friendship. "He was a remarkable person and was a lot of fun to be around," Patterson said. Blount was an Army Air Forces pilot in WWII and was training to fly B-29s when the war ended. An aviation enthusiast, he owned his own plane and would sometimes call on the spur of the moment and ask the governor to join him on a weekend getaway. One Saturday they flew to South Bend, Indiana, to see a Notre Dame-Army football game, and then on to Chicago on Sunday to see the Bears play the San Francisco 49ers. "First and only professional football game I've ever seen," Patterson said.[6]

Blount's company plane was the same model as the one owned by the state, a twin Beechcraft. Blount was looking at a new twin-engine turbo-prop executive aircraft that Howard Aero in San Antonio, Texas, was selling, and Howard flew to Montgomery for a demonstration. Blount called the governor and said, "Let's go with Mr. Howard in his plane to Jackson Hole, Wyoming, and hunt some moose." Patterson had never been moose hunting, so he thought that was a good idea. He needed to get away and relax for a couple of days. The governor, Charlie Meriwether, and John Overton, a business acquaintance in Montgomery, joined the hunting party.[7]

As they were leaving to go to the airport, Blount's wife Mary Katherine ran out of the house carrying her husband's rifle. "Wait a minute, Red. You forgot your gun." That was the first inkling Patterson had that "Red didn't intend to go hunting moose after all." On the way to Wyoming they decided to lay over in Las Vegas, and fly to Jackson Hole the next day. They stayed at the Desert Inn, which was owned by a wealthy Alabamian named Billy Harrigan, who also owned the Scotch Lumber Company at Vredenburgh, Alabama.[8]

"Of course, Harrigan knew we were coming. Red let him know, so we were entertained royally," Patterson laughed. "Our money was no good there." Four days later they were still at the Desert Inn. "Even though we had our rifles and gear in the plane we never made it to Jackson Hole. Always wanted to go. But

I've never been there." Word back home was they got weathered in by a blizzard. That story suited the governor just fine.[9]

"When Red Blount did things he did them up right," Patterson said, recalling that when they left Reno Blount told the pilot to fly over the Grand Canyon. It was a clear day. They dropped down into the Grand Canyon at the upper end and flew for miles below the rim of the canyon before pulling up. "I have never in my life experienced anything that was as thrilling as that was. That was a sight to see. I won't ever forget that."[10]

The governor had only the one spat with Blount, and it was not lasting. He had received complaints that stringent licensing criteria kept young people fresh out of college from breaking into the construction business. "The board classified contractors on the size of the jobs they bid, money-wise," Patterson explained. "At the lower end were the young guys coming right out of college trying to get into the business, trying to get started. The board didn't cut them no slack, and as they worked their way up the ladder they couldn't bid on a job without putting up a bond, and to get the bond they had to have resources, which the guys just starting out didn't have." It was a vicious cycle for the new businesses, and they complained to the governor. When he took the complaints to the board and asked that restrictions be eased on businesses just starting out, they argued and Blount resigned as board chairman.[11]

Grover Hall, sensing a Patterson nosebleed, charged in the evening *Journal* that the governor had forced Blount's resignation in "a petty political act reflecting no credit upon his judgment." He accused the governor of "not thinking soundly" because he had "gone so completely hog wild about Kennedy and Johnson and is so desperately eager for them to carry Alabama." Hall continued the harangue in the morning *Advertiser*, describing the governor as "Caesar P," a harsh and vengeful partisan," and "hickory-headed." Hall also dragged in an unrelated incident, accusing Patterson of playing politics in the resignation of John Kohn as chairman of the milk control board.[12]

Blount was quoted as saying he believed his "forced resignation" as board chairman was politically inspired. While Patterson and Blount were on different sides in the presidential race (Blount was a Republican) the governor would not be drawn into a public airing of their dispute. He denied that politics had anything to do with Kohn's resignation, but he refused to challenge Blount's version of events, stating only that "Mr. Blount submitted his resignation. He is a very close friend of mine and a very close supporter." "That was the only disagreement he and I ever had," Patterson said. "But we got over that and remained friends. There were no hard feelings about it."[13]

The flare-up between the governor and Blount occurred in October, near the end of the hotly contested 1960 presidential race. More than a year had passed since Patterson first endorsed John F. Kennedy, and if he ever had any doubts about the Kennedy-Johnson ticket after the roll call was over at the Democratic Convention in Los Angeles in July, he never let it show. Later that month in Chicago, the Republicans nominated Vice President Richard M. Nixon and UN Ambassador Henry Cabot Lodge, Jr., of Massachusetts as their standard bearers. Blount, who had served as chairman of Alabama Citizens for Eisenhower in 1952, became the chairman for Richard Nixon's campaign in the Southeast.

When he was first asked to work for Nixon's election, Blount went to the governor and offered his resignation as chairman of the contractors board. Having supported Patterson in the gubernatorial race, Blount said he "did not want to embarrass him in anyway." Since the governor refused to accept the resignation at that time, his recollection of events leading to Blount's eventual departure just short of election day makes sense. Nevertheless, Blount chose to make the dispute a political issue at the time and assailed the governor for backing the Democratic ticket. The governor refused to answer in kind, allowing the awkward moment between two friends to recede into the slipstream of Alabama history.[14]

For more than a year Patterson had taken political heat for his support of John F. Kennedy. He hadn't lost sleep over that, and a few more days or weeks until the election was over wouldn't make any difference. He knew the race was tight, but he was confident about the outcome, particularly as far as Alabama was concerned. Alabama was still a Democratic state, and with a Southerner, Senator Lyndon Baines Johnson of Texas, on the ticket, even closet Vatican haters weren't likely to cross over. Alabama's delegates hadn't voted with their feet in Los Angeles, as some diehards back home wanted them to do. Now, Alabama's voters would either back the Democratic ticket in the general election, or sit this one out.

The governor and his cabinet had their collective ear to the ground and had a good idea what people around the state were saying. In November 1959 Patterson had introduced an innovative policy of "visiting the various communities of the state and bringing the governor's office closer to the people." With the 1959 legislative session out of the way, he announced that as soon as he returned from the "moose-hunting" trip with Winton Blount, his administration was going to concentrate on management. He said he planned "to get out into the field more where we can see exactly what is going on. I want to look at the new roads and bridges we are building."[15]

Elaborating on the field inspection trips following his return, he stated the purpose was to take the state government out to the people "to determine if the taxpayers are getting their money's worth, if state projects are progressing satisfactorily, and if state services and operations can be streamlined to increase efficiency." A few critics lampooned "the Patterson pageant" as it wound through the countryside, but even they applauded the governor's "idea of going into the various counties, for a day, visiting their industries, looking at their roads, and talking with the people." They praised not only "the energy and devotion he has given to his job," but his equal "consideration to a community or a county whether it opposed him or supported him."[16]

Taking the governor's office to the people was not a "hit-and-miss, piece-meal" proposition, but a well-planned, orchestrated calendar of events reaching out to all sixty-seven counties by the end of his four-year term. Planned weeks in advance, the visits and the cabinet members who accompanied the governor were tailored to the special character and needs of individual counties. A typical visit to Barbour County, the heart of George Wallace country, in October 1960 was timed to coincide with the Eufaula Chamber of Commerce's annual meeting and barbecue. State Docks Director Earl McGowin went with the governor to announce a decision "to buy up ninety acres along the Chattahoochee River for a new inland docks site."[17]

McGowin's news was a reflection that the Patterson administration was for all of the people, and that the governor held no grudges against those who didn't vote for him. Inland docks development in the state was financed from a $10 million bond issue approved a few years earlier. McGowin explained to the cheering crowd that engineers had reported favorably on the Eufaula site, "with access to water, rail and highway transportation," and the administration was moving ahead with plans "to acquire the land and get the show on the road as quickly as possible."[18]

Former Governor Chauncey Sparks of Eufaula introduced Patterson as a governor who "has given Alabama a wide-awake administration." Patterson replied that the Sparks administration "was known for honesty and integrity, and we have drawn on the policies and programs of that administration for assistance and guidance." The governor got in six speeches during the Barbour County tour, which lasted all day and into the night.[19]

The thrust of the county tours was not political stumping, but to open the lines of communication and strengthen the ties between the local communities and their state government. By law, Governor Patterson could not run to succeed himself in 1962, and he had no designs on other public office at the time. The outings taken during the 1960 presidential campaign did provide opportunities to speak out for the Democratic ticket of John Kennedy and Lyndon Johnson, however, and the governor promoted the ticket in his speeches and his discussions with local officials everywhere he went.[20]

When the governor went to Los Angeles with Alabama's delegates in July, the furor over his early endorsement of Kennedy for president had receded. Only an occasional political column mentioned the endorsement as being premature, or chided the governor for giving away any leverage he might have used at the national convention. Patterson shrugged off the criticism. Admitting to some degree of naivete, the governor said he wasn't looking for political leverage. He was simply throwing his support behind the person he believed would be the next president of the United States.

By convention time, Patterson had established himself as one of Alabama's most progressive governors. Rarely a day passed that the governor's office (braced by the first-class publicity team of Marcato, Harper, Cook, and Giles) failed to make the news. The youthful administration was always on the move. They would come back to their busy desks from visits to the field, only to head back out on trips serving Alabama's interests outside the state. The governor jumped at every chance to tell others about the assets and opportunities his state had to offer—all in the interest of promoting economic growth, tourism, and industrial development at home.

On one such trip in early 1960 the governor and State Docks Director Earl McGowin led a Port of Mobile trade mission to Puerto Rico. The purpose of the mission—growing out of initiatives from the National Governor's Conference at San Juan, Puerto Rico, the previous August—was to increase Latin American shipping trade at the Mobile port where Puerto Rican ships already accounted for "about 350,000 tons of cargo, worth some five million dollars" annually. The state yacht *Jamelle* (named for Folsom's wife) was sent to the Caribbean island to entertain business and political leaders while state officials were visiting.[21]

Patterson flew back from the Caribbean early, leaving McGowin and his staff to complete the trade mission. He believed the mission was successful in winning friends for the port of Mobile and would increase shipping trade, but felt his presence was no longer required.[22] Other pressing matters awaited him back at the office. Among them were nagging education and race problems that he knew were not going away.

GOVERNOR PATTERSON WAS THE toast of the town to educators at the end of 1959. They had not backed him during the 1958 campaign, but now they welcomed him down from Mount Olympus. The Alabama Education Association, in the October issue of its monthly magazine, had ranked him "along with past great friends of education"—Governors Braxton Bragg Comer (1907–11), Thomas Kilby (1919–23), and Bibb Graves (1927–31 and 1935–39). But by late winter and early spring of 1960, Patterson and educators had crossed swords over managing the $100 million school construction program and a shortfall in education revenues; the governor's feet had turned to clay. At times the confrontation overheated, prompting a quip from Bob Ingram that the governor was "now going through the graduate school of politics" and all he had to do "to get his degree, with honors" was "come out alive."[23]

A priority concern was that the state get maximum return on the $100 million bond issue for building new schools and classrooms, and that the money be spent wisely. In February Patterson and Finance Director Meriwether went to New York and convinced rating agencies to rate the bonds as "Class AA"—said to be the first time such a high rating had been given a state revenue bond issue. Securing the favorable rating would save the state an estimated $4 million in interest, Meriwether said.[24]

Patterson had persuaded the legislature to pass the bond issue based on the urgent need for new schools and new classrooms in all of Alabama's 120 school districts. To emphasize the rundown condition of Alabama's schools he told legislators about visiting "the worst high school he had ever seen" when he stopped on the campaign trail in West Blocton, a small mining town between Tuscaloosa and Birmingham. "You've heard about people going to school in chicken houses," he said. "Well, in West Blocton they really are." He had promised voters there that if he became governor he would build a new high school in West Blocton, and he meant to keep the promise.[25]

A conflict arose when state educators proposed to divide the $100 million equally among the districts and let them spend the money as they wished. Patterson would not agree to that. Each school district had submitted a list of building priorities. Upon review the governor found that the districts were primarily interested in building new gymnasiums and cafeterias, instead of classrooms. "You had to go way down on the priority list before you got to a classroom," Patterson said. Conspicuously omitted were new facilities for black students, although they had been promised separate but equal schools. He had specifically asked that a new high school for West Blocton be included. It too was left off the list.[26]

In later years Patterson said he was convinced that millions of dollars from that bond issue would be frittered away or sitting in banks across the state drawing interest if he had left the matter in the hands of school administrators. "No, sir, we're going to build school houses," he told State Superintendent Stewart. To resolve the problem he moved to "centrally control and supervise" spending of the $100 million dollars for new schools. At the governor's insistance, the Alabama Education Authority adopted a resolution giving the State Building Commission overall supervision of planning and building new schools with the bond money. Stewart protested, but reluctantly went along with the resolution.[27]

When asked if West Blocton got its new high school the governor said, "Yes, and here's how we did it." While preparing to build new schools, which took time, the state invested a large part of the $100 million in U.S. Treasury bonds and other interest-bearing bonds. Part of that interest was used to build the new high school at West Blocton. "The school folks couldn't object to that," Patterson said. "They didn't want to do it, but they couldn't object to it either."[28]

Patterson also kept his promise to the black community by insisting that the bond money "be spent equally on the black schools as well as the white schools." The bond money also paid for building new vocational or trade schools. One was the John M. Patterson Technical School in Montgomery. Four decades later the facility was merged with another technical school and the name changed to the H. Council Trenholm State Technical College in honor of a distinguished African American educator and former president of Alabama State University. The technical college maintained two campuses, the Patterson campus and the Trenholm campus.[29]

"I learned quickly, as governor, that the people responsible for building roads, bridges, and schools weren't nearly as important as the fact they were built," Patterson remarked. When he was governor he cut ribbons on numerous projects begun by Folsom, just as Wallace got credit for a lot of Patterson programs after he left office. "We started a number of bridges and buildings, and George Wallace who followed me in office cut the ribbon on them and took the credit," he laughed. "And by that time the public had forgotten who built them anyway."

A vignette about the Auburn University library illustrated his point. Soon after Patterson was elected governor, Auburn's president Ralph Draughon invited him over for a tour of the campus. Dr. Draughon took him by the university's ramshackle library facilities, partly housed in quonset huts. "Isn't that pitiful for a major university to have a library like that?" Draughon asked. "I want you to help me build a library at Auburn while you're governor." "Yessir' we'll do that for you," Patterson promised. The money for a new library "came off the top of the hundred million dollars."

Patterson was there for the ground-breaking, and was invited back for the ribbon-cutting after he left office. He sat on the back row "behind a potted plant" with his friend John Overton while Governor Wallace cut the ribbon and took credit for the new library. Draughon knew the story, of course, and asked Patterson to come by the president's house after the ceremony. Draughon took his guest into the den and said, "You know, I really appreciate all you've done and I want you to have a drink with me." He went over to the liquor cabinet and brought out a bottle of rare Old Overholt rye whiskey. "I've been saving this a long time for a special occasion. This is the occasion. The new library."

Patterson was a Scotch on the rocks man, but he wasn't about to spoil the moment by turning his host down. "Just me and him," Patterson recalled, relishing the memory. "He pours us a glass of Old Overholt and a chaser. And we took that drink, and he says, 'Let's have one more.' So we had another one." Then Dr. Draughon put the stopper back in the bottle, and he said, "All right. I'm going to save the rest of this for the night after we beat Alabama in that football game."[30]

Draughon was unaware of the political cudgel required to get the new library. The governor had used the power of his office to make certain the proceeds from the $100 million bond issue were not frittered away, but had to override protests from the state superintendent and the board of education in the process. Superintendent Stewart had agreed reluctantly to the state's oversight, but the embers of a feud still smoldered when state revenues, pinched by a nationwide steel strike and a slump in the economy, fell short of the $148 million appropriated to run the schools.

Faced with a 10 percent proration for the 1959–60 fiscal year, giving teachers a 5 percent raise instead of the promised 15 percent, the school boards and administrators leaped on the governor and state legislators "with a vengeance."[31]

The alternative to proration, the governor warned state educators, was to close the schools six weeks to two months early. At a meeting on March 3 state school board members voted to postpone consideration of the revised budget, while Stewart urged the governor to call a special legislative session "to raise more money for schools." Pressure mounted, but the governor stood firm. "The demand for a special session includes the demand for more taxes," he pointed out, and he was opposed to "raising state taxes or adding on any new taxes."[32]

He could have passed the burden off to the legislature but was not going to waste the state's time and money on an extraordinary session when he knew the outcome. This made the fourth straight year that Alabama's educational funds had been prorated. Taxes were not raised to resolve the school crises in the past, and legislators could not be expected to raise them now against the wishes of the people. Governors who preceded him had brought the question of school taxes up for a vote, and the people of Alabama had rejected them.[33]

A proposal to levy temporary taxes to provide emergency relief for education was opposed by the governor. "Temporary measures have a way of becoming permanent," Patterson said. He pointed out that the sales tax law itself originally was intended as an emergency measure, but had been in effect nearly thirty years. A plea the governor made to a general session of the Alabama Educational Association in Birmingham to accept proration without a teacher walkout or school closures was ignored. The AEA, Superintendent Stewart, and the state school board (where Patterson appointees were outvoted 7-to-4) worked against the governor in trying to resolve the crisis.[34]

Near the end of March the governor called another meeting of the board to decide on a final course of action for keeping the schools open. The board voted 7-to-4 against accepting a 10 percent cutback, which meant that city and county school systems would continue to operate under the current budget with no reductions in teacher salaries. The burden was on the local school boards to keep the schools open. The governor believed the local boards could mostly offset the loss by diverting other funds to teachers' salaries. While the governor had received minimal cooperation from educators on the question of proration, a full-blown crisis had been averted.[35]

For a change the capitol reporters took the governor's side in the dispute. Bob Ingram reminded readers that no recent governor had "gone further out on the political limb . . . to help improve education's lot than Patterson," and he felt that Patterson had "every reason to be vexed by the conduct of the school people." The popular columnist needled state educators: "They no doubt have many scholastic degrees but if any of them majored in diplomacy they have long since forgot what they learned."[36]

Patterson learned from the crisis, putting the disagreements behind him. Healthy political exchange was the vital spark of public discourse, while learning in the Patterson household was a dawn-to-dusk endeavor and teaching a family tradition. The state's public school system and higher education in Alabama remained high on John Patterson's list of priorities, before, during, and after his term as governor.

CLOUDING THE EDUCATION PICTURE were the thunderheads of pending racial desegregation and the fog of the public schools system's future in Alabama. At the end of 1959 Patterson, having pledged to close the schoolhouse doors in the face of forced desegregation, warned that the people of the South were "kidding themselves" if they believed they could maintain segregated public schools in the long run. Their only recourse, he said, was to make a choice between private and public schools.[37]

To abandon the public schools would penalize poor families, both blacks and whites, but was a sacrifice many Southern politicians worried they might have to make to avert racial violence and bloodshed. A central point of Patterson's strategy since his days as attorney general was to stave off the inevitable mixing of the public schools by contesting desegregation in the courts, while counting on the threat of school closures to deter or delay federal action. This strategy apparently succeeded in the short term since no Alabama schools were forced to integrate while he was governor.[38]

Had Justice Department officials been more astute they might have called the governor's bluff. Nearly a year had passed since Governor Lindsay Almond threw in the towel on dismantling Virginia's public school system. Almond was Patterson's friend and mentor on resistance to federal desegregation. Perhaps Patterson, like Almond, could have closed the doors of one or two schools as a show of defiance, but he knew that nailing the doors shut was a hollow threat. Alabama's public school system was not a pawn in the state's standoff with the federal government, and he knew it. Keeping the federal officials guessing gave the state a slight edge in delaying school desegregation until after he left office in January 1963.

The threat to close the public schools had been a staple of Patterson's political speeches since he decided to run for governor in 1958. Concerned citizens actually set up the machinery to operate private segregated schools, but education officials were never enthusiastic about this solution.[39] Patterson publicly endorsed private schools as a last resort, and had shown that he was a man of his word. But the governor was also a practical person. He had not fought tooth and nail for a bond issue to build new schools just to close them down. No one explained that to the U.S. Justice Department.

In November 1959, Justice announced that it was looking into integrating an elementary school in Huntsville attended by military dependents at Redstone Arsenal. While there had been no complaints from Huntsville, the school there was among "the last holdouts of segregation among institutions attended exclusively by children of military personnel." A government spokesman described the Huntsville situation as a special problem because there was "no telling what Governor Patterson will do." "He might close all the schools in the district," the spokesman said.[40]

Arriving in Muscle Shoals for dedication of the new Wilson Lock and Dam on the day the announcement was made, the governor told reporters waiting at the airport that any move to integrate Huntsville would force him to close down the schools, adding that if government officials used force they would "find their troops guarding empty school houses." Back in Montgomery Reverend Martin Luther King, Jr., was prepared to call the governor's bluff. King sent a telegram to U.S. Attorney General William Rogers urging him to follow through with the school integration plan at Huntsville: "A retreat at this point would only confirm state officials in their undemocratic defiance of the law and make them more determined in their resistance."[41]

King announced earlier that civil rights leaders had asked the state school board to submit an integration plan and were prepared to go into court if necessary to achieve their goal. In the wake of these announcements the governor signed into law a bill authorizing state funds for financing private schools. He had considered vetoing the bill, patterned after an old law permitting state appropriations for private colleges, but played it as another trump card to counter the rising clamor over school desegregation. A law authorizing the use of state funds to subsidize private schools where public schools were closed or turned over to citizen groups was already on the books.[42]

As his first year in office drew to a close, Patterson stated at a press conference that he was pleased there were no school integration cases pending in the courts in Alabama, but admitted to being "fearful of what might come in 1960." "We have been hearing some rumblings and we might well have some cases by next September," he said. The U.S. Supreme Court had ruled in 1958 that Alabama's school placement law was constitutional on its face, but Patterson said that he was sure the first time the law was used to preserve segregation the high court would strike it down.[43]

For much of 1959 the civil rights movement in Alabama had been marked by restraint. Contested actions were in the courts where the governor said they belonged. In March the state felt somewhat vindicated when U.S. Middle District Judge Frank M. Johnson, Jr., dismissed a Justice Department lawsuit asking for a permanent injunction against the Macon County board of registrars for voting rights violations and seeking "to prohibit alleged discrimination against Negroes because of race or color." The grounds for dismissal were that the Civil Rights Act of 1957 was a "compromise measure" and did not give the government authority to sue states "allegedly guilty of violating Negro-voting rights."[44]

The appeals process bought time for the state, but was little more than a stumbling block to the forward march of the civil rights movement. Late in the year the civil rights commission issued its report recommending that federal registrars be appointed at places in the South where people were denied the right to vote because of race. In October, Patterson announced that federal agents had reopened investigations into voter complaints in Alabama.[45]

The governor condemned the commission's report as "a slander on the integrity of Alabama and its local officials." Senator Lister Hill called the report "one of the most indefensible and irresponsible statements of a public agency" he had ever seen. Patterson also tore into the federal investigators—charging that their tactics of "harrassment and intimidation" were politically inspired and were likely to continue until next year's presidential election. He urged state officials to give no help to investigators, and promised he would "pack them out of the state" as soon as he could.[46]

In February, the governor testified before the U.S. Senate rules committee on the commission's report and its "carpet bag registrars" proposals. He argued that proposed new voting rights legislation would usurp the powers of the states and "lead to chaos and bitterness." The commission's actions had "damaged race relations in the South" and exacerbated already strained relations between the states and the federal government, he charged—reiterating his oft-stated dictum that problems in race relations could "only be solved through local people working together in a spirit of cooperation without outside interference and agitation."[47]

Two months later he appeared before two congressional subcommittees conducting separate hearings on civil rights legislation, and told them "flatly" that Alabama would not "tolerate" integrated schools. The governor's words resonated with the white majority back home, but were given a wink and a nod by the U.S. Congress. Representative Emanuel Cellar (D., N.Y.) said he would look into the complaints about the civil rights commission, but nothing came of it. Soon thereafter, with the Democratic and Republican national conventions on the horizon, President Eisenhower signed a new civil rights bill authorizing federal inspection of voter registration rolls and establishing penalties for obstructing voter registration or actual voting. Patterson charged that "the interference from Washington" was politically motivated, and was an "attempt to win votes" for Vice President Nixon.[48]

Both political parties vied for African American votes, yet dragged their feet on securing minority voting rights. Studies estimated that the two Eisenhower civil rights acts (1957 and 1960) brought only an additional three percent of black voters to the polls in the 1960 presidential election. Six years had gone by since *Brown v. Board* and three since the ugly violence at Little Rock. Many African Americans were still denied voting rights. The public schools in Alabama and other Deep South states were no closer to accepting desegregation, and showed no signs of giving ground.

With civil rights advocates losing patience and the political conventions coming up in the summer of 1960, the climate was ripe for racial unrest, which erupted among students on the campuses of black colleges in the South. Starting with a lunch counter sit in by four students in Greensboro, North Carolina, on February 1, the spontaneous protests soon spread to other states, reaching Alabama toward the end of the month.

Meanwhile, Governor Patterson had made a decision (later described by him as "dumb," "mule-headed," and "wrong") to have Reverend King indicted and brought to trial on perjury charges for allegedly failing to report honorariums on tax returns he filed for 1956 and 1958 as a resident of Alabama. In November, King had announced that he was leaving the pulpit at Montgomery's Dexter Avenue Baptist Church to be co-pastor with his father at the Ebenezer Baptist Church in Atlanta. King departed amid rumors, which he denied, that he was leaving because black teachers opposed his efforts to integrate Montgomery's schools.[49]

King, whose image personified the civil rights movement in Montgomery, had taken his message beyond the cradle of freedom onto the national stage. King explained that his moving to Atlanta would facilitate directing the Southern Christian Leadership Conference (which he and other ministers had founded in 1957) and its campaign for racial equality throughout the South. On a return visit to the capital city in late February to sign papers relating to his indictment by a Montgomery grand jury, King spoke at a rally at Alabama State College where a student sit-in demonstration and a wave of campus protests were making headlines.[50]

While King and the SCLC had not instigated "the student protest now sweeping the South," the *New York Times* reported that the civil rights leader's teaching was believed to have inspired the student movement. King's presence undoubtedly gave heart to those who were demonstrating in Montgomery.[51] The first sign of campus unrest in the capital city occurred during a slack lunch hour in late February. It was a slow, do-nothing Thursday. Governor Patterson was at his desk clearing out the in-basket before flying to Cincinnati to open the Alabama exhibit at the Ohio Valley Travel Show. Ruth Richardson cracked the door to tell the governor that Floyd Mann needed to see him about a disturbance down at the courthouse.

Mann reported that some thirty-five black college students had crowded into the privately-operated grill in the courthouse basement and asked to be served. The proprietor shut the business down for the day, warned the students they were trespassing, and asked them to leave. Mingling around in the basement corridor for about an hour under the watchful eye of city police and Sheriff Mac Sim Butler's deputies, the students exited the building and dispersed. No arrests were made. Mann had state troopers at the scene, but they did not interfere. Keeping the peace was the city's responsibility, unless the troopers were invited in or the situation got out of hand.[52]

Patterson was confident that Sheriff Butler (described by the governor as "a class act") would keep the lid on violence in the county, but was less certain what Police Commissioner L. B. Sullivan would do "when push came to shove." The former public safety director was a seasoned lawman, but he was a hard-line segregationist and had a reputation for being hard-nosed and overly protective of law enforcement—he had stood up for Russell County's corrupt system in the impeachment trial of Sheriff Matthews in 1953 and testified for the defense in Deputy Fuller's murder trial in 1955. Still, the state had to rely on the city police force to do its job. Mann had his people monitoring the situation. If the city failed to establish control Mann was ready to send his troopers in.

Acting to head off violence, the governor ordered the president of Alabama State, Dr. H. Council Trenholm, to conduct a full investigation with the aim of stopping more disturbances and expelling the troublemakers. Trenholm, a distinguished educator who had served as president of the college for thirty-five years and was a faculty member before that, was clearly shaken by the student disturbance and the conflict it posed between the moral rightness of the students' cause and his own need to protect the college. "The citizens of this state do not intend to spend their tax money to educate law violators and race agitators," Patterson warned. "If you do not put a stop to it you might well find yourself out of public school funds."[53]

While in Cincinnati to open the Alabama exhibit, the governor kept in "close touch with the situation" at home through his legal adviser, Robert Bradley, and other members of the staff. On Friday several hundred Alabama State students appeared at the courthouse for the trial of a classmate accused of making a false statement when he had tried to register to vote. When they were returning to the campus—"walking two by two back to the college some two miles across town"— one student was ticketed for jaywalking, a charge that was almost never enforced. When President Trenholm broke up a rally on campus, protest leaders threatened a mass march on the capitol if any students were expelled.[54]

The student demonstrations were disruptive, but were nonviolent in line with Reverend King's teaching. Governor Patterson's main concern (and that of Mann and other law enforcement officials) was that the protests, overtly defiant and confrontational, would provoke a violent response from angry white citizens. Early Saturday morning those fears became real when city and state police observed carloads of white men from out of town gathering at the city ball park. Highway patrol chief Joe Smelley (former state investigator who was promoted after being taken off the Patterson murder case in 1954) stated that the men had been questioned and said they were in town "to stand by if needed but were not going to cause any trouble."[55]

Later in the day about two dozen white men were seen roaming the downtown sidewalks carrying miniature baseball bats in paper sacks. Their presence was not menacing until one of the men struck a black woman (who was not a student) on the head. A brief scuffle between the races ensued, but ended before the police could step in. The white assailant was not taken into custody. Afterward, about eight hundred Alabama State students held a four-hour rally at the Hutchinson Street Baptist Church, under the watchful eye of Reverend Ralph D. Abernathy, who had succeeded King as president of the Montgomery Improvement Association.[56]

Abernathy told the students that the club-carrying men "were reported to be members of the Ku Klux Klan," and that "a state of terror prevailed on downtown streets." Although not advocating a boycott, the clergyman urged black citizens to avoid the business district until their safety was assured. After the rally student spokesmen issued a prepared statement appealing to Patterson "to back down from his threat to have them expelled."[57]

Patterson had returned from Cincinnati, but the statehouse was closed in observance of Mardi Gras Day, when Alabama State student body president Bernard Lee led a protest march of about six hundred students from the college to the steps of the state capitol on Monday morning. The students, who were encouraged by Reverends King and Abernathy to continue their campaign, held a rally on the capitol steps where Lee repeated a call for a mass walkout from the college in the event any of the demonstrators was expelled.[58]

Trenholm appeared at a state board of education meeting on Wednesday and identified nine students as leaders of the local protests. Five, including Lee, were from out of state, an irrelevant fact that unhappily fed the views of whites that all black protests against segregation could only be the result of "outside agitators." Only one was from Montgomery. Trenholm recommended that all of the students involved be reprimanded and placed on probation. The board, however, unanimously approved a motion by Patterson to expel the nine ringleaders and to place the other twenty students on probation "pending good behavior."[59]

Patterson explained that the campus leaders were unrepentant, citing as evidence a telegram from Lee to him saying the students had "no sense of shame or regret for their conduct." As to probation for the others, he said they might have been influenced by civil rights leaders. "Some of them are very young and possibly there were mitigating circumstances," he said. When asked, Trenholm agreed that the students were "obsessed with obligation and conviction" and did not believe they had done "anything wrong." Reverends King and Abernathy said they had consulted with the students since the protests started, but denied any inspiration of the movement.[60]

No matter how righteous their cause, the governor said the students were going about things the wrong way. Their conduct was detrimental to the college, he said, and threatened bloodshed in Montgomery. Trenholm feared that expulsions might serve as "pretexts" for "other things," but Patterson disagreed. "If we ever bow to a mob . . . that could only lead to worse," he said. "We ought not to do anything as a result of a threat." He demanded the ringleaders' expulsion "without further hesitation."[61]

The expelled student leaders were defiant, however, and had the support of their two thousand classmates who all joined in a mass walkout from school two days later. Their youthful defiance was emboldened by adult leaders in the community. At an off-campus rally Reverend Abernathy denounced the state board's expulsion order as "the greatest blunder in the history of education in Alabama." Reassuring "the cheering audience" of the black community's support, Abernathy pledged "financial and moral" support if students were expelled or arrested.[62]

Abernathy avoided any criticism of the Alabama State president, stating that he had "continued faith and confidence" in Trenholm, who was "seeking to be loyal to his superiors as well as his school and students." He knew that Trenholm, highly regarded on both sides of the racial divide, walked a thin line between being labeled an "Uncle Tom" or losing his job. But, then the elected state and city officials weren't operating in a vacuum either. At the state board meeting Trenholm had replied "yes," when the governor asked, "Don't you think we can ask for a higher degree of conduct from college students than ordinary people?" Patterson told Trenholm that it was "inescapable that the board must look to you to maintain order."[63]

King briefly addressed another student meeting at Beulah Baptist Church on Friday night and promised "a wildly cheering crowd" of the SCLC's full support. King said his organization would provide scholarships for the nine expelled students. Abernathy announced that congregations of all the city's black churches would march to the front steps of the capitol on Sunday afternoon for a prayer meeting. Students shouted their endorsement of a strike at Alabama State when the spring quarter registration began on Monday.[64]

On Saturday morning Patterson watched from a window in his office in the north wing of the capitol as "a parade of about thirty carloads of unidentified white men and women drove through downtown Montgomery . . . with signs calling on whites to fire their Negro employees." Afterward, Police Commissioner Sullivan issued a prepared statement that the city would allow "no further demonstration by whites or Negroes . . . that would tend to create further racial tensions." Therefore, he said the city police would prohibit any mass protest at the capitol such as the one proposed for Sunday "under the guise of a religious service."[65]

"No one wants to deprive any human being of the privilege of worshiping God," Sullivan said, "However, we feel that the Negroes, like the white people, have their churches for this purpose. Further if the Negroes want to hold a combined service, they have the campus, athletic field, and facilities of Alabama State College for such use."[66]

In the midst of the turmoil, a rash of threats against the governor and his family convinced Mann to post an additional highway patrolmen to guard the official residence. Mann said an anonymous caller warned that "something bad is going to happen" at the mansion. A guard who answered the phone identified the voice as that of a black man. Other ominous calls included a bomb threat telephoned to the mansion by a white male over the weekend.[67]

On Sunday the black churches yielded to the police commissioner's directive and revised plans for holding a mass prayer service on the capitol steps. They congregated instead at the historic Dexter Avenue Baptist Church a block away. While a cordon of city, county and state police blocked entry onto the capitol grounds, more than five hundred riot policemen and city firemen with fire hoses stood by, ready to swing into action if a disturbance broke out. Their strong presence didn't seem to intimidate a surly group of several hundred white men who had gathered across from the church. An estimated five thousand spectators stood back, looking on from surrounding areas. Trouble was in the air.[68]

When the service was over and the congregation poured out of the church, the mob of white troublemakers charged across the street toward them. A formation of mounted sheriff's deputies (a special force highly trained by Sheriff Butler) moved in quickly between the two groups, forcing the congregation back into the church and driving the angry whites away. Keeping the would-be attackers at bay, the deputies watched over the black churchgoers as they departed the area in small groups. Governor Patterson, looking out from his office window, breathed a sigh of relief. What could have been a violent scene had been avoided.[69]

The governor knew things were under control when Floyd Mann looked up from the capitol grounds and gave him the high sign. He left the office and walked down to where Mann was standing. "Floyd we got to get you some of those trained horses," he said. "They're really something." Mann got a call on his walkie-talkie and headed back to headquarters. The governor looked around and shook a few hands before heading down to the Elite Cafe for one of Mr. Pete's special cups of Sunday coffee.

On Tuesday a crowd of Alabama State students and some faculty members staged a demonstration near the capitol, defying Trenholm's guidance and the police commissioner's warning against further demonstrations. The police dispersed the crowd and thirty-seven protesters, mostly students, were jailed on charges of disorderly conduct and refusal to obey an officer. Faced with continued racial demonstrations and an "apparent lack of cooperation . . . by faculty and students," the police commissioner recommended to the governor and the board of education that the black college be closed. "Alabama State College is a state tax-supported institution," Sullivan stated, "and I believe that with the tense racial situation . . . as well as the current financial crisis of our state educational system, the tax dollars paid by Alabamians could be put to better use than that of financing an institution turning out graduates of hate and racial bitterness."[70]

Patterson asked State Education Superintendent Frank Stewart to make a "full investigation of the school, faculty and students" at the college. He said college officials "must maintain order and discipline at the school" and could not allow "a handful of agitators to disrupt classes, assault school officials, and prevent conscientious students from studying." Trenholm said the students had been "getting some bad advice from some of their adult leaders," but declined to elaborate. He expressed belief that some of the "emotional feelings" had died down, and was hopeful that no further student demonstrations would be held. A college source also reported that faculty members had called a meeting to guide the students out of "the recent emotional conflict," and that two-thirds of the student body had decided to halt all demonstrations and "disassociate themselves from any future agitative moves."[71]

In his "investigation" of Alabama State, Stewart learned that at least eleven members of the faculty "had not been loyal to the school" and had not cooperated with the president "in trying to get things straightened out." Three of the professors had taken part in the attempted mass meeting near the capitol on Sunday. Stewart said he had information that the student demonstrations were ordered by "out-of-state agitators." Stewart said there was evidence that the Congress of Racial Equality (CORE) in New York had distributed instructions "in how to carry out sit-in demonstrations." The board subsequently instructed Trenholm "to fire any faculty member who encourages student protests and to maintain order on the campus." Trenholm said he would cooperate with the superintendent to purge the college of "disloyal" faculty members.[72]

There were racial disturbances elsewhere in the state, but they were mild compared to those in Montgomery. Governor Patterson expected criticism from all sides, and he wasn't disappointed. Civil rights activists wanted him to ease off on restrictions and leave the college alone. Hardliners wanted him to close the college. In the final analysis the state's role in the situation, as he saw it, was to prevent racial violence, to calm the troubled waters, and to keep the campus disturbance from flaring up again. That neither the civil rights activists nor the hardliners would be happy with the results was a given.

By the end of the spring break the worst was behind. In the aftermath there were no violent reprisals as there had been during the Montgomery bus boycott when King's parsonage and black homes and churches were bombed by assailants who were never arrested or tried. In retrospect, the charges against the demonstrators under the dying throes of Jim Crow justice do not appear to have been unduly harsh. A blatant sign of the double standard in local law enforcement, however, was the fact that city policemen arrested no white lawbreakers—not even the man who clubbed the black woman over the head—for their thuggery. A white photographer with the *Montgomery Advertiser* was arrested for taking pictures of the Sunday disturbance near the capitol.[73]

The group of thirty-one students and a faculty member arrested the following Tuesday were convicted on charges of disorderly conduct and failure to obey police officers who ordered them to disperse. Each was fined one hundred dollars and costs. The college placed the students on probation. Of the Alabama State professors alleged to have been "disloyal," only one was eventually dismissed for being "a disturbing influence on the campus." A dossier from the Fulton County Bureau of Criminal Investigation in Atlanta had linked the fired professor to a number of subversive organizations.[74]

Montgomery attorney Fred Gray (aided by a staff attorney for the NAACP Legal Defense Fund) added to his string of civil rights victories in the courtroom when the federal court, in *St. John Dixon v. Alabama State Board of Education*, set aside the expulsion of the nine Alabama State students. Patterson and state school officials had defended before U.S. District Judge Frank Johnson, Jr., their order to expel the students. Johnson ruled in the state's favor. On appeal, however, the U.S. Fifth Circuit Court of Appeals in New Orleans reversed the ruling and remanded Johnson's refusal to issue an injunction.[75]

The news media, for the most part, provided evenhanded treatment of the 1960 student protests in Montgomery. Network television flexed its new muscle on the streets of Montgomery during the protests. Patterson and eight other witnesses accused NBC-TV correspondent Sandor Vanocur of staging the incident in which thirty-one students were arrested on 1 March. Vanocur was observed directing the actions of students to produce more sensational camera footage. Public Service Commissioner Ralph Smith (Patterson's former legal adviser) referred the matter to the Federal Communications Commission and the Justice Department for investigation, but nothing came of it.[76]

On March 29 a full-page ad published in the *New York Times* vilified Patterson and other Alabama officials, wrongly accusing them of such outrages as "padlocking the dining hall of the Negro Alabama State College in an attempt to starve Negro students into submission." The ad was paid for by "The Committee to Defend Martin Luther King and the Struggle for Freedom in the South." The purpose of the ad (the signers included Mrs. Eleanor Roosevelt and celebrities Marlon Brando, Shelly Winters, Eartha Kitt and Harry Belafonte) was to raise money for Reverend King's legal defense in his upcoming trial "on charges of falsifying state income tax returns."[77]

The *Times* ad also raised funds "to finance the student demonstrations that were then spreading across the South." Bayard Rustin, a New York civil rights activist and former associate of King, spearheaded the fund drive. King himself, while approving the general aim of the *Times* ad, was not apprised of its contents prior to publication. The names of Reverends Ralph Abernathy and Solomon S. Seay, Sr. of Montgomery, Joseph E. Lowery of Mobile, and Fred Shuttlesworth of Birmingham appeared in the ad, but they too denied prior knowledge or approval of the contents.[78]

Three city officials, including Police Commissioner Sullivan, sued the *Times* for libel. The plaintiffs retained the Montgomery firm of Steiner, Crum & Baker, with Roland Nachman, Jr., serving as lead counsel. Eric Embry with the Birmingham firm of Beddow, Embry & Beddow was lead counsel for the *New York Times*. Montgomery attorneys Fred Gray and Solomon S. Seay, Jr., along with Vernon Crawford of Mobile, represented the Alabama ministers whose names appeared in the ad and were listed as co-defendants in the three lawsuits.[79]

Patterson, soon after the ad appeared, had demanded a retraction. The *Times* apologized to the governor for the inaccuracies in the ad and printed a partial retraction in mid-May. Finding the halfhearted response unsatisfactory, the governor, acting on the advice of the attorney general's office, filed his own libel suit. In a prepared statement accompanying the suit, Patterson said if he received a judgment he would donate the money to the state "for the construction of a modern, well-equipped nursing home for our needy old folks."[80]

Sullivan's suit went to trial first and he predictably won a judgment in Montgomery County Circuit Court in November. Pending appeal, the *New York Times* filed a bond in the amount of one million dollars to stop a levy against its assets, but the black ministers did not have the resources to post such a bond. In obvious retaliation for their civil rights activities, Sullivan placed a levy on their property without awaiting the outcome of the appeal. [81]

It took four years for *Times v. Sullivan* to be resolved by the high court, but when it came in 1964 the opinion rewrote case law on libel in the United States. Under the new standard a public official seeking to recover damages "for a defamatory falsehood relating to his official conduct" had to prove "actual malice" on the part of the defendant. In his concurring opinion in the case, Justice Hugo Black, an Alabamian, wrote, "An unconditional right to say what one pleases about public affairs is what I consider to be the minimum guarantee of the First Amendment."

Patterson had been out of office over a year when the justices ruled on the case. He had his attorney negotiate with the *Times* lawyers, who agreed to pay the court costs of $17,000 in return for his dropping the suit.[82] L. B. Sullivan, meanwhile, had to return the money he had received from his earlier hasty sale of the black ministers' property.

King's tax trial, the incentive for the *Times* ad, had long since been decided in favor of the defendant. In May 1960 the defense team of three Alabama attorneys (Gray, Seay, and Arthur Shores) and two from out of state (Hubert T. Delaney of New York and Robert Ming of Chicago) won a not-guilty verdict from an all-white jury in Montgomery. Looking back on the King verdict, Patterson said that he was wrong in having the civil rights leader brought to trial and that the jury "took the high ground" in acquitting him.[83]

King had a special gift for uplifting the spirits while calming the troubled seas. When he appeared at the rousing church rally in March, several speakers were so harshly critical of Patterson that King admonished them: "Nobody here must hate Governor Patterson. We must still believe that he is a child of God and can be transformed from a segregationist into an integrationist."[84]

Soon after he was elected governor, Patterson was introduced to Roy Wilkins, by now the executive director of the NAACP, during a trip to Washington. He had stopped by the clerk's office in the Supreme Court Building and Wilkins was there. A distinctive and articulate man, Wilkins was Patterson's elder by twenty years. "Patterson, you should come over to our side," Wilkins said. "We admire your stand on law and order and for honoring your father's legacy. But you're a mystery to us. We just don't understand you." Patterson smiled and said, "Mr. Wilkins, that's because you aren't running for my job."

The governor told CBS commentator Richard C. Hottelet—in Montgomery to give a lecture at the Air War College—that Southern officials had to resist integration even if they personally believed otherwise, because "the people insist on it." "For some reason the people in Washington can't seem to get it into their heads why public officials down here don't knuckle down to the *Brown* decision," Patterson added. "If they did bow down to it, it would be their last term in office." He also told Hottelet there was "grave danger of violence over integration efforts in Alabama," but promised to do all in his power to prevent it.[85]

FORMER BASEBALL STAR JACKIE Robinson, speaking at a rally in North Carolina in May, declared that Senator Kennedy would not have the NAACP's support as long as he had the endorsement of Alabama's Governor Patterson, whom he reviled as the "worst segregationist in the country."[86] Patterson shrugged off this and other personal attacks, which had grown in number since announcing his endorsement of Kennedy. While the governor did not sling mud back at his attackers, he knew it was part of the price one paid for going into politics.

Still, he worried that the negative response from civil rights organizations to his working for the senator's campaign in the South could be "of some difficulty and embarrassment" to the Kennedy camp. At no time during the campaign, however, did Senator Kennedy or any of his people say anything to the governor about the South's racial troubles or about his growing role as a spokesman for the Southern cause. Nor had Patterson raised the racial issue with them.[87]

Patterson knew his support for Kennedy was not going to help him with the segregation battle in Alabama. That never entered his mind. He did admit to thinking that if Kennedy "ever had to put his foot on us as president because of the segregation issue, he might because of our relationship put his foot on us lightly instead of heavily."[88]

The governor met with Senator Kennedy on occasion, but he and his staff worked mostly with Stephen Smith, Kennedy's brother-in-law and "chief administrator and money man," in New York. They (Patterson, Meriwether, Engelhardt, and Montgomery businessman John Overton, a friend of Kennedy's) raised money for the senator's campaign in the Wisconsin and West Virginia primaries. The governor also made available two of his key staff members, press secretary Harry Cook and television whiz Roy Marcato, to work directly with the Kennedy campaign. Cook worked in the national headquarters in New York. Marcato traveled with Kennedy assisting with televising the senator's campaign stops and disseminating film to make the evening news. [89]

Patterson made some speeches for the candidate, including the keynote address kicking off the Democratic campaign in Louisiana. Senator Russell Long was a strong Kennedy supporter, so he and other Louisiana Democrats invited Patterson there to boost the Kennedy ticket. Much of Patterson's pre-convention effort was spent lining up Kennedy delegates in Los Angeles that July. Reminded of Folsom's embarrassing defeat when he ran as a delegate to the 1948 national convention, Patterson decided his and Engelhardt's time would be better spent trying to elect a pro-Kennedy delegation rather than running as a delegate himself.[90]

Kennedy's toughest rival for the Democratic nomination was Senator Lyndon Baines Johnson of Texas. Patterson recalled that the election of delegates, which was divided between the Kennedy forces and the states' righters (the "old Dixiecrat crowd"), was "pretty bitter" in Alabama. The old political organization was for Johnson, who had a lot of friends in the state. Lady Bird Johnson spent her childhood years on a large farm in Billingsley, and still had kinfolks in Autauga County.[91]

The Johnson forces, including people sent into the state to undermine the effort for Kennedy, ran Attorney General MacDonald Gallion to try and get the chairmanship of the delegation going to the convention. Kennedy's supporters, led by Patterson, were able to get their person seated as chairman instead. The election of delegates—some were elected by district and others were delegates at large—was a Byzantine affair. Patterson said they made a special effort to run pro-Kennedy candidates whose surnames started at the front of the alphabet. Names on the ballots at that time were printed alphabetically, and voters had shown a propensity for checking the names at the top of the ballot.[92]

Finding people who were willing to serve as delegates was part of the intrigue. The delegates, who were not paid for their services, ran the gamut from dilettantes who dabbled in politics to professionals who attended the conventions religiously. Patterson recalled that some of the pro-Kennedy delegates had no money. "We paid to fly some delegates out there, and even bought suits of clothes for some of them. When we got to Los Angeles we had a split delegation, split right down the middle between Gallion's crowd for LBJ and ours." Alabama had 56 half-vote delegate seats, for a total of 28 votes. Fourteen votes (28 delegates) were pledged to Kennedy.[93]

"Keeping them in line was a difficult task," Patterson said. The convention consisted of three days of back-room maneuvering before the roll call voting took place. The candidates wined and dined the delegates, and "weren't beyond putting young starlets on them too"—making it difficult to hold younger delegates in line. "You could go to bed at night confident of a certain number of votes and wake up the next morning with half that," Patterson said. "You'd have to go get the rest of them back again."[94]

He told a story about a delegate who was a young truck driver and had the same name as a former governor of Alabama. The former governor was still living and "got madder than hell" when they qualified this man with his name as a statewide delegate. They flew him out to Los Angeles, put him up in a hotel, and gave him spending money. He was committed to vote for Kennedy, but Johnson's crowd worked on him trying to change his mind. He took full advantage of all the things that were offered to him, and Patterson had someone checking constantly to make sure he had not been proselyted by the other side.[95]

"It's funny how that young fellow got more important every day," Patterson recalled. "He began to project his voice out like a senator, you know." One night they were having a drink in a bar near the convention hall when the delegate nudged Patterson and said, "You know, that governor who's got the same name as me. He cost me a million votes when I ran for this job." "Anyway, he stayed hitched, and after the thing was over we flew him home and I've never seen him or heard from him since," Patterson said. "But, for once in his life he was up there on top of the mountain."[96]

There was tremendous pressure from home for the delegates not to cast their vote for Kennedy. Some received long telegrams with hundreds of names of prominent people in their town telling them if they voted for a Catholic, not to come home. Big Jim Folsom, an LBJ supporter and a Baptist, described a vote for Kennedy "as a vote for integration of church and state," and appealed to Alabamians at home to try to stop delegates from voting for Kennedy. Patterson was alone among elected public officials from Alabama carrying the banner for

Kennedy. Conspicuously absent was Alabama's congressional delegation. Not a single congressman or U.S. senator from the state showed up in Los Angeles, although all were Democrats.[97]

As the state delegations gathered on the floor for the voting to start, Robert Kennedy (who was his brother's floor leader at the convention) came to Patterson and asked how many votes he had. "Fourteen," Patterson replied. They were getting ready to poll the states in alphabetical order, and the Alabama delegation was to be called first. Kennedy said, "I want you to cast only three or four." "Wait a minute now," Patterson protested.

Kennedy explained: "Get the others to vote for somebody else the first time. If we go all the way through the alphabet and come back to Alabama and we don't have a majority, then you go to fourteen. That will demonstrate a shift and the impetus will help us with the other states."

"Man, that's a tough order. These folks caught hell for supporting your brother, and you want me to ask them not to vote for the man. Don't know whether they'll do it or not." But Patterson reluctantly agreed to try. They held a caucus in a stairwell, and he presented Robert Kennedy's proposal to them. Patterson convinced them to cast only four votes for JFK on the first roll call. The rest were to vote for other people. "You never heard such grumbling and carrying on," Patterson said. "People were mad as hell." Several asked how Senator Kennedy would know that they were ready to vote for him? "Don't worry about that. I'll take care of that," he said.[98]

The delegates did as he asked, and Kennedy got a majority without having to repeat the roll call of state votes. "Those people never got to change their vote," he said. "Some of them are mad to this day about that." The next night the votes were cast to nominate the vice president. Kennedy sent Steve Smith to ask Patterson if he had any objection to Lyndon Johnson. He immediately sent word back that he had no objection. In fact he was very pleased with the selection because over half of the Alabama delegation was for LBJ anyway. They all agreed, and voted Lyndon Johnson the nominee.[99]

Patterson said he would never, under any circumstances, put himself through anything like that again. There were a few interesting moments, but that was the extent of it. On the second night of the convention he had met actress Arlene Dahl at a party on Mulholland Drive. Later she was seated in the balcony at the convention hall when the roll call of delegates began. A waiter brought the governor a message from the actress suggesting they "cut out of here and go have a drink somewhere." He sent a note back saying that he was sorry, but he had to stay on the floor because they were getting ready to nominate the next president of the United States. "I kicked my butt for that when it was all over. The rest of the event wasn't worth the trouble. It really wasn't."[100]

HAVING LYNDON JOHNSON ON the ticket with Kennedy in the general election helped mend party fences. Alabama's senators and congressmen in Washington no longer hung back. They actively promoted the Democratic ticket and came home to speak at several rallies across the state. No one worked harder in support of the ticket than the governor and his people.

Charles Adams of Alexander City, who was probate judge of Tallapoosa County and had been House speaker when Patterson's programs were passed in 1959, served as chairman of the campaign in Alabama. He was a loyal Democrat and a leader in Alabama politics, Patterson said. The assistant to Adams in the campaign was Charles Cashion, a businessman from Vina, Alabama. They were helped by Patterson's administration, by the state Democratic machinery, and by Sam Engelhardt as chairman of the state Democratic Committee. "We had pretty well the support of the rank and file of the county and city officials all over the state," Patterson said. "The major opposition was in south Alabama in the area we call the Black Belt, and the major support for Mr. Kennedy was in north Alabama, in the Tennessee Valley regions and in the heavy industrial areas where the people are essentially Democratic."[101]

At a post-convention news conference Patterson pledged to "do everything possible to help the Kennedy-Johnson ticket." He said he would stump the state, if necessary, "to insure a Democratic victory in the November general election." When questioned about a reported move by Mississippi Governor Ross Barnett to bolt the party over the strong civil rights plank adopted at the convention, Patterson called any Southern revolt "unwise." He refused to comment on Barnett's political views, but said the South should not dissipate its future strength by forming splinter groups. Forming a third party would mean giving up vital chairmanships and vice chairmanships where the battles counted the most. "The chief executive of this nation can only enforce the laws that Congress passes," he said.[102]

On October 10, Kennedy flew into LaGrange, Georgia, near the Alabama-Georgia line, to make a campaign speech. Patterson joined the presidential candidate at LaGrange and traveled with him to Warm Springs, Georgia, the vacation spot made famous by FDR when he was president. At Warm Springs, Kennedy spoke from the steps of the Little White House, the vacation cottage where President Roosevelt suffered a stroke and died in 1945. Kennedy, with assurances from Patterson that failing to make a personal appearance would not hurt his chances in Alabama, agreed to have former President Harry S. Truman come and speak in his place.[103]

The band struck up "I'm Just Wild About Harry," when the seventy-six-year-old former chief executive stepped jauntily down from the plane at Pryor Field in Decatur and took a deep breath of Alabama sunshine. Governor Patterson had sent the state's twin-engine Beechcraft to Independence, Missouri, to bring the honored guest to Decatur. Angry Alabama Democrats had bolted the party in 1948 when Truman was nominated for president, but that was then. This was now, and "acres and acres of people" came out to welcome "Give 'Em Hell Harry" to "the Heart of Dixie."[104]

The thousands who packed the schoolhouse to hear Truman speak gave their governor confidence that his call for party unity had been heard and they would vote the Democratic ticket in the November election just two weeks away. A remark made earlier in the year by Truman that Communists were behind the sit-in strikes in the South had angered civil rights groups, but convinced Southern political leaders that he understood their problems. "It was a great experience to get to meet the former president," Patterson said. "And he made a tremendous speech late in the afternoon."[105]

On hand with the governor to welcome the former president were U.S. senators Lister Hill and John Sparkman, along with congressmen Albert Rains and Robert E. Jones. At a press conference immediately preceding his fiery speech, Truman was asked about school desegregation and responded that "no matter which party is in there, they will have to be integrated. It's the law of the land." He hurled a "no guts" charge at the Republican administration in answer to reporters' questions about Cuba. "If we'd had somebody in there with guts we wouldn't have this trouble in Cuba," he said. "All they had to do was enforce the Monroe Doctrine." He spent the night in Decatur and left early the next morning for Louisiana where he said he would continue "to give 'em hell."[106]

Patterson said he really liked Truman. "After he got back, and sometime later, he wrote me, and we started corresponding. What a great fellow he was." Patterson had to bite his tongue when Truman accused the Republicans of not doing anything about Fidel Castro and the Red menace on America's doorstep.

He was sworn to secrecy about a meeting he recently had with a high-ranking spook from the CIA. The topic of conversation had been plans to form a small liberation air force to support a forthcoming invasion of Cuba at the Bay of Pigs.[107]

Brigadier General George Reid Doster commanded the Air Guard's 117th Tactical Reconnaissance Wing headquartered in Birmingham. The wing had flying units in Montgomery and Birmingham, as well as Meridian, Mississippi, and Fort Smith, Arkansas. Doster called Governor Patterson one day and said he would like to bring a visitor from the CIA down from Birmingham to see the governor. Doster said their business was hush-hush and the CIA man did not want to be seen around the state capitol. Patterson set a time to meet with them at the governor's mansion.[108]

For once the extroverted Doster (a cigar-chomping general in the Curtis LeMay mold) let someone else do the talking. The spook was dressed in civilian clothes, but flashed an I.D. showing that he too was a general officer and out-ranked Doster. He told Governor Patterson that the agency was training a brigade of 1500 Cuban exiles in Guatemala to invade their homeland and needed an air arm. The Air Force had agreed to equip the air arm with refurbished Douglas B-26 Invaders from the mothball fleet at Davis-Monthan AFB in Tucson, Arizona. Since the Birmingham wing was the last USAF unit to fly B-26s, the CIA wanted the governor to agree for the agency to recruit Alabama guardsmen to go to Guatemala to organize and train the small liberation air force.[109]

The CIA official assured the governor that no Alabama guardsmen would fly combat missions in the invasion. "Your boys won't be in harm's way. They'll just be training the exiles to fly the hot missions."

Patterson wanted to know if the old man knew about this, referring to President Eisenhower. The agent assured him the president had blessed the operation, and Patterson agreed to it. "Keep me informed," the governor told Doster.

A sizeable contingent from the 117th Wing, including Doster, volunteered and went to Guatemala to train the Cuban exiles. They wore civilian clothing and were given fake papers identifying them as employees of Double-Chek Corporation (a CIA front), which was testing military aircraft at sea. The CIA paid the men "handsomely" and they were insured by Lloyd's of London in case anything happened to them.[110]

As the training progressed Doster made frequent flights back to Birmingham, and would stop to refuel at Dannelly Field in Montgomery so he could go to the capitol and brief Patterson on how things were going. On one of these trips shortly before the general election in November, Doster was pumped up with adrenaline and boasted to the governor: "Any morning now you're going to pick up the morning paper, and the headline's gonna' be that we've invaded Cuba. It's gonna' be a whopping success! The Cubans will welcome the invasion with open arms. There's no way we can fail in this thing."[111]

After Doster left, the governor thought long and hard about the political consequences of the CIA operation. The timing, if Doster was right about the invasion being imminent, was suspicious to say the least. The presidential election was just around the corner and Vice President Nixon was chairman of the National Security Council. Nixon and the NSC had to be privy to it. If the invasion kicked off before November and was the "great success" Doster said it would be, how would that affect the election? The race appeared to be close, and a CIA-sponsored overthrow of the Castro regime could throw the election to Nixon.[112]

Patterson called Steve Smith in New York and said that he had to talk to Senator Kennedy and would meet him anywhere they wanted. Smith checked the senator's itinerary and gave the governor an appointed day and time to come to New York and meet with Kennedy at the Barkley Hotel. "I went to the Barkley at ten o'clock one evening as arranged," Patterson recalled. "Kennedy came and shut the door. Just me and him talking. I told him what I knew about the Bay of Pigs operation. Now don't you ever breathe a word about this to anybody, I said. You know there's lives at stake here."[113]

Patterson studied Kennedy carefully to see if he already knew about the pending invasion. "I got no indication whether he knew or didn't know. He thanked me and went on his way." As things turned out, the invasion did not come off as early as Doster had projected, and was inherited by Kennedy when he won the election and took office in January. Patterson did note that after their talk Kennedy had altered his speeches "a little bit" to address the need to do something about the Cuban situation.[114]

A highlight of the presidential campaign for many Alabamians was seeing LBJ's special "Democratic Victory Train" roll through the state in mid-October. Johnson launched the thirteen-car whistle-stop special in Washington and rolled south into Florida. With the vice president-nominee was his wife Lady Bird and their teenage daughters, Lucy Baines and Lynda Bird. Patterson and members of his staff boarded the train in Pensacola, Florida, with other dignitaries. They made ten stops in eight counties during the 350-mile trip across Alabama, with LBJ or Lady Bird addressing the crowds at each stop from the train's rear platform. Patterson, in his role as master of ceremonies, "got rousing cheers at every stop" as he introduced LBJ and Lady Bird to the welcoming crowds.[115]

On Thursday the 13th, they made stops at Brewton, Evergreen, Greenville, Montgomery, Clanton, and on to Birmingham where they spent the night. At each station public officials from the next stop on the agenda boarded the train to talk with Senator Johnson on the way to their town. Johnson made a television appearance soon after arriving in Birmingham, and then left the train Friday morning to fly to Macon, Georgia, to speak at Mercer College.[116]

Mrs. Johnson spoke for her husband during stops at Tuscaloosa, Eutaw, Livingston, and York before the Senate majority leader rejoined the train in Meridian, Mississippi. Patterson remained on board to accompany her on the swing through west Alabama. He said farewell to the Johnsons in Meridian and returned to Montgomery. The trip had been exhausting but was well-organized and went like clockwork for the most part. There were a couple of glitches, the governor admitted.[117]

On Thursday morning Frank Boykin, the Mobile congressman, was standing with Patterson on the platform in Pensacola waiting for the arrival of Johnson's train. Their first stop after crossing into Alabama at Flomaton was Brewton, which was in Boykin's district. "Let me introduce Lyndon in Brewton," Boykin pleaded. "That's my district. Let me make the introduction." Patterson said, "Well, all right, go ahead." They were on a very tight schedule. Boykin was long-winded and got carried away. He was still talking when the train pulled out. "Boykin didn't finish the introduction, and the folks at Brewton to this day don't know what Johnson was going to say to them. LBJ was madder than hell."[118]

When the train rolled into Montgomery there was a "sea of faces" waiting at the railroad station to greet the Johnsons. The governor had declared a state holiday and encouraged all the state employees to go to the rally. One thing they hadn't counted on, the governor said, was all of Lady Bird's relatives. When the train pulled into the station all of her relatives were there and got on the train to see her. "There was all that hugging and carrying on, and we couldn't get them off the train. The train pulled out on time and carried them all to Birmingham. We were up all night using the state troopers to get Lady Bird's kinfolks back home."[119]

WHEN THE KENNEDY-JOHNSON TICKET prevailed in the November election, one of the first observations made by Patterson was that apparently the religious issue "had very little effect" on the election outcome in Alabama. "It is encouraging that this matter is behind us," he said. "I hope that religious prejudice and bigotry will not rear its head again."[120]

Kennedy swept the state by about 72,000 popular votes in a record turnout. Approximately 500,000 of the state's estimated 850,000 registered voters went to the polls to "set a record for a presidential election in Alabama." The state's eleven electors were on the ballot, and voters assumed that when the electoral college met in December that all eleven votes would be cast for the candidate who carried the general election. Not necessarily so, Patterson pointed out. By law the Alabama electors were not pledged to the winner of the popular vote. To nearly everyone's surprise, when the body of electors met at the secretary of state's office at the capitol to cast their ballots, six voted for Harry Byrd of Virginia and five voted for Kennedy. All eleven electors cast their votes for Lyndon Johnson as vice president.[121]

The ballots for Byrd were protest votes. "The Dixiecrat crowd had elected over half of our electors, and we didn't even know it until the election was over," the governor said. He did his utmost to persuade the electors not to split their vote, telling them "it would be a great embarrassment" to the state, but they wouldn't listen. "They didn't like a liberal and they didn't like a Catholic and they didn't like a guy from Massachusetts. They were still smarting over Lyndon Johnson losing to Kennedy, even though Lyndon would be the vice-president." The Dixiecrats described Johnson as "their kind of man," implying that if he was from Texas he was a segregationist. Nothing was further from the truth.[122]

Patterson recalled that the Dixiecrats, by dividing the electors, had allowed Richard Nixon a wry moment at the state's expense. Nixon, as vice president, presided over the joint session of Congress in January when the electoral votes were formally canvassed and announced. The votes were tallied state-by-state for president and vice president. The clerk read off Alabama's votes first: "Alabama. Six votes for Harry Byrd. Five votes for John F. Kennedy." Nixon, without the hint of a smile, announced that Harry Byrd was now leading in the race for president.[123]

A trend emerged in the 1960 campaign that Alabama could no longer be taken for granted as a "one-party" state. The state Republicans, led by chairman Claude O. Vardaman, made a strong impression on the electorate. Richard

Nixon campaigned in Alabama, followed closely by Arizona's ultra-conservative Senator Barry Goldwater who gave "rip-roaring speeches" in Montgomery and Birmingham. "Rival camps were trading heavy punches, conducting large-scale direct mail drives, ringing doorbells, keeping telephone lines hot and carrying on numerous other vote-seeking activities never before witnessed in a national campaign in the state," a reporter wrote. Patterson attributed the record Republican vote "to the influence of the big daily newspapers, especially in Birmingham and Montgomery, where the GOP candidates for presidential elector ran in front of the Democrats."[124]

The civil rights question was not an issue in the election, according to a UPI reporter, since most Alabama voters generally considered both the Democratic and Republican planks "equally obnoxious." That was debatable. The civil rights movement itself was an unseen guest at both national conventions, and its voice was heard in the election. Kennedy had called for a strong civil rights plank and said, "I want our party to speak with courage and candor on every issue, and that includes civil rights." Representative Adam Clayton Powell (D-NY), who broke party lines to support Eisenhower against Adlai Stevenson in 1956, had attacked Kennedy all year long for having accepted the Alabama governor's support and falsely accused Patterson of doing "business with the KKK."[125]

The congressman's comments were chalked up to politics as usual, but intemperate personal attacks by Jackie Robinson, former star of the Brooklyn Dodgers baseball team, whom Patterson had seen play at Ebbetts Field, were harder to take. Robinson, like Powell, denounced Senator Kennedy for meeting with Governor Patterson and for accepting his support. The governor declined to repay the favor when Kennedy met with Robinson a year later to reassure him of a strong stand on civil rights. Kennedy said he favored "an end to all discrimination—in voting, in education, in housing, in employment, in the administration of justice, and in public facilities including lunch counters." Kennedy's overtures did not persuade Robinson, who supported the Republican ticket in the election.[126]

A month after the election, in mid-December, Robinson "unloosed a vitriolic attack" on Patterson in a speech in Montgomery. Speaking before an audience of two thousand African Americans to conclude a week-long institute on nonviolence, Robinson called the governor "stupid" and said it was "a disgrace for a state like Alabama to be represented by a man like that." He also spoke "derisively" of Governor Jimmie Davis of Louisiana, saying that "men like Davis and Patterson are hurting America in the United Nations."[127]

Robinson followed up with a swing at president-elect Kennedy. He expressed concern about Kennedy's popularity with black voters in the election, attributing it to the Democratic nominee's call of support to Coretta Scott King when police had arrested her renowned husband in Atlanta during the presidential campaign. Robinson said he was distressed that "Negroes would be influenced by an emotional incident." Kennedy's cabinet appointments drew criticism from Robinson before they were even made.[128]

The barbs from Powell and Robinson got more national press coverage than other political bricks thrown the governor's way because of his support for John F. Kennedy. When reporters asked if he thought his backing of Kennedy had hurt him politically in Alabama, Patterson said: "I haven't thought so much of my own political ambitions as I have of doing the best thing I could for the country as well as Alabama. I was motivated by the fact that Kennedy was the best possible choice we could make for the nominee, considering all things." After a pensive moment he added, "I think the people of Alabama are looking to our administration to carry out our program and . . . I think we are doing pretty good. That is where my administration will be judged."[129]

15

"It's a Hell of a Job"

"One presidential inaugural in a lifetime is enough for anybody," Governor Patterson said, then added with a smile, "Of course, the person who's taking the oath of office thinks differently about that." A large delegation from Alabama was invited, and stayed at the Washington Hotel owned by Mobile's congressman Frank Boykin. The governor had a front-row seat in the reviewing stand. Alabama's first lady sat directly behind President Kennedy. The president's stirring inaugural address was "worth the price of admission," Patterson said, but other events celebrating the occasion were lost in the maddening crush of people, the sea of honking horns, and the whirlwind pace of events. Adding to the confusion, the D.C. area was paralyzed the night before the inaugural when a winter storm blanketed the Eastern seaboard with nearly a foot of snow.[1]

At the governors' reception Kennedy took Patterson aside and asked would he mind if they took Charlie Meriwether away from him. Kennedy said he wanted to appoint Meriwether to the board of the Export-Import Bank of the United States. This was the first the governor had heard about Meriwether leaving. He told the president that Charlie was essentially the leading member of his cabinet and he would hate to see him go, but said "no, he didn't mind."[2]

Earlier, in a discussion after winning the election, Kennedy had raised the subject of federal appointments in Alabama and asked if Patterson was interested in filling any of them. He had to give the matter some thought because patronage had not been a condition of his support in the campaign. When he subsequently expressed an interest in three federal appointments, he was told to submit portfolios on the three prospects. The positions of interest were the head of the Federal Housing Administration (FHA), the customs collector for the port of Mobile, and a Treasury Department office that was in charge of selling government bonds. Having state Democratic stalwarts in those key positions would help if Patterson decided to run for public office again. The FHA appointment could also bring legal business his way after he returned to private practice.[3]

Months went by without any word, until one morning he read in the *Advertiser* where people other than the ones he recommended had been appointed to the coveted positions. Since President Kennedy had made the overture, not him, Patterson felt someone in the administration "had dropped the ball." He had to go to Washington on other business, so he took the opportunity to visit the White House and raise the issue with the president. Kennedy asked Lawrence O'Brien (a key aide who handled legislative liaison) to set up an appointment with the two Alabama senators "to discuss some way of working out the situation."[4]

Senator Sparkman was out of the country at the time, so they sat down with Senator Hill and discussed the protocol of patronage appointments. "They were extremely nice to me and polite, but informed me that it was too late, of course, to do anything about it now," Patterson recalled. Senators were the ones to clear federal patronage through, he was told, while a governor's prerogatives rested in state matters. "I got brushed off," he laughed. He joked about having to work through people who were nowhere to be found at the national convention in 1960. "Everybody had a good laugh, and I didn't feel too badly about it."[5]

Patterson said they told him the same thing he used to tell county officials when they wanted to know why he hadn't appointed their cousin, uncle, or drinking buddy to some state position. The pat answer, he said, was, "Well, I had to do that because I've got to get that legislative support for our program, and I hope you understand." The governor got the same treatment except on a higher level. "I understood it all right," he laughed. "I had no hard feelings about that."[6]

THE GILT EDGES OF Camelot began to rub off early in the governor's relations with the Kennedy administration. The Kennedy doctrine, with the ink not dry on plans for the New Frontier and flexible response, was off to a sputtering start. Three months after the inaugural, Patterson was jolted awake one morning by the news that the CIA's invasion of Cuba had gone terribly wrong. The brigade of Cuban exiles had put up a fight, but never made it off the beachhead at the Bay of Pigs. Those who were not killed had been captured by Fidel Castro's soldiers.

His first thoughts were for the men of the Alabama Guard who had gone to Guatemala to equip and train the brigade air arm. He knew some of the men personally, and all were friends of Joe Robertson's from the 117th Wing in Birmingham. Reid Doster and the CIA officer had assured him that the Alabama volunteers would be used strictly as training cadre and would not be put in harm's way. Still the governor felt uneasy. He soon knew why—the failed invasion at the Bay of Pigs had cost the lives of four Alabama air guardsmen.[7]

News accounts gave an inkling of the mistakes that were made in planning and executing the Cuban invasion. They painted an unflattering picture of an elitist, monolithic CIA blinded by past successes and a vacillating White House learning to cope with global challenges. Patterson did not know how badly things had gone until Doster flew back and briefed him on the high-level snafus leading to the invasion's failure and the loss of the Alabama aircrews. All through the fall and spring Doster had given the governor glowing progress reports about the covert operation. He had been so cocksure of victory. How could he have been so wrong?[8]

Papa Doster, the stars on his epaulets sparkling in the sunlight streaming through the blinds in the governor's office, had a weary, hangdog look as he plopped into the proffered chair and filled in the blanks on what had gone wrong with the invasion. Doster's CIA sources told him that President Kennedy had misgivings about the Cuban invasion from the start, and would have called things off had it not already progressed to the jumping-off point. Kennedy had inherited a "done deal" with fifteen hundred gung-ho Cuban exiles waiting in the mountains of Guatemala and felt he had no political recourse except to go forward with the mission.[9]

Had Kennedy seen the raw data in a Joint Chiefs of Staff study giving the invasion only a 30 percent chance of success, things might have been different. Typical of consensus papers, a euphemistic conclusion by the JCS chairman that the invasion stood a fair chance of success crossed the president's desk instead. Military experts knew that the element of surprise was paramount and that Castro's third-rate air force had to be eliminated, but no one bluntly hammered these critical points home to the president. The heart of the plan envisioned the brigade, under the protection of sustained air cover, going ashore near the city of Trinidad where anti-Castro groups were known to be active. If the plan went sour, the Cuban exiles could melt into the nearby Escambria Mountains and join resistance forces still holding out against Castro's army.[10]

To informed journalists, the CIA's fingerprints were all over the botched operation, but the White House still showed more concern for masking the U.S. role than assuring the Cuban brigade's success. In February the CIA prepared to move the invasion force from Guatemala to the staging base in Nicaragua. Then President Kennedy postponed the D-Day of March 5. From there the tightly wound plan unraveled, from the top down. A fateful order from the president changed the beachhead from the more strategic Trinidad area to the Bay of Pigs, a swamp-infested mousetrap with no route of escape. Indecision became the order of the day as the deadline then slipped from April 5 to April 15, and finally to April 17.[11]

Arbitrary restrictions on the brigade's already meager air support drove the final nail in the coffin. Doster said he knew the invasion was doomed when the order came down from the White House arbitrarily reducing the strikes against Cuban airfields. Pre-invasion airstrikes by the small force of sixteen unescorted B-26 bombers were reduced to half, and follow-up strikes were cancelled. Only a handful of Castro's fighters survived the scaled-down attacks, but those were enough to turn the tactical advantage decisively in favor of the Cuban defenders.[12]

When the Brigade lost a third of its bombers to Castro's fighters and was pinned down on the beachhead, the CIA obtained permission for U.S. advisers to fly into combat. Seven Alabama guardsmen and one CIA crew member volunteered to fly four B-26 missions into Cuba at daybreak in a desperate gamble to save the brigade. Four of the guardsmen did not return. They were killed when two of the B-26s were hit and went down. One bomber piloted by Major Riley Shamburger crashed into the sea off the Bay of Pigs. The other one flown by Captain Pete Ray made a crash landing far inland of the beachhead. Ray and flight engineer Leo Baker survived the crash, but were killed by Castro's soldiers.[13]

The high level of secrecy surrounding the mission precluded communicating with the families of the slain guardsmen, but the governor wanted assurances that federal authorities would take care of them. The CIA notified the widows, but gave them a phony cover story about the circumstances. A Miami attorney for the Double-Chek Corporation (a CIA cover operation) flew to Birmingham to see the families and to arrange for insurance payments. The families were informed that their loved ones had been shot down off the Cuban coast while flying a cargo mission for a wealthy anti-Castro group. Lieutenant Colonel Joseph Shannon, who flew one of the hot missions over Cuba and made it back, said that keeping the secret and not telling the families the truth was the hardest thing he had ever done.[14]

Doster blamed the Kennedy White House for everything that went wrong with the invasion, and the president of course shouldered full responsibility in his address to the American people. But Patterson knew there had to be more to the story. He imagined Kennedy agonizing over the decisions he made concerning the CIA debacle, and figured the president's biggest mistake had been not to call the ill-conceived invasion off. The president drank a bitter draught from the defeat, but his leadership had grown in stature when the USSR tested the nation's mettle in the Berlin crisis later in the year and in the Cuban missile crisis of 1962.[15]

Patterson always considered Kennedy to be a caring leader. That compassion was reflected in the great lengths Kennedy went to gain the freedom of the captured Cuban brigade members from Castro's prisons. Patterson said the president never forgot the Alabama guardsmen who gave their lives at the Bay of Pigs. The governor was in Washington several times in the spring of 1961 and went by the White House to see Kennedy. On one occasion after the Bay of Pigs, he and seven other governors were at the White House for the signing of the Appalachian relief bill. They had lunch with the president in a small executive dining room.[16]

As they talked at the luncheon table, the president turned to Patterson and said, "You know, I hope I live long enough to do something for those four boys from Alabama who lost their lives in the Bay of Pigs invasion." The governor grew pensive whenever he recalled the conversation with Kennedy. "Of course he never lived long enough to recognize them or do anything about it," Patterson said. "But he did bring it up at that luncheon."[17]

To A STATE STILL mourning the loss of its airmen in a tragedy Papa Doster credited to amateur hour at the White House, President Kennedy's decision to send hundreds of federal marshals to Montgomery during the "Freedom Rider" crisis a month later struck a raw nerve in Alabama. The Justice Department's involvement after violence erupted against the Freedom Riders in Anniston and Birmingham reached its climax a few days later in Montgomery. Patterson, stung by the brusque treatment and political grandstanding of the president's younger brother, Bobby, vigorously opposed the attorney general's intervention—insisting that it was not needed and inflamed an already tense and violent situation. When the crisis was over, although he still admired the president and considered him a friend, the governor now said laconically, "He couldn't get enough votes in Alabama to wad a shotgun."[18]

Patterson had feared the worst in March when the Congress of Racial Equality announced plans to send a biracial group of student activists into Southern states to test "the Supreme Court's ruling in *Boynton v. Virginia* (1960) that segregation in interstate bus and rail stations was unconstitutional." He had not anticipated the Justice Department's support of the Freedom Rides or its "implied sponsorship" of CORE's tactics, however. In CORE's own words, the Freedom Ride tactics were calculated to create a crisis in the South, so the Kennedy administration would be "compelled to enforce the law."[19]

CORE director James Farmer stated afterwards: "When we began the ride, I think all of us were prepared for as much violence as could be thrown at us. We were prepared for the possibility of death." Since Farmer was not a foot soldier in the movement, his statement smacked of bravado. But he too gained stature from having participated in the Freedom Ride when a valiant female student later shamed Farmer (who admitted he was "scared shitless") into boarding the bus in Montgomery to face the unknown perils awaiting them across the Mississippi line.[20]

The Freedom Ride started on May 4 when seven blacks and six whites left Washington, D.C., on a pair of Greyhound and Trailways buses. They were scheduled to go south through Virginia and the Carolinas to Atlanta, then cut across Alabama and Mississippi down to New Orleans. The trip went without serious incident until 9 May when the Greyhound bus pulled into Rock Hill, South Carolina, where racial tensions were high. Two members of the group were assaulted by local thugs when they attempted to enter the white waiting room. Another rider was arrested for going inside a barbershop that served whites only. The violence at Rock Hill drew widespread news coverage, achieving precisely what CORE intended.[21]

The other states kept Patterson and public safety director Floyd Mann informed about the Freedom Ride's progress. In public the governor took the position that the Freedom Riders were outside agitators and "when people go looking for trouble, they usually find it," but when alone with Mann and other department heads he worried that they were sitting on a powder keg. That CORE hoped to stir up trouble for its own purposes seemed obvious to Alabama's white officials. The organization had recruited the student activists and trained them with the knowledge, even the expectancy, they would be placed in harm's way.[22]

From the governor's perspective, CORE was exploiting the student activists, using them to promote the organization's agenda. Theirs was a role the students eagerly sought, however. They were young, idealistic, and inspired by the justice of their cause. Since the prior year's sit-ins the students had become a vital new dimension of the civil rights movement. With or without them, change was coming. It was the law of the land, as former President Truman said. But what had a hundred years in Beulah Land brought their people, except a seat at the back of the bus? For the Freedom Riders, their journey was a religious pilgrimage. For the workaday white Southerner, the pilgrimage was annoying, disruptive, widely resented and generally misunderstood.

Truman had advice for both sides. He believed the nation was "making good progress toward integration, but not moving fast enough." A major step forward would be the removal of racial signs from Southern waiting rooms, he said. His advice to the Freedom Riders was to "stay up North and let the South work out its own problems." In the final analysis the racial problems could be solved only with "common sense and good will" by both blacks and whites.[23]

Not all of the Freedom Riders were outsiders. In fact, the movement had its roots in the South, and many of the young black activists were Southern-born and Southern-raised. One of the student leaders was twenty-one-year-old John Lewis, a seminarian who would become a driving force in the movement and later serve two decades in the U.S. Congress. Few Alabamians who watched the civil rights drama unfold on TV or in the morning papers that spring were aware that Lewis—beaten by white toughs at bus stations in Alabama and South Carolina—had grown up in Pike County, Alabama, near the town of Troy and only a few miles of dusty road south of Montgomery.[24]

The white riders were cut of a different cloth. Some were older. Most, but not all, came from the North. Two or three were throwbacks to the rampant dissent on college campuses of the fifties where civil disobedience to some white students (weaned off Chubby Checker, chug-a-lugging and panty raids) had become, if not a career, then surely something more than an avocation. Political activism was not new to white New Yorker James Peck, who was badly beaten by a mob lying in wait for the Freedom Riders in Birmingham. Peck had been a WWII dissenter and in 1948 had chained himself to a gate at the White House to protest the military draft. A month after the Freedom Ride his name was back in the news for accosting former President Truman on one of his morning walks, calling on him to clarify his characterization of the Freedom Riders as agitators.[25]

When the Freedom Riders arrived in Atlanta for an overnight stop, Reverend King and other civil rights leaders met them for dinner. King warned a black reporter with the group that they would "never make it through Alabama." At a meeting in the governor's office in Montgomery, Patterson and Mann had the same concern. They sent a plainclothesman named E. L. Cowling to Atlanta to board the Greyhound bus carrying ten of the Freedom Riders to Birmingham so he could keep an eye out for trouble. State troopers were on alert along the stretch of highway leading through Anniston to Birmingham.[26]

The riders resumed their journey the following morning, on Mother's Day, May 14. One group had tickets on a Trailways bus which departed Atlanta and made its first stop across the state line at Anniston (an industrial city of 38,000 in the Alabama hill country) before noon. Not surprisingly—Anniston was a Klan hotbed—an angry mob was waiting when the bus pulled into the terminal. The passengers were not allowed off the bus, and the Anniston police had to clear an escape lane for the bus to leave. When the other riders arrived on the Greyhound bus a short time later, the welcome party had grown larger and more menacing and the station was closed. A raging crowd surrounded the bus, smashing windows and slashing tires. Once more the police came to the rescue, dispersing attackers and clearing the way for the bus to leave.[27]

Outside of town a flat tire, either slashed or shot, forced the bus to pull off the road near a country store. A string of cars had followed them out of Anniston and pulled in behind the crippled bus. When a frenzied mob poured out of the cars and converged on the bus, officer Cowling stood in the door and brandished his revolver to hold them back. One of the attackers sent a Molotov cocktail crashing through a rear window and set the interior of the bus on fire. The flames spread rapidly. When Cowling collapsed, overcome by fumes, the frantic passengers pushed past him gasping for air.[28]

The riders and their assailants fell back and stared spellbound at the white-hot flames and sparks exploding from the sizzling hulk of white-hot metal, and black plumes of smoke shooting skyward. The gutted bus, engulfed in flames, could be seen for miles. State highway patrol cars, with blue lights flashing and sirens screaming, sped to the scene. The troopers, with pistols drawn, helped their fallen comrade to his feet and broke up the unruly crowd. A witness who was on the bus later testified in federal court that E. L. Cowling and the other state troopers had saved their lives. The witness described Cowling as "one of the bravest men" he had ever seen.[29]

Mann immediately informed the governor about the burned-out bus and told him that the Trailways liner which left Atlanta earlier in the morning would soon arrive in Birmingham. Neither Patterson nor Mann trusted Birmingham's defiantly segregationist police commissioner Eugene "Bull" Connor, who was a political enemy and no friend of the governor's, but they never imagined he would stand back and let the Freedom Riders be mobbed in his city. In Birmingham, Connor was the law. The city had a huge police force, with more uniformed officers than the state had highway patrolmen. Keeping the peace on his turf was Connor's responsibility, unless of course there was a complete breakdown in law and order like that in Phenix City in 1954 when the governor's father was murdered, or if the police commissioner called on the state for help.[30]

Bull Connor not only failed to keep the peace in the Freedom Rider crisis, but he had secretly made a deal with United Klans' leader Robert Shelton. When the bus arrived at the Trailways terminal in Birmingham, not a single police uniform was in view. Instead of police protection they found a mob of unrobed Klansmen awaiting them. Wielding chains and clubs, the raging Klansmen jumped their helpless victims when they got off the bus. Only later did word leak out that Klansman Gary Thomas Rowe was an FBI informant and had been present when Bull Connor agreed to keep the police away while the Klan carried out the beatings. Rowe had reported the conspiracy to his FBI contacts, but was told to go ahead and beat up the Freedom Riders. When reporters wanted to know why the police were absent, the commissioner replied with a lopsided grin that he had given them the day off because it was Mother's Day.[31]

CORE officials were ready to call off the Freedom Ride after the bloody welcome in Birmingham, but the students insisted on seeing the journey through to New Orleans. At this juncture Bobby Kennedy and his people got involved. Rumors spread that the Justice Department had been in on CORE's plans for the Freedom Rides from the beginning, a charge which the attorney general denied. He emphasized in a press interview that he never knew of the Freedom Rider trip "until after they were in Alabama and violence had occurred."[32] With the civil rights division under him and newsmen all over the story after the South Carolina incident, how could he not have known?

From their initial conversations about protecting the Freedom Riders, Patterson informed the attorney general that the state did not need any help, the state did not want any help, and the federal government's intrusion would only make matters worse. He assured Kennedy that the Freedom Riders would get the same protection all interstate passengers received, but the state was not going to nursemaid them. Kennedy was adamant about the Justice Department's role in the unfolding drama. "This was a state problem, obviously," he noted later, "but they were traveling in interstate commerce, so we had a responsibility."[33]

Over the next several days Kennedy's office was described as "a command post," where he kept the phone lines humming with calls to the governor's office and to Justice Department officials he had dispatched to "the war zone." These included John Doar and John Seigenthaler, who tried unsuccessfully to persuade the riders not to continue their trip, and later deputy attorney general Byron "Whizzer" White, who flew to Montgomery and set up headquarters at nearby Maxwell Field. As tensions rose the attorney general's calls to the governor became more frequent and more demanding, the conversations between them more rancorous. "He would talk to us like we were privates in his army," Patterson said. "It was irritating. It really was."[34]

The governor said every time they finished a conversation, he would read about it in the morning paper. Kennedy gave the impression of wanting to reflect a White House that was decisive and in control after the debacle at the Bay of Pigs. The governor and the attorney general each accused the other of becoming hysterical during their discussions. At one point the governor became so exasperated he slammed the phone down on the attorney general, and then refused to take a call from the president. Lieutenant Governor Boutwell took the call instead, but would make no commitments without the governor's approval. When he finally got back to the attorney general, Patterson suggested that Kennedy send a liaison to Montgomery to work with him and Floyd Mann.[35]

"Look, every time we talk you hold a press conference and say things that hurt us here in Alabama," Patterson said. "You twist my words. You and I can't talk. Why don't you send somebody down here to stay with us and report back to you." Kennedy agreed and had assistant John Seigenthaler go to Montgomery to represent him. Seigenthaler, a thirty-two-year-old journalist from Nashville, was a former newspaper editor who now worked for the Justice Department.[36]

Meanwhile, the black citizens of Birmingham seethed with rage. The bloodied riders—aided by Reverend Fred Shuttlesworth and other civil rights leaders—were stitched up and replacements were brought in. Among the refreshed riders was John Lewis, who had temporarily left the group coming out of South Carolina on a pressing personal matter. Upon arrival in Birmingham, Lewis and the others were arrested and tossed in jail. Bull Connor told them to get out of Alabama and personally escorted them to the Tennessee line, only to have the students return to Birmingham the next day more determined than ever not to give in.[37]

Before the riders could leave Birmingham and continue their journey, they had to find a bus driver who was willing to take them. Patterson agreed to give the riders protection en route to Montgomery, but the company's regular drivers feared there would be more violence and refused to make the trip. When he learned of this, Robert Kennedy got on the phone to the Greyhound superintendent in Birmingham and told him the government "would be very upset" if the group was not able to continue their ride. "Greyhound had better make arrangements immediately," he ordered.[38]

Kennedy suggested the superintendent find a black driver if necessary, but was told none were available. "Well, hell, you can look for one, can't you," Kennedy said. Then in a fit of pique, he snapped, "Why, hell, can't Mr. Greyhound get out and drive one of 'em?"

Finally one of the regular drivers was convinced to make the run to Montgomery. The bus left Birmingham escorted by state troopers. John Lewis describes the "surreal trip" in his memoir *Walking with the Wind*:

> Arrangements had been made for a state patrol car to be stationed every fifteen miles between Birmingham and Montgomery, and the highway patrol provided our escort, handing us off along the way. Overhead, a highway patrol airplane pointed the way as we raced down the highway, doing about ninety miles an hour.
>
> In less than two hours we reached the Montgomery city limits, and suddenly, as if on cue, the patrol cars turned away, the airplane banked off toward the horizon, and we were on the road alone.[39]

The governor had been assured there would be no problems at the bus station. Police commissioner Sullivan gave his word that the Montgomery police could and would protect the riders inside the city limits. He turned down the offer of help from the state. As added insurance, the governor had Floyd Mann bring in extra state troopers and have them ready just in case. Mann notified Sullivan when the bus carrying the freedom riders reached Prattville, about ten miles out of Montgomery. Sullivan was committed to take it from there.[40]

Lewis recalled the strange feeling he had when they pulled into Montgomery. In Birmingham a squadron of Bull Connor's police cruisers had escorted them to the city limits, but there were no police cars waiting to lead them into Montgomery. For a Saturday morning, it was eerily quiet. No other cars were on the road as they made the slow turn onto the street leading to the bus station. Floyd Mann, who approached the terminal from a different direction, sensed something was wrong. He and his assistant Bill Jones arrived shortly after the bus pulled into the Greyhound terminal and the passengers disembarked. From out of nowhere a howling mob of white men and women wielding clubs, metal pipes, and purses with bricks inside descended on the riders. Where were the blue uniforms? Mann swore under his breath. That damned Sullivan had gone back on his word.[41]

ANY OTHER SATURDAY MORNING would have been a routine day at the office for John Patterson. A time to catch up on unfinished business. The governor was known to keep a neat desk. Cluttered desk, cluttered mind, he'd been taught. This Saturday, the 20th of May, was different. His thoughts were occupied with getting the Freedom Riders into Montgomery and out of Alabama in one piece before their presence stirred up more trouble for the state or got somebody killed. The lawlessness at Anniston and Birmingham had already given the state a black eye, and the governor didn't want another one. No need to be uneasy, he thought to himself. L. B. Sullivan had promised full cooperation, and Floyd Mann would see that he carried through. Then the phone rang. Tommy Giles was on the line. All hell had broken loose down at the bus station!

Riots seem to last forever, but are usually over in minutes. State photographer Giles had gone to the bus station with the thought of taking pictures, but almost got caught in the melee as the rioters lashed out at anything and everything in sight. The mob assaulted one news photographer and smashed his camera. Giles backed off to a phone booth and called the governor. With an unobstructed view of the mayhem, Giles reported that passengers from the bus had been knocked to the ground and were still being pummeled as they lay bleeding on the spattered cement. Off to his right the Justice Department's John Seigenthaler had been hit in the head with a lead pipe and lay unconscious in the gutter. He had been clubbed while trying to rescue a female Freedom Rider from the mob.

The door to the phone booth rattled and shook. Giles at first thought he was being attacked, but then recognized a wire service reporter trying to get to the phone. Giles waved him away. He continued surveying the scene for the governor, while Floyd Mann was busy protecting the Freedom Riders. The police commissioner was there, but the Montgomery police had made no move to break up the riots. Giles saw Mann wade into the mob, grab one rioter by the neck and pull him off an unconscious rider, while brandishing his pistol to stop the mayhem. Calling in the state troopers, Mann had restored a semblance of order when the Montgomery police arrived late on the scene. When white ambulances failed to respond, other means were found to transport the severely beaten victims to the hospital. The remaining Freedom Riders eventually were escorted away from the bus station and were looked after by Reverend Ralph Abernathy and members of the black community.[42]

Judge Frank Johnson, when he later presided over a hearing into the riots, castigated the Birmingham and Montgomery police for having "virtually abdicated their responsibility." They stood by and allowed the bus terminal rampages to take place unimpeded in their cities. "Bull Connor didn't do a thing," he said. "Then six days went by and the Montgomery police knew the riders were coming. They had six days to get ready. Six days. And didn't do a thing." Johnson credited Floyd Mann for taking charge with his men and doing "the job the Montgomery police should have done." "If it hadn't been for Floyd Mann, there would have been some folks killed that day," the judge said. "Instead of protecting people, the police were directing traffic."[43]

Johnson revealed that the Justice Department had FBI agents with a movie camera parked in a van near the Greyhound terminal. Mindful of informant Gary Rowe's instructions to go ahead with the beating in Birmingham, the FBI agents were not there to shield the Freedom Riders. Patterson, who well remembered the FBI turning a blind eye to Phenix City vice and gambling at the impeachment trial of Sheriff Matthews in 1952 and then refusing to help investigate his father's murder, had little confidence in what the federal agency said or did. Judge Johnson commented on the "incredible coincidence" that all the footage from the FBI's three movie cameras that Saturday morning "had been exposed and ruined." The only pictures available to the court had been taken by an ATF agent looking down on the melee at the terminal from his office in the federal building. [44]

Even after the police quelled the initial wave of violence, rioting spread to another downtown section of the capital city. The rioters were wildly reported to number from two hundred to one thousand, with the police having to resort to tear gas to subdue them.

With the hot sun bearing down around mid-day the violence subsided, but the peace which settled over the cluttered downtown streets was an uneasy one. Patterson went on radio and television to announce that he would "not allow any group to take the law into their hands." "We are fully able to enforce the laws of this state," he stated. "We have the duty and the desire to protect human lives no matter who is involved, and to safeguard personal property and to keep order."[45]

The governor's phones rang off the hook. More trouble was brewing. Reverend King had cancelled a speaking engagement in Chicago and was flying into Montgomery to speak at a mass rally in support of the Freedom Riders. A busload of "American Nazi" leader George Lincoln Rockwell's followers was reported to be en route to Alabama to exploit the racial strife. Klansmen had already moved in from around the state. Robert Kennedy threatened to send in federal marshals. Patterson fired back that his state was already under invasion, and Kennedy's interference would only make matters worse.[46]

The phone lines between the governor's office and Washington sizzled with as much heat as the racial tensions percolating around the capital city. The attorney general barked orders like a drill sergeant, while the governor gave as good as he got. Patterson told the attorney general if he truly wanted to help ease the tensions in Alabama he would pull his people out of Alabama and would convince King to stay in Chicago. Alabama could handle its own problems, Patterson insisted, adding that Kennedy's sending federal marshals to Montgomery would only "worsen the situation and make our job of law enforcement more difficult."

Patterson (with Mann, state attorney general McDonald Gallion, and members of the press in attendance) repeated the state's position in a meeting on Sunday morning with assistant U.S. Attorney General Byron White. The governor made it clear that he believed White's presence and the Justice Department's act of political grandstanding in sending federal marshals to Alabama was unconstitutional, was unwarranted, and would "only further complicate and aggravate the situation and worsen federal-state relations." He accused the administration of sending "your forces here ostensibly to quell a disturbance that you, yourselves, have helped create."[47]

Patterson said he personally liked Byron White, but thought at the time that "we ought to be very clear that we did not need federal intervention in maintaining order in Alabama." White, whose calls from Maxwell AFB were monitored by a friendly telephone operator, was overheard telling Kennedy that he believed the state was fully capable of handling the situation. He recommended pulling the federal marshals out. Kennedy disagreed. Pulling the marshals out now would look as if the administration had backed down.[48]

Patterson's concern grew by the minute as he and his staff assessed the situation. He was told that the five hundred or so federal marshals were a mixed lot brought in from various federal court systems around the country and were not trained in crowd control. The presence of the marshals, the rally that Reverend Abernathy had scheduled at his First Baptist Church for Sunday evening, and King's arrival in the afternoon were magnets pulling a horde of white hecklers and troublemakers into downtown Montgomery. When King arrived at the airport, federal marshals escorted him into town to Abernathy's church where a large congregation was waiting. A throng of reporters and television cameramen tagged along, scurrying to make the evening news.

As nightfall approached, radio announcers were pleading for listeners to stay away from downtown and not to come near the church where King was to speak. The public announcements had the opposite effect, attracting not only racist troublemakers but every young tough and curiosity seeker from miles around. Patterson and his staff had seen the trouble brewing through the day and prepared to deal with it. Kate Simmons had typed a proclamation of martial law and had it on the governor's desk for his signature if needed. Major General Henry Graham assigned Colonel Rufus Sheppard to stay with the governor and serve as a liaison with the National Guard. The general moved Guard units into Montgomery and had them on standby at the Dixie Graves Armory.

The Guard units (the equivalent of a regimental combat team) were comprised primarily of infantrymen and two military police battalions that were trained in riot control. They were not allowed to have live ammunition. They had fixed bayonets, with orders not to use them except in a life or death situation. "I didn't want anybody to get killed out there, if we could avoid it," Patterson explained. "We knew those marshals couldn't hold off that mob, if things got bad down at the church. Our guardsmen could. They were well-trained, they were tough, and they were ready. No concerns about that."

When night fell the marshals formed a ring around the church. Standing back on the perimeter, a few city policemen swapped jokes as the gathering mob grew larger and bolder under the cover of darkness. Mann and the governor's aide, state trooper Tom Posey, were on the scene with Henry Graham watching and listening. Tommy Giles was there. "Every few minutes they would call me from a pay phone down there and tell me what was going on," the governor said. The open fields fronting the church were overflowing with spectators and disorderly troublemakers aching for a fight.

Violence broke out with sudden fury as the surly mob swarmed into the streets taunting the marshals and setting fire to a car parked down from the church. The car belonged to Virginia Durr, a well-known Montgomerian who, with her at-torney husband, Clifford, were among the few local whites who were sympathetic to civil rights activities. Mrs. Durr was the sister-in-law of U.S. Supreme Court Justice Hugo Black. Her friend, British writer Nancy Mitford, had borrowed the Durrs' car to drive to the church to interview Dr. King. Mitford was inside the church when stones and bottles flew and the rioters, cursing and howling racial slurs, charged toward the marshals. "When the bottles started flying the marshals covered up to protect themselves, and the crowd ran right over them," the gov-ernor recalled. "Floyd moved in quickly with state troopers and Henry Graham ordered in squads of infantry with rifles in diamond formation and stopped the rioters before they could break down the door of the church. Our troops beating on a few of them broke it up real quick. That was the end of it."

When Tom Posey called and said "Guv'ner, you'd better call 'em out," Pat-terson had given the order to commit the troops and signed the proclamation of limited martial law. Graham and Mann decided that even with armed soldiers patrolling the city streets, the situation was still too dangerous for King and the others in the church to leave before daylight. Fearing that people leaving the church would be set upon individually or in small groups as they walked home in the dark, Graham and Mann convinced them to remain overnight and then had them escorted to their homes after the sun came up.

The National Guard patrols kept order in the capital city until the Freedom Riders left the Montgomery terminal in a pair of buses a few days later heading through Selma to the Mississippi line. A convoy of three planes, two helicopters, and seventeen highway patrol cars escorted them to the state line where Governor Ross Barnett's highway patrolmen took over. To keep from repeating the violence inflicted on the riders in Alabama, the Mississippi governor had the Freedom Riders arrested in Jackson for violating state laws. They were incarcerated in the state penitentiary at Parchman Farm for three weeks.[49] The immediate Freedom Rider crisis was over, but King noted that the rides and the sit-ins "dramatized the new militancy of Southern Negroes, particularly young people," and were a turning point in the civil rights movement. Together they were on a venture to change the moral compass of the nation.

ROBERT KENNEDY, IN A jocular mood after the Freedom Riders left Alabama, told reporters at a Washington press conference, "You know what Seigenthaler said to me after he saw Governor Patterson about this. He said, 'Don't you ever run for governor of Alabama. It's a hell of a job.'"[50]

All sides in the controversy spun the story to their advantage. In his meeting with the press on Tuesday, Attorney General Kennedy took full credit for putting down the riot in Montgomery on Sunday night and saving those crowded into Reverend Abernathy's church. Kennedy claimed that newsmen, who were present in Montgomery, reported that "if the marshals had not been present the church would have been burned to the ground with great loss of life."[51] The attorney general didn't bother to mention the governor's proclamation of limited martial law and the National Guard's pivotal role in resolving the crisis.

Kennedy insisted that the marshals were sent in "only as a last resort, and with great reluctance." He referred to the discussion Seigenthaler had with Patterson on Friday. The governor had given his assurance that the state could control the situation without "outside help." "Twelve hours later, Mr. Seigenthaler was lying unconscious in a street in Montgomery after having attempted to rescue a young girl from another armed mob," Kennedy said.[52]

King, in his speech at the Sunday night rally, laid the blame for the violence "at the doorstep of the governor." The governor's words and actions had "created the atmosphere in which violence could thrive," King said. Yet, the civil rights icon's own hyperbole brought more fervor than calm to a volatile situation. "Alabama," he said, "has sunk to a level of barbarity comparable to the tragic days of Hitler's Germany."[53] King indicated that he planned "to capitalize on the drama and the national and international attention now trained on the South" by stepping up "the tempo of protest against racial segregation in such states as Alabama and Mississippi."[54]

Patterson had a contrasting view of King's and the Justice Department's roles in the crisis. He too met with the press on Tuesday, but blamed the Sunday night riot on the federal marshals. "The riot Sunday night was caused by federal marshals bringing Martin Luther King into the city to address a large rally," he stated. He believed the Kennedy administration's intervention in the crisis had made a bad situation worse, but insisted that he still admired the president and considered him a friend. He reemphasized that the federal marshals were not needed in Alabama, and if they really wanted "to contribute to law and order they should go home."[55]

If he had not declared limited martial law and called out the National Guard when he did, the governor believed the rioters would have overrun the marshals and stormed the church. General Graham and Floyd Mann agreed. Even Byron

White, years later when he was on the U.S. Supreme Court, acknowledged "being 'very happy' when the National Guard arrived just when it appeared the marshals might be overrun."[56]

Inside the church King had had an open phone line to Robert Kennedy in Washington. The attendees at the mass meeting cheered wildly when informed about 9:15 P.M. of the proclamation of limited martial law. Attorney Fred Gray, a longtime and able courtroom adversary in the state's civil rights cases, expressed dismay to a reporter, "commenting that he thought it gave Patterson the initiative over federal authority in the situation." The governor's power under martial law permitted banning mass meetings like the one at the besieged church.[57]

Patterson called on the federal government to use its "prestige and power" to persuade the Freedom Riders to leave. "At least the administration could take a public position against them," he said. John Seigenthaler had tried but failed to convince the riders not to continue after the violence in Birmingham. Robert Kennedy belatedly called for a "cooling-off period" after the riders left Alabama and were arrested in Mississippi. Federal intervention in the crisis was widely believed to have been politically motivated—the administration did not want to lose the African American vote, which many analysts believed had been shifted from its historical allegiance to the party of Lincoln to the Democrats in 1960 by John F. Kennedy's timely call to King's wife when King was jailed in Georgia just before the election.[58]

Politics was also a factor in Patterson's response to the crisis. Even if he had wanted federal assistance, which he didn't, the governor would not have asked for it. A majority of white Alabama voters did not condone mob violence, but they resented outside interference as well. Few white Southern advocates of racial equality—they were growing in number by 1961—thought it prudent to defend the Freedom Riders' methods. Patterson could not succeed himself as governor, but had not ruled out running for public office at some future date. As shown in his early and persistent support of Kennedy's campaign for president, however, the governor's decisions could and did transcend political ambitions when he believed they were best for the state. The same could be said for the Kennedys where the interests of the nation were at stake.

Patterson's stand on the Freedom Riders was supported seventy-five to one by his mail, according to executive secretary Joe Robertson. Other Southern governors were behind him. Predictably, with the exception of Grover Hall and a few editors who opposed Patterson politically, Alabama's newspapers backed the governor. The *Birmingham News* cagily attacked Patterson one day and took Kennedy and King to task the next day. The South's influential *Atlanta Constitution* boldly supported the Freedom Riders, while blaming the Alabama governor for the violence in his state.[59]

Patterson made the cover of *Time* in the June 2 issue. The cover photograph was a good likeness of the governor, complete with a white carnation which he wore in the lapel of his coat each day. On the inside pages, however, *Time* gave readers a one-dimensional caricature of a segregationist governor of a segregationist state whose cultural mindset was to deny African Americans their constitutional rights and to preserve the antebellum South. The theme of the article was that black Americans were due all the rights and privileges of every other citizen in the U.S., and it framed a message to desegregation diehards: "That time cannot come too swiftly for young Negroes of 1961—and the John Pattersons of the South can do little to stop them."[60]

Not surprisingly, Rebe Gosdin (the talented musician whose Sunshine Valley Boys gave a special twang to Patterson's gubernatorial campaign) saw a humorous side to the Freedom Rider story that *Time* overlooked. The fiddle and bow are the South's parlor music. Even those who don't like it pretend they do. The dangling feet of some who pretend they don't are seen swinging in rhythm to a toe-tapping tune. In mid-June the governor took a lot of ribbing on Saturday night when Gosdin's TV show featured a new song about the contentious relations with Bobby Kennedy during the Freedom Rider crisis. Rebe wrote the parody and set it to music to the tune of the hillbilly ballad, "No Help Wanted." A typical verse and chorus went like this:

> Them riders came here stirring up hate,
> Arrived at the capitol, met their fate;
> Law was there, soon quelled the resistance,
> But Bob Kennedy was on long distance.
>
> Do you need any help? (No help wanted.)
> I'll send you some help . . . (no help wanted)
> If you need any help . . . If you need any help.
> (We can handle this job all by ourselves.)[61]

Judge Frank Johnson (a man King said "gave true meaning to the word 'justice'") convened hearings into the Freedom Rider violence on May 29. The Justice Department's Doar and White, on the morning following the riots at Reverend Abernathy's church, had filed a motion at the U.S. courthouse in Montgomery seeking a permanent injunction against the KKK and the Montgomery Police Department. Earlier, Circuit Judge Walter B. Jones, at the request of the state attorney general, had issued an injunction forbidding CORE and any of its followers from testing bus segregation laws in Alabama.[62]

After four days of hearings Judge Johnson worked late into the night on June 1 to prepare his findings, which he handed down the following day. Johnson, as expected, came down hard on the three KKK groups (the United Klans, Knights of the Ku Klux Klan, and the Alabama Knights of the Ku Klux Klan) for the racial violence in Anniston and Birmingham on May 14, and in Montgomery on May 20. He issued a court order enjoining the KKK from "conspiring to interfere with the travel of passengers, committing acts of violence upon, or threatening or otherwise obstructing, impeding, or interfering with the free movement of interstate commerce."[63]

Montgomery's finest anticipated that they too would be rebuked by the court. Johnson did not disappoint them. The court specifically found that the Montgomery Police Department under the direction of commissioner Sullivan and chief G. J. Ruppenthal "willfully and deliberately failed to take measures to ensure the safety of the students and to prevent unlawful acts of violence upon their persons." They were the subject of a preliminary injunction for "refusing to provide protection for all persons traveling in interstate commerce."[64]

While deliberate inaction by the Montgomery police was public knowledge, witnesses were reluctant to testify against them. Even Floyd Mann, who was recognized by the court for taking the necessary precautions and saving lives at the bus terminal, was faltering in his testimony and shrank from criticizing fellow police officers. Johnson emphasized that Mann and the state highway patrol had done more than asked of them. They had stepped in and done what the municipal police forces were paid to do in preventing further violence outside Anniston and at the bus terminal in Montgomery.[65]

Judge Johnson surprised the courtroom by placing a temporary restraining order against those involved in "sponsoring, financing, assisting or encouraging" organized tests of segregation in Alabama. Specifically mentioned in the court order were CORE, the Southern Christian Leadership Conference, Reverends Abernathy, Shuttlesworth, King, Seay, and Wyatt Tee Walker, and other civil rights groups. Recognizing that the organized Freedom Rides "were agitation within the law of the United States," the court found that sponsoring these "bonafide trips" caused "an undue burden and restraint upon interstate carriers" and "upon the free flow of interstate commerce." Johnson later clarified that the court order was directed to the riders' backers, not to the riders themselves since they were free to travel wherever they wished.[66]

Judge Johnson explained in the court opinion that he felt the Freedom Riders "went about pursuing their rights in the wrong way," and "when they ran into trouble in Anniston . . . they should have quit and come to the courts." "That's why we have courts," he said. Their decision to continue the rides "created strife," "interfered with the other passengers who were riding buses," and "impeded the normal flow of interstate commerce."[67]

At the same time Johnson enjoined state attorney general Gallion from enforcing the injunction he had obtained from the state circuit court against the Freedom Riders (an injunction Gallion had personally and infamously served at the bus station that Saturday morning on John Lewis as he lay bleeding on the ground). Johnson found that one of the attorney general's "primary purposes was to enforce segregation contrary to the federal law, a law he was duty bound to uphold." He said the attorney general should have been advising local authorities that interstate passengers "were entitled to use bus terminal facilities . . . on a nonsegregated basis."[68] The court opinion also found that the U.S. Attorney General did not have to push as hard as he did in his demands on the Greyhound bus officials.[69]

There was "total silence except for the quiet hum of the air conditioning" in the courtroom when Judge Johnson read the court order. Before starting he had fixed his eyes on the principals seated at the tables in front of him. To preclude any misunderstanding of his findings and conclusions, or the injunction and restraining order, Johnson said they simply meant that the court would tolerate no other occasions like the ones in this case, and if there were other such occasions he was "going to put some Klansmen, some city officials, and some policemen, and some Negro preachers, in the U.S. penitentiary in Atlanta."[70]

16

Building Highways, Building Bridges

The Freedom Rider controversy was off the front pages but still in the public eye when the National Conference of Governors convened in Honolulu on June 25–28, 1961. Patterson learned beforehand that Republican governors, led by Nelson Rockefeller of New York, proposed to capitalize on the South's problems with the Freedom Riders to introduce a civil rights resolution at the conference. He said he was distressed to read where Governor Rockefeller "praised the Freedom Riders and encouraged more of them to invade our state." This was not the way to build bridges between their two states.[1]

To counter what he saw as unfair criticism by Northern politicians "who wink at shameful conditions in their own back yards," Patterson prepared a lengthy rebuttal calling on the conferees "to reaffirm the sovereign right of states" in the face of growing encroachment by the federal government. When the bus burst into flames outside Anniston, the Freedom Rider situation "had ceased quickly to be a protest civil rights demonstration and became a law enforcement matter." Robert Kennedy failed to grasp this, Patterson said, and showed no understanding for the federal-state or state-municipal relationships when it came to enforcing the law. "Nobody ever would have dreamed that a group of people would stop a bus on the highway outside of Anniston, Alabama, in the United States today and burn a bus," he later recalled.[2]

He believed Judge Johnson "had the Freedom Rider thing about right." Patterson liked and respected Frank Johnson, even though his own political doctrine on state sovereignty and the desegregation issue was more philosophically aligned with Judge Walter B. Jones, the antithesis of Johnson on and off the bench. The governor had tremendous respect for Judge Jones, never forgetting the powerful symbol of justice the judge came to represent in Phenix City during his family's darkest days of 1954. That Johnson the federal district judge and Jones the state circuit judge were poles apart in their legal opinions on racial equality and civil rights did not lessen his regard for either man. Both were men of honor and respect for the rule of law.[3]

Patterson thought of himself as more centrist on the race issue than his public image conveyed. The "unfortunate Freedom Rider situation," as he described it in a 1967 interview, had ramifications other than intended. Instead of reading into the experience a sense of urgency in righting the South's racial wrongs, he seemed more determined than before that Alabama needed time to adjust to social reform and that he was right in holding the line on gradual desegregation through the end of his term as governor. Nothing occurred at the Honolulu conference to change his mind. When pushed, as he had been in the sit-ins and the Freedom Rides, Patterson had a natural inclination to push back. He went on the offensive in Hawaii.[4]

On their way to the Honolulu conference the governor's party stayed overnight at the Jack Tar Hotel in San Francisco, where CORE protestors picketed outside. The next day about seventy-five protesters staged a rally at the airport terminal and took contributions to help bail out the Freedom Riders jailed in Mississippi. California Governor Edmund (Pat) Brown reportedly contributed $100. An affable Patterson told reporters he found most Californians hospitable. "I certainly am going to obey the laws of California while I'm here," he said, "and I feel that we in Alabama have a right to expect the same of visitors to our state."[5]

On the flight from San Francisco he took some good-natured ribbing from Governors Brown and Rockefeller. They were having a drink together in the back of the plane, when the other two governors kidded him about their having contributed money to CORE. Patterson laughed and told them, "Now that you've got your racial problems solved, you can turn your attention to Alabama." It was all in fun, Patterson said. He liked Nelson Rockefeller, who had thrown "a big bash" for the other governors at their previous conference in San Juan, and Pat Brown. They had their constituencies, and Patterson had his. This was politics.[6]

When Governor and Mrs. Patterson deplaned in Honolulu they were offered "a back way out" of the airport to avoid protesters waiting there, but he "refused to duck the pickets." Receiving a warm welcome from Hawaii's Governor William Quinn and an Oahu beauty queen, Patterson traded his customary white carnation for a traditional island lei. Responding to reporters' questions about the Freedom Rider violence in Alabama, Patterson commented that Hawaii's good race relations "were a tribute to the Hawaiian people" and an example for other states to follow. He stressed that individual states had to "work out their own problems as Hawaii did," and that nothing could be accomplished by force. "Court injunctions, federal troops and federal marshals will only worsen relations," he stated.[7]

Before addressing his fellow governors, Patterson held a press conference and was invited to appear on Honolulu television to talk about states' rights and the Freedom Riders issue. He pointed out that the Freedom Riders, by their own admission, rode into the South to stir up trouble and they succeeded. Their aim was to force federal intervention, and they achieved that goal when Robert Kennedy obliged them by sending federal marshals to Montgomery. He called on the governors to band together to preserve states' rights and warned that federal force could be used in their states as it had been in Alabama.[8]

Patterson outlined "recent progress in Alabama," and urged that the state "be allowed to work out its problems on its own schedule, in its own way." "The customs of generations are not changed in a single year or perhaps even in decades," he declared. If "the pretty boy politicians" in Washington pushed integration by force, he feared the Southern states could be "engaged in a full scale 'cold war' with our own government."[9]

During his TV appearance, described by the *Honolulu Star* as a "near-perfect" showing, Patterson was questioned by John Gailbraith, KHVH news director, William H. Ewing, *Honolulu Star-Bulletin* editor, and William J. Lederer, author of *A Nation of Sheep* and co-author of *The Ugly American*. The governor favorably impressed the panel and the viewers. An editorial in the *Honolulu Star-Bulletin* the next day suggested that the U.S. State Department invite the Alabama governor to go to non-Caucasian countries "to explain what's been going on in his state."[10]

The idea of sending Patterson abroad to speak and answer questions about the South originated with Lederer, who noted that the governor represented a point of view that was not widely supported, but that existed in the United States. "He understands it; he is articulate in a rare degree, he can express it," the editorial stated. "Furthermore, he could explain something which foreigners never seem quite able to grasp—the dual sovereignty of the Federal and State governments."[11]

One Southern newspaper described the Hawaii conference, with the exception of Patterson's appearance on TV, as "a pep rally for the New Frontier" and a "big disappointment." The Alabama governor charged that the president's younger brother was "getting too big for his britches." "Mr. Kennedy called me up on the telephone in the middle of the night and issued orders like I was a private in his army. That's not what I am and that's not the way I do business." While he was not a cheerleader for the administration, Patterson said that his opposition to federal intervention did not mean "a split between himself and the president." As a loyal Democrat he still supported the president and his policies. Patterson said he would be "most willing" to travel throughout the world explaining the Southern viewpoint on race relations, but he knew the odds of the State Department inviting him to do so were "slim to none."[12]

Unified Southern opposition caused the conferees to back away from a strong civil rights resolution. Democratic National Chairman John Bailey, speaking for the Kennedy administration, heatedly insisted that the Democrats could not afford to be outdone on civil rights by minority Republicans. He urged adoption of a tougher Democratic resolution regardless of how Southerners might react. Three days of secret maneuvers and compromises resulted in the adoption of "a mild statement studiously omitting any reference to civil rights." An exasperated Northern governor was overheard to say, "We've got to have something, even if it says nothing."[13]

The tenuous display of Southern unity at the Hawaii conference lasted no longer than it took the delicate Hilo orchids on the governors' souvenir leis to wither. Three weeks after the island junket hawkish Ross Barnett of Mississippi invited eleven regional governors to Jackson for a meeting on states rights and racial integration, and only three "found it convenient to come." "Florida, Georgia, Louisiana, and Kentucky sent lesser officials while Tennessee, Virginia, North Carolina, and Texas sent none." Barnett admitted to reporters there was no such thing as Southern unity on the need for greater "self determination" in the civil rights field, but said it was "long overdue."[14]

Patterson, bouyed by the reception in Hawaii, joined Barnett, Ernest F. Hollings of South Carolina, and Orval Faubus of Arkansas, and the attorney generals of Georgia and Louisiana at the discussions in Jackson. The group proposed a follow-up session in Montgomery, which never came off. In September Governor Buford Ellington of Tennessee hosted the annual Southern Governors Conference in Nashville where moderate chief executives shied away from any discussion of "Southern unity to combat racial integration and federal intervention." Patterson defended this to reporters, explaining that the conference traditionally "stays away from controversy."[15]

Patterson boldly proclaimed, however, that as Alabama's governor he dealt in controversy. He had made up his mind to stand fast with the strategy of resistance and "to ride this thing out" for the year and a few months he had left in office. He told reporters in September that Attorney General Kennedy's suits against Alabama officials had hurt the Democratic Party. Resentment in Alabama against his brother's actions to force integration in Alabama, the governor said, had people so "sore" at the president he "couldn't possibly carry Alabama if he runs in 1964." He said a recent Interstate Commerce Commission order to desegregate bus stations might "force buses to let passengers 'out on the highways under the trees' in his state."[16]

When Ralph Smith stepped down as the governor's special counsel and returned to private practice, he was retained to represent the state on legal matters including racial desegregation cases in the federal courts. In *Brown v. Board*, the U.S. Supreme Court had referenced scientific evidence in Swedish economist Gunnar Myrdal's landmark book *An American Dilemma: The Negro Problem and Modern Democracy*. Alabama now sought equivalent evidence that the learning environment for children of both races might be enhanced by separate but equal schools. In 1962, at Smith's suggestion, Patterson commissioned a book, *The Biology of the Race Problem* by Dr. Wesley Critz George, to assist in making the state's argument.[17]

George, seventy-two-year-old professor emeritus and former department chair at the University of North Carolina Medical School, was an internationally recognized researcher on the genetics of race. When Patterson commissioned the study, he was unaware that the professor's racial views were so extreme they were repudiated by his former colleagues in academe. Afterward George came to the governor with a story about being destitute and needing a job. Touched by the professor's story, Patterson called Dr. Frank Rose and asked if the University of Alabama could use someone with George's credentials. Rose exclaimed, "God, John, I can't do that. If I hired that man every faculty member at Alabama would leave tomorrow."[18]

THE GOVERNOR WAS PERSONA non grata at the White House after his falling-out with Robert Kennedy. "I did not get invited back anymore. We did not communicate with each other anymore. So that was it. That ended my relationship with the Kennedy administration." Afterwards, in the time left to him as governor, he recalled that the Justice Department did the talking for the administration with an onslaught of legal actions against the few diehard Southern states still resisting federal directives on civil rights and desegregation.[19]

Patterson said what he should have done in the Freedom Rider situation was to "have rounded up all the Klansmen in the vicinity of Anniston the day they burned that bus and put their asses in jail." "Any of them we missed there we would of got at the Birmingham bus station," he said. "If I had it to do all over again I would crack down on them unmercifully from the very beginning." That would have bagged Gary Thomas Rowe, too, he said, and the FBI would have been scurrying to get their informant out of jail. There would have been "a hue and cry about violating people's rights," but he thought that could have been handled at the time without "too much flak," and was "what we should have done."[20]

Patterson said he probably should have handled Robert Kennedy differently. "The first time I got a call from Bobby Kennedy, knowing what I do today, I would say, 'Yes, sir, Mr. Kennedy, you tell me what you want me to do, and I will do it. But I want it in writing, and you're going to have to be responsible if it don't work.'" If he had simply called Kennedy's hand that way, he believed that might have been the end of it. "We, of course, will never know," he said.[21]

Looking back on that troubled period, Patterson said the U.S. Department of Justice's actions made it increasingly clear that buying time for the South on desegregation meant buying trouble. Over the next year and continuing into George Wallace's administration, the Justice Department unrelentingly turned up the heat on Alabama and other recalcitrant Southern states. [22]

While CORE and NAACP officials assailed Patterson verbally—Roy Wilkins said other governors were not "as much in earnest, as deadly, as fanatical as Barnett . . . in Mississippi or Patterson in Alabama"—the civil rights organizations refrained from further testing the state's resolve until after he left office. There were racial flare-ups around the state, but the only known activity organized and sponsored by CORE field representatives at the time were sit-ins in the Huntsville area in January 1962. Located in northeast Alabama in the middle of the Tennessee Valley, Huntsville was home to Redstone Arsenal and the new Marshall Space Flight Center. As a hub of federal activity and one of Alabama's most progressive cities (growing from a small town of 13,150 inhabitants in 1940 to a thriving community of 72,000 by 1960) Huntsville was liberal on the race issue compared to other areas of the state.[23]

Of the hundred or so youthful demonstrators engaged in the Huntsville sit-ins, approximately one-third were students of Alabama Agricultural & Mechanical College. Administrators at the college posted notice that A&M did not condone the off-campus activity and asked CORE representatives to cease activities on the campus. Working with the new Superintendent of Education, W. A. LeCroy, the governor used the earlier problems at Alabama State to resolve those at A&M. He was concerned that both schools, having failed to meet academic standards, had been dropped from the approved list for accreditation by the Southern Association of Colleges and Schools in December. Neither college had ever been fully accredited.[24]

Having taken a special interest in improving "the administration and teaching programs at both our state Negro colleges and to get them accredited," Patterson told LeCroy "to push" to get accreditation and to take measures "to see that students that go to state colleges behave themselves and obey our laws and study their books." The governor said he "would hate to see the general public which supports this college lose interest in it and lose respect for it because of the bad behavior of some of the students."[25]

GOVERNOR PATTERSON HAD TAKEN a special interest in seeing Alabama's institutions of higher learning grow and prosper. An example of this was the support he gave Dr. Wernher von Braun and Dr. Frank Rose in their efforts to create the University of Alabama research center at Huntsville. Patterson had become acquainted with von Braun when NASA's Marshall Space Flight Center was dedicated in 1960. The renowned German rocket scientist, who had been with the Army Ballistic Missile Agency at Redstone Arsenal since 1950, was director of the new space center.[26]

President Eisenhower flew down for the dedication and was greeted at the Redstone Arsenal airstrip by Patterson, von Braun, and other dignitaries. Eisenhower and Patterson rode through Redstone Arsenal on the way to the dedication and chatted for a few minutes inside the space center. They reminisced about the governor's service as a young lieutenant in Eisenhower's headquarters in London and later in Algiers during WWII, and "about the president's days at West Point, and about the war."[27]

Patterson joked to reporters before the president arrived that he thought about "wearing his Kennedy button" but decided against it. Eisenhower's brief stay at Redstone caused a stir since he was the first sitting president to visit Alabama since Franklin D. Roosevelt's trip to Jasper in 1940 "to pay final respects to a stalwart Democratic leader, House Speaker William B. Bankhead." The *Advertiser* ran a colorful account of an earlier FDR visit to the capital city in 1933 when he was president-elect: "Roosevelt rode in a state car with Gov. B. M. Miller up to Court Square . . . Along Dexter avenue, bands played his campaign song, 'Happy Days are Here Again,' and he tipped his hat and waved as he passed the Advertiser building, then located at Dexter and Lawrence."[28]

When he addressed admiring Montgomerians from the capitol steps, FDR said, "It's a great privilege to stand on this sacred spot where a great American took the oath of office as president of the Confederacy." The president-elect "smiled broadly as he observed the colorful, cheering throng." "Isn't that beautiful," he said. "I want to come here again." In a 1939 visit to Tuskegee Institute FDR said he was fulfilling an "ancient promise" to Booker T. Washington. Later that day he had given a speech at nearby Auburn and "urged the South to 'get itself out of hock to the North' by using its own resources to establish its own enterprises."[29]

Reading the *Advertiser* article, Patterson was reminded of how much his father and his Uncle Lafayette had admired FDR. He believed Roosevelt would have been proud to see the progress Alabama had made since his visits to the state. The Huntsville area was a showcase of that progress. When von Braun and Rose came to see Patterson about support for an extension of the University of Alabama in Huntsville, he was ready to do all he could to help them. Von Braun explained that if they did not get a university facility in Huntsville where young scientists who came there to work on the Saturn rocket project could further their education, they would go elsewhere. "They won't stay here," he said, "and we will lose the Center."[30]

The governor talked to his floor leaders and key legislators, and they invited von Braun to address a joint session. "He came and made a tremendous appeal to the legislature," Patterson said. Afterward the governor and first lady hosted a luncheon at the mansion. When the legislators got back to the capitol they met and unanimously approved creating the University of Alabama at Huntsville and appropriated the money for it. The Marshall Space Center was one year old, and already making an impact on Alabama's industry and economy.[31]

During a visit to Jasper in October 1962, at the dedication of the Whiteway bearing his name, Patterson pointed to the Unversity of Alabama Research Center, now under construction in Huntsville, as an indicator that the state (already gaining "about one industrial plant per week") was "on the verge of great economic growth." In three months he would leave the governor's office. He laid down a challenge to those who followed him: "Don't be afraid of big superhighway programs, big educational programs or any other program for the well-being of the state. Being conservative in these things is not wise, for it takes some daring to build this state as it should be built."[32]

IN THE WINTER OF 1960–61 the *Birmingham News* ran a series of articles by staff writer James E. Jacobson appraising the Patterson administration's progress at midterm. The series purported to give a balanced look at how the administration measured up against the campaign pledges Patterson had made, to assess both accomplishments and setbacks, and to survey what the next two years held "for the people of Alabama." The progress made in the state's highway construction program was described by Jacobson as nothing short of "spectacular."[33]

On the eve of WWII, when the effort to "Get Alabama Out of the Mud" gained momentum, the state had less than five thousand miles of paved roads. Eighteen years later, when Folsom left office for the second and final time, "the figures had passed twenty-two thousand miles on all systems, federal, state and county." "It is now in the neighborhood of thirty thousand miles," Jacobson wrote. "Thus, in two years, Gov. Patterson has already neared the eighty-five hundred miles of construction which he set as a four-year goal to be achieved without any new tax increase."[34]

As the largest state agency (5,550 employees representing 43 percent of the state payroll), the highway department in the past had been open to abuse, and was used as a political patronage plum with reports of "handsome profits on road deals." Patterson had cracked down on the abuses while he was attorney general, but he credited the success of the highway program during his administration to having picked the right department head, Sam Engelhardt. While under attack for chairing the State Democratic Executive committee, alleged by the federal Civil Service Commission to be a violation of the Hatch Act, Engelhardt had "pushed diligently a highway construction program of near-astounding proportions." The Civil Service Commission's charge didn't amount "to a hill of beans," Patterson said, and was just another way for the federal government to harass his administration.[35]

Two years later the governor's report on the affairs of state reminded legislators that their approval of his $60 million bond issue for highway construction in 1959 and the $500 million in federal matching funds had been the engine driving the success of his other programs and Alabama's thriving economy for the past four years. The administration had spent record amounts—some $200 million above the previous four years—on county and farm-to-market roads, on the interstate system, and on maintenance. The new highways not only benefited Alabama travelers, but were an incentive for bringing new industries into Alabama and attracting out-of-state tourists.[36]

Critics were surprised that the Freedom Rider turbulence had little impact on tourism in Alabama. The administration reported that the travel industry had added $270 million to the state economy in 1961. Giving much of the credit to the State Bureau of Publicity and Information under Bob Harper, the governor noted that the state had attracted eighteen million visitors during the year, many on leisure trips. To make the state even more attractive to visitors, the administration had developed the Tennessee Valley, the mid-Alabama lakes region, and Gulf Shores-Dauphin Island beaches as major tourist recreational areas.[37]

Concerns that the state's racial troubles might discourage industrial development also proved unfounded. The governor reported "unprecedented industrial growth" under his administration. "Our State has acquired 430 new plants representing a capital investment of $190.9 million," he stated, "and 642 existing industries have invested an additional $472.5 million to expand their facilities." Industrial expansion in the past four years had created 49,800 new jobs for Alabama's work force. Patterson singled out his old friend Leland Jones, head of the planning and industrial development board, as the man who had assisted in this growth.[38]

Another magnet pulling new industry into Alabama was an expansion of aviation facilities. The Department of Aeronautics, under director Asa Rountree, Jr., administered a dynamic airport development program, financed by a tax on aviation gasoline. The governor reported in January 1963 that in the past fiscal year twenty-six new airports were authorized. "In this age of business and executive flying, an industry will rarely locate in a community without airport facilities," he explained. "And more Alabama areas have good airports—with paved landing strips long enough to handle twin-engine aircraft—than any other state in this area can claim."[39]

Of course, the more Alabama became involved in the federal highway program, aviation, and interstate commerce the more it was subject to oversight by federal agencies. One favorable aspect of the federal highway program, Patterson said, was that it had taken "the politics out of road-building." Only on one occasion while he was governor did Patterson hear of the federal authorities yielding to political pressure in administering the highway program in Alabama, and this was after the Kennedy administration took office. In the fall of 1961 the Federal Bureau of Roads directed the state to reroute a segment of Interstate 85, running east-west through Montgomery, to keep from going through property owned by prominent black residents of the city.[40]

White House officials denied having influenced the rerouting decision, but reporters turned up a link suggesting otherwise. In a roundabout way allegations of racial discrimination made to Eleanor Roosevelt reached the White House and were passed down through Secretary of Commerce Luther Hodges to the Bureau of Public Roads. The Civil Rights Commission became involved in the controversy and asked that the right-of-way be changed to avoid displacing "Negro leaders of importance not only to the South but to the North." The Bureau of Roads agreed, and the highway was rerouted.[41]

One of the structures the black community wanted to keep from tearing down was a historic church. Reflecting on this bit of history concerning his highway program, Patterson recalled: "If you drive out on the interstate today, when you get close to Jackson Hospital there is a bend where the highway was rerouted. Sitting up on the hill there is the little old church. They could have taken the church and given them enough money to build a cathedral. But it wouldn't have been the same, would it?"[42]

THE GOVERNOR PERSONALLY MONITORED the road-building program across the state while going into the counties with Sam Engelhardt and other cabinet members, taking the government directly to the people. The visits to the counties were as popular at the end of his four-year term as they had been when he started them the first year he was in office. Most of the time he and selected cabinet members drove out to the rural areas and spent the whole day visiting with legislators, county officials, and a host of people discussing their problems and how the state could be of help.

Tommy Giles, the state photographer, went on many of these trips. "We also brought one of the state yachts up the Tombigbee River and made home port visits," Giles recalled. "Never will forget we brought the yacht up to Demopolis and kept it there for nearly a week. Busloads of school children came to see the yacht." The crew set up a table in the parking lot and served punch and cookies to the school children. Marine police, game wardens, and highway patrolmen were there to help the public. "Later we took a yacht up the Tennessee River and made several port calls along the way," Giles said.[43]

Many of the tours were made on the weekends. Bob Ingram went along once or twice, and reported that "Patterson thrives on them." He noted that the governor's belt "has been let out several inches" since the 1958 campaign, but he could "still outdo any member of his cabinet." On a tour of Conecuh County, the governor's caravan arrived at mid-morning in Evergreen and he "immediately set out on a fast-paced tour." "By noon most of the pack following him were wilted and gasping, the broiling sun taking its toll," Ingram wrote. "Not Patterson. He never shed his coat. Nor did he slow down."[44]

After presiding over a luncheon and granting a forty-five-minute interview at a local radio station, the governor stopped off at the motel where his cabinet members were taking a breather. "Patterson came hustling into the motel room, paused only long enough to rinse off his face, voiced an observation that the room 'looks like Castro's suit' and was off and running again. The cabinet members muttered profanity under their breaths and then followed their leader." Their prayers that the governor might relax before his banquet address that night went unanswered.[45]

Some county tours were more exciting than others. New airport dedications had become biweekly events under Patterson's administration, with the communities often hosting fly-ins for aircraft from around the state. On one such occasion, Patterson and members of his cabinet arrived at the Abbeville airport early in the state plane. Several hundred people had gathered to meet the governor and hear him speak. Minutes before the dedication ceremony was scheduled to begin, Tommy Giles looked up and said, "Governor, there's Ed Azar coming in on that new plane they bought."[46]

The Alabama ABC Board had recently purchased a Cessna 170 aircraft for its enforcement division to use in hunting down moonshiners. Azar had flown to Abbeville in the small craft with his assistant Billy Vickers and Porter Howell, assistant director of the State Planning and Industrial Development Board. Bill Sellers, an Air Guardsman and full-time employee of the liquor board, piloted the four-seater plane. The newly paved 2,900-foot runway was built along the backside of a cotton field. Sitting in the middle of the field was "a great big old tenant house with these high ceilings, an old rural farmhouse." Giles recalled that the windows were open, and "all these people were sitting in the windows watching what was going on over at the airfield."[47]

All eyes were on the Cessna since it was the last flight cleared to land before the ceremony got underway. As the plane touched down it got caught in a crosswind and spun to one side. One wingtip hit the ground sending the plane crashing toward the startled onlookers in the windows of the old farmhouse. The Cessna skidded past the farmhouse, barely made it under some power lines, and crashed into another cottonfield across the highway. The undercarriage of the plane was torn off and the propeller was badly twisted, but the pilot and passengers escaped with minor bruises and scratches. Floyd Mann went to the crash scene and reported back to the governor that except for Billy Vickers swallowing his cigar everyone was fine.[48]

Giles delighted in telling another story about one of the first trips out to the counties. State Senator John E. Gaither had invited the governor to Heflin to crown the poultry queen. The delegation left from the State Capitol early on Saturday morning in a long line of cars, with four highway patrol motorcycles leading the way and Chief Joe Smelley's patrol car bringing up the rear. In Clay County, the governor stopped at the town squares in Ashland and Lineville to shake hands with people before proceeding on to Heflin. When the day's events in Heflin were over, Patterson said he wanted to go through Cheaha State Park on the return to Montgomery. There were still a few hours of daylight left, so they headed up the Clay County side of Cheaha Mountain.[49]

As they wound their way up the highest peak in Alabama, Tom Posey had to turn off the air conditioner to keep the old Cadillac limousine, which had seen service in two Folsom administrations, from stalling out. "I looked out at those deep drop-offs and we're trying to chug up that mountain," Giles recalled. "The engine sputtered and spit, and I didn't think we were going to make it." "We're not gonna have to get out and push, are we, Tom?" the governor asked. "God, I hope not, Governor," Posey said. He knew who would be doing most of the pushing if they did. They slowed to about twenty miles an hour, but finally made it to the top. Joe Robertson was riding shotgun on the front seat with Posey. Patterson told him, "Joe, the first damned thing out of the gate Monday morning, I want you to buy us a new state car."[50]

An hour or two later, motorcycle helmets and new motorcycles for the highway patrol were added to Robertson's list. The trooper's motorcycles were also old and also had barely made it to the top of Cheaha Mountain. On the way back to Montgomery, as the procession came down a hill leading into Wetumpka, one of the troopers had moved out ahead to stop the traffic at an intersection. "We came down that hill with the sirens blowing, and Trooper Gray had all the traffic stopped. Everybody's looking to see who's coming and all eyes are on this long line of cars and these motorcycles."[51]

There was a sharp turn at the intersection, and the lead trooper, Kenneth Rush, skidded and fell, going down beside the governor's car. Chief Smelley stopped to check on Rush, who was not hurt, while the motorcade pressed on. "On down the road I hear Chief Smelley come on the radio, '219 to State Motor One. Y'all slow down a little bit. Rush is coming.' All of sudden here comes Rush roaring by us on that motorcycle. They didn't have helmets in those day. They wore baseball caps, and the hat was going up and down, and the governor says, 'Joe, we're buying those motorcycle men some helmets Monday morning. And we're buying them four new motorcycles.'"[52]

The old Cadillac limousine may have been gone, but the Southern comedian Dave Gardner made certain it was not forgotten. "Brother Dave," whose song "White Silver Sands" was a hit the year Patterson was elected governor, was one of his favorite performers. Whenever the comedy star came to town the governor sent the state limousine to pick him up at the airport. Brother Dave got to know Tom Posey and other members of the governor's staff, and he added to his comic repertoire a skit about "the governor's big black limousine with its big old antenna going swish, swish, swish."[53]

Their acquaintance with Gardner nearly caused Patterson and Ralph Smith a world of embarrassment, or worse, one night in Atlanta. They were in Atlanta on business, staying at the King's Inn Motel, and decided to catch Brother Dave's performance that night in the basement club of the old Imperial Hotel where he was a regular. It was a little after midnight when they arrived, and they got a table way in the back in the shadows so they wouldn't be recognized. Otherwise they knew he would put the spotlight on them or have them up on the stage.[54]

Brother Dave was in rare form. Having been a one-semester ministerial student in college, he spiced up his routines with a generous sprinkling of backsliding pulpit humor. "Y'all know the difference between a Nawthun Baptist and a Southern Baptist?" he would ask, and then he would tell them the difference. "A Nawthun Bapist says there ain't no hell. A Southern Baptist says the hell there ain't." When the act was over Brother Dave started table-hopping, spotted Patterson and Smith sitting back in the corner, and came over to them.

"What are y'all doing back here? Wish y'all woulda told me you was here, so I coulda introduced you."

"That's why we didn't tell you. We didn't wanna be part of the act."

He insisted they come on up to his room and have a drink. He and his wife were staying at the Imperial that night. They went up to the hotel room and had just poured a drink when the phone rang. Brother Dave picked up the phone and said, "Yeah. Yeah. Uh-huh. Yeah. Yeah." Then he hung up the phone and said, "Guv'na, you and Ralph have to leave. I'm sorry but I'll be seeing you some other time." He rushed them over to the window. "Would you mind taking the fire escape on your way out? Hurry up. Y'all don't wanna be seen in here." They didn't know whether it was one of Brother Dave's crazy jokes or what, but they went down the rickety fire escape and hailed a cab.[55]

"Early the next day Ralph came in with the morning paper," Patterson said, "and splashed across the front page was the headline that the feds had raided Brother Dave Gardner's room in the Imperial Hotel and seized some marijuana." Patterson and Smith were flabbergasted. Realizing they had a close call and that Brother Dave had done them a great favor, the governor said they got in touch with him as soon as they could and thanked him profusely for getting them out of there. The arrest for marijuana possession sent Brother Dave's television and recording career into a tailspin from which he never fully recovered. Patterson said sadly their paths never crossed again.[56]

PATTERSON HAD URGED HIS cabinet not to let racial tensions and the controversy swirling around the Freedom Riders distract their departments and hinder progress toward the administration's goals. He had taken stock midway into his administration and, while there had been mistakes, was pleased with what he saw. History would serve his administration well, he believed. The media coverage—although he like Big Jim had crossed swords with "those lyin' newspapers" on more than one occasion—seemed to agree.

Jacobson, in his series for the *Birmingham News*, found that despite falling short in some programs the administration had "indeed been a progressive one," and that the governor had already fulfilled many of his campaign pledges or was on the way to doing so. Ingram summed up his assessment of Patterson's midway progress with a lengthy column in the *Montgomery Advertiser*. "The first two years of the Patterson administration have been marked with a number of outstanding achievements coupled with a number of incidents which Patterson would most probably like to forget."[57]

Overarching the concrete achievements (passage of the small-loan law, the record school budget and the $100 million bond issue for school construction, and an unparalleled highway construction program, etc), Ingram wrote, was "the overall good state government" and "the dignity which Patterson has returned to the office of governor; an element totally lacking in the previous administration." Both Ingram and Jacobson had high praise for the Patterson cabinet, which Ingram considered "the best collection of department heads assembled by any governor in recent years." Jacobson described the cabinet members as totally loyal to the governor and molded in his image—"young, vigorous, determined to make a record for their four years in office."[58]

Among the few Alabama journalists remaining sour on the administration was *Montgomery Advertiser* editor Grover Hall, Jr., who had never forgiven Patterson for trouncing his candidate in 1958. Patterson could do no right. Wallace could do no wrong. When the capital paper attacked his younger brother Maurice after he replaced Meriwether as finance director, Patterson commented that his brother must be doing a good job "since the *Advertiser* jumped on him so early." Told that his brother threatened to get in a fist fight with Bob Ingram over a story in the *Advertiser*, Patterson said, "There are a bunch of folks you'd like to whip, but being a public official you have to laugh such things off and just go on trying to do the best you can."[59]

If Hall had no legitimate beef with the governor, he could always make one up. In July 1961 the dapper editor penned an editorial excoriating the Patterson administration for "two horticultural scandals." It was unfitting, he wrote, for there not to be a single Confederate Jasmine vine on the grounds of the First White House of the Confederacy. "Second, the great rose bed on the southeast greensward of the Capitol shames the administration. The state of this rose bed proclaims laziness or incompetence, perhaps both." Then Hall, who considered himself an expert on growing roses, went to great lengths to explain how they should be planted, fertilized, and cultivated.[60]

The prison trusties who had been caring for the rose beds took a lot of ribbing about the war of the roses. They were amused to hear that the governor told the editor that if he thought he could do better, the job was his. Hall accepted the dare, and the governor turned the trusties and the rose garden over to him. They dug up the dead rose bushes and rearranged the garden. Hall personally selected the roses and helped the inmates plant them. One afternoon the governor sent Tommy Giles down to photograph the gardeners at work. Apparently the governor had spotted Hall, wearing old clothes and a straw hat, down on his knees slaving in the hot sun. The seat of his pants had ripped and his undershorts were showing through. When Giles started shooting, Hall stuck his backside in the air and mooned the camera. "Heah. Take my picture and give it to John. Tell him that's what I think about his horticultural skills."[61]

Keeping his administration motivated was not a problem. Reining in the state legislature, however, was like "driving a team of spirited horses, without blinders, and all pulling in separate directions." Patterson, ever mindful of the quote attributed to pre-WWII governor Bibb Graves that "a setting sun gives off little heat," prepared studiously for the final legislative session of his term. The legislature had been in session two days when the Freedom Ride buses rolled south on May 4. There was already a chill in the air and talk of an early frost on Goat Hill.[62]

Interviewed by the *Birmingham News* in February, Patterson reaffirmed that his policy was to "work with the Legislature as a team." The governor believed this was "absolutely essential" if they were to get much accomplished. Old hands were predicting a turbulent legislative session that "could be one long filibuster after another." Patterson appeared confident in the face of this growing pessimism. The legislature was essentially the same one he had worked with in the last session. He didn't agree with those who said the upcoming session would be a "do-nothing" legislature, because he didn't believe most of the legislators were "do-nothing" people.[63]

Reapportionment was at the top of the agenda. The governor had no illusions that the looming reapportionment battles would be easily won. Since the last session the need for the state legislature to reapportion itself (as required by the Constitution and long overdue) was overshadowed by notification that Alabama would lose a congressional seat based on population figures from the 1960 census—thereby reducing the state's U.S. House of Representatives delegation from nine to eight members. Having studied the history of previous administrations he knew the state had lost only one seat in Congress since the turn of the century, and that occurred in 1931 when the Fifth District was redrawn to the detriment of his Uncle Lafayette. He found it interesting that the political hassle had been no less intense when the state gained a congressional seat in 1911.[64]

Patterson decided to stay out of the congressional muddle and to concentrate his energies on reapportioning the legislature. Black Belt members had succeeded in blocking legislation in previous sessions, despite repeated warnings that the courts would step in and order reapportionment if the legislature took no action. To renew the effort in 1961, the governor worked with his team to draft a bill calculated to appeal to as many non-Black Belt legislators as possible. Under the proposed bill, ten counties in rural south Alabama lost representation. The remaining fifty-seven counties gained strength, or kept what they had. The governor was braced for "a do-or-die battle" with the Black Belt legislators when the regular session (dubbed a "powder-keg legislature" by the *Birmingham News*) opened on May 2.[65]

Addressing the joint session, the governor called reapportionment "one of the most serious problems facing us." The lawmaking body's continuous failure to reapportion itself, as required by the Constitution, now made it possible "for about 28 per cent of the people . . . to elect a majority of the members of both Houses." "There exist grossly unfair variations in the number of people a legislator represents," Patterson charged, "and a large majority of the citizens . . . do not have a fair voice in the passage of laws under which they must live." He challenged the lawmakers "to give every Alabamian a fair voice in his government" through reapportionment or to call a constitutional convention and give the people a chance to decide.[66]

The session got off to a promising start for the administration when Virgis M. Ashworth of Bibb was elected speaker of the House of Representatives over Albert Brewer of Morgan. The vacancy occurred when Patterson's friend and former Speaker Charles C. Adams resigned from the legislature. Patterson had "backed Ashworth to the hilt," but the wide margin of victory (82-22) surprised even him. Support for the governor's legislative agenda looked favorable ten days into the session when the Haltom Bill (sponsored by Senator Bert Haltom of Florence) for legislative reapportionment cleared the House Judiciary Committee by a one-vote margin, but the bill quickly bogged down in "factional strife, plots, and counter-schemes" on the House floor.[67]

"An old-timer says he's never seen anything like it in his many years around the Capitol—and the session began only two weeks ago," a reporter wrote, citing congressional redistricting and legislative reapportionment as "the two explosive, trouble-causing issues." Patterson fought hard for the Haltom Bill, at one point broadcasting a special report to the people over a number of Alabama radio stations, but he failed to break the logjam in the legislature. The regular legislative session adjourned September 1 after four tumultuous months. Bob Ingram wrote that the 1961 session would "be remembered for what it did not do rather than what was accomplished."[68]

The final night brought an end to a ninety-six-hour filibuster—the "longest in state history." Hundreds of bills were left to die "on the calendar"—the two most prominent ones being the congressional redistricting bill and the $43.5 million general appropriations bill. The failure to pass a general appropriation bill had never happened before. Legislators went home fully expecting to be called back into special session to pass an appropriations bill, and possibly to take up congressional redistricting as well. Reapportionment was generally regarded as "dead for this session."[69]

Patterson did not keep the legislators waiting. He called them back into session the second week in September to pass the general appropriations act to keep the state operating. He challenged the legislative body to find common ground on other pending legislation, including the so-called 9-8 redistricting bill which retained the existing nine congressional districts for the time being, by eliminating the district nominee receiving the least votes in the general election. Around the country stores and the courthouse squares across the state the checkerboard sages stroked their chins and opined that Guv'na John was right to call a special session. It couldn't be "as big a farce as the past one."[70]

The legislators surprised everyone by working "like a colony of beavers" in the week-long session. While the Hill got overheated at times—a brief fist-fight broke out on the Senate floor between Joe Robertson and Tallapoosa Representative Charles Reynolds—the legislators quickly passed the general appropriations act and enacted into law the 9-8 plan for congressional redistricting. They passed the hundreds of other bills left over from the regular session, and Patterson immediately signed them into law. Mobile's *Press-Register* reported that the lawmakers had gone back to their homes "after the busiest five-day special session in history—but with cries for more school money still ringing in their ears."[71]

Education leaders had lobbied hard for more school revenue, but the governor remained firmly opposed to levying new statewide taxes. A majority of the legislators went along with him. Still very much an education governor, Patterson said the bill he was happiest to sign was one the legislature passed allowing Alabama localities to levy additional property taxes for their schools. Some of the bills now appear archaic in light of a half-century of progress. One was an act providing income and property tax deductions for families who built fallout shelters.[72]

The legislature's continued failure to reapportion itself was a big disappointment to the governor. The picture he had painted of the federal courts stepping in and doing the job for them was already becoming reality. In mid-August, while Black Belt filibustering thwarted efforts to bring reapportionment to a vote, a group of citizens filed a class-action suit in federal district court asking that members be elected at-large until the legislature abided by its constitutional mandate. The U.S. Supreme Court historically had refused to hear lawsuits challenging legislative districting, but reversed course in 1962 by ruling in the landmark Tennessee case of *Baker v. Carr* that the cases were reviewable by federal courts. Judge Frank Johnson then ordered the Alabama legislature to reapportion itself by July 16, or the court would do it for them.[73]

Patterson called a special session in June to comply with the district court's order. Meeting for eighteen grueling days, the legislature hammered out a reapportionment package for review by a three-judge federal panel. Although the measures enacted were not the ones Patterson had recommended, he publicly commended "their courage in facing up to our problems" and for their "determination to work out a solution." Pointing out that the legislature faced "an almost impossible task" that was without precedent in Alabama history, the governor said he was convinced the lawmakers produced the most liberal reapportionment plan they could have.[74]

The legislature's measures called for a senator-for-every-county constitutional amendment that would reshuffle House membership within existing limits— "solidifying small-county control in the Senate and giving the large counties a greater voice in the House than they now have." A backup plan favoring the status quo was to become effective if the state's voters failed to approve the "sixty-seven-senator amendment." The federal court panel handed down a decision on reapportionment on July 22, surprising the legislature and the governor with the quickness of its decision. The federal panel accepted portions of the state plan, but ordered immediate implementation of its revised plan calling for representation more evenly based on population rather than by counties.[75]

After consulting with legislators and Assistant Attorney General Gordon Madison, who had presented the leading arguments for the state before the federal court, Patterson accepted the decision without appealing it to the U.S. Supreme Court. Madison had served as a specialist on reapportionment for the governor during the special session of the legislature. The governor concurred with Madison's position that "both the legislature and the federal court have done well in moving to the solution of a difficult problem" and with his recommendation not to appeal. Patterson said he felt the federal judges "could have dealt with us more severely" than they did. Moreover, the measures ordered by the court were a partial resolution of the problem. The matter would need to be revisited by the state legislature and the courts in 1963.[76]

The lawmakers dealt with other legislation during the special session. One that the governor let die by pocket veto was a bill by Jefferson Representative Hugh Locke establishing a State Commission on Constitutional Government. The so-called sovereignty commission created by Locke's bill was to have been given the power to deal with other states and even the federal government on the issue of maintaining segregation in the public schools. There had been earlier attempts (supported by the KKK and citizens rights groups) to create a sovereignty commission. Patterson had steadfastly refused to abdicate this responsibility to any such commission. "I cannot believe that the people of Alabama would want such vital issues as school segregation left in the hands of fifteen individuals whose personal whims and attitudes are unknown to the public. They would be free to make any kind of deals and would not be accountable for their actions. For these reasons, I am opposed to the creation of such a commission."[77]

Two measures killed in the session "would have required labeling by race of all blood stored in blood banks and changing Alabama's jury laws to reduce the number of Negroes who could qualify for jury duty by making only registered voters eligible to serve."[78] The defeat of the two measures implied some progress within the state legislature toward enacting laws that would stand the scrutiny of the federal courts. That the measures were even brought to the floor for a vote, however, manifested a lingering defiance of the federal statutes and a racial bias that statutes alone could not overcome.

LOOKING BACK ON 1961 the *Montgomery Advertiser* reported that racial issues had kept Alabama in the national spotlight. The violence inflicted on the Freedom Riders erupted "in nation-girdling headlines" in May, but other racial troubles simmered through the year. The governor's rebuke of the Interstate Commerce Commission ruling on bus station integration in November captured a few passing headlines, but was then forgotten.[79]

Patterson said he believed the ICC was wrong in issuing such a ruling, because it was not what the people wanted. "We already are facing the closing of many bus stations," he added. "The bus company is having to sell tickets on the street, and people are having to relieve themselves behind the bushes." He called the ruling another "attempt to do by executive order what the majority of the people don't want."[80]

The governor's denouncement of the ICC ruling was perfunctory. In the wake of the Freedom Rider experience, to contest the ruling was a waste of everybody's time. The *Advertiser* noted that at year's end, the "White" and "Colored" signs at the bus station waiting rooms were gone. Proving the axiom that old habits are hard to break, "white and colored passengers continued to segregate themselves during stopovers just as if the signs were there." Almost unnoticed, the facilities at Montgomery's Union Station railroad terminal had been "quietly integrated four weeks before the public announcement was made in Washington."[81]

By the end of 1961 political analysts observed that the importance of the race issue as a "decisive political factor" in the South had ebbed—particularly in those states where some desegregation had occurred. An analysis in the *Washington Post* at year's end pointed to the changed political climate in Virginia after Governor Almond ended the state's resistance to desegregation of the public schools. In the most recent statewide election Virginia's candidates conspicuously avoided using race as a campaign issue. In Arkansas, Governor Faubus had quietly softened his stand against desegregation since the Little Rock crisis of 1957. Other regional governors followed suit. Only Patterson of Alabama and Barnett of Mississippi were seen as not retreating before the federal onslaught of desegregation.[82]

The *Post* article singled out Patterson and Faubus as two "relatively good governors" whose national image had been hurt because they were among those who had to "be immoderate at times to stay in office." That image diluted their "influence on the national scene" and confined their political fortunes to the boundaries of their respective states. Having vowed to close schools before he would allow them to be desegregated, Patterson was described as "sweating out the next six months." "Alabama law prevents a governor from serving consecutive terms, and Patterson knows that some desegregation somewhere is coming to Alabama soon. If he can escape it until state attention is drawn to the gubernatorial primaries next spring, he can run for governor again four years hence and boast that desegregation did not come while he was in office."[83]

Weeks before the Christmas holidays—when five hundred guests crowded the governor's mansion for a gala Christmas party—the 1962 gubernatorial race was already shaping up. Former Governor Folsom was touted by some as a shoo-in for a third term when he led a successful campaign to defeat the proposed $10 million bond issue to finance a prison rebuilding program. Patterson had supported the bond issue, and the legislature had approved putting it on the ballot for a statewide vote on December 5.[84]

Starting with a speech at Talladega in November, Folsom voiced opposition to building a "prison palace" while Alabama's schools were "in dire need of funds." Patterson struck back, calling the bond issue "a humanitarian piece of legislation" and criticizing those seeking to make it a "political issue." When the vote went Folsom's way the former governor declined to speculate on how it might affect his political future, but a spokesman observed, "It never hurts to be a winner."[85]

It was that time again. Patterson knew it was open season. The candidates would be gunning for him, just as he had fired the verbal shotgun at Big Jim's administration when he was attorney general. He took it in stride, but refused to be drawn into the campaign to elect his successor and also cautioned his department heads to stay out of the political arena. He urged that they concentrate their efforts fully on doing the people's business and meeting the administration's goals. Despite the uproar over the Freedom Riders and racial strife in general, the state had made "impressive gains" during the past year. Signs of progress—new schools, agriculture, businesses, industry, airports, highways, tourism and a thriving economy—brightened the landscape from the Tennessee Valley down through the Piedmont to the Black Belt, and on to the Wiregrass, to the white silver sands of Gulf Shores and to the endless blue of the Gulf of Mexico.[86]

Nowhere was that progress more meaningful for the governor than in Phenix City. On a sunny day in October the proud citizens of Russell County rolled out the red carpet to honor him on "John Patterson Day" in Phenix City. He gave several speeches, warmly praising the community spirit and enterprise which had "transformed Phenix City into a modern, bustling metropolis of thirty thousand happy, forward-looking people." "On a tour of the rejuvenated city the governor saw new highways, including a by-pass and four-lane bridge over the Chattahoochee River, new factories and shopping centers, new homes and churches, new schools under construction (including Central High School, the state's first campus-style, air-conditioned school)."[87]

"Signs of rapid advance were everywhere," an observer noted, all having been encouraged and aided by the governor. Patterson said he was not only greatly impressed with the material gains "but also with the fine attitude of the local people." He described his hometown as "a new Phenix City" that was "really on the move." "The change is more than meets the eye," he said. [88] As the day wore on the memories of the old Phenix City came flooding back with haunting clarity. The progress was a fitting tribute to his father's memory. To the community, it was a bridge to the future.

17

When Evening Shadows Fall

I used to think that the last year would be the easiest one," Governor Patterson said to Bob Ingram in the spring of 1962. "I figured at this stage we would sorta be coasting in. I'm finding out that the last year is the toughest year." Ingram, knowing that resting on his laurels was not the governor's style, let the comment pass. Earlier word to Patterson's cabinet that he did not intend for the administration "to coast during our last year in office" was more in character.[1]

Patterson stated that he and his people would "work hard right up to our last hour." Anyone who wanted to run for office had to resign their state jobs, he told cabinet members. He hoped there wouldn't be too many jumping ship, however, since finding suitable replacements during the final year was next to impossible.[2]

Ingram had been invited to the governor's office for the signing of a proclamation setting aside a World Day of Prayer in Alabama. Patterson mentioned wanting to speak with him after the signing. Having recently ruffled the governor by exposing a cabinet member's extracurricular activities on state time, Ingram said he didn't know what to expect when he followed Preacher Swearingen and three local ladies into the inner sanctum. He had seen the governor lash out in anger over something you wrote that he didn't like, then charm the pants off you the next time you saw him. Ingram took it in stride. Good news this morning. The governor was his charming best.

Ingram recalled Ruth Richardson looking up from her desk in mock surprise when he started into the office. He mentioned "facetiously" that he was going in "to pray with the governor." She quipped that it was about time. "I couldn't have agreed more," Ingram later wrote in his Sunday column. After the signing he hung back to see what was on the governor's mind.

Patterson didn't challenge what Ingram had written, but wanted to explain the employee's side. He spoke of the problem "keeping cabinet members on the job in the final months of the administration." "It is hard to take a man away from his business or practice for four years, then cut him off," Patterson said. "These men make real sacrifices." Younger members who were just getting started

372

in life knew their jobs "would soon be over" and were anxious "to get started in their own endeavors." The governor said he wanted to help them anyway he could, and not hold them back.

Ingram left their meeting relieved that he and the governor were back on good terms. He said to Ruth Richardson on the way out, "Don't tell me prayers don't work."[3]

INGRAM AND THE GOVERNOR chatted briefly about the Democratic primary which was heating up. Lieutenant Governor Albert Boutwell had thrown his hat in the ring for governor, but no one in Patterson's cabinet had entered the race. Sam Engelhardt's name had been mentioned as a likely candidate, but he chose not to run. The highway director was under fire from the Civil Service Commission (unfairly so, according to the governor) for heading up the Democratic committee in Alabama while serving as highway director, but this would not have hurt his chances. Engelhardt placed fifth in a *South* magazine survey of gubernatorial favorites even though he was not a candidate.

The survey came out a week before the campaign officially opened and had Big Jim Folsom leading the field by a wide margin. George Wallace was in second place and Albert Boutwell third, with MacDonald Gallion and Ryan deGraffenreid close on their heels. The pecking order was much the same when the "political circus" officially opened in mid-January. Trailing in the nine-man race was Birmingham's public safety commissioner Eugene "Bull" Connor, who had conspired with the Klan in the Freedom Rider beatings of 1961 and whose image would become synonymous with police brutality against civil rights protesters in 1963.[4]

Like other governors before him, Patterson made no endorsement. He told reporters he had a lot of friends in the race (Bull Connor was not one of them, he emphasized) and "it's going to be hard for me to decide how to cast my vote. I'm not going to take an active part in campaigning for the election of my successor." He pointed out that none of the candidates had asked for his endorsement. Alabama history showed that usually "when the incumbent governor gets out and beats the bushes for somebody he gets beat." Back in 1911 Governor Braxton Bragg Comer "might have influenced the election of his successor," but that was an exception to the rule.[5]

Knowing that the campaign mud would start flying, Patterson said he intended "to steer free of controversy with any gubernatorial candidate who would choose to attack his administration." "The occasion might arise when I would want to set the record straight. But I don't intend to dignify attacks by politicians seeking to get votes by getting involved in any arguments." He did on occasion lash back at his critics when seeing a need to protect his people or the administration. As a general rule, however, he let the record speak for itself.[6]

Patterson expected political rivals to declare open season on his administration, just as he had gone after the Folsom crowd in 1958. As attorney general and governor he had stood up to the Big Mule and Black Belt lobbyists and put his foot on the loan sharks and corrupt public officials. Four years of a progressive, reform-minded administration that had stepped on well-polished wing tips, along with his strong support of John F. Kennedy for president, made him a prime target. Cast as the white knight of Alabama politics, everything he or his administration did was subject to closer scrutiny and more running political commentary than lame-duck governors might normally expect.

Folsom was first to "square off" on the administration. Patterson figured Big Jim "had a right." "He [Patterson] said he was going to stop up the holes in the bucket," Folsom prodded. "Then he turned right around and busted the bottom out of the thang." Folsom's barbs were long on generalities and short on specifics. They poked fun for the most part, and did no harm to Patterson's record or anyone else's. The towering Folsom, his silver-streaked hair and crinkled face showing age and the scars of public life, kicked off his campaign in north Alabama, passing around collection bags he called ham sacks while accusing the incumbent administration of "frying too much gravy out of the ham." "Y'all put in the meat, and I'll do the grinding," he told the cheering crowds.[7]

Folsom admitted he had made mistakes during his two terms in office, but promised to do better the third time around. His soft-shoe approach to the issue of the day, racial integration, nudged people's consciences without offending them. He mixed up many of the same lines he had used on audiences throughout his career. In his Black Belt appearances, which were few and far between, he delighted in needling mostly white crowds about the segregation issue, mentioning on occasion that he saw many light-skinned black brethren as he drove through the county. His earthy punch line, "and if that ain't integrating, I don't know what is," never failed to soften up an audience.[8]

Wallace insiders smiled knowingly when their candidate promised audiences on the campaign trail that he would "improve state government administration if he became governor." Voters, however, wouldn't find out that "administering the state's affairs" was not Wallace's strong suit until after he took office. Candidate Wallace borrowed freely from Patterson's 1958 playbook during the 1962 campaign. He made a calculated move to go after the side-lined governor's constituents while sniping at his policies. "I'll stop political payoffs by abolishing liquor agents," Wallace declared. "We're going to tie up those two state yachts at Mobile and leave them there."[9]

Wallace neglected to mention that the Patterson administration had neither purchased the yachts nor retained them for pleasure cruises, but had used them primarily to attract new business and industry to Alabama. Their recent tour of inland ports had served "to demonstrate the accessibility of landlocked cities to the seaboard through the extensive development of waterways." The ninety-six-foot *Jamelle* was purchased for $144,000 in 1947 during Folsom's first term. The eighty-foot *Alice* cost approximately $100,000 when purchased by the Persons administration in 1952. Both vessels were offered for sale in 1958 by Folsom, but the high bids of $30,005 and $30,000 were rejected. As for doing away with the liquor agents, Ed Azar had explained there would be no benefit to the state coffers. The distillers had long paid a total of $450,000 annually to agents at no cost to the state.[10]

As the campaign heated up, Wallace, in a backhanded reference to the Adam Clayton Powell affair and Folsom's well-known appetite for drink, vowed not to serve liquor in the governor's mansion if he won the election. Critics said Wallace did not abstain from drinking because he was a teetotaler, but because he couldn't hold his liquor. On the night of May 29th when Wallace trounced deGraffenreid in the run-off to win the Democratic nomination, the liquor agents pretended to run for cover, but not the imbibers. A reporter for the *Columbus Ledger* wrote that "a potpourri of frantically happy people" packed the lobby of the Greystone Hotel where Wallace was "hidden in an upper floor above the madness below." "A sign on the mezzanine said, 'We're drinking coffee—by George' and from the fumes this wasn't all they were 'drinking.'"[11]

Other candidates in the race had been loath to attack the incumbent administration. Patterson didn't act like a lame-duck governor, and he was still popular with the people. In March he led a delegation on a fifteen-day trade mission to Latin America. Returning from the tour he immediately called a special session of the legislature to deal with reapportionment. At its annual meeting in April, the Alabama League of Municipalities presented Patterson with its Distinguished Service Award—one of the few times in the league's history the honor had been bestowed on a sitting governor. Making the occasion more remarkable, the league honored a governor it had tried mightily to defeat four years earlier.[12]

In his acceptance speech Patterson made light of what little mud was thrown his way. He reminded the municipal officials that they would "hear charges and counter charges," and joked that a couple of the candidates "are recovering things that haven't even been stolen yet." As for the future, Patterson said it was going to be nice "to read a newspaper in the morning . . . and not have to go down to the office and deny everything that has happened the last twenty-four hours."[13]

After the field of would-be successors had narrowed to Wallace and deGraffenried, Patterson still declined to pick a winner. He said the only commitment he wanted to make with his successor was "to look after my tomcat, Tar Baby." The black Persian was given to the family as a kitten, and had lived in the mansion since the Pattersons moved there in January 1959. "I don't think he's going to want to leave the mansion," the governor said. "He likes that high living."[14]

ON THE DAY AFTER Wallace won the May 29 run-off in a landslide, political analysts were already predicting a Patterson-deGraffenried race in 1966. The two men were friends. No one fought harder for Governor Patterson's legislative programs than deGraffenried. The Tuscaloosa senator helped push through the small-loan law, aid for the schools, and bills to raise the old age pensions and a medical program for the aged. If they were the top contenders in 1966, the voters were assured of a fair, hard-fought gentleman's race.[15]

Would the fourth estate stand for such a race? Too much to ask from a profession that disgruntled politicians accused of bottom-feeding and worse? Garden parties don't sell newspapers. As for partisanship, anyone conversant in Alabama politics would have spotted the same critics who flayed Patterson for not renouncing the Klan's support in the 1958 campaign giving Wallace a pass on the same issue in 1962. Wallace not only demagogued the race issue more than Patterson had in 1958, but he flaunted the Klan's endorsement when he brought in Asa Earl Carter, a talented but virulent white supremacist and race-baiter, as his speechwriter. Carter is credited with the defiant lines in Wallace's 1963 inaugural address: "Segregation today, segregation tomorrow, segregation forever."[16]

While the candidates found little about the Patterson administration to criticize, a wave of acrimonious press attacks after Wallace won the nomination had Patterson wondering if Grover Hall, Jr., now bearing the grand title of editorial vice president of the *Montgomery Advertiser* and *Alabama Journal*, was out for blood or just milking anti-Patterson stories for all they were worth. Hall's infatuation with Wallace—"he was just gang-busters about Wallace," Ingram said—and his personal animus toward Patterson were obvious to readers who sipped their morning coffee while browsing the editorial pages of the *Advertiser*.

Ingram, known across the state for his hard-hitting but nonpartisan coverage of the capital, said of Hall, "I loved him. He was my mentor," but admitted that Hall could be "arrogant as hell" and "a pompous ass." At times he "could just be mean," unnecessarily so.[17] Perhaps these attributes obscured his vision and diluted the journalistic courage which had made his father famous as the *Advertiser*'s editor in the 1920s. Ray Jenkins, who moved from the *Columbus Ledger* to the *Advertiser* city desk in 1959 and eventually replaced Hall as editor, was surprised that "no one at the newspaper had any contact at all with Martin Luther King." With Montgomery "almost the epicenter of the civil rights movement" and King "a world-wide figure by this time," Jenkins found it odd that the *Advertiser* editor had never met King, whose church was only a couple of blocks up the street.[18]

Had Hall Jr. missed the one opportunity fate had given him to follow in his father's footsteps and win a Pulitzer? Were his horizons skewed by cultural biases or the political libido of a man who even then envisioned using the governor's office as a launching pad to the White House? In July 1962, on the heels of an *Advertiser* expose credited to an anonymous tip, the attorney general's office rocked the outgoing administration with the nearest thing to a political scandal it had faced. The stage was set for editor Hall to crown his candidate's landslide victory in the primary with a coup de theatre against Governor Patterson as he made his exit. Enter a Tobacco Road cast of characters in search of a plot.

Patterson had learned from the Battle of El Guettar that nothing knots up the stomach like waking to find that the enemy has sneaked up on you in the dark of night. He had a similar gut reaction the morning he unfolded the *Advertiser* to read that Attorney General Gallion had charged officials in his administration of conspiring with a contractor "to violate the law in letting a contract to paint lines on Alabama highways." The charges were made in a petition for injunction to halt further payments on the contract. Gallion had assigned the case to a circuit solicitor to determine if criminal prosecution was in order.[19]

Under the contract in question the state had paid almost $900,000 over a two-year period to Barton's Alabama Marking & Sign Company for painting the stripes on Alabama's highways. A middleman named Joe Barton was said to have operated the company from his home and subcontracted the work out for half what he was paid, allegedly as part of a profiteering scheme involving state officials. Reassured by his staff that the contract had been let on a competitive bid and the attorney general's charges were without basis, the governor issued a statement that he had high regard for MacDonald Gallion, but believed he was being used "by others bent on political revenge." The involvement of the partisan *Advertiser* and individuals figuring prominently in Alabama gubernatorial politics made him believe the charges were the opening salvo in the next governor's race.[20]

At a brief hearing in August, Circuit Judge Eugene W. Carter declined to issue the injunction requested by the attorney general after administration officials promised no further striping would be done without the court's permission. The judge told Gallion, "They've agreed to do everything you asked. It's much ado about nothing." Outside the courtroom the attorney general informed newsmen that his investigation would continue, and that he would likely take further legal action to recover the payments for the striping work.[21]

Meanwhile, an incident at the Patterson farm in Tallapoosa County the week after the attorney general made the road striping charges aroused concerns even more. After becoming governor Patterson had purchased the old family homeplace in Goldville from his Uncle Lafayette and later added acreage when it became available. A farm cabin was located in the woods some distance from the nearest road. One morning in July the governor's state trooper aide, Lieutenant Tom Posey, caught *Advertiser* reporter Charles McWilliams and Joe Malone, a member of the attorney general's staff, snooping around the property.

The governor and his family had spent the night at the farm and were on their way back to Montgomery. Posey had stayed behind to lock up and check security when he spotted the intruders. As he approached the pair, the man later identified as Malone ran into the woods and hid. Posey confronted McWilliams who was peering into the windows of the cabin and snapping pictures. He asked the reporter what he was doing there, and was told, "None of your business." When McWilliams refused to leave, the big state trooper assisted the reporter back into his car and sent him on his way.

Posey and a neighbor followed McWilliams. When he stopped to pick up his companion who was hiding in the woods, Posey went up to the car and asked the second prowler to identify himself. The man, later identified as Malone, refused.

Posey reported the incident to the governor, who expressed dismay that "a member of the attorney general's staff would be in the company of a reporter of the *Montgomery Advertiser* engaged in an unlawful activity." Malone obviously was embarrassed about being caught spying on the governor. Patterson had brought Malone on board as a special investigator when he was attorney general, and liked the man. The first lady filed trespassing charges, then dropped them.

If the governor had any doubts that the *Advertiser*, working in concert with others, was out to smear him and injure him politically, the trespassing incident and subsequent revelations erased them. When he and Posey went over to talk with the attorney general about the trespassing incident, they ran into McWilliams coming out of Gallion's office. Instead of an apology, the governor got a denial in the morning paper that Malone was acting under orders from the attorney general when he participated in "the alleged acts."[22]

With family, friends, and staff harried by an overly aggressive reporter and with editorial barbs staring him in the face each morning, the governor had no objections when informed that supporters had retained a Birmingham detective agency to investigate the investigators. Fred J. Bodecker of the National Detective Agency announced in late August that he was looking into purported irregular expenditures of gubernatorial candidates in the Democratic primary and other political irregularities. He stated that private citizens called for the investigation and that no state officials or state funds were involved.[23]

During the course of the investigation an operative from the detective agency went to Montgomery and checked into the Jeff Davis Hotel. Hanging around the hotel bar, he became acquainted with various politicians and reporters, including McWilliams. Two fellow reporters, Bob Raymond and Don Martin with the United Press International in Montgomery, volunteered information that Grover Hall hired McWilliams in December to use exclusively "as a hatchet man on the Patterson administration." They expressed disapproval of the arrangement, and thought Hall would let McWilliams go when Patterson left office in January because he would have served the newspaper's purpose.[24]

McWilliams made an easy target. Puffed up with self-importance he forgot that a good reporter must be a good listener. He drank too much. He talked too much. The more he drank the more he talked. It didn't take long (a few meetings at the bar and a little flattery) for the skilled operative to worm his way into the reporter's confidence. McWilliams was described as being very disrespectful of Patterson and boasted that his whole job was to dig up dirt to embarrass the governor. He claimed full credit for the paint-striping case, saying that "we don't much expect to ever get a conviction but if we get a grand jury indictment . . . then that will smear the Patterson administration." "Most people don't know the difference between a grand jury indictment and conviction in court," he added.[25]

McWilliams beamed proudly when a *Newsweek* article labeled him the "Barracuda" for his attacks on the Patterson administration. He not only claimed to have a key to the attorney general's office, but he revealed that a disgruntled Patterson department head was unlawfully slipping him copies of personal income tax information on individuals. The boastful reporter contradicted earlier denials, asserting that the attorney general's office had authorized Malone's visit with him to the governor's farm, as well as other assignments to spy on Patterson's family and friends.

From the operative's report, if McWilliams was to be believed, the attacks on the governor were motivated more by politics and personal pique than concern for the public good. When asked if his boss Grover Hall was sore at Patterson, McWilliams replied, "Hell, yes, he is and always will be!" His sophomoric description of a party attended by the attorney general at Hall's house put an exclamation mark on the editor's personal grudge against the governor. "All of us were out at Hall's house and everybody got drunk and let their hair down and for awhile it seemed to be a contest to see who could cuss Patterson and his crowd the most."[26]

Meanwhile, the judicial mill ground slowly. No indictments were handed down in the paint-striping case before Patterson left office in mid-January 1963, but his detractors got what they wanted from a Montgomery County Grand Jury report made public in December. Five days before Christmas the grand jury, after month-long deliberations, returned a true bill denouncing the Barton contract "as a fraud" and asking that governor-elect Wallace continue the investigation after he took office on January 14. No early resolution of the case meant that the outgoing administration, after six months of unfavorable publicity, would leave office under a cloud of innuendo and suspicion.

As for the Hall-McWilliams connection, the two United Press reporters at the bar called it right. When Patterson turned the state reins over to Wallace, the Barracuda's ties with the *Montgomery Advertiser* were severed. McWilliams had confided to the operative from Birmingham that he and Mr. Hall were certain that the attorney general was "going to play ball with them" to get the indictments in the road-striping case, and when that was done "he would have served their purpose."[27] Now, so had McWilliams. Before he pulled up stakes, no one thought to ask if the man behind the stories was the story.

Another six months went by before indictments were handed down in the paint-striping case. In July 1963 the grand jury indicted assistant highway director Walter Craig of Selma on a charge of bribery. Barton had skipped town, but returned under indictment. He and *South* magazine publisher Hubert Baughn, who was also implicated in the case, were given full immunity for turning state's evidence against Craig. In November the new attorney general, Richmond Flowers, brought charges against Craig in circuit court. When a juror reported receiving threats to his life ("They'll find you floating in the Alabama River," a caller warned), Judge Carter declared a mistrial. At a new trial in February 1964 the jury, "in less time than it takes to smoke a cigarette," deliberated and filed back into the courtroom with a not-guilty verdict.[28]

Attorney General Flowers dropped all criminal charges in the case in May. A civil suit seeking to recover damages remained pending until February 1965 when it too was dismissed by Judge Carter at Flowers's request. The only loser in the case was Hubert Baughn, who with Barton had escaped prosecution by turning state's evidence. Craig's attorneys turned their testimony against Baughn and Barton when they admitted lying about alleged kickbacks to their client in sworn statements to income tax agents. "Baughn lost his reputation, health, and magazine," Patterson said. "Barton, no friend of mine, had no reputation to lose."[29]

Patterson chalked the experience up to partisan politics and put it behind him. Ingram noted that observers who had written the former governor off because of the paint-striping scandal now saw his stock rising in the polls. Instead of the affair becoming a weapon to be used against the former governor, it had become a weapon in the Patterson arsenal instead. "The same observers who a few months back were asking if Patterson could possibly be elected governor in 1966 were all of sudden asking if he could possibly be defeated in his certain bid for a second term."[30] Others wondered. The months of unfavorable publicity and the lingering acrimony over Patterson's support for the Kennedy ticket had poisoned the air. For how long was anybody's guess.

As inauguration day 1963 drew closer wags were saying that Governor Patterson should integrate Alabama's public schools to keep his successor from going to jail. In late October the UPI's Don Martin reported that George Wallace's "pledge to go to jail rather than permit integration of a single Alabama school has come back to haunt him three months before he begins pulling the reins of state government." Martin noted that the pressure had been building since the start of the academic year when Mississippi Governor Ross Barnett's defiance, and violence on the Ole Miss campus, failed to stop James Meredith from enrolling as the first black student at the University of Mississippi.[31]

Grover Hall admitted that his friend George Wallace now found himself in the unenviable position of "having to break his pledge in the interest of sanity." In a Sunday editorial he revealed: "Wallace has repeatedly said in private that he will disperse the mob and confront the marshals in solitary fashion. He has conceded he can't halt integration. He simply thinks it worthwhile for a governor to go to jail."[32] Plans were already being laid for what would become the infamous "stand in the schoolhouse door." History shows that the incoming governor, who had turned a confrontation with Judge Frank Johnson to his advantage four years earlier, had no intention of going to jail over the integration of Alabama's schools.

Hall had acknowledged that "the inevitable showdown between the United States government and the Alabama government was coming on at an accelerated pace." Hall stated that the Patterson administration had "borne a charmed life," but this could end "with a court order for September integration in Birmingham." A suit to force admission of blacks to Birmingham public schools was pending in federal district court. "It is possible that if the wall is breached on Patterson's time, Wallace will take the position that surrender occurred before he took command," Hall wrote.[33]

When September came and went, it was clear that the federal government would wait Patterson out before acting to desegregate Alabama's public schools. The shooting death of two students at Ole Miss had put a somber face on President Kennedy's order sending federal marshals to escort Meredith onto the campus. A riot broke out and the students were killed before the National Guard arrived to reinforce the marshals. Alabama's entire congressional delegation joined Patterson, Wallace, state legislators, and countless Alabamians in serving notice that "Mississippi's fight is Alabama's fight." Wallace defiantly sent word to Barnett, "The Justice Department and the federal government dare not put their filthy hands on you. If they do the people will answer in the proper manner. We shall stand up also in Alabama."[34]

Patterson had sent a telegram to President Kennedy urging that he not turn the Ole Miss campus into a another Little Rock by using federal troops. He reminded the president's brother Robert of a pledge he made at the Democratic National Convention that federal troops "would never be used against the Southern states."[35] The reminder was a pointless gesture since the attorney general had shown by his earlier actions in the Freedom Rider crisis that political expediency trumped political promises. The governor had no illusions about Bobby Kennedy keeping his word.

Patterson condemned both the use of federal force and the riots at Ole Miss. Wanting to head off any Alabamians or other outsiders who might be going into the neighboring state to create more trouble, he ordered Public Safety Director Floyd Mann to put Alabama's four hundred state troopers on alert and to station uniformed officers at the main routes leading into northeast Mississippi. They were instructed to report any unusual activity and to turn back any automobile caravans headed toward the riot-torn university town of Oxford.[36]

In the wake of Meredith's enrollment, Dr. Martin Luther King, Jr., announced there would be a second attempt at breaking down racial barriers at the University of Alabama. The university had remained segregated since Autherine Lucy's brief attendance in 1956. Neither Patterson nor Wallace commented on King's announcement. A spokesman for the governor said he did not want "to engage in a word battle with King." Patterson was said to be taking a "wait-and-see" attitude while keeping abreast of the situation. Wallace's friends attributed his silence to not wanting "to be accused of interfering with Gov. John Patterson."[37]

Three black students applied for admission to the University of Alabama, but their applications were still pending when Patterson left office. Meanwhile, Southern governors and the Southern press generally reflected growing acceptance of the high court's desegregation mandate. "Heretofore, it has been political suicide in Alabama even to suggest that the state yield to integration edicts, either by law or court order," a reporter wrote. "Responsible groups and high state officials, shaken by the bloodshed and disorder at the University of Mississippi are (now) making public proclamations for law and order." In early December, State Democratic Chairman Roy Mayhall declared that he favored enforcing the law even if it meant integration. He called for "a calm, restrained leadership."[38]

State leaders were calm, but restraint in the face of violence was seen as neither a tradition nor a virtue. The groundswell of public resistance to violence did not mean that Alabama had surrendered, a reporter observed. Governor-elect Wallace was committed to fight integration "by whatever means necessary." Sources close to the incoming governor said Reverend King's announced plans to have black students apply for admission to the University of Alabama had stiffened Wallace's determination to create a state militia (apart from the National Guard) under his control "to meet violence in racial integration."[39]

The bombing of the Bethel Baptist Church and four neighboring homes in Birmingham the week before Christmas sent a chill through the community of white leaders calling for a responsible, nonviolent resolution of the race problem. The bombers had hurled sticks of dynamite from a car and then sped off into the darkness of a shattered Friday night. Over the weekend, Jefferson County Solicitor Emmett Perry posted a $5,000 reward for information in the case. The money had come from contributors, including a state reward of $1,000 (the maximum allowable) approved by Patterson.[40]

Fortunately no one was killed in the blast, which police believed was aimed at the Reverend Fred Shuttlesworth, civil rights leader and former pastor at the church, who months earlier had moved to Cincinnati. The senseless bombing, followed by a Wallace inaugural address that was more defiant, more bellicose than his predecessor's, did not bode well for peaceful transition of civil rights under the incoming administration. Words, too, are weapons when they incite violence.

When Shuttlesworth returned to Birmingham the following May and joined with King and Reverend Ralph Abernathy to lead a protest march, he found a more hostile environment than when he left. The civil rights leaders were arrested, and while in solitary confinement King wrote his famous "Letter from Birmingham Jail." A few months later, in the autumn of 1963 members of Robert Shelton's United Klans of America dynamited the Sixteenth Street Baptist Church, killing four young girls and earning the city the noxious name of "Bombingham." The senseless murders shocked the nation and left a scar on Southern justice matched only by Klan blood lust in the neighboring state of Mississippi. Escaping justice, the murders were a harbinger of violence yet to come.

Objective scholars have given the Patterson administration high marks for its programs, with the exception of the governor's record on civil rights. A tendency to survey that record through the lens of today's camera risks overlooking context and overstating the obvious. Perhaps journalist Ray Jenkins explained the Southern white culture best when he said: "I went through the entirely segregated school system from kindergarten through graduation at the state university, and during that entire time, it never occurred to me in a million years that a black might want to go to this college. It was just something that . . . no one thought about. I think there's a line in Goethe, 'We are all so inclined to accept that which is commonplace,' and that's what we all did."[41]

Patterson's record on civil rights was the offspring of political reality. The governor did what he was elected to do. Wallace's landslide victory in 1962 showed that majority attitudes had not changed. The white voters simply were not going to elect a governor who was weak on segregation. Patterson credited "constant work, diligence and attention," for keeping the schools from being integrated during his administration, while critics contended that "a combination of legal maneuvering and sheer luck on the governor's part" had been in play. Whatever the reasons, holding the line on school desegregation dropped the problem in Wallace's lap and left the door open for Patterson should he choose to run again in 1966.[42]

A decade later, in an interview for Tuskegee Institute's History Series, the former governor himself posed the question of "how could Alabama produce a Jim Folsom in 1955 and produce a John Patterson and a George Wallace four years later?" Alabama was traditionally a liberal state and Jim Folsom, in his opinion, was "one of the most liberal governors economically as well as racially" that the state ever had. Had it been left up to Folsom, Patterson believed that "he might very well have solved many of the problems of race earlier than they were ultimately solved."[43]

However, Patterson pointed out, Folsom was hamstrung in what he could do because there was no support in the legislature and little in the state at large. Racial desegregation became a political issue because of polarization and the push for change, he said. "I think the racial problems in Alabama created a polarization of feeling. And it got even worse after Folsom because of this polarization and made it even more difficult to do anything toward letting down the racial barriers."[44]

In a 1972 letter, Patterson went further, saying he thought "the *Brown* decision, the 'massive resistance' in Virginia, the actions of the federal courts, such incidents as Central High School in Little Rock and Clinton, Tennessee, the bus boycott in Montgomery and the pushing by Negro groups coupled with counter activity by the citizens' councils, Klan groups and the white population generally tended to polarize the people" and made it impossible for anyone considered moderate on the segregation issue to be elected governor of Alabama at the time. "I think this accounts for the change in attitude, if indeed there was one, of the people between 1954 and 1958—the difference between the stated views of a Folsom on one hand and a Patterson and a Wallace on the other," he wrote. "In retrospect I do not see how this period could have been avoided. It was an experience which we obviously had to endure."[45]

After Patterson left office, the policy on desegregating the state's schools "changed from one of avoiding confrontation to one of confrontation." His strategy, coming out of the Birmingham meeting of December 1958, had been "to gain time for adjustment so that change would come so gradually that there would be no trouble and violence." Part of this strategy had been to decentralize authority among the school districts so "that when they took us on, they would have to take us on one district at a time." "There'd be hundreds of suits instead of one, you see." When the policy changed back to centralized authority under the succeeding administration, the court integrated all of Alabama's schools with a single "stroke of the pen."[46]

A reporter sent to Alabama by the Boston-based *Christian Science Monitor* arrived expecting to find the state darkly draped in racial strife "like so much stifling moss on a live-oak tree." He found instead a progressive, thriving economy in which a "mimosa-scented, leisurely mood of southern tradition gives way to pioneering rocket technology at Huntsville; port development at Mobile; industrial expansion and diversification at Birmingham (and in almost every county of the state); and state governmental reform at Montgomery, the capital." Civil rights progress was "arduously slow," but evidences of progress in other areas were "apparent everywhere."[47]

As the curtain came down on the Patterson years, the governor got ahead of the naysayers by disseminating the administration's record in the form of a message to the legislature. With the facts up front for the world to see, even the *Birmingham News* viewed the record as "one of substantial accomplishment, of tangible achievement, of service to the state" and said it would be hard for the severest critics to paint the Patterson administration—try as they may—anything much less than good." The *News* pointed to the administration's unprecedented progress in support of public education, highway construction, operation of the state docks at Mobile, construction of more inland dock facilities, industrial growth, and increased benefits to pensioners, including the state's first program of medical care for the elderly. Other accomplishments included:

> Passage of a strict small-loan law; renewed attention to mental health prob-
> lems; efficient administration of the often politically troublesome liquor system;
> capital improvements; law enforcement; conservation. The list goes on.[48]

Interviewed about the record, Patterson said he was most proud of the increases in public assistance. When he went into office the state's elderly people
were drawing about $38 a month in old-age pensions. When he left office they had
started to get $75 monthly. Added boons were medicare and medicaid plans for
both pensioners and the indigent, and additional benefits for dependent children,
the blind, and the physically handicapped.[49] The *Birmingham News* concluded
that the administration's overall record was one on which the governor "could
base a healthy campaign for a second term" if he chose to run again.[50]

This balanced critique by a perennial critic must have been sweet music to the
administration. Even more so the parting shot from the icy *Advertiser*'s warmer
evening counterpart, the *Alabama Journal*: "The Patterson quadrennium has been
a period of remarkable progress along all lines, and much of the record is due to
the men and women who carried on public affairs under the leadership of the
youngest governor Alabama has ever before put into office." To that summation,
the paper added the vox populi that the Patterson administration's four years had
"constituted one of the great periods in state history."[51]

THERE WAS UNFINISHED BUSINESS Patterson wanted to revisit if he served a
second term. Prison reform was at the top of the list. Although prison reform
was not part of the administration's program when he took office, a legislative
study convinced him of "the need for overhauling Alabama's prison system." The
physical plant was in bad shape, and prison facilities were seriously overcrowded.
Having worked with lawmakers to get the $10 million bond issue through the
legislature, he was disappointed when the public voted the prison reform amendment down in December 1961.[52]

Folsom's opposition to spending more tax dollars on prisons, which helped
defeat the amendment, was legend. Patterson disagreed with his predecessor's
liberal views on prison reform, but understood the complexities of the issue and
why Folsom thought as he did. Big Jim believed that the criminal justice system
was inherently unfair to the poor and disadvantaged, that too many prisoners

were incarcerated who shouldn't be there, and that the prisons should be emptied out. His first term had been marred by a pardon and parole scandal that overshadowed his positive accomplishments. His liberalism apparently blinded him to the fact that the pardon and parole board was indiscriminately selling pardons and paroles.[53]

Patterson was not unsympathetic to the abuses in the criminal justice system, but he felt each case had to be reviewed on its merits. He remembered from his days as attorney general how Folsom agonized over commuting the death sentences that came before him. "I reviewed all the death penalty records and Jim would occasionally ask my advice on someone coming up for execution. We had a lot more capital crimes and executions then than we have now. Rape, murder, and armed robbery were capital offenses."[54]

When Patterson moved into the governor's mansion one of the first things that caught his eye was a red phone with a direct line to the warden at Kilby Prison. Folsom had watched the old movies where the warden got a call from the governor at the last minute, "seconds before midnight," sparing the life of a prisoner who was about to be executed, and he had a hotline put in from Kilby Prison to the mansion. There were always pickets outside the mansion on the night of an execution. "Folsom would be inside the mansion drinking. He would agonize over the pending execution like they did in the movies, and it wasn't uncommon for him to pick up the red phone and call the warden just before midnight and reprieve the person."[55]

An apocryphal story about Folsom's last-minute reprieves gave pause even to uncompromising proponents of the death penalty. As the story goes, the board of corrections had scheduled a grim double feature at Kilby that had pickets protesting the death penalty out in force. The convicts facing execution were both black males. The crimes that put them on death row were rankly disparate. One had been sentenced to die for raping a white woman in her home out in the country below Phenix City and the other for the gruesome murder of his drunk friend (he poured gasoline over the man and burned him alive) in Montgomery.

The record of the convicted rapist's trial raised questions about the capital sentence in the case. The presiding judge and jurors in the case were said to have second thoughts about the severity of the sentence, and appealed to the governor for clemency. The young black male had been incarcerated in Columbus, Georgia, on a lesser crime. He escaped and swam across the Chattahoochee River to the Alabama side, where he walked up to a lonely farmhouse and forced his way inside. A young white woman was there alone with her baby. She testified that he threatened to kill the baby if she did not have sex with him. At her request he used a prophylactic. Afterward, she cooked him breakfast and he went on his way.

On the night the chaplain prayed with the two men in their cells and they ate their last meals, Folsom agonized over whether to pick up the red phone and stay the executions. At the eleventh hour, the warden received a call from the governor to spare the life of one of the convicts. He commuted the sentence of the man who murdered his friend to life in prison. The man convicted of rape was executed. No one knew for sure, but given the disparity of the two crimes and Folsom's reputation for fairness on the race issue the question lingered in people's minds, had the governor mistakenly commuted the wrong sentence?[56]

Bearing "the awesome power of life or death for a human being" rests heavy on a governor's shoulders. Patterson, although not required to do so, presided over clemency hearings to give prisoners a final opportunity to present testimony helpful to their cause. Early in his administration Patterson said he made the mistake of opening a hearing to the public. "There were so many people who wanted to be heard that I held the hearing in the Senate chamber. It was like a Roman orgy. I almost lost control of it. After that I always held them across the hall in a small office where they couldn't get enough people in to have a demonstration."[57]

Ingram, covering the event for his paper, commended the governor for the manner in which he performed "this most unpleasant of gubernatorial duties," noting that he "was plainly in pain throughout the long hearing." Ingram described the hearing as a painful drama, "containing the public-determined necessary ingredients of love, hate, passion, hysteria, sex, and finally death." The spectacle gave vent to the feelings of a growing number of people who wanted to abolish capital punishment in Alabama. While Ingram did not propose this as a solution to the problem, he thought it deserved serious study and "would be done almost overnight if every Alabamian witnessed an execution."[58]

Crimes of passion have historically cried out for leniency. People who commit the crimes are normally not repeat offenders and are good prospects for having their sentences commuted to life. Governor Patterson remembered one such case involving an elderly black man named Jesse, who was married to a much younger woman who was running around on him. One night she came home, and he was mad drunk. They had a "knock-down-and-drag-out" fight which woke the neighborhood. Jesse stabbed his young wife with a butcher knife and killed her. A jury found him guilty, and he was sentenced to die for the crime.

A few days before the execution date, Patterson received a call from a white man in New Orleans who said he felt obligated to come to Montgomery and testify for Jesse. The man said he was an engineer on an L&N freight train out of Birmingham for forty years, and Jesse was his fireman. "In all that time Jesse never missed a day's work. I never heard him raise his voice or use a bad word. He was the kindest, gentlest man I ever knew. Guv'na, I feel obligated to come up there and tell you that." "Well, come ahead." He was the only person who showed up at the clemency hearing and testified for Jesse, the governor said.

When the man finished testifying, the governor asked the prisoner, "Jesse, you got anything you want to say?" He thought for a moment and raised up out of his seat. "Guv'na, that was the meanest woman you ever saw in yo' life," he said. "She treated me like a dog. She run around with other men right in front of me, and just treated me like a dog. Guv'na, you jus' wouldn't believe it." Patterson said he felt so sorry for that man he didn't know what to say. He closed the hearing and promised to let him "know something right away."

Patterson went back to his office and had Joe Robertson go get the man from New Orleans. "I really appreciate you coming all the way up here to testify on Jesse's behalf," he said. "I wanna tell you now, before you go back, that I'm going to commute his sentence to life imprisonment. He strikes me as a good man, who don't deserve to die."

Patterson and Folsom were the last Alabama governors to commute a death sentence until 1999 when Fob James commuted the sentence of convicted murderess Judith Ann Neely on his last night in office. Patterson presided over a dozen or so clemency hearings while he was governor, and he commuted about half of those. "I handled them all myself. I figured that was an important enough matter for the governor to listen to them personally." The hearings were not easy on a governor or anyone else involved, but he believed they were a just and necessary part of the process. The governor has the common law power of granting clemency. "We don't want to take that responsibility away from the governor. It's the last resort for prisoners on death row. We don't want to take that final ray of hope away from them."[59]

MONTHS BEFORE LEAVING OFFICE Patterson announced plans to practice law when his term ended in January 1963. "My present intention is to remain in

Montgomery," he told a morning news conference in the summer of 1960. "I like it very much. It's one of the nicest places I've ever lived."

"Despite the daily press?" a city reporter asked. The governor smiled. "Oh, I read the *Advertiser* every morning and the *Alabama Journal* every night. Don't know how I could do without them."

He declined to talk about future political plans, noting that he would be an ex-attorney general and an ex-governor at forty-one years of age. "I'm peaking a little too early in life. But, I've enjoyed it. I deeply appreciate the confidence the people have expressed in me."[60]

Spoken like a true politician. State law prevented him from running for office until he had been out of the chief executive's chair for a year, but he already had his eye on the next gubernatorial race in 1966. Meanwhile, he laid plans to "quietly practice law with his good and trusted friend, Ralph Smith, Jr., in the same office suite once occupied by his successor, George Wallace, in the Washington Building just across the street from the county courthouse."[61]

WHEN TIME CAME, THE Pattersons vacated the mansion early to give the Wallace family more time to prepare for inauguration day. To guard against items missing during the transition, as had happened in previous years, Tom Posey stayed at the mansion until the Wallaces moved in and the property could be signed over to the incoming administration. The Pattersons moved only a few blocks away, settling into their new residence at 210 Felder Avenue, a stately five-bedroom home and grounds of approximately two acres.[62]

"It was an old brick Georgian home, probably the nicest and best-built house in Montgomery," Patterson mused. "Four-car brick garage, five or six bedrooms, four baths, half-basement, slate roof, a wonderful home." They purchased the property for $52,750 from the estate of the late Dr. John Blue, a noted Montgomery surgeon. "Nobody should own a place like that," he added. "The price was right, but it was a real money pit. Something needed repair all the time."[63]

But Mary Joe had her heart set on buying the home. One of the first things she did was to have camellias planted near the entrance gate. Soon after becoming Alabama's first lady she had been given a large degree of credit for her husband signing the bill into law replacing the sneeze-provoking goldenrod with the camellia as the state's official flower. Ingram reported at the time there was scant opposition "after a group of formidable-appearing lady camellia growers from the 'Camellia City' of Greenville marched on the capitol in support of the bill."[64]

"The strongest argument in support of the camellia came from one of the co-sponsors of the bill—Rep. F. LaMont Glass of Butler," Ingram wrote. "He stated emphatically that the goldenrod was merely a weed which had been transplanted in Alabama by Yankee invaders. After that charge it was but a matter of time before the bill was passed."[65]

The Pattersons' new home at 210 Felder was ideal for two active children and a menagerie of family pets. The location was convenient for Albert, now thirteen, and nine-year-old Barbara (still called "Babel" by family and friends) to continue attending the same public schools. They remained in the Montgomery public school system until their graduations from high school. Albert impressed guests with "an amazing array of hobbies" and extracurricula activities which included modeling ships and scouting. A room overflowing with equine figurines of all shapes and sizes reflected Barbara's special interest in horses which continued into adulthood.[66]

Barbara remembers her father telling them they could not have dogs while living in the governor's mansion. Someone gave them a toy Manchester Terrior named Martini, and Barbara slipped it into the house and hid it in the bathroom. "The guard would call when Daddy was coming up the driveway. He would say, 'Papa's home,' and we would run and put Martini in the bathroom." Then one evening Papa was entertaining guests, and the dog jumped up in the arm chair and sat down beside him. He said to his guests, "Have any of you ever seen a toy Manchester?" He had known about the dog all along. Then Tom Posey gave Albert and Barbara a Collie they named Sheba. "She ended up being Daddy's dog too," Barbara laughed.[67]

The transition into the new home at 210 Felder was smooth. Patterson mentioned that he was the only member of the family having trouble adapting to the new regimen and the new surroundings. Then he remembered Tar Baby. The black Persian cat had been spoiled rotten by the kitchen staff at the executive mansion. For the longest time Tar Baby kept disappearing and ending up back at the mansion's kitchen door. He just never got over that high living, the governor said.

18

WHITE KNIGHT ON A DARK HORSE

With the return to private life, Patterson's waking hours were soon taken up with "lawyering to pay the bills" and preparing to campaign again in 1966. If records counted for anything, supporters expected him to be a leading contender in the next gubernatorial election. "Charlie Meriwether was still in Washington, but we began to work to keep our organization together as best we could, to try and stay active politically, and to lay the groundwork to run again in four years. For some reason I had to hoe that row on out, and see what the outcome would be."[1]

The first year out of office he lost a trusted friend and adviser when Judge Walter B. Jones died from cancer of the throat after a long illness. Since the Phenix City cleanup Judge Jones had supported him with a wellspring of political and judicial wisdom. "I admired him tremendously," Patterson said. "He loved to take a drink in the evening. He liked Haig & Haig Scotch. I'd been by his home many times in the evening and had a drink with him. When I was governor and had control of the liquor system, I made certain Santa Claus put a case of Haig & Haig under his tree every Christmas."[2]

When the doorbell rang at 210 Felder one afternoon in 1963, Barbara opened the door and called out, "Daddy, someone's here to see you." He went to the door, and the judge's long-time bailiff was standing there. "Judge Jones is out in the car," Eddie Lacey said. "He's not able to come in, but he wants you to come out to the car." Patterson walked out to the curb. Jones apologized for not coming in, and explained that he didn't have long to live. "I'm going around town today saying farewell to some of my friends," he said. "And I wanted to come by and tell you good-bye, and tell you how much I enjoyed my association with you." Two days later he was dead.[3]

"He left a letter of instructions for his funeral, and named me one of his six active pallbearers. I tell you that was one of the great honors of my life to be named one of his pallbearers." Many times over the years since then, Patterson reflected on how Judge Jones had influenced his life, particularly during the cleanup in Phenix City after his father's murder: "If the Lord had picked a man to send over there to do that job it would have been Judge Jones. It was a unique thing that you would have a combination of people like Walter B. Jones, Bernard Sykes, MacDonald Gallion, General Hanna, and all the others. It was a remarkable group at a critical time, and they delivered."[4]

As he reflected on the old and the new Phenix City, everything about his life since was tied to the umbilical cord of that terrible summer of 1954. As attorney general and governor he had played a pivotal role in not letting Phenix City slide back into its old ways. Later governors George Wallace, Lurleen Wallace, and Albert Brewer felt the same way he did about keeping the criminal elements from returning. "Folks like Sheriff Lamar Murphy, Bill Benton, and all the decent folks of Phenix City deserve the credit. They wanted to raise their families in a decent community. Now they have it. I don't think it will ever go back."[5]

ACQUIRING THE OLD PATTERSON place in Goldville from his Uncle Lafayette had allowed him to preserve the family's roots in Tallapoosa County. With politics and a law practice vying for his attention, taking care of the farm was too much for a weekend commuter. The farm was not just the thick forest passersby saw on the paved county road once fronted by the old Patterson home. Inside the gated property was a sheltered glen off to the right of the mile-long drive which snaked through the woods to the hunting-lodge-like cabin looking out over a fifteen-acre lake stocked with bream and bass. A few pampered horses and a herd of Angus brood cows—their calves were sold each year at the Roanoke stockyards—grazed in the secluded pasture under the possessive care of a prize hornless bull named Tonto.

Gracing the far side of the county road, a stand of company-managed timber helped the farm earn its keep. While still governor, Patterson had looked around for someone to manage the place. Billy Vickers said, "I know just the man you need. Works for Mr. Albert Barnes. Name's Earmon Glenn. Folks call him Wolf. One of the finest people in Tallapoosa County." The governor knew the Barnes family well. He and Mr. Albert's son Woodrow had served together in the 17th Field Artillery during WWII. Mr. Albert, a present county commissioner, was "a mighty fine man." The governor paid him a courtesy call and said he was thinking of asking Glenn to come work for him. "You go right ahead. It'll be a good thing for you and Wolf both. You tell him I'm delighted."

That night Patterson went with Billy Vickers to see Glenn. The Glenn family (Wolf's wife, Nellie B., a young daughter, and twin sons) lived in a shotgun house on a hill overlooking New Site. Glenn was a large, powerfully built man who was a few years older than the governor. He, too, was a WWII veteran, and he and Nellie B. were leaders in the black community. They sat around the kitchen table, and the governor put the proposition to him:

"I told him that I would like for him to come to work for me as my farm manager, that I would furnish him a vehicle and salary, and he could help me look after my place up here. He agreed to it, and that was the beginning of a very fine relationship," Patterson recalled. "He and I became great friends. I would venture to say at the time he died that he was the best friend that I had in the world. We spent many days together, many hours working on this place. We traveled places together. We loved to come up here and fish. He took over this place as if it was his own, and he looked after it as if it was his own place. We had a tremendous relationship."[6]

When he hired Glenn, the governor learned that no previous employer had ever deducted social security for him. "So I set him up so he would eventually get his ten quarters in and be eligible for social security someday." At first there was no house on the farm where the Glenn family could live. The old Patterson home had fallen down and was beyond repair. The governor later acquired the adjacent Foreman property, which had a residence on it. "He moved his family there, and we fixed it up, put a bathroom in the house and everything, and he lived there until he died."

Patterson recalled Earmon Glenn's death in the summer of 1991 as "the end of an era." They had been together for three decades. Every year the Glenn family had a reunion. "They always invited us, and we participated in the activities." Wolf called on family and friends when extra help was needed at the farm. There were men like Glenn's uncle Gaines Wykoff and cousin Rufus Wykoff, who managed the farm after Wolf died. "All of them were friends of mine. And they've all died off now. They were older than me, and they've all died off." Thinking of Wolf, he said, "It's a sad thing to lose a close friend. We enjoyed each other's company. I'll tell you we had a great time, he and I."

Then Patterson reflected on the cultural inequalities that had prevented Wolf and other elders in the black community from reaching their full potential. "Wolf had the ability . . . he could have done anything that he wanted to do. If he'd had the privilege of a good education, there ain't nothing this man could not have done. But, unfortunately at that particular time in history, the segregated school system was not an equal system." He elaborated:

"The black school was back in the country. It was totally inadequate. Had outdoor toilets. Had no plumbing. The facilities weren't anywhere near equal to the white facilities, and the people just were not able to get a good education under the system. A few broke out and left, and were able to do it, but not many. Finally, when the black school here was consolidated with the white school in New Site, and they closed up that black school out there, that was one of the greatest things that ever happened around here. Made it possible for black children to get a better education, and helped a lot of them tremendously. Helped the whole community."[7]

His thoughts turned to local politics. Wolf and Nellie B. were leaders in all this, he said. They were the "leading black citizens in this part of the county," and had a "tremendous reputation." Nellie B. was on the board of voter registrars. Patterson claimed the Glenns controlled more votes in the community than he did. "They controlled probably seven hundred to a thousand votes themselves. When candidates were running for office [in Tallapoosa County], they didn't come to see me. They went to see Wolf and Nellie B."[8]

PATTERSON NEVER DREAMED THAT he would be a dark horse in the next campaign for governor, or that the election would be a crossroads to his political future. Political columnists seemed to agree that his early and enthusiastic backing for John F. Kennedy had been the former governor's only stumbling block of any consequence, and that this had ceased to be a handicap after the nation's nightmare in Dallas in November 1963. Ingram observed that "in wake of the Dallas tragedy, Kennedy no longer was a cussword in any Alabama political quarter."[9]

Others were not so sure. Mississippi's former governor James P. Coleman had paid a price for his support of JFK. In that state's off-year gubernatorial campaign in 1963, the once popular Coleman lost to Paul B. Johnson, Jr., whose father he had defeated in 1955. The younger Johnson painted Coleman as a racial moderate and a tool of the Kennedy administration. Johnson's campaign staff spread a fictitious story that Coleman "had allowed candidate JFK to sleep in the governor's mansion in the bed of white supremacist Theodore Bilbo."[10]

Coleman's drubbing at the polls took place just before President Kennedy was assassinated but was still seen as an indicator of what might befall Patterson's attempt to retake the governor's office in Alabama. Patterson's concern, however, was not with deciphering the message sent by voters in Mississippi, but with winning Alabama's voters back from George Wallace. He and Wallace drew their support essentially from the same people and, despite different governing styles, both were populists and wanted to better the lives of all Alabamians. Wallace's campaign in 1962 had mirrored Patterson's winning run four years earlier. Wallace had even added Rebe Gosdin's country band to his entourage.

The contrast between the two men and their governing styles was obvious. Patterson the reluctant lawyer drawn into the political arena by his father's murder versus the Willy Stark incarnate who fed on grits and political power as if they were the breakfast of champions. Patterson, disciplined lawyer, soldier and administrator, looked after the affairs of state as he would his own, while Wallace the high-octane campaigner put politics ahead of the state's business and had little patience for checkbook stubs, staff meetings, or who was minding the store.

Both men, yielding to the traditional base of Alabama voters, became voices of a cause they knew was lost. Patterson's strategy on the race issue essentially sought to avert trouble in the streets by waging a delaying action in the courts, thus successfully fending off federally ordered desegregation of the public schools while he was in office. Although school integration began under Wallace's administration with the choreographed "stand in the schoolhouse door" and the opening of white schools to blacks in Macon County, his fiery rhetoric stirred racial passions and waved a red flag to hotheaded white extremists. The nationally televised police brutality against civil rights marchers in Birmingham and the murder of the four young churchgoers by KKK bombers in 1963 marked an upsurge in violence and a flagrant abuse of police power.

In the mob violence inflicted on the Freedom Riders in Anniston, Birmingham, and Montgomery in 1961, the city police were accused of being in collusion with the KKK when standing by and allowing the Freedom Riders to be savagely attacked by white mobs. Having no direct authority over municipal law enforcement, Governor Patterson had relied on the disciplined state highway patrol force under Floyd Mann and the mobilized national guardsmen under General Henry Graham to quell the violence. His declaration of limited martial law and mobilization of the guardsmen saved lives, while perhaps costing him as many votes as had his support for JFK.

Unlike the backroom collusion in the Klan's assaults on the Freedom Riders, Birmingham's notorious Bull Connor, with his political ally George Wallace in the governor's chair, showed no restraint in unleashing his uniformed policemen on peaceful black demonstrators. The use of police dogs, fire hoses, and cattle prods against helpless civil rights protesters placed police brutality on the front pages with Klan violence. Matched only by racial strife in neighboring Mississippi (where local law enforcement and the KKK also often were one and the same), the Klan lawlessness in Alabama, culminating in the cowardly Sabbath murder of the four girls in Birmingham, went unchecked and unpunished. Wallace never formed a special militia to deal with racial unrest as he had threatened, but he didn't have to; he gave that role to "hard-nosed and impulsive" Colonel Al Lingo, his head of the Alabama highway patrol.[11]

Lingo put his state troopers in uniforms emblazoned with Confederate flags. This misappropriation of the Rebel flag and the intimidation of black citizens was offensive to thinking Alabamians and it made caricatures of Southern law officers who became the objects of revulsion and even the butt of jokes from coast to coast. Alabama's citizens witnessed a return to McCarthyism when an anti-subversive unit, a sovereignty commission and a Commission to Preserve the Peace were created during Wallace's first term to root out Communist ties to the civil rights movement.[12] For multiracial American forces who were fighting for the Free World in Southeast Asia and other trouble spots around the globe, the suppression of liberties at home had more to do with aiding the enemy's cause than any metaphoric Red affiliation to the peaceful struggle for civil rights.

Wallace trampled on the lines between state and municipal authority when he ordered Lingo's state troopers to Birmingham to put down protests against Klan bombings in the black community, and later to Selma to forcefully halt a planned civil rights march to Montgomery. Lingo earned the world's condemnation for his actions on the day that became known as "Bloody Sunday" in Selma. On orders from the governor to use force if necessary to halt the peaceful march, the state troopers (and local deputies) met the marchers at the Edmund Pettus Bridge and brutally drove them back. At the front of the line with Hosea Williams (an SCLC staffer) was John Lewis, who had been clubbed by the white mob at the Montgomery bus station in the 1961 Freedom Rider incident.[13]

Judge Frank Johnson, described as "visibly disgusted" at subsequent hearings on the police brutality in Selma, then ordered Governor Wallace to protect the marchers on their way to Montgomery. The state complied, but on the night the procession concluded, a carload of Klansmen shot and killed Viola Gregg Liuzzo on a desolate stretch of road between Montgomery and Selma. Liuzzo, thirty-nine, was the wife of a Detroit Teamsters official and mother of four who had come to Alabama to participate in the march. Her accused killers were arrested within twelve hours of the crime, fingered by FBI informant Gary Thomas Rowe, who had been in the Klan car when Liuzzo was shot. Once more, Rowe's "planning and participation in the violence he was reporting to the FBI" raised questions about the Bureau's failure to act on prior knowledge of a crime.[14]

ALABAMA MAY HAVE GOTTEN a black eye from the Selma violence, but Wallace himself may have enjoyed the attention. In the Wallace camp, only a few close advisers such as Seymore Trammell, editor Grover Hall, Jr., and arch segregationist John Kohn knew their candidate hungered for national prominence after his spectacular win in 1962. With the exception of Trammell perhaps, even these insiders blinked at the audacity of Wallace positioning himself for a run at the U.S. presidency. Were his political ambitions whetted by the national spotlight on Patterson during the Freedom Rider crisis, or was it the public opinion polls indicating a backlash of working class voters against the incessant drumbeat for civil rights? In 1964 Wallace made a surprising debut in Maryland and other presidential primaries, but did not poll enough votes to keep him in the race.[15]

As his term as governor began to run down, Wallace toyed with the idea of challenging John Sparkman for his seat in the U.S. Senate, but decided he needed to hold on to the power and prestige of the governor's office if he hoped to build a national constituency. Besides, he did not want to lose momentum by turning the governor's office over to Patterson or some other political rival who might pose a threat to his "avarice of power." His showing in the 1962 governor's race had given Wallace a lock on the Patterson base, which he did not intend to relinquish. The only way he could succeed himself in 1966 would be to amend the state constitution. In 1965 he called the legislature into special session to try to get an amendment passed and submitted to the people before the next election.[16]

Wallace twisted enough arms to get the bill through the House, but ran into trouble in the Senate. Senators Ryan deGraffenried and Robert Gilchrist were interested in running for governor and did not want Wallace in the race. They formed a coalition with Patterson and Vaughn Hill Robison in opposition to the amendment and led the fight in the Senate to defeat it. Folsom called Patterson up during the Senate fight and said, "John, that thang's gonna backfire on you boys. Y'all oughta come out in favor of it. Go ahead and support the amendment. Try to pass it. That'll make people suspicious. It's gotta go to the people before it's adopted."

"Why would we wanna do that, Jim?"

"Y'all could git yo' people out during the statewide vote and defeat it. If folks vote overwhelmingly in favor of it anyways, that means George is too hot to handle. Then don't run this time. The office ain't goin' nowhere. Stay out and wait another four years 'fore you run again."

Folsom's words went unheeded, and weeks of hardball politicking by Wallace failed to turn the Senate vote in his favor. "We won that battle, but lost the war. Turned out that Big Jim was right," Patterson later said. "His words were very prophetic. That would have been awfully good advice for us, but we wouldn't listen."[17]

Bob Ingram recalled that one of the fascinating things to come out of the succession battle in the Senate was that "every state senator save one who opposed the amendment was never elected to a public office again." "Wallace just destroyed anybody who opposed him. There were some good men and some powerful men in that group. But only one out of the nineteen or twenty that opposed Wallace in the Senate on succession was ever heard from again."[18]

WITH WALLACE UNABLE TO run, Patterson and deGraffenried emerged as front-runners at the outset of the election year. Patterson appeared to have the edge because he and Wallace drew their support from the same voters. The former governor knew, however, that deGraffenried was an attractive candidate and had a strong following, particularly in north Alabama. Rebe Gosdin and his band had rejoined the Patterson campaign for the kick-off at New Site High School, and at first it looked like 1958 all over again. After the enthusiastic send-off in New Site, however, Patterson's campaign failed to catch fire. He did not have the war chest he had four years earlier, and the untimely death of Ryan deGraffenried in a plane crash in February changed everything.[19]

"Ryan's death was a great shock to everyone," Patterson recalled, "and it put a completely different complexion on that campaign." The popular candidate started his campaign early on Sand Mountain and hopped from one rally to another around northeast Alabama by helicopter. On the day he was killed he and a pilot had taken off from Fort Payne in a twin-engine Cessna to fly to a political rally in Gadsden. The weather was bad and the pilot flew into a mountain, killing the pilot and deGraffenried. "That plane crash was a terrible loss, and may well have taken the life of the man who was going to be the next governor," Patterson said.[20]

A week after the crash Wallace shocked everyone with the announcement that his wife Lurleen would be a candidate: "We were gonna support deGraffenried, but since he's out of it and I can't run, Lurleen has agreed to run in my place." Wallace had been pressing his wife to run, and she finally agreed. "We all sorta laughed it off, you know," Patterson said, "but as the deadline approached, sure enough, Lurleen qualified to run for governor. The rest, as they say, is history."[21]

Patterson's standing in the race had suddenly shifted from odds-on favorite to dark horse. Starting with rallies in south Alabama, the campaign to elect Lurleen to succeed her husband caught on like wildfire. The Wallace caravan, featuring Lurleen and George, crisscrossed the state drawing massive crowds "like you've never seen." "Within two or three days it was quite obvious that she was very, very popular and this was going to be a big thing," Patterson said. "From that point on, our campaign went downhill."[22]

He had some people following the Wallace caravan. They came back in a few days and told him, "John, you ain't never seen nothin' like this. When George introduces her, she gets up and says a few words and points to George, 'This is the fella who's going to run things for me.' Then folks just go wild. They run at her, wanting to touch her and to shake her hand. John, you got to see this to believe it. This is awful."

Patterson's "high hopes" for a second term faded quickly. He didn't have the organization he had in 1958, and the people who had put him over the top then were now pledged to Wallace. He knew he was in a race he couldn't win, but he could not bring himself to withdraw. He had raised $300,000, which was already committed to advertising agencies. He couldn't give the money back, and he couldn't back out. He described the futility: "When you are running a losing campaign for governor, it's hard to keep that from your people. It's hard to keep their spirits up. The candidate is the first to know, but is the last one who can show any signs of defeatism. With every piece of bad news your folks start to disappear on you. Ultimately, when the campaign really gets in bad shape, you find you're out there on the road by yourself. There's a difference in friends and political friends. The political friends disappear very quickly when the going gets tough."[23]

Timing can mean everything in politics. This was Lurleen's time. She won the Democratic primary in an unprecedented landslide, polling 480,000 votes and becoming the party nominee without a runoff. Patterson polled only 31,000 votes and came in sixth. "All of the people who supported me in 1958 became

Wallace supporters, and they stayed with Wallace and stayed with Lurleen. She was even more popular than him, and she beat us all."[24]

Outside of war, there are few defeats more bitter than a hard-fought political campaign. Losing candidates have to go through the motions of swallowing their pride and consoling their supporters. In Birmingham the tearful scene at the Molton Hotel on election night bore no resemblance to the wild victory party of eight years ago. "The crowd was not large. There was a good bit of drinking, and by nine o'clock we were whipped and everybody knew it. Women started crying and carrying on. An awful scene. I just couldn't stand that any longer, so I packed my stuff and me and Neil Keller, a friend of mine, slipped out of the hotel and drove down to the farm in Goldville."

He built a big fire in the fireplace after midnight. Somebody had emptied the Haig & Haig bottle. So he poured a double shot of bourbon before going to bed. "If you must eat crow, and I don't recommend it as a steady diet, it's more digestible with a nightcap." There in the glow of the crackling fire and the bourbon, he made the decision never to put himself, or his family and friends, through the strain of another race for governor. Early the next morning he woke up with a slight hangover, drove down to Montgomery "and went back to practicing law." First, he walked over to the courthouse when it opened and went around to all of the offices and shook hands with people and told them he was glad to be back. "That did me a world of good, and also helped me in my law practice."

Patterson called the Wallaces and congratulated them on Lurleen's tremendous victory. "George invited me to the inauguration, and I went." He had wanted for some time to mend fences between himself and Wallace, and this was a start. His father and Wallace had been friends and had worked on key legislation together when they were in the legislature. Since they "drew water from the same well" and both had the interests of the working families at heart, Patterson decided since he was not going to run for governor again that he would actively support Wallace in future elections.

Lurleen's death from cancer in May 1968 was a terrible loss to the Wallace family and to all Alabamians. Lieutenant Governor Albert Brewer took over the affairs of state and served out her term. In a moment of grief and in gratitude for Brewer's many kindnesses to Lurleen, Wallace said he would not run for governor in 1970 and promised to support Brewer's candidacy. Later, in the wake of a disappointing showing in the 1968 presidential election, Wallace reneged on his promise and entered the governor's race. Stung by finishing second to Brewer in the first primary, Wallace stormed into the runoff and returned to the governor's office by running one of the "nastiest" campaigns in state history.[25]

The assassinations of Martin Luther King, Jr., in April 1968 and Robert F. Kennedy that June added to the keen sense of loss Americans had felt when President Kennedy was felled by an assassin's bullets five years earlier. Occurring in the backdrop of the Vietnam War, where President Ngo Dinh Diem and his brother Ngo Dinh Nhu were assassinated in November 1963 following a military coup, the murders of the Kennedys and King scarred the nation's psyche and might have influenced the outcome of the 1968 presidential election. Subsequently, the crippling shots fired at George Wallace by a would-be assassin at a campaign appearance in Maryland in May 1972 brought the nation's trauma home to Alabama.

These shootings were repulsive to Patterson, and personal. Two decades since his father was gunned down in Phenix City, memories of the tragedy sometimes jarred him awake after midnight to reflect on the dying embers in the fireplace or the shadows on the wall. The loss of his mother in the summer of 1983 brought no closure to the family's tragedy. On one of his visits with her at the nursing home in Birmingham not long before she died, they sat outside in the late afternoon shade of a hickory tree and reminisced about his father. She was frail, but her mind and voice were strong. "Was it worth it, Mama?" he asked. She thought for a long while before answering. "No," she said, softly. "No, it wasn't."[26]

Having put his own gubernatorial aspirations aside, Patterson worked in Wallace's subsequent campaigns for governor and president. When Wallace ran as an Independent candidate in 1968, with General "Bombs Away" Curtis LeMay as his running mate, the Wallace-LeMay ticket carried only five Southern states and 13 percent of the vote. Wallace's stirring speeches against the political left and the government's mishandling of the Vietnam War pulled in huge crowds, however. The crowds grew in later campaigns, after Wallace was shot and had dumped LeMay. Patterson traveled some with Wallace in Florida and spent a week helping manage the candidate's office in Fort Worth, Texas. "I introduced him one night in Houston, Texas, at a stadium which seated fifteen thousand people, and by God every seat was taken," Patterson recalled. "I never saw anything like that in my whole life."[27]

While Wallace's popularity among working class voters sent tremors through the national political landscape, the fortunes of his friend and adviser Grover

Hall, Jr., had gone downhill. When the *Montgomery Advertiser* came under new management in 1963, Wallace lost the paper's unqualified support and Hall's stock went with him. After a rancorous four-year relationship the new owner fired Hall on the eve of the general election in 1966. Accepting a position with the *Richmond News Leader*, Hall moved to Virginia and went to work with editor James J. Kilpatrick on New Year's Day. Months of "downright obstreperous" relations with colleagues forced Hall to leave the *Leader* for Washington, D.C., where he wrote a syndicated column.[28]

Hall was not the Wallace lapdog that some critics portrayed, but he never gave up on Wallace, nor Wallace on him. Wallace had offered him a job when he was fired by the *Advertiser*, but Hall's pride would not let him accept a staff position. In September 1970, homesick and despondent, he agreed to return to Alabama to manage Wallace's campaign publications. On the way home he became disoriented and was picked up by police in Charlotte, North Carolina, when they observed him weaving on and off the road. He passed a sobriety test but was delirious and had no identification on him. A reporter recognized Hall and notified the family, who had him transported to University Hospital in Birmingham where he underwent surgery for a malignant brain tumor. He was terminally ill and died a year later in Montgomery.[29]

Patterson had joined in the search efforts (calling friends and state officials along the route from Washington, D.C.) when he learned Hall was missing on the way back to Alabama. Hall's personal attacks remained a mystery to Patterson. He shrugged them off as Garden District snobbery which was nothing to lose sleep over. A governor before him called the *Advertiser* "the best damn fish-wrapping paper in the world." Patterson wouldn't go that far, but he had more than his share of differences with the paper while Hall was there.

The autumn of Hall's ill-fated return to Alabama coincided with a decision by Patterson to test the political waters one more time. Patterson was resigned not to run for governor again, but he had not given up on a long-held dream to one day sit on the state's highest court. When he learned that Chief Justice Ed Livingston was not up for reelection (the seventy-eight-year-old jurist had held the position since 1951), Patterson qualified to run for chief justice.[30]

"I qualified first and early. Figured I would scare everybody else out. At first it looked like I had done that. Then at the last minute, in fact the last day, Howell Heflin qualified to run against me." Heflin was the last person Patterson expected to face. The thickset, good-natured lawyer from Tuscumbia (Colbert

County) was a friend from law school and had supported Patterson in his gubernatorial campaigns. A decorated Marine officer in WWII, Heflin had a thriving law practice and came from a prominent Alabama family. His uncle, J. Thomas "Cotton Tom" Heflin, a notorious white supremacist who practiced law in LaFayette (Chambers County), served twenty-four years in the U.S. Congress beginning in 1904.[31]

Heflin, who was far more liberal on the race issue than his famous uncle, was a formidable opponent. As the handpicked candidate of the Alabama trial lawyers, he was heavily favored in the race. Patterson was not active in the state bar association. When he announced for chief justice, the establishment legal community looked around for someone to run against him. A friend who worked for Francis Hare's law firm told Patterson that Hare did not want him to be chief justice because he "would do violence to the system," whatever that meant. Patterson opponents approached Heflin who had recently served as president of the state bar association. He expressed reluctance, but finally agreed to run. Heflin's entry into the race had Patterson scrambling for campaign funds. At that time the man on the street was not in the habit of contributing large sums to candidates for the bench. He was able to raise only a little over ten thousand dollars in campaign contributions.[32]

In contrast, several of the top trial lawyers—"T. B. Hill in Montgomery and Francis Hare in Birmingham, and about six or seven others"—put up ten thousand dollars each for Heflin. They went all out to get Heflin elected. In one ad alone, four hundred practicing lawyers in Jefferson County endorsed Heflin and "strongly" recommended his election. Among them were Lamar Reid, who had allowed the vote tally to be changed in the 1954 attorney general's race, and the Beddows (father and son), who had defended Albert Fuller when he was on trial for murdering Patterson's father.[33]

Patterson lost to Heflin by a two-to-one margin—550,000 to 287,000. He did not rule out running for a seat on the bench at a later date, but for now he took the defeat in stride and went back to work at the law firm. "Me and Ted Rinehart made some money," he said.[34]

WHEN PATTERSON LOST THE governor's race in 1966, his law partner Ralph Smith decided he had enough of the capital city and moved back to his hometown of Guntersville. Patterson then formed a partnership with Ted Rinehart and opened a law office in the Bell Building. Rinehart had returned to Montgomery from Birmingham where he had joined a law firm after stepping down as state insurance commissioner.

By the time Patterson made the unsuccessful bid for chief justice, he and Rinehart had a lucrative practice. "Ted was a smart lawyer. The more we practiced, the more we became an insurance practice representing the insurance companies." Patterson's biggest payday came in the settlement of a case against a handful of drug companies who had conspired to set the price of a new antibiotic drug. He and Nick Hare, a lawyer in Monroeville, represented the states of Mississippi, Kentucky, Louisiana, and Texas in the case, which was an antitrust and class action suit consolidated for trial in New York. "Ultimately we settled the case for a hundred million dollars," Patterson said. "I made the biggest fee I've ever made practicing law."[35]

Patterson took his money and put it in the bank. "I kept right on practicing law and coming up here to the farm working with Wolf and riding old pickup trucks around," Patterson recalled. "Nick Hare, a great fellow and a bachelor, took a trip around the world and had a good time with his." One day Patterson got a call from Hare. He was with Jack Gremillion, a mutual friend and attorney general of Louisiana. "Guv'na, I'm down here on the Delta Queen. We're tied up at Baton Rouge. Get you a plane and come on down heah. We got women and whiskey on board, and having a grand old time." Patterson said he responded, "Sorry Nick, old buddy. I got me two brood cows ready to drop their calves. Y'all are welcome to come on up and give me a hand."

Patterson's travels in the antitrust suit carried him all over the Rio Grande Valley in Texas and the state of Kentucky looking up people who had filed claims against the drug companies involved in the case. The last claimant he called on was a country lawyer living in Olive Hill, Kentucky, nestled in the northeast corner of the state. He filled up at a two-pump gas station, where a Goober look-alike, resplendent in oil-soaked overalls and a faded blue Wildcats jersey, informed him that he had now entered the hometown of famous country songwriter Tom T. Hall and that the claimant he was asking about was the only lawyer in town.

Following the man's directions Patterson drove slowly into the town square where he spotted a barbershop and next to it the shuttered windows and the lawyer's shingle hanging lopsidedly over the door. Inside the hole in the wall, the lawyer was expecting him. The station attendant had called ahead, and by now every telephone owner in Carter County knew a big shot attorney had come to town. Patterson introduced himself to the middle-aged man sprawled behind a desk cluttered with stacks of paper. There was no secretary, and from the appearance of things the attorney was not in a hurry to advertise for one.

On the wall behind the desk a framed charcoal drawing captured Patterson's attention. The drawing depicted two hobos lying with their hands behind their heads on a hillside overlooking a train track. Fields of clover and daffodils announced that spring was in the air. A puff of smoke in the distance indicated that a lazy ride to anywhere was on its way. In the caption to the drawing, one hobo said to the other, "You know, every spring about this time, I think of the many years that I frittered away practicing law."

"I just got to have that picture," Patterson said to the man. "What'll you take for it? Name your price." The attorney quickly replied, "No. No. I wouldn't sell that picture for nothing!" The picture was a prized possession, having been drawn for him by a dear friend, and no amount of money could persuade him to part with it. Tom T. Hall's "Old Dogs and Children and Watermelon Wine" had not been released yet, but when the song hit the charts a few years later Patterson was often reminded of his visit to the small hometown where Hall's father used to preach, of the two hobos in the drawing, and of its laid-back owner who was the only lawyer in town.

Many of the cases Patterson and Rinehart handled were settled out of court, and the others were generally devoid of courtroom drama. Few professions are more fraught with surprises, however, and the potential for drama was ever present with trial lawyers not knowing what to expect from the bench, the jury box, or the witness stand. From 1967 to 1968, his youngest brother Jack made life in the courtroom interesting for the family after he accepted a position in Montgomery as assistant U.S. Attorney for the Middle District of Alabama. Jack was proud of John and had campaigned hard for him in all of his political races, but this did not keep him from "giving it his all" when they squared off against each other in the courtroom.

Jack won the first case he tried against his big brother. The U.S. Attorney brought charges against several defendants in Tallapoosa County for possession of illegal whiskey. One of the accused moonshiners was a third cousin of the Pattersons. He and his co-defendants retained cousin John and Alexander City attorney Tom Radney to represent them. The case was tried in the federal courthouse in Opelika. Concerned about how it might look if the government lost, Jack offered to stay out of the case but the U.S. attorney insisted he handle it—explaining that he did not want lawbreakers to think they could influence the government's position by the person they picked to defend them. The U.S. attorney said he knew Jack would give it his best, and if the verdict went in favor of the defendants, so be it.

The courtroom usually emptied when an ordinary criminal case was on the docket, but for this particular trial the courtroom overflowed with spectators wanting to see the Patterson show—brother against brother with a cousin in the middle. Jack knew he had a problem with jury selection when the jurors were asked if any of them were acquainted with the lawyers in the case. "About two-thirds of the jury raised their hands, and in response to questioning said they were friends of John Patterson's. Nobody knew me, but they all knew John. Some were close friends. One juror even said that he had dinner with John the previous night."

Each time Jack struck one of the jurors for being a friend of his brother's, the courtroom erupted in laughter. The last juror he challenged was John's dinner companion of the previous evening. Needless to say, the juror was excused. The trial was "a real scrap," but when it was over the jury returned convictions against all of the defendants. "I know John was disappointed at losing the case, but I think he was also proud of me for winning," Jack recalled.

Being the governor's brother had its awkward moments. Before joining the U.S. attorney's office in Montgomery, Jack practiced law in Birmingham and Huntsville. He soon found out that people didn't refer to him by name. He was "just the governor's brother." One night in Birmingham after George Wallace won the 1962 gubernatorial election, Jack walked into a hotel lobby downtown where a group of people were talking. He recognized some people in the group and walked over to them. An acquaintance said, "Hey guys I want all of you to meet the governor's brother." One of the fellows standing there—"I didn't know him, obviously he didn't know me"—pumped his hand and enthused: "Proud to shake yo' hand, fella. Yo' brother Gawge got my vote. Sho' hope he keeps his pledge to clean up after that rotten Patterson bunch.[36]

While in Montgomery, Jack tried a number of federal cases in Judge Frank Johnson's court and had high regard for the fairness and impartiality of Johnson's decisions. Jack was aware that his older brother, while in office and afterward, had numerous contacts with Johnson, officially and socially, and considered him a friend. Johnson's father had supported Patterson when he ran for governor. The former governor believed that the judge was destined for greater things, and was not surprised to learn, during Richard Nixon's first term in office, that the judge was on the short list of nominees for a seat on the U.S. Supreme Court.

Word leaked out that opposition by U.S. Congressman William L. Dickinson was a major obstacle standing in the way of the Johnson appointment. Dickinson, as Alabama's only Republican congressman in Washington at the time, carried a lot of weight with the Nixon administration. His refusal to go along with the appointment (he threatened to make it a point of personal privilege in Congress) forced Nixon to reconsider. Patterson and Dickinson were friends. They had gone to law school together, and Ralph Smith had worked for Dickinson for a while after leaving Montgomery and returning to Guntersville. Patterson thought highly of Johnson as well, however, and was certain "he would have made a great contribution" if he'd been confirmed to sit on the U.S. Supreme Court.

In the middle of the controversy, Frank Johnson's brother Jimmy called on Patterson one night and said, "Frank asked me to come over and talk to you." Jimmy and another brother were in the finance business in Montgomery. They had not always been on the friendliest terms with Patterson, who had sued one of them when he was attorney general and took on the small loan operators. Jimmy asked Patterson if he would mind "getting hold of Bill Dickinson" and seeing if he could persuade the congressman to back off from his opposition to the appointment. "All he has to do is tell the president he won't fight it. He don't have to approve it. Just don't fight it."

"Yeah. I'll do that for Frank," Patterson said. He went to see Dickinson and said, "Bill, don't you think you oughta go ahead and back this appointment. It'll be good for the state." Dickinson wasn't buying it. He said, "Look. I'm not gonna be a martyr for Frank Johnson. If I were to back off and not oppose this appointment, it'll prove to everybody in Alabama that George Wallace is right that there's not a dime's worth of difference between the Democrats and the Republicans." He was adamant.

Reverse psychology didn't work. "Think about it, Bill. He's the darling of the liberals, but he's not who they think he is. Frank Johnson is a disciplinarian. He's a straight shooter. He upholds the law. He'll help a guy in trouble one time, but if he comes back to his court again he's a goner. The liberals think he's one of them because he stood firm on civil rights, but they don't have a clue to what he's really like. He's a tough bird. They'll rue the day he gets up there. You ought to agree to it on that basis alone." Dickinson shook his head no. Patterson pushed. "Think about it. If for no other reason, it would get him out of Alabama. Maybe we'll get a more favorable judge in his place." Dickinson was not persuaded. Patterson regretted having to report back that his mission had failed.

On a later occasion Patterson offered Judge Johnson some unsolicited advice that he too chose to ignore. When Jimmy Carter became president in 1977, he and Attorney General Griffin Bell approached Judge Johnson about taking the post of FBI Director. Patterson went by to see Johnson the morning the news came out that President Carter had invited the judge to Atlanta to discuss the offer. "Can I give you a little unsolicited advice?" he asked. Johnson said, "Fire away." Patterson said, "Don't take that FBI job. It's an executive position. If you take that thing and don't last long there, you may never get back to the bench." He reminded Johnson what happened in 1965 when President Johnson convinced Arthur Goldberg to resign his seat on the court to replace the late Adlai Stevenson as the U.S. Ambassador to the United Nations.

Goldberg reluctantly accepted the position after much prodding from Johnson, only to clash later with the president over his handling of the Vietnam War. He longed to return to the bench and left the UN post after three frustrating years. Subsequently passed over for chief justice when Earl Warren retired, Goldberg never made it back to the court. Johnson, of course, was familiar with Goldberg's misgivings about leaving the court, but was noncommittal in his discussion with Patterson.

Patterson thought one of his old Army buddies could have been right when he said, "Free advice is worth about what you pay for it." Johnson kept his appointment in Atlanta the next day, but a heart aneurysm prevented him from accepting the nomination as FBI director. President Carter then nominated him to a new seat on the United States Court of Appeals for the Fifth Circuit. Patterson said, "Frank Johnson was tough. He was straight. And he and I were friends. No question about it."[37]

Patterson later heard about Sam Engelhardt going up to Judge Johnson on the street and saying that he (Engelhardt) and other segregationists had been wrong and Johnson had been right all along. "I didn't want to die without telling you that, Judge," Engelhardt said.[38] Patterson saw this as further evidence that Sam Engelhardt was a decent and honorable man. He knew that people thought he had picked Engelhardt to head the highway department and backed him to chair the state Democratic Executive Committee, because he was head of the White Citizens' Council and a staunch segregationist. That had nothing to do with the selection. Patterson said he picked Engelhardt because he had been an effective state legislator and manager, because he trusted him, and because he was the right person for the job.[39]

BY THE ONSET OF the 1970s, the former governor's marriage was in trouble. Like everything else he and Mary Joe did, their private life was public fare. Word of the divorce came as a shock to their daughter Barbara, who got the news over the car radio as she drove to morning classes in Tuscaloosa. Graduating from Lanier High School in the spring of 1971, she had enrolled at the University of Alabama that September. When her parents divorced Barbara was completing her undergraduate studies. She graduated in 1975, and was awarded a teaching assistantship. Two years later she earned her master's degree.[40]

The year 1971 had been a milestone for her brother Albert who graduated near the top of his class at the U.S. Military Academy. When he boarded a Delta twin-engine prop plane for New York four years earlier, Albert was seventeen. There was never a question of him not making the grade when he said good-bye to his parents at Dannelly Field. "I'd been given this appointment to go up there from Alabama, and I sort of carried the burden of do not fail." With the Vietnam War taking its toll of fellow officers, Albert was more determined than ever to make the U.S. Army a career.[41]

In 1975 Patterson married the former Florentina Brachert, known to family and friends as Tina. He and Tina met while he was still governor. Tina had two daughters, Christa and Maria, by a previous marriage. Once during a class visit to the governor's mansion while in elementary school, Maria knew she was special when the governor removed the white carnation from his lapel and pinned it on her sweater. Not until her mother and the former governor were wed in 1975 did she fully understand the poignancy of that childhood memory.[42]

After their wedding John and Tina Patterson moved into a townhouse in Montgomery, but they spent much time at their second home on the old family place near New Site in Tallapoosa County.

Four years later, Bob Ingram wrote in one of his columns that the two Patterson offspring, who had been small children when they lived in the governor's mansion, were now grown and married. Albert, twenty-nine, was a captain in the Army. His wife was expecting their first child, and would make the former governor a grandfather "early next year." Twenty-six-year-old Barbara had recently married.[43]

During much of the 1970s, the Patterson and Rinehart offices in the Bell

Building were down the hall from those of Ingram, still the hard-hitting, non-partisan commentator on Alabama politics, but mellower perhaps after his own political stint in the Brewer administration. Unhappy with the management, Ingram had left the *Advertiser* shortly before Grover Hall's firing in the sixties. When Lurleen Wallace died, he became finance director in the Brewer cabinet and served through the end of that abbreviated term. Afterward he bought *South*, formerly published in Birmingham by Hubert Baughn, changed the name back to *Alabama*, and published the magazine for fifteen years in the capital city. His syndicated columns appeared in many Alabama papers, while nightly appearances on Channel 12 News with his "that's the way we see it" candor made him better known than the politicians he reported on.[44]

Patterson and Ingram saw each other on a daily basis at the Bell Building, and they got together "fairly often" for lunch. Ingram said his wife Edith got to know Patterson well while they were in the Bell Building, "thought he was a class act, and couldn't understand why I had not liked John in the past." Ingram admitted to their having problems when Patterson was governor, "partly because the *Advertiser* had been so close to Wallace," but said they "laughed about it in recent years." That was old newsprint to both men. "Either he's changed a lot or I've changed a lot because I am so fond of John," Ingram said.[45]

Patterson's relations with the *Advertiser* improved markedly after Ray Jenkins replaced Hall as editor. Jenkins routinely traded verbal punches with George Wallace, who in a turnabout from earlier times railed against Montgomery's *Advertiser* and *Journal* "as liberal, left-wing socialist" rags and ridiculed the respected editor for being a "snooty" Nieman Fellow from Harvard. Patterson and Ingram had been friends with Jenkins from his days with the *Columbus Ledger* and his reporting on Phenix City's lawless past. Jenkins often joined them for lunch. Patterson sometimes found himself defending Wallace's political prowess, to the amusement of his luncheon companions.[46]

In the November 1979 issue of *Alabama*, Ingram ran a feature on the fifty-eight-year-old former governor, portraying him as someone who, after a life of political and personal highs and lows, appeared "to have found what all aspire for: contentment." Patterson never spoke ill of a political opponent, and showed no bitterness toward any of the people who had opposed him in the political arena. "Life's too short for that," he said to Ingram. "There are some people I don't like . . . I could count them all on one hand . . . and I hope to live long enough to forgive them, too." In addition to what he called a "good but it could be better" law practice with Ted Rinehart, Patterson had also started teaching a class one night a week at Troy State in local/state government. "He thoroughly enjoys his teaching assignment," Ingram wrote.[47]

Ingram detected a deep sense of public service ingrained in Patterson. "He feels a very strong obligation to the people of Alabama for having elected him governor, and because of this, he makes it a point to go where former governors should go, and do what former governors should do. It is time-consuming, it also costs him money, but it is a debt he feels he owes." Patterson told Ingram that he could foresee no circumstance that would draw him back into the political arena as a candidate, but confided that he still had a yearning to serve on the Alabama Supreme Court. "To me it is the highest honor that a lawyer could have."[48]

FOUR YEARS LATER, GEORGE Wallace was elected governor for an unprecedented fourth term. He knew of Patterson's interest in the Supreme Court, and when Judge John Paul DeCarlo left the Court of Criminal Appeals to become district attorney of Jefferson County, the people around Wallace expected him to appoint Patterson to the vacant position. Judge John C. Tyson III, a good friend on the court at the time, called Patterson to come over and see his new offices. Patterson said, "Naw, John, I'm superstitious as hell, and I'm not coming over there until I get that paper."[49]

"Sure enough, George appointed his brother-in-law Hubert Taylor, who was a prominent lawyer and former state legislator from Gadsden," Patterson recalled. "I went to see George and said I understood about him appointing Hubert, but if he got another one, I'd really like to have it." Wallace said, "Okay, you got it. If I get another one, I'll appoint you." A year went by. Wallace called him one day and said, "John, you still want to serve on the appellate court?"

"Well, yeah, but you don't have a vacancy."

"Come Monday I will."

"How's that?"

"Hubert don't like it down heah. Wants to go back home."

Under Alabama law, a special election would be held in the fall to elect someone to serve the remaining four years of DeCarlo's six-year term. Wallace wanted Patterson's promise that, if he were appointed, he would run in the special election. "Well, all right," Patterson said.

Wallace explained that his brother-in-law was going to hand in his resignation on Monday morning at nine o'clock. "I want you to be there, and when he gives me his resignation I'll appoint you to take his place. Don't tell nobody about this. I don't want folks givin' me hell or harassin' me about this thing. It'll be a done deal before anybody knows anything about it."

Patterson had to let his law partner know he would be leaving. At the close of business on Friday, he went into Rinehart's office and closed the door. "Ted, I'm going to be appointed to the Court of Criminal Appeals on Monday morning at nine o'clock. George expects me to start sitting on cases Tuesday. I'll have to run for reelection in the fall. I've agreed to all this. So I'll be leaving here today, and I won't be coming back. Don't tell nobody now. He wants it kept secret."

He handed Rinehart the keys to the office. "You can have everything, all the furniture, the files, all the pending cases. It's all yours." Patterson left on Friday afternoon and didn't go back. "Boy, that's the way to get rid of a law practice," he said.[50]

Governor Wallace's announcement that he had appointed Patterson a judge on the Court of Criminal Appeals was well received by colleagues across the state. The still-trim sixty-two-year-old Patterson got a late start on the bench, but, as Wallace noted, the former governor and attorney general brought to the court a depth of experience that would be an asset to the jurisprudence system and to the state of Alabama. Patterson called the appointment "a culmination of an ambition I've always had since I was a little boy to become a judge." He professed to have no "particular philosophical views" that would affect his decisions on the court. "My job, as I conceive it, is to review cases that come up on appeal and apply the proper laws as I see them."[51]

The public investiture ceremony was held in the Supreme Court room the following Monday. Patterson took the oath of office from Alabama Supreme Court Chief Justice C. C. "Bo" Torbert, Jr., a longtime friend and colleague from Opelika. In his comments after the ceremony, Patterson called the swearing-in "one of the most important moments" of his life. "I've wanted always to be a lawyer and judge," he said. "Being an attorney general and a governor were just a sidetrack."[52]

Among colleagues paying tribute to the new judge, Circuit Court Judge Paul Jack Miller, who grew up with Patterson in Phenix City, described him "as a scholarly, caring man" who related "as well to a millionaire as a man wearing patches walking down the street." Henry C. Chappell, Jr., president of the Montgomery County Bar Association, said Patterson was a "skilled and professional attorney" with a sense of fairness. William B. Hairston, Jr., president of the

Alabama State Bar, predicted Patterson would add "luster" to the five-member appellate court.[53]

Ingram, commenting over WSFA-TV, said his reaction to the Patterson appointment was that "occasionally something happens in politics that makes you feel a little better about human nature . . . something that gives you a warm feeling." Noting that out of grudging respect between Wallace and Patterson had come "a warm friendship," he found it "reassuring that things like this can happen . . . even in politics." He commended Wallace for the appointment, and said he thought Governor Patterson would serve well as Judge Patterson.[54]

Those attending the investiture ceremony were mostly white, but there were black guests in the audience as well. Among them was pioneer civil rights leader E. D. Nixon, who had become a supporter of Wallace's when the former segregationist publicly apologized to blacks and "openly courted the black vote" in the 1982 campaign. Others included Bert Morell, bell captain at the Whitley Hotel, and a young man named Melvin "Choo Choo" Hamlin who shined shoes in the Whitley barber shop. Morell had known Patterson's father when he was a state senator and stayed at the hotel. Patterson had befriended Melvin, and a close bond was formed between the bootblack and the former governor.[55]

On one occasion Patterson became concerned when a prankster called the barbershop pretending to be George Wallace's secretary and invited Melvin to lunch with the governor. Melvin had dressed for the occasion, only to arrive at the appointed time and find out that the invitation was a hoax. While getting a haircut, Patterson overheard him being teased about the incident. Afterward he got together with Wallace, who sent his chauffeur to the barbershop to pick Melvin up in the limousine and bring him to the governor's office for lunch. The teasing stopped. A few days after Patterson's investiture, a colleague wrote him that he was in the barbershop, and Melvin was sharing with everyone how he was invited and took part in helping Judge Patterson put on his new black robe. "You cannot imagine what this has done for that young man. To me this is another evidence of your genuine love for people."[56]

When Wallace appointed Patterson to the criminal appeals court, a single dissenting voice was heard. State Representative Alvin Holmes of Montgomery, an outspoken civil rights activist, protested the appointment and sent a telegram to the Alabama Court of the Judiciary asking that Patterson's record be investigated "to determine whether he is fit to serve as an appellate court judge." Holmes charged that the former governor spread "hatred and racism upon this state to a level unknown to mankind," and questioned whether he could serve "fairly, equally and impartially on this court, or any court in the entire free world?" Claiming to have received more than two thousand telephone calls and letters protesting the appointment, Holmes expressed concern that "unlike Wallace, Patterson has never made a public apology to blacks."[57]

Patterson was not personally acquainted with Holmes, but attorney Alvin Prestwood (former commissioner of the Department of Pensions and Security in the Patterson administration) had formed "a pretty good relationship" with the Montgomery legislator. They shared the same first name, and Prestwood said Holmes "kidded me about being his namesake." In his relations with Holmes, Prestwood had found him to be a man of his word, that if he told you he was going to do something, "you could pretty well take it to the bank."[58]

Prestwood and his wife Sue had helped with Patterson's investiture ceremony. When they discussed the objections made by Holmes, Prestwood offered to go see the legislator and try to smooth things over. On a number of occasions Patterson had expressed regret about the segregationist stand he took as governor, and wished that he had done more to support black citizens in their struggle for equal rights. "By all means, go right ahead," he said to Prestwood.[59]

So Prestwood called Holmes and went by to see him. Prestwood explained that Patterson's segregationist policies as governor were a political expedient. Not once had Patterson made derogatory statements about African Americans in his presence, Prestwood said. It would have been out of character. He cited examples of what the governor had done to help elderly and needy people regardless of their race. After their discussion, Holmes agreed to drop his opposition to Patterson's appointment to the state court if Prestwood could show him evidence that the former governor had apologized publicly for the stand his administration had taken against racial desegregation.[60]

Prestwood had cut out and saved copies of newspaper articles in which Patterson had apologized for not doing more to help black citizens in their struggle for civil rights. He particularly regretted not taking steps to remove obstacles denying them the right to vote, and not doing more to bring them into the political process. Prestwood made copies of the articles and sent them over to Holmes. "I never heard back from him, but Patterson had no opposition in the fall election," Prestwood said. Holmes kept his word, as Prestwood knew he would.[61]

The realization of a dream is a time for quiet celebration and reflection. Judge Patterson and Tina made their weekend pilgrimage to the farm. He went out in the fields on Saturday and worked up a sweat with Wolf and Rufus Wykoff and Gaines Wykoff. To work at the things he loved, the earth and the law, what more could a person ask, he said to Tina. That evening he stoked a fire in the fireplace. It was mid-April, but in the Tallapoosa hill country there remained a chill in the air. He and Tina sat together near the crackling fire.

They spent so many Sundays at the farm that he'd been thinking about transferring membership from the Saint James Methodist Church in Montgomery to one closer to Goldville. He had been a Methodist all his life, but thought about becoming a member of the New Salem Baptist Church because the church was nearby and he liked the minister. When the minister told him that he would have to be baptized by immersion in a tank of water before the church congregation, Patterson changed his mind. "We'd be glad to have you, John," the minister said, "but you're going to have to be baptized."

"The hell you say," Patterson exclaimed.

"That's right, John."

"Precisely what does that entail?"

"Well, we have a tank up there under the pulpit."

"You don't say."

"Some Sunday we'll open that thing up and submerge you in it."

Patterson protested mildly. "Don't think I wanna' do that," he said. "Can't you make an exception in my case?" The minister's reply was uncompromising—leaving the former governor, for one of the few times in his adult life, at a loss for words

"Sorry, John. We didn't make one for Christ," the minister said.[62]

19

The Lectern and the Law

How sweet the Confederate jasmine, the wisteria, and the honeysuckle around Dexter Avenue when Tina dropped him off in the cool of the morning at the judicial building. As the day wore on the weathered, granite-like edifice warmed in the sun like an old friend. The office he now occupied as an appellate judge had been the attorney general's library when he held that position prior to becoming governor. He was at home in the familial embrace of the law books—"reading and studying were life's passions"—undisturbed by a family of mockingbirds nesting outside his window in the high fork of a crape myrtle.

He had spotted the nest while hanging his father's portrait on the wall behind his desk, flanked on either side by two great windows. The sighting conjured up images from Harper Lee's novel—she had been a student at the university when he was there—and his father's admonition not to harm nesting birds when he and his brothers awoke their first Christmas morning in the house on Pine Circle in Phenix City to find a Daisy air rifle beneath the tree. He remembered that his father had stopped by the judicial building to visit with criminal appeals court clerk Mollie Sue Jordan on the day he made the trip to Montgomery before being gunned down upon his return to Phenix City.

Judge Patterson knew that the old building's days as a beacon of the Alabama judicial system were numbered. Chief Justice Bo Torbert had persuaded former colleagues in the legislature that a modern structure housing the Supreme Court, the Courts of Civil and Criminal Appeals, the State Law Library, and the Administrative Office of Courts was needed. Much had to be done (including the purchase of a city block fronting Dexter), however, before the project could get underway. Construction of the new building carried over into the term of Chief Justice Sonny Hornsby, who assumed office in January 1989. Until that move, the portrait of his father, which had previously hung in the offices of the attorney general and the governor, remained centered on the wall of his chambers in the old building. "It's there to remind me every day how I got there, and the price that was paid," he told a *Huntsville Times* reporter. "It's always given me a reason to try to do better, and to never do anything to dishonor my office."[1]

The two decades the portrait hung above Judge Patterson's desk at the Court of Criminal Appeals were a culmination of his life's work. When his second term was up in 1996 he was seventy-five and, by state law, could not run for reelection. Retiring in January 1997 he continued to serve with the appellate court as a supernumerary judge for another eight years.

When the new Alabama Judicial Building, a block west and across Dexter Avenue from the old one, opened in 1993, Tina began volunteering as a docent, greeting visitors and giving them information about the state's court system. One afternoon when she was conducting a tour for a high school senior class from Birmingham, Judge Patterson slipped out onto the second floor balcony and listened to her presentation in the rotunda below. "She was outstanding," he said. "She really was."[2]

Miss Mollie Jordan was still clerk of the court when Governor Wallace appointed Patterson to the bench. She was the court's institutional memory, having come to work there in 1936 at a time when women were not even allowed to sit on juries in Alabama. When she died in 1996 Montgomery attorney Roland Nachman called her a "leader of judicial reform" and the "preeminent woman in Alabama government." Judge Patterson delivered the eulogy, remembering her as a person of "complete integrity" who had been a trusted friend to both him and his father.[3]

He followed her advice when she recommended to him that he keep a bright young attorney named Jennifer Garrett on his staff at the Court of Criminal Appeals. "That was the smart thing to do all right," Patterson said. "She said 'you'll never regret it' and I never did." He brought the secretary, Diane Illarmo, from his and Rinehart's law offices in the Bell Building with him. She and Jenny became the judge's right arm during his time on the bench. They started together as a team in the spring of 1984 and left the Court of Criminal Appeals together near the end of 2003 after twenty years of faithful service.[4]

TEACHING WAS AS MUCH a part of the Patterson heritage as his love for the law. For a number of years before his appointment to the appellate court, Patterson's Monday evenings were reserved for teaching a two-hour class on state and local government at Troy University. He continued to teach the class while serving on the court. Part of the time he also taught a course in political theory. One year he taught a political science course for officers at Maxwell Field's Air War College. He missed only one class while teaching at Troy, and on that occasion Tina (who accompanied him to the main campus on Monday nights) went in his stead and gave the final exam.[5]

He had taken on the teaching assignment in the mid-1970s at the personal request of Dr. Ralph W. Adams, Troy's "dynamic and innovative" president and later chancellor. A towering figure in higher education in Alabama, Adams built Troy from "a relatively small teacher's college to an outstanding state university with international renown." He was said to be the only acquaintance close enough to George Wallace to go to the mansion unannounced in the middle of the night and visit at the governor's bedside. Adams and Wallace had known each other since before WWII, and were as tight as two friends could be. When Adams prevailed on Patterson to teach a class at Troy, the judge readily accepted. A love for the law and the lectern were handed down from his parents. "Besides, I needed the extra money," he said.[6]

Adams, who brought a host of notable and sometimes controversial figures to the Troy campus to teach and lecture, considered the school's arrangement with Patterson a bargain. "Our goal was to bring in the best, the top people in their fields," he wrote in his memoirs. "The former governor of Alabama, John Patterson, taught political science at our Troy campus for [nearly] seventeen years. Can you imagine what a great experience that was for our students?"[7]

Working with the students was just as rewarding for the former governor. Young people of all races and nationalities flocked to his classes. He drew between forty to sixty students "every Monday night for two hours." "These were young, interested students who were serious about getting through college and going out into the business world," he said. "Many of them wanted to get involved in politics in some way." He did a lot of counseling. When classes were over, students lined up to talk with him about their personal aspirations. "I enjoyed working with these young people because I think it's very important . . . that the interested and certainly the educated people take an active role in the affairs of their community and their state."[8]

At the turn of the century, Patterson could look with pride at what his former students had achieved in their careers. Some were in the legislature. Some were circuit judges. Judge Lex Short from Andalusia had served two years as a law clerk with Judge Patterson. He was just out of law school, had a wife and child, and needed a job. Now Judge Patterson was writing an opinion on one of his cases, which had come before the appellate court. "He was a very bright young man, and now he's a circuit judge down at Andalusia deciding cases, and I think deciding them correctly."[9]

A commencement address Judge Patterson delivered at Troy in the summer of 1985 is as timely today as then. He encouraged the graduates to exercise self-discipline, to adhere to time-honored moral principles, and to always work to better themselves. "And, when you have reached a position of authority, seek then to advance the welfare of others looking to you for leadership. This, in my opinion, is the key to success in all fields of endeavor." He urged them "not to abandon the time-tested values of honesty, integrity, fair-dealing, compassion, and even-handedness," warning that "if you do, you will most certainly be unhappy in your life, and you will have failed to meet your responsibilities as a citizen and a graduate of this institution."

He believed this to be equally true of the nation, that in a democracy the state must hold to the same principles of law as those incumbent upon its citizens. Breaching those principles places the nation's moral compass and its moral authority at risk. In his lifetime he had observed a decline in the ability of "our democratic system to exercise self-discipline" and "the apparent drift of our country away from the moral principles upon which it was founded, and to which, I think, we owe our success." He spoke of a nation that was unable to control its borders—"we have no idea who lives in our country"—where violent crime and drug trafficking were rampant, the public schools were "not meeting the challenge of the new age," and the trend toward winning at any cost under-mined the national heritage.

Revelations of excesses in the CIA's undercover operations and "the break-down of discipline" in the Vietnam War "as evidenced by the My Lai massacre and the Lieutenant [William] Calley case" were signs of a disturbing trend. If we adopt the methods of the enemy, are we any better than them? "The answer is obvious: we must find a way to protect our interests, but it must not be at the price of sacrificing our honor. If we do not abandon the moral principles upon which our nation was founded, we have a good chance of enduring permanently, if we can learn to discipline ourselves. However, if we abandon our moral prin-ciples, we will most certainly perish as a nation and society, whether we learn to discipline ourselves or not."[10]

WHILE TEACHING AT TROY, Judge Patterson supported the school in other ways.

In 1974, he accompanied members of the Council on Postsecondary Education on an inspection tour of the university's military education program in Europe. Criticism of Troy's far-flung extension campuses (located at U.S. military bases around the world) by a Harvard professor had precipitated the inspection. Patterson made the trip as a personal favor to Chancellor Adams.

Dr. James D. Robinson, a retired Air Force colonel, headed up Troy's European operation. Under his direction, the programs had attracted quality teachers who were on sabbatical leaves from prestigious universities. The inspectors returned home with "nothing but glowing praise" for the university's contribution overseas. "John Patterson was the person responsible for this reaction," Dr. Adams wrote in his memoir. "They were impressed that an ex-governor of a state would be teaching, involved and interested enough to go to Europe and talk to people who were concerned about our extension educational program. We came out smelling like a rose."[11]

Patterson said the inspection team took a thorough look at the quality of classes on U.S. bases in England, before flying to Germany to inspect the military education program there. They worked out of Wiesbaden, where they had lodgings at the General Von Steuben Hotel run by U.S. armed forces. While the inspection group was in Germany the host officer and his wife drove Patterson to Gelnhausen and to Frankfurt where he had served after being recalled into the Army during the Korean War.

At Frankfurt the 4th Infantry Division had been replaced by the 3rd Armored Division, but the garrison looked the same. He went inside the headquarters building and walked down to his former office in the JAG section. Nothing had changed. Same old G.I. furniture. Same old olive drab. Same old problems. Just more of them. The drain of the Vietnam War had taken its toll on the disciplined Army he knew. He introduced himself to a captain sitting behind the desk and said, "You know, I used to sit at that desk twenty-five years ago doing exactly what you're doing now." Patterson asked if there was anyone around who would have been there in the fifties. The captain thought for a moment and said, "There's a German interpreter named Werner Keil who might have been here then."

"God, you mean to tell me he's still here?"

"Yep. He's still around."

"Would you call and tell him I'd like to see him?"

The captain made the call, and Werner Keil burst into the room a short time later. "He came up there and we had a big reunion," Patterson said. "Werner was a very fine fellow. We had worked together on a lot of criminal cases, preparing them for trial. He traveled all over the American zone with me interviewing witnesses and acting as my interpreter. He still lives in Germany, and I've corresponded with him for years." Back at the Von Steuben Hotel that night he jotted down a few notes. There would be a lot of stories to share with Ted Rinehart and Fred Rothstein when the trip was over, and the notes would jog his memory.[12]

He saw Rinehart about every other day, but didn't get to sit down as often with Rothstein, who lived in New York City. They had remained close through the years. Rothstein not only supported Patterson in his political campaigns, but became president of Manhattan Shirt Company and was instrumental in locating a shirt company in Andalusia, Alabama. They talked often on the phone, and the Rothsteins were always welcome guests at the Patterson farm.[13]

Patterson's comrades from World War II were special to him. In 1981, he co-hosted a reunion of the 17th Field Artillery with Colonel Tom Shackleford and Dr. George Kenmore, both of Montgomery. Shackleford had been the executive officer in the 17th and Kenmore, who became a veterinarian after the war, had been the S-3. The reunion was held in Montgomery, and was "a great event." For a number of years he was too pressed for time to attend the reunions, but he had started going to them after he and Tina married.

Two hundred or three hundred of the 17th artillerymen and their wives and sometimes their children would attend the reunions. "They were the most enjoyable things I ever attended," Patterson said. "I never enjoyed anything more. We'd meet every other year, try to drink up everything in town, and never go to bed. We'd sit up and talk all night and day. By the third day we had lost our voices and were so exhausted we had to go home." Tina, who as a young girl had lived through the Allied bombing of her hometown of Augsburg, enjoyed the memories and the camaraderie as much as he did.

Two of his closest friends from the war were Paul Frank and John Waggoner, both from Ohio. The three had toughed it out together in the 17th Field Artillery, from the hellholes of North Africa, Sicily, and Italy through the final campaigns in France and Germany. Waggoner was from Fremont, Ohio. They corresponded after the war, but were getting started in life and busy with their own pursuits. When Patterson was on the reviewing stand at his inauguration for governor, he looked down and saw John Waggoner in the crowd snapping his picture. First time he'd seen him since the war. He had the family whisked out of the crowd and brought up to the reviewing stand. "John died just a few years ago," Patterson said in a 2007 interview. "He used to come down every year and visit. We were very, very close friends."

Paul Frank also died not long ago. He was in a nursing facility in Canton, Ohio. "He visited down here and I visited up there," Patterson said. "He and I would call each other occasionally. Always started out by saying, 'Hey buddy, I got a fire mission for you.'" Early one morning Paul Frank was on his mind. He picked up the telephone and called him: "Hey buddy, I got a fire mission for you." Frank started laughing. Patterson asked what he was doing. Frank said, "I'm sitting here in a wheelchair looking out the window." "Whataya see?" "A parking lot full of cars with snow up to the windows."

The following morning he got a call that Paul Frank was dead. The old soldiers from "the greatest generation" were leaving us. Frank's death left Patterson as the only surviving officer who served with the 17th Field Artillery in WWII. Sometimes when he would read gripping WWII battle narratives like Rick Atkinson's *An Army at Dawn* or Matthew Parker's *Monte Cassino,* the nostalgia was overpowering. Now there was no one left for him to call and say, "Old buddy, I got a fire mission for you."[14]

JUDGE PATTERSON TAKES GREAT pleasure in reading military history and biography. He remarked how time stands still when he is reading a good book. With the turn of a page, one fights with the Highlanders at Culloden Moor, crosses the Delaware with Washington's army, stands beside Grant and Lee at Appomattox, and sits with Oliver Wendell Holmes, Jr., on the highest court of the land. His favorite biography is *Yankee from Olympus*, Catherine Drinker Bowen's classic portrait of Chief Justice Holmes. Admiration for Holmes was instilled in him by his father and grandfather, and grew with his law studies at the university. For a work in progress, what better sculptor than the Yankee from Olympus?

Patterson referred to Holmes as "my favorite American," and to Holmes's small groundbreaking volume *The Common Law* (a reworking of various essays, articles, and lectures published in 1881) as "one of the best books written on the law." Patterson relishes the study of law. While a student at the university, he had a key to the library and access to the stacks. "I liked nothing better than to spend a whole weekend by myself in the stacks in the law library with nobody else around." Even today he enjoys researching and writing—a luxury carried over from two decades on the appellate court.

"Most of the work on the appellate court is mundane, but occasionally you get a case in which you have to really be a judge," he said, explaining in lay terms that not all law is based on precedent. "Every now and then you are confronted with having to make a decision arising out of certain facts that has not been done before. This requires a deeper study and application of the law in making your decision." There is an eroding of confidence in the bench when we have Judge Roy Beans making decisions "by the seat of their britches, or by hunches," or for reasons other than logic and the law, he explained. He added that "a little common sense thrown in for good measure" mixes sugar with the vinegar.

Delving into the occasional case of first impression that came to the court for review intrigued him the most about preserving the intellectual integrity and fairness of the law. "There should always be a methodical approach leading to a logical decision, but this becomes more intriguing in a case of first impression. You have to write an opinion in which you set out the reasoning for deciding the way you did. These opinions are published in the law books where people read them and they can serve as precedent."

He took pride in the opinions he wrote. "When I work on an opinion, I want to write the opinion where it makes sense. I want it to be logically correct, and I want it to be understandable by anyone who reads it." He believed that Justice Holmes's opinions were "certainly a model to follow." They were clear, concise, and to the point—"the shortest and briefest of anybody who ever served on the Supreme Court." Patterson sought to ingrain a similar intellectual approach and pride of authorship in the law clerks he brought under his wing at the Court of Criminal Appeals.

He had two law clerk positions authorized. Approximately fifteen different lawyers clerked for him during his years on the court. He preferred not to keep a clerk longer than one or two years, unless there was good reason for their staying. Usually, after a year, it was better for them to start looking elsewhere and to get on with their legal careers. Judge Patterson remained flexible, however. If a law clerk was not ready to leave after the first or second year, "he didn't see any sense in rushing anybody out the door."[15]

His philosophy was to make their assignments meaningful learning experiences that would help them in their legal careers. "Some judges put their law clerks off in a corner and ignored them, but not Judge Patterson. He put us to work on cases and made us members of his team. He was always accessible and was interested in our ideas and opinions. He meant for it to be a career-enriching experience, and it was." This was the consensus of a group of former law clerks who sat around a table at Jennifer Garrett's home in 2004 and reminisced about their experiences with Judge Patterson.[16]

"He was not a yes or no person," a member of the group said. "If a question was deserving of an answer, it deserved explication. He was living history. He had a story for every occasion." When the staff approached Judge Patterson about letting them dress casual for work on Fridays, he told them about General Patton's order that his officers wear ties in the sweltering heat of North Africa or about the stern instructions Dr. Masters gave his law students at the university requiring them to wear ties to his classes. "Judge Patterson didn't say no, but we left his office knowing that casual Fridays were out."

If the young lawyers became too personally wrapped up in a case, he might bring them back to reality with a humorous story about the time he went with Jimmy Faulkner of Bay Minette on a fund-raising quest in support of Jones Law School. Faulkner, who had become close friends with both Patterson and Wallace since the hotly contested 1958 gubernatorial race, had become a highly successful businessman and philanthropist. Faulkner was the largest contributor to Montgomery's Alabama Christian College—where Jones Law School was located—and the institution was renamed Faulkner University in his honor.

When he was asked to help raise money for a new building to house the law school, Faulkner asked Patterson to go with him to Birmingham to talk with a wealthy contributor, John Harbert of Harbert Construction Company. "Jimmy picked me up in his airplane. We flew to Birmingham and went over to see Mr. Harbert. Mr. Harbert said he might consider giving Faulkner University some money, but not the law school. Mr. Harbert said, 'Absolutely not. I despise lawyers. I wouldn't contribute a thin dime to educate a lawyer.'" Judge Patterson said he didn't take it personally.[17]

Who could forget the bottle of Hennessy that appeared on Judge Patterson's desk to celebrate special occasions? "When something important happened, like when we finished an important case or got our scores back from the bar exam, he would break out a bottle of Hennessy and the brandy snifters he kept in the office. On these rare occasions, he'd lock the door and we'd go in at the end of the day and just sit there and have a cognac and talk. He made you feel good about being a lawyer. You knew you'd made the team."

He took the law clerks with him to special events outside the court, ranging in social diversity from Francis Stallworth's famous annual swamp suppers in Monroe County to the induction of new members into the Alabama Academy of Honor (which Judge Patterson chaired)." These were opportunities for him to introduce them to prominent people from around the state. "Judge Patterson gave you comfort by just being around him—comfort in what you were doing and confidence in your own abilities."[18]

"He was always gracious and generous with his time," another admirer recalled. "Some law clerks never saw their judge, never wrote opinions. Judge Patterson was always available. He was genuinely interested in us, what we were doing, and our ideas." Respect for the law and the rights of the defendant were sine qua non. Whenever they worked on a case, he drilled into them "that no matter how heinous the crime" the person accused of the crime had the same rights under the constitution as any other individual. It was their duty as lawyers to put their personal feelings aside and to defend their client to the best of their ability.

"He was a firm believer in the Fourth Amendment, the search and seizure law," attorney Dee Miles recalled. He had seen enough of the other side of justice in the old Phenix City days to know the consequences when the courts failed in their duty to protect the rights of the people. "When I left the court I had a good understanding of the Fourth Amendment because he was such a firm believer in the rights of everybody. Their rights had to be protected. That stayed with me more than anything."

That belief that the law was for everybody and not a privileged few sparked Randall Houston's interest in search and seizure cases when he went to work with Judge Patterson in 1984. Today Houston is the district attorney for the Nineteenth Judicial Circuit, which encompasses Chilton and Elmore counties. "I basically became a search and seizure expert working for Judge Patterson," Houston said. "His advice to me was to be honest with yourself and to be honest with the public. Treat everybody fairly. Honor and integrity are the words I think of when I think of Judge Patterson."

"He was a calming influence, never condescending," Jennifer Garrett said of their long professional relationship. He always led by example. Elizabeth Dressler said he "commanded your respect, because he respected you." The group as a whole said Judge Patterson taught them to work hard at solving problems and "to get it right," but that "we all make mistakes, and should have the courage to admit them when we're wrong." Human frailty and the law is a study in itself.

A CASE IN POINT arose out of an incident in 1993 when flamboyant District Attorney Chris N. Galanos of Mobile County called a press conference to attack a reversal of one of his cases by the Court of Criminal Appeals. Galanos caused a stir in the black community when he referred to the Criminal Appeals Court "as the five dumbest white men on earth." One indignant appellate judge came to Patterson's office and wanted to cite Galanos for contempt, which Patterson as presiding judge refused to do. The tempest blew over as quickly as it blew in.

Three years later Patterson presided over an appellate review overturning another case from Mobile County. In a footnote to its opinion, the court cited Galanos's office for "egregious error" in sustaining multiple reversals on the same issue. Galanos, meanwhile, had vacated the district attorney position for a seat on the bench as a judge of the Thirteenth Circuit. He bristled at the footnote citation, which contained mistakes in its references to other cases, and filed a complaint suggesting that the court's criticism might be payback for his earlier "intemperate and inappropriate" comments about the court.[19]

On the presumption that his public slur against the court and the court's subsequent actions formed a basis for real or perceived bias against him, Galanos requested that Judge Patterson recuse himself from any pending or future cases coming before the appellate court in which he had participated as either a prosecutor or a judge. Upon further review, Judge Patterson concluded there indeed were "inexcusable" errors in the footnote to the court's opinion. He made other members of the court aware of Galanos's concerns, and took immediate action to have the "inappropriate" footnote removed from the published opinion.[20]

In a letter of apology, Patterson offered assurances that Galanos's criticism of the court was not a basis for any bias toward the aggrieved Mobile judge. He noted that when Galanos's comment about the court was first reported by the press, he had dismissed it as "an incautious comment made on the spur of the moment" and "probably regretted ... as soon as it was said." Noting that he too "regretted incautious remarks" made on occasions when he was "frustrated by some situation," Patterson assured Galanos that he held no "personal bias or ill feeling" toward him that would necessitate recusing himself from cases in which Galanos was involved."[21]

During Judge Patterson's two decades on the bench the Court of Criminal Appeals handled between 1,800 to 2,500 new cases each year, which was one of the heaviest state appellate caseloads in the nation. With only five judges sitting on the court, and each of their offices minimally staffed, a backlog was built into the system. Due to time constraints alone the court could hear oral arguments in no more than ten percent of the criminal appeals. About the same percentage of convictions appealed to the court resulted in reversals.

Judge Patterson explained that the appellate court's affirmations or reversals derived solely from the evidentiary material in the case record and were based on case law. The court had no investigatory power, and could not consider evidence that was not in the case record. Allegations of reversible error or prosecutorial misconduct not supported by the case record, for instance, were not a basis for reversing a lower court's ruling or overturning a conviction. The appellate court's findings, pro or con, had to be reached on the basis of material evidence brought forward in the appeal and supported by case law.

The law required that all death penalty cases in Alabama be appealed to the state appellate court. The U.S. Supreme Court had banned capital punishment in 1972, but in 1976 authorized states to resume the practice after state laws had been revised to conform to federal guidelines. Most of the prisoners on death row were indigent and had to rely upon a court-appointed lawyer. Judge Patterson credited pro bono efforts by trial lawyers within the private sector as a critical factor in assisting these defendants attain equal justice under the law. He pointed to progress made in criminal justice in Alabama by committed attorneys such as veteran civil rights lawyer J. L. Chestnut, Jr., of Selma and pro bono lawyer Bryan Stevenson, who founded the Montgomery-based Equal Justice Initiative, a nonprofit firm for handling death penalty cases, in 1989.[22]

These attorneys knew from their years of courtroom experience that every man's nightmare of ending up on death row for a crime one did not commit was more real than a complacent public might think. Two appellate court reversals— the overturning of a life imprisonment conviction, *Knight v. State* in the 1980s, and a death penalty conviction, *McMillian v. State* in the 1990s—made their point. In the first of the two cases, Patterson was the presiding judge in October 1985 when the Court of Criminal Appeals reversed the conviction of defendant James Selma Knight for burglary and theft in the first degree, and remanded the case to the circuit court in Macon County for a new trial.[23]

The circuit court had sentenced Knight, a habitual offender, to life without parole in the state penitentiary. A mistrial was declared on a more serious charge of rape. Knight confessed to the police while under interrogation, but the evidence, including the victim's description of her assailant (she had been raped and her house burglarized after returning home from a party hosted by the mayor), pointed to someone other than Knight having committed the crime.[24]

The Court of Criminal Appeals based its reversal on the finding that the prosecutor withheld forensic test results proving that half-smoked cigarettes left at the crime scene by the rapist were not the defendant's. The court ruled that prosecution's failure to produce this exculpatory evidence had violated the defendant's right to due process. The alleged confession constituted "the totality of the evidence" against Knight, and appeared to have been coerced. The illiterate defendant had been interrogated without the presence of an attorney (although he had asked for one) and without being allowed to eat.[25]

The jury in the remanded trial—either uninformed of the appellate court's reversal of the first trial or overlooking the court's doubts about the "voluntariness" of the defendant's confession—convicted Knight for the second time, and he was again given a life sentence. Judge Patterson's opinion in the appeal of the second conviction upheld the court's earlier finding that all evidence of guilt apart from the "alleged confession" pointed to the defendant's innocence and cast doubt upon the credibility of the confession itself. The trial court's admission of this confession was deemed to be "contrary to the weight of the evidence and manifestly wrong." Ruling that the trial court committed reversible error in admitting the confession into evidence, the appellate court again reversed the conviction and remanded the case. Arguments by the state attorney general for a rehearing failed to persuade the court to alter its decision. Knight was a free man.[26]

The stakes in the appeal of Walter McMillian's conviction in 1988 were higher since he was sentenced to die for the murder of a store clerk during a robbery in Monroe County. McMillian, a black man, was tried and convicted in Baldwin County on a change of venue. The victim was Ronda Morrison, an eighteen-year-old white college student who worked part-time at Jackson Cleaners in Monroeville. The only evidence against McMillian was testimony by witnesses, principally that of a white man named Ralph Myers who "told the court McMillian had gone with him to the cleaners, shot Morrison, and brought a wad of money back out of the cleaners."[27]

The appellate court affirmed the conviction in 1991, but new district attorney Tommy Chapman, who took office two years after McMillian was convicted, had doubts about the case. There was no physical evidence tying McMillian to the crime. According to Chapman the police had bungled the case by moving the body, contaminating the crime scene, and smudging fingerprints before forensic tests could be made. Myers, a convicted felon, had an unsavory reputation, as did two other state witnesses who testified against McMillian.[28]

Attorney Bryan Stevenson and the Equal Justice Initiative took the case, and with cooperation by the new district attorney succeeded in winning a reversal. Stevenson "unearthed statements and documents never seen at trial" and found witnesses "who knocked big holes" in testimony given at trial. Based on these discoveries, McMillian was granted another appeal. At an appeals court hearing in 1992, Myers admitted that he had never seen McMillian on the day Morrison was killed, and the other two witnesses recanted their testimony. Far more damaging to the prosecution's case, Stevenson discovered the authorities had suppressed exculpatory evidence that would have helped clear McMillian.[29]

Myers's admission that he had falsely testified against McMillian was supported by hospital records at Taylor Hardin Secure Medical Facility showing that, "several months prior to the appellant's trial, Myers told four hospital staff doctors at separate times that he was being pressured by police officers to testify falsely against the appellant and that he knew nothing of the crime." At the appellate hearing, presided over by Judge Patterson, the court found that the prosecutor's failure to disclose the hospital records and other exculpatory evidence "created reasonable probability that trial result would have been different had evidence been disclosed and, thus, required reversal of defendant's conviction and sentence."[30]

Had Bryan Stevenson and his non-profit organization not entered the picture, would the discovery of "police bungling" (in the words of the new district attorney) and overzealous prosecution in the Walter McMillian case have ever seen the light of day? The alternative would have seen a middle-aged African American, who had only one previous arrest (for a speeding ticket) on his record, still languishing on Alabama's death row or already strapped in the electric chair known as "Yellow Mama." No one empathized more than Judge Patterson with justice for the slain victim in the case, whose senseless murder devastated her family and left an Alabama community in shock and anger. He was ever mindful, however, that convicting someone for a crime he or she did not commit denies justice to the victim, and a new victim is born. Everyone loses.

Clarity in a court opinion is golden. The longer the opinion, the more room for obfuscation. He recalled a lengthy opinion one of his law clerks turned in that was beautifully written, but hard to understand. "Hell, I couldn't understand it," he recalled. He looked up at the law clerk and said, "I don't understand this, but it sure sounds good. Let's just go ahead and release that." He laughed. "That's the Alabama rule now. Everybody understands it except me."[31]

Asked what his imprimatur on a court opinion would mean to criminal justice in Alabama, Judge Patterson said he hoped it stood for "intellectual honesty." He had done his utmost to render "fair and equitable" decisions to the appellant, regardless of race, creed, or standing in life. "I think that my worst enemies, if I haven't outlived them all, would tell you that John Patterson was intellectually honest about his decisions," he said. "They knew that I would reverse a case in a heartbeat, regardless of who the parties were, if I thought the appellant didn't get a fair trial. If you do what you think is right in making your decisions, you can always defend that successfully, anywhere, anytime. I have always conscientiously tried to do that."[32]

Judge Patterson's tenure on the Court of Criminal Appeals came to a close when the legislature reduced funding for the judiciary in fiscal year 2004. He had just celebrated his eighty-second birthday. "I wasn't ready to go," he said. "I was the only temporary employee working for the court, so it was only natural that I would be the first to go. But they also laid off seven law clerks, and I hated that. Some of those folks were married and had children."

His name came off the personnel rolls on the 30th of September. He stayed two more weeks without pay to get rid of the backlog. Before leaving he was delighted to learn that Governor Bob Riley had accepted his recommendation to appoint Jenny Garrett to a seat on the Pardon and Parole Board. On the day he and his staff left the court he administered the oath of office to her, and they walked out of the judicial building together. He turned his building pass in at the guard desk, and he and Tina drove out the parking ramp, turned right on McDonough Street and took the familiar route back to Goldville and their farm.

Farewell to the judiciary. His robe had been cleaned and put away. The portrait of his father, carefully wrapped, was placed on the backseat of the car. His papers had been accessioned into the state archives. He was nostalgic, but felt surprisingly carefree as they passed through the streets of Alexander City where he had sold newspapers so many years ago. For the first time since he wore knee pants, John Patterson was without a job. He was out of the fishbowl of state politics. He could devote his energies full-time to his studies and to family, friends, and the care of the animals on his farm.

But not for long.

Back in Montgomery storm clouds swirled around Chief Justice Roy Moore's losing battle over the 5,280-pound granite monument of the Ten Commandments he had placed in the rotunda of the judicial building. Moore had the monument installed late on the night of July 31, 2001, without consulting the other justices, and the next morning he called a press conference where he unveiled the monument to great fanfare. Since a smaller, but similar flap had propelled Moore to the highest judicial seat in the state, critics naturally assumed that the public unveiling was the first step in his campaign for governor.[33]

Lawyers offended by Moore's placing the monument in the rotunda of the judicial building filed lawsuits and, in November 2002, U.S. District Judge Myron Thompson ruled that the granite display was an unconstitutional state endorsement of religion and ordered it removed. In August 2003, when the U.S. Supreme Court rejected an emergency plea by Moore, he announced his intention to disobey Judge Thompson's order. The Alabama Judicial Inquiry Commission charged him with violating six judicial canons of ethics. Moore was suspended and the eight other members of the Alabama Supreme Court intervened and had the monument removed from the rotunda and placed it in a storage area. Nearly three months later, after a one-day trial, the Court of the Judiciary found the chief justice guilty of willfully disobeying a federal court order and removed him from office.[34]

Moore's supporters rallied to his defense. Large demonstrations were held in front of the judicial building "featuring speakers such as [former ambassador] Alan Keyes, the Reverend Jerry Falwell, and Moore himself." Emotions ran high, but the rallies were peaceful and those on the other side of the issue refrained from holding counter-demonstrations. Before Judge Thompson's ruling, African American politicians had petitioned Moore to install a monument honoring Dr. Martin Luther King Jr.'s "I have a dream" speech in the rotunda alongside the Ten Commandments monument, but Moore had rejected the proposal.[35]

Later, when Moore appealed his ouster, Acting Chief Justice Gorman Houston and the other supreme court members recused themselves. In December, Judge Patterson (who had been away from the court less than three months) and six other retired judges agreed to hear the appeal. The names of the retired judges were randomly picked, Houston said, and were submitted to Governor Riley for his approval. Riley called Patterson, who said, yes he would serve, but thought the governor should appoint former justice Janie L. Shores as chief justice of the special court. She had served on the Alabama Supreme Court for twenty-five years and was senior to him. Riley insisted, "No, she's a fine person and a fine judge, but I want you to do it."[36]

Early in 2004 the seven retired judges were sworn in to serve as the temporary Supreme Court charged with hearing Moore's appeal. The other six judges were Janie L. Shores, Kenneth F. Ingram, Harry J. Wilters, Jr., Braxton Kittrell, J. Richmond Pearson, and Dwight Fay, Jr. Their combined experience on the bench totaled 139 years. On the day he moved into the chief justice's office, Judge Patterson brought his father's portrait back from Goldville to hang on the wall behind his desk until their work on the Moore case was done.[37]

After weeks of careful study and the hearing of oral arguments, the special court rendered its decision in the Moore case. In his appeal Moore contended that he was unlawfully removed from office because the federal court order mandating removal of the Ten Commandments monument was unlawful, and violated his oath of office "to acknowledge God." This argument failed to sway the special court, which denied Moore's appeal to regain his job. Finding that Chief Justice Moore cited "no authority that provides an exception to the rule of law that one must obey a court order or that would allow disobedience to a court order on the basis of one's religious beliefs," the court ruled unanimously that the Court of the Judiciary "could hardly have done otherwise than to impose the penalty of removal from office."[38]

The outcry was predictable. Moore lashed out at the special court of retired justices, calling them "an illegally appointed, politically selected court." Retired Alabama Supreme Court Justice Terry L. Butts, a Moore spokesman, reacted angrily, "I think that the atheists, the agnostics, the ACLU, the Southern Poverty Law Center and those that think like they do, that if their rear ends were as narrow as their minds they could all sit in the same rocking chair."[39] Others saw narrow minds, and perhaps politics, hard at work in Moore's behalf.

In 2005 when the former chief justice announced for governor and lost to incumbent governor Bob Riley in the primary, Moore's critics believed they had been right all along—that politics was an underlying reason for installing the Ten Commandments monument in the rotunda of the judicial building from the outset. When a pair of religious zealots (one black and one white) confronted Selma attorney J. L. Chestnut, Jr., over something he had written about Moore's political ambitions, Chestnut wryly compared them to "Alabama's equivalent of the intolerable Taliban in Afghanistan."[40]

The former chief justice's political ambitions had no bearing on the decision rendered by the special court. Perhaps even they wondered what role, if any, politics had played in Moore's defiance of the federal law. Had convictions not blinded political vision, Moore could easily have copied George Wallace's stand in the schoolhouse door, thus making his point loud and clear without forfeiting his job. Whether the motives were more Moses or more Machiavellian, Shakespearean tragedies have survived the ages on plots less contrived. But that is a story for another day.

From the veranda outside the chief justice's office, historic Dexter Avenue was a street of memories. A sense of deja vu was in the air whenever protests rocked the capital city. The crowd of protesters supporting Moore and the Ten Commandments display paled in comparison to the swell of civil rights marchers of the fifties and sixties. Where was the Moore group's Martin Luther King, Jr., with his impassioned speech at the conclusion of the Selma march? Where was their John Lewis with his iron will and fearless determination? Where were their Rosa Parks, their E. D. Nixon, and the countless others whose march to freedom put down roots on Dexter Avenue and changed a nation?

The civil rights movement had no equal in American history. The movement was evangelical, and forgiveness was as biblical as the righteousness of their cause. Alabama's resulting political and social transformation was personified in the forgiveness shown to George Wallace. Nearly as many blacks as whites were among the estimated twenty-five thousand mourners who paid their last respects when George Wallace lay in state at the Capitol in September 1998. Former Governor Patterson noted at the time that Wallace was a populist who "did more to improve the lives of the people of Alabama than any other person in our state." The Reverend Franklin Graham (son of evangelist Billy Graham), led the funeral services and closed with a variation of Wallace's famous inaugural quote, "Jesus Christ today. Jesus Christ tomorrow. Jesus Christ forever."[41]

WITH THE DECISION RENDERED in the Moore case, Judge Patterson and Tina could return their full attention to family, friends, and the farm. The capital city had been too great a part of their lives, however, for them to stay away for long periods at a time. Judge Patterson was still active in a variety of organizations, including the Alabama Academy of Honor, which he formerly chaired, and the board of trustees at Lyman Ward Military Academy, which he still chaired.

The induction of attorney Fred D. Gray of Tuskegee into the Academy of Honor in 2005 was a nostalgic moment for both Gray and Patterson. Fifty years had passed since Patterson (as attorney general) and Gray (as a young civil rights lawyer) faced off in the courtroom over the NAACP injunction and Tuskegee boycott cases in the turbulent fifties. Gray, a nationally recognized civil rights attorney, had risen to the top of his profession. Among a lifetime of achievements and honors, in 2002 he became the first African American to be elected president of the Alabama Bar Association. Decatur attorney John A. Caddell, a 1977 Academy of Honor inductee, said Gray "has made the light shine on our state."[42]

In July 2004, Governor Riley called on former Governor Patterson to speak at a commemorative ceremony honoring his father, Judge Walter B. Jones, General Walter Hanna, the Alabama National Guard, and the citizens of Phenix City. The occasion marked the fiftieth anniversary of the restoration of law and order to Phenix City. Governor Riley spoke of the wave of moral outrage that swept Alabama after Albert Patterson's assassination and sounded the death knell for the criminals that controlled Phenix City.

He pointed to the "fifty years of remarkable progress" that had been achieved by Phenix City's citizens and community leaders as a lesson in history to all of Alabama—a lesson that John Patterson had stressed continuously since his father's murder. That lesson, Governor Riley said, was this: "Tolerating evil leads only to more evil. And when good people stand by and do nothing while wickedness reigns, their communities will be consumed."[43]

Patterson's three brothers (Maurice, Sam, and Jack) were recognized during the ceremony. Also in attendance was the former governor's son, Albert Patterson III, who had retired from the Army as a colonel and was now president of Navigator Development Group, Inc., based in Enterprise, Alabama. Two years later, a proud father was on hand when his son's company was among the first eight recipients of the Governor's Trade of Excellence Award. Navigator owners Patterson and Keith Gay had ventured into the international market and were doing a thriving business overseas.[44]

On June 16, 2006, the former governor brought the portrait of his father home to Phenix City. The Russell County Commission and the Russell County Historical Commission had made arrangements for the portrait to hang permanently in the foyer of the county courthouse. The portrait and a historical marker honoring the late Albert Patterson were unveiled at a ceremony on the courthouse lawn. The historical marker was later moved to a spot outside the Coulter Building where Albert Patterson was slain fifty-two years ago.[45]

Patterson recalled that his father was aware of the dangers he faced in trying to clean up Phenix City, "but was dedicated to carrying it out and making this city and county a better place." William Benton, director of the Russell County

Historical Commission and a longtime family friend, echoed this sentiment, saying, "Phenix City is a better place because of what happened back then. We've made a lot of progress and it's been positive." Russell County commissioner Gentry Lee noted that the assassination changed not only Phenix City and Russell County, but the politics in the state of Alabama.[46]

With his brothers at his side, John Patterson said that the best monument to their father was "a Phenix City free of the organized crime influence he had fought to end." "You have already given the greatest tribute that could be made to Albert Patterson," he said. "Immediately after my father's death, the people from Phenix City, with some initial outside assistance, rose up and restored law and order to his community and it has been free of organized vice and crime since that day. Since that time and today it is a progressive, growing city. Clean, a good place to live and raise a family and prosper. . . . That's the lasting monument to Albert Patterson that really counts."[47]

More than two hundred people braved a heat wave to attend the ceremony. Family members were there in force. John Patterson's daughter Barbara and his brother Jack were among those flying in from out of state. More than forty Patterson family members joined local citizens and public officials for dinner. When John and Tina drove back to the farm that afternoon, the temperature dropped into the eighties as they made their way into the hill country of north Tallapoosa County. A refreshing pitcher of iced tea topped off a near-perfect day.

Before dark John Patterson drove alone in the truck down through the pasture, and with the cows trailing him to the fence line, went through the gate to the ruins of the old Patterson place. Whenever he wanted to be alone with the past, this is where he came. He walked over to the old boarded-up well where as a child he had drawn water and let it warm in the sun so he could bathe in the evening before going to bed. He bent down and dug his fingers into the soil, crumbled the dirt in his hand, and sifted the timeless grains back onto the ground that had once been his grandmother's flower bed. Climbing back into the truck he drove on up the road past the rise where he had played as a child and had looked out into the distance and wondered what grand adventures lay ahead of him. He had gone away, but his father's assassination brought home to him a half century ago that this was where he had always belonged. He turned the truck around and headed back to the house to join the family.

EPILOGUE

Had he heard the young man right? Did he really say that old Governor Patterson was buried there? That morning he had driven a visiting historian over to where his great-grandfather's seven hundred-acre "Leander Farm" once sprawled across the rolling hills outside of Hackneyville. John Love Patterson ("the miller") was buried in a small graveyard on the old place, which long ago had been broken up into plots and sold by his widow and their five daughters, now all deceased.

From the roadside they were unable to reach the grave site which was overgrown with briars and kudzu vines. Pulling up to the nearest residence Patterson inquired about the property and learned that it had recently changed hands. The new owner had moved to the area and now resided in Alexander City. He got the man's phone number and called him that evening at home. "I'm John Patterson from Goldville," he said, and explained that he had kin buried in the cemetery. He asked the owner's permission to go onto the property and clean up the grave site.

The owner was expecting the call. He had been contacted by the friendly neighbor whom Patterson had seen that morning, although some particulars of their conversation had obviously become garbled. The owner was amiable and wanted to help. "Yes, sir. You go right ahead. Been meaning to clean the place up myself."

Patterson thanked him. "It's a very historic spot, you know."

"So I hear. I understand old Governor Patterson is buried there."

A moment of awkward silence. Then Patterson laughed and said, "Oh, hell no. You heard wrong. This is old Governor Patterson talking to you on the telephone."

THAT VERY DAY HE had mentioned to Tina that he wasn't going "to move into no retirement home near Disneyland or Cape Canaveral where people don't even know me." "I got nothing against them places you understand, but I wouldn't

438

want to live among strangers where you have to hire people to be your pallbearers when you die. I prefer to live and die right here amongst family and friends."

Not long before, Bob Ingram had reminded Channel 32 viewers that "Alabama's oldest living governor" was still alive and well, and gave them a rare glimpse at his life on the farm. "If what Tina and John Patterson have in rural Tallapoosa County near Goldville is your typical retirement home, well I can't wait to be put out to pasture," he said in his lead-in to the TV special.[1]

He explained that the Patterson farm was named "Timbergut" because a spring on the property serves as the headwaters for Timbergut Creek, which runs through the wooded countryside all the way down to the Tallapoosa River. The spring, surrounded by twelve hundred acres of timber, also feeds the scenic fifteen-acre lake behind the Patterson home. "It's a scene that would make for a wonderful picture postcard," Ingram reported.[2]

In the camera's eye, Patterson and Ingram were as comfortable together as two old political warriors are apt to be. With the black Channel 32 van trailing at a distance, they climbed into Patterson's old truck and drove out to the fenced-in pasture where five pampered horses ran free near the stable and tack room. Jessie "Just a Fool" was a twenty-four-year-old racehorse that Barbara had owned in New Jersey and brought to the farm to live out her years. The other four were quarter horses named Sioux Fran, Clover Honey Lady, Tequila Sunrise, and Kenwood's Babe. Across the pasture, Macedon Tonto, the prize polled Angus bull, moved closer to his inquisitive herd of twenty-four brood cows.[3]

Patterson had learned cattle farming from scratch. His next-door neighbor when he was attorney general was Ham Wilson, the improbably named executive director of the Alabama Cattleman's Association. Wilson got him interested in the cattle business, he said. Later, after Patterson added acreage to the farm, a doctor friend who was a big cattleman down in Greenville gave him a young Angus heifer named Belvedere Lass. "Belvedere had to have company so we bought four more from a fellow over at Opelika. Then we bought a bull. First thing you know we were in the cattle business."[4]

With the cameras rolling, Ingram said: "The Pattersons are not only living the good life, but it's a healthy one as well." Patterson nodded. "My health is good. I don't have any problems. I don't take any pills." "He credits his good condition to his lifestyle," Ingram said. Patterson explained, "I run the tractor and bush-hog and all that kind of stuff myself. I do my own feeding, have my own hay. That's a lot of exercise. So I'm in good health."[5]

Later, on the evening news, Ingram told viewers that he couldn't resist asking the former governor to rate the chief executives he had known. Ingram said he had not expected Patterson to do it, and he didn't. "You're not asking me to rate them, are you? I guess you know I wouldn't do that," Patterson said. "They might rate me."[6]

Today the former governor retains an interest in Alabama politics that reflects his lifelong concern for good government and good law enforcement. "I'm very disturbed when I see things going on in government that I would not have tolerated," he said. "When I see things creeping into Alabama that make me believe there's some signs of organized crime coming back into our state. This concerns me, but I'm concerned from a distance."

But not from too great a distance. There are no teenagers at home, but the telephone still rings all day long. He and Tina don't mind. In fact they would be at a loss without Ma Bell's tinny accompaniment to the chorus of honking geese that make the placid lake their home. If the caller is not a family member, it is likely a friend or colleague. Of course it could be farm business or a former student or even a political acquaintance seeking the former governor's counsel or support. "I wouldn't know what to do if the phone stopped ringing. It's a terrible thing to become irrelevant. I think one of the worst things that can happen to a person is for folks to quit calling them for advice."

He lauds the progress Alabama has made in the economic and political arenas over the past fifty years since he was governor. The contributions made by minorities and women are enormous. Ever mindful that the ballot box is where good government begins, he has expressed regret numerous times for not having done more as governor "to bring Alabama's black citizens into the political process, to give them the power of the vote. "Now [the Klan] would have burned crosses on my lawn and all that kind of stuff, and I wouldn't have been reelected. But I didn't get reelected anyway, so it really wouldn't of made any difference."

Speaking of those turbulent times, Patterson has been quoted as saying, "Politically, we couldn't solve segregation. The federal courts solved it and it was a good thing. People went ahead and cussed the federal judges and the politicians could survive." He admits that if it were not for the civil rights movement, the politicians would have dragged their feet "until the cows came home" if that's what it took to hold on to their political base.[7]

His advice to young politicians is "do your job the way you conscientiously believe you oughta do it, and you will probably get reelected." "If you constantly think about reelection and you weigh your decisions based on whether you think they are going to get you reelected or not, you are making a terrible mistake. You've got to be true to yourself and true to the people. If you're not, you probably won't be reelected."[8]

His long service with the Alabama Court of Criminal Appeals has made him keenly aware of the contributions women and minorities have made to the system of justice in Alabama. He believes the accomplishments of women judges in recent years will inspire even more young and talented women to pursue legal and political careers. "Women judges I have known are incorruptible," Patterson said. "Whatever they do, they do from their own intellect and their own conscience."[9]

What truer testament than when Sue Bell Cobb, a friend and colleague on the Court of Criminal Appeals, was elected Alabama's first female chief justice in November 2006. The bonds she and Patterson had formed on the court and their mutual respect led to his administering her oath of office. Chief Justice Cobb took the oath with her hand on his grandfather Delona Patterson's Bible, which was used when he was sworn in as Alabama's youngest governor in January 1959. A half century of change and consequence was encapsulated in the poignant moment.

That evening, when he and Tina topped the hill outside Wetumpka on the way home, Patterson grew reflective. The day had been long, but invigorating. He smiled, recalling that Alabama's trial lawyers, who were among Sue Bell Cobb's staunchest supporters, had been the ones who frustrated his chances of becoming chief justice in 1970. History often has an odd way of evening things out.

The state couldn't do better than Sue Bell Cobb, in his estimation. If they'd had magistrates of her caliber meting out justice in his father's time, the Russell County of old would surely have seen its "bought-and-paid-for" sheriff impeached and the lawless conditions there cleaned up without his father being murdered. He was momentarily jarred out of his reverie when Tina applied the brakes and slowed the Mercedes passing through Santuck, where the frame buildings and empty booths of its famous flea market were boarded up for the winter.

Last spring an acquaintance had run across one of his old campaign buttons at the flea market in Santuck and sent it to him. "Nobody But the People for John Patterson." "You don't see many of these around anymore," the man wrote in an accompanying note to the former governor. "Scarce as hen's teeth," the note said. The note acknowledged that Nobody But the People had been more than a campaign slogan when it swept Patterson into office as the state's youngest elected governor. It spoke for the way his administration did business when he was governor, and the way he lived his life afterward.

Were the days of the populists over in Alabama politics? Maybe, but Patterson didn't think so. Look at the gains the state had made over the past half-century since that tragic night in Phenix City had driven him to reluctantly step forward to fill his father's shoes as Alabama's attorney general and then governor. The substantial progress the state had made since that turbulent time was reflected in the day's swearing-in ceremony in Montgomery. His role in that progress? Well, he'd leave that to the historians.

ACKNOWLEDGMENTS

The road to completing this biography would have been a beggar's journey were it not for the assistance of so many gracious and generous people. Dr. Ed Bridges and his staff at the Alabama Department of Archives and History were unflagging in their support of the project. I am grateful to Frazine Taylor, Norwood Kerr, John Hardin, Mark Palmer, Ken Tilley, Willie Maryland, Jerome Wiley, Mary Jo Scott, Rickie Bruner, Margaret Cleveland, and Pat Wilson for their guidance and many kindnesses when I was doing research at the state archives starting in the winter of 2002–2003.

Other repositories, private collections, and individuals who granted interviews or provided documents and photographs for the Patterson biography breathed life into the story. I could not have done without their support. I owe a special word of thanks to Bill Benton and the Russell County Historical Commission, and to the following individuals who gave generously of their time and expertise: Hoyt Allen, Edward Azar, Geraldine Blair, Elizabeth Thomson Bressler, Ruth Benson Cole, Harry Cook, Hilda Coulter, Eric Davis, Christa Frangiamore, George MacDonald Gallion, Jennifer Garrett, Tommy Giles, Carrie Gosdin, Fred Gray, Pete Hanna, Sibyl (Burnette) Hanson), Richard Heinzman, Randall Houston, Diane Illarmo, Robert Ingram, Dorothy Johnson, Conley Knott, McDowell Lee, Floyd McGowin, W. Daniel Miles III, Maria Florentina Mixon, Simon Partner, Albert Patterson II, Jack Patterson, Maurice Patterson, Alvin T. Prestwood, Edmon Rinehart, Joseph G. Robertson, Fred H. Rothstein, Barbara Louise Scholl, Dr. Nancy Smith, Mose Stuart IV, Charles Volz, Adelia Warren, Johnny Warren, and William Younger.

I owe special thanks to Randall Williams, Suzanne La Rosa, and Brian Seidman of NewSouth Books, and to my son Tom. Their contributions have made this a far better book. To all who lent their support, I am deeply appreciative.

NOTES

Prologue

1. K. A. Turner, "All politicians should keep us in mind," *Alexander City Outlook*, Jan. 7–8, 1995, sec. Opinion, 4.
2. General Order Number 51, HQ VI Corps, U.S. Army, June 26, 1945; *The Heritage of Tallapoosa County*, Heritage Publishing Consultants, Inc., 2000, 54–55; Order No. 15.249, The Marshal, Commander in Chief of the French Armies of the East, Petain, Apr. 1, 1919.
3. Bob Ingram, "John Malcolm Patterson," *Alabama Magazine*, Nov. 1979, 6–8.
4. "Nobody's For John Patterson . . . But The People," *Greene County Democrat*, Apr. 10, 1958, 1.
5. Ingram, 6–8; Shelton Foss, "Alabama's 'Boy Governor,'" *Montgomery Advertiser* and *Alabama Journal-Old Newsboys Day*, Dec. 6, 1988, 5.
6. Foss, 5.
7. "Send Gov. Patterson on tour," *Birmingham News*, July 2, 1961, 16.
8. Ingram, 6–8.
9. Philip Rawls, "Patterson has three key regrets about his term," *Birmingham Post-Herald*, Jan. 19, 1984, sec. State, C4.
10. Linda Dean, "Memories with Governor John Patterson," *Lake Martin Living*, July 2001, 22–24.
11. Ingram, 6–8.
12. Ibid.; Marshall Frady, *Wallace* (New York: Random House, 1968), 131; Dan T. Carter, *The Politics of Rage: George Wallace, The Origins of the New Conservatism, and the Transformation of American Politics* (Baton Rouge: Louisiana State University Press, 1995), 96n, 267, 268.
13. Ingram, 6–8; Frady, 193–196; Carter, 274–292.
14. Phillip Rawls, "Retiring judge is a lesson in history," *Montgomery Advertiser*, Dec. 26, 1996, 1A, 4A.
15. Philip Rawls, "Patterson has three key regrets about his term," *Birmingham Post-Herald*, Jan. 19, 1984, sec. State, C4.
16. Ibid.
17. Ibid.; Statement, John Patterson to author, Apr. 13, 2003.
18. Mike Marshall, "Former governor recalls his family's legacy, tries to reshape reputation," *Huntsville Times*, Oct. 27, 2002, unknown.
19. Dean, *Lake Martin Living*, 22–24.
20. Turner, *Alexander City Outlook*, 4.
21. Alvin Benn, "John Patterson Has Farming on His Mind," *Cooperative Farming News*, Decatur, AL, July 2007, 1, 22–24.

Chapter 1, Barefoot in Tallapoosa

1. Heritage Publishing Consultants, *The Heritage of Tallapoosa County, Alabama* (Clanton, AL: Walsworth Publishing Company, 2000), 4, 294.
2. Ibid., 1.
3. Interview, Gov. John M. Patterson by author, Sept. 18, 2002; Arthur Schlesinger, Jr., "Andrew Jackson," in *The World Book Encyclopedia*, Vol 11 (Chicago: 1975), 6–13.
4. Interview, Gov. John M. Patterson by author, Oct. 19, 2001.
5. Ibid. Not uncommon for this period, various sources such as the headstone at his grave site, obituaries, political bios, military records, and *Who's Who in the South and Southwest* list conflicting dates for Albert Patterson's birth. The birth date of January 27, 1891, is consistent with the Federal census records for 1900, on file in the State of Alabama Department of Archives and History.
6. Patterson Interview, Sept. 18, 2002.
7. Patterson Interview, Oct. 19, 2001; Bob Ingram, "John Malcolm Patterson," *Alabama Magazine*, Nov. 1979, 6–8.
8. Patterson Interview, Oct. 19, 2001.
9. Biography of Albert L. Patterson in *Who's Who in the South and Southwest*, undated; Statement by Jack Patterson, Sept. 29, 2003.
10. Ibid.; Biography of Albert L. Patterson, on file in Gov. John M. Patterson papers, State of Alabama Dept. of Archives and History, undated.
11. Order No. 15.249, The Marshal, Commander in Chief of the French Armies of the

East, Petain, Apr. 1, 1919.

12. Patterson Interview, Oct. 19, 2001.

13. Ibid., *The Heritage of Tallapoosa County*, 294–5, 297; Notes provided by Dr. Nancy Smith, Enterprise, AL, Aug. 27, 2003; Sarah Townsend, "Alex City's only congressman remembers term of 50 years ago," *Alexander City Outlook*, no date.

14. Notes by Dr. Smith; Nick Lackeos, "Ex-solon Patterson, 91, Recalls First Speech,"*Alabama Journal*, Aug. 27, 1979, 1A.

15. Patterson Interview, Oct. 19, 2001; Ltr, John Patterson to Mrs. Lois Phillips, Sept. 18, 1972.

16. Ibid.; "John Keeps With Early Principles," *Phenix City Citizen*, Feb. 13, 1958, 1.

17. *The Heritage of Tallapoosa County*, 294.

18. Ibid.; Patterson Interview, Oct. 19, 2001.

19. Description of John Love Patterson by Ben F. Ray, Birmingham, AL, Feb. 18, 1960.

20. Patterson Interview, Oct. 19, 2001; Interview with Dr. Nancy Smith, Enterprise, AL, Aug. 27, 2003; Interview with Mrs. Geraldine Blair, Birmingham, AL, Oct. 1, 2003.

21. Ibid.; "Young John Patterson Was Fond Of Farm Life and Work," *Alexander City Outlook*, Jan. 23, 1958, 1, 4.

22. Patterson Interview, Sept. 18, 2002.

23. Interview with Sibil Burnett Hanson, New Site, AL, Oct. 23, 2003.

24. Ibid.

25. Patterson Interview, Oct. 19, 2001.

26. Ibid.; Lackeos, *Alabama Journal*, Aug. 27, 1979.

27. Patterson Interview, Oct. 19, 2001.

28. *Alexander City Outlook*, Jan. 23, 1958.

29. Patterson Interview, Oct. 19, 2001.

30. Patterson Interview, Sept. 25, 2003.

31. Smith Interview, Aug. 27, 2003; Blair Interview, Oct. 1, 2003.

32. Patterson Interview, Sept. 25, 2003.

33. Patterson Interview, Oct. 19, 2001.

34. Interview with Hoyt Allen, New Site, AL, Oct. 23, 2003.

35. Ibid.

36. Patterson Interview, Oct. 19, 2001; Patterson Interview, Sept. 25, 2003.

37. Patterson Interview, Oct. 19, 2001.

38. Ibid.; *Alexander City Outlook*, Jan. 23, 1958.

39. Patterson Interview, Oct. 19, 2001.

40. *Alexander City Outlook*, Jan. 23, 1958; Ltr, John Patterson, Goldville, AL, to Mr. A. L. Patterson, Phenix City, AL, Sept. 4, 1936.

41. Patterson Interview, Oct. 19, 2001.

Chapter 2, When All the Leaves Were Green

1. "Remembering The Old Rockford Grammar School," *Coosa County News*, July 20, 2001, 6.

2. Interview with John Patterson, Dec. 1, 2003; Interview with Dr. Nancy Smith, Enterprise, AL, Aug. 27, 2003.

3. Patterson Interview, Oct. 19, 2001.

4. *Coosa County News*, 6.

5. Patterson Interview, Oct. 2, 2002.

6. *Alexander City Outlook*, May 22, 1930, 1.

7. "Attorney Patterson Moving to Alex City," *Outlook*, Jan. 21, 1929, 8; "Rockford News," *Outlook*, Mar. 21, 1929.

8. Patterson Interview, Oct. 23, 2003.

9. Ibid.

10. Ibid.

11. Ibid.

12. "Graves and Lovelace Winners for Representative," *Outlook*, Aug. 14, 1930, 1.

13. "Alabamans Pledge a Roosevelt Drive," *New York Times*, Nov. 30, 1931; Ltr, C. J. Coley to Dr. Edwin C. Bridges, Dir., Alabama Department of Archives and History, Jan. 3, 1989.

14. "John Keeps With Early Principles," *Phenix City Citizen*, Feb. 13, 1958.

15. Ibid.

16. Patterson Interview, June 29, 203; Patterson Interview, Oct. 23, 2003.

17. Patterson Interview, Oct. 23, 2003.

18. Ibid.

19. *Phenix City Citizen*, Feb. 15, 1958.

20. Ibid.; Patterson Interview, Oct. 19, 2001.

21. Patterson Interview, Dec. 1, 2003; *Alexander City Outlook*, 1929 and 1930.

22. Patterson Interview, Dec. 1, 2003.

23. Patterson Interview, Oct. 23, 2003.

24. Ibid.

25. Ibid.

26. Ibid.

27. Linda Dean, "Memories with Governor John Patterson," *Lake Martin Living*, July 2001, 23.

28. Patterson Interview, Oct. 23, 2003.

29. Patterson Interview, June 29, 2003.

30. Ibid.

31. Patterson Interview, Sept. 25, 2003.

32. Ibid.

33. Ibid.

34. Ibid.

35. Patterson Interview, Dec. 13, 2003.

36. Interview with Geraldine Blair, Birmingham, AL, Oct. 1, 2003.

37. Patterson Interview, Dec. 13, 2003.

38. Ibid.

39. Jerrold M. Packard, *American Nightmare: History of Jim Crow* (New York: St. Martin's Press, 2002), 73–78; "Digest of Jim-Crow Laws Affecting Passengers in Interstate Travel," Extract from Internet.

40. Patterson Interview, Oct. 25, 2002; Patterson Interview, June 29, 2003; Patterson Interview, Oct. 23, 2003.

41. Memorial Obituary of Lafayette L. Patterson, Mar. 5, 1988; Mary Reeves, "90-year-old in March of Dimes Walkathon," *Montgomery Advertiser-Journal*, Apr. 1, 1978, 3; E. J. Parkins, "Ex-Raleighite to be recognized in Congress," *Raleigh Times*, May 25, 1978, 5-B.

42. Memorial Obituary; Parkins, *Raleigh Times*; Al Fox, "Whatever happened to Lafayette Patterson," News clipping in Gov. Patterson's files, newspaper and date unknown.

43. Parkins, *Raleigh Times*; "Funeral To Be Held Day He Was To Wed," News clipping in Gov. Patterson's files, newspaper and date unknown.

44. Interview with Gov. Patterson, Feb. 5, 2004.

Chapter 3, Across the Chattahoochee

1. Interview with Gov. Patterson, Oct. 2, 2002; Shelton Foss, "Alabama's 'boy governor,'" *Montgomery Advertiser* and *Alabama Journal-Old Newsboys Day*, Dec. 6, 1988, 5.

2. Interview with Gov. Patterson, Dec. 13, 2002.

3. Margaret Anne Barnes, *The Tragedy and Triumph of Phenix City, Alabama* (Macon, GA; Mercer University Press, 1998), 8, 11.

4. Ibid., 11, 12; Interview with Gov. Patterson, Dec. 13, 2002.

5. Barnes, 13–15.

6. Barnes, 13; Hugh W. Sparrow, "Sinful as red-haired siren, screwy as Brooklyn Dodg-

ers," *Birmingham News*, July 6, 1954, 13; Gene Wortsman, "Gambling Not Easy, 'Boss' Shepherd Says," *Birmingham Post-Herald*, July 24, 1954, 1.

7. Interview with Gov. Patterson, Oct. 2, 2002.

8. Ibid.

9. Ibid.

10. Brief bios of Albert L. Patterson, undated; A statement about Albert Patterson appearing in *Who's Who in the South and Southwest*. Docs were in Albert Patterson's office files at time of his murder in 1954.

11. Interview with Gov. Patterson, Oct. 25, 2002. FDR was the last president inaugurated on March 4 and the first inaugurated on January 20 four years later.

12. Interview with Gov. Patterson, Oct. 2, 2002.

13. Ibid.; Oral History with Gov. Patterson, Oct. 19, 2001.

14. Foss, "Alabama's 'boy governor,'" 5.

15. Interview with Gov. Patterson, Oct. 2, 2002.

16. Ibid.

17. Interview with Dorothy Johnson, Phenix City, AL, Sept. 26, 2003.

18. Ibid.

19. Ibid.

20. Interview with Gov. Patterson, Oct. 2, 2002.

21. Ibid.

22. Patterson Oral History, Oct. 19, 2001; Barnes, 14.

23. Ibid.

24. Ibid.

25. Interview with Gov. Patterson, Oct. 2, 2002.

26. Ibid.; Central HS report cards, John Patterson, 1936–37, 1937–38, 1938–39.

27. Interview with Gov. Patterson, Oct. 2, 2002.

28. Ibid.; Ray Jenkins, "Patterson Praises Phenix City Spirit," *Alabama Journal*, Oct. 5, 1961, 1.

29. Interview with Mrs. Geraldine Blair, Oct. 1, 2003.

30. Interview with Dr. Nancy Smith, Aug. 27, 2003.

31. Oral History, Gov. Patterson, Apr. 3, 2002.

32. Interview with Gov. Patterson, Oct. 2, 2002.

33. Oral History, Gov. Patterson, Oct. 19, 2001.

34. Interview with Gov. Patterson, Oct. 2, 2002.

35. Clancy Lake, "'How long, oh Lord? How long?' was Patterson's cry . . . ," *Birmingham News*, June 20, 1954, 7c.

36. Ibid.

37. Barnes, 17, 18.

Chapter 4, March to the Sound of the Guns

1. Interview with Gov. Patterson, Oct. 19, 2001.

2. Ibid.; Statement by Gov. Patterson, June 29, 2003.

3. Statement by Gov. Patterson, June 1, 2004.

4. Ltr to his mother, Feb. 6, 1942.

5. Ltr to his father, June 7, 1942.

6. Ltr to his parents, Aug. 23, 1942.

7. Interview, Oct. 19, 2001; War Department I.D., AGO Form No. 65-1, 2d Lt. John M. Patterson, Sept. 1942. (The I.D. describes his eyes as brown, while others describe them as blue. He has hazel eyes.)

8. Interview, Oct. 19, 2001.

9. Statement by Gov. Patterson, Feb. 28, 2004.

10. Interview, Oct. 19, 2001.

11. Ibid.; Rick Atkinson, *An Army at Dawn: The War in North Africa, 1942–1943* (New York: Henry Holt and Company, LLC, 2002), 195.

12. Interview, Oct. 19, 2001; Geoffrey Perret, *Eisenhower* (New York: Random House, 1999), 213–17.

13. Interview, June 1, 2004; Christopher Chant, *Compendium of Armaments and Military Hardware* (London: Routledge & Kegan Paul, 1987), 97–99.

14. Interview, Oct. 19, 2001.

15. Ibid.; Interview, June 1, 2004.

16. Interview, Oct. 19, 2001.

17. Ibid.; The Honorable John Patterson, "Starting Off on the Right Foot," *Field Artillery*, Oct. 1990, 31–34.

18. Patterson, "Starting Off on the Right Foot," 31–32.

19. Interview, Oct. 19, 2001.

20. Atkinson, *An Army at Dawn*, 402.

21. Statement by Gov. Patterson, June 14, 2004; Journal, 1st Bn 17th Regt, Mar. 1943.

22. Atkinson, *An Army at Dawn*, 434; Statement by Gov. Patterson, June 14, 2004; Journal, 1st Bn 17th FA Regt, Mar. 1943.

23. Atkinson, 402.

24. Ibid.; Interview, Oct. 19, 2001.

25. Interview, Oct. 19, 2001.

26. Tapes with Gov. Patterson, June 1 and 12, 2004.

27. William O. Darby with William H. Baumer, *Darby's Rangers: We Led the Way* (New York: Ballantine Books, 1980), 80–94; Atkinson, 431–43.

Chapter 5, Long Road Home from El Guettar

1. Interview, Oct. 19, 2001.

2. Ibid.; Atkinson, 442; The Honorable John Patterson, "Starting Off on the Right Foot," *Field Artillery*, Oct. 1990, 31–34.

3. Atkinson, 442; Patterson, 33.

4. Patterson, 33.

5. William O. Darby and William H. Baumer, *Darby's Rangers: We Led the Way* (Novato, CA: Presidio, 1980), 91.

6. Tape with Gov. Patterson, June 1, 2004.

7. Ibid.

8. Patterson, 33.

9. Atkinson, 442–43.

10. Patterson, 33.

11. Interview, Oct. 19, 2001.

12. Tape, June 1, 2004.

13. Tape, June 12, 2004.

14. Tape, June 1, 2004.

15. Staff writer, "Yanks, British 8th Army Meet; Allies Swing North After Rommel," *The Stars and Stripes*, Africa, Fri., Apr. 9, 1943, 1.

16. Ltr, 1st Lt. Patterson to his father, Apr. 5, 1943.

17. Tape, June 12, 2004.

18. Ibid.; Joseph R. Couch, "WWII Soldier Recalls Wine A Spoil of War," *Alexandria Gazette*, Dec. 27, 1979, 6.

19. A Combat Record of the 17th Field Artillery Gp, Aug. 15, 1945, 5; Atkinson, 536–37.

20. Story by Lt. Col. Joseph Couch at Reunion of the 17th Field Artillery Assn, Fort Bragg, NC, 1985.

21. A Combat Record of the 17th Field Artillery Gp, Aug. 15, 1945.
22. Tape, June 1, 2004.
23. Interview, Oct. 19, 2001.
24. Ibid., Journal, 1st Battalion, 17th Field Artillery Gp, 1943.
25. "The 666 Days," a combat record of the 17th F.A. Gp, undated.
26. Tape with Gov. Patterson, June 12, 2004.
27. Ibid.
28. Interview, Oct. 19, 2001; Ltrs, Lt. Patterson to his mother, Nov. 27 and 30, 1943.
29. Ltrs, Lt. Patterson to his mother, Nov. 30, 1943 and Dec. 27, 1943.
30. Tape with Gov. Patterson, Dec. 13, 2002.
31. Ibid.
32. Interview, Oct. 19, 2001.
33. S.O. No. 93, Certificate of Promotion, North African Theater of Operations, Apr. 5, 1944; Eric Morris, *Circles of Hell: The War in Italy, 1943–1945* (New York: Crown Publishers, Inc., 1993), 279, 313–25, 335–39.
34. Patterson tape, June 1, 2004.
35. Historical Report, HQ 17th Field Artillery Bn, May 1944.
36. Patterson tapes, June 1 and 12, 2004.
37. Patterson tape, June 12, 2004.
38. Ibid.
39. Ibid.; A combat history of the 17th FA in WWII, undated.
40. Combat history of the 17th FA; Morris, *Circles of Hell*, 364–65.
41. Combat history of the 17th FA.
42. Ibid.
43. Ibid.; Tape with Gov. Patterson, June 12, 2004.
44. Ltr, Capt. Patterson to his mother, Nov. 29, 1944.
45. Carlo D'Este, *Patton: A Genius for War* (New York: HarperCollins, 1995), 703–712.
46. Interview, Oct. 19, 2001.

Chapter 6, Another Lawyer in the Family

1. Interview, author with Jack Patterson, Sept. 25, 2003.
2. Interview, author with John Patterson, Oct. 19, 2001; Final decree, *Gladys Broadwater Patterson v. John M. Patterson*, Circuit Court of Tuscaloosa County, AL, Jan. 28, 1946.
3. Interview with Patterson, Oct. 19, 2001.
4. Bob Ingram, "UA Friendship Leads To Job With Patterson," *Tuscaloosa Graphic*, Oct. 9, 1958.
5. Interview with Patterson, Oct. 19, 2001.
6. Interview, author with Joe Robertson, June 29, 2003.
7. Interview with Patterson, Oct. 19, 2001.
8. Ibid.
9. Interview, author with Maurice Patterson, June 29, 2003.
10. Interview with Jack Patterson, Sept. 25, 2003.
11. Interview with Patterson, Oct. 19, 2001.
12. Interview with Jack Patterson, Sept. 25, 2003.
13. Interview with Patterson, Oct. 19, 2001.
14. Statement by John Patterson, Aug. 13, 2004.
15. Ibid.; Barnes, *The Tragedy and Triumph of Phenix City, Alabama*, 54–74.
16. Interview with Jack Patterson, Sept. 25, 2003.
17. Barnes, *The Tragedy and Triumph of Phenix City, Alabama*, 54–74.
18. Ibid., 49.
19. Ibid., 74.
20. Interview with Jack Patterson, Sept. 25, 2003; Interview with John Patterson, Oct. 2, 2002.
21. Barnes, 75, 76; Interview, Oct. 19, 2001.
22. Barnes, 78–88.
23. Interview with John Patterson, Dec. 13, 2002. Also see Barnes, 106–113, for complete account of the story.
24. Ibid.
25. Ibid.
26. Clancy Lake, "Calls allege Ferrell oft-mentioned 'boss,'" *Birmingham News*, July 22, 1954, 1.
27. Douglass Cater, "The Wide-open Town On the Chattahoochee," *Reporter*, Feb. 24, 1955, 22–27.
28. Lake, *Birmingham News*, July 22, 1954, 1.
29. Cater, *Reporter*, Feb. 24, 1955, 23; Website, "Phenix City, the Fight For the Soul of a Small Southern Town," Bouldree, University of Florida Education, Fall 2002; Edwin Strickland and Gene Wortsman, *Phenix City* (Birmingham, AL: Vulcan Press, 1955), 223–27.

30. Barnes, *The Tragedy and Triumph of Phenix City, Alabama*, 91–93.

31. Ibid., 98–100.

32. Lake, *Birmingham News*, July 22, 1954, 1.

33. Clancy Lake and Ed Strickland, "Wire tap discs tell story of plot reaching capital," *Birmingham News*, A1, A2; Strickland and Wortsman, *Phenix City*, 125.

34. "Wire taps allege czar no Patterson admirer," *Birmingham News*, July 21, 1954, 6.

35. Interview with Patterson, Oct. 19, 2001.

36. Interview with Fred Rothstein, May 1, 2004.

37. Interview with Patterson, Oct. 19, 2001.

38. Ibid.

39. Ibid.

40. Ibid.

41. Ibid.

42. Report of Birth, Barbara Louise Patterson, by American consulate in Frankfurt, Ger., June 15, 1953; Interview with Barbara Louise Patterson by author, Aug. 21, 2002.

43. Ltr, Maj. John M. Patterson to the Adjutant General, Dept. of the Army, subj: Relief from Active Duty, Aug. 8, 1953; Interview with Patterson, Oct. 19, 2001.

Chapter 7, No More Darkness, No More Night

1. Interview with Governor Patterson, Jan. 18, 2002.

2. Ibid.; Interview with Maurice Patterson, June 29, 2003; Interview with Jack Patterson, Sept. 25, 2003.

3. Strickland and Wortsman, *Phenix City*, 206, 207; Barnes, *The Tragedy and the Triumph of Phenix City, Alabama*, 100, 101.

4. Interview with Patterson, Oct. 2, 2002; Barnes, 101.

5. Interview with Patterson, Oct. 19, 2001; Jack Patterson email, subj: 1952 Democratic Convention, Aug. 11, 2004.

6. Jack Patterson email, Aug. 11, 2004.

7. James Free, "Kefauver suggests state set up crime commission to down Phenix rackets," *Birmingham News*, July 22, 1954, 50.

8. Barnes, 121.

9. "Efforts of Blind Negro Fail To Save Russell Judge's Life," *Montgomery Advertiser*, June 17, 1956, 1.

10. Interview with Patterson, Oct. 2, 2002.

11. Barnes, 121, 122; Strickland and Wortsman, 189, 190; Certificate of Incorporation, Russell Betterment Association and the Gall Club, signed and notarized on Oct. 26, 1951, and filed with Judge of Probate on Oct. 27, 1951.

12. William Slocum, "America's Wickedest City," *Look*, Oct. 5, 1954, 33–37.

13. Barnes, 123.

14. Ibid., 125, 126; Slocum, 36.

15. Alan Grady, *When Good Men Do Nothing: The Assassination of Albert Patterson* (Tuscaloosa: University of Alabama Press, 2003), 94.

16. Barnes, 128.

17. Slocum, 36.

18. Roland Joseph Page, "The *Columbus Ledger* and the Phenix City Story: On Winning a Pulitzer Prize," Graduate Thesis, Florida State Univ., Dec. 1966, 48.

19. Interview with Jack Patterson, Sept. 25, 2003; Barnes, 133, 134.

20. Ibid.; Strickland and Wortsman, 192.

21. Barnes, 136, 137.

22. Interview with Patterson, Apr. 3, 2002.

23. Barnes, 137.

24. Barnes, 143; Strickland and Wortsman, 190.

25. Barnes, 143; Interview with Patterson, Apr. 3, 2002.

26. Interview with Patterson; Strickland and Wortsman, 191.

27. Barnes, 154; Strickland and Wortsman, 191.

28. Strickland and Wortsman, 191; Slocum, 36; Interview with Patterson.

29. Interview with Patterson.

30. Ibid.; Fred Taylor, "Porter and Patterson slug in attorney general race," *Birmingham News*, May 23, 1954.

31. Interview with Gov. Patterson, Oct. 2, 2002.

32. Interview with Patterson, Apr. 3, 2002; Page thesis, 77.

33. Interview with Patterson; Tel. conversation with Gov. Patterson by author, Sept. 9, 2004.

34. Bob Ingram, "Commentary," *Montgomery Independent*, Aug. 8, 2002, 5.

35. Interview with Patterson.

36. Page thesis, 78; John M. Patterson, as told

to Furman Bisher, "I'll Get the Gangs That Killed My Father!" *Saturday Evening Post*, Nov. 27, 1954, 62.

37. Page thesis, 78.

38. Ibid.

39. Barnes, 160.

40. Emmett Perry, "The Story Behind Phenix City: The Struggle for Law in a Modern Sodom," *American Bar Association Journal*, Dec. 1956, 1149.

41. Page thesis, 79; George E. Sims, *The Little Man's Big Friend: James E. Folsom in Alabama Politics 1946–1958* (Tuscaloosa: The University of Alabama Press, 1985), 138; Carl Grafton and Anne Permaloff, *Big Mules and Branchheads: James E. Folsom and Political Power in Alabama* (Athens: The University of Georgia Press, 1985), 176.

42. Grafton and Permaloff, *Big Mules and Branchheads*, 175; Sims, *The Little Man's Big Friend*, 138, 139.

43. Patterson, "I'll Get the Gangs That Killed My Father," 62, 63; Page thesis, 79.

44. Patterson, 63.

45. Page thesis, 79.

46. Strickland and Wortsman, 156–158.

47. Ibid.

48. Ibid.; Interview with Gov. Patterson, Oct. 19, 2001.

49. Douglass Cater, "The Wide-open Town On the Chattahoochee," *Reporter*, Feb. 24, 1955, 22.

50. Interview with Patterson; Barnes, 165, 166.

51. Ibid.

52. Perry, "The Story Behind Phenix City," 1149.

53. Ibid.; Cater, "The Wide-open Town," 22.

54. Statement by John Patterson, Sept 27, 2004.

55. Patterson, "I'll Get the Gangs That Killed My Father," 60; Cater, 22, 23; Barnes, 187.

56. Statement by Patterson, Sept 27, 2004.

57. Ibid.

58. Ibid.; Barnes, 188, 189.

59. Statement by Patterson, Sept 27, 2004.

60. John Patterson, as told to Erin Simpson, "A story 50 years in the making," *Columbus Ledger-Enquirer*, June 18, 2004, A8.

61. Statement by Patterson, Sept 27, 2004; Barnes, 189.

62. Barnes, 190.

63. Simpson, "A story 50 years in the making," A8.

Chapter 8, Big Trouble in River City

1. Interview with Gov. Patterson, Apr. 17, 2002.

2. Ibid.; Interview with Jack Patterson, Sept. 25, 2003.

3. Interview with William Benton, Nov. 19, 2003; Barnes, *The Tragedy and the Triumph*, 200.

4. Interview with Morgan Reynolds, July 29, 2004; Interview with Gov. Patterson, Apr. 17, 2002.

5. Interview with William Benton, Nov. 19, 2003.

6. Interview with Bob Ingram, Jan. 7, 2003.

7. Grady, *When Good Men Do Nothing*, 84, 85.

8. Fred Taylor, "John Patterson is 'available' for post won by slain father," *Birmingham News*, June 21, 1954.

9. Clancy Lake and Ed Strickland, "Patterson laid to rest, a rallying point in fight against crime," *Birmingham News*, June 22, 1954, 1.

10. Ibid.

11. Ibid.

12. Andrew Tully, Scripps-Howard staff writer, "Son Seeking U.S. Aid in Killer Hunt," *Birmingham Post-Herald*, June 25, 1954, 1.

13. Ibid.

14. "Sykes Bars Solicitor Ferrell From Patterson Murder Probe, *Birmingham Post-Herald*, June 25, 1954, 1.

15. "Patterson Murder Spurs State To Crush Phenix City Vice," *Alabama*, June 25, 1954, 5.

16. Martin Waldron, "Grand Jury Findings Today May Link Killing, Vote Theft," *Birmingham Post-Herald*, June 25, 1954, 1.

17. Barnes, *The Tragedy and the Triumph*, 209–10.

18. Ibid., "Sykes Bars Solicitor Ferrell From Patterson Murder Probe," *Birmingham Post-Herald*, June 25, 1954, 1.

19. Fred Taylor, "Demos ponder whether to call special election or name Patterson successor," *Birmingham News*, June 20, 1954, 1A.

20. "Pernicious Practice," *Alabama*, Aug. 13, 1954, 5.

21. "Phenix Vice Fight Lost 'Til Law Officers Ousted," *Birmingham News*, July 21, 1954, 2A.

22. Ibid.; Ray Jenkins, "Public Feeling Brought Drastic Steps To Track Down Patterson's Murderer," *Sunday Ledger-Enquirer (Columbus, GA)*, Jan. 2, 1955, C4.

23. "Demand For Murder Solution Rises to An Impatient Pitch," *Alabama*, July 23, 1954, 5.

24. Ibid.

25. "Nominee," *Alabama*, July 9, 1954, 7.

26. Interview with Gov. Patterson, Apr. 3, 2002.

27. "Nominee," *Alabama*, July 9, 1954, 7.

28. Interview with Gov. Patterson, Apr. 3, 2002.

29. Tom Sellers, "Patterson Martyred in Justice's Cause," *Sunday Ledger-Enquirer*, Jan. 2, 1955, C1.

30. "Action At Last?" *Alabama*, July 30, 1954, 6.

31. "Demand For Murder Solution Rises To An Impatient Pitch," *Alabama*, July 23, 1954, 5.

32. Interview, author with George MacDonald Gallion, Jan. 25, 2002; News release, Bill Pryor, Alabama Atty Gen, "Macdonald Gallion Tells of Service to State; Former Attorney General Celebrates 89th Birthday," Apr. 10, 2002.

33. Ibid.

34. Ibid.

35. Barnes, 210, 211.

36. "Garrett Bonded In Vote Fraud, Faces August Sanity Hearing," *Alabama*, July 16, 1954, 5.

37. Ibid., 6.

38. Ibid.

39. "Phenix City clerk out on $1500 bond after damaging News lensman's camera," *Birmingham News*, Aug. 12, 1954, 14.

40. Dr. John Eidsmore, *Legalized Gambling, America's Bad Bet* (Lafayette, LA: Huntington House Publishers, 1994), 1–6.

41. Ibid.; "History of T. G. Jones School of Law," Faulkner University, Internet 2004.

42. Interview with Benson, Nov. 19, 2005; Eidsmore, 5.

43. Grady, 164; Interview with John Patterson.

44. Interview with Benson, Nov. 19, 2005.

45. Ibid.

46. Ibid.

Chapter 9, Bittersweet Refrain in Birmingham

1. Erin Simpson, "A Story 50 Years in the Making," *Columbus Ledger-Enquirer*, June 23, 2003, 1.

2. Gordon Cooksey, "New Phenix City," *Ledger-Enquirer East Alabama Today*, Apr. 5, 1979, 6; Alan Grady, "When Good Men Do Nothing: The Murder of Albert Patterson," *Alabama Heritage*, Winter 1996, 6–21.

3. "Not Guilty," *Alabama*, May 13, 1955, 13.

4. Ibid.

5. Grady, *When Good Men Do Nothing*, 221, 227.

6. Grady, *When Good Men Do Nothing*, 31, 32.

7. Interview, Gov. Patterson by author, Apr. 3, 2002.

8. Ibid.

9. Edwin Strickland, "Mathews' cheerful smile fades as Deason asks the questions," *Birmingham News*, Mar. 5, 1955, 12.

10. Affidavit by Johnny Frank Griffin, Sept. 25, 1954.

11. Clancy Lake, "The state rests; here's the evidence prosecution offered against Fuller," *Birmingham News*, Feb. 27, 1955, 17-A.

12. Ibid.

13. Ibid.

14. Patterson Interview, Apr. 3, 2002.

15. Ibid.

16. Ibid.

17. Patterson Interview, Apr. 3, 2002.

18. Arnold Snow, "State Launches Strong Onslaught Against Alibi Claims For Fuller," *Alabama Journal*, Mar. 8, 1955, 1; Editorial, "The Patterson Murder—XIX," *Montgomery Advertiser*, Mar. 8, 1955, 4-A.

19. Ibid.

20. Patterson Interview, Apr. 3, 2002.

21. Gerry Lee, "Fuller Gets Himself Crossed Up Three Times On Witness Stand," *Montgomery Advertiser*, Mar. 6, 1955, 1-A.

22. Harry Cook, "Garrett's 'death night' dinner party here again scrutinized," *Birmingham News*, July 31, 1954, 2.

23. "Mathews Says Victim Offered Defendant Post," *Montgomery Advertiser*, Mar. 5, 1955, 7-A.

24. Ibid.

25. Patterson Interview.

26. Ibid.; "Not Guilty," *Alabama*, May 13, 1955, 13; Telephone conversation with Judge Patterson, Mar. 16, 2005.

27. *Alabama*, May 13, 1955, 13.

28. News clippings, "State law group disbars Arch Ferrell," undated; "Arch Ferrell Is Disbarred From Practice," undated; "Bar Reviews, Move To Oust Arch Ferrell," Apr. 19, 1955. loc. in Sheriff Lamar Murphy's files.

29. "Ferrell Arrested After Auto Chase," *Montgomery Advertiser*, Aug. 4, 1957; Ferrell Takes Mental Tests After Two Tiffs," *Montgomery Advertiser*, May 27, 1958, 1.

30. *Montgomery Advertiser*, May 27, 1958, 1.

31. Interview with William Benton, Nov. 19, 2003.

32. Patterson Interview, Apr. 3, 2002; Grady, *When Good Men Do Nothing*, 227.

33. "Slapped In Jail At Phenix City After Surrender," *Tuscaloosa News*, Oct. 11, 1955, 1; "Si Garrett Surrenders To Face Murder Count," *Valley Daily Times-News*, Oct. 11, 1955, 1.

34. Patterson Interview, Apr. 3, 2002; "Psychiatrist Doubts Garrett's Sanity," *Tri-Cities*, Oct. 21, 1955, 1.

35. Ray Jenkins, "Patterson in PC 'Working on Case,'" *Columbus Ledger*, Oct. 21, 1955, 1.

36. Patterson Interview, Dec. 13, 2002.

37. Edwin Strickland, "Garrett trial decision up to son of victim," *Birmingham News*, Oct. 10, 1958, 1.

38. "Si Garrett Murder Indictment Dropped," *Birmingham Post-Herald*, July 16, 1963, 1.

39. Patterson Interview, Apr. 3, 2002.

40. "The Patterson Murder-II," *Montgomery Advertiser*, Feb. 15, 1955.

41. Patterson Interview, Apr. 3, 2002; Memorandum by Gov. John Patterson, July 10, 1959.

42. Grady, 207; Katherine McDuffie, "Mrs. Fuller Sends Out Word That She Has 'No Comment,'" *Columbus Enquirer*, Mar. 12, 1955, 1.

43. "Fuller taken to Kilby to begin sentence," *Birmingham News*, June 17, 1955, 1.

44. "Si Garrett May Face Trial As Fuller Loses Appeal," *Birmingham Post-Herald*, Jan. 12, 1960, 1.

45. Bob Ingram, "Fuller Vows To Seek Patterson Slayer," *Montgomery Advertiser*, June 17, 1956, 1.

46. Ltrs, Avon Fuller to Grover Hall, June 20, 1955 and June 16, 1956; Ltr, Grover Hall to Avon Fuller, July 19, 1955; Ltr, Grover Hall to Albert Fuller, Jan. 14, 1959.

47. Sid Thomas, "Pensive Albert Fuller longs to be free," *Birmingham News*, June 17, 1956, 17-A.

48. Bob Brown, "Fuller Appears Sure of Freedom" and "Will Appeal Show New Facts," *Columbus Ledger*, Nov. 13 and 14, 1956, 5.

49. "Albert Fuller Waits, Hopes," *Montgomery Advertiser*," July 13, 1957, 1.

50. Memorandum by Atty Gen John Patterson, May 2, 1957.

51. Patterson Interview, Apr. 3, 2002.

52. Ibid.; Ltr, Johnny Benefield to C.O. "Head" Revel, Jan. 1, 1957.

53. See note above.

54. Patterson Interview, Apr. 3, 2002; Memo to John Patterson from J. Noel Baker, subj: Further information from John Benefield, Jan. 24, 1957.

55. Grady, 226, 227.

56. Memorandum by Gov. Patterson, July 10, 1959.

57. Ibid.

58. Patterson Interview, Apr. 3, 2002.

59. Ibid.; Grady, 227; Barnes, 307.

60. Patterson Interview, Apr. 3, 2002; Grady, 227; "Ex-Convict Fuller Hospitalized, Has Had 3 Operations on Brain," *Montgomery Advertiser*, date unknown.

61. See note above.

62. See note above.

63. Patterson Interview, Apr. 3, 2002.

64. Ibid.

65. Ibid.

66. "Racketeers Trying For Control in Phenix, John Patterson Says," *Alabama Journal*, Mar. 23, 1955, 1.

Chapter 10, New Blood and Old Political Wars

1. Hugh Sparrow, "Patterson pledges his office will help prosecute men accused of slaying father," *Birmingham News*, Jan. 18, 1955, 1; "Patterson Takes Office For Which Father Died," *Birmingham Post-Herald*, Jan. 17, 1955, 1.

2. Sparrow, Jan. 18, 1955, 1.

3. "John Has Bright Future," *Phenix Citizen*,

Sept. 29, 1955; Interview with John Patterson by author, Apr. 17, 2002.

4. Ibid.

5. Ibid.; Sparrow, Jan. 18, 1955, 1.

6. "Patterson Warns PC Of Rackets Comeback," *Columbus Ledger*, Jan. 17, 1955, 1.

7. "Patterson Says Folsom Will Do The Right Thing," *Columbus Ledger*, Jan. 19, 1955, 1.

8. "Mobile Groups Hear State Attorney General," *Mobile Register*, Nov. 10, 1955, 6B; James W. Smith, Jr., "Attorney General Warns Citizens To Run City, Or Others Will Take Over," *Gadsden Times*, Nov. 1955, 1.

9. "Slain Albert Patterson Gets LaGuardia Award," *Birmingham Post-Herald*, Dec. 1, 1955; 1; Frederick M. Winship, "Widow of Sin City Victim Warns All to Vote At Every Opportunity," *Bridgeport Post (Conn)*, Dec. 12, 1955, 1.

10. Ray Jenkins, "Patterson Aides Eye Phenix City Elections," *Columbus Ledger*, Sept. 19, 1955, 1.

11. "Patterson Fears Bid by 'Rackets,'" *Columbus Ledger*, Sept. 20.

12. Ray Jenkins, "Joy and Despair Separated By Closed Courthouse Doors," *Columbus Ledger*, Sept. 20, 1955, 1.

13. "Mims Says Patterson 'Scared Voters Away,'" *Columbus Ledger*, Sept. 21, 1955.

14. Patterson Interview, Apr. 17, 2002.

15. Grady, 229–31; "Mrs. Albert Patterson sues CBS for Studio One TV Show," *Birmingham News*, Nov. 29, 1955; "The Phenix City Story Is Arousing Excitement," *Tri-Cities*, Oct. 13, 1955.

16. Edwin Strickland, "Patterson denies he's a resident of Georgia," *Birmingham News*, Sept. 29, 1954, 1.

17. News clipping in Sheriff Murphy's scrapbook entitled "Machine Is Attempting To Come Back," date unknown; Patterson Interview.

18. Interview with Jack Patterson.

19. Patterson Interview, Apr. 17, 2002; Grady, 228–29; "Phenix Janitor Gets State Job," *Montgomery Advertiser*, Nov. 11, 1955, 1; "Padgett 'Pay' Story Denied By Patterson," *Alabama Journal*, June 22, 1961, 1.

20. Mildred Grimes, "Turbulent Events, Far-Reaching Changes Swept Through Phenix City," *Montgomery Advertiser*, Dec. 31, 1955.

21. Tom Sellers, "All-America Award Gives Phenix Most Jubilant Day," *Sunday Ledger-Enquirer*, Jan. 8, 1956, D-2.

22. Ibid.

23. Grimes, *Montgomery Advertiser*, Dec. 31, 1955; "Two-Year Anniversary of Crusader's Murder," *Mobile Press-Register*, June 17, 1956, 1; "Racket Empire Appears Crushed In Phenix City," *Gadsden Times*, June 17, 1956, 1.

24. *South Magazine*, Oct. 1, 1956, 6, 7; "Gov. Folsom, Lt. Gov. Hardwick Clash Over Auditing Issue," *Opelika Daily News*, Oct. 18, 1956, 1.

25. *South Magazine*, Dec. 10, 1956, 7.

26. Patterson Interview.

27. Ibid.

28. "Jones Upholds Payment Block," *Gadsden Times*, Sept. 26, 1956, 1; "Jones Upholds Road Work Payment Ban," *Birmingham Post-Herald*, Sept. 26, 1956, 1; *South Magazine*, Oct. 8, 1956, 7.

29. *Birmingham Post-Herald*, Sept. 26, 1956; Bob Ingram, "Paterson Delays Cash For Glencoe," *Montgomery Advertiser*, Mar. 3, 1957, 1.

30. "Supreme Court Gets State Purchasing Method Test Case," *Dothan Eagle*, Dec. 21, 1956, 1; "Under His Skin," *Birmingham Post-Herald*, Sept. 23, 1956.

31. Bob Ingram, "Folsom's Jubilant, Patterson Wounded," *Advertiser-Journal*, Feb. 24, 1957; Bob Lee, "Folsom Wins Glencoe Paving Verdict," *Columbus Ledger*, Feb. 25, 1957, 1A; Remer Tyson and Herschel Cribb, "Patterson, Reform Bloc Score in '56," *Ledger-Enquirer*, Jan. 1, 1957.

32. Patterson Interview.

33. Ibid.

34. Ibid.; "John Halts Folsom Project," *Columbus Ledger*, Sept. 7, 1956; Bob Lee, "Folsom's Free-Spending Reign Blasted," Sept. 10, 1956.

35. Patterson Interview.

36. Ibid.; Frank Sikora, "Deal in mid-50s nearly deprived state of millions," *Birmingham News*, June 10, 1984, 6A.

37. See note above.

38. See note above.

39. See note above.

40. Patterson Interview.

41. Ibid.; Frye Gaillard, *Cradle of Freedom: Alabama and the Movement That Changed America* (Tuscaloosa: The University of Alabama Press,

2004), 79; Paul Hogan, "A governor seen Demo '60 leader," *Birmingham News*, Mar. 22, 1957, 39.

42. Patterson Interview; "Patterson Fights Loan Sharks," *Anniston Star*, Sept 1955, 1.

43. Patterson Interview.

44. Patterson Interview.

45. Ibid.; "Attorney General Patterson's Loan Shark Victory," *Montgomery Advertiser*, Sept. 26, 1955.

46. "Loan Company Ordered To Halt High Charges," Associated Press news release, Sept. 23, 1955.

47. "Loan Firms Face Widened Crusade," *Selma Times-Journal*, Nov. 15, 1957; Clarke Stallworth, *Birmingham Post-Herald*, Nov. 15, 1957.

48. "Senator Declares Alabama Nation's Small Loan Capital," *Tuscaloosa News*, Sept. 19, 1957; "Alabama Labeled 'Loan Shark State,'" *Dothan Eagle*, Sept. 19, 1957, 1.

49. "Patterson Testifies At Loan Firm Probe," *Huntsville Times*, Sept. 19, 1957; Patterson Interview.

50. "Finance Lobbyists To Appear Before Committee," *Tri-Cities Daily*, Sept. 20, 1957.

51. Clarke Stallworth, "Loan Situation Called 'Very Bad,'" *Birmingham Post-Herald*, Sept. 21, 1957.

52. Clarke Stallworth, "Military Digging Into Loan Problem," *Birmingham Post-Herald*, Jan. 31, 1958, 1.

53. "Acts To Keep State Records From Court," *Birmingham Post-Herald*, Feb. 21, 1958; Cody Hall, "Jim Is Seen As 'Off Base' By Lawyers," *Anniston Star*, Feb. 21, 1958, 1.

54. Patterson Interview.

55. "Guy Sparks Appointed For 'Loan Shark' Probe," *Anniston Star*, Dec. 14, 1951, 1; Patterson Interview.

56. Patterson Interview.

57. Interview with Jack Patterson; Gaillard, *Cradle of Freedom*, 80.

58. Patterson Interview.

59. Ibid.; GCH, Jr., "The Patterson Murder," *Montgomery Advertiser*, Mar. 8, 1955, 4-A.

60. Patterson Interview.

61. Grafton and Permaloff, *Big Mules and Branchheads*, 192–201; Patterson Interview.

62. Patterson Interview; Interview with John Patterson by Norman Lumpkin, oral history project, Tuskegee Institute History Series, May 22, 1973.

63. Patterson Interview.

64. Ibid.

65. Robert E. Baker, "Race Issue Ebb in Importance," *Washington Post*, Dec. 11, 1961.

66. See note above.

67. See note above.

68. Edwin Strickland, "Bus boycott and Lucy case among reasons," *Birmingham News*, June 1, 1966; "Attorney General Sets Action in Montgomery," *Anniston Star*, June 1, 1956; "NAACP To Respect Order, Leaders Say," *Gadsden Times*, June 2, 1956.

69. "Judge Jones Orders Halt Of Activity," *Birmingham Post-Herald*, June 2, 1956; "White Citizens Hail NAACP Ban," *Florence Times*, June 2, 1956; "Folsom Says Race Mixing In State Schools Is Out," *Mobile Press*, June 13, 1956.

70. "Hearing starts in suit to open NAACP books," *Birmingham News*, July 9, 1956; "Hearing Set For Expose of NAACP," *Selma Times-Journal*, July 6, 1956.

71. "NAACP Gets Ears Boxed For Defying Judge Jones," *Mobile Register*, July 27, 1956; "Alabama NAACP Facing $100,000 Deadline Today," *Advertiser-Journal*, July 30, 1956.

72. "NAACP Vows To Fight Order," *Birmingham Post-Herald*, July 27, 1956; "NAACP Snubs Order To List State Members," *Huntsville Times*, July 30, 1956.

73. "$100,000 Fine Against Group Allowed To Stand," *Birmingham Post-Herald*, July 31, 1956; "NAACP Asks High Court To Stay $100,000 Fine," *Decatur Daily*, July 31, 1956.

74. "Alabama, NAACP go before Supreme Court," *Birmingham News*, Jan. 16, 1958, 1A; James Free, "Ruling could end NAACP in South," *Birmingham News*, Jan. 17, 1958, 1A; Brief and Argument for Respondent, in the Supreme Court of the United States, October Term 1957, No. 91, *National Association for the Advancement of Colored People, A Corporation, Petitioner, v. State of Alabama, ex rel. John Patterson Attorney General*.

75. "Alabama Winds Up Arguments In NAACP Washington Hearing," *Huntsville Times*, Jan. 17, 1958; "Supreme Court Rulings 2 to 1 Against Negroes," *Gadsden Times*, July 2, 1958.

76. Patterson Interview.

77. "Alabama Success," *Southerner*, Nov. 28, 1957; Louis Kraar, "NAACP Setbacks," *Wall Street Journal*, Vol. CLI. No. 21, undated; "Last Ditch Battle Set By NAACP," *Montgomery Advertiser*, Sept. 23, 1957, 1.

78. Ibid.

79. Ibid.; Interview, author with Attorney Fred D. Gray, Apr. 30, 2003.

80. Gray Interview; Fred D. Gray, *Bus Ride to Justice* (NewSouth Books: Montgomery, 2002), 3, 4; Darlene Clark Hine, John A. Hannah Professor of History, Michigan State University, in Foreword to *Bus Ride to Justice*, ix.

81. "Bus Boycott Group Files Incorporation," *Alabama Journal*, June 6, 1956.

82. "Negroes Form New Group Replacing Banned NAACP," *Alabama Journal*, June 6, 1956.

83. Ibid.; Henry S. Bradsher, "Negroes Hail Bus Decision," *Alabama Journal*, Nov. 14, 1956; "Court Ruling Branded Unlawful Interference With Rights Of States," *Selma Times-Journal*, Nov. 14, 1956.

84. Gray, 112; "Boycott Probe Resumes Monday," *Tuscaloosa News*, July 28, 1957; "State Resumes Boycott Probe," *Dothan Eagle*, July 28, 1957; "Alabama Senate Approves Amendment Abolishing Nego-Dominated Macon," *Tri-Cities Daily*, Aug. 24, 1957.

85. Patterson Interview.

86. Gray, 115, 116; "Boycott Office Papers Seized," *Tuscaloosa News*, July 26, 1957; Stuart Culpepper, "Gray Weighing Legal Attack Against Seizure of Records," *Montgomery Advertiser*, July 31, 1957; "Court Issues Injunction In Boycott at Tuskegee," *Mobile Press*, Aug. 16, 1957.

87. "Tuskegee Negroes Form Racial Trade Organization," *Florence Times*, Aug. 7, 1957; Stuart Culpepper, "Negro Merchants Battle For Tuskegee Customers," *Montgomery Advertiser*, Aug. 7, 1957.

88. "Patterson Seeking Extended Injunction," *Phenix City Herald*, Jan. 31, 1958; Gray, *Bus Ride to Justice*, 115.

89. "TCA Defense Calls Attorney General In Boycott Trial," *Montgomery Advertiser*, Jan. 23, 1958.

90. "Judge Walton In 'No Rush' To Rule in Tuskegee Case," *Opelika Daily News*, Jan. 23, 1958; Gray, *Bus Ride to Justice*.

91. Patterson Interview.

92. "12 In Running In Governor's Race," *Clayton Record*, Jan. 31, 1958; Patterson Interview by Lumpkin, May 22, 1973; Ray Jenkins, "Albert Patterson Had Eye on Chair Son Seeks in Tomorrow's Election," *Columbus Ledger*, June 2, 1958.

93. "Hurry, Hurry! The Big Show's About To —," *Moulton Advertiser*, Jan. 24, 1957; "Patterson link with convicted loan firm made," *Birmingham News*, Dec. 12, 1957; Clarke Stallworth, "Smear Effort Won't Deter Doing Job," *Birmingham Post-Herald*, Dec. 12, 1957.

94. "Banking Chief Answers Patterson Smear Charge," *Birmingham Post-Herald*, Dec. 14, 1957; "Alabama: Of Interest," *South Magazine*, Dec. 16–30, 1957, 15, 16.

95. See note above; "Patterson 'Innocent Victim' in P.C. Bank," *Muscle Shoals Morning Sun*, Dec. 12, 1957.

96. *South*, Dec. 16–30, 1957, 16; Bob Lee, "Patterson Loan Firm Stock Ownership Deals Damaging Blow to His Campaign," *Columbus Ledger*, Dec. 16, 1957, 1-A.

Chapter 11, The Jingle, the Rumble, the Roar

1. "Patterson Enters Race As Governor Candidate," *Montgomery Advertiser*, Jan. 29, 1958, 1; Clarke Stallworth, "Patterson Enters Race Hits Graft," *Birmingham Post-Herald*, Jan. 29, 1958, 1.

2. "County Man Has Perfect Record Of Forecasting," *Pickens County Herald*, May 2, 1957.

3. "Patterson Leads Governor Poll," *South Magazine*, Sept. 23, 1957.

4. "Hurry, Hurry! The Big Show's About To—," *Moulton Advertiser*, Jan. 24, 1957; Patterson Interview, May 1, 2002.

5. Patterson Interview, Apr. 17, 2002; Clyde Bolton, "Patterson 'Considers' Running For Governor," *Gadsden Times*, Aug. 8, 1957, 1.

6. Patterson Interview, Apr. 17, 2002.

7. Bob Ingram, "Charlie Meriwether: A Success Story," *Montgomery Advertiser*, Mar. 12, 1961.

8. Ibid.

9. Patterson Interview, May 1, 2002.

10. Ibid.

11. Ibid.

12. Ibid.

13. Interview with Jack Patterson, Sept. 25, 2003; Interview with Maurice Patterson, June 29, 2003.

14. Grafton and Permaloff, *Big Mules and Branchheads*, 59.

15. Patterson Interview, May 1, 2002; Grafton and Permaloff, 7–9.

16. Patterson Interview, May 1, 2002.

17. Ibid.

18. Ibid.; Grafton and Permaloff, 56.

19. Patterson Interview; Interview, author with Carrie Gosdin, Feb. 10, 2003; George Prentice, "Patterson Opens Campaign With Vow Against NAACP," *Montgomery Advertiser*, Feb. 11, 1958; "New Site Rally Attracts 1500; Lanett Talk Set For Friday," *Phenix City Citizen*, Feb. 13, 1958, 1.

20. Prentice, *Montgomery Advertiser*, Feb. 11, 1958.

21. Ibid.; Interview, author with Judge Patterson, July 20, 2005.

22. Prentice, *Montgomery Advertiser*, Feb. 11, 1958; *Phenix City Citizen*, Feb. 13, 1958; Patterson Interview, Apr. 17, 2002.

23. Fred Taylor, *Birmingham News* staff writer, "Patterson promises $75 old age check," *Centreville Press*, Feb. 13, 1958, 1.

24. Ibid.; *Phenix City Citizen*, Feb. 13, 1958.

25. See note above; "Patterson Opens Campaign, Opposes School Integration," *Columbus Enquirer*, Feb. 11, 1958.

26. Prentice, *Montgomery Advertiser*, Feb. 11, 1958; Patterson Interview, May 1, 2002.

27. "Nobody's For John Patterson . . . But The People," *Greene County Democrat*, reprinted in the *Centreville Press*, Apr. 24, 1958.

28. Ibid.; Patterson Interview, May 1, 2002.

29. Millard Grimes, "Patterson Talks Sense at Rallies," *Sunday Ledger-Enquirer*, Mar. 16, 1958.

30. Ibid.; Stan Zuckerman, "Patterson Vows Vice Is Through," *Columbus Enquirer*, Mar. 14, 1958.

31. Grimes, *Sunday Ledger-Enquirer*, Mar. 16, 1958.

32. Ben Knight, "There's Nothing Wrong With A Little Entertainment In Gubernatorial Race," *Florence Times*, Mar. 25, 1958; "Entertainment Marks State Political Campaigns," *Tuscaloosa News*, June 1, 1958.

33. Ibid.

34. Patterson Interview, May 1, 2002.

35. "Attorney General John Patterson Spoke To Large Crowds in Hundreds of Alabama Cities," *Phenix-Girard Journal*, June 2, 1958; Patterson Interview.

36. "Patterson Keeps Tabs On Public," *Huntsville Times*, May 24, 1958.

37. Bob Ingram, "J Birds Looking For A Roost," *Montgomery Advertiser*, date unknown, 3B.

38. Ibid.

39. Grafton and Permaloff, *Big Mules and Branchheads*, 194; Carter, *Politics of Rage*, 84, 85.

40. Carter, 84.

41. Grafton and Permaloff, 194; Carter, 84, 85; "Shorty" Price, *Alabama Politics—Tell It Like It Is* (New York: Vantage Press, 1973), 139; "Political Mud Flies," *Muscle Shoals Sun*, Apr. 12, 1958.

42. Fred Taylor, "Wallace pledges full segregation," *Birmingham News*, Feb. 15, 1958; "The Negro Vote in Alabama," *Phenix City Citizen*, Apr. 24, 1958; Price, *Alabama Politics*, 140.

43. Interview, author with Gov. Patterson, July 20, 2005.

44. "The Negro Vote In Alabama," *Phenix City Citizen*, Apr. 24, 1958.

45. "Indians Support John Patterson For Governor," *Phenix City Citizen*, Apr. 10, 1958.

46. Bob Ingram, "Grand Dragon's Aid Story True, Says Patterson," *Montgomery Advertiser*, May 22, 1958.

47. Patterson Interview, May 1, 2002.

48. Interview, author with Carrie Gosdin, Feb. 10, 2003.

49. Ibid.

50. Tape, author with Patterson, Oct. 23, 2003.

51. Ibid.; Alabama Department of Archives and History, "Alabama's Supreme Court Chief Justices," May 10, 2002.

52. Bob Ingram, "10,000 In Scottsboro Hear Election Pleas," *Montgomery Advertiser*, Apr. 8, 1958.

53. Ibid.

54. Fred Taylor, "Todd, Faulkner get big ovations," *Birmingham News*, Apr. 8, 1958.

55. Ingram, *Montgomery Advertiser*, Apr. 8, 1958.

56. Fred Taylor, "Persons' withdrawal opens

up governor's race," *Birmingham News*, 1957; Hugh Sparrow, "Gubernatorial race appears wide open," *Birmingham News*, Jan. 26, 1958; Rex Thomas, "Segregation Spotlighted By All Gubernatorial Candidates," *Tri-Cities Daily*, Apr. 8, 1958.

57. "Wallace Has Big Lead In New Poll," *Hartselle Enquirer*, May 1, 1958; Bob Ingram, "Ingram Finds It Is A Wallace-Faulkner-Patterson Race In Tennessee Valley," *Advertiser-Journal*, May 1, 1951.

58. Ingram, *Advertiser-Journal*, May 1, 1958; "Crowd of 7,000 Cheers For John," *Phenix City Citizen*, Apr. 24, 1958.

59. Bob Ingram, "Two Candidates Change Their Style," *Advertiser-Journal*, Apr. 27, 1958.

60. Bob Ingram, "Three-Way Battle Shapes Up For Governor Runoff Spots," *Advertiser-Journal*, Apr. 13, 1958.

61. Associated Press, "Wallace Given New Challenge For Debate," *Mobile Press*, Apr. 12, 1958; "Schedule Conflicts Force Wallace To Decline Debate," *Montgomery Advertiser*, Apr. 11, 1958.

62. Clarke Stallworth, "People Apparently Believe What Patterson Tells Them," *Birmingham Post-Herald*, Apr. 22, 1958.

63. Ibid.

64. Ibid.

65. "60 Years in Review: Democratic Gubernatorial Elections in Alabama," *Alabama Magazine*, Mar. 1982, 12, 13; "Runoff For Governor Rare Thing In Alabama Politics," reprinted from *Birmingham News*, *Clayton Record*, May 16, 1958.

66. "Faulkner Studies Action In Gubernatorial Runoff," *Advertiser-Journal*, May 8, 1958.

67. "Judge Wallace Promise To Lay The Facts On The Line In Second Primary," *Labor Journal*, May 16, 1958; "Wallace Scores Patterson As Weak On Segregation," *Jackson County Sentinel*, May 15, 1958.

68. "Patterson Thanks Voters in State," *Atmore Advance*, May 15, 1958; "Patterson Repeats Segregation Stand," *Tuscaloosa News*, Apr. 28, 1958.

69. Patterson Interview, Oct. 2, 2002; Bob Ingram, "Charlie Meriwether: A Success Story," *Montgomery Advertiser*, Mar. 12, 1961.

70. Roger Thames, News radio-TV editor, "First Part of 'King's Men' well done," *Birmingham News*, May 16, 1958.

71. Carter, *Politics of Rage*, 91.

72. "The Facts of the Matter," *South, The News Magazine of Dixie*, May 19, 1958, 1; "Two Alabama TV Stations Give Wallace 'Time,'" *Decatur Daily*, May 21, 1958; "Wallace Asserts Patterson Win May Revive Klan," *Advertiser-Journal*, May 17, 1958.

73. Bob Ingram, "Klan Aids Patterson," *Montgomery Advertiser*, May 15, 1958, 1; "KKK Dragon Seen At Hqs Of Patterson," *Advertiser-Journal*, May 15, 1958; Clarke Stallworth, "Patterson Answers Question On Klan," *Birmingham Post-Herald*, May 22, 1958.

74. Ingram, *Montgomery Advertiser*, May 15, 1958; Stallworth, *Birmingham Post-Herald*, May 22, 1958.

75. Trudy Cargile, "Patterson now says he knew Klan chief only as individual," *Birmingham News*, May 22, 1958; "The *Huntsville Times* For Wallace," *Montgomery Advertiser*, May 31, 1958.

76. Patterson Interview, Oct. 2, 2002; "Patterson Gets Run-Off Backing of Engelhardt," *Gadsden Times*, May 28, 1958; Carter, *Politics of Rage*, 107.

77. Grover C. Hall Jr., "Alabama Klan Pushing Patterson Victory?" *Montgomery Advertiser*, June 1, 1958.

78. "The Klan Issue Tomorrow," *Huntsville Times*, June 2, 1958; Drew Pearson, "Klan Revival Is Seen In Patterson Victory," *Anniston Star*, June 3, 1958.

79. Ibid.; Patterson Interview, Oct. 2, 2002.

80. Bob Ingram, "Grand Dragon's Aid Story True, Says Patterson," *Montgomery Advertiser*, May 22, 1958.

81. Ibid.

82. Carter, *Politics of Rage*, 96; "Patterson Scores Solid Victory Over Wallace," *Childersburg News*, June 5, 1958, 1.

83. Edwin Strickland, "Patterson, in victory, shatters old traditions," *Birmingham News*, June 4, 1958; "Democratic Gubernatorial Elections in Alabama," *Alabama Magazine*, Mar. 1982; "Patterson Is Youngest Elected Governor," *Evergreen Courant*, Aug. 28, 1958.

84. "State Righters Gain Control; 500,000 Vote," *Troy Messenger*, June 4, 1958, 1; *Alabama Magazine*, Mar. 1982.

85. "Minority Bow," *Montgomery Advertiser*, June 5, 1958.

86. Edwin Strickland, "Patterson in victory, shatters old traditions," *Birmingham News*, June 4, 1958.

87. Hugh W. Sparrow, "Many troublesome problems face next governor of state," *Birmingham News*, June 8, 1958.

88. Bob Lee, "John Patterson Strong Favorite As Runoff Voting Day Approaches," *Columbus Ledger*, June 2, 1958; "Folsom Says Patterson's Campaign Style Like His," *Talladega Daily Home*, July 10, 1958.

Chapter 12, Sweeter Than Muscadine Wine

1. Interview with John Patterson, Sept. 30, 2005.
2. Ibid.
3. Ibid.
4. Ibid.; Interview with John Patterson, May 15, 2002.
5. See note above.
6. Patterson Interview, Sept. 30, 2005.
7. Ibid.
8. Video tape of Judge John Patterson, July 30, 1998.
9. Ibid.
10. Patterson Interview, Sept. 30, 2005.
11. Ibid.
12. Interview with McDowell Lee, Sec. of the Alabama Senate, Dec. 10, 2003.
13. Ibid.
14. Patterson Interview, Sept. 30, 2005.
15. Ibid.
16. Ibid.; Grafton and Permaloff, *Big Mules and Branchheads*, 82.
17. Grafton and Permaloff, 82.
18. Ibid., 82, 164–65.
19. Ibid.
20. Patterson Interview, Sept. 30, 2005.
21. Ibid.
22. Ibid.
23. Patterson Interview, Sept. 30, 2005; Interview with Maurice Patterson, June 29, 2003.
24. See note above.
25. Patterson Interview, Sept. 30, 2005.
26. Ibid.
27. Ibid.; Millard Grimes, "Patterson Ate A Late Supper," *Columbus Ledger-Enquirer*, June 8, 1958, A-4.
28. Grimes, *Ledger-Enquirer*, June 8, 1958.
29. Edwin Strickland, "Patterson, in victory, shatters old traditions," *Birmingham News*, June 4, 1958.

30. Hugh W. Sparrow, "Many troublesome problems face next governor of state," *Birmingham News*, June 8, 1958, 1A; Lynne Brannen, "Patterson to Skip Vacation To Catch Up on His Work," Associated Press release, undated.
31. Brannen, "Patterson to Skip Vacation . . . ," Associated Press release, undated.
32. "New Site plans fete for Patterson," *Birmingham News*, June 23, 1958; "Patterson Gives Outline Of His Four-Year Plan," *Huntsville Times*, July 11, 1958; "Patterson Talks of Big Bond Issue," *Dothan Eagle*, Aug. 14, 1958.
33. *Huntsville Times*, July 11, 1958; Patterson Interview, Sept. 30, 2005; Patterson Interview, May 15, 2002.
34. Patterson Interview, May 15, 2002.
35. *Huntsville Times*, July 11, 1958.
36. Video tape of Judge Patterson, July 30, 1998.
37. Clarke Stallworth, "Patterson Seeks Close U.S.-Alabama Ties," *Birmingham Post-Herald*, July 24, 1958; "John Patterson Going To Washington," *Phenix Journal*, July 11, 1958.
38. Phillip Kyle, "Wheeler Co-Op Hears Patterson Promise 'Get' Race Agitators," *Decatur Daily*, Aug. 14, 1958.
39. "Patterson Admits He Eyes Arkansas, Virginia Cases," *Huntsville Times*, Aug. 27, 1958.
40. Fred Taylor, "Patterson warns mixing will ruin state's schools," *Birmingham News*, Aug. 23, 1958.
41. "Patterson Admits He Eyes Arkansas, Virginia Cases," *Huntsville Times*, Aug. 27, 1958; "Patterson Lauds School Decision," *Birmingham Post-Herald*, June 23, 1958.
42. "Patterson Sees More Strife To Follow Court's Decision," *Montgomery Advertiser*, Sept. 13, 1958; "Patterson vows: No integration," *Birmingham News*, Sept. 13, 1958.
43. See note above.
44. "Patterson Ready to Protect State Against Court-Integrated Schools," *Mobile Press-Register*, Aug. 31, 1958.
45. Patterson Interview, Sept. 30, 2005.
46. "Patterson's Cabinet Is Shaping Up," reprinted from *South Magazine*, *Centreville Press*, Aug. 14, 1958.
47. Patterson Interview, May 15, 2002.

48. Ibid.; Crystal Bonvillian, "Love of law filled his life," *Montgomery Advertiser*, Aug. 24, 2005, 1B.

49. Patterson Interview, Sept. 30, 2005.

50. Ibid.

51. Ibid.

52. Ibid.; Biographical sketch of Earl Mason McGowin, Alabama Academy of Honor, Feb. 26, 1998.

53. Patterson Interview, Sept. 30, 2005; James E. Jacobson, "Kelley move angers some; condition good," *Birmingham News*, Feb. 22, 1961.

54. "Patterson Appoints 3 To Fill ABC Positions," *Montgomery Advertiser*, Jan. 20, 1959; "It's Official: Azar Heads ABC," *Alabama Journal*, Jan. 20, 1959.

55. Patterson Interview, May 15, 2002.

56. Bob Ingram, "Ted Rinehart, Converted Rebel," *Montgomery Advertiser*, Sept. 24, 1958.

57. Video tape of Judge John Patterson, July 30, 1998; Patterson Interview, May 15, 2002.

58. Ibid.

59. Associated Press, "Patterson Blasts Federal 'Invasion' Of States Rights," *Birmingham Post-Herald*, Sept. 12, 1958.

60. Associated Press, "Patterson Terms Probe 'Invasion,'" *Anniston Star*, Sept. 11, 1958; Associated Press, "Patterson blasts civil rights probe," *Birmingham News*, Sept. 12, 1958.

61. "Looks Like Fireworks In Civil Rights Probe," *Dothan Eagle*, Nov. 30, 1958; Rex Thomas, "Alabama May Be Test Ground," *Huntsville Times*, Nov. 30, 1958.

62. See note above.

63. "Civil Rights Group Ends Hearing," *Thomasville Times*, Dec. 11, 1958.

64. "State Resistance," *Mobile Press*, Dec. 10, 1958.

65. "Civil Rights Group Ends Hearing," *Thomasville Times*, Dec. 11, 1958; "Showdown on Lists' Impounding Delayed," *Dothan Eagle*, Dec. 8, 1958.

66. See note above; "Six Refuse To Testify About Work," *Mobile Register*, Dec. 9, 1958; "Probers Plan Legal Moves," *Mobile Register*, Dec. 10, 1958.

67. See note above; "Voter Registration Inquiry Hits Snag," *Valley Daily Times-News*, Dec. 10, 1958.

68. "Refusal To Cooperate Held 'Tactical Error' By Battle," *Montgomery Advertiser*, Dec. 10, 1958.

69. "Patterson's Rights Statement Released," *Montgomery Advertiser*, Dec. 11, 1958.

70. Ibid.; "Department of Justice Assigns Two Aides To Voting Records Battle," *Selma Times-Journal*, Dec. 11, 1958.

71. "Let's Stick to Legal Route; Patterson's Advice Is Good," *Advertiser-Journal*, Dec. 10, 1958.

72. "State Resistance," *Mobile Press*, Dec. 10, 1958.

73. "Voter Registration Inquiry Hits Snag," *Valley Daily Times-News*, Dec. 10, 1958.

74. Interview with McDowell Lee, Dec. 10, 2003.

75. Ted Pearson, "2 Alabamians Who Lost In Elections Emerge In Even Greater State Roles," *Mobile Press-Register*, Dec. 14, 1958.

76. "A Natural Alliance," *Montgomery Advertiser-Journal*, Dec. 18, 1958.

77. Carter, *Politics of Rage*, 99.

78. Allen Gunn, "Judge Asked To Recall Order For Voter Files," *Montgomery Advertiser*, Dec. 17, 1958; Donald F. Martin, UPI, "Hearing Date Set On Records," *Mobile Register*, Dec. 18, 1958.

79. "Wallace Mum On Agreement Over Records," *Montgomery Advertiser*, Jan. 6, 1959; Carter, *Politics of Rage*, 98.

80. "Alabama Wins A Good Deal," *Birmingham Post-Herald*, Jan. 6, 1959.

81. Interview with Gov. Patterson, Sept. 30, 2005.

82. Ibid.; Jack Bass, *Taming the Storm* (New York: Doubleday, 1993), 189, 190.

83. See note above; Carter, *Politics of Rage*, 103.142–51.

84. "No Negro Bands At Inauguration," *Selma Times-Journal*, Dec. 28, 1958; "Negro Marchers Will Not Receive Inauguration Bid," Dec. 28, 1958.

85. Telephone conversation with former Governor John Patterson, Jan. 4, 2006.

86. "Klan Chief Says Bloodshed To Follow School Mixing," *Montgomery Advertiser*, Jan. 5, 1959.

87. Fred Taylor, "Urges South-wide segregation parley," *Birmingham News*, Sept 17, 1958; Fred Taylor, "Passes up big API session to make trip," *Birmingham News*, Feb. 12, 1959.

88. Fred Taylor, "Dixie leaders pressing drive,"

Birmingham News, Dec. 2, 1958.

89. Ibid.

90. Ibid.; Patterson Interview.

91. "Patterson Asks Appeasement End in Racial Fight," *Birmingham Post-Herald*, Mar. 18, 1959.

92. Ibid.

93. Interview with Alvin T. Prestwood, May 29, 2003.

94. Ibid.

95. Ibid.

Chapter 13, The People's Governor

1. Interview, author with Gov. Patterson, May 15, 2002; "500 Units To March In Inaugural Parade," *Birmingham Post-Herald*, Jan. 9, 1959.

2. Patterson Interview, May 15, 2002.

3. W. J. Mahoney Jr., "Mahoney—'As I See It,'" *Alabama Journal*, Jan. 19, 1959, 4-A.

4. "Text Of Patterson's Inaugural Address," *Alabama Journal*, Jan. 19, 1959, 1A; Giles Interview, Sept. 5, 2003.

5. "Patterson Warns Negro Citizens," *Alabama Journal*, Jan. 19, 1959, 1A.

6. Ibid.

7. "Patterson Will Learn Negro Is Not Scared," reprinted from *Houston Texas Informer*, *Alabama Citizen*, Feb. 2, 1959.

8. "Patterson To Encourage Industry," *Troy Messenger*, Jan. 6, 1959.

9. "Text of Patterson's Inaugural Address," Jan. 19, 1959.

10. Ibid.

11. "Governor's grandmother dies in Dadeville at 93," *Birmingham News*, Feb. 2, 1959.

12. Patterson Interview, May 15, 2002.

13. Ibid.

14. Jim Shaw, "'I've had enough,' says Cullman man, back home again," *Birmingham News*, Jan. 25, 1959.

15. Interview with Joe Robertson, by author, June 29, 2003.

16. Patterson Interview.

17. Interview with Albert Patterson (Col., USA ret.) by author, Aug. 27, 2003.

18. Ibid.

19. Jim Shaw, "'I've had enough,' says Cullman man, back home again," *Birmingham News*, Jan. 25, 1959.

20. Ibid.; Bob Ingram, "Folsom Shows Charity At Term End," *Montgomery Advertiser*, Jan. 5, 1959.

21. "Administration Steps in Quietly," *Florala News*, Jan. 22, 1959; "Patterson Order to New Cabinet: Cut Out Waste," *Birmingham Post-Herald*, Jan. 21, 1959; "Patterson Tells His Cabinet There Will Be No Favorites," *Birmingham Post-Herald*, Mar. 12, 1959.

22. Interview with Gov. Patterson, May 15, 2002; Alvin Benn, "Mann stood tall through turbulent time," *Montgomery Advertiser*, May 12, 2001.

23. Patterson Interview, May 15, 2002.

24. "Politics Out In Operation Of ABC Unit, Azar Says," *Montgomery Advertiser*, Jan. 24, 1959, 6-A.

25. Bob Ingram, "ABC's Ed Azar: He Prefers Coffee," *Montgomery Advertiser*, Dec. 18, 1960.

26. "Enforcement, Not Revenue, Chief ABC Mission—Azar," *Alabama Journal*, May 10, 1961.

27. Ibid.

28. Ingram, *Montgomery Advertiser*, Dec. 18, 1960.

29. Ibid.

30. Bob Ingram, "Patterson, Reid Feud," *Graphic*, Apr. 2, 1959.

31. Bob Ingram, "Patterson Arrives Early, Remains Late At Office," date unknown.

32. "Gov. Patterson Adopts New Open Door Policy," *Montgomery Advertiser*, May 7, 1959.

33. Ibid.

34. Patterson Interview; Clarke Stallworth, "Patterson Scores in Legislature," *Birmingham Post-Herald*, Aug. 29, 1959.

35. Patterson Interview, May 15, 2002; Press release, Gov. John Patterson, for week of Jan. 26, 1959.

36. Patterson Interview.

37. "Record Breaking Legislature," *Tuscaloosa News*, Nov. 15, 1959.

38. Bob Ingram, "Session 'Tempest' Seen," *Advertiser-Journal*, May 3, 1959; "The Humid Season Opens," *Dothan Eagle*, May 6, 1959.

39. Rex Thomas, "Meet Crisis, Is Challenge," *Anniston Star*, May 5, 1959.

40. Forrest Castleberry, "Black Belters Lead In Open Defiance," *Alabama Journal*, May 6, 1959; Bob Ingram and Herschel Cribb, "House Kills Bid To Halt Filibustering," *Montgomery*

Advertiser, May 9, 1959.

41. "Black Belters Force Reading 'Just In Case,'" *Dothan Eagle*, May 5, 1959; "Hale Solon Warns Of Delay Tactics," *Alabama Journal*, May 8, 1959.

42. "Lawmakers Return To Work," *South Magazine*, June 1, 1959, 5.

43. Clarke Stallworth, "State Legislators Spar To Keep Controlling Hand," *Birmingham Post-Herald*, May 8, 1959.

44. Herschel Cribb and Bob Ingram, "Senate Filibusters; House Ends Logjam," *Montgomery Advertiser*, May 13, 1959; "Only 2 Votes Cast Against Measure," *Birmingham Post-Herald*, June 3, 1959.

45. "Appropriation Bill Passed by Legislature After A Compromise," *Huntsville Times*, June 19, 1959.

46. Clarke Stallworth, "Patterson Scores In Legislature," *Birmingham Post-Herald*, Aug. 29, 1959.

47. Ibid.; Patterson Interview.

48. Msg to the Legislature by Gov. John Patterson, June 24, 1959; Clarke Stallworth, "Governor Improves Docks, Pushes Good Loan Law," *Birmingham Post-Herald*, Feb. 13, 1961; Bailey Leopard, "Governor's Office Responds," *Limestone Democrat*, Aug. 24, 1961; Patterson Interview.

49. "Bill Gives $148 Million In 1st Year," *Anniston Star*, Aug. 14, 1959; Bob Ingram, "Patterson Administration Notes Shining Victory, Blushing Defeat," *Montgomery Advertiser*, Aug. 14, 1959.

50. See note above.

51. Clarke Stallworth, "Calls Opponents of Sales Tax Plan 'Big Mules,'" *Birmingham Post-Herald*, July 21, 1959.

52. Ibid.; "Farmer-Big Mule Group Shines In Revenue Fight," *Advertiser-Journal*, July 19, 1959; "Speech by 'Big Mule' rouses Alabama tax committee," *Sylacauga News*, July 30, 1959.

53. "Rose Asks All-Out Education Drive," *Montgomery Advertiser*, May 18, 1959.

54. "Drew Pearson Lauds Courage of Patterson," *Montgomery Advertiser*, July 27, 1959; "Patterson blasts columnist," *Birmingham News*, Feb. 16, 1961.

55. Stallworth, "Patterson Scores In Legislature," *Birmingham Post-Herald*, Aug. 29, 1959.

56. "Frowns and Smiles," *South Magazine*, Sept. 7, 1959, 6.

57. Grafton and Permaloff, *Big Mules and Branchheads*, 102.

58. Don Henry, "Session Was Progressive Oden Claims," *Russellville Times*, Nov. 17, 1959; Rex Thomas, "Governor Salutes Bodies Despite Inaction On Bills," *Birmingham News*, Nov. 17, 1959.

59. Grafton and Permaloff, 95–98; 151–52.

60. Ibid., 95–98; Rex Thomas, "New Projects Are Pondered By Patterson," *Anniston Star*, Aug. 23, 1959.

61. Grafton and Permaloff, 186–87.

62. "Haden Will Direct Revenue Agency," *Advertiser-Journal*, Nov. 23, 1958; "Keen Student Label Given To Patterson," *Montgomery Advertiser*, Jan. 20, 1959.

63. Patterson Interview, May 15, 2002; Sam Jones, "Haden Talks At Meeting Of Bar Unit," *Anniston Star*, Apr. 17, 1959.

64. See note above; Ingram, *Montgomery Advertiser*, Aug. 14, 1959.

65. James E. Jacobson, "Key keeper controversial tax gatherer," *Birmingham News*, Feb. 23, 1961.

66. Ibid.

67. Hugh W. Sparrow, "Patterson, Legislature may fight on assessments," *Birmingham News*, Apr. 12, 1959; "Solons Open Fight To Kill 30 Pct. Tax," *Dothan Eagle*, June 5, 1959.

68. Jacobson, *Birmingham News*, Feb. 23, 1961.

69. Ibid.; Patterson Interview, May 15, 2002.

70. Don Henry, "Session Was Progressive Oden Claims," *Russellville Times*, Nov. 17, 1959; Herschel Cribb, "Alabama Legislature Logged Record in '59," *Montgomery Advertiser*, Nov. 17, 1959.

71. "Lawmakers Return To Work," *South*, June 1, 1959.

72. Patterson Interview, Oct. 19, 2001. *The Dictionary of Alabama Biography* shows that the state's fourth governor John Murphy was born about 1785 to Neil Murphy and a Miss Downing.

73. Interview with Alvin T. Prestwood, May 29, 2003; Rex Thomas, "Governor Salutes Bodies Despite Inaction On Bills," *Birmingham News*, Nov. 15, 1959.

74. "Patterson Asks For Old Age Aid and Laws Controlling Loan Sharks," *Sumter County*

Journal, May 7, 1959; Rex Thomas, "Governor Salutes Bodies Despite Inaction On Bills," *Birmingham News*, Nov. 15, 1959.

75. "Record-Breaking Legislature," *Tuscaloosa News*, Nov. 15, 1959.

76. "Senate gives fast OK on appointments," *Birmingham News*, May 9, 1959.

77. Clarke Stallworth, "Patterson May Visit Coleman In Squabble," *Birmingham Post-Herald*, Jan. 30, 1959.

78. John Goheen, "Phenix Raised," *National Guard Magazine*, Aug. 2004.

79. Statement of Governor John Patterson, Jan. 29, 1959.

80. "Gov. Coleman Insists He Is Opposing Hanna For 'Excellent Reason,'" *Decatur Daily*, Jan. 27, 1959.

81. "Guard Bureau Is Hands Off In 31st Feud," *Alabama Journal*, Apr. 24, 1959.

82. "Alabama, Mississippi Military Leaders Discuss 31st Today," *Opelika Daily News*, Jan. 28, 1959; "State National Guard Will Get Face-Lifting," *Montgomery Advertiser*, Apr. 7, 1959.

83. "Coleman Leaves Guard Decision Up to Patterson," *Tuscaloosa News*, June 18, 1959.

84. "Sides Named Guard Chief," *Mobile Press*, Aug. 19, 1959; "Guard Wrangle Ended," *Anniston Star*, Aug. 21, 1959.

85. Ltr, Maj. Gen. Henry V. Graham, Adjutant General, to Gen. Herbert B. Powell, CG Third US Army, Oct. 3, 1960; Ltr, Gov John Patterson to Gov Ross Barnett, Aug. 2, 1961; Ltr, Gov. Ross Barnett to Gov John Patterson, Aug. 24, 1961; Special Order No. 176, Office of the Adjutant General, Sept. 13, 1961; Patterson Interview, May 15, 2002.

86. Patterson Interview, May 15, 2002.

87. Oral History Interview (OHI) with John Patterson, by John Stewart, for the John F. Kennedy Library, May 26, 1967.

88. Ibid.

89. Ibid.; Ltr., Sen. John F. Kennedy to Gov. John Patterson, Mar. 2, 1959.

90. "Kennedy Seals 1960 Covenant With Patterson," *Montgomery Advertiser*, June 16, 1959.

91. Ibid.; James Free, "Patterson to back Kennedy Demo bid," *Birmingham News*, June 16, 1959.

92. Gene Wortsman, "Democratic And NAACP Spokesmen Say Kennedy Hurt By Patterson,"

Birmingham Post-Herald, July 3, 1959; James Free, "Powell flays Patterson aid for Kennedy," *Birmingham News*, June 29, 1959; "Word's In Hand: Powell's Spoken," *Birmingham News*, June 30, 1959.

93. Patterson OHI by Stewart, May 26, 1967.

94. "Kennedy Seals 1960 Covenent With Patterson," *Montgomery Advertiser*, June 16, 1959.

95. "Patterson's Backing of Kennedy Draws Few Press Comments," *Decatur Daily*, June 28, 1959.

96. "Patterson Feels Kennedy's Religion Won't Affect Chances At Presidency," *Montgomery Advertiser*, June 29, 1959.

97. "Southern Affairs," *South Magazine*, Aug. 24, 1959, 7, 8; "Quiz Group Spokesman Is Called Klan Leader," *Birmingham Post-Herald*, Aug. 18, 1959; "All Things To All People," *Greensboro Watchman*, Aug. 13, 1959.

98. See note above; Patterson Interview, May 15, 2002; Interview with Fred Rothstein.

99. "All Things To All People," *Greensboro Watchman*, Aug. 13, 1959.

100. Ibid.

Chapter 14, All the Way with JFK and LBJ

1. Albert M. Colegrove, Scripps-Howard, "Johnson Backers Press Patterson," *Birmingham Post-Herald*, June 28, 1960.

2. Interview with Gov. Patterson by author, May 15, 2002.

3. "Statue Dedicated Of A. L. Patterson," *Advertiser-Journal*, date unknown.

4. Interview with Gov. Patterson by author, Oct. 25, 2002.

5. Ibid.

6. Ibid.

7. Ibid.; "Patterson going to Wyoming for moose hunt," *Birmingham News*, Nov. 14, 1959.

8. Patterson Interview, Oct. 25, 2002.

9. "No Reno Likely Here," *Opelika Daily News*, Nov. 20, 1959.

10. Ibid.

11. Ibid.

12. Editorial, "Petty Politics By Governor," *Alabama Journal*, Oct. 20 1960; Editorial, "Caesar P.," *Montgomery Advertiser*, Oct. 21, 1960.

13. "Patterson Denies Politics Caused Kohn's Resignation," *Montgomery Advertiser*, Oct. 26, 1960; "Blount Charges Political Differences Moved Patterson To Force His Ouster," *Montgomery Advertiser*, Oct. 31, 1960.

14. See note above; Patterson Interview, Oct. 25, 2002.

15. "Governor Plans To Concentrate On 'Managing,'" *Alabama Journal*, Nov. 14, 1959.

16. Editorial, "The Patterson Pageant," *Selma Times-Journal*, June 24, 1960.

17. "Patterson To Talk Here Dec. 6," *Phenix City Citizen*, Nov. 24, 1959; Al Stanton, "Patterson, Barbour puff on 'peace pipe,'" *Birmingham News*, Oct. 12, 1960.

18. Stanton, *Birmingham News*, Oct. 12, 1960.

19. Ibid.

20. Ibid.

21. "Patterson Calls Mission To Carib Isle 'Success,'" *Mobile Press*, Apr. 18, 1960.

22. Ibid.

23. "Editorial: In Appreciation," *Alabama School Journal*, October 1959, 16, 17; "Patterson Added To List Of Education Governors," *Sylacauga Advance*, Oct. 29, 1959; Bob Ingram, "The School 'Crisis': A Hero Turned Heel," *Advertiser-Journal*, Mar. 20, 1960.

24. "$20 Mllion In School Bonds For Sale; Governor Expects Low Interest Rate," *Sylacauga Advance*, Feb. 18, 1960; Bob Ingram, "Salesman J.P. Scores in N.Y.C.," *Advertiser-Journal*, Feb. 28, 1960.

25. Interview with Gov. Patterson, May 15, 2002.

26. Ibid.

27. Ibid.; Herschel Cribb, "School Plans Control Asked By Governor," *Montgomery Advertiser*, Feb. 6, 1960.

28. Patterson Interview.

29. Ibid.; Website, "College Information," Trenholm State Technical College, 2006.

30. Patterson Interview.

31. Bob Ingram, "The School 'Crisis': A Hero Turned Heel," *Advertiser-Journal*, Mar. 20, 1960.

32. "School Board Delays Action On Salary Cut," *Huntsville Times*, Mar. 3, 1960; Allison Stanton, "Board bucks Patterson by majority vote," *Birmingham News*, Mar. 3, 1960; Governor Rejects Legislature Call," *Huntsville Times*, Mar. 9, 1960.

33. Editorial, "School Crisis Again," *Huntsville Times*, Mar. 7, 1960; Bob Ingram, "Capitol Report," *Sand Mountain Reporter*, Mar. 22, 1960.

34. Clarke Stallworth, "Governor Opposes Temporary Levy," *Birmingham News*, Mar. 16, 1960; William O. Tome, "Accept Cut, Is Appeal To Teachers," *Anniston Star*, Mar. 18, 1960; "School Administrators Ignore Governor's Word," *Tri-Cities Daily*, Mar. 19, 1960.

35. "Governor Challenges Educational Leaders On School Finances," *Birmingham Post-Herald*, Mar. 25, 1960; "School Board Rejects Pay Cut," *Alabama Journal*, Mar. 26, 1960.

36. Ingram, "The School 'Crisis' . . . ," *Advertiser-Journal*, Mar. 20, 1960.

37. Bob Ingram, "Patterson Sees School Close Ahead," *Montgomery Advertiser*, Dec. 31, 1959; "Violence in Integration Certain, Says Governor," *Dothan Eagle*, Dec. 30, 1959.

38. See note above; Patterson Interview by Norman Lumpkin, May 22, 1973.

39. "Endowment Plan Would Provide Necessary Funds," *Gadsden Times*, Oct. 10, 1958; "Private Plan For Schools Gains Force," *Montgomery Advertiser*, Oct. 12, 1958.

40. "Alabama School Is One Of Last Mix Holdouts," *Mobile Register*, Nov. 9, 1959.

41. Lorene Frederick, "Patterson Hits Mixing Try In Remarks Here," *Tri-Cities Daily*, Nov. 11, 1959; Clark Stallworth, "Patterson Vows To Close School," *Birmingham Post-Herald*, Nov. 11, 1959; "Rev. King Backs Huntsville Plan," *Alabama Journal*, Nov. 20, 1959.

42. "King Denies Patterson Statement," *Anniston Star*, Dec. 31, 1959; "Governor Signs Private Schools, Registration Bills Into Law Friday," *Opelika Daily News*, Nov. 21, 1959; "State Funds For Children Are Involved," *Alabama Journal*, Nov. 20, 1959.

43. Ingram, "Patterson Sees School Close Ahead," *Montgomery Advertiser*, Dec. 31, 1959.

44. Donald F. Martin, "State's War On Mixing Successful," *Mobile Register*, Jan. 14, 1960.

45. "Patterson, Hill Blast Civil Rights Report; Call It Slander On Alabama," *Tri-Cities Daily*, Sept. 9, 1959.

46. Ibid.; Ted Pearson, "Patterson Says Move Political," *Mobile Register*, Oct. 30, 1959; Martin, "State's War On Mixing Successful," *Mobile Register*, Jan. 14, 1960.

47. "Insulting Registrar Bills Lambasted by

Gov. Patterson," *Birmingham Post-Herald*, Feb. 3, 1960; "Federal Vote Registrars Could Wreck Election Machinery, Patterson Warns," *Sylacauga Advance*, Feb. 4, 1960; Editorial, "Carpetbaggers Will Not Help," *Birmingham Post-Herald*, Feb. 3, 1960.

48. "Patterson Vows Rights Fight," *Alabama Journal*, Apr. 28, 1960; "Civil Rights Act of 1960," Wikipedia, the Internet encyclopedia, the Wikimedia Foundation, Inc.

49. Patterson Interview; Edgar Dyer, draft article, "A 'Triumph of Justice' in Alabama: The 1960 Perjury Trial of Martin Luther King, Jr.," Dec. 16, 2002; "Negro Rift On Mixing Is Reported," *Birmingham Post-Herald*, Dec. 31, 1959; "King Denies Patterson Statement," *Anniston Star*, Dec. 31, 1959.

50. *Anniston Star*, Dec. 31, 1959; Dyer, draft article, Dec. 16, 2002.

51. See note above.

52. "City Leaders Issue Words Of Warning," *Montgomery Advertiser*, Feb. 26, 1960; "Take Action College Told By Patterson," *Birmingham Post-Herald*, Feb. 26, 1960.

53. Dick Hines and Bob Ingram, "Alabama State President Given Mandate In Governor's Office," *Montgomery Advertiser*, Feb. 26, 1960; Allison Stanton, "Governor Orders Negroes Expelled," *Birmingham News*, Feb. 26, 1960.

54. "Capital Negroes Threaten To Seek 'Bama, AU Entry,'" *Birmingham Post-Herald*, Feb. 27, 1960; Allison Stanton, "Negroes stage mass protest at Capital," *Birmingham News*, Feb. 26, 1960.

55. "State of Terror Exists, Says MIA After Violence," *Tuscaloosa News*, Feb. 28, 1960.

56. Ibid.

57. Ibid.

58. "Negroes March In Montgomery, Protesting Ban," *Gadsden Times*, Mar. 1, 1960; "Brief Rally Staged At Close Capitol By Students of Negro College," *Selma Times-Journal*, Mar. 1, 1960.

59. "9 Expelled, 20 Given Probation," *Montgomery Advertiser*, Mar. 3, 1960.

60. Ibid.; "Expulsion Very Light Penalty, Says Governor," *Birmingham Post-Herald*, Mar. 1, 1960.

61. See note above.

62. Trudy Cargile and Allison Stanton, "Students at Alabama State quit classes in new protest," *Birmingham News*, Mar. 3, 1960.

63. Ibid.

64. "Negroes Back School Strike," *Tuscaloosa News*, Mar. 5, 1960.

65. "Police To Prohibit Negro Mass Meet," *Tuscaloosa News*, Mar. 6, 1960.

66. Ibid.

67. "Negro College Closing Urged By Sullivan," *Dothan Eagle*, Mar. 10, 1960.

68. "Negro Gathering Almost Provokes Clash In Streets Of Montgomery," *Mobile Register*, Mar. 7, 1960.

69. Ibid.

70. "Close of Negro College Asked," *Decatur Daily*, Mar. 10, 1960.

71. "Patterson Orders Probe Of School After Official Suggests Shutdown," *Mobile Register*, Mar. 11, 1960; "Demonstrators marched into Capital court," *Birmingham News*, Mar. 11, 1960.

72. "'Disloyal' Teachers At Negro College Ordered Fired," *Birmingham Post-Herald*, Mar. 26, 1960; "Purge Is Ordered At State College," *Anniston Star*, Mar. 27, 1960; "Negro Faculty To Be 'Purged,'" *Dothan Eagle*, Mar. 27, 1960.

73. "Negro Gathering . . . ," *Mobile Register*, Mar. 7, 1960.

74. "Negro Faculty To Be 'Purged,'" *Dothan Eagle*, Mar. 27, 1960; "Fired Nego Says Charge is Political," *Mobile Register*, June 16, 1960.

75. "Court Rules Expulsion Of 6 In Sit-In Illegal," *Mobile Press*, Aug. 5, 1961; Gray, *Bus Ride to Justice*, 175, 176.

76. "Congress Unit Slates Probe In Montgomery," *Mobile Press*, June 14, 1960.

77. "Governor Maps Ruling On Plea To Sue Times," *Alabama Journal*, Apr. 21, 1960.

78. Gray, *Bus Ride to Justice*, 152, 153; "King Denies Authorizing *Times* Ad," *Montgomery Advertiser*, June 14, 1961.

79. Gray, 162, 163.

80. "*Times* Sued By Patterson For Million," *Birmingham Post-Herald*, May 31, 1960.

81. Gray, 168, 169.

82. Ibid., 170; Interview with John Patterson, Mar. 31, 2006.

83. Edgar Dyer, "A 'Triumph of Justice' in Alabama," 2002.

84. "Negroes Back School Strike," *Tuscaloosa News*, Mar. 5, 1960; "King Says Governor Can Be Converted," *Selma Times-Journal*, Mar. 7, 1960.

85. "Patterson Sees Violence Danger," *Huntsville Times*, May 27, 1959.

86. "Jackie Robinson Takes Crack At Gov. Patterson," *Centreville Press*, May 5, 1960.

87. OHI with John Patterson by John Stewart for the John F. Kennedy Library, May 26, 1967.

88. Patterson Interview, May 15, 2002.

89. Ibid.; Patterson OHI by Stewart, May 26, 1967.

90. See note above; "Patterson Criticized For Kennedy Backing," *Dothan Eagle*, June 16, 1959.

91. Patterson OHI by Stewart; Patterson Interview, May 15, 2002.

92. See note above.

93. Patterson Interview.

94. Ibid.

95. Ibid.

96. Ibid.

97. Ibid.; Patterson OHI by Stewart; "Folsom Describes Vote For Kennedy," *Dothan Eagle*, July 12, 1960; Grover C. Hall, Jr., "Governor Failed In Push To Give Kennedy Majority," *Montgomery Advertiser*, July 11, 1960.

98. Patterson Interview.

99. Ibid.

100. Ibid.

101. Patterson OHI with Stewart.

102. "3rd Party Talk Is Denounced By Patterson," *Mobile Press*, July 21, 1960.

103. Patterson Interview; "Kennedy May Visit Alabama Oct. 10," *Alabama Journal*, Oct. 3, 1960.

104. Patterson Interview; Bob Ingram, "State Democratic Brass 'Just Wild About Harry,'" *Montgomery Advertiser*, Oct. 22, 1960.

105. See note above.

106. Al Fox, "Truman Hurls No-Guts Charge," *Gadsden Times*, Oct. 22, 1960.

107. Patterson Interview.

108. Ibid.; Warren Trest and Don Dodd, *Wings of Denial* (Montgomery: NewSouth Books, 2001), 16, 17.

109. Patterson Interview; Trest and Dodd, 17–20.

110. Patterson Interview; Trest and Dodd, 93.

111. Patterson Interview.

112. Ibid.

113. Ibid.

114. Ibid.

115. "LBJ Train Rolls Today In Alabama," *Montgomery Advertiser*, Oct. 13, 1960; Bob Ingram, "LBJ, Former Outcast Is Saluted In Alabama," *Advertiser-Journal*, Oct. 16, 1960.

116. See note above.

117. "Gov. Patterson, Others To Accompany Johnson," *Gadsden Times*, Oct. 11, 1960; "Democrats Counting On Johnson's Talks In S. Alabama To Boost Sagging Strength," *Tuscaloosa News*, Oct. 9, 1960; Patterson Interview.

118. Patterson Interview.

119. Ibid.

120. "Bright Days Ahead, Patterson Predicts," *Birmingham Post-Herald*, Nov. 10, 1960.

121. Patterson Interview; Patterson OHI by Stewart.

122. See note above.

123. Patterson Interview.

124. "Demos, GOP Tiff As If Alabama Vote Is Pivotal," *South Magazine*, Oct. 3, 1960, 5; "Toe-To-Toe Battle Indicates Heavy Alabama Vote Turnout," *South Magazine*, Oct. 17, 1960, 7; "Bright Days Ahead, Patterson Predicts," *Birmingham Post-Herald*, Nov. 10, 1960.

125. Donald F. Martin, UPI, "Dems Take Ala. In Record Vote," *Daily Mountain Eagle*, Nov. 10, 1960; Joe Lewis, "Adam Powell Incensed At Alabama Governor," *Alabama Journal*, July 11, 1960; Gene Wortsman, "Rep. Powell Warns King Not To Split Unity," *Birmingham Post-Herald*, June 22, 1960.

126. Anthony Lewis, "Kennedy Pledges to Stand Firm In Support of Negroes' Rights," *New York Times*, July 2, 1960.

127. "Patterson, Kennedy Rebuked By Robinson," *Alabama Journal*, Dec. 12, 1960.

128. Ibid.

129. Bob Ingram, "Gleeful Governor Happy With World," *Montgomery Advertiser*, July 16, 1960.

Chapter 15, "It's a Hell of a Job"

1. Patterson Interview, May 15, 2002.

2. Ibid.; OHI with Patterson by Stewart, May 26, 1967.

3. OHI with Patterson by Stewart.

4. Ibid.

5. Ibid.

6. Ibid.

7. Patterson Interview.

8. Ibid.

9. Ibid.

10. Trest and Dodd, *Wings of Denial*, 38, 52.

11. Ibid., 53, 54.

12. Ibid., 53–57.

13. Ibid., 78–85.

14. Ibid., 93.

15. Patterson Interview.

16. Ibid.

17. Ibid.

18. Judd Arnett, "Washington Will Bring Chaos—Patterson," *Miami Herald*, June 5, 1961.

19. Ibid.; Online history of CORE-Congress of Racial Equality, 1960.

20. Jerrold M. Packard, *American Nightmare. The History of Jim Crow* (New York: St. Martin's Press, 2002), 263; John Lewis with Michael D'Orso, *Walking With The Wind. A Memoir of the Movement* (New York: Harcourt Brace & Company, 1998), 163, 166.

21. Lewis with D'Orso, *Walking with the Wind*, 136–138; Frye Gaillard, *Cradle of Freedom. Alabama and the Movement That Changed America* (Tuscaloosa: The University of Alabama Press, 2004), 77, 78.

22. Ibid.; Patterson Interview.

23. "Yankee Stay Home, Truman Tells 'Rider,'" *Birmingham Post-Herald*, June 6, 1961.

24. Lewis with D'Orso, *Walking with the Wind*, 1–6.

25. Ibid., 132; "Yankee Stay Home . . . ," *Post-Herald*, June 6, 1961.

26. Ibid., 140; Gaillard, *Cradle of Freedom*, 79, 80; Frank Sikora, *The Judge: The Life & Opinions of Alabama's Frank M. Johnson, Jr.* (Montgomery: The Black Belt Press, 1992), 104.

27. Sikora, *The Judge*, 104.

28. Ibid., 104, 105; Gaillard, 81.

29. Sikora, 105, 106, 130.

30. Patterson Interview.

31. Sikora, 106, 107; Jack Bass, *Taming the Storm: The Life and Times of Judge Frank M. Johnson, Jr. and the South's Fight Over Civil Rights* (New York: Doubleday, 1993), 174.

32. Lewis with D'Orso, 144; "More Light On The 'Freedom Rides,'" *U.S. News & World Report*, Oct. 30, 1961, 70.

33. See note above.

34. Associated Press, "Justice Chief's Office Like a Command Post," press clipping, source and date unknown; Patterson Interview.

35. Patterson Interview.

36. Ibid.

37. Lewis with D'Orso, 147–151; "Connor Deports Riders," *Tuscaloosa News*, May 19, 1961.

38. "RFK's Plea For Negro To Drive 'Riders' Bus Is Told At Hearing," *Birmingham Post-Herald*, June 1, 1961.

39. Lewis with D'Orso, 154.

40. Patterson Interview; "RFK's Plea For Negro To Drive . . . ," *Post-Herald*, June 1, 1961.

41. Lewis with D'Orso, 154.

42. Patterson Interview; Giles Interview.

43. Sikora, 148, 149.

44. Ibid.

45. Associated Press, "Patterson Vows To Uphold Laws," May 20, 1961.

46. "Violence Breaks Out," *Mobile Press-Register*, May 21, 1961.

47. Transcript of conference, Sunday, May 21, 1961, between Governor John Patterson, Attorney General McDonald Gallion, Assistant U.S. Attorney General Byron White and Director of Public Safety Floyd Mann.

48. Patterson Interview.

49. Cliff Sessions, UPI, "Freedom Riders Jailed in Miss.," *Los Angeles Mirror*, May 24, 1961; Lewis with D'Orso, 168–172; "The South: Crisis in Civil Rights," *Time*, June 2, 1961, 15.

50. Associated Press, "Justice Chief's Office Like a Command Post."

51. Gardner L. Bridge, Associated Press, "Attorney General Says Marshals Prevented Costly, Bloody Rioting," *Mobile Register*, May 24, 1961.

52. Ibid.

53. "King Lays Violence Blame on Governor," *Decatur Daily*, May 22, 1961.

54. News clipping, Dan Oberdorfer, Washington Bureau Staff, "King Plans to Step Up Protests of Segregation," undated.

55. Bob Ingram, "Patterson Blames Marshals For Riots; Says JFK Still Friend Despite 'Error,'" *Montgomery Advertiser*, May 24, 1961; "Patterson Blames Riot On U.S. Government," *Mobile Register*, May 24, 1961.

56. Bass, *Taming the Storm*, 180.

57. "Patterson Says Law Rests in Local Units,"

Alabama Journal, May 22, 1961.

58. Stanley Meisler, Associated Press, "Kennedy Wants 'Freedom Rides' Ended in Alabama, Mississippi," *Mobile Register*, May 25, 1961; News clipping, Don Oberdorfer, Washington Bureau Staff, "King Plans to Step Up Protests of Segregation," undated.

59. "Governor Backed 75 to 1 In Mail On Racial Stand," *Alabama Journal*, May 25, 1961; Trudy Cargile, "Dixie governors back up Patterson," *Birmingham News*, May 23, 1961; "We asked for Federal intervention—we got it," *Birmingham News*, May 23, 1961; "Mr. Kennedy: Why aren't King, 'riders' held in check?" *Birmingham News*, May 24, 1961; "Alabama Governor Fails State, Nation," *Atlanta Constitution*, May 22, 1961.

60. "The South: Crisis in Civil Rights," *Time*, June 2, 1961, 14–18.

61. "Patterson's 'Rider' Stand Set To Music," *Birmingham Post-Herald*, June 21, 1961.

62. Bass, 3; Sikora, 110; "Bitter KKK Rivals Named In Conjunction," *Montgomery Advertiser*, May 22, 1961; "Riders Face An Injunction," *Decatur Daily*, May 20, 1961.

63. Sikora, 146.

64. Ibid.; Bass, 179.

65. Sikora, 146, 148.

66. Ibid., 147; "Judge Johnson's 'Rider' Clarification," *Birmingham News*, June 7, 1961.

67. Bass, 3; Sikora, 147.

68. Bass, 183.

69. Sikora, 148.

70. Bass, 182; Sikora, 145.

Chapter 16, Building Highways, Building Bridges

1. "The Breach in Federal-State Relations," Statement of Honorable John Patterson, Governor of Alabama, at National Conference of Governors, Honolulu, HI, June 25–28 1961.

2. Ibid.; Patterson OHI by John Stewart for the JFK Library, May 26, 1967.

3. Patterson Interview.

4. Ibid.

5. "Patterson Picketed in San Francisco," *Alabama Journal*, June 24, 1961; Brian Casey, "Bob Kennedy 'Hysterical' On Riders, Says Patterson," *Honolulu Advertiser*, June 27, 1961.

6. Telephone Interview with John Patterson by author, June 20, 2006.

7. "Conference Highlights," *Honolulu Star-Bulletin*, June 27, 1961; "Patterson To Air 'Rider' Issue," *Mobile Register*, June 26, 1961; "Pickets Jeer Patterson in Hawaii," *Montgomery Advertiser*, June 25, 1961.

8. "Patterson Warns Of 'Cold War' Against Federal Interference," *Montgomery Advertiser*, June 29, 1961; Patterson statement to governors' conference, June 25–28, 1961.

9. See note above.

10. Editorial, "Explanation, Not Apology," *Honolulu Star-Bulletin*, June 28, 1961.

11. Ibid.

12. "Governors, Not Leaders," *Alabama Journal*, July 7, 1961; "Patterson Would Travel World to Explain Views," *Montgomery Advertiser*, July 2, 1961; Patterson Interview.

13. "Governors' Parley Skips Civil Rights," *New York Herald Tribune*, July 8, 1961.

14. "Governors Plan Second Unity Event," *Anniston Star*, July 20, 1961.

15. Gavin Scott, "States Rights Issue Threat To Conference," *Florence Times*, Sept. 25, 1961.

16. "Patterson Raps Bob Kennedy," *Tuscaloosa News*, Sept. 26, 1961.

17. "Governor Patterson Hires Expert To Prove Negro Race Inferior," *Selma Times-Journal*, Nov. 12, 1961.

18. Ibid.; Wesley Critz George Papers, Ms Dept., Library of the University of North Carolina, undated; Patterson Interview.

19. Patterson Interview; "How Kennedys Punish Alabama," *Alabama Journal*, Sept. 8, 1961.

20. Patterson Interview.

21. Ibid.

22. Patterson Interview.

23. "NAACP'er Calls State 'Pretty Bad,'" *Birmingham Post-Herald*, Oct. 8, 1962.

24. Case report, Dir. of Public Safety Floyd H. Mann to Gov. John Patterson, Feb. 12, 1962; Karl Portera, "Bitter Storm Follows College Head's Ouster," *Montgomery Advertiser*, Feb. 16, 1962.

25. Case report, Mann to Patterson, Feb. 12, 1962; Ltr, Gov. John Patterson to Hon. W. A. LeCroy, Supt of Ed, Feb. 1, 1962.

26. Press release, "President, Governor Reminisce During Redstone Arsenal Visit," Sept. 14, 1960.

27. Clarke Stallworth, "Patterson Served In Ike's Command," *Birmingham Post-Herald*, Sept. 9, 1960.

28. Dick Hines, "Visit of President . . . ," *Advertiser-Journal*, Sept. 11, 1960.

29. Ibid.

30. Patterson Interview.

31. Ibid.; Ltr, Wernher von Braun to Gov. Patterson, June 29, 1961; Ltr, Patterson to von Braun, July 11, 1961.

32. Bill Jones, "Patterson predicts Alabama growth as Space Age center," *Birmingham News*, Oct. 27, 1962.

33. James E. Jacobson, "Road building pace in state is spectacular," *Birmingham News*, Feb. 13, 1961.

34. Ibid.

35. Ibid.; Patterson Interview.

36. "The Patterson Years," A message by Governor John Patterson to the State Legislature assembled at Montgomery, Alabama, Jan. 8, 1963.

37. Ibid.

38. Ibid.

39. Ibid.

40. Patterson Interview; Walling Keith, "Somebody fumbled political ball in highway skirmish," *Birmingham News*, Oct. 29, 1961.

41. Charles Grainger, "Roosevelts, JFK linked to dispute over road routing," *Birmingham News*, Oct. 25, 1961; "Finagling Denied By White House," *Birmingham Post-Herald*, Oct. 26, 1961; Walling Keith, "Somebody fumbled political ball in highway skirmish," *Birmingham News*, Oct. 29, 1961.

42. Patterson Interview.

43. Interview with Tommy Giles, Sept. 5, 2003.

44. Bob Ingram, "Indefatigible JP Poops His Men," *Montgomery Advertiser*, Sept. 25, 1960.

45. Ibid.

46. Giles Interview, Sept. 5, 2003.

47. Ibid.; "Azar Unhurt In Abbeville Crash," *Alabama Journal*, Sept. 12, 1960.

48. See note above; "Plane flying state officials cracks up," *Birmingham Post-Herald*, Sept. 12, 1960.

49. Giles Interview.

50. Ibid.

51. Ibid.

52. Ibid.

53. Ibid.

54. Patterson Interview.

55. Ibid.

56. Ibid.

57. James E. Jacobson, "Solid growth in first half fulfills goals," *Birmingham News*, Feb. 24, 1961; Bob Ingram, "Patterson Took Governor Oath Two Years Ago," *Montgomery Advertiser*, Jan. 19, 1961.

58. See note above.

59. Ramona Allison, "Governor Hurls Blast At Press," *Alabama Journal*, Apr. 4, 1961; Hugh Sparrow, "Newspapermen lectured by irate Patterson," *Birmingham News*, Apr. 5, 1961.

60. "JP's 200 failures," *Montgomery Advertiser*, July 4, 1961.

61. Giles Interview.

62. Patterson Interview.

63. James E. Jacobson, "Governor says it takes team to run state," *Birmingham News*, Feb. 25, 1961; "Governor Has Some Surprises," *Birmingham Post-Herald*, Apr. 27, 1961.

64. See note above.

65. Rex Thomas, "One Filibuster After Another Is The Outlook," *Tri-Cities Daily*, Apr. 16, 1961.

66. Charlie Grainger, *Birmingham News*, May 2, 1961.

67. Don Martin, UPI, "Group Okays Reapportionment Bill," *Daily Mountain Eagle*, May 13, 1961; Dan Coggin, "House Torn By Schemes, Strife, Plots," *Decatur Daily*, May 14, 1961.

68. Bob Ingram, "Filibuster Drowns Stormy Session," *Advertiser-Journal*, Sept. 3, 1961.

69. Ibid.; Bob Ingram, "The 1961 Legislature, An Abysmal Flop," *Advertiser-Journal*, Sept. 3, 1961.

70. Carl Coggins, "Montgomery Report," *Daily Mountain Eagle*, Sept. 13, 1931.

71. Carl Coggins, "Capitol Report . . . Comments," *Daily Mountain Eagle*, Sept. 17, 1961; Ted Pearson, "Solon Resemble Band of Beavers," *Press-Register*, Sept. 17, 1961.

72. Clarke Stallworth, "Patterson Signs '9-8', Money Bill," *Birmingham Post-Herald*, Sept. 18, 1961.

73. Paper, "A History of 20th and 21st Century Redistricting and Reapportionment in the State of Alabama," Legislative Reapportionment Office, undated.

74. Ted Pearson, "Patterson praises legislators, court's verdict is awaited," *Birmingham News*, July 15, 1962.

75. Ibid.; "Governor Says Judges Could Have 'Dealt More Severely,'" *Montgomery Advertiser*, July 23, 1962.

76. "Election Bill Is Signed," *Tuscaloosa News*, 23 July 1962.

77. "Patterson sees Dumas bill as 'strictly a local matter,'" *Birmingham News*, July 26, 1962.

78. Ibid.

79. "Conflict Over Racial Issues Keeps Alabama In Spotlight During 1961," *Montgomery Advertiser*, Jan. 2, 1962.

80. "Patterson Sees Terminal Closings," *Alabama Journal*, Nov. 11, 1961; "Governor Sees ICC Bus Ruling Being 'Wrong,'" *Florence Times*, Nov. 11, 1961.

81. "Conflict Over Racial Issues . . . ," *Montgomery Advertiser*, Jan. 2, 1962.

82. Robert E. Baker, "Race Issue Ebbs in Importance," *Washington Post*, Dec. 11, 1961.

83. Ibid.

84. "State VIPs guests at Patterson party," *Birmingham News*, Dec. 23, 1961; "Prison Victory Boosts Folsom," *Tuscaloosa News*, Dec. 7, 1961.

85. "Prison Modernization Program Gaining Broad State Support," *South*, Nov. 13, 1961, 5; Charles Grainger, "Prison head gives amendment views," *Birmingham News*, Nov. 26, 1961.

86. Hugh W. Sparrow, "Gov. Patterson's report notes impressive gains in Alabama," *Birmingham News*, Dec. 12, 1961; "Progess Mars Alabama In '61 In Business, Agriculture, Schools," Dec. 25, 1961, 5.

87. "Patterson's Day," *South*, Oct. 16, 1961, 5.

88. Ibid.

Chapter 17, When Evening Shadows Fall

1. Bob Ingram, "The Last Year Is The Toughest," *Advertiser-Journal*, Mar. 11, 1962; "Patterson Doesn't Intend To Coast During Last Year," *Opelika Daily News*, Feb. 6, 1962.

2. "Sound Ruling," *Birmingham Post-Herald*, Jan. 18, 1962.

3. Ingram, *Advertiser-Journal*, Mar. 11, 1962.

4. "Folsom Leads Governor Poll; Gets 34% in Statewide Survey," *South*, Jan. 8, 1962, 5; Bob Ingram, "Folsom seeking unprecedented third term as political circus underway," *Shades Valley Sun*, Jan. 18, 1962; Patterson Interview.

5. Bob Ingram, "Governor Patterson's Press Conferences," *Alabama Journal*, Nov. 20, 1961.

6. Charlie Grainger, "Patterson to avoid any clashes with candidates," *Birmingham News*, Jan. 12, 1962; "Folsom Charges Patterson, Others Speeded Mixing," *Birmingham Post-Herald*, Feb. 15, 1962.

7. "Ex-governor squares off on Patterson," *Birmingham News*, Feb. 2, 1962; "Folsom Pledges To Do Better Job," *Tuscaloosa News*, Jan. 13, 1962.

8. Grafton and Permaloff, *Big Mules and Branchheads*, 68.

9. Glenn T. Eskew, Wallace essay in Samuel L. Webb and Margaret E. Armbrester, eds., *Alabama Governors* (Tuscaloosa and London: The University of Alabama Press, 2001), 221; Donald F. Martin, UPI, "Patterson Receives Criticism," *Daily Mountain Eagle*, Mar. 7, 1962.

10. "Wallace Stands Pat On Pledges: Drydock Yachts, Liquor Agents," *South*, Nov. 26, 1962, 5.

11. Jo Anne Singley, "Voters Brave Heat, Rain," *Columbus Ledger*, 30 May 1962.

12. Elvin Stanton, UPI, "Patterson Begins Tour," *Birmingham Post-Herald*, Mar. 31, 1962; "Parleys Set Up By John," *Anniston Star*, Apr. 16, 1962; "Mayor Presents Patterson With Service Award," *Sumter County Journal*, Apr. 12, 1962.

13. "Mayor Presents . . . ," *Journal*, Apr. 12, 1962.

14. "Please take care of Tar Baby, next governor urged," *Birmingham News*, May 10, 1962.

15. Clarke Stallworth, "Governor's Race For '66 Shaping," *Birmingham Post-Herald*, May 31, 1962.

16. Carter, *Politics of Rage*, 107, 109.

17. Interview, author with Robert B. Ingram, Jan. 7, 2003.

18. Oral history Interview of Ray Jenkins by Barbara Fought, undated.

19. "Tempers Hot In Montgomery After Patterson Named In Striping Deal," *Northwest Alabamian*, July 13, 1962.

20. Ted Pearson, "Gallion charge of conspiracy stirs governo," *Birmingham News*, July 12, 1962.

21. "Highway Striping Contract Stopped, Gallion Says Repayment Should Come," *Daily Times-Democrat*, Aug. 8, 1962.

22. "Governor Says Reporter 'Snooping' On Property," *Alabama Journal*, July 20, 1962.

23. "Private Eye Investigates Gubernatorial Candidates," *Alabama Journal*, Aug. 17, 1962.

24. Confidential Report regarding Charles McWilliams, by Fred J. Bodeker, Oct. 10, 1962.

25. Report from Mr. Fred Bodeker, continued, Nov. 1, 1962.

26. Confidential Report regarding Charles McWilliams, Oct. 10, 1962.

27. Ltr, Charles McWilliams to J. W. Oakley Sr., *Centreville Press*, Jan. 5, 1963; Additional report regarding Charles McWilliams, Fred Bodeker, Nov. 20, 1962.

28. Bob Ingram, "There's a Comeback in Patterson's Stock," *Huntsville Times*, Mar. 1, 1954; Arthur Osgoode, "Craig Ruled Innocent of Road Stripe Bribe," *Montgomery Advertiser*, Feb. 27, 1964.

29. Osgoode, *Montgomery Advertiser*, Feb. 27, 1964; Ltr, John Patterson to Gene Howard, Mar. 27, 1992.

30. Ingram, *Huntsville Times*, Mar. 1, 1964.

31. Donald F. Martin, "Wallace Race Issue Stand Comes Back To Haunt Him," *Gadsden Times*, Oct. 23, 1962.

32. Ibid.

33. Grover C. Hall Jr., "Patterson, Wallace Shying From U.S. Integration Orders," *Atlanta Constitution*, July 6, 1962.

34. Ibid.; James Marlow Associated Press, "Only Two States Left Unintegrated," *Huntsville Times*, Oct. 4, 1962; Carl Goggins, "Wallace Criticized On Barnett Support," *Eufala Tribune*, Sept. 27, 1962; "Alabama's Elected Officials Feel Mississippi's Fight Is Alabama's," *Anniston Star*, Sept. 30, 1962.

35. "Patterson Pleads With White House," *Montgomery Advertiser*, Sept. 28, 1962; "Patterson Urges JFK To Refrain From Troop Use," Sept. 28, 1962; Associated Press, "Patterson Tells RFK Of Promise," *Press-Register*, Sept. 30, 1962.

36. "Patrol guards roads going to Mississippi," *Birmingham News*, Oct. 1, 1962.

37. Martin, "Wallace Race Issue . . . ," *Gadsden Times*, Oct. 23, 1962.

38. Ross M. Hagen, "State Sees Groundswell Of Violence Resistance," *Alabama Journal*, Dec. 14, 1962.

39. Ibid.; "State militia expected to be organized," *Birmingham News*, Oct. 21, 1962.

40. "Bombing Rewards Mount To $5000," *Birmingham Post-Herald*, Dec. 20, 1962; "Blast Rewards Total $5,000," *Alabama Journal*, Dec. 20, 1962.

41. Permaloff and Grafton in *Alabama Governors* edited by Webb and Armbrester, 210–215; Oral history interview of Ray Jenkins by Barbara Fought, undated.

42. "A Look Back, A Look Ahead," *Birmingham News*, Jan. 15, 1963.

43. Patterson Interview by Lumpkin, May 22, 1973.

44. Ibid.

45. Ltr, John Patterson to Tom Gilliam, Pensacola Junior College, Apr. 6, 1972.

46. Ibid.

47. Robert Elson, Christian Science Monitor, "Alabama Borders On Dawn Of 'New Day,'" *Alabama Journal*, Sept. 10, 1962.

48. "A Look Back, A Look Ahead," *Birmingham News*, Jan. 15, 1963.

49. "Governor Patterson Tells Of His Record," *Coosa Valley News*, Aug. 23, 1962; "Gov. Patterson Cites Gains Of Administration," *Advertiser-Journal*, Oct. 21, 1962.

50. *Birmingham News*, Jan. 15, 1963.

51. "The Patterson Four Years," *Alabama Journal*, Jan. 10, 1963.

52. "Allison Stanton, "Governor backs prison study," *Birmingham News*, Nov. 29, 1959; Ltr, A. Frank Lee, Board of Corrections, to Gov. John Patterson, Dec. 7, 1961.

53. Grafton and Permaloff, *Big Mules and Branchheads*, 154–60.

54. Patterson Interview, May 1, 2002.

55. Ibid.

56. Ingram Interview, Jan. 7, 2003.

57. Patterson Interview; Bob Ingram, "Clemency Hearings: Painful Spectacle," *Advertiser-Journal*, Dec. 13, 1959.

58. Ingram, *Advertiser-Journal*, Dec. 13, 1959.

59. Patterson Interview.

60. "Governor Pondering Law Practice Here," *Alabama Journal*, June 9, 1960; "Patterson Talks About '63 Plans," *Birmingham Post-Herald*, June 9, 1960.

61. Ted Pearson, "Patterson quietly waiting for next governor's race," *Birmingham News*, Oct. 15, 1963.

62. "It was moving day for John Pattersons," *Birmingham News*, Jan. 11, 1963.

63. Patterson Interview, May 15, 2002.

64. Bob Ingram, "Camellia State Flower," *Montgomery Advertiser*, Mar. 19, 1959.

65. Ibid.

66. Jane Marxer, "Refreshing Glimpses Of Childhood," *Advertiser-Journal*, Jan. 14, 1962.

67. Interview with Barbara Scholl, Aug. 21, 2002.

Chapter 18, White Knight on a Dark Horse

1. Patterson Interview, May 15, 2002.

2. Patterson Interview, Dec. 13, 2002.

3. Ibid.

4. Ibid.

5. Ibid.

6. Patterson Interview, June 5, 2002.

7. Ibid.

8. Ibid.

9. "Politics Laid On '63 Shelf But Rights Issue Looms in 1964," *South*, Dec. 9, 1963, 5; Bob Ingram, "Patterson's Stock Given Big Boost," *Commercial Dispatch (Columbus, MS)*, Mar. 1, 1964.

10. Wikipedia, the Internet encyclopedia, the Wikimedia Foundation, Inc.

11. Webb and Armbrester, eds, *Alabama Governors: A Political History of the State* (Tuscaloosa and London: The University of Alabama Press, 2001), 221.

12. Ibid., 221; Carter, *Politics of Rage*, 230–35.

13. Webb and Armbrester, 221; Carter, 247–52; Lewis, *Walking with the Wind*, 335–62.

14. Michael T. Kaufman, "Gary T. Rowe, 64, Klansman and Informer In Killing of Civil Rights Worker, Is Dead," *New York Times*, Oct. 4, 1998.

15. Eskew in Webb and Armbrester, 222.

16. Ibid.; Patterson Interview, May 15, 2002.

17. Patterson Interview.

18. Interview with Bob Ingram, Jan. 7, 2003.

19. Ibid.; Carter, 280.

20. Patterson Interview.

21. Ibid.

22. Ibid.

23. Ibid.; "John Malcolm Patterson," *Alabama Magazine*, Nov. 1979, 7.

24. Patterson Interview.

25. Eskew in Webb and Armbrester, 223–24.

26. Patterson Interview.

27. Ibid.

28. Daniel Webster Hollis III, *An Alabama Newspaper Tradition: Grover C. Hall and the Hall Family* (Tuscaloosa: University of Alabama Press, 1983), 126–29.

29. Ibid., 131–32.

30. Patterson Interview.

31. Ibid.; John Hayman with Clara Ruth Hayman, *A Judge in the Senate: Howell Heflin's Career of Politics and Principle* (Montgomery: NewSouth Books, 2001), 9, 158–62.

32. See note above.

33. Patterson Interview.

34. Ibid.

35. Ibid.

36. Interview with Jack Patterson, Sept. 25, 2003.

37. Patterson Interview.

38. Sikora, *The Judge*, 321.

39. Patterson Interview.

40. Interview with Barbara Patterson, Aug. 21, 2002.

41. Interview with Albert Patterson, Aug. 27, 2002.

42. Interview with Maria Florentina Mixen, Sept. 8, 2005.

43. Ingram, "John Malcolm Patterson," *Alabama News Magazine*, Nov. 1979, 6–8.

44. Bob Ingram Interview.

45. Ibid.

46. Carter, 282–83; Ingram Interview; Patterson Interview.

47. Ingram, "John Malcolm Patterson," *Alabama News Magazine*, Nov. 1979, 6–8.

48. Ibid.

49. Patterson Interview.

50. Ibid.

51. "Wallace Picks Patterson For Appellate Court," *Alabama Journal*, Apr. 3, 1984; Linda Funderburk, "Patterson says judgeship fulfills

lifelong ambition," *Advertiser*, Apr. 4, 1984.

52. Mark Smith, "Patterson sworn in as appellate judge," *Advertiser*, Apr. 10, 1984.

53. Bessie Ford, "Patterson takes spot on court," *Birmingham Post-Herald*, Apr. 10, 1984.

54. Bob Ingram, "Judge John Patterson," WSFA-TV Channel 12, Montgomery, Apr. 4, 1984.

55. Ford, *Birmingham Post-Herald*, Apr. 10, 1984; Story by Charlie Rogers, Dec. 2006.

56. Rogers, Dec. 2006; Ltr, Jesse M. Williams, III, to Hon. John Patterson, Apr. 16, 1984.

57. Ford, *Birmingham Post-Herald*, Apr. 10, 1984; Smith, *Advertiser*, Apr. 10, 1984.

58. Interview, author with Attorney Alvin T. Prestwood, May 29, 2003.

59. Ibid.

60. Ibid.

61. Ibid.

62. Patterson Interview.

Chapter 19, The Lectern and the Law

1. Mike Marshall, "Former governor recall his family's legacy, tries to reshape reputation," *Huntsville Times*, Oct. 27, 2002.

2. Tape with Gov. Patterson, Jan. 8, 2007.

3. Obituary, Ms. Mollie Jordon, Dec. 1996; Eulogy by Judge Patterson at memorial service for Mollie Jordon, Dec. 6, 1996.

4. Patterson tape, Jan. 8, 2007.

5. Ibid.

6. Ibid.

7. Ralph W. Adams, *Retrospect: An Autobiographical Reveille and Taps* (Montgomery, AL: Black Belt Communications Group, 1995), 85.

8. Patterson Interview, May 15, 2002.

9. Ibid.

10. 1985 Summer Commencement at Troy University, by the Honorable John Patterson, delivered August 2, 1985.

11. Adams, *Retrospect*, 95, 96.

12. Tape with Gov. Patterson, Jan. 8, 2007.

13. Ibid.

14. Ibid.

15. Tape discussion with law clerks at Jennifer Garrett's residence, Nov. 11, 2004.

16. Ibid.

17. Interview with Gov. Patterson, Sept. 18, 2002.

18. Interview with Conley Knott, Nov. 11, 2004.

19. Ltr, Circuit Judge Chris N. Galanos to Judge John Patterson, Oct. 18, 1996.

20. Ibid.

21. Ltr, Judge Patterson to Judge Galanos, Oct. 28, 1996.

22. Telephone Interview with Gov. Patterson, Feb. 20, 2007.

23. *Knight v. StateAla.Cr.App.*, 1985.

24. Ibid.

25. Ibid.

26. *Knight v. StateAla.Cr.App.*, 1987.

27. *McMillian v. StateAla.Cr.App.*, 1991; Taylor Bright, "Love letters almost fatal," *Birmingham Post-Herald*, Dec. 2001.

28. Bright, *Post-Herald*.

29. Ibid.; Tape with Judge Patterson, Nov. 2, 2002; *McMillian v. StateAla.Cr.App.*, 1993.

30. See note above.

31. Story by Judge Patterson, Nov. 11, 2004.

32. Patterson Interview, May 15, 2002.

33. Michael Evans, "The Decalogue in Montgomery," *Religion in the News*, Spring 2003, Vol. 6, No. 1.

34. Jannell McGrew, "Judicial Building reopens," *Montgomery Advertiser*, Sept. 6, 2003; Jannell McGrew, "Ten Commandments monument on tour," *Montgomery Advertiser*, July 20, 2004.

35. Todd Kleffman, "Judge evicts Commandments display," *Montgomery Advertiser*, Nov. 19, 2002.

36. Jessica M. Walker, "7 retired judges may hear appeal," *Montgomery Advertiser*, Dec. 16, 2003; Patterson Interview, Nov. 11, 2004.

37. Jessica M. Walker, "Appeal justices sworn in to positions," *Montgomery Advertiser*, Jan. 27, 2004.

38. Jessica M. Walker, "Moore loses bid to regain job," *Montgomery Advertiser*, May 1, 2004.

39. Ibid.; Jessica M. Walker, "Decision stirs both sides of issue," *Montgomery Advertiser*, May 1, 2004.

40. J. L. Chestnutt, Jr., "Judge Roy Moore, Preachers and Dixie Hypocrisy: Alabama's Taliban," *Counterpunch*, Dec. 2, 2005.

41. Sue Anne Pressley, "At Wallace Funeral, a Redemptive Tone," *Washington Post*, Sept. 17, 1998; CNN, "Wallace remembered as man with 'courage to change,'" Sept. 1998.

42. Bio of Fred David Gray, Alabama Academy of Honor, 2005; M. J. Ellington, "Academy of Honor adds 4," *Decatur Daily*, Aug. 23, 2005.

43. Speech by Governor Bob Riley, "Commemorating the 50th Anniversary of the Restoration of Law and Order to Phenix City," July 27, 2004.

44. "Governor honors Navigator with award, Montgomery, Ala.," *NDGI News*, Mar. 8, 2006.

45. Jerry F. Rutledge, "Right reaction: *Columbus Ledger-Inquirer*," June 17, 2006.

46. Alvin Benn, "Phenix City martyr's legacy lives on," *Montgomery Advertiser*, June 17, 2006.

47. Rutledge, "Right reaction: *Columbus Ledger-Inquirer*," June 17, 2006.

Epilogue

1. TV script, Bob Ingram with John and Tina Patterson, for *Channel 32 News*, Jan. 31, 2001.

2. Ibid.

3. Patterson Interview, Sept. 18, 2002.

4. Ibid.

5. Ingram TV script, Jan. 31, 2001.

6. Ibid.

7. Patterson Interview, May 2, 2002; Phillip Rawls, Associated Press, "Retiring judge is a lesson in history," *Montgomery Advertiser*, Dec. 26, 1996.

8. Patterson Interview, May 2, 2002.

9. Discussion at Jennifer Garrett's residence, Nov. 11, 2004.

BIBLIOGRAPHY

Books

Adams, Dr. Ralph W. *Retrospect: An Autobiographical Reveille and Taps*. Montgomery: Black Belt Communications Group, 1995.

Arsenault, Raymond. *Freedom Riders: 1961 and the Struggle for Racial Justice*. Oxford: Oxford University Press, 2006.

Atkinson, Rick. *An Army at Dawn: The War in North Africa 1942-1943*. New York: Henry Holt and Company, 2002.

Barnes, Margaret Anne. *The Tragedy and the Triumph of Phenix City, Alabama*. Macon, GA: Mercer University Press, 1998.

Bartley, Numan V. *The Rise of Massive Resistance: Race and Politics in the South During the 1950s*. Baton Rouge: Louisiana State University Press, 1969.

Bass, Jack. *Taming the Storm: The Life and Times of Judge Frank M. Johnson, Jr. and the South's Fight Over Civil Rights*. New York: Doubleday, 1993.

Branch, Taylor. *Parting the Waters: America in the King Years 1954-63*. New York: Simon & Schuster Inc., 1988.

Bryant, Nick. *The Bystander: John F. Kennedy and the Struggle for Black Equality*. New York: Basic Books, 2006.

Burns, Stewart, ed. *Daybreak of Freedom: The Montgomery Bus Boycott*. Chapel Hill: University of North Carolina Press, 1997.

Carter, Dan T. *The Politics of Rage: George Wallace, the Origins of the New Conservatism, and the Transformation of American Politics*. Baton Rouge: Louisiana State University Press, 1995.

Chant, Christopher. *Compendium of Armaments and Military Hardware*. London: Routledge and Kegan Paul, 1987.

Chestnutt, J. L., Jr. and Julia Cass. *Black in Selma: The Uncommon Life of J. L. Chestnut, Jr.* New York: Farrar, Straus and Giroux, 1990.

Darby, William O. with William H. Baumer. *Darby's Rangers: We Led the Way*. New York: Ballantine Books, 1980.

Davis, Townsend. *Weary Feet, Rested Souls: A Guided History of the Civil Rights Movement*. New York: W. W. Norton & Company, Inc., 1998.

D'este, Carlo. *Patton: A Genius for War*. New York: HarperCollins, 1985.

Eidsmore, Dr. John. *Legalized Gambling: America's Bad Bet*. Lafayette, LA: Huntington House Publishers, 1994.

Frady, Marshall. *Wallace: The Classic Portrait of Alabama Governor George Wallace*. New York: Random House, 1968.

Gaillard, Frye. *Cradle of Freedom: Alabama and the Movement That Changed America*. Tuscaloosa: University of Alabama Press, 2004.

Grady, Alan. *When Good Men Do Nothing: The Assassination of Albert Patterson*.

Tuscaloosa: University of Alabama Press, 2003.

Grafton, Carl and Anne Permaloff. *Big Mules and Branchheads: James E. Folsom and Political Power in Alabama.* Athens: University of Georgia Press, 1985.

Gray, Fred. *Bus Ride to Justice: Changing the System by the System: The Life and Works of Fred D. Gray.* Montgomery: NewSouth Books, 1995.

Great Issue 1985: A Forum on Important Questions Facing the American Public. Volume 16. Troy, AL: Troy State University Press, 1985.

Hayman, John with Clara Ruth Hayman. *A Judge in the Senate: Howell Heflin's Career of Politics and Principle.* Montgomery: NewSouth Books, 2001.

Hersh, Seymour M. *The Dark Side of Camelot.* Boston: Little, Brown and Company, 1997.

Hollis, Daniel Webster III. *An Alabama Newspaper Tradition: Grover C. Hall and the Hall Family.* Tuscaloosa: University of Alabama Press, 1983.

Kimbrell, Fuller. *From the Farm House to the State House: The Life and Times of Fuller Kimbrell.* Tuscaloosa: Word Way Press, Inc., 2001.

Klein, Patricia H., Dr. Donald B. Dodd and Dr. W. Stewart Harris. *Twentieth Century Alabama: Its History and Geography.* Montgomery: Clairmont Press, 1993.

Lesher, Stephan. *George Wallace: American Populist.* Reading, MA: Addison-Wesley, 1993.

Lewis, John with Michael D'Orso. *Walking with the Wind: A Memoir of the Movement.* San Diego: Harcourt Brace & Company, 1998.

Martin, David L. *Alabama's State and Local Governments.* Dubuque, Iowa: Kendall/ Hunt Publishing Company, 1975.

McWhorter, Diane. *Carry Me Home: Birmingham, Alabama, the Climatic Battle of the Civil Rights Revolution.* New York: Simon & Schuster, 2001.

Morris, Eric. *Circles of Hell: The War in Italy 1943-1945.* New York: Crown Publishers, Inc., 1993.

Packard, Jerrold M. *American Nightmare: The History of Jim Crow.* New York: St. Martin's Press, 2002.

Patterson, John. *Messages and Addresses of John Patterson, Governor of Alabama, 1959-1963*; Attorney General of Alabama, 1955-1959. Montgomery: Brown Printing Co., 1963.

Perret, Geoffrey. *Eisenhower.* New York: Random House, 1999.

Price, Shorty. *Alabama Politics: Tell It Like It Is.* New York: Vantage Press, 1973.

Russell County Historical Commission. *History of Russell County.* Dallas: National Sharegraphics, 1982.

Sarratt, Reed. *The Ordeal of Desegregation.* New York: Harper & Row, 1966.

Sikora, Frank. *The Judge: The Life & Opinions of Alabama's Frank M. Johnson, Jr.* Montgomery: Black Belt Press, 1992.

Sims, George E. *The Little Man's Big Friend: James E. Folsom and Political Power in Alabama.* Tuscaloosa: University of Alabama Press, 1985.

Smith, Starr. *Only the Days Are Long: Reports of a Journalist and World Traveler.* Oxford, MS: Yoknapatawpha Press, 1986.

Sorensen, Theodore C. *Kennedy.* New York: Konecky & Konecky, 1965.

Stanton, Elvin. *Faith and Works: The Business, Politics, and Philanthropy of Alabama's Jimmy Faulkner.* Montgomery: NewSouth Books, 2002.

Starr, Lt. Col. Chester G., ed. *From Salerno to the Alps: A History of the Fifth Army, 1943–1945.* Nashville: Battery Press, Inc., 1986.

Strickland, Edwin and Gene Wortsman. *Phenix City: The Wickedest City in America.* Birmingham: Vulcan Press, 1955.

The Heritage of Tallapoosa County. Heritage Publishing Consultants, Inc., 2000.

Trest, Warren and Don Dodd. *Wings of Denial.* Montgomery: NewSouth Books, 2001.

Walker, Anne Kendrick. *Russell County in Retrospect: An Epic of the Far Southeast.* Richmond, VA: Dietz Press, 1950.

Webb, Samuel L. and Margaret E. Armbrester, ed. *Alabama Governors.* Tuscaloosa: University of Alabama Press, 2001.

Articles

Allen, Brig. Gen. Richard F. AUS retired. "The Alabama National Guard in Phenix City—A High Watermark." *Army*, Aug 2005: 50-55.

"Bloodless Triumph (Part II)." *The National Guardsman*, May 1955: 2-4.

Cannel, Ward. "Death of Albert Patterson: Hell Fell On Alabama!" *Headquarters Detective*, November 1954, 36-41: 70, 71.

Cater, Douglass. "The Wide-Open Town on the Chattahoochee." *The Reporter*, February 24, 1955: 22-27.

Coley, C. J. "History of the Alabama Academy of Honor." *Alabama Historical Quarterly*, Spring 1976: 69-80.

"Crisis in Civil Rights." *Time* 77. June 2, 1961: 14-18.

Dean, Linda. "Memories with Governor John Patterson." *Lake Martin Living*, July 2001: 22-24.

Dyer, Edgar. "A 'Triumph of Justice' in Alabama: The 1960 Perjury Trial of Martin Luther King, Jr." *Journal of African American History*, June 22, 2003: 245-267.

Grady, Alan. "When Good Men Do Nothing: The Murder of Albert Patterson." *Alabama Heritage*, Winter 1996: 7-21.

Grafton, Carl and Anne Permaloff. "The Big Mule Alliance's Last Good Year: Thwarting the Patterson Reforms." *Alabama Review*, Oct 1994: 243-266.

Heerey, Peter (The Hon Mr. Justice). "Away Down South in Dixie." *Australian Law Journal*, September 1994: 641-648.

Laklan, Carli. "Report On Phenix City." *Real Detective*, August 1955: 50, 51, 63, 64.

McGlasson, Colonel W. D. "Phenix City 1954: Putting Out the Flames of Corruption." *National Guard*, June 1961: 8-13, 29.

Patterson, John. "Starting Off on the Right Foot." *Field Artillery*, October 1990: 31-34.

Patterson, John with Furman Bisher. "I'll Get the Gangs That Killed My Father!" *Saturday Evening Post*, November 27, 1954: 20-21, 60-64.

Perry, Emmett. "The Story behind Phenix City: The Struggle for Law in a Modern Sodom." *American Bar Association Journal* 42 (December 1956): 1146-49, 1178-79.

Sparrow, Hugh and W. W. Ward. "Alabama's Attorney General: The Man Who Inherited Dynamite." *Front Page Detective*, 1957: 56-61, 67.

Slocum, William. "America's Wickedest City." *Look*, October 5, 1954: 33-37.

Unpublished Theses

Grady, Edwin Alan. "The Campaign for Decency: John Patterson as Alabama Attorney General, 1955-1959." M.A. thesis, University of Alabama in Huntsville, 1992.

McLean, William Campbell IV. "From the Ashes: Phenix City, Alabama and Its Struggle With Memory." M.A. thesis, Emory University, 1995.

Page, Roland Joseph. "The Columbus Ledger and the Phenix City Story: On Winning a Pulitzer Prize." M.A. thesis, Florida State University, 1966.

Interviews by Author

Hoyt Allen, October 23, 2003.

Edward Azar, June 30, 2003.

William Benton, November 19, 2005.

Geraldine Blair, October 1, 2003.

Elizabeth Thomson Bressler, November 11, 2004.

Ruth Benson Cole, October 1, 2003.

Harry Cook, July 15 and August 14, 2003

Hilda Coulter, August 2004 (telephone)

Eric C. Davis, November 11, 2004.

John Henry East, November 19, 2005.

Christa S. Frangiamore, April 11, 2005.

George MacDonald Gallion, January 25, 2002.

Jennifer Garrett, November 11, 2004.

Tommy Giles, September 5 and September 12, 2003.

Carrie Gosdin, February 10, 2003.

Fred David Gray, April 30, 2003.

Pete Hanna, August 2004 (telephone)

Sibil Burnette Hanson, October 23, 2003.

Richard R. Heinzman, November 11, 2004.

Randall V. Houston, November 11, 2004.

Robert B. "Bob" Ingram, January 7, 2003.

Dorothy Hilyer Johnson, Sep 26, 2003.

Conley W. Knott, November 11, 2004.

McDowell Lee, December 10, 2003.

Floyd McGowan, February 20, 2003.

W. Daniel Miles III, November 11, 2004.

Maria Florentina Mixon, September 8, 2005.

Simon Partner, April 13, 2003.

Albert Patterson II, August 27, 2003.

John M. Patterson, October 19 and November 26, 2001; January 18, March 15, April 3, 17, May 1, 15, 29, and June 5, 12, 2002; June 29 and September 25, 2003; June 1, 12, and September 27, 2004; July 20 and 30, 2005.

Florentina Patterson, September 20, 2005.

Maurice Patterson, June 29, 2003.

Alvin T. Prestwood, May 29, 2003.

Morgan Reynolds, July 29, 2004 (Telephone).

Edmon L. Rinehart, August 15, 16, and September 3, 2003.

Joseph G. Robertson, June 29, 2003.

Fred Rothstein, May 1, 2004.

Barbara Louise Scholl, August 21, 2002.

Nancy Smith, August 27, 2003.

Mose Stuart IV, November 11, 2004.

CharlesVolz, June 13, 2003.

Adelia Warren, March 28, 2004.

Johnny Warren, March 28, 2004.

William C. Younger, July 8, 16, and 31, 2003.

Other Interviews

Alabama Public Telivision interviews, 1985

Ray Jenkins, by Barbara Fought, April 24, 2004 (Newhouse Civil Rights and the Press Symposium)

John Patterson, by Norman Lumpkin, May 22, 1973 (Tuskegee Institute History Series)

John Patterson, by John Stewart, May 26, 1967 (John F. Kennedy Library)

Newspapers and Periodicals

Alabama Citizen	*Look*
Alabama Heritage	*Los Angeles Mirror*
Alabama Journal	*Miami Herald*
Alabama Magazine	*Mobile Press*
Alabama News Magazine	*Mobile Register*
Alexander City Outlook	*Montgomery Advertiser*
American Bar Association Journal	*Montgomery Independent*

Anniston Star
Atlanta Constitution
Atmore Advance
Birmingham News
Birmingham Post-Herald
Bridgeport (Conn.) Post
Centreville Press
Childersburg News
Christian Science Monitor
Clayton Record
Columbus (Ga.) Enquirer
Columbus (Ga.) Ledger
Commercial Dispatch (Miss.)
Coosa County News
Counterpunch
Daily Mountain Eagle
Decatur Daily
Dothan Eagle
Eufala Tribune
Field Artillery
Florala News
Florence Times
Gadsden Times
Greene County Democrat
Greensboro Watchman
Honolulu Advertiser
Honolulu Star-Bulletin
Huntsville Times
Jackson County Sentinel
Lake Martin Living
Limestone Democrat

Moulton Advertiser
Muscle Shoals Morning Sun
National Guard Magazine
New York Herald Tribune
New York Times
Northwest Alabamian
Opelika Daily News
Phenix City Citizen
Phenix-Girard Journal
Pickens County Herald
Raleigh (N.C.) Times
Russellville Times
Sand Mountain Reporter
Saturday Evening Post
Selma Times-Journal
Shades Valley Sun
South Magazine
Sumter Co. Joural
Sylacauga News
Talladega Daily Home
The Reporter
Thomasville Times
Time
Tri-Cities Daily
Troy Messenger
Tuscaloosa Graphic
Tuscaloosa News
U.S. News & World Report
Valley Daily Times-News
Wall Street Journal

Films

Big Jim Folsom: The Two Faces of Populism. Produced and directed by Robert Clem. A Waterfront Pictures Release, 1997.

George Wallace: Setting the Woods on Fire. Directed by Daniel McCabe and Paul Steckler for PBS, 2000.

John Patterson: In the Wake of the Assassins. Directed by Robert Clem. A Waterfront Pictures Release, produced by Russell County Historical Commission, 2007.

The Phenix City Story. Directed by Phil Karlson. An Allied Artists Pictures Corporation film, 1955.

INDEX